Idaho, Montana & Wyoming

S0-ABZ-453

Published by AAA Publishing
1000 AAA Drive, Heathrow, FL 32746-5063
Copyright AAA 2015, All rights reserved

Advertising Rate and Circulation Information: (407) 444-8280

Printed in the USA by Quad/Graphics

This book is printed on paper certified by third-party standards for sustainably managed forestry and production.

Printed on recyclable paper.
Please recycle whenever possible.

Stock #4611

CONTENTS

Attractions, hotels, restaurants and other travel experience information are all grouped under the alphabetical listing of the city in which those experiences are physically located—or the nearest recognized city.

Featured Information

Idaho

Montana

Wyoming

Going the Extra Mile

Every year AAA experts travel North America to check out places for members to see, stay, dine and play.

Professional Inspectors - conduct in-person hotel and restaurant evaluations, providing ratings, notes and tips to guide your decisions.

Seasoned Travel Writers - gather destination insight, providing itineraries and top picks including AAA GEM attractions.

A to Z City Listings

Cities and places are listed alphabetically within each state or province. Attractions, hotels and restaurants are listed once — under the city in which they are physically located.

Cities that are considered part of a larger destination city or area have an expanded city header. The header identifies the larger region and cross-references pages that contain shared trip planning resources:

- Destination map – outline map of the cities that comprise a destination city or area
- Attraction spotting map – regional street map marked with attraction locations
- Hotel/restaurant spotting map and index – regional street map numbered with hotel and restaurant locations identified in an accompanying index

Cities that are not considered part of a larger destination city or area but have a significant number of listings may have these resources within the individual city section:

- Attraction spotting map
- Hotel/restaurant spotting map and index

Location Abbreviations

Directions are from the center of town unless otherwise specified, using these highway abbreviations:

Bus. Rte.=business route
CR=county road
FM=farm to market
FR=forest road
Hwy.=Canadian highway
I=interstate highway
LR=legislative route
R.R.=rural route
SR/PR=state or provincial route
US=federal highway

Maps

Use the navigable road maps and accompanying legend in the Atlas Section for route planning. Check the destination maps for general location reference. In select cities only, refer to the mass transit overview maps to cross-reference station names and numbers. For attraction and hotel/restaurant spotting maps, see the legend below to identify symbols and color coding.

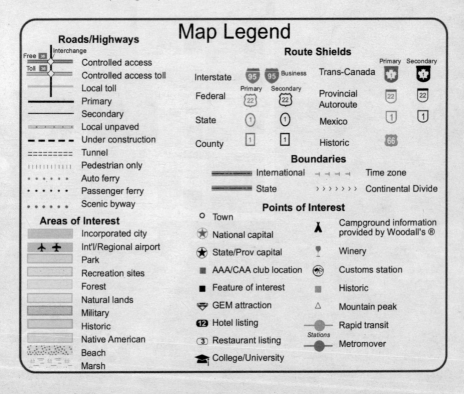

Map Legend

Roads/Highways

Free / Interchange	
Toll	
	Controlled access
	Controlled access toll
	Local toll
	Primary
	Secondary
	Local unpaved
	Under construction
	Tunnel
	Pedestrian only
	Auto ferry
	Passenger ferry
	Scenic byway

Areas of Interest

- Incorporated city
- Int'l/Regional airport
- Park
- Recreation sites
- Forest
- Natural lands
- Military
- Historic
- Native American
- Beach
- Marsh

Route Shields

	Primary	Secondary	
Interstate	95	95 Business	Trans-Canada
Federal	Primary 22	Secondary 22	Provincial Autoroute
State	1	1	Mexico
County	1	1	Historic 66

Trans-Canada: Primary / Secondary

Boundaries

- International
- State
- Time zone
- Continental Divide

Points of Interest

- ○ Town
- ⭐ National capital
- ⭐ State/Prov capital
- ■ AAA/CAA club location
- ■ Feature of interest
- ⬇ GEM attraction
- 12 Hotel listing
- 3 Restaurant listing
- 🎓 College/University
- ⚑ Campground information provided by Woodall's ®
- ⚐ Winery
- Customs station
- ■ Historic
- △ Mountain peak
- Rapid transit
- Stations / Metromover

About Listed Establishments

AAA/CAA Approved hotels and restaurants are listed on the basis of merit alone after careful evaluation and approval by full-time, professionally trained AAA/CAA inspectors. An establishment's decision to advertise in the TourBook guide has no bearing on its evaluation or rating; nor does inclusion of advertising imply AAA endorsement of products and services.

Information in this guide was believed accurate at the time of publication. However, since changes inevitably occur between annual editions, please contact your AAA travel professional, visit AAA.com or download the AAA mobile app to confirm prices and schedules.

Attraction Listings

ATTRACTION NAME, 3 mi. n. off SR 20A (Main Ave.), consists of 250 acres with Olmsted-designed gardens, a 205-foot marble and coquina bell tower and a Mediterranean-style mansion. One of the state's oldest attractions, the tower and gardens were dedicated to the American people in 1929 by President Calvin Coolidge on behalf of their founder, a Dutch immigrant.

Hours: Gardens daily 8-6. Last admission 1 hour before closing. Visitor center daily 9-5. Estate tours are given at noon and 2. Carillon concerts are given at 1 and 3. Phone ahead to confirm schedule. **Cost:** $10; $3 (ages 5-12). Gardens and estate $16; $8 (ages 5-12). **Phone:** (555) 555-5555.

⌁ GT ⊤⊤ ⫪ 🚇 Dupont Circle,13

AAA/CAA travel experts may designate an attraction of exceptional interest and quality as a AAA GEM — a *Great Experience for Members®. See GEM Attraction Index (listed on CONTENTS page) for a complete list of locations.*

Consult the online travel guides at AAA.com or visit AAA Mobile for additional things to do if you have time.

Cost

Prices are quoted without sales tax in the local currency (U.S. or Canadian dollars). Children under the lowest age specified are admitted free when accompanied by an adult. Most establishments accept credit cards, but a small number require cash, so please call ahead to verify.

Adventure Travel

Activities such as air tours, hiking, skiing and white-water rafting are listed to provide member information and do not imply AAA/CAA endorsement. For your safety, be aware of inherent risks and adhere to all safety instructions.

Icons

SAVE AAA Discounts & Rewards® member discount

⌁ Electric vehicle charging station on premises. Domestic station information provided by the U.S. Department of Energy. Canadian station information provided by Plug'n Drive Ontario.

GT Guided Tours available

A Camping facilities

⊤⊤ Food on premises

🞩 Recreational activities

🐾 Pets on leash allowed

⫪ Picnicking allowed

In select cities only:

🚇 Mass transit station within 1 mile. Icon is followed by station name and AAA/CAA designated station number within listing.

Information-Only Attraction Listings

Bulleted listings, which include the following categories, are listed for informational purposes as a service to members:

- **Gambling establishments** (even if located in a AAA/CAA Approved hotel)
- **Participatory recreational activities** (those requiring physical exertion or special skills)
- **Wineries that offer tours and tastings**

Mobile Tags

Scan QR codes throughout the TourBook guide to see online offers, menus, videos and more on your smartphone or tablet. If you need a QR scanner app, download one for free from your app store.

If you see a non-QR code in an ad, check the nearby text for details on which app you'll need to scan it.

Hotel and Restaurant Listings

1 Diamond Rating – AAA/CAA Approved hotels and restaurants are assigned a rating of one to five Diamonds. Red Diamonds distinguish establishments that participate in the AAA/CAA logo licensing program. For details, see p. 11 or AAA.com/Diamonds.

fyl indicates hotels and restaurants that are not AAA/CAA Approved and/or Diamond Rated but are listed to provide additional choices for members:

- **Hotels** may be unrated if they are too new to rate, under construction, under major renovation or have not yet been evaluated; or if they do not meet all AAA requirements. Hotels that do not meet all AAA requirements may be included if they offer member value or are the only option; details are noted in the listing.
- **Restaurants** may be unrated if they have not yet been evaluated by AAA.

2 Classification or Cuisine Type – Noted after the Diamond Rating.

- **Hotel Classifications** indicate the style of operation, overall concept and service level. Subclassifications may also be added. (See p. 12.)
- **Restaurant Cuisine Types** identify the food concept from more than 100 categories. If applicable, a classification may also be added. (See p. 13.)

3 Dollar Amounts – Quoted without sales tax in the local currency (U.S. or Canadian dollars), rounded up to the nearest dollar. Most establishments accept credit cards, but a small number require cash, so please call ahead to verify.

- **Hotel Rates** indicate the publicly available two-person rate or rate range for a standard room, applicable all year.
- **Restaurant Prices** represent the minimum and maximum entrée cost per person. Exceptions may include one-of-a-kind or special market priced items.

4 Spotting Symbol – Ovals containing numbers correspond with numbered location markings on hotel and restaurant spotting maps.

5 Parking – Unless otherwise noted, parking is free, on-site self parking.

6 Hotel Value Nationwide – Blue boxes highlight member benefits available at AAA/CAA Approved locations across a hotel chain. (See Just For Members section for details.)

7 Hotel Unit Limited Availability – Unit types, amenities and room features preceded by "some" are available on a limited basis, potentially as few as one.

8 Hotel Terms – Cancellation and minimum stay policies are listed. Unless otherwise noted, most properties offer a full deposit refund with cancellations received at least 48 hours before standard check-in. Properties that require advance payment may not refund the difference for early departures. "Resort fee" indicates a charge may apply above and beyond the quoted room rate.

9 Hotel Check-in/Check-out – Unless otherwise noted, check-in is after 3 p.m. and check-out is before 10 a.m.

10 Restaurant Dress Code – Unless otherwise noted, dress is casual or dressy casual.

11 Restaurant Menu – Where indicated, menus may be viewed in a secure online environment at AAA.com or, if a mobile tag is provided, via the restaurant's website.

12 Hotel Icons – May be preceded by CALL and/or SOME UNITS.

Member Information:

SAVE Member rates: discounted standard room rate or lowest public rate available at time of booking for dates of stay.

ECO Eco-certified by government or private organization.

⊞ Electric vehicle charging station on premises. Domestic station information provided by the U.S. Department of Energy. Canadian station information provided by Plug'n Drive Ontario.

⊠ Smoke-free premises

In select cities only:

🚇 Mass transit station within 1 mile. Icon is followed by station name and AAA/CAA designated station number within listing.

Services:

⊀ Airport transportation

🐾 Pets allowed (Call property for restrictions.)

🐾 Pets allowed (Call property for restrictions and fees.)

🍽 Restaurant on premises

🍽⁺ Restaurant off premises

🛎 Room service for 2 or more meals

🍷 Full bar

HOTEL LISTING

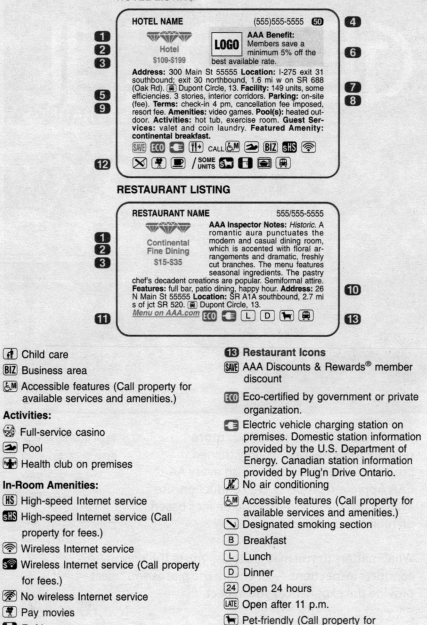

HOTEL NAME (555)555-5555 **50** **4**

1
2
3

Hotel
$109-$199

LOGO **AAA Benefit:** Members save a minimum 5% off the best available rate. **6**

5
9

Address: 300 Main St 55555 **Location:** I-275 exit 31 southbound; exit 30 northbound, 1.6 mi w on SR 688 (Oak Rd). Dupont Circle, 13. **Facility:** 149 units, some efficiencies. 3 stories, interior corridors. **Parking:** on-site (fee). **Terms:** check-in 4 pm, cancellation fee imposed, resort fee. **Amenities:** video games. **Pool(s):** heated outdoor. **Activities:** hot tub, exercise room. **Guest Services:** valet and coin laundry. **Featured Amenity:** continental breakfast. **7** **8**

12 CALL /SOME UNITS

RESTAURANT LISTING

RESTAURANT NAME 555/555-5555

1
2
3

Continental
Fine Dining

$15-$35

AAA Inspector Notes: *Historic.* A romantic aura punctuates the modern and casual dining room, which is accented with floral arrangements and dramatic, freshly cut branches. The menu features seasonal ingredients. The pastry chef's decadent creations are popular. Semiformal attire. **Features:** full bar, patio dining, happy hour. **Address:** 26 N Main St 55555 **Location:** SR A1A southbound, 2.7 mi s of jct SR 520. Dupont Circle, 13. **10**

11 *Menu on AAA.com* ECO L D **13**

🚼 Child care

BIZ Business area

♿M Accessible features (Call property for available services and amenities.)

Activities:

🎰 Full-service casino

🏊 Pool

💪 Health club on premises

In-Room Amenities:

HS High-speed Internet service

sHS High-speed Internet service (Call property for fees.)

📶 Wireless Internet service

s📶 Wireless Internet service (Call property for fees.)

📶 No wireless Internet service

🎬 Pay movies

🧊 Refrigerator

📟 Microwave

☕ Coffee maker

🅐 No air conditioning

📺 No TV

☎ No telephones

13 Restaurant Icons

SAVE AAA Discounts & Rewards® member discount

ECO Eco-certified by government or private organization.

🔌 Electric vehicle charging station on premises. Domestic station information provided by the U.S. Department of Energy. Canadian station information provided by Plug'n Drive Ontario.

🅐 No air conditioning

♿M Accessible features (Call property for available services and amenities.)

🚭 Designated smoking section

B Breakfast

L Lunch

D Dinner

24 Open 24 hours

LATE Open after 11 p.m.

🛏 Pet-friendly (Call property for restrictions.)

In select cities only:

🚃 Mass transit station within 1 mile. Icon is followed by station name and AAA/CAA designated station number within listing.

Just For Members

Understanding the Diamond Ratings

Hotel and restaurant evaluations are unscheduled to ensure our professionally trained inspectors encounter the same experience members do.

- When an establishment is Diamond Rated, it means members can expect a good fit with their needs. The inspector assigns a rating that indicates the type of experience to expect.
- While establishments at high levels must offer increasingly complex personalized services, establishments at every level are subject to the same basic requirements for cleanliness, comfort and hospitality. Learn more at AAA.com/Diamonds.

Hotels

Budget-oriented, offering basic comfort and hospitality.

Affordable, with modestly enhanced facilities, décor and amenities.

Distinguished, multifaceted with enhanced physical attributes, amenities and guest comforts.

Refined, stylish with upscale physical attributes, extensive amenities and high degree of hospitality, service and attention to detail.

Ultimate luxury, sophistication and comfort with extraordinary physical attributes, meticulous personalized service, extensive amenities and impeccable standards of excellence.

Restaurants

Simple, economical food, often self-service, in a functional environment.

Familiar food, often cooked to order, served in relaxed surroundings.

Popular cuisine, skillfully prepared and served, with expanded beverage options, in enhanced setting.

Imaginative, market-fresh food creatively prepared and skillfully served, often with wine steward, amid upscale ambience.

Cutting-edge cuisine of the finest ingredients, uniquely prepared by an acclaimed chef, served by expert service staff led by maître d' in extraordinary surroundings.

What's the difference?

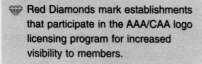 Red Diamonds mark establishments that participate in the AAA/CAA logo licensing program for increased visibility to members.

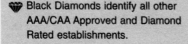 Black Diamonds identify all other AAA/CAA Approved and Diamond Rated establishments.

Hotel Classifications

Quality and comfort are usually consistent across each Diamond Rating level, but décor, facilities and service levels vary by classification.

Berry Manor Inn, Rockland, ME

Bed & Breakfast — Typically owner-operated with a high degree of personal touches. Guests are encouraged to interact during evening and breakfast hours. A continental or full, hot breakfast is included in the room rate.

Killarney Lodge, Algonquin Provincial Park, ON

Cabin — Often located in wooded, rural or waterfront locations. Freestanding units are typically rustic and of basic design. As a rule, essential cleaning supplies, kitchen utensils and complete bed and bath linens are supplied.

Hyatt Regency Clearwater Beach Resort & Spa, Clearwater Beach, FL

Condominium — Apartment-style accommodations of varying design or décor, units often contain one or more bedrooms, a living room, full kitchen and an eating area. As a rule, essential cleaning supplies, kitchen utensils and complete bed and bath linens are supplied.

Montpelier Plantation and Beach, St. Kitts and Nevis

Cottage — Often located in wooded, rural, or waterfront locations. Freestanding units are typically home-style in design and décor. As a rule, essential cleaning supplies, kitchen utensils and complete bed and bath linens are supplied.

Nottoway Plantation & Resort, White Castle, LA

Country Inn — Although similar in definition to a bed and breakfast, country inns are usually larger in scale with spacious public areas and offer a dining facility that serves breakfast and dinner.

The Shores Resort & Spa, Daytona Beach Shores, FL

Hotel — Typically a multistory property with interior room entrances and a variety of guest unit styles. The magnitude of the public areas is determined by the overall theme, location and service level, but may include a variety of facilities such as a restaurant, shops, a fitness center, a spa, a business center and meeting rooms.

All Star Vacation Homes, Kissimmee, FL

House — Freestanding units of varying home-style design. Typically larger scale, often containing two or more bedrooms, a living room, a full kitchen, a dining room and multiple bathrooms. As a rule, essential cleaning supplies, kitchen utensils and complete bed and bath linens are supplied.

Bryce View Lodge, Bryce Canyon City, UT

Motel — A one- or two-story roadside property with exterior room entrances and drive up parking. Public areas and facilities are often limited in size and/or availability.

Vista Verde Guest Ranch, Clark, CO

Ranch — Typically a working ranch featuring an obvious rustic, Western theme, equestrian-related activities and a variety of guest unit styles.

Hotel Subclassifications

These additional descriptives may be added to the classification for more information:

- **Boutique** — Often thematic, typically informal yet highly personalized; may have a luxurious or quirky style that is fashionable or unique.

- **Casino** — Extensive gambling facilities are available, such as blackjack, craps, keno and slot machines.

- **Classic** — Renowned and landmark properties, older than 50 years, well known for their unique style and ambience.

- **Contemporary** — Overall theme reflects characteristics of present mainstream trends.

- **Extended Stay** — Offers a predominance of long-term accommodations with a designated full-service kitchen area within each unit.

- **Historic** — More than 75 years old with one of the following documented historical features: Maintains the integrity of the historical nature, listed on the National Register of Historic Places, designated a National Historic Landmark or located in a National Register Historic District.

- **Resort** — Extensive recreational facilities and programs may include golf, tennis, skiing, fishing, water sports, spa

treatments or professionally guided activities.

- **Retro** — Overall theme reflects a contemporary design that reinterprets styles from a past era.

- **Vacation Rental** — Typically houses, condos, cottages or cabins; these properties are "home away from home" self-catering accommodations.

- **Vintage** — Overall theme reflects upon and maintains the authentic traits and experience of a past era.

Restaurant Classifications

If applicable, in addition to the cuisine type noted under the Diamond Rating, restaurant listings may also include one or both classifications:

- **Classic** — Renowned and landmark operation in business for 25 plus years; unique style and ambience.

- **Historic** — Meets one of the following: Listed on National Register of Historic Places, designated a National Historic Landmark or located in a National Register Historic District.

Service Animals

Under the Americans with Disabilities Act (ADA), U.S. businesses that serve the public must allow people with disabilities to bring their service animals into all areas of the facility where customers are normally allowed to go.

Businesses may ask if an animal is a service animal and what tasks the animal has been trained to perform. Businesses may not ask about the person's disability, require special identification for the animal or request removal of the animal from the premises except in limited cases that require alternate assistance. Businesses may not charge extra fees for service animals, including standard pet fees, but may charge for damage caused by service animals if guests are normally charged for damage they cause.

Call the U.S. Department of Justice ADA Information Line: (800) 514-0301 or TTY (800) 514-0383, or visit ada.gov. Regulations may differ in Canada.

AAA/CAA Approved Hotels

For members, AAA/CAA Approved means quality assured.

- Only properties that meet basic requirements for cleanliness, comfort and hospitality pass inspection.
- Approved hotels receive a Diamond Rating that tells members the type of experience to expect.

Guest Safety

Inspectors view a sampling of rooms during evaluations and, therefore, AAA/CAA cannot guarantee the presence of working locks and operational fire safety equipment in every guest unit.

Member Rates

AAA/CAA members can generally expect to pay no more than the maximum TourBook listed rate for a standard room. Member discounts apply to rates quoted within the rate range and are applicable at the time of booking. Listed rates are usually based on last standard room availability. Rates may fluctuate within the range and vary by season and room type. Obtain current AAA/CAA member rates and make reservations at AAA.com.

Exceptions

- Rates for properties operating as concessionaires for the U.S. National Park Service are not guaranteed due to governing regulations.
- Special advertised rates and short-term promotional rates below the rate range are not subject to additional member discounts.
- During special events, hotels may temporarily increase room rates, not recognize discounts or modify pricing policies. Special events may include Mardi Gras, the Kentucky Derby (including pre-Derby events), college football games, holidays, holiday periods and state fairs. Although some special events are listed in the TourBook guides and on AAA.com, it's always wise to check in advance with AAA travel professionals for specific dates.

If you are charged more than the maximum TourBook listed rate, question the additional charge. If an exception is not in effect and management refuses to adhere to the published rate, pay for the room and contact AAA/CAA. The amount paid above the stated maximum will be refunded if our investigation indicates an unjustified charge.

Reservations and Cancellations

When making your reservation, identify yourself as a AAA/CAA member and request written confirmation of your room type, rate, dates of stay, and cancellation and refund policies. At registration, show your membership card.

To cancel, contact the hotel, your AAA/CAA club office or AAA.com, depending on how you booked your reservation. Request a cancellation number or proof of cancellation.

If your room is not as specified and you have written confirmation of your reservation for a specific room type, you should be given the option of choosing a different room or receiving a refund. If management refuses to issue a refund, contact AAA/CAA.

Contacting AAA/CAA About Approved Properties

If your visit to a AAA/CAA Approved attraction, hotel or restaurant doesn't meet your expectations, please tell us about it — **during your visit or within 30 days**. Be sure to save your receipts and other documentation for reference.

Use the easy online form at AAA.com/TourBookComments to send us the details.

Alternatively, you can email your comments to: memberrelations@national.aaa.com or submit them via postal mail to: AAA Member Comments, 1000 AAA Dr., Box 61, Heathrow, FL 32746.

AAA/CAA Preferred Hotels

All AAA/CAA Approved hotels are committed to providing quality, value and member service. In addition, those designated as AAA/CAA Preferred Hotels also offer these extra values at Approved locations nationwide. Valid AAA/CAA membership required.

- **Best AAA/CAA member rates for your dates of stay.**
- **Seasonal promotions and special member offers.** Visit AAA.com to view current offers.
- **Member benefit.** See the blue boxes in hotel listings for the chains shown in the right-hand column below to find values offered at AAA/CAA Approved locations nationwide, subject to availability. Details valid at the time of publication and may change without notice.

- **Total satisfaction guarantee.** If you book your stay with AAA/CAA Travel and your stay fails to meet your expectations, you can apply for a full refund. Bring the complaint to the hotel's attention during the stay and request resolution; if the complaint is not resolved by the hotel, ask your AAA/CAA travel agent to request resolution through the AAA/CAA Assured Stay program.

BEST WESTERN®, BEST WESTERN PLUS®, EXECUTIVE RESIDENCY, Vib, BEST WESTERN PREMIER® and BW Premier Collection℠

Hilton Hotels & Resorts, Waldorf Astoria™ Hotels & Resorts, Conrad® Hotels & Resorts, Canopy by Hilton, Curio - A Collection by Hilton™, DoubleTree by Hilton™, Embassy Suites Hotels™, Hilton Garden Inn™, Hampton Inn™, Homewood Suites by Hilton™, Home2 Suites by Hilton™ and Hilton Grand Vacations™

Park Hyatt®, Andaz®, Grand Hyatt®, Hyatt Centric®, Hyatt®, Hyatt Regency®, Hyatt Place®, HYATT house®, Hyatt Zilara® and Hyatt Ziva®

JW Marriott®, Autograph Collection® Hotels, Renaissance® Hotels, Marriott Hotels®, Delta Hotels and Resorts®, Gaylord Hotels®, AC Hotels by Marriott®, Courtyard®, Residence Inn®, SpringHill Suites®, Fairfield Inn & Suites® and TownePlace Suites®

Bellagio®, ARIA®, Vdara®, MGM Grand®, The Signature at MGM Grand®, Mandalay Bay®, Delano™ Las Vegas, The Mirage®, Monte Carlo™, New York-New York®, Luxor®, Excalibur® and Circus Circus® Las Vegas

starwood
Hotels and
Resorts

St. Regis®, The Luxury Collection®, W®, Westin®, Le Méridien®, Sheraton®, Four Points® by Sheraton, Aloft®, element® and Tribute Portfolio™

Landry's Seafood House, The Crab House, Chart House, Oceanaire, Saltgrass Steak House, Muer Seafood Restaurants and Aquarium Restaurants

Member Discounts

Visit AAA.com/searchfordiscounts to find locations and available member discounts. Your AAA/CAA club may offer even greater discounts on theme park tickets. Amtrak and theme park discounts may be used for up to six tickets; restaurant savings may be used for up to six patrons. Other restrictions may apply. All offers subject to change. For complete restrictions, visit your AAA office or AAA.com/restrictions.

- Save 10% on food and nonalcoholic beverages at all of the above restaurants.

- Save 10% on merchandise at Aquarium, Downtown Aquarium and Rainforest Cafe restaurants.

ATTRACTIONS

Six Flags

- Save on admission at the gate, participating AAA/CAA offices or AAA.com/SixFlags.

- Save 10% on merchandise of $15 or more at in-park stores.

Universal Orlando Resort and Universal Studios Hollywood

- Save on tickets at select AAA/CAA offices or AAA.com/Universal. In-park savings available in FL.

- Save 10% on Blue Man Group tickets and at select food and merchandise venues at Universal CityWalk®.

DINING

Hard Rock Cafe

- Save 10% on food, nonalcoholic beverages and merchandise at all locations in the U.S. and Canada, plus select international locations. Visit AAA.com/HardRock for full listing.

SHOPPING

adidas Outlet

- Save 20% on the entire purchase. Visit AAA.com/adidasoutlet for list of locations.

Reebok & Rockport Outlet

- Save 20% on the entire purchase. Visit AAA.com/Reebok for list of locations.

Tanger Outlet Centers

- Receive a free coupon book with discounts up to 50% at select merchants.

TRANSPORTATION

Amtrak

- Save 10% on rail fare booked at least three days in advance of travel date at AAA.com/Amtrak.

Hertz

- Save on daily, weekend, weekly and monthly rentals at AAA.com/Hertz or (800) 654-3080.

RACK UP THE REWARDS

Make membership an even more rewarding experience.

The AAA Member Rewards Visa® credit card lets you earn reward points on all of your purchases. Apply for an account today and let the rewards start rolling in!

 Earn 1 point for every $1 in purchases with your AAA Member Rewards Visa® card!*

 Earn 2X points for gas, grocery and drug store purchases!

 Earn 3X points on qualifying AAA and travel purchases!

 Redeem for cash or get a AAA Voucher that gives you up to 40% more value!**

 Exclusive rewards to make you smile!

VISIT AAA.com/creditcard   **STOP BY** any AAA branch

Schweitzer Mountain Resort, Sandpoint

Idaho

Visit Idaho and you'll need an oxygen mask; the scenery is that breathtaking. From the serrated granite peaks of the Sawtooth Mountains at the state's core to the towering Seven Devils flanking Hells Canyon, Idaho features some of the country's most stunning high-altitude panoramas. And if the views don't steal your breath away, the thin air at these lofty elevations just might.

Fortunately, there's no better place to deeply inhale than within the state's numerous unspoiled wilderness areas. Clean air and peaceful solitude attract urbanites from around the country seeking refuge from pollution and stress. They come to places like the Selway-Bitterroot Wilderness or Craters of the Moon National Monument and Preserve.

Expel that fresh air in a shout of triumph as you conquer exhilarating white water along the Snake, Selway or Salmon rivers. Whoop

Fly-fish in one of the many northern lakes

with excitement while flying down a powder-covered slope in Sun Valley or on Schweitzer Mountain. Scream with delight at the discovery of a star garnet near Coeur d'Alene, the only place outside of India you can find one and just one reason Idaho's nickname—the Gem State—is appropriate.

The Call of the Wild West

Idaho remains one of the country's most isolated and rugged regions. To early explorers and entrepreneurs—from Meriwether Lewis and William Clark to adventurous traders and prospectors—the territory was practically impenetrable. But with a determination undaunted come Hells Canyon or high water, they journeyed west. Follow their lead, and you, too, will be struck by this land's power to inspire.

Idaho counts plenty of contemporary dreamers and doers on its dossier. The memorial marking one of Ernest Hemingway's favorite fly-fishing spots is half-hidden near a shady stream in Sun Valley's outskirts. And astronaut Alan Shepard and his crew trained for a lunar landing at the aptly named Craters of the Moon National Monument and Preserve, an eerie volcanic landscape outside Arco.

As you shop and stroll in the resort towns of Ketchum and Hailey, keep a covert eye out for famous faces; a who's who of movie stars and Olympic athletes lives here part time. Still, Idaho's allure sways more than celebrities. The state is home to one of the world's largest concentrations of nesting hawks, falcons, owls and other raptors; spy on some of these magnificent birds at Boise's World Center for Birds of Prey.

Not For Your Eyes Only

So, what *is* all the fuss about? Mountains, mostly. Three of Idaho's borders wear crowns topping 9,000 feet. From Bruneau River Canyon's Goliath-like stone shoulders to the Precambrian pillars of City of Rocks National Reserve, grandiose mountain scenery dominates this state.

Not that less rugged diversions are lacking. State capital Boise offers a fine orchestra and opera. Coeur d'Alene reinforces its resort image with a fun theme park and a golf course featuring one offshore green. In Sandpoint, the focal point is a city bridge-turned-popular downtown market.

But it's the outdoors that beckon. Here you can watch the slow, mesmerizing spiral of a golden eagle poised on a canyon-channeled thermal of mountain air, or paddle through a fast, furious white-water spin cycle with a boatful of cohorts. The offerings are as vast as the mountains.

Recreation

An abundance of publicly held land and wilderness area is set aside in scenic Idaho—all the better for play in any season.

Thousands of miles of groomed trails—as well as millions of acres of forest land and backcountry—provide fast snowmobiling fun in the chilly winter air. Best bets include Clearwater, Idaho Panhandle and Nez Perce national forests.

For downhill skiing, Bogus Basin, 16 miles north of Boise; Silver Mountain, south of Kellogg; and Sun Valley will satisfy your need for speed. If you prefer cross-country skiing or snowshoeing, outfitters plan overnight treks through the Boulder, Pioneer, Sawtooth and Teton mountains. Skiers of moderate ability enjoy Fish Creek Meadows and Lolo Pass in Nez Perce National Forest; the scenic trails in Farragut State Park; and the paths winding throughout Sawtooth National Recreation Area.

Idaho's waterways provide thrills of their own. Class III and IV rapids, with names like Split Rock and Whiplash, may explain how the Salmon got its nickname as the "River of No Return." Rafting and kayaking also are wild and woolly on the Middle Fork of the Salmon and the Owyhee, Payette and Lochsa rivers, the last of which is a Nez Perce Indian word for "rough water." Jet boats zip along the Snake River through Hells Canyon.

Want to take it slowly? Go canoeing between the cliffs rising around the Snake River at Hagerman Fossil Beds National Monument in Hagerman, or watch eagles, ospreys and mink as you enjoy a leisurely float trip down the placid Boise River.

Dories and drift boats take anglers to favorite fishing waters on the Clearwater, Salmon and Snake rivers, where hardy steelhead thrive. Meanwhile, the upper St. Joe River is a haven for cutthroat.

Anglers find the northern lakes no less exciting. Coeur d'Alene, Pend Oreille and Priest lakes teem with chinook and kokanee salmon, Kamloops trout and northern pike.

Equestrian activities abound in the Grand Tetons and near Coeur d'Alene, Sun Valley and Yellowstone, while ridgelines across such ranges as the Bitterroot, Cougar and Salmon afford outstanding panoramas for mountain bikers.

Climbing expeditions tackle Slick Rock, near McCall; City of Rocks National Reserve, near Almo; and the state's highest peak, Mount Borah. For a less rugged experience, go hiking or backpacking or make your way up mountains around McCall and Sun Valley on a llama. Only pack trains and hikers penetrate the unspoiled terrain of the Frank Church-River of No Return, Sawtooth and Selway-Bitterroot wilderness areas, which blanket more than 2 million acres.

City of Rocks National Reserve, Almo

Historic Timeline

1805   Meriwether Lewis and William Clark explore what is now Idaho.

1860   Mormons establish Franklin, the first permanent white settlement in Idaho.

1874   The railroad first reaches Idaho at Franklin.

1890   Idaho becomes the 43rd state.

1951   An Atomic Energy Commission testing station near Idaho Falls first uses fission to generate electricity.

1968   Engineers complete three dams to harness the power of the Snake River.

1983   An earthquake registering 7.3 on the Richter scale shakes central Idaho.

1988   Congress establishes Hagerman Fossil Beds National Monument and the City of Rocks National Reserve.

1995   Idaho native Picabo Street becomes the first American to win a World Cup season title in a speed event.

1999   University of Idaho graduate Jeffrey S. Ashby pilots the space shuttle *Columbia*.

2009   Native American Larry EchoHawk, a former Idaho attorney general, becomes head of the U.S. Bureau of Indian Affairs.

What To Pack

Temperature Averages Maximum/Minimum	JANUARY	FEBRUARY	MARCH	APRIL	MAY	JUNE	JULY	AUGUST	SEPTEMBER	OCTOBER	NOVEMBER	DECEMBER
Boise	36/21	42/26	52/31	62/37	71/45	79/51	90/59	88/57	78/49	65/40	48/30	39/25
Idaho Falls	28/3	33/8	42/18	58/29	68/38	76/44	88/50	86/47	75/38	62/28	43/17	33/9
Lewiston	38/24	44/28	53/33	63/39	71/46	78/52	90/58	88/56	78/49	64/40	48/32	42/28
Pocatello	32/13	37/18	46/26	60/33	69/41	78/48	90/55	87/53	77/44	64/34	45/25	36/19
Salmon	28/9	37/15	50/25	60/32	69/40	78/46	87/51	86/48	75/40	60/30	41/21	29/11
Sandpoint	32/19	38/23	46/28	56/34	65/41	72/47	80/50	80/49	70/41	56/33	40/28	32/21

From the records of The Weather Channel Interactive, Inc.

Good Facts To Know

ABOUT THE STATE

POPULATION: 1,567,582.

AREA: 83,569 square miles; ranks 14th.

CAPITAL: Boise.

HIGHEST POINT: 12,662 ft., Borah Peak.

LOWEST POINT: 710 ft., Snake River at Lewiston.

TIME ZONE(S): Mountain/Pacific. DST.

GAMBLING

MINIMUM AGE FOR GAMBLING: 18 (for lotto/scratch-off tickets).

REGULATIONS

TEEN DRIVING LAWS: No more than one passenger under age 17 (excluding family members) is permitted for the first 6 months. Driving is not permitted daily dusk-dawn. The minimum age for an unrestricted driver's license is 16. Phone (208) 334-8735 for more information about Idaho driver's license regulations.

SEAT BELT/CHILD RESTRAINT LAWS: Seat belts are required for driver and all passengers ages 7 and older. Children under age 7 are required to be in a child restraint. AAA recommends the use of seat belts and appropriate child restraints for the driver and all passengers.

CELLPHONE RESTRICTIONS: Text messaging while driving is prohibited for all drivers.

HELMETS FOR MOTORCYCLISTS: Required for riders under 18.

RADAR DETECTORS: Permitted. Prohibited for use by commercial vehicles.

MOVE OVER LAW: Driver is required to slow down and vacate lane nearest stopped police, fire and rescue vehicles using audible or flashing signals. The law also includes tow trucks.

FIREARMS LAWS: Vary by state and/or county. Contact Idaho Attorney General's Office, 700 W. Jefferson St., Suite 210, P.O. Box 83720, Boise ID 83720-0010; phone (208) 334-2400.

HOLIDAYS

HOLIDAYS: Jan. 1 ▪ Martin Luther King Jr. Day, Jan. (3rd Mon.) ▪ Washington's Birthday/Presidents Day, Feb. (3rd Mon.) ▪ Memorial Day, May (last Mon.) ▪ July 4 ▪ Labor Day, Sept. (1st Mon.) ▪ Columbus Day, Oct. (2nd Mon.) ▪ Veterans Day, Nov. 11 ▪ Thanksgiving, Nov. (4th Thurs.) ▪ Christmas, Dec. 25.

MONEY

TAXES: Idaho's statewide sales tax is 6 percent. There is a 2 percent Travel & Convention Tax on lodgings, with local options to levy up to an additional 5 percent.

VISITOR INFORMATION

INFORMATION CENTERS: State welcome centers that provide details about state attractions, accommodations, historic sites, parks and events as well as road and ski reports are at Fruitland I-84E, Milepost 1 ▪ 6 miles south of Malad City on I-15N ▪ and along I-90E at Post Falls.

FURTHER INFORMATION FOR VISITORS:
Idaho Department of Commerce—Tourism Division
700 W. State St.
P.O. Box 83720
Boise, ID 83720
(208) 334-2470
(800) 847-4843 *(See ad p. 321.)*

NATIONAL FOREST INFORMATION:
U.S. Forest Service, Idaho Panhandle National Forests
3815 Schreiber Way
Coeur d'Alene, ID 83815-8363
(208) 765-7223
(877) 444-6777 (reservations)
TTY (877) 833-6777

USDA Forest Service, Ogden Ranger District
507 25th St.
Ogden, UT 84401
(801) 625-5112
(877) 444-6777 (reservations)

FISHING AND HUNTING REGULATIONS:
Idaho Department of Fish and Game
600 S. Walnut St.
Boise, ID 83712
(208) 334-3700

RECREATION INFORMATION:
Idaho State Department of Parks and Recreation
5657 Warm Springs Ave.
Boise, ID 83716
(208) 334-4199

Get maps, travel information and road service
with the AAA and CAA Mobile apps

Idaho Annual Events
Please call ahead to confirm event details.

JANUARY

- Soda Springs Winter Carnival, Fishing Derby and Cross Country Ski Race Soda Springs 208-547-4516
- Winter Carnival / McCall 208-634-7631
- WinterFest / Island Park 208-558-7755

FEBRUARY

- Lionel Hampton Jazz Festival / Moscow 208-885-6765
- American Dog Derby Ashton 208-360-0988
- Pierce Winter Festival Pierce 208-464-2171

MARCH

- Boise Flower and Garden Show / Boise 503-335-3336
- St. Patrick's Day Parade Coeur d'Alene 208-415-0116
- Chrome in the Dome Car and Bike Show / Pocatello 208-282-3605

APRIL

- Dogwood Festival of the Lewis-Clark Valley Lewiston 208-743-3531
- Salmon River Jet Boat Races / Riggins 208-628-3320
- Gene Harris Jazz Festival Boise 208-426-1711

MAY

- Sun Valley Wellness Festival / Sun Valley 208-726-2777
- Lost in the '50s / Sandpoint 208-263-9321
- Riggins Rodeo and Parade Riggins 208-628-4084

JUNE

- Emmett Cherry Festival Emmett 208-365-3485
- National Oldtime Fiddlers' Contest and Festival Weiser 800-437-1280
- Meridian Dairy Days Festival and Marketplace Meridian 208-888-2817

JULY

- Idaho International SummerFest / Rexburg 888-463-6880
- Eagle Rock Art Guild Sidewalk Show / Idaho Falls 208-523-1010
- Snake River Stampede and Snake River Dayz / Nampa 208-466-4641

AUGUST

- Festival at Sandpoint Sandpoint 208-263-6858
- Black Daisy Arts and Crafts Festival / Mackay 208-588-2693
- Huckleberry Heritage Festival / Wallace 208-753-7151

SEPTEMBER

- Eastern Idaho State Fair Blackfoot 208-785-2480
- Idaho State Draft Horse and Mule International Show / Sandpoint 208-263-8414
- Spirit of Boise Balloon Classic / Boise 208-375-0512

OCTOBER

- Fall Harvest Festival / Boise 208-343-8649
- Sun Valley Jazz Jamboree Sun Valley 208-726-3423
- Trailing of the Sheep Ketchum 800-634-3347

NOVEMBER

- Boise Holiday Parade Boise 208-433-5675
- Kootenai Health Foundation Festival of Trees Coeur d'Alene 208-625-4433
- Winter Garden aGlow at the Idaho Botanical Garden Boise 208-343-8649

DECEMBER

- Holiday Pops / Nampa 208-344-7849
- Yuletide Celebration and Lighting Festival / Wallace 208-753-7151
- Famous Idaho Potato Bowl Boise 208-424-1011

Spirit of Boise Balloon
Classic, Boise

Dome of the State Capitol, Boise

Fort Sherman Chapel,
Coeur d'Alene

Idaho Panhandle National Forests

Fort Hall Replica, Pocatello

Index: Great Experience for Members

AAA editor's picks of exceptional note

Yellowstone National Park

Craters of the Moon National Monument and Preserve

Silverwood

Discovery Center of Idaho

See Orientation map on p. 30 for corresponding grid coordinates, if applicable.

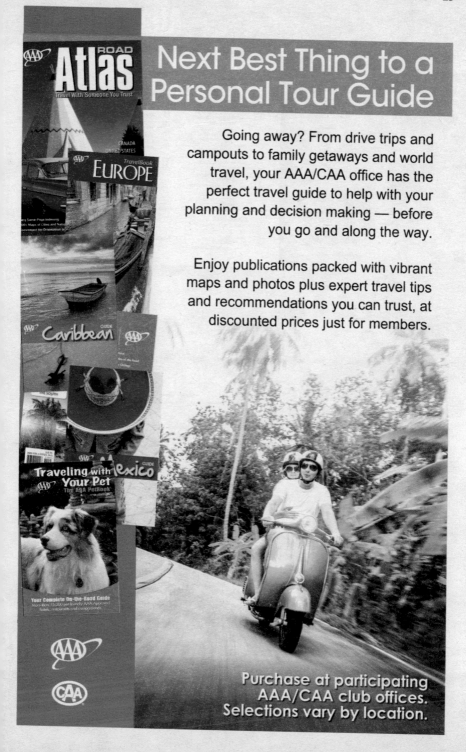

Idaho
Atlas Section

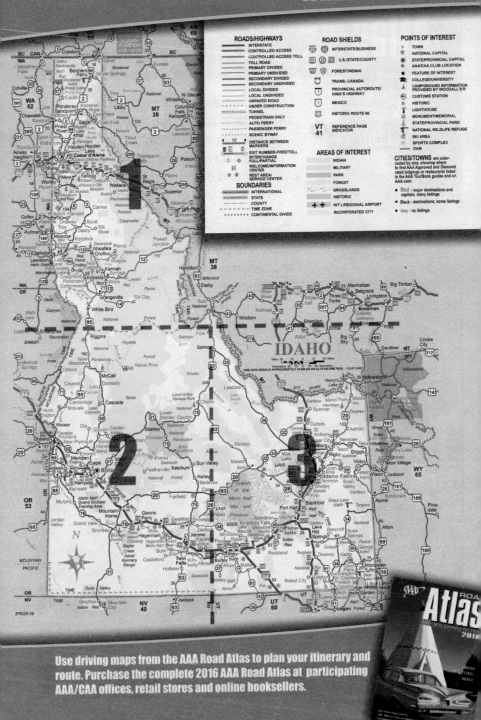

ROADS/HIGHWAYS

INTERSTATE
CONTROLLED ACCESS
CONTROLLED ACCESS TOLL
TOLL ROAD
PRIMARY DIVIDED
PRIMARY UNDIVIDED
SECONDARY DIVIDED
SECONDARY UNDIVIDED
LOCAL DIVIDED
LOCAL UNDIVIDED
UNPAVED ROAD
UNDER CONSTRUCTION
TUNNEL
PEDESTRIAN ONLY
AUTO FERRY
PASSENGER FERRY
SCENIC BYWAY
DISTANCE BETWEEN MARKERS
EXIT NUMBER-FREE/TOLL
INTERCHANGE FULL/PARTIAL
WELCOME/INFORMATION CENTER
REST AREA/ SERVICE CENTER

BOUNDARIES

INTERNATIONAL
STATE
COUNTY
TIME ZONE
CONTINENTAL DIVIDE

ROAD SHIELDS

INTERSTATE/BUSINESS
U.S./STATE/COUNTY
FOREST/INDIAN
TRANS- CANADA
PROVINCIAL AUTOROUTE/ KING'S HIGHWAY
MEXICO
HISTORIC ROUTE 66
REFERENCE PAGE INDICATOR

AREAS OF INTEREST

INDIAN
MILITARY
PARK
FOREST
GRASSLANDS
HISTORIC
INT'L/REGIONAL AIRPORT
INCORPORATED CITY

POINTS OF INTEREST

TOWN
NATIONAL CAPITAL
STATE/PROVINCIAL CAPITAL
AAA/CAA CLUB LOCATION
FEATURE OF INTEREST
COLLEGE/UNIVERSITY
CAMPGROUND INFORMATION PROVIDED BY WOODALL'S®
CUSTOMS STATION
HISTORIC
LIGHTHOUSE
MONUMENT/MEMORIAL
STATE/PROVINCIAL PARK
NATIONAL WILDLIFE REFUGE
SKI AREA
SPORTS COMPLEX
DAM

CITIES/TOWNS are color-coded by size, showing where to find AAA Approved and Diamond rated lodgings or restaurants listed in the AAA TourBook guides and on AAA.com:

- **Red** - major destinations and capitals; many listings
- **Black** - destinations; some listings
- **Grey** - no listings

ER020-16

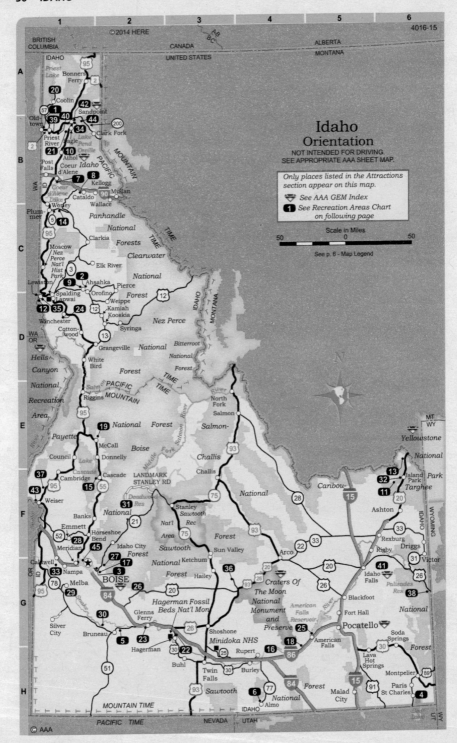

Idaho
Orientation
NOT INTENDED FOR DRIVING.
SEE APPROPRIATE AAA SHEET MAP.

*Only places listed in the Attractions
section appear on this map.*

See AAA GEM Index

See Recreation Areas Chart
on following page

Scale in Miles
50   0   50

See p. 6 - Map Legend

©2014 HERE

4016-15

BRITISH
COLUMBIA
IDAHO
CANADA
UNITED STATES
ALBERTA
MONTANA

Priest Lake
Bonners Ferry
Coolin
Sandpoint
Oldtown
Priest River
Clark Fork
Eagle
Athol
Post Falls
Coeur d'Alene
Idaho
Kellogg
Mullan
Cataldo
Wallace
Worley
Plummer
Panhandle National Forests
Clarkia
Moscow
Nez Perce Nat'l Hist Park
Elk River
Clearwater
Lewiston
Ahsahka
Pierce
Spalding
Orofino
National
Lapwai
Weippe
Kamiah
Winchester
Kooskia
Syringa
Forest
Cottonwood
Nez Perce
Grangeville
Bitterroot National Forest
White Bird
Hells Canyon National Recreation Area
Riggins
North Fork
Salmon
National Forest
Payette
McCall
Boise
Salmon-
Council
Donnelly
Challis
Cambridge
Cascade
LANDMARK STANLEY RD
Challis
Weiser
National
Emmett
Banks
Stanley
Sawtooth Rec
Caribou-
Ashton
Horseshoe Bend
National
Nat'l Area
Rexburg
Meridian
Idaho City
Forest
Sun Valley
Arco
Risby
Caldwell
Nampa
Ketchum
Driggs
Melba
BOISE
Hailey
Idaho Falls
Victor
Silver City
Hagerman Fossil Beds Nat'l Mon
Glenns Ferry
Sawtooth
Blackfoot
Bruneau
Shoshone
Craters Of The Moon National Monument and Preserve
Fort Hall
Hagerman
Minidoka NHS
Rupert
American Falls
Pocatello
Soda Springs
Buhl
Twin Falls
Burley
Lava Hot Springs
Montpelier
MOUNTAIN TIME
Sawtooth
National
Almo
Malad City
Paris
St Charles
PACIFIC TIME
NEVADA
UTAH
IDAHO

© AAA

Recreation Areas Chart

The map location numerals in column 2 show an area's location on the preceding map.

	MAP LOCATION	CAMPING	PICNICKING	HIKING TRAILS	BOATING	BOAT RAMP	BOAT RENTAL	FISHING	SWIMMING	PETS ON LEASH	BICYCLE TRAILS	WINTER SPORTS	VISITOR CENTER	LODGE/CABINS	FOOD SERVICE
NATIONAL FORESTS *(See place listings.)*															
Boise **(E-2)** 2,612,000 acres. South-central Idaho.		•	•	•	•	•		•	•	•	•	•		•	
Caribou-Targhee **(F-5)** 3,000,000 acres. Southeastern Idaho.		•	•	•	•	•	•	•	•	•	•	•		•	
Clearwater **(C-2)** 1.8 million acres. Northeastern Idaho.		•	•	•	•	•		•	•	•	•			•	•
Idaho Panhandle **(B-1)** 2,495,517 acres. Northern Idaho.		•	•	•	•	•		•	•	•	•	•		•	
Nez Perce **(D-2)** 2,223,594 acres. North-central Idaho.		•	•	•	•	•		•	•	•	•			•	
Payette **(E-1)** 2,307,897 acres. West-central Idaho.		•	•	•	•	•	•	•	•	•	•	•		•	
Salmon-Challis **(E-3)** 4,300,000 acres. East-central Idaho.		•	•	•	•	•		•	•	•	•	•		•	
Sawtooth **(F-3)** 2,101,422 acres. South-central Idaho. Horse rental.		•	•	•	•	•		•	•	•	•	•		•	•
NATIONAL RECREATION AREAS *(See place listings.)*															
Hells Canyon **(D-1)** 652,977 acres in northeastern Oregon and western Idaho. Horse rental.		•	•	•	•	•		•		•		•	•		•
Sawtooth **(F-3)** 756,000 acres in south-central Idaho.		•	•	•	•	•	•	•	•	•	•	•		•	•
ARMY CORPS OF ENGINEERS															
Albeni Cove **(A-1)** 20 acres 1 mi. e. of Oldtown on a county road. Water skiing.	**1**	•	•	•	•	•		•	•	•					
Dworshak Reservoir **(C-1)** 19,823 acres 7 mi. n. of Orofino. Bird-watching, water skiing.	**2**	•	•	•	•	•	•	•	•	•			•		
Lucky Peak Lake **(G-2)** 237 acres 9 mi. s.e. of Boise on SR 21. Water skiing.	**3**	•	•	•	•	•		•	•	•					
STATE															
Bear Lake **(H-6)** 966 acres just e. of St. Charles on E. Shore Rd. Snowmobiling, water skiing. *(See St. Charles p. 95.)*	**4**	•	•	•	•	•		•	•			•	•	•	•
Bruneau Dunes **(G-2)** 4,800 acres 5 mi. n. of Bruneau on SR 51/78, then 2 mi. e. on SR 78. Equestrian trails, sand dunes. No motorized boats. *(See Bruneau p. 51.)*	**5**	•	•	•	•	•		•	•	•			•		
Castle Rocks **(H-4)** 1,440 acres 2 mi. n. of Almo on Elba-Almo Rd., then 1.4 mi. w. on 2800 S. (Big Cove Ranch Rd.). Bird-watching, horseback riding, rock climbing, snowshoeing.	**6**	•	•	•					•	•		•	•	•	
Coeur d'Alene Parkway **(B-1)** 34 acres e. of Coeur d'Alene off I-90 exit 15 on Coeur d'Alene Lake Dr.	**7**		•	•				•		•	•				
Coeur d'Alene's Old Mission **(B-1)** 18 acres 11 mi. w. off I-90 exit 39. Historic. *(See Cataldo p. 54.)*	**8**		•	•				•		•			•		
Dworshak **(C-1)** 850 acres 26 mi. n.w. of Orofino.	**9**	•	•	•	•	•		•	•	•			•	•	
Farragut **(B-1)** 4,000 acres 4.9 mi. e. of Athol on SR 54. Historic. Cross-country skiing, snowmobiling. Museum. *(See Athol p. 34.)*	**10**	•	•	•	•	•		•	•	•	•	•	•		
Harriman **(F-6)** 11,000 acres 9 mi. s. of Island Park via US 20 at 3489 Green Canyon Rd. Bird-watching, boating (no motors), cross-country skiing, mountain biking, snowshoeing; horse rental, wildlife viewing. *(See Island Park p. 71.)*	**11**		•	•	•			•		•	•	•	•	•	
Hells Gate **(D-1)** 360 acres 4 mi. s. of Lewiston off Snake River Ave. Water skiing. Interpretive centers. *(See Lewiston p. 77.)*	**12**	•	•	•	•	•		•	•	•	•		•		
Henrys Lake **(F-6)** 586 acres 15 mi. w. of West Yellowstone off US 20. Bird-watching, canoeing, kayaking, water skiing.	**13**	•	•	•	•	•		•		•					
Heyburn **(C-1)** 7,825 acres 5 mi. e. of Plummer on SR 5. Canoeing, cross-country skiing, horseback riding, ice fishing, water skiing. *(See Plummer p. 89.)*	**14**	•	•	•	•	•	•	•	•	•	•	•	•	•	•
Lake Cascade **(F-1)** 4,450 acres just n.w. of Cascade. Bird-watching, cross-country skiing, ice fishing, snowmobiling; horse-shoe pits. *(See Cascade p. 54.)*	**15**	•	•	•	•	•		•	•	•		•			
Lake Walcott **(H-4)** 65 acres 11 mi. n.e. of Rupert off SR 24. *(See Rupert p. 95.)*	**16**	•	•	•	•	•		•	•	•			•		
Lucky Peak **(G-2)** 240 acres 10 mi. s.e. of Boise off SR 21. Marina; boat moorage.	**17**		•	•	•	•		•	•	•			•		
Massacre Rocks **(G-4)** 990 acres 10 mi. s.w. of American Falls off I-86. Historic. Canoeing, disc golf, kayaking. *(See American Falls p. 33.)*	**18**	•	•	•	•	•		•		•	•		•	•	

Recreation Areas Chart

The map location numerals in column 2 show an area's location on the preceding map.

	MAP LOCATION	CAMPING	PICNICKING	HIKING TRAILS	BOATING	BOAT RAMP	BOAT RENTAL	FISHING	SWIMMING	PETS ON LEASH	BICYCLE TRAILS	WINTER SPORTS	VISITOR CENTER	LODGE/CABINS	FOOD SERVICE
Ponderosa (E-2) 1,470 acres 2 mi. n.e. of McCall via Park St. and Thompson Ave. at 1920 N. Davis Ave. Canoeing, cross-country skiing, snowshoeing. *(See McCall p. 79.)*	19	•	•	•	•	•	•	•	•	•	•	•	•	•	
Priest Lake (A-1) 463 acres 11 mi. n. of Coolin. Cross-country skiing, ice fishing, snowmobiling.	20	•	•	•	•	•	•	•	•	•		•		•	•
Round Lake (B-1) 142 acres 10 mi. s. of Sandpoint off US 95 on Dufort Rd. Cross-country skiing, ice fishing, ice-skating, sledding, snowshoeing. No motorized boats.	21	•	•	•	•			•	•	•		•			
Thousand Springs (H-3) 1,500 acres .2 mi. s. off I-84 exit 147, then .2 mi. w. following signs to the welcome kiosk at Malad Gorge. Canoeing, kayaking, horseback riding. *(See Hagerman p. 64.)*	22		•	•				•		•	•		•		
Three Island Crossing (G-2) 513 acres 1 mi. w. of Glenns Ferry via S. Commercial St. and W. Madison Ave. Historic. *(See Glenns Ferry p. 63.)*	23	•	•	•				•		•		•	•	•	
Winchester Lake (D-1) 318 acres .25 mi. s. of Winchester on US 95 Bus. Rte. Cross-country skiing, ice fishing, ice-skating, sledding. No motorized boats (except with electric motors).	24	•	•	•	•	•	•	•		•		•	•	•	
OTHER															
American Falls Reservoir (G-4) 59,893 acres .2 mi. n. of American Falls on I-15. Historic.	25	•	•		•	•		•	•	•			•		•
Anderson Ranch Reservoir (G-2) 5,000 acres 30 mi. n.e. of Mountain Home on SR 20 and FR 61.	26	•	•		•	•		•	•	•		•		•	•
Arrowrock Reservoir (F-2) 4,000 acres 16 mi. e. of Boise on SR 21 and FR 268.	27	•	•		•	•		•	•	•					
Black Canyon Reservoir (F-1) 2,364 acres 8 mi. n.e. of Emmett on SR 52.	28	•	•		•	•		•	•	•					
Celebration Park (G-1) 84 acres 8.1 mi. s. of Melba at 6530 Hot Spot Ln. Historic. Scenic. Bird-watching, horseback riding; interpretive programs. *(See Melba p. 80.)*	29	•	•	•		•		•		•	•		•		
C.J. Strike Reservoir (G-2) 7,500 acres n.w. of Bruneau via SR 78. *(See Bruneau p. 51.)*	30	•	•		•	•		•	•	•					
Deadwood Reservoir (F-2) 3,000 acres 34 mi. n.e. of Garden Valley on FR 555.	31	•	•		•	•		•	•	•					
Island Park Reservoir (F-6) 7,800 acres 27 mi. n. of Ashton off US 20. Snowmobiling.	32	•	•		•	•	•	•		•				•	•
Lake Lowell (G-1) 10,587 acres 8 mi. s. of Caldwell via 10th Ave. or SR 55. Bird-watching; water skiing.	33	•	•		•	•		•	•	•					
Lake Pend Oreille (B-1) 94,600 acres s. and e. of Sandpoint. *(See Sandpoint p. 97.)*	34	•	•		•	•	•	•	•	•				•	•
Lake Waha (D-1) 100 acres 18 mi. s.e. of Lewiston on Thain Rd.	35		•	•	•			•	•	•					
Little Wood River Reservoir (G-3) 976 acres 11 mi. n. of Carey on access road.	36	•	•		•	•		•	•	•					
Mann Creek Reservoir (F-1) 4 acres 9 mi. n. of Weiser on US 95. Water skiing.	37	•	•		•	•		•	•	•					
Palisades Reservoir (G-6) 27,845 acres 50 mi. s.e. of Idaho Falls on US 26.	38	•	•		•	•		•	•	•			•		
Priest River (B-1) 20 acres .5 mi. e. of Priest River off US 2. Bird-watching, water skiing.	39	•	•	•	•	•		•	•	•					
Riley Creek (B-1) 45 acres 1 mi. s. of US 2 at Laclede on Riley Creek Rd. Water skiing.	40	•	•	•	•	•		•	•	•					
Ririe Reservoir (G-6) 6,069 acres 20 mi. n.e. of Idaho Falls on US 26.	41	•	•		•	•		•	•	•		•			
Springy Point (A-1) 13 acres 3.2 mi. w. of US 95 at Sandpoint on Lakeshore Dr. Water skiing.	42	•	•	•	•	•		•	•	•	•				
Steck Park (F-1) 20 mi. n.w. of Weiser via SR 70 on the Snake River.	43	•	•		•	•	•	•		•	•				
Trestle Creek (B-1) 2 acres n.w. of Hope on SR 200. Water skiing.	44		•		•	•		•	•	•					
Veterans Memorial (F-1) 80 acres on SR 44 at 36th St. in Boise. Bird-watching. Playground. No motorized boats.	45		•	•	•			•	•	•	•	•			

AHSAHKA (C-1) elev. 1,001'

CLEARWATER FISH HATCHERY is at 118 Hatchery Roe Dr. Interpretive panels throughout the complex describe the life cycles of steelhead, or rainbow trout, and chinook salmon, both of which are raised at the hatchery. A 1.8-mile pipeline delivers a constant flow of cool, clear water from Dworshak Dam to the facility. Smolts are released from mid-March through late April. Visitors can see adult chinook at the hatchery from mid-July to mid-September. A pond contains large rainbow trout.

Time: Allow 30 minutes minimum. **Hours:** Daily 7:30-4. Visitor center closed holidays; no fish in raceways the last 2 weeks in April. **Cost:** Free. **Phone:** (208) 476-3331. ⌦

DWORSHAK DAM VISITOR CENTER 1842 Viewpoint Rd., is 3 mi. e. on SR 7, following signs, on the North Fork of the Clearwater River. The visitor center overlooks the 717-foot dam, one of the highest straight-axis concrete gravity dams in North America. Behind the dam, Dworshak Reservoir *(see Recreation Areas Chart)* extends 54 miles into wild, rugged timberland.

Interpretive displays are available. Audiovisual presentations are shown in the theater upon request. **Hours:** Visitor center daily 8:30-4:30, Memorial Day weekend-Labor Day; Mon.-Fri. 8:30-4:30, rest of year. Ninety-minute guided tours are available daily at 9, 11:30 and 2:30, Memorial Day weekend-Labor Day. Closed winter holidays and Christmas-Jan. 1. Phone ahead to confirm schedule. **Cost:** Free. **Phone:** (208) 476-1255. ⌦

DWORSHAK NATIONAL FISH HATCHERY, s.e. on SR 7 at the confluence of the North Fork and Main Stem Clearwater rivers, just below Dworshak Dam. About 2.1 million steelhead trout, 1.5 million Chinook salmon and 400,000 coho salmon are raised in environmentally controlled ponds. The best time to see the adult steelhead is November through April; the returning salmon brood stock July through October.

Displays, a viewing balcony above the spawning room and 126 outdoor ponds are on-site. A self-guiding tour is available. **Time:** Allow 30 minutes minimum. **Hours:** Grounds daily dawn-dusk. Main building daily 7:30-4; hatchery building closed major holidays. **Cost:** Free. **Phone:** (208) 476-4591.

HIGH COUNTRY INN OROFINO/AHSAHKA

(208)476-7570

▼▼▼
Bed & Breakfast
$99-$450

Address: 70 High Country Ln 83520 **Location:** 0.5 mi w to Dworshak Visitors Center Rd, 2 mi n, then 1 mi w, follow signs. **Facility:** Located above a river valley midst ponderosa pines, this charming and inviting inn boasts sweeping views, is close to the Dworshak Reservoir recreation area and offers a nice selection of rooms and cabins. 6 units, some cabins. 1-2 stories (no elevator), interior/exterior corridors. **Terms:** 7 day cancellation notice, resort fee. **Activities:** hot tub, picnic facilities. **Guest Services:** coin laundry. **Featured Amenity:** full hot breakfast.

SAVE 🛜 ⌧ 𝐖 🚭 ▤ / SOME UNITS 🆘 🔋

ALMO (H-4) elev. 5,390'

CITY OF ROCKS NATIONAL RESERVE is .25 mi. s. on Almo-Elba Rd. and 1 mi. w. on City Rocks Rd., on unpaved roads. Within the 14,407-acre reserve are massive granite rocks, some 2.5 billion years old, eroded into shapes resembling the ruins of an ancient city. Inscriptions written in axle grease and scratched into the rocks by pioneers traversing the Oregon and California trails afford insights into emigrant trail history. Rock climbing, sightseeing and hiking through high deserts are possible.

Hours: Visitor center daily 8-4:30, mid-Apr. to mid-Oct.; Tues.-Sat. 8-4:30, rest of year. Closed major holidays. **Cost:** Day use free. Campsite fee $12. Only eight people and two tents per site are permitted. **Phone:** (208) 824-5901. ⛺ ⌦

AMERICAN FALLS (G-5) pop. 4,457, elev. 4,330'

The "Idaho Gem Community" of American Falls, an early campsite on the old Oregon Trail, is the center of irrigation projects that enable the cultivation of thousands of acres of farmland. The American Falls Reservoir *(see Recreation Areas Chart)*, the largest on the Snake River, provides excellent opportunities for boating, sailing, water skiing and rainbow trout fishing.

MASSACRE ROCKS STATE PARK is off I-86 exit 28 at 3592 N. Park Ln. Once a popular stop along the Oregon Trail, this area along the Snake River is rich in pioneer and geological history. Travelers called the rocky gorge "Devil's Gate" and "Gate of Death" as it seemed a likely spot for an ambush. Inscriptions made by Oregon Trail emigrants can be seen at Register Rock, 2 miles west of I-86 exit 28.

The 1,000-acre state park offers six hiking trails. One leads beneath the freeway to Oregon Trail ruts. Guided interpretive programs are offered summer weekends. Canoe and kayak rentals are available, and two disc golf courses are on-site.

The large boulders scattered about the area were deposited by the Bonneville Flood, a months-long deluge that occurred 14,500 years ago that drained much of ancient Lake Bonneville, the predecessor of Great Salt Lake. *See Recreation Areas Chart.* **Time:** Allow 1 hour minimum. **Hours:** Daily dawn-dusk. **Cost:** $5 (per private vehicle). **Phone:** (208) 548-2672. ⛺ ⌧ 🏕 ⌦

ARCO (G-4) pop. 995, elev. 5,320'

EXPERIMENTAL BREEDER REACTOR #1 is 20 mi. e. on US 20 at the Idaho National Laboratory. On Dec. 20, 1951, the reactor became the first nuclear reactor to generate a usable amount of electricity. Exhibits document the facility's history, and free 45- to 60-minute guided tours are conducted as needed by trained guides. Self-guiding tour pamphlets describing the nuclear reactors, a reactor control room and detection devices are available.

Time: Allow 1 hour minimum. **Hours:** Daily 9-5, Memorial Day weekend-Labor Day. Last tour begins 1 hour before closing. **Cost:** Free. **Phone:** (208) 526-2029 or (208) 526-0050.

ASHTON (F-6) pop. 1,127, elev. 5,259'

Located in the northeast corner of the Snake River Plain, Ashton was established in 1906 by the Oregon Short Line Railroad. The district is today the world's largest producer of seed potatoes and also grows wheat, barley, hay, peas and canola. Off to the southeast, the ragged profile of the Teton Range is visible on the horizon.

MESA FALLS RECREATION AREA is 15 mi. n.e. via SR 47 and Mesa Falls Scenic Byway. Henry's Fork of the Snake River carved a canyon here in tuff and basalt rock forming two scenic waterfalls. Upper Mesa Falls plunges 114 feet over a 200-foot-wide precipice. An interpretive boardwalk loops down for close-up views of the falls and canyon. Big Falls Inn, a 1916 roadhouse, serves as a visitor center that offers exhibits about plants and animals, the geology of the falls and the inn's history. Trails cut through the area, including one departing from a roadside pullout .8 miles south that leads to 65-foot Lower Mesa Falls and a 2-mile nature trail starting at the visitor center parking lot.

Time: Allow 1 hour minimum. **Hours:** Recreation area daily 24 hours. Visitor center daily 9:30-5:30, Memorial Day to mid-Sept.; Sat.-Sun. 10-3, early Jan. to mid-Mar. Scenic byway typically closed to traffic late Oct.-Apr. 30. **Cost:** $5 (per private vehicle); $1 (per motorcycle). **Phone:** (208) 558-4207.

ATHOL (B-1) pop. 692, elev. 2,391'

In a region rich with timber, Athol developed around a sawmill established at the turn of the 20th century. The town is in a popular summer recreation area centered on Lake Pend Oreille *(see Sandpoint p. 97).*

FARRAGUT STATE PARK is 4.9 mi. e. on SR 54. On the site of a former U.S. Navy training center built in 1942, the 4,000-acre park borders Lake Pend Oreille and is a popular boating, fishing and recreation area. Features include an extensive hiking and biking trail system, groomed trails for cross-country skiing and a visitor center with exhibits. Wildlife includes deer, bear, elk, mountain goats and a diverse bird population. *See Recreation Areas Chart.*

Time: Allow 1 hour minimum. **Hours:** Park open daily dawn-dusk. Visitor center open daily 8 a.m.-9 p.m. Phone ahead to confirm schedule. **Cost:** Park $5 (per private vehicle). Camping $20-$38.60. **Phone:** (208) 683-2425.

Museum at the Brig is at 13550 E. SR 54 in Farragut State Park. Exhibits housed in the former brig of Farragut Naval Training Station chronicle events of World War II and activities at the naval station during the period. Topics include boot camp, bunk quarters, health care and German prisoners of war. Displays feature memorabilia donated by military personnel. **Time:** Allow 30 minutes minimum. **Hours:** Daily 10-5, Memorial Day-Labor Day. **Cost:** Free with Farragut State Park admission of $5 (per private vehicle). **Phone:** (208) 683-2425.

SILVERWOOD 3 mi. s. of Athol on US 95. One of the Northwest's largest theme parks, Silverwood covers 221 acres and offers more than 70 rides, slides, shows and attractions. Aftershock is a 191-foot-tall steel roller coaster that travels forward and backward through a cobra loop at speeds exceeding 65 mph. SpinCycle is a 104-foot-tall thrill ride that swings upside down like a giant pendulum with riders strapped into a cylinder on the other end that spins 360 degrees.

Other rides include two wooden coasters: the 55-mph Timber Terror and Tremors, which reaches speeds of 63 mph during a 103-foot drop; the 140-foot-tall Panic Plunge drop tower; the Thunder Canyon white-water ride and a 1915 steam-powered train. Garfield's Summer Camp has 10 family-friendly rides for kids. The park also has dozens of traditional amusement rides. Entertainment includes a magic show, a staged train robbery, and appearances by Garfield and Odie.

Time: Allow 6 hours minimum. **Hours:** Open daily, late May-Labor Day; Sat.-Sun., early-late May and day after Labor Day-late Sept. Hours vary for special events; phone ahead. **Cost:** One-day pass $46.99; $23.99 (ages 3-7 and 65+). One-day pass after 5 p.m. $23.99. Two-day pass $74.99; $36.99 (ages 3-7 and 65+). All passes include Boulder Beach Water Park when open. **Parking:** $5. **Phone:** (208) 683-3400.

Boulder Beach Water Park 2 mi. s. on US 95 at Silverwood to 27843 N. US 95. Rides include two gigantic wave pools, four tube slides, three high-velocity body slides, two family raft rides, a lazy river and two play areas for children. **Time:** Allow 4 hours minimum. **Hours:** Opens daily at 11, early June-Labor Day. Closing times vary; phone ahead. **Cost:** (includes Silverwood) $46.99; $23.99 (ages 3-7 and 65+). Discounted admission is offered after 5 p.m. **Parking:** $5. **Phone:** (208) 683-3400.

LOG SPIRIT BED & BREAKFAST   208/683-4722

Bed & Breakfast
$140-$200

Address: 31328 N Tiara Ln 83801 **Location:** US 95, just e on SR 54 to Howard Rd, 1.8 mi n, then 0.5 mi e. **Facility:** The grounds of this log B&B offers a small bridge with a waterfall, gardens, and small farm animals. Rooms and bathrooms are large with wood floors and luxurious bedding. 6 units. 2 stories (no elevator), interior corridors. **Parking:** winter plug-ins. **Terms:** 2 night minimum stay - weekends, 14 day cancellation notice-fee imposed. **Activities:** trails. **Guest Services:** coin laundry. **Featured Amenity:** full hot breakfast.

BANKS (F-1) pop. 17, elev. 2,840'

At the confluence of the North and South forks of the Payette River, Banks is popular with kayakers and white-water rafters and lies along the 112-mile Payette River Scenic Byway (SR 55), which connects Boise, at the southern terminus, with New Meadows, to the north.

RECREATIONAL ACTIVITIES
White-water Rafting
• **Bear Valley Rafting Co.** meets downstairs from the Banks Store and Cafe on SR 55 for transportation to departure points. **Hours:** Daily 9-6, May-Sept. **Phone:** (208) 793-2272 or (800) 235-2327.

BITTERROOT NATIONAL FOREST—See Montana p. 140

BLACKFOOT (G-5) pop. 11,899, elev. 4,497'

At the northern end of the Snake River Valley, land is key. In the 19th century the fertile lava soil helped establish Blackfoot as an important agricultural center, with the russet potato eventually becoming the town's main crop. Visit the Idaho Potato Museum *(see attraction listing)* to learn why Blackfoot is known as the "Potato Capital of the World," then head next door to Depot Park for a self-guiding walking tour past antique potato harvesting devices. Remnants of the past also are exhibited at Veterans Park, which features army tanks and other military equipment.

Stemming from Blackfoot's agricultural roots, the Eastern Idaho State Fair attracts tens of thousands of revelers with livestock shows as well as mouthwatering foodstuffs—from Indian tacos to (what else?) loaded baked potatoes. The weeklong end-of-summer party takes place around Labor Day. Watch a bull riding competition or marvel over fine equestrian specimens; browse antiques and charming quilt displays; or sniff out the best recipes for such tasty bites as hash browns, brownies and peanut butter cookies.

Although residents have been tapping Blackfoot's natural resources since the late 1880s, the area still boasts striking, untouched terrain. You'll discover year-round recreational opportunities in and around town. In warm weather, you can hike, fish or get drenched white-water rafting at Wolverine Canyon, about 19 miles northeast. When temperatures drop there are still plenty of outdoor activities to enjoy, including cross-country skiing and snowmobiling.

Wildlife viewing is popular throughout the region. Blackfoot River Canyon—home to golden eagles, prairie falcons, red-tailed hawks and great horned owls—is especially breathtaking. In summer swimmers and boaters crowd 55-acre Jensen Lake at Jensen Grove; nearby you'll find such man-made recreational features as a skate park and a 2-mile paved walking path. Abutting Jensen Lake's northern bank at 3115 Teeples Dr. is the 18-hole Blackfoot Golf Course; phone (208) 785-9960.

Greater Blackfoot Area Chamber of Commerce: 130 N.W. Main St., P.O. Box 801, Blackfoot, ID 83221. **Phone:** (208) 785-0510.

BINGHAM COUNTY HISTORICAL MUSEUM, 190 N. Shilling Ave., is in a renovated 1905 Southern mansion built of lava rock and lumber. The museum displays period furnishings, clothing, photographs, dolls and other historical items. **Time:** Allow 30 minutes minimum. **Hours:** Wed.-Fri. noon-5, late May-Aug. **Cost:** $2. **Phone:** (208) 785-9906.

 IDAHO POTATO MUSEUM, 130 N.W. Main St., presents a variety of exhibits related to the potato, including antique machinery and tools, gunnysack clothing and, at 24 by 14 inches, the "Guinness World Records" world's largest potato crisp. Each visitor is offered a free potato product. Videos about the potato industry and production processes are shown. Phone for special tour arrangements. **Time:** Allow 1 hour minimum. **Hours:** Mon.-Sat. 9:30-5, Apr.-Sept.; Mon.-Fri. 9:30-3, rest of year. Closed Thanksgiving and Dec. 24-Jan. 2. **Cost:** $3; $2.50 (military with ID and senior citizens); $1 (ages 6-12). **Phone:** (208) 785-2517.

BEST WESTERN BLACKFOOT INN   (208)785-4144

Hotel
$72-$93

AAA Benefit: Save 10% or more every day and earn 10% bonus points!

Address: 750 Jensen Grove Dr 83221 **Location:** I-15 exit 93, 0.3 mi e to Parkway Dr, then 0.4 mi n. **Facility:** 60 units. 2 stories (no elevator), interior corridors. **Parking:** winter plug-ins. **Pool(s):** heated indoor. **Activities:** hot tub. **Guest Services:** coin laundry.

SUPER 8   (208)785-9333

Hotel $51-$79 **Address:** 1279 Parkway Dr 83221 **Location:** I-15 exit 93, just se, then just w. **Facility:** 61 units. 2 stories (no elevator), interior corridors. **Guest Services:** coin laundry.

WHERE TO EAT

TOMMY VAUGHN'S GRILL   208/785-6400

American. Casual Dining. $7-$20 **AAA Inspector Notes:** Wood-framed flat-screen TVs adorn the walls throughout this comfortable eatery. Menu items include a tasty steak salad, a popular appetizer sampler, burgers, a few pasta selections, grilled shrimp skewers and beer-battered fish and chips. Do not hesitate to share a piece of red velvet cake. Gluten-free items are available. **Features:** full bar, patio dining, early bird specials, senior menu, happy hour. **Address:** 850 Jensen Grove Dr 83221 **Location:** I-15 exit 93, 0.3 mi e to Parkway Dr, then 0.7 mi ne. L D

AAA Vacations® packages ...

exciting itineraries

and exclusive values

BOISE (G-1) pop. 205,671, elev. 2,739'
• Hotels p. 43 • Restaurants p. 46
• Hotels & Restaurants map & index p. 40

The woods lining the Boise River were a welcome sight for French-Canadian trappers who were grateful to reach a forest again after trudging across the territory's semiarid plain. As a result, they named the area *Boisé*, meaning "wooded." The city, however, was not founded until 1863, a year after the gold rush reached the Boise Basin.

"The City of Trees," Boise is Idaho's capital and largest metropolitan area. The first sessions of the territorial government were held during 1863 in Lewiston, then moved to this population center the following year. The new territorial capital was the center of commerce and culture for miners and traders from nearby mountain boomtowns. Built in 1863, the O'Farrell Cabin on Fort Street is one of the city's oldest buildings.

The quality of life, low cost of living and liberal tax advantages as well as the city's role as state capital and transportation hub, account for Boise's steady economic growth. Many national and multinational firms have their headquarters in Boise, and light industry flourishes. The city also is the home of Boise State University *(see attraction listing)*, where the Broncos play football on the blue field of Albertsons Stadium from early September to early December; the 🏈 Famous Idaho Potato Bowl takes place at the stadium after football season ends. In addition, the Boise Philharmonic plays in the university's Velma V. Morrison Center for the Performing Arts. Entertaining audiences since 1998, the 🎷 Gene Harris Jazz Festival takes place at the college in April.

Boise is the southwest terminus of SR 21, the Ponderosa Pine Scenic Route. The route passes through part of Sawtooth National Forest before ending in Stanley; depending on weather conditions, portions of SR 21 may be closed in winter.

Protected from unduly harsh winter weather by the Owyhee Mountains, the capital enjoys year-round opportunities for leisure and recreation. Ann Morrison Park, 153 acres between Americana and Capital boulevards, offers picnicking, playgrounds, ball fields and tennis courts as well as the 🎈 Spirit of Boise Balloon Classic, held in August.

A novel way to reach Ann Morrison Park is by floating down the Boise River on a rental raft or inner tube from Barber Park, which is on the southeast edge of town; at the junction of Warm Springs Avenue and SR 21 turn onto Eckert to reach the park. Rentals are available daily mid-June through Labor Day, river flows permitting; a return shuttle bus is available. Phone (208) 577-4584.

Kathryn Albertson Park is a 41-acre downtown wildlife sanctuary across Americana Boulevard from Ann Morrison Park. Paved footpaths meander past gazebos, ponds and fountains while offering glimpses of waterfowl and other wildlife. The park

also provides nearby access to the Boise Greenbelt, a 25-mile path following the Boise River. A favorite place to walk, jog, skate or ride a bicycle, the greenbelt connects 12 area parks.

The Idaho Shakespeare Festival presents five plays in repertory from the last weekend in May through September at an outdoor amphitheater at 5657 Warm Springs Ave.; phone (208) 336-9221.

Once used as a Native American lookout, Table Rock rises 1,100 feet above the valley east of Boise. Its flat summit, surmounted by an illuminated cross that can be seen for miles, affords a view of the city and a pioneer route south of the river.

In the 1921 St. Paul Baptist Church building at 508 Julia Davis Dr. in Julia Davis Park, the Idaho Black History Museum presents changing educational exhibits about the history and culture of African-Americans in Idaho; phone (208) 433-0017.

To the southeast, 12 miles south of Kuna, the Morley Nelson Snake River Birds of Prey National Conservation Area provides a 600,000-acre haven for two dozen species of raptors. The area represents one of the world's densest concentrations of birds of prey; phone (208) 384-3300.

Boise Convention & Visitors Bureau: 250 S. Fifth St., Suite 300, Boise, ID 83702. **Phone:** (208) 344-7777 or (800) 635-5240.

Self-guiding tours: A map showcasing downtown Boise's public art displays and historical points of interest is available from information kiosks at 8th and Idaho streets, 8th and Broad streets and the city hall front entrance.

Shopping: Boise Factory Outlets, I-84 exit Gowen Road, offers such factory stores as Eddie Bauer, Levi's Outlet and Reebok. Boise Towne Square Mall, Milwaukee and Franklin streets, features Dillard's, JCPenney, Macy's and Sears. Downtown shopping includes BoDo (short for Boise Downtown), a former late-1890s warehouse district at 8th and Front streets; Hyde Park on N. 13th Street; and Old Boise Historic District on Main Street between Capitol and 4th streets. The 85 vendors comprising the gift shop at the State Capitol *(see attraction listing)* specialize in items made in Idaho, including jewelry that uses semi-precious stones from the state.

BASQUE MUSEUM AND CULTURAL CENTER, 611 Grove St., on the Basque block, celebrates the legacy of the Basques and is the only museum in the country dedicated to the ethnic group. Permanent and temporary exhibits focus on the history and culture of these modern people with ancient roots. Basque traditions are further depicted through a cultural center and a restored Basque boarding house. **Time:** Allow 30 minutes minimum. **Hours:** Tues.-Fri. 10-4, Sat. 11-3. Closed major holidays. **Cost:** $5; $4 (ages 65+ and students with ID); $3 (ages 6-12). **Phone:** (208) 343-2671.

(See map & index p. 40.)

BOISE STATE UNIVERSITY, 1910 University Dr. along the Boise River, is the state's largest institution of higher learning, with more than 200 fields of study in seven colleges. Established in 1932, the university has approximately 22,000 students enrolled in graduate and undergraduate programs.

Highlights of the campus include the Velma V. Morrison Center for the Performing Arts. Bronco Stadium is noted for its blue artificial turf. **Hours:** Public tours of the university are offered Mon.-Fri. at 10 and 1, during the academic year; at 10, in summer. **Cost:** Free. Reservations are recommended. **Phone:** (208) 426-1156.

BOISE TROLLEY TOURS departs from Joe's Crab Shack restaurant, 2288 N. Garden St., on the riverfront. The tour, aboard a replica open-air trolley car, includes a 75-minute historical narration covering downtown Boise, the State Capitol and other government buildings, Harrison Boulevard and Warm Springs-area mansions, Hyde Park and the Old Idaho Penitentiary State Historic Site. **Time:** Allow 1 hour minimum. **Hours:** Tours depart Mon.-Fri. at 11, Sat.-Sun. at 2, May-Sept. Halloween tours Fri.-Sat. at 8 in Oct. Holiday Lights tours nightly, early Dec.-late Dec. **Cost:** $20; $18 (ages 65+, military and students with ID); $10 (ages 3-12); $5 (ages 0-2). Reservations are recommended. **Phone:** (208) 433-0849.

(See map & index p. 40.)

DISCOVERY CENTER OF IDAHO, GEM SAVE 131 W. Myrtle St., is a hands-on museum with more than 160 exhibits relating to science, math and technology. Visitors can use the Whisper Dish exhibit to carry on a quiet conversation across the room; squeeze clay with 24,000 pounds of force at the Make a Rock exhibit; generate electricity using the Pedal Generator; and experiment with electric arcs at the Electric Flame exhibit.

Other displays designed to encourage interaction with natural science phenomena include Touch the Spring, Disappearing Glass Rods, Pedaling Legs and Air Brake. In-house featured exhibits rotate approximately every six months. **Time:** Allow 1 hour minimum. **Hours:** Mon.-Sat. 9:30-5, Sun. noon-5. Closed Jan. 1, Easter, Thanksgiving and Christmas. **Cost:** $10; $8 (ages 65+); $7 (ages 3-17); Members free. **Phone:** (208) 343-9895.

FIRST UNITED METHODIST CHURCH occupies a city block bordered by 11th, 12th, Franklin and Hay sts.; the entrance is on 11th St. Known as the Cathedral of the Rockies, the church dates from 1872. The present Gothic structure, the third building used by the congregation, contains impressive stained glass windows and hand-painted murals. **Hours:** Mon.-Fri. 9-4:30. **Cost:** Free. **Phone:** (208) 343-7511.

IDAHO ANNE FRANK HUMAN RIGHTS MEMORIAL, at 777 S. 8th St. in a park behind the Boise Public Library, is dedicated to the importance of human rights. The life of Frank, the well-known Holocaust victim whose published diary became the basis for several plays and films, is highlighted. Benches are scattered throughout the memorial, which includes a life-size bronze statue of Frank, a wall engraved with more than 60 quotes from humanitarian leaders, and informational placards.

The site's water features are intended to mimic the canals of Amsterdam, where Frank and her family lived in hiding for many years. Other natural elements such as stone and native plants also are incorporated into the design. **Time:** Allow 1 hour minimum. **Hours:** Daily dawn-dusk. **Cost:** Free. **Phone:** (208) 345-0304.

IDAHO BOTANICAL GARDEN, 2.5 mi. e. on SAVE Main St. and Warm Springs Ave., then n. on N. Penitentiary Rd., offers 14 specialty gardens on 33 acres of the former Idaho Penitentiary. The sandstone walls provide a historic backdrop for theme gardens, garden art and a labyrinth. The Lewis and Clark Native Plant Garden features a bronze likeness of Sacagawea and has examples of period plants catalogued by the explorers; it also offers views of Treasure Valley.

Time: Allow 1 hour minimum. **Hours:** Mon.-Thurs. 9-5, Fri.-Sun. 9-7, mid-Mar. to mid-Jun.; Mon.-Thurs. 9-5, Fri.-Sun. 9-8, mid-June to mid-Nov.

Cost: $7; $5 (ages 5-12 and 65+). **Phone:** (208) 343-8649.

THE IDAHO MILITARY HISTORY MUSEUM is at 4692 W. Harvard St. Weapons, photographs, artifacts, military guidons and small arms chronicle the participation of various Idaho military units in conflicts ranging from the Civil War to current events including items from the Philippine Insurrection, Operation Iraqi Freedom and Operation Enduring Freedom. Armored vehicles and aircraft are displayed outdoors. **Time:** Allow 1 hour minimum. **Hours:** Tues.-Sat. noon-4. Closed major holidays. **Cost:** Donations. **Phone:** (208) 272-4841.

IDAHO MUSEUM OF MINING & GEOLOGY (IMMG), 2455 Old Penitentiary Rd., documents the state's geologic history and mining heritage through models, dioramas, maps, a working seismography and microscope for examining samples. Rocks, minerals, fossils, photographs and historical artifacts are displayed in five themed exhibit areas. Topics discussed include mining districts of the Northwest, Ice Age floods and lakes, and the everyday uses of minerals. Professors and geologists lead field trips to such locations as the Bruneau Algal Reef and area mining districts. **Time:** Allow 45 minutes minimum. **Hours:** Wed.-Sun. noon-5, Apr.-Oct. **Cost:** Donations. Field trips $15. **Phone:** (208) 368-9876.

JULIA DAVIS PARK, with entrances on Capitol Blvd. or Third St. off Myrtle St., contains within its 89-acre expanse the Boise Art Museum; the Idaho Historical Museum; the Idaho Black History Museum; Zoo Boise; and the Discovery Center of Idaho, which offers hands-on exhibits *(see attraction listing this page)*. A lagoon, a rose garden, a playground, a tennis complex, the R.A. and Annette Bloch Cancer Survivor Plaza and a band shell are within the park; a portion of the Boise River Greenbelt runs through the park as well. **Hours:** Daily dawn-midnight; hours may be extended for events at Boise State University. **Cost:** Free. **Phone:** (208) 608-7600.

Boise Art Museum, 670 Julia Davis Dr. at the SAVE Julia Davis Park entrance, displays more than 15 changing art exhibitions annually. **Time:** Allow 1 hour minimum. **Hours:** Tues.-Sat. 10-5 (also first Thurs. of the month 5-8), Sun. noon-5. Closed Jan. 1, Easter, Thanksgiving and Christmas. **Cost:** $6; $4 (ages 62+); $3 (students in grades 1-12 and college students with ID); donations (first Thurs. of the month). **Phone:** (208) 345-8330.

Idaho Historical Museum, 610 Julia Davis Dr., provides an overview of the state's history. Displays include a 19th-century saloon as well as artifacts of early Idaho. **Note:** The museum is closed for renovations and is expected to reopen in 2017. A few exhibits may be available with limited hours at its temporary administrative office and store at 214 Broadway in Boise. **Time:** Allow 1 hour minimum. **Hours:** Tues.-Fri. 9-5, Sat.-Sun. 10-5, May-Sept.;

(See map & index p. 40.)

Tues.-Fri. 9-5, Sat. 10-5, rest of year. Closed Jan. 1, Thanksgiving and Christmas. Phone ahead to confirm schedule. **Cost:** $5; $4 (ages 60+); $3 (ages 6-12 and students with ID). **Phone:** (208) 334-2120.

Zoo Boise, .5 mi. s. off Capitol Blvd. in Julia Davis Park, has more than 300 animals from around the world, including Amur tigers, zebras, snow leopards, Magellanic penguins, lions, giraffes and red pandas. Small Animal Kingdom spotlights animals and plants indigenous to islands, deserts and rainforests. Conservation Action Stations feature seasonal activities including giraffe feeding, a sloth bear encounter, a zoo farm and a conservation cruise. **Hours:** Daily 9-5, May-Sept.; 10-5, rest of year. Closed Jan. 1, Thanksgiving and Christmas. **Cost:** May-Sept. $10; $8 (ages 62+); $7 (ages 3-11). Rest of year $7; $4.50 (ages 62+); $4.25 (ages 3-11). Prices may vary. **Phone:** (208) 608-7760. ⑪

MORRISON KNUDSEN NATURE CENTER is 2.5 mi. off I-84 exit 54 (Broadway Ave.); cross the Boise River, turn e. onto Park Blvd. then head .5 mi. e. to 600 S. Walnut St., following signs. This 4.5-acre area features a sampling of Idaho's ecosystems. Walking trails pass a mountain stream with logjams and waterfalls, a wetlands pond and a high desert plain with sagebrush and lava rock. Along the way are plants and wildlife indigenous to each area. Windows along the stream walk offer "face-to-fish" viewing opportunities and lessons on stream ecology.

The visitor center features exhibits and offers educational programs. **Time:** Allow 1 hour minimum. **Hours:** Outdoor area daily dawn-dusk. Visitor center Tues.-Fri. 9-5, Sat.-Sun. 11-5. **Cost:** Free. **Phone:** (208) 334-2225.

SAVE **OLD IDAHO PENITENTIARY STATE HISTORIC SITE,** 1.5 mi. e. of Broadway and Warm Springs Ave. at 2445 Old Penitentiary Rd., was used 1872-1973 as Idaho's state penitentiary. Additions to the complex were constructed by prisoners with sandstone they quarried and cut. Exhibits include historical weapons and vehicles; an explanation of the history of tattoos; and a video presentation recalling prison history, notorious inmates and conditions of prison life.

Guided tours are offered on weekends and during summer months. Visitors should wear comfortable shoes and dress for an outdoor experience. Picnicking is permitted outside the prison walls. **Time:** Allow 2 hours minimum. **Hours:** Daily 10-5, Memorial Day-Labor Day; noon-5, rest of year. Last admission 45 minutes before closing. Closed major holidays. Phone ahead to confirm schedule. **Cost:** $6; $4 (ages 60+); $3 (ages 6-12). **Phone:** (208) 334-2844.

STATE CAPITOL, bordered by Jefferson, W. State, 6th and 8th sts., is Boise's most treasured public building. The Idaho sandstone exterior base is carved to resemble logs—a tribute to pioneer cabins. Vermont and Georgian marble and hand-crafted scagliola (imitation marble) dominate the bright interior spaces of all four floors of the rotunda.

Begun in 1905, the five-part neoclassical building that motorists see while approaching from Capitol Boulevard was finished in 1920. A restored 5-foot-tall statue of a golden eagle sits atop the Capitol dome 208 feet above street level. **Hours:** Mon.-Fri. 6-6 (also 6-10 p.m., during legislative sessions), Sat.-Sun. 9-5. **Cost:** Free. **Phone:** (208) 332-1000 during legislative sessions, (208) 332-1012 in the interim between sessions or (800) 626-0471. ⒼⓉ

SAVE **WORLD CENTER FOR BIRDS OF PREY** is 7 mi. s. at 5668 W. Flying Hawk Ln.; take I-84 exit 50 to S. Cole Rd., then s. 6 mi. and w. on Flying Hawk Ln. to the top of the hill. The world headquarters of the Peregrine Fund—an organization dedicated to the conservation of birds of prey—includes a 7,200-square-foot interpretive center. Exhibits about wildlife, biology and ecology are featured, and live birds, such as falcons, California condors and eagles, can be seen. Outdoor flight demonstrations are offered Friday through Sunday in October. Docents are available to answer questions and to lead tours of the interpretive center.

Hours: Tues.-Sun. 10-5, March-Oct.; Tues.-Sun. 10-4, rest of year. Last admission 45 minutes before closing. Closed major holidays. **Cost:** $7; $6 (ages 62+); $5 (ages 4-16). **Phone:** (208) 362-8687.

RECREATIONAL ACTIVITIES

Skiing

• **Bogus Basin Mountain Recreation Area** is 16 mi. n. at 2600 N. Bogus Basin Rd. **Hours:** Mon.-Fri. 10-10, Sat.-Sun. and holidays 9 a.m.-10 p.m., Thanksgiving-late Mar. (weather permitting). Phone ahead to confirm schedule. **Phone:** (208) 332-5100 or (800) 367-4397.

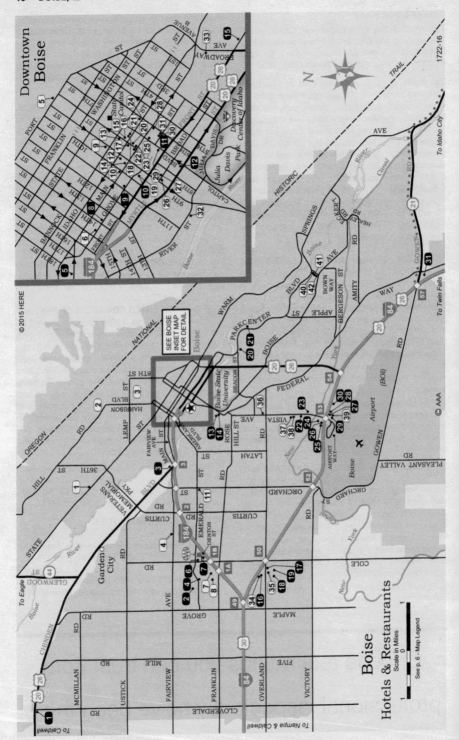

Downtown Boise

© 2015 HERE

Boise
Hotels & Restaurants

Scale in Miles
0   1

See p. 6 - Map Legend

1722-16

✈ Airport Hotels

Map Page	BOISE AIRPORT (Maximum driving distance from airport: 1.0 mi)	Diamond Rated	Rate Range	Page
27 p. 40	BEST WESTERN Airport Inn, 0.5 mi	◈◈	$80-$150 SAVE	43
29 p. 40	BEST WESTERN Vista Inn at the Airport, 0.5 mi	◈◈◈	$81-$125 SAVE	43
23 p. 40	Comfort Suites - Airport, 0.9 mi	◈◈◈	$85-$300	43
25 p. 40	Fairfield Inn by Marriott - Airport, 0.9 mi	◈◈◈	$85-$178	44
26 p. 40	Hampton Inn - Airport, 0.8 mi	◈◈◈	$89-$179	44
24 p. 40	Holiday Inn Boise - Airport, 0.8 mi	◈◈◈	Rates not provided	44
30 p. 40	Inn America - Airport, 0.7 mi	◈◈	$59-$76	45
22 p. 40	La Quinta Inn & Suites Boise Airport, 1.0 mi	◈◈	$75-$185 SAVE	45
28 p. 40	Quality Inn - Airport, 0.6 mi	◈◈	$58-$300 SAVE	46

Boise

This index helps you "spot" where approved hotels and restaurants are located on the corresponding detailed maps. Hotel daily rate range is for comparison only. Restaurant price range is a combination of lunch and/or dinner. Turn to the listing page for more detailed rate and price information and consult display ads for special promotions.

BOISE

Map Page	Hotels	Diamond Rated	Rate Range	Page
1 p. 40	SpringHill Suites by Marriott - Boise/Eagle	◈◈◈	$92-$174	46
2 p. 40	Hyatt Place - Boise Towne Square (See ad p. 45.)	◈◈◈	$79-$219 SAVE	45
3 p. 40	The Riverside Hotel	◈◈◈	$119-$189	46
4 p. 40	La Quinta Inn & Suites - Boise Towne Square	◈◈◈	$82-$240	45
5 p. 40	Red Lion Hotel Boise Downtowner	◈◈◈	Rates not provided	46
6 p. 40	Candlewood Suites - Boise Towne Square	◈◈◈	Rates not provided	43
7 p. 40	Residence Inn by Marriott - Boise Town Square	◈◈◈	$91-$209	46
8 p. 40	Modern Hotel & Bar	◈◈	Rates not provided	45
9 p. 40	Safari Inn Downtown	◈◈	$89-$119	46
10 p. 40	Hotel 43	◈◈◈	Rates not provided SAVE	45
11 p. 40	The Grove Hotel	◈◈◈◈	$139-$349 SAVE	44
12 p. 40	Hampton Inn & Suites - Boise/Downtown	◈◈◈	$159-$299	44
13 p. 40	Residence Inn by Marriott - Boise/Downtown	◈◈	$113-$212	46
14 p. 40	TownePlace Suites by Marriott - Downtown	◈◈◈	$98-$188	46
15 p. 40	Courtyard by Marriott - Downtown	◈◈◈	$98-$270 SAVE	44
16 p. 40	Oxford Suites Boise	◈◈◈	$95-$229 SAVE	46
17 p. 40	Hampton Inn & Suites - Boise Spectrum	◈◈◈	$94-$169	44
18 p. 40	Homewood Suites by Hilton - Boise Spectrum	◈◈◈	$99-$309	44
19 p. 40	Hilton Garden Inn - Boise Spectrum	◈◈◈	$99-$229	44
20 p. 40	Holiday Inn Express - Boise/University Area	◈◈◈	Rates not provided	44
21 p. 40	SpringHill Suites by Marriott - Boise/Parkcenter	◈◈◈	$96-$199	46

BOISE (cont'd)

Map Page	Hotels (cont'd)	Diamond Rated	Rate Range	Page
22 p. 40	**La Quinta Inn & Suites Boise Airport**	◆◆	$75-$185 SAVE	45
23 p. 40	Comfort Suites - Airport	◆◆◆	$85-$300	43
24 p. 40	Holiday Inn Boise - Airport	◆◆◆	Rates not provided	44
25 p. 40	Fairfield Inn by Marriott - Airport	◆◆◆	$85-$178	44
26 p. 40	Hampton Inn - Airport	◆◆◆	$89-$179	44
27 p. 40	**BEST WESTERN Airport Inn**	◆◆	$80-$150 SAVE	43
28 p. 40	**Quality Inn - Airport**	◆◆	$58-$300 SAVE	46
29 p. 40	**BEST WESTERN Vista Inn at the Airport**	◆◆◆	$81-$125 SAVE	43
30 p. 40	Inn America - Airport	◆◆	$59-$76	45
31 p. 40	**BEST WESTERN Northwest Lodge**	◆◆◆	$89-$139 SAVE	43

Map Page	Restaurants	Diamond Rated	Cuisine	Price Range	Page
1 p. 40	Flying Pie Pizzaria State	◆	Pizza	$7-$29	48
2 p. 40	Highlands Hollow Brewhouse	◆◆	American	$7-$17	48
3 p. 40	Java Hyde Park	◆	Breakfast Sandwiches	$6-$9	48
4 p. 40	Flying Pie Pizzaria Fairview	◆	Pizza	$7-$29	48
5 p. 40	Cafe Vicino	◆◆◆	Mediterranean	$10-$28	47
6 p. 40	Big City Coffee & Cafe - Linen District	◆	Breakfast Sandwiches	$5-$12	47
7 p. 40	The Cheesecake Factory	◆◆◆	International	$11-$30	47
8 p. 40	Cafe Ole Restaurant & Cantina	◆◆	Mexican	$8-$14	47
9 p. 40	Yen Ching	◆◆	Chinese	$7-$18	50
10 p. 40	Asiago's Restaurant & Winebar	◆◆◆	Italian	$7-$25	46
11 p. 40	Tango's Subs & Empanadas	◆	Argentine	$3-$7	49
12 p. 40	Berryhill & Co.	◆◆◆	American	$9-$37	47
13 p. 40	Zeppole Downtown	◆	Breads/Pastries Deli	$5-$7	50
14 p. 40	Bombay Grill	◆◆	Indian	$9-$20	47
15 p. 40	Red Feather	◆◆◆	American	$7-$22	49
16 p. 40	Bittercreek Alehouse	◆◆	Pacific Northwest	$9-$25	47
17 p. 40	Fork	◆◆◆	American	$12-$28	48
18 p. 40	Mai Thai Modern Asian Cuisine	◆◆◆	Thai	$8-$30	49
19 p. 40	Chandlers Steakhouse	◆◆◆	Steak Seafood	$29-$75	47
20 p. 40	Shige Japanese Cuisine	◆◆	Japanese	$11-$30	49
21 p. 40	Moon's Kitchen	◆	American	$7-$12	49
22 p. 40	Flatbread Community Oven Pizzeria & Wine Bar - Downtown	◆◆	Pizza Sandwiches	$8-$17	48
23 p. 40	Piper Pub & Grill	◆◆	Scottish	$10-$19	49
24 p. 40	Java Downtown	◆	Breakfast Sandwiches	$5-$9	48
25 p. 40	Goldy's Breakfast Bistro	◆◆	Breakfast Sandwiches	$8-$13	48

Map Page	Restaurants (cont'd)	Diamond Rated	Cuisine	Price Range	Page
26 p. 40	Bonefish Grill	▽▽▽	Seafood	$10-$29	47
27 p. 40	Happy Fish Sushi & Martini Bar	▽▽	Sushi	$11-$21	48
28 p. 40	Reef	▽▽	Polynesian	$8-$24	49
29 p. 40	Emilio's at The Grove Hotel	▽▽▽	New American	$24-$36	48
30 p. 40	Bardenay Restaurant & Distillery	▽▽	American	$6-$23	47
31 p. 40	Leku Ona	▽▽	Basque	$7-$28	49
32 p. 40	Cottonwood Grille	▽▽▽	American	$9-$37	47
33 p. 40	Boise Fry Company	▽	Specialty Burgers	$6-$12	47
34 p. 40	Tucanos Brazilian Grill	▽▽	Brazilian	$9-$23	50
35 p. 40	Legends Pub & Grill	▽▽	American	$7-$19	49
36 p. 40	Cucina di Paolo	▽▽	Italian	$8-$11	48
37 p. 40	Willowcreek Grill	▽▽	American	$9-$22	50
38 p. 40	RAW Sushi	▽▽	Sushi	$8-$23	49
39 p. 40	Kopper Kitchen Pub & Grill	▽▽	American	$7-$19	48
40 p. 40	Bier: Thirty Bottle & Bistro	▽	German	$8-$11	47
41 p. 40	Tavern at Bown Crossing	▽▽	American	$11-$42	50
42 p. 40	Flatbread Community Oven Pizzeria & Wine Bar - Bown Crossing	▽▽	Pizza Sandwiches	$8-$17	48

BEST WESTERN AIRPORT INN   (208)384-5000 27
Motel $80-$150

AAA Benefit: Save 10% or more every day and earn 10% bonus points!
Address: 2660 Airport Way 83705 **Location:** I-84 exit 53 (Vista Ave), just se. **Facility:** 50 units. 2 stories (no elevator), exterior corridors. **Terms:** cancellation fee imposed. **Pool(s):** heated outdoor. **Guest Services:** coin laundry. **Featured Amenity: continental breakfast.**

BEST WESTERN NORTHWEST LODGE   (208)287-2300 31
Hotel $89-$139
AAA Benefit: Save 10% or more every day and earn 10% bonus points!
Address: 6989 Federal Way 83716 **Location:** I-84 exit 57 (Gowen Rd/Idaho City), just e, then just s. **Facility:** 69 units. 3 stories, interior corridors. **Pool(s):** heated indoor. **Activities:** hot tub, exercise room. **Guest Services:** valet and coin laundry. **Featured Amenity: full hot breakfast.**

BEST WESTERN VISTA INN AT THE AIRPORT   (208)336-8100 29
Hotel $81-$125

AAA Benefit: Save 10% or more every day and earn 10% bonus points!
Address: 2645 Airport Way 83705 **Location:** I-84 exit 53 (Vista Ave), just s. **Facility:** 85 units. 2 stories (no elevator), interior/exterior corridors. **Pool(s):** heated indoor. **Activities:** hot tub, exercise room. **Guest Services:** valet and coin laundry. **Featured Amenity: full hot breakfast.**

CANDLEWOOD SUITES - BOISE TOWNE SQUARE   208/322-4300 6
▽▽▽ Extended Stay Hotel. Rates not provided. **Address:** 700 N Cole Rd 83704 **Location:** I-84 exit 50A westbound; exit 50B eastbound, 2 mi n on Cole Rd, then just w. **Facility:** 84 efficiencies. 3 stories, interior corridors. **Activities:** picnic facilities, exercise room. **Guest Services:** complimentary and valet laundry.

COMFORT SUITES - AIRPORT   (208)472-1222 23
▽▽▽ Hotel $85-$300 **Address:** 2906 Vista Ave 83705 **Location:** I-84 exit 53 (Vista Ave), 0.5 mi n. **Facility:** 83 units. 3 stories, interior corridors. **Amenities:** safes. **Pool(s):** heated indoor. **Activities:** exercise room. **Guest Services:** valet and coin laundry.

(See map & index p. 40.)

COURTYARD BY MARRIOTT - DOWNTOWN
(208)331-2700 **15**

COURTYARD Marriott

Hotel $98-$270

AAA Benefit: Members save 5% or more!

Address: 222 S Broadway Ave 83702 **Location:** I-84 exit 54 (Broadway Ave), 3 mi n. **Facility:** 162 units. 4 stories, interior corridors. **Pool(s):** heated indoor. **Activities:** hot tub, picnic facilities, exercise room. **Guest Services:** valet and coin laundry, boarding pass kiosk.

[SAVE] [+] [Y] CALL [&M] [≈] [BIZ]
[HS] [≈] [X] [B] [▣]
/SOME UNITS [▣]

FAIRFIELD INN BY MARRIOTT - AIRPORT
(208)331-5656 **25**

Hotel $85-$178 **Address:** 3300 S Shoshone St 83705 **Location:** I-84 exit 53 (Vista Ave), just n to Elder St, then just w. **Facility:** 63 units. 3 stories, interior corridors. **Pool(s):** heated indoor.

AAA Benefit: Members save 5% or more!

Activities: hot tub, limited exercise equipment. **Guest Services:** valet and coin laundry.

[+] [T+] CALL [&M] [≈] [BIZ] [≈] [X] [B] [▣] [▣]
/SOME UNITS [S]

THE GROVE HOTEL
(208)333-8000 **11**

Boutique Hotel $139-$349

Address: 245 S Capitol Blvd 83702 **Location:** At Front St and S Capitol Blvd; downtown. **Facility:** This impressive high-rise hotel has a strikingly sophisticated lobby featuring a nightly piano player. Guest rooms are beautifully appointed with a large desk and multiple upscale bedding accents. 250 units. 16 stories, interior corridors. **Parking:** on-site (fee) and valet. **Terms:** cancellation fee imposed. **Dining:** Emilio's at The Grove Hotel, see separate listing, entertainment. **Pool(s):** heated indoor. **Activities:** sauna, hot tub, spa. **Guest Services:** valet laundry.

[SAVE] [+] [T+] [Y] CALL [&M] [≈] [Y+] [BIZ] [≈]
[X] [Y] [B] [▣]

HAMPTON INN - AIRPORT
(208)331-5600 **26**

Hotel $89-$179 **Address:** 3270 S Shoshone St 83705 **Location:** I-84 exit 53 (Vista Ave), just n to Elder St, then just w. **Facility:** 63 units. 3 stories, interior corridors. **Terms:** 1-7 night minimum stay, cancellation fee imposed. **Pool(s):** heated indoor. **Activities:** hot tub, exercise room. **Guest Services:** valet laundry.

AAA Benefit: Members save up to 10%!

[+] [T+] CALL [&M] [≈] [BIZ] [≈] [B] [▣] [▣]
/SOME UNITS [🐾]

HAMPTON INN & SUITES - BOISE/DOWNTOWN
(208)331-1900 **12**

Hotel $159-$299 **Address:** 495 S Capitol Blvd 83702 **Location:** I-84 exit 53 (Vista Ave), 2.2 mi n, then 0.8 mi ne; at W Myrtle St and S Capitol Blvd. **Facility:** 186 units. 11 stories, interior corridors. **Parking:** on-site (fee). **Terms:** 1-7 night minimum stay, cancellation fee imposed. **Pool(s):** heated indoor. **Activities:** hot tub, bicycles, exercise room. **Guest Services:** valet and coin laundry.

AAA Benefit: Members save up to 10%!

[+] [T+] CALL [&M] [≈] [BIZ] [HS] [≈] [X] [Y] [B]
[▣] /SOME UNITS [▣]

HAMPTON INN & SUITES - BOISE SPECTRUM
(208)323-2500 **17**

Hotel $94-$169 **Address:** 7499 W Overland Rd 83709 **Location:** I-84 exit 50A westbound; exit 50B eastbound, just s. **Facility:** 133 units, some two bedrooms and efficiencies. 4 stories, interior corridors. **Terms:** 1-7 night minimum stay, cancellation fee imposed. **Pool(s):** heated indoor. **Activities:** hot tub, exercise room. **Guest Services:** valet and coin laundry, area transportation.

AAA Benefit: Members save up to 10%!

[+] [T+] CALL [&M] [≈] [BIZ] [HS] [≈] [X] [B] [▣]
/SOME UNITS [▣]

HILTON GARDEN INN - BOISE SPECTRUM
(208)376-1000 **19**

Contemporary Hotel $99-$229 **Address:** 7699 W Spectrum Way 83709 **Location:** I-84 exit 50A westbound; exit 50B eastbound, just s, then just w. **Facility:** 137 units. 4 stories, interior corridors. **Terms:** 1-7 night minimum stay, cancellation fee imposed. **Pool(s):** heated indoor. **Activities:** hot tub, exercise room. **Guest Services:** valet and coin laundry.

AAA Benefit: Members save up to 10%!

[+] [T+] CALL [&M] [≈] [BIZ] [HS] [≈] [B] [▣] [▣]

HOLIDAY INN BOISE - AIRPORT
208/344-7444 **24**

Hotel. Rates not provided. **Address:** 2970 W Elder St 83705 **Location:** I-84 exit 53 (Vista Ave), just n to Elder St, then just w. **Facility:** 119 units, some two bedrooms. 4 stories, interior corridors. **Amenities:** safes. **Pool(s):** heated indoor. **Activities:** hot tub, exercise room. **Guest Services:** valet and coin laundry.

[+] [T] [Y] CALL [&M] [≈] [BIZ] [HS] [≈] [X] [B]
[▣] [▣] /SOME UNITS [S]

HOLIDAY INN EXPRESS - BOISE/UNIVERSITY AREA
208/345-2002 **20**

Hotel. Rates not provided. **Address:** 475 W Parkcenter Blvd 83706 **Location:** I-84 exit 54 (Broadway Ave), 2.3 mi n to Beacon St, then 0.3 mi e. Next to Boise River Greenbelt. **Facility:** 159 units. 6 stories, interior corridors. **Pool(s):** heated outdoor. **Activities:** hot tub, bicycles, game room, trails, exercise room. **Guest Services:** valet and coin laundry, area transportation.

[+] [T+] CALL [&M] [≈] [BIZ] [≈] [X] [B] [▣] [▣]
/SOME UNITS [S]

HOMEWOOD SUITES BY HILTON - BOISE SPECTRUM
(208)375-8500 **18**

Extended Stay Contemporary Hotel $99-$309 **Address:** 7957 W Spectrum Way 83709 **Location:** I-84 exit 50A westbound; exit 50B eastbound, just s, then just w. **Facility:** 110 efficiencies, some two bedrooms. 4 stories, interior corridors. **Terms:** 1-7 night minimum stay, cancellation fee imposed. **Pool(s):** heated indoor. **Activities:** hot tub, game room, picnic facilities, exercise room. **Guest Services:** valet and coin laundry.

AAA Benefit: Members save up to 10%!

[+] [T+] CALL [&M] [≈] [BIZ] [HS] [≈] [Y] [B] [▣]
[▣]

(See map & index p. 40.)

HOTEL 43

208-342-4622 **10**

◆◆◆
Boutique
Contemporary
Hotel
Rates not provided

Address: 981 W Grove St 83702 **Location:** At 10th and W Grove sts; downtown. **Facility:** This northwest boutique hotel is on the 43rd parallel in the 43rd state and boasts artfully designed guest rooms offering a variety of city views and a unique and modern décor style throughout. 112 units. 6 stories, interior corridors. **Parking:** on-site (fee) and valet. **Terms:** check-in 4 pm. **Dining:** Chandlers Steakhouse, see separate listing. **Activities:** exercise room. **Guest Services:** valet laundry, boarding pass kiosk, area transportation.

HYATT PLACE - BOISE TOWNE SQUARE

(208)375-1200 **2**

◆◆◆
Contemporary
Hotel
$79-$219

AAA Benefit: Members save 10%!

Address: 925 N Milwaukee St 83704 **Location:** I-84 exit 49 (Franklin St), just w, then 0.5 mi n. Located in a residential area. **Facility:** 127 units. 4 stories, interior corridors. **Terms:** cancellation fee imposed. **Amenities:** safes. **Pool(s):** heated indoor. **Activities:** exercise room. **Guest Services:** valet laundry, area transportation. **Featured Amenity:** breakfast buffet. *(See ad this page.)*

INN AMERICA - AIRPORT

(208)389-9800 **30**

◆◆ Hotel $59-$76 **Address:** 2275 Airport Way 83705 **Location:** I-84 exit 53 (Vista Ave), 0.3 mi se. **Facility:** 73 units. 3 stories, interior corridors. **Terms:** cancellation fee imposed. **Pool(s):** heated outdoor. **Guest Services:** valet and coin laundry.

LA QUINTA INN & SUITES BOISE AIRPORT

(208)388-0800 **22**

◆◆◆
Hotel
$75-$185

Address: 2613 S Vista Ave 83705 **Location:** I-84 exit 53 (Vista Ave), 0.6 mi n. Located in residential neighborhood. **Facility:** 63 units. 3 stories, interior corridors. **Pool(s):** heated indoor. **Activities:** hot tub, exercise room. **Guest Services:** valet and coin laundry. **Featured Amenity:** full hot breakfast.

LA QUINTA INN & SUITES - BOISE TOWNE SQUARE

(208)378-7000 **4**

◆◆◆ Hotel $82-$240 **Address:** 7965 W Emerald St 83704 **Location:** I-84 exit 49 (Franklin St), just w, 0.5 mi n on Milwaukee St to Emerald St, then just e. **Facility:** 124 units, some efficiencies. 4 stories, interior corridors. **Pool(s):** heated indoor. **Activities:** hot tub, exercise room. **Guest Services:** valet and coin laundry.

MODERN HOTEL & BAR

208/424-8244 **8**

◆◆ Boutique Motel. Rates not provided. **Address:** 1314 W Grove St 83702 **Location:** At 13th and W Grove sts; downtown. **Facility:** If you are looking for a fun experience and luxury bedding, including pressed sheets, this retro boutique motel is like none other in the area. Some rooms have a private balcony. 39 units. 2 stories (no elevator), interior/exterior corridors. **Parking:** on-site and street. **Activities:** bicycles. **Guest Services:** valet laundry.

▼ See AAA listing this page ▼

(See map & index p. 40.)

OXFORD SUITES BOISE

(208)322-8000 **16**

Hotel
$95-$229

Address: 1426 S Entertainment Ave 83709 **Location:** I-84 exit 50A, just s to Spectrum Way, just w, then just n. **Facility:** 132 units, some efficiencies. 4 stories, interior corridors. **Terms:** 3 day cancellation notice-fee imposed, resort fee. **Pool(s):** heated indoor. **Activities:** sauna, hot tub, steamroom, exercise room. **Guest Services:** valet and coin laundry. **Featured Amenity:** breakfast buffet.

[SAVE] [⊁] [¶¶♦] CALL [&M] [⇌] [BIZ] [HS] [🛜] [✕] [🖥] [🗄] / SOME UNITS [S🛏]

QUALITY INN - AIRPORT

(208)336-0077 **28**

Hotel
$58-$300

Address: 2526 Airport Way 83705 **Location:** I-84 exit 53 (Vista Ave), just se. **Facility:** 61 units. 2 stories (no elevator), interior/exterior corridors. **Pool(s):** heated indoor. **Activities:** hot tub, limited exercise equipment. **Guest Services:** valet and coin laundry. **Featured Amenity:** continental breakfast.

[SAVE] [⊁] [¶¶♦] [⇌] [BIZ] [🛜] [✕] [🖥] [🗄] / SOME UNITS [S🛏] [🖨]

RED LION HOTEL BOISE DOWNTOWNER

208/344-7691 **5**

Hotel. Rates not provided. **Address:** 1800 Fairview Ave 83702 **Location:** I-84 exit 3 (Fairview Ave), 1 mi n. **Facility:** 182 units. 3-7 stories, interior corridors. **Pool(s):** heated outdoor. **Activities:** hot tub, bicycles, exercise room. **Guest Services:** valet laundry, area transportation.

[⊁] [¶¶] [Y] CALL [&M] [⇌] [BIZ] [🛜] [✕] [🖥] [🗄] / SOME UNITS [S🛏]

RESIDENCE INN BY MARRIOTT - BOISE/DOWNTOWN

(208)344-1200 **13**

Extended Stay Hotel $113-$212 **Address:** 1401 S Lusk Pl 83706 **Location:** I-84 exit 53 (Vista Ave), 2.4 mi n, just w on Ann Morrison Park Dr, then just s on Lois Ave. **Facility:** 104 units, some two bedrooms, efficiencies and kitchens. 2 stories (no elevator), exterior corridors. **Pool(s):** heated outdoor. **Activities:** hot tub, picnic facilities, limited exercise equipment. **Guest Services:** valet and coin laundry, area transportation.

AAA Benefit: Members save 5% or more!

[⊁] [¶¶♦] [⇌] [BIZ] [🛜] [✕] [🖥] [🗄] [🖨] / SOME UNITS [S🛏] [HS]

RESIDENCE INN BY MARRIOTT - BOISE TOWN SQUARE

(208)385-9000 **7**

Extended Stay Hotel $91-$209 **Address:** 7303 W Denton St 83704 **Location:** I-84 exit 50A westbound; exit 50B eastbound, 2 mi n on Cole Rd, then just w. **Facility:** 104 units, some two bedrooms, efficiencies and kitchens. 4 stories, interior corridors. **Pool(s):** heated outdoor. **Activities:** hot tub, exercise room. **Guest Services:** valet and coin laundry, boarding pass kiosk.

AAA Benefit: Members save 5% or more!

[⊁] [¶¶♦] CALL [⇌] [HS] [🛜] [✕] [🖥] [🗄] [🖨] / SOME UNITS [S🛏]

THE RIVERSIDE HOTEL

(208)343-1871 **3**

Hotel $119-$189 **Address:** 2900 W Chinden Blvd 83714 **Location:** I-84 exit 49 (Franklin Rd), 2.7 mi ne on I-184 exit 3 (Fairview Ave), just n, then just w. Adjoining the Boise Greenbelt. **Facility:** 303 units, some two bedrooms. 2 stories, interior corridors. **Terms:** cancellation fee imposed. **Dining:** 2 restaurants. **Pool(s):** heated outdoor. **Activities:** hot tub, bicycles, lawn sports, trails, exercise room. **Guest Services:** valet and coin laundry, area transportation.

[ECO] [⊁] [¶¶] [Y] CALL [&M] [⇌] [BIZ] [🛜] [🗄] [🖥] / SOME UNITS [S🛏] [HS] [🖨]

SAFARI INN DOWNTOWN

(208)344-6556 **9**

Hotel $89-$119 **Address:** 1070 Grove St 83702 **Location:** At 11th and Grove sts. **Facility:** 103 units. 3 stories, interior corridors. **Terms:** 3 day cancellation notice. **Amenities:** safes. **Pool(s):** heated outdoor. **Activities:** sauna, hot tub, exercise room. **Guest Services:** valet and coin laundry.

[¶¶♦] [⇌] [BIZ] [HS] [🛜] [✕] [🖥] [🗄] [🖨] / SOME UNITS [S🛏]

SPRINGHILL SUITES BY MARRIOTT - BOISE/EAGLE

(208)939-8266 **1**

Hotel $92-$174 **Address:** 6325 N Cloverdale Rd 83713 **Location:** I-84 exit 46 (Eagle Rd), 4.5 mi n to Chinden Blvd, 1 mi e, then just s. **Facility:** 119 units. 4 stories, interior corridors. **Pool(s):** heated indoor. **Activities:** exercise room. **Guest Services:** valet and coin laundry, area transportation.

AAA Benefit: Members save 5% or more!

[⊁] [¶¶♦] CALL [&M] [⇌] [BIZ] [HS] [🛜] [✕] [🎥] [🖥] [🗄] [🖨] / SOME UNITS [S🛏]

SPRINGHILL SUITES BY MARRIOTT - BOISE/PARKCENTER

(208)342-1044 **21**

Hotel $96-$199 **Address:** 424 E Parkcenter Blvd 83706 **Location:** I-84 exit 54 (Broadway Ave), 2.3 mi n to Beacon St, 0.3 mi e, then 0.7 mi se. Near Boise River Greenbelt. **Facility:** 230 units. 3 stories, interior corridors. **Pool(s):** heated outdoor. **Activities:** hot tub, bicycles, trails, exercise room. **Guest Services:** valet and coin laundry, area transportation.

AAA Benefit: Members save 5% or more!

[⊁] [¶¶♦] CALL [&M] [⇌] [BIZ] [🛜] [✕] [🖥] [🗄] [🖨] / SOME UNITS [S🛏]

TOWNEPLACE SUITES BY MARRIOTT - DOWNTOWN

(208)429-8881 **14**

Extended Stay Hotel $98-$188 **Address:** 1455 S Capitol Blvd 83706 **Location:** I-84 exit 53 (Vista Ave), 2.4 mi n. **Facility:** 121 units, some two bedrooms, efficiencies and kitchens. 4 stories, interior corridors. **Terms:** check-in 4 pm. **Pool(s):** heated indoor. **Activities:** hot tub, picnic facilities, exercise room. **Guest Services:** valet and coin laundry.

AAA Benefit: Members save 5% or more!

[⊁] [¶¶♦] CALL [&M] [⇌] [BIZ] [HS] [🛜] [✕] [🖥] [🗄] [🖨] / SOME UNITS [S🛏]

WHERE TO EAT

ASIAGO'S RESTAURANT & WINEBAR

208/336-5552 **10**

Italian. Casual Dining. $7-$25 AAA Inspector Notes: The warm ambience found here mixes Old World designs with modern accents. The creative menu features walnut-pesto risotto cakes, chicken breast stuffed with prosciutto, beef tenderloin with bacon-balsamic onion crust over whiskey-horseradish sauce and crisp gremolata eggplant filets. Equally imaginative are mouth-watering desserts such as sour cream-rum cake with spiced pecans, chocolate-espresso flourless torte and a lime-mascarpone tart. **Features:** beer & wine, patio dining. **Reservations:** suggested. **Address:** 1002 Main St 83701 **Location:** At 10th and Main sts; downtown. **Parking:** on-site (fee) and street. [L] [D]

(See map & index p. 40.)

BARDENAY RESTAURANT & DISTILLERY 208/426-0538 (30)
▼▼▼ American. Casual Dining. $6-$23 **AAA Inspector Notes:** This spot was the first in the country licensed to operate its own distillery. Vodka, rum and gin are produced on the premises. The restaurant is appropriately named--bardenay is a term sailors use loosely in place of the word cocktail. A wide variety of dishes is served including chicken, beef and pork satay, Thai salmon cakes, Oriental chicken salad, meatloaf sandwich, Hagerman trout and burgers. **Features:** full bar, patio dining, Sunday brunch, happy hour. **Address:** 610 Grove St 83702 **Location:** Between Capitol and 6th sts; downtown. **Parking:** street only. L D

BERRYHILL & CO. 208/387-3553 (12)
▼▼ American. Fine Dining. $9-$37 **AAA Inspector Notes:** This restaurant began as a tasting room for the catering business, and after much positive response and some urging from clients, the restaurant was born. Fresh food focuses on as much local produce as possible and an extensive wine list pairs with creative and appealing dishes for lunch and dinner. The pan-seared ginger Kobe wontons melt in your mouth, while the chile chocolate soufflé is spot on with a cup of coffee. **Features:** full bar, patio dining, Sunday brunch. **Reservations:** suggested, for dinner. **Address:** 121 N 9th St 83702 **Location:** Downtown; in Plaza 121. **Parking:** street only. L D

BIER: THIRTY BOTTLE & BISTRO 208/342-1916 (40)
▼ German. Gastropub. $8-$11 **AAA Inspector Notes:** In the East Side, this little gastropub offers more than 400 craft beers and imported bottles. Menu items include schnitzel tacos, bier broth mussels, barley pasta salad and an Alaskan amber hummus plate with olive salad and sun-dried tomato pesto—too good to share. Vegan and vegetarian items are available. **Features:** beer & wine, patio dining, happy hour. **Address:** 3073 S Bown Way 83706 **Location:** I-84 exit 54 (Broadway Ave), 1 mi n to Linden St, 1 mi e to Boise Ave, just se to Apple St, 0.3 mi n to Parkcenter Blvd, then 1 mi se to Bown Way. **Parking:** on-site and street. L D

BIG CITY COFFEE & CAFE - LINEN DISTRICT
208/345-3145 (6)
▼ Breakfast Sandwiches. Quick Serve. $5-$12 **AAA Inspector Notes:** You have not experienced Boise culture until you have experienced this eclectic cafe. Enjoy fresh-baked pastries, award-winning quiche and delicious wraps and sandwiches. Surrounded by antiques and brightly colored walls and fixtures, your eyes are sure to discover something new with each visit. **Features:** patio dining. **Address:** 1416 W Grove St 83702 **Location:** Between 14th and 15th sts; downtown. **Parking:** street only. B L CALL M

BITTERCREEK ALEHOUSE 208/345-1813 (16)
▼▼ Pacific Northwest. Gastropub. $9-$25 **AAA Inspector Notes:** From the pasture-raised ground chuck to the Alaskan salmon, Pacific cod and Idaho trout, this pub offers great entrées with all of the drink pairings that one could imagine. Locals seem to favor the ground chuck and brisket burger and the fish and chips. Guests may end up with a weekly yearning for bacon and sage popcorn or polenta logs with cumin-lime aioli. Seating is tight and it gets noisy. **Features:** full bar, patio dining, Sunday brunch, happy hour. **Address:** 246 N 8th St 83702 **Location:** Jct Idaho and 8th sts; downtown. **Parking:** street only. L D LATE CALL M

BOISE FRY COMPANY 208/495-3858 (33)
▼ Specialty Burgers. Quick Serve. $6-$12 **AAA Inspector Notes:** Fries are the main event here and they are treated with respect. Pick a potato (gold, purple, russet, sweet, white or yam) and then choose the cut (regular, wide or curly). Order a side, such as a bison burger, house vegan patty or quinoa salad, to go with it. You have to see the seasoning and dipping stations to believe it. Do not miss fry happy hour. Be advised in advance, this eatery is addictive. **Features:** beer only, happy hour. **Address:** 111 S Broadway Ave, Suite 111 83702 **Location:** I-84 exit 54 (Broadway Ave), 3.1 mi n. L D

BOMBAY GRILL 208/345-7888 (14)
▼▼ Indian. Casual Dining. $9-$20 **AAA Inspector Notes:** Located near shops and a movie theater, this grill is inside the historic Idanha Building which served as a hotel in the early 1900s catering to guests such as Theodore Roosevelt and Ethel Barrymore. Menu highlights include a long list of chicken, lamb and tandoori specialties. Expect a line at the popular lunch buffet. **Features:** beer & wine. **Address:** 928 W Main St 83702 **Location:** At 10th St. **Parking:** street only. L D

BONEFISH GRILL 208/433-1234 (26)
▼▼ Seafood. Fine Dining. $10-$29 **AAA Inspector Notes:** Fish is the house specialty, and the menu and nightly specials offer a variety of choices. Well-prepared food is cooked to perfection. Service is casual in nature, and the staff is skilled and attentive. **Features:** full bar. **Reservations:** suggested. **Address:** 855 W Broad St 83702 **Location:** Jct Broad and 9th sts; downtown. **Parking:** street only. L D CALL M

CAFE OLE RESTAURANT & CANTINA 208/322-0222 (8)
▼▼ Mexican. Casual Dining. $8-$14 **AAA Inspector Notes:** Set eyes on this white stucco, Spanish-style building and entry-way water fountain and you'll know immediately that you're about to experience authentic Mexican cuisine. Genuine dishes are served boasting loads of flavor. If you're in the mood for a margarita, be ready to choose from over 20 different types of tequila. **Features:** full bar. **Address:** 210 N Milwaukee Rd 83704 **Location:** I-84 exit 49 (Franklin Rd), just w, then just n. L D

CAFE VICINO 208/472-1463 (5)
▼▼▼ Mediterranean. Fine Dining. $10-$28 **AAA Inspector Notes:** Located in the historic North End, this quaint Mediterranean-style bistro serves up tasteful, innovative dishes. The menu changes seasonally and always features a variety of pasta, seafood and steak. **Features:** beer & wine, patio dining. **Reservations:** suggested. **Address:** 808 W Fort St 83702 **Location:** Between 7th and 8th sts. **Parking:** on-site and street. L D

CHANDLERS STEAKHOUSE 208/383-4300 (19)
▼▼▼ Steak Seafood. Fine Dining. $29-$75 **AAA Inspector Notes:** Specializing in Prime steaks and seafood dishes with a regional flair, this modern and elegant restaurant is known for its extensive wine list, creative cocktails and martinis and live nightly jazz performances. Patrons enjoy dinner at candlelit tables surrounded by flowers. **Features:** full bar, patio dining. **Reservations:** suggested. **Address:** 981 W Grove St 83702 **Location:** Corner of 10th and W Grove sts; downtown; in Hotel 43. **Parking:** valet and street only. D CALL M

THE CHEESECAKE FACTORY 208/377-4466 (7)
▼▼▼ International. Casual Dining. $11-$30 **AAA Inspector Notes:** What started as a small bakery in Los Angeles in the 1970s has since blossomed into one of the most recognizable restaurant chains today. Known for their large portion sizes and seemingly never-ending menu, this restaurant features over 200 selections to choose from! The "SkinnyLicious" menu options may appeal to those counting calories. **Features:** full bar, patio dining, Sunday brunch. **Address:** 330 N Milwaukee St 83704 **Location:** I-84 exit 49 (Franklin Rd), just w, then just n. L D CALL M

COTTONWOOD GRILLE 208/333-9800 (32)
▼▼▼ American. Fine Dining. $9-$37 **AAA Inspector Notes:** This restaurant features riverfront dining in lush surroundings alongside the Boise River. Inside, the main dining room features an enormous stone fireplace. Menu items include a variety of elk, premium buffalo, grilled pheasant, rack of lamb, juicy steaks and a nice selection of fresh fish and shellfish. Diners may want to share the large seasonal and decadent desserts. **Features:** full bar, patio dining, Sunday brunch, happy hour. **Reservations:** suggested. **Address:** 913 W River St 83702 **Location:** I-84 exit 53 (Vista Ave), 2.8 mi n, then just w. L D

Upgrade to Plus or Premier membership
for *more* of the benefits you need most

(See map & index p. 40.)

CUCINA DI PAOLO   208/345-7150 (36)
WW Italian. Casual Dining. $8-$11 **AAA Inspector Notes:**
Using as many local producers and farmers as possible, this cozy
eatery offers tasty food in an adorable setting. Some menu items include lasagna, chicken pot pie, seasonal soups, attractively prepared
salads and sandwiches. Try the triple crème Danish Brie and merlot
wine jelly on grilled crostini. Mouth-watering desserts are lined up in
a glass case just waiting to tempt guests. **Features:** beer & wine,
patio dining. **Address:** 1504 S Vista Ave 83702 **Location:** I-84 exit
53 (Vista Ave), 1.4 mi n. [L]

EMILIO'S AT THE GROVE HOTEL   208/333-8002 (29)
WWW New American. Fine Dining. $24-$36 **AAA Inspector
Notes:** Relax in the upscale atmosphere of this restaurant while savoring an innovative seasonal menu. Beautifully prepared items may
include crab cakes with a not-to-be-forgotten tomato-chive jam, tama-
rind rack of lamb, roasted chicken breast served with cheddar polenta
fries or miso-glazed salmon with roasted edamame ragout. **Features:** full bar. **Reservations:** suggested, for dinner. **Address:** 245 S
Capitol Blvd 83702 **Location:** At Front St and S Capitol Blvd; downtown; in The Grove Hotel. **Parking:** on-site and valet.

[B] [L] [D] CALL [&M]

**FLATBREAD COMMUNITY OVEN PIZZERIA & WINE BAR -
BOWN CROSSING**   208/343-4177 (42)
WW Pizza Sandwiches. Casual Dining. $8-$17 **AAA Inspector
Notes:** Tucked away in a quaint community, this certified Neopolitan
pizzeria always is packed with returning fans. Choose from a variety
of distinctive pizza, pasta and sandwich choices while enjoying the
bright ambience that the patio fire pits and candlelit walls create.
Gluten-free items are available. **Features:** full bar, happy hour. **Ad-
dress:** 3139 S Bown Way 83706 **Location:** I-84 exit 54 (Broadway
Ave), 1.2 mi n, 1.1 mi e, then just n. **Parking:** street only.

[L] [D]

**FLATBREAD COMMUNITY OVEN PIZZERIA & WINE BAR -
DOWNTOWN**   208/287-4757 (22)
WW Pizza Sandwiches. Casual Dining. $8-$17 **AAA Inspector
Notes:** This certified Neopolitan pizzeria always is packed with returning fans. Choose from a variety of specialty pizza, salads and
sandwiches while enjoying the bright ambience that this streetside location offers. **Features:** full bar, happy hour. **Address:** 800 W Main
St 83702 **Location:** Corner of 8th and Main sts. **Parking:** street
only. [L] [D]

FLYING PIE PIZZARIA FAIRVIEW   208/345-0000 (4)
W Pizza. Quick Serve. $7-$29 **AAA Inspector Notes:** From the
eclectic décor and distinctive pizza pies, it is no wonder this local favorite has become famous. Dining at this restaurant is sure to be a
new experience for each and every customer with a variety of contests and hands-on activities ranging from hands-on pizza tours to the
rotating It's Your Day contest. Vegetarian pizzas are available. **Features:** beer & wine. **Address:** 6508 Fairview Ave 83704 **Location:**
I-184 exit 2 (Curtis Ave), just n, then 0.5 mi w. [L] [D]

FLYING PIE PIZZARIA STATE   208/384-0000 (1)
W Pizza. Quick Serve. $7-$29 **AAA Inspector Notes:** From the
eclectic décor and distinctive pizza pies, it is no wonder this local favorite has become whirled famous. Dining at this restaurant is sure to
be a new experience for each and every customer with a variety of
contests and hands-on activities ranging from hands-on pizza tours to
the rotating It's Your Day contest. Vegetarian pizzas also are available. **Features:** beer & wine. **Address:** 4320 W State St 83703 **Location:** 3 mi nw of downtown; jct Willow Ln. [L] [D]

FORK   208/287-1700 (17)
WWW American. Casual Dining. $12-$28 **AAA Inspector
Notes:** Put this loyal-to-locals, farm-to-fork restaurant on your to-do
list. The variety of menu items makes it hard to make a selection, but
diners will go back again. The salads are creative and large. Entrées
and appetizers such as the cast iron buttermilk fried chicken and
cheddar waffle, blackened catfish tacos and pork tenderloin in a bran-
died cherry sauce are filled with flavor, as are the grilled jumbo artichoke and lean braised pork belly set in pozole verde. **Features:** full
bar, patio dining. **Address:** 199 N 8th St 83702 **Location:** At 8th and
W Idaho sts; downtown. **Parking:** street only. [L] [D]

GOLDY'S BREAKFAST BISTRO   208/345-4100 (25)
WW Breakfast Sandwiches. Casual Dining. $8-$13 **AAA Inspector Notes:** Within a few blocks of excellent shopping and a
movie theater, this small but mighty café features a wide variety of
freshly prepared waffles, stuffed French toast, frittatas and killer Hollandaise specialties. Create-your-own combination plates offer a dizzying array of choices. My favorite is the bacon, basil and tomato on
toasted focaccia bread. A distinctive ceiling light fixture adds visual
appeal in the bi-level dining room. A long wait for a table is a given.
Features: beer & wine. **Address:** 108 S Capitol Blvd 83702 **Location:** At Main St; downtown. **Parking:** street only. [B] [L]

GOODWOOD BARBECUE COMPANY   208/658-7173
WW Barbecue. Family Dining. $10-$26 **AAA Inspector Notes:**
This lively, casual, family-friendly restaurant specializes in traditional
barbecue fare, as well as new twists on such old favorites as smoked
prime rib. The menu lists comfort food at its best. Barbecue lovers
should not miss this place. **Features:** full bar. **Address:** 7849 W
Spectrum St 83709 **Location:** I-84 exit 50A westbound; exit 50B
eastbound, just s, then just w. [L] [D] CALL [&M]

HAPPY FISH SUSHI & MARTINI BAR   208/343-4810 (27)
WW Sushi. Casual Dining. $11-$21 **AAA Inspector Notes:**
This eatery is located in the popular BoDo District, within walking distance of a comedy club, concert venue and movie theater. They
serve a wide variety of nigiri, sashimi, traditional Japanese maki and
specialty maki rolls. Along with great sushi and rice bowls, the contemporary restaurant is also known for their innovative martini creations such as the James Bond, Slippery Slope and Happy Ginger
Lemon Drop. **Features:** full bar, patio dining, happy hour. **Address:**
855 Broad St, Suite 250 83702 **Location:** Downtown. **Parking:** street
only. [L] [D]

HIGHLANDS HOLLOW BREWHOUSE   208/343-6820 (2)
WW American. Casual Dining. $7-$17 **AAA Inspector Notes:**
This eatery serves up traditional comfort food with a splash of Boise's
North End eclectic style. Some favorites include the chicken cordon
bleu sandwich, lightly breaded halibut and chips, and the chocolate
chunk snow-capped cookie for dessert. Portions are hearty, so bring
an appetite. Be sure to try one of their flavorful beers from the on-site
brewery. **Features:** beer & wine, patio dining. **Address:** 2455 Harrison Hollow Ln 83703 **Location:** I-184 exit River St, 0.8 mi n on 15th
St, just w on Hays St, 1 mi n on Harrison Blvd, then just w.
[L] [D]

JAVA DOWNTOWN   208/345-0777 (24)
W Breakfast Sandwiches. Quick Serve. $5-$9 **AAA Inspector
Notes:** This casual, yet eccentric, café is located on one of the
busiest street corners in downtown Boise, making dining in or taking
your food to go both appealing options. They offer only Fair Trade
Certified organic coffee and homemade baked goods, soups, sandwiches and wraps made with fresh local ingredients. **Address:** 223 N
6th St 83702 **Location:** Jct Idaho St. **Parking:** street only.

[B] [L]

JAVA HYDE PARK   208/345-4777 (3)
W Breakfast Sandwiches. Quick Serve. $6-$9 **AAA Inspector
Notes:** Fair Trade Certified organic coffee couples with homemade
baked goods, soups and sandwiches made from fresh local ingredients at this casual, eccentric café. Try the grilled cheese sandwich
with a bowl of fruit and their signature "bowl of soul" made with
Mexican chocolate. **Features:** patio dining. **Address:** 1612 N 13th St
83702 **Location:** Jct 13th and Eastman sts; in Hyde Park District.
Parking: on-site and street. [B] [L]

KOPPER KITCHEN PUB & GRILL   208/344-4271 (39)
WW American. Casual Dining. $7-$19 **AAA Inspector Notes:**
This restaurant appeals to travelers looking for a convenient place to
eat a good meal and offers an inviting pub to relax in before or after
a meal. The menu offers a full breakfast, sandwiches and several
steak, chicken and pasta dishes. Try the carrot cake! **Features:** full
bar, happy hour. **Address:** 2661 Airport Way 83705 **Location:** I-84
exit 53 (Vista Ave), just s. [B] [L] [D]

(See map & index p. 40.)

LEGENDS PUB & GRILL
208/377-1819 ③⑤

◆◆ American. Casual Dining. $7-$19 **AAA Inspector Notes:** This popular sports-themed restaurant offers a variety of steaks, poultry, pasta, seafood, salads, sandwiches and pizza. Patio seating overlooks a frequented sand volleyball court. **Features:** full bar, happy hour. **Address:** 7609 W Overland Rd, Suite 100 83709 **Location:** I-84 exit 50A westbound; exit 50B eastbound, just s.

Ⓛ Ⓓ

LEKU ONA
208/345-6665 ③①

◆◆ Basque. Casual Dining. $7-$28 **AAA Inspector Notes:** With a name meaning good place, this eatery serves traditional fare from the Basque region of Spain. The dining room resembles a quaint country cottage with pictures of cultural events adorning the walls, and menu items hard to pronounce but deliciously identifiable. Favorites include red bean soup with chorizo, homemade meatballs, pork chops and grilled salmon. **Features:** full bar, patio dining. **Address:** 117 S 6th St 83702 **Location:** At 6th and Grove sts; downtown; in Basque Center. **Parking:** street only.

Ⓛ Ⓓ CALL ⑤Ⓜ

MAI THAI MODERN ASIAN CUISINE
208/344-8424 ①⑧

◆◆◆ Thai. Casual Dining. $8-$30 **AAA Inspector Notes:** This contemporary restaurant is known for their modern approach to traditional Thai cuisine and sushi. Guests can enjoy their meal surrounded by multiple calming water features, candle light and distinctive and ornate wall appointments. Vegetarian options are available. **Features:** full bar, happy hour. **Reservations:** suggested, for dinner. **Address:** 750 W Idaho St 83702 **Location:** Just nw of Capitol Blvd and W Idaho St; downtown. **Parking:** street only. Ⓛ Ⓓ

MCGRATH'S FISH HOUSE
208/375-6300

◆◆ Seafood. Casual Dining. $8-$30 **AAA Inspector Notes:** The popular chain specializes in fresh Pacific Northwest seafood, including dishes grilled over a wood fire and items from the daily fresh sheet. Also on the menu are steaks, chicken, pasta and gourmet burgers. **Features:** full bar. **Address:** 1749 S Cole Rd 83709 **Location:** I-84 exit 50A westbound; exit 50B eastbound, just s, then just w. Ⓛ Ⓓ CALL ⑤Ⓜ

MOON'S KITCHEN
208/385-0472 ②①

◆ American. Casual Dining. $7-$12 **AAA Inspector Notes:** Step back in time to the 1950s when the traditional soda fountain and sandwich shop was the social gathering spot. This eatery specializes in flavorful shakes, sirloin burgers, chicken, sandwiches and big, home-style breakfasts including fluffy omelets. Expect a wait during peak dining times. Early-bird breakfast specials and gluten-free bread are available. **Features:** early bird specials. **Address:** 712 W Idaho St 83702 **Location:** Between N Capitol Blvd and 8th St. **Parking:** street only. Ⓑ Ⓛ

PIPER PUB & GRILL
208/343-2444 ②③

◆ Scottish. Casual Dining. $10-$19 **AAA Inspector Notes:** This gathering place serves the largest selection of single-malt scotch in Idaho. Popular menu items include blackened salmon sliders, IPA flank steak, Guinness black and tan corned beef, the whiskey or elk burger, shepherd's pie served in a bread bowl, and fried chicken and waffles with Jim Beam maple pecan syrup. A bustling atmosphere predominates with live music on most weekends. **Features:** full bar, patio dining, Sunday brunch, happy hour. **Address:** 150 N 8th St, Suite 200 83702 **Location:** Jct 8th and Main sts; downtown. **Parking:** street only. Ⓛ Ⓓ Ⓛ̲A̲T̲E̲

PROTO'S PIZZERIA NAPOLETANA
208/331-1400

◆◆ Pizza. Casual Dining. $5-$22 **AAA Inspector Notes:** Known for fresh ingredients, eclectic style and friendly service, this pizzeria always is bustling. Try the cannoli or tiramisu, but be prepared to wait in line for a table during peak dining hours. **Features:** full bar, patio dining. **Address:** 345 S 8th St 83702 **Location:** Downtown; in BoDo District. **Parking:** street only.

Ⓛ Ⓓ

RAM RESTAURANT AND BREWERY
208/345-2929

◆◆ American. Casual Dining. $9-$24 **AAA Inspector Notes:** The enormous restaurant features high ceilings, huge television screens, large sports-themed banners and a brew pub area. The menu is equally enormous, with steaks, poultry, pasta, seafood, salads, sandwiches and pizza. The on-site brewery turns out a large selection of microbrews. **Features:** full bar, happy hour. **Address:** 709 E Park Blvd 83712 **Location:** I-84 exit 54 (Broadway Ave), 2.8 mi n. Ⓛ Ⓓ CALL ⑤Ⓜ

RAW SUSHI
208/343-0270 ③⑧

◆ Sushi. Casual Dining. $8-$23 **AAA Inspector Notes:** Relaxing, Zen-like décor surrounds diners at this eatery while the friendly and knowledgeable servers add to the dining experience. Guests can sit at the sushi bar, a table, booth or cozy banquette. The menu offers a wide variety of attractively presented sushi, sashimi and maki. **Features:** beer & wine. **Address:** 2273 S Vista Ave 83705 **Location:** I-84 exit 53 (Vista Ave), 0.9 mi n. Ⓛ Ⓓ

RED FEATHER
208/429-6340 ①⑤

◆◆◆ American. Casual Dining. $7-$22 **AAA Inspector Notes:** This dimly lit, contemporary eatery offers innovative American cuisine ranging from flat-bread pizzas to short ribs and Asiago-encrusted calamari. Unique martinis along with a wide variety of wines can be found on the drink menu. **Features:** full bar, Sunday brunch, happy hour. **Reservations:** suggested. **Address:** 246 N 8th St 83702 **Location:** Between Idaho and Main sts; downtown. **Parking:** street only. Ⓛ Ⓓ CALL ⑤Ⓜ

REEF
208/287-9200 ②⑧

◆◆ Polynesian. Casual Dining. $8-$24 **AAA Inspector Notes:** Guests feel as though they are entering a Hawaiian luau as they arrive at this second-story eatery. In a setting with tiki-adorned walls, thatch roofs and flowers, a wide variety of Hawaiian and Polynesian dishes are served here. Try the coconut chicken or the pupu platter. On the patio, patrons can sit in personal tiki huts when the weather permits. **Features:** full bar, patio dining, happy hour. **Address:** 105 S 6th St 83702 **Location:** Jct 6th and Main sts; downtown. **Parking:** street only. Ⓛ Ⓓ

SHIGE JAPANESE CUISINE
208/338-8423 ②⓪

◆◆ Japanese. Casual Dining. $11-$30 **AAA Inspector Notes:** Boise's original Japanese restaurant is still voted one of the best places for sushi and traditional Japanese cuisine. A variety of bento boxes, rice bowls and maki rolls are available. If fast sashimi is your style, try out Shige Express near the back of the restaurant. **Features:** beer & wine. **Address:** 100 N 8th St, Suite 215 83702 **Location:** At 8th and Main sts; center. **Parking:** street only.

Ⓛ Ⓓ

SMOKY MOUNTAIN PIZZERIA GRILL
208/387-2727

◆◆ Italian. Casual Dining. $7-$27 **AAA Inspector Notes:** Built into an old house in the city's historic district, this local favorite is adorned with eclectic decor from the past 40 years and is perfect for a family get-together. Worth noticing here are the rotating beer taps and creative seasonal drinks. **Features:** beer & wine, patio dining. **Address:** 1805 W State St 83702 **Location:** Jct 18th and State sts.

Ⓛ Ⓓ

SMOKY MOUNTAIN PIZZERIA GRILL
208/429-0011

◆◆ Italian. Casual Dining. $7-$27 **AAA Inspector Notes:** This local favorite is perfect for a family get-together. Be sure to enjoy rotating beer taps, monthly pizza specials and creative seasonal salads and drinks. Gluten-free penne pasta items are available. **Features:** beer & wine, patio dining, happy hour. **Address:** 415 E Parkcenter Blvd 83706 **Location:** I-84 exit 54 (Broadway Ave), 2.4 mi s, then 0.7 mi e on Park Blvd (which becomes Parkcenter Blvd).

Ⓛ Ⓓ

TANGO'S SUBS & EMPANADAS
208/322-3090 ①①

◆ Argentine. Quick Serve. $3-$7 **AAA Inspector Notes:** From Argentina to Idaho, stop in at this cute family-run eatery for a tasty selection of addictive savory or sweet empanadas. **Features:** patio dining. **Address:** 701 N Orchard St 83706 **Location:** Just s of N Orchard and Fairmont sts. Ⓛ Ⓓ

(See map & index p. 40.)

TAVERN AT BOWN CROSSING   208/345-2277   (41)
▼▼ American. Casual Dining. $11-$42 **AAA Inspector Notes:** This popular eastside eatery features tasty USDA Prime steak, distinctive sushi rolls and fresh seafood. Enjoy a seat inside among the eclectic décor or, if the weather allows, enjoy the meal on the second floor patio with fire pits and amazing views of the mountains. The pot roast nachos are one of the favored appetizers. **Features:** full bar, patio dining, Sunday brunch. **Reservations:** suggested. **Address:** 3111 S Bown Way 83706 **Location:** I-84 exit 54 (Broadway Ave), 1.7 mi n, 2.3 mi e on Boise Ave, then just n. **Parking:** street only.

L   D

TUCANOS BRAZILIAN GRILL   208/343-5588   (34)
▼▼ Brazilian. Casual Dining. $9-$23 **AAA Inspector Notes:** This eatery serves up fresh cuisine using the Brazilian tradition of grilling (churrasco). Be sure not to fill up on the extensive salad bar, as most entrées feature endless meats. **Features:** full bar. **Reservations:** suggested. **Address:** 1388 S Entertainment Ave 83709 **Location:** I-84 exit 50A eastbound; exit 50B westbound, just w on Overland Blvd. L   D   CALL   M

WILLOWCREEK GRILL   208/343-5544   (37)
▼▼ American. Casual Dining. $9-$22 **AAA Inspector Notes:** Tasty entrées at this grill include Idaho rib-eye, Atlantic salmon and seared ahi. Most dinners are coupled with Willowcreek twigs, also known as sweet potato fries. The chicken, broccoli and feta salad is a home run. **Features:** beer & wine. **Address:** 2273 S Vista Ave, Suite 150 83705 **Location:** I-84 exit 53 (Vista Ave), 1 mi n.

L   D

YEN CHING   208/384-0384   (9)
▼▼ Chinese. Casual Dining. $7-$18 **AAA Inspector Notes:** Located in the bustling downtown corridor, this popular eatery has been dubbed by locals as having some of the best Chinese food in town. Serving up traditional favorites, the menu features chow mein, egg foo young, fried rice and a variety of chicken, pork, beef and seafood entrées. **Features:** full bar, patio dining. **Address:** 305 N 9th St 83702 **Location:** At 9th and Bannock sts; downtown. **Parking:** street only. L   D

ZEPPOLE DOWNTOWN   208/345-2149   (13)
▼ Breads/Pastries Deli. Quick Serve. $5-$7 **AAA Inspector Notes:** Known for their variety of breads made from only the best all-natural and fresh ingredients, this soup and sandwich shop always is bustling during the lunch hour. In addition, the menu offers salads and pastries. **Address:** 217 N 8th St 83702 **Location:** Between Bannock and Idaho sts. **Parking:** street only. B   L

BOISE NATIONAL FOREST (E-2)

Elevations in the forest range from 2,860 ft. at Lucky Peak Reservoir to 10,751 ft. at Thomason Peak. Refer to AAA maps for additional elevation information.

In south-central Idaho, lakes, abandoned mines and ghost towns amid ponderosa pine and Douglas fir dot the 2,612,000 acres of mountainous terrain that make up the Boise National Forest. Large areas of the forest serve as summer range for big game. Black bears, wolves, mountain goats, bighorn sheep, mule deer and elk inhabit the woods. Upland game birds including chukars, sage grouse, Hungarian partridges and turkeys roam the backcountry. Salmon, trout and bass thrive in the cold, clear rivers, streams and reservoirs.

Deep canyons, rugged peaks exceeding 9,000 feet and high meadows offer an abundance of recreation opportunities year-round. Cross-country skiing and snowmobiling are popular during the winter. The forest offers more than 900 miles of hiking trails.

Scenic drives wind through the canyons and along the edge of the Sawtooth Wilderness; only trails enter the Frank Church-River of No Return Wilderness in the northeast section. Lake Cascade recreation facilities include camping; phone for more information about special facilities and amenities.

Additional information can be obtained from the Boise National Forest Visitor Center, 1387 S. Vinnell Way, Boise, ID 83709; phone (208) 373-4100, (208) 373-4039 or (208) 373-4007. *See Recreation Areas Chart.*

BONNERS FERRY (A-1) pop. 2,543, elev. 1,773'

Although trappers David Thompson and Finan McDonald were drawn to the banks of the Kootenai River and established a fur trading post in 1808, it was not until 1864 that a permanent settlement was founded. It was in that year that E.L. Bonner's ferry replaced the canoes of Native Americans, who the previous year had carried gold miners rushing to the Canadian Wild Horse lode.

Trapping and river transportation no longer dominate the commerce of Bonners Ferry; today the town, 25 miles south of Canada, maintains a resource-oriented economy of lumbering and farming.

The mountainous terrain of northern Idaho and the gorge cut by the Kootenai River make the Bonners Ferry region popular for its beauty. Katka View Point, 9 miles east on CR 24, provides a view of the Kootenai Valley, the Selkirk Mountains and the proposed Selkirk Crest National Wilderness area. Another popular and easy-to-reach spot to enjoy mountain scenery is near the junction of US 95 and SR 1.

Greater Bonners Ferry Visitor Center: 6373 Bonner St., Bonners Ferry, ID 83805. **Phone:** (208) 267-5922.

BOUNDARY COUNTY HISTORICAL MUSEUM is at 7229 Main St. Themed exhibit areas showcase Native American and pioneer artifacts, an early post office, a doctor's office, household items, and logging equipment and tools. Historical photos and a digital photo display also are featured. Inside the main hall is a replica of the White Caribou Bar, a Main Street landmark that operated 1905-09 and was known for featuring a mounted white caribou in its storefront window. While the caribou has been at the museum for more than 20 years, it is now back in its rightful place in the bar's window.

Behind the museum, the Historic Railroad Courtyard includes a railway semaphore signal and interpretive plaques describing the three railroads that once served the area. **Time:** Allow 30 minutes minimum. **Hours:** Tues.-Sat. 10-4, Apr.-Sept.; Fri.-Sat. 10-4, rest of year. Closed major holidays. **Cost:** $2. **Phone:** (208) 267-7720.

KOOTENAI NATIONAL WILDLIFE REFUGE is 5 mi. w. on Riverside St. along the south shore of the Kootenai River. Almost 3,000 acres along the river provide feeding, resting and breeding areas for migratory birds. Tundra swans are common in spring; Canada geese and ducks are most numerous in fall. White-tailed and mule deer, moose, black bears and coyotes also use the refuge.

One vehicle route, foot trails and three observation areas are maintained for visitors. **Hours:** Refuge daily dawn-dusk. **Cost:** Free. **Phone:** (208) 267-3888.

GAMBLING ESTABLISHMENTS

- **Kootenai River Inn Casino & Spa** is at 7169 Plaza St. **Hours:** Daily 24 hours. **Phone:** (208) 267-8511 or (800) 346-5668.

BEST WESTERN PLUS KOOTENAI RIVER INN CASINO & SPA (208)267-8511

Hotel
$119-$209

AAA Benefit: Save 10% or more every day and earn 10% bonus points!

Address: 7169 Plaza St 83805 **Location:** On US 95; City Center. **Facility:** The hotel's restaurant and most guest rooms overlook the river. A recent addition houses very spacious rooms with upscale furnishings. 103 units. 3 stories, interior corridors. **Terms:** check-in 4 pm, resort fee. **Amenities:** safes. **Pool(s):** heated indoor. **Activities:** sauna, hot tub, game room, exercise room, spa. **Guest Services:** coin laundry. **Featured Amenity: full hot breakfast.**

BONNERS FERRY LOG INN 208/267-3986

Motel
$82-$100

Address: 43 Tobe Way 83805 **Location:** 2.5 mi n on US 95. **Facility:** 22 units. 1 story, exterior corridors. *Bath:* shower only. **Parking:** winter plug-ins. **Terms:** cancellation fee imposed. **Activities:** hot tub. **Featured Amenity:** continental breakfast.

NORTHSIDE SCHOOL BED & BREAKFAST (208)267-1826

Historic Boutique Bed & Breakfast $80-$140 **Address:** 6497 Comanche St 83805 **Location:** US 95, w on Chinook St, just n on Bingham St, then just e. Located in a quiet rural area. **Facility:** Located in a historic schoolhouse, these charming guest rooms are located in what used to be classrooms and the principal's office, each with their own unique theme. You may even find a blackboard. 9 units. 2 stories (no elevator), interior corridors. **Pool(s):** heated outdoor. **Activities:** hot tub.

MUGSY'S TAVERN AND GRILL 208/267-8059

American. Casual Dining. $9-$20 **AAA Inspector Notes:** The friendly staff offers up daily specials at this tavern where a large selection of beer is offered. **Features:** full bar, patio dining. **Address:** 7161 Main St 83805 **Location:** On US 95; City Center.

BRUNEAU (G-2) elev. 2,525'

Bruneau, the French name first given the brownwater river that skirts the northern edge of the Great Basin Desert, was founded by 19th-century French-Canadian trappers.

BRUNEAU CANYON OVERLOOK is 15 mi. s.e. via a paved and gravel road, then 3 mi. w. on a dirt road, following signs. The Bruneau River courses through a narrow canyon whose vertical walls consist of layers of volcanic rhyolite and basalt that are 800 feet high in places. The overlook provides a panoramic vista of this deep and rugged canyon.

BRUNEAU DUNES STATE PARK is 5 mi. n. on SR 51/78, then 2 mi. e. on SR 78 to 27608 Sand Dunes Rd. Windblown sands have collected in this swale for about 15,000 years. The relatively constant winds have formed what is said to be the tallest single-structured sand dune in North America; its peak towers 470 feet above two shallow lakes at its base.

A visitor center features natural history displays, while The Bruneau Observatory, one of the largest public facilities of its kind in the Northwest, boasts a 25-inch reflector telescope. *See Recreation Areas Chart.*

Interpretive programs are available by appointment. The 4,800-acre park also has hiking and equestrian trails, as well as lakes for fishing and non-motorized boating. Summer temperatures in the park occasionally reach 100 F, and winter lows can fall below zero. Walking on the dunes is permitted, but vehicles must stay on the roads at all times. **Time:** Allow 1 hour minimum. **Hours:** Park open daily 7 a.m.-10 p.m. Visitor center open daily 9-5, Apr. 1 to mid-Oct.; hours vary rest of year. Observatory open Fri.-Sat. 7 p.m.-midnight, early Apr. to mid-Oct. Visitor center closed winter holidays. **Cost:** Park admission $5 (per private vehicle). Observatory $3; free (ages 0-5). **Phone:** (208) 366-7919.

C.J. STRIKE DAM AND RESERVOIR is n.w. via SR 78 on the Snake River. The 7,500-acre reservoir offers opportunities for boating, swimming and fishing. *See Recreation Areas Chart.* **Hours:** Daily 24 hours. **Cost:** Day-use access free. Camping Apr.-Oct. $8 (tent); $10 (RV). Camping rest of year $4 (tent); $5 (RV). **Phone:** (208) 388-6691, or (208) 388-2231 Mon.-Fri. 8-4.

BUHL (H-3) pop. 4,122, elev. 3,800'

Buhl (BEWL) is on the Snake River, at the western end of a valley that grew little but sagebrush until 1906, when irrigation transformed the desert into lush farmland. Agriculture and aquaculture are the bases of Buhl's present economy. Tourism and the raising of sheep and beef and dairy cattle are important. The surrounding area produces barley, sugar beets, corn, dry beans, alfalfa, grains, sugar snap peas, seed crops and potatoes.

Buhl is said to be the rainbow trout capital of the United States, since the town is a leader in trout research and production. Trout farms raise and process rainbow trout that are shipped throughout the world; similar farms produce catfish, tilapia and salmon. The products of dirt farms and local craftsmen are available Wednesday 4:30-6 p.m., mid-July through early October, at the farmers market in the parking lot of the senior citizens' center at 1010 Main St.

An oddity of nature called the Balanced Rock can be seen by taking a short drive south to Castleford, then 6 miles west. The 40-foot-high rock is perched on a base only a few feet in diameter.

Buhl Chamber of Commerce: 716 US 30E, Buhl, ID 83316. **Phone:** (208) 543-6682.

BURLEY (H-4) pop. 10,345, elev. 4,165'

Hydroplanes, super stock and other powerful racing craft churn up Burley's Snake River waterfront during the month of June, when such national speedboat championships as the Idaho Regatta take place.

CASSIA COUNTY HISTORICAL SOCIETY MUSEUM, E. Main St. and Hiland Ave., contains collections of fossils; an early railroad car and caboose; local history items; a World War II exhibit; and tools and wagons of the miners, trappers, loggers and farmers who settled southern Idaho. Audiovisual displays chart the pioneer trails that led emigrants to the Pacific Northwest.

On the museum grounds are a replica sheepherder's wagon and furnished reproductions of a one-room cabin, a general store, a schoolhouse and a barbershop. **Time:** Allow 1 hour minimum. **Hours:** Tues.-Sat. 10-5, Apr. 15-Oct. 15. Closed major holidays. **Cost:** Donations. **Phone:** (208) 678-7172.

BEST WESTERN PLUS BURLEY INN & CONVENTION CENTER (208)678-3501

Hotel
$89-$129

AAA Benefit: Save 10% or more every day and earn 10% bonus points!

Address: 800 N Overland Ave 83318 **Location:** I-84 exit 208, just s. **Facility:** 124 units. 2 stories (no elevator), interior/exterior corridors. **Parking:** winter plug-ins. **Pool(s):** heated outdoor. **Activities:** exercise room. **Guest Services:** valet and coin laundry. **Featured Amenity:** full hot breakfast.

FAIRFIELD INN & SUITES BY MARRIOTT (208)677-5000

Hotel
$93-$155

AAA Benefit: Members save 5% or more!

Address: 230 W 7th St N 83318 **Location:** I-84 exit 208, just sw. **Facility:** 81 units. 3 stories, interior corridors. **Pool(s):** heated indoor. **Activities:** hot tub, exercise room. **Guest Services:** valet and coin laundry. **Featured Amenity:** full hot breakfast.

SUPER 8 BURLEY (208)678-7000

 Hotel $75-$116 **Address:** 336 S 600 W 83318 **Location:** I-84 exit 208, just n. **Facility:** 68 units. 3 stories, interior corridors. **Parking:** winter plug-ins. **Pool(s):** heated indoor. **Activities:** hot tub, exercise room. **Guest Services:** coin laundry.

WHERE TO EAT

STEVO'S 208/679-3887

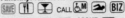 American. Casual Dining. $6-$20 **AAA Inspector Notes:** In addition to popular burgers and sandwiches, this family-run restaurant offers thick lamb chops, juicy steaks, and seven different types of Idaho super spuds. **Features:** beer & wine. **Address:** 290 S 600 W 83336 **Location:** I-84 exit 208, 0.3 mi n. L D

CALDWELL (F-1) pop. 46,237, elev. 2,367'

On the Boise River, Caldwell was established in the late 19th century. The community, which began as a construction camp for the Oregon Short Line Railroad, is now associated with the processing and distribution of farm products. Boone Science Hall, near the corner of 20th and Fillmore streets on the 800-student College of Idaho campus, houses the Orma J. Smith Museum of Natural History, the Evans Gem and Mineral Collection and the Whittenberger Planetarium; phone (208) 459-5011.

Caldwell Chamber of Commerce: 704 Blaine St., Caldwell, ID 83606. **Phone:** (208) 459-7493.

WINERIES

- **Ste. Chapelle Winery** is 8 mi. s.w. on SR 55, then .5 mi. e., following signs. **Hours:** Mon.-Sat. 10-5,

Sun. noon-5, Memorial Day-Labor Day; Sun.-Fri. noon-5, Sat. 10-5, rest of year. Closed Easter, Thanksgiving and Christmas. **Phone:** (208) 453-7843. GT

BEST WESTERN PLUS CALDWELL INN & SUITES
(208)454-7225

Hotel
$79-$139

AAA Benefit: Save 10% or more every day and earn 10% bonus points!

Address: 908 Specht Ave 83605 **Location:** I-84 exit 29, just s. **Facility:** 69 units. 3 stories, interior corridors. **Pool(s):** heated indoor. **Activities:** hot tub, picnic facilities, exercise room. **Guest Services:** valet and coin laundry.

LA QUINTA INN CALDWELL
(208)454-2222

Hotel $64-$235 **Address:** 901 Specht Ave 83605 **Location:** I-84 exit 29, just s. **Facility:** 65 units, some kitchens. 3 stories (no elevator), interior corridors. **Pool(s):** heated indoor. **Activities:** hot tub, exercise room. **Guest Services:** coin laundry.

WILD ROSE MANOR BED & BREAKFAST
(208)454-3331

Bed & Breakfast $139-$189 **Address:** 5800 Oasis Rd 83607 **Location:** I-84 exit 17 (Sand Hollow), just w, then 0.5 mi nw, follow signs. **Facility:** This picturesque property offers beautifully appointed and themed guest rooms. It's perfect for a single special night or a three-day weekend. 4 units. 2 stories (no elevator), interior corridors. **Terms:** check-in 4 pm, 3 day cancellation notice-fee imposed. **Activities:** hot tub, game room.

WHERE TO EAT

MR. V'S FAMILY RESTAURANT
208/454-9778

American. Family Dining. $6-$15 **AAA Inspector Notes:** Serving up home-style favorites since 1971, you can expect pot roast, a twist on a seasonal chicken pot pie, roasted turkey and chicken-fried steak along with the friendliness and charm of a small town diner. Ask your server if they have the toasted coconut cream pie. If they do, order it quick! **Address:** 407 N 10th Ave 83605 **Location:** I-84 exit 28 (10th Ave), just s.

CAMBRIDGE (F-1) pop. 328, elev. 2,739'

CAMBRIDGE MUSEUM, jct. US 95 and SR 71, provides information about area heritage, from the arrival of the first settlers in 1869 through the 1930s. Displays focus on geology, farming, Native American life and the community's pioneer days. A blacksmith shop and a replica schoolroom with historical items can be seen. A reproduction of a mine entrance features illustrations demonstrating dynamiting techniques.

A genealogy library is available by appointment. **Time:** Allow 30 minutes minimum. **Hours:** Museum Wed.-Sat. 10-4, June-Aug. Phone ahead to confirm schedule. **Cost:** Donations. **Phone:** (208) 257-3485.

RECREATIONAL ACTIVITIES

White-water Rafting

- **Hughes River Expeditions** departs from various locations depending on trip. **Hours:** Schedule varies; phone ahead. **Phone:** (208) 257-3477 or (800) 262-1882.
- **ROW Adventures** departs from the Frontier Motel at 240 S. Superior St. **Hours:** Snake River trips are offered May-Sept. Schedule varies; phone ahead. **Phone:** (208) 765-0841 or (800) 451-6034.

CARIBOU-TARGHEE NATIONAL FOREST (F-5)

Elevations in the forest range from 4,700 ft. at Curlew Campground to 12,197 ft. at Diamond Peak. Refer to AAA maps for additional elevation information.

In southeast Idaho extending into Wyoming and Utah, Caribou-Targhee National Forest covers more than 3 million acres. The Caribou unit is noted for rugged scenery marked by towering mountain ranges and beautiful valleys. Drives along the Snake River and through the many canyons provide scenic vistas. A few traces of the ghost towns of Keenan and Caribou City recall the gold rush days.

Named for Tygee, a Bannock Indian chief, the Targhee section is in the Lemhi, Beaverhead, Teton, Centennial, Palisades and Caribou ranges and extends in a semicircle around the headwaters of Henry's Fork of the Snake River. The Continental Divide forms most of the northern boundary; Yellowstone and Grand Teton national parks make up most of the eastern border. Canyons, high peaks and desert add to the picturesque scenery.

Minnetonka Cave *(see St. Charles p. 95)* in St. Charles Canyon is one of two accessible caves and features interesting geological formations. Ice never melts in Paris Cave, a small, undeveloped cave in nearby Paris Canyon.

Water is abundant throughout the Targhee. Big Springs, one of the largest springs in the United States, is reached by SR 59 from US 20 at Macks Inn. It issues from the base of a high plateau at a constant 52 F and is the headwaters of Henry's Fork, which is the north fork of the Snake River.

A 3- to 5-hour canoe/float trip can be taken along a 5-mile national recreation water trail just below Big Springs. Moose, trumpeter swans, ospreys and bald eagles can often be seen. Further down Henry's Fork, boaters must portage around several sections of dangerous water between Macks Inn and Ashton.

Upper and Lower Mesa falls are east of US 20 and north of Ashton on Mesa Falls Scenic Byway. The Upper Mesa Falls is 114 feet high; the Lower Mesa Falls is 65 to 70 feet high.

Trout fishing is excellent, most notably at Palisades Reservoir, Henry's Lake, Island Park Reservoir, Henry's Fork and South Fork of the Snake River.

Winter sports activity areas near Ashton, Driggs, Heise, Island Park, Montpelier and Pocatello contain miles of groomed snowmobile and cross-country skiing trails as well as downhill ski resorts. More than 1,100 miles of hiking, horse and mountain bike trails provide a variety of summer backcountry experiences.

Camping is available from Memorial Day weekend to Labor Day (weather permitting). Fees for developed camping areas range from $10 to $36 at single-family campgrounds, depending on the level of service at each facility. Group camping facilities also are available. Phone (877) 444-6777 for campsite reservations.

Brochures are available at the visitor center, 425 N. Capitol Ave. in Idaho Falls, open year-round. For more information contact the Forest Supervisor's Office, Caribou-Targhee National Forest, 1405 Hollipark Dr., Idaho Falls, ID 83401; phone (208) 524-7500. *See Recreation Areas Chart.*

CASCADE (F-2) pop. 939

Though logging has historically been an important industry for Cascade, tourism has increasingly contributed to the local economy. The town is a jumping-off point for travel to millions of acres of mountainous backcountry and wilderness, where snowmobiling and Nordic skiing are popular cold weather pursuits.

In addition, the community is located in Long Valley near the southern end of Lake Cascade, a 30,000-acre reservoir formed in 1948. Boating, sailing, kayaking, water skiing and some of the state's best perch fishing can be enjoyed on the body of water, and in winter, ice fishing is added to the long list of recreational activities. Lake Cascade State Park, 4,450 acres off SR 55, offers camping facilities and six boat ramps *(see Recreation Areas Chart).*

Cascade Chamber of Commerce: P.O. Box 571, Cascade, ID 83611. **Phone:** (208) 382-3833.

RECREATIONAL ACTIVITIES
White-water Rafting
- **Kelly's Whitewater Park** is 1 mi. s. on SR 55. Stretching along 1,800 feet of the Payette River, the park features four sets of rapids suitable for kayaking, tubing and stand-up paddling enthusiasts of all ages and skill levels. A sloping lawn offers the perfect spot to dry off after a run on the river. Also on-site is a 2.5-mile trail, volleyball and bocce courts, horseshoe pits and a welcome center. **Time:** Allow 30 minutes minimum. **Hours:** Daily 10-7; Memorial Day weekend-Sept. 30. **Cost:** Donations. **Phone:** (208) 405-3000.

🍴 🏕

THE ASHLEY INN   (208)382-5621

♦♦♦ **Boutique Hotel** $154-$322 **Address:** 500 N Main St 83611 **Location:** 0.3 mi n of center on SR 55 (Main St). **Facility:** Located along a river bend with panoramic mountain views, the tastefully appointed decor in every section of this hotel has to be seen to be appreciated. The guest rooms and bathrooms are spacious. 67 units. 3 stories, interior corridors. **Parking:** winter plug-ins. **Terms:** cancellation fee imposed. **Pool(s):** heated indoor. **Activities:** hot tub, lawn sports, picnic facilities, limited exercise equipment. **Guest Services:** coin laundry.

🅟 CALL 🔊ᴹ 🔁 BIZ HS 📶 ✖ 💻
/SOME UNITS 🛡 🖼

CATALDO (B-1) elev. 2,150'

COEUR D'ALENE'S OLD MISSION STATE PARK, off I-90 exit 39, is named for the restored Old Sacred Heart Mission, built 1848-53 by Coeur d'Alene Indians under the guidance of Jesuit priest Father Antonio Ravalli. It is reputedly the oldest standing structure in the state. The 18-inch-thick mission walls were built of woven grass and adobe mud without nails. The Sacred Encounters exhibit documents the meeting of the Jesuit missionaries and the Coeur d'Alene and Salish tribes and the effects the encounter had on both cultures.

Video presentations, mission tours and a visitor center are available. The park also is the headquarters for the state-run portion of the Trail of the Coeur d'Alenes; the 56-mile section runs between Mullan and Harrison. *See Recreation Areas Chart.* **Hours:** Daily 9-5, Apr.-Oct.; 10-3, rest of year. Closed Jan. 1, Thanksgiving and Christmas. **Cost:** Park admission $5 (per private vehicle). Sacred Encounters exhibit $5; $10 (family). **Phone:** (208) 682-3814.

✖ 🐾 🏕

CHALLIS (F-3) pop. 1,081, elev. 5,288'

LAND OF THE YANKEE FORK STATE PARK AND HISTORIC AREA has its interpretive center at jct. US 93 and SR 75. The center offers dioramas, artifacts and photographs of the mines and miners from 1870-1920 as well as an audiovisual program about mining and ghost town history.

A 91-mile scenic loop, the Custer Motorway Adventure Road (FR 70), begins in Challis on a narrow, gravel and dirt road, and runs past stage stations, ghost towns and abandoned mines, the Yankee Fork Gold Dredge, the Custer Museum and Sunbeam Dam Interpretive Site. The loop's return road is paved SR 75 (the Salmon River Scenic Byway).

The Custer Museum features mining artifacts and early pioneer belongings. Once a thriving mining town, Custer is now a ghost town providing insights into what life was like in the 1880s. At Sunbeam Dam Interpretive Site, information about the historic area, Sawtooth National Recreation Area and the dam is available.

Several recreational trails offer opportunities for hiking and biking; some are open to all-terrain vehicles and motorbikes. Bayhorse, a ghost town noted for its former silver mines, is a trailhead for a system of motorcycle/ATV trails. Access is via a well-maintained gravel road that accommodates trailers and motorhomes about 4 miles off SR 75.

Note: The Custer Motorway Adventure Road is not recommended for vehicles with low clearance, trailers or motor homes. Allow 30 minutes for the interpretive center. Allow 3 hours for the loop. **Hours:** Interpretive center open daily 9-5, May-Oct.; Wed.-Sat. 10-4, rest of year. The Custer Motorway Adventure Road may be closed by snow Oct. 1 to mid-June. Yankee Fork Gold Dredge open for tours Memorial Day-Labor Day. Custer Museum open Memorial Day-Labor Day. **Cost:** Park, interpretive centers and museum $2; $5 (family). Trails or ghost town $5. Gold dredge tour $5; $1 (ages 6-12). **Phone:** (208) 879-5244 or (208) 838-2529. 🐾

CHALLIS NATIONAL FOREST—See
Salmon-Challis National Forest p. 96

CLARK FORK (B-1) pop. 536, elev. 2,084'

Clark Fork lies at the foot of the Cabinet Mountains, just northeast of Lake Pend Oreille. The town is on the lake's main tributary, the Clark Fork River, just before it flows into the lake. This location experiences unusually warm winters and cool summers.

The town sprang up in the 1880s when the main line of the Northern Pacific Railroad cut through the Bitterroot and Cabinet mountains. The railroad made lumbering profitable, and lumberjacks began arriving on the area's first steam tugboats. Soon nearby trappers were giving up their trade and joining the timber camps. Today the area attracts hikers, anglers and other outdoor enthusiasts.

Lake Pend Oreille is a focal point of the Pend Oreille Scenic Byway (SR 200), which runs northwest from the Montana border to Sandpoint.

CABINET GORGE DAM, 8 mi. e. on SR 200, on the Clark Fork River, is a horseshoe-shaped dam in a scenic setting. A lookout point affords an excellent view of the project. **Hours:** Viewpoint open Apr.-Sept. (weather permitting).

CABINET GORGE HATCHERY, 8 mi. s.e. on River Rd., then n. on Cabinet Gorge Rd. following signs, raises up to 16 million kokanee salmon annually for release into Lake Pend Oreille in June. Self-guiding tours provide opportunities to see salmon and other fish species in various stages of development. Viewing is best November through June. **Time:** Allow 30 minutes minimum. **Hours:** Daily 8-4. Closed Jan. 1, Thanksgiving and Christmas. Phone ahead to confirm schedule. **Cost:** Free. **Phone:** (208) 266-1431.

CLARKIA (C-1)

The area surrounding Clarkia (CLAR-key) is rich in gemstones, particularly star garnets and fossils. Fossil digging is permitted at the Clarkia Miocene Site, south on SR 3.

EMERALD CREEK GARNET AREA is 7 mi. n. on SR 3, then 8 mi. w. on gravel FR 447. A .5-mile uphill trail leads to 281 Gulch, one of only two places in the world where star garnets exist (the other is in India). Visitors sluice for the 12-sided crystals using buckets, shovels and screen boxes furnished onsite. **Time:** Allow 2 hours minimum. **Hours:** Fri.-Tues. 9-4:30, Fri. before Memorial Day weekend-Labor Day. **Cost:** $10; $5 (ages 6-12). **Phone:** (208) 245-2531. 🏕

CLEARWATER NATIONAL FOREST (C-2)

Elevations in the forest range from 1,200 ft. to 8,820 ft. at Ranger Peak. Refer to AAA maps for additional elevation information.

In the northeastern part of the state, large stands of tall trees and many miles of clear, fast-running streams and rivers characterize the rugged, mountainous Clearwater National Forest. Scenic Lewis and Clark Highway (US 12) runs a few miles south of but roughly parallel to the Lolo Trail, the Native American route across the Bitterroots to buffalo-hunting country.

A portion of the Selway-Bitterroot Wilderness, the second largest wilderness area in the continental United States, makes up part of Clearwater's 1.8 million acres. US 12 follows the rugged Lochsa Wild and Scenic River, where kayak and raft enthusiasts challenge the stream's white water. Recreation information is available at ranger stations in Kooskia, Orofino, Potlatch and Powell.

Lolo Pass Visitors Center, along US 12 at the crest of the Bitterroots on the Idaho-Montana border, and the restored Lochsa Historical Ranger Station, halfway between Powell and Kooskia on US 12, are open Memorial Day weekend through late September. For further information, contact the North Fork Ranger's Office, 12730 US 12, Orofino, ID 83544; phone (208) 476-8267. *See Recreation Areas Chart.*

COEUR D'ALENE (B-1) pop. 44,137, elev. 2,157'
• Hotels p. 56 • Restaurants p. 58

The largest city in northern Idaho takes its name from the local tribe of Native Americans. French trappers dubbed them Coeur d'Alene (CORE-dah-LANE), meaning "heart of the awl," a vernacular phrase describing them as shrewd traders.

Gen. William Tecumseh Sherman established an Army post in 1878 at the point where the Spokane River drains Lake Coeur d'Alene. Fort Sherman became the nucleus of a settlement that was named for the lake. The 1880s mining boom in the Silver Valley brought prosperity, as Coeur d'Alene became an important shipping point. For a period it was the busiest steamboat port west of the Mississippi River. By 1900 boats were carrying tourists on excursion cruises.

North Idaho College now occupies the old fort site, and Fort Sherman Chapel survives at the corner of Hubbard Street and Woodland Drive. The community college has an enrollment of 4,600; phone (208) 769-3300.

Idaho's "Lake City" remains a popular resort. In summer the city's beaches, parks and docks throng with outdoor enthusiasts. Boating, houseboating, swimming, water skiing, parasailing and fishing are popular activities.

Downtown on the shores of Lake Coeur d'Alene is forested Tubbs Hill, a 120-acre preserve featuring trails to secluded coves and beaches, and to the summit for panoramic views. Also along the waterfront, The Coeur d'Alene Resort Golf Course is a par 71 distinguished by its floating, 15,000-square-foot island green; phone (208) 667-4653 or (800) 935-6283.

What is said to be the world's longest floating boardwalk runs 3,300 feet from Independence Point in City Park to the foot of Third Street, around The Coeur d'Alene Resort. The park offers a large public beach as well as a playground designed after Fort Sherman. Here, walkers, bicyclists and skaters also find access to the North Idaho Centennial Trail. The paved pathway extends 24 miles from Higgens Point, east of Coeur d'Alene, west to the Idaho/Washington border, where it connects with Spokane's Centennial Trail.

Coeur d'Alene Visitor Bureau: 105 N. 1st St., Suite 100, Coeur d'Alene, ID 83814. **Phone:** (208) 664-3194 or (877) 782-9232.

Shopping: Downtown Coeur d'Alene, along Sherman Avenue, is home to a number of art galleries and retail outlets offering clothing, custom jewelry and housewares. Silver Lake Mall, 3.5 miles north on US 95, offers JCPenney, Macy's and Sears. Antiques can be found at Coeur d'Alene Antique Mall, 408 Haycraft, and at Government Way Antique Mall, 3650 N. Government Way.

HUMAN RIGHTS EDUCATION INSTITUTE is at 414 W. Mullan Rd. in the historic 1902 Spokane & Inland Empire Electric Railway substation building in the northeast corner of Coeur d'Alene City Park. The cultural organization educates and raises awareness about various human rights issues; its exhibit galleries host changing displays that support these goals. The Peace Lives Here Gallery showcases artwork illustrating human rights principles and responsibilities. Interactive activities for children are offered.

Time: Allow 30 minutes minimum. **Hours:** Mon.-Fri. 10-5. Closed major holidays. Phone ahead to confirm schedule. **Cost:** Free. **Phone:** (208) 292-2359. GT

LAKE COEUR D'ALENE is s. of town. Once called one of the five most beautiful lakes in the world by *National Geographic*, it is surrounded by mountains and a lush forest. Twenty-five miles long, it averages 2.5 miles in width and has a 135-mile-long shoreline. It has one of the nation's largest populations of osprey, and bald eagles can be seen diving into the lake to catch salmon in winter. Power boating, sailing and fishing are popular summer sports.

LAKE COEUR D'ALENE CRUISES departs from the Coeur d'Alene city dock at Independence Point. A 90-minute, narrated lake cruise provides glimpses of wildlife and local scenery. Brunch, sunset, full-day and themed cruises also are available. **Time:** Allow 2 hours minimum. **Hours:** Narrated lake cruises depart daily, late Apr.-late Oct. Departure times vary; phone ahead. **Cost:** $23.75; $21.75 (ages 55+); $15.75 (ages 6-12). **Phone:** (208) 765-4000, ext. 21.

MUSEUM OF NORTH IDAHO, 115 Northwest Blvd., explores the history of the Coeur d'Alene region. Exhibits about exploration, transportation, early settlers, firefighting, logging and lumbering are included. Rotating seasonal exhibits and a 20-minute video presentation relating the history of the Coeur d'Alene region also are offered. **Time:** Allow 30 minutes minimum. **Hours:** Tues.-Sat. 11-5, Apr.-Oct. Closed July 4. **Cost:** $4; $1 (ages 6-16); $10 (family, two adults and children ages 0-16). **Phone:** (208) 664-3448.

 SILVERWOOD—see Athol p. 34.

RECREATIONAL ACTIVITIES
White-water Rafting

- **ROW Adventures** offers trips on the Grande Ronde, Owyhee and Snake rivers from various departure points. **Hours:** Trips are offered mid-May to mid-Sept. Schedule varies; phone ahead. **Phone:** (208) 765-0841 or (800) 451-6034.

Ziplines

- **Timberline Adventures** is at 210 Sherman Ave. #131. Trips depart from the office for the canopy course located 12 miles east of Coeur d'Alene. It features 7 lines and three sky bridges overlooking Beauty Bay. It takes 2-2.5 hours to complete the course. **Note:** Riders must be 7 years old, weigh no more than 270 lbs. and sign a waiver. Riders under 18 will need guardian's written permission. Closed-toe shoes required. **Time:** Allow 4 hours minimum. **Hours:** Mon.-Sat. 9-5, May-Dec. Tours run every 30 minutes. **Cost:** $95. Reservations are required. **Phone:** (208) 820-2080.

BAYMONT INN & SUITES COEUR D'ALENE   208/667-6777

▼▼ ▼▼ **Hotel.** Rates not provided. **Address:** 2209 E Sherman Ave 83814 **Location:** I-90 exit 15 (Sherman Ave), just s. **Facility:** 62 units, some kitchens. 3 stories (no elevator), interior corridors. **Pool(s):** heated indoor. **Activities:** hot tub. **Guest Services:** valet and coin laundry.

CALL   BIZ   / SOME UNITS

BEST WESTERN PLUS COEUR D'ALENE INN
(208)765-3200

Hotel
$129-$234

AAA Benefit: Save 10% or more every day and earn 10% bonus points!

Address: 506 W Appleway Ave 83814 **Location:** I-90 exit 12, just nw. **Facility:** 122 units. 2 stories, interior corridors. **Parking:** winter plug-ins. **Terms:** check-in 4 pm, resort fee. **Pool(s):** heated indoor. **Activities:** hot tub, exercise room. **Guest Services:** valet laundry, area transportation.

THE COEUR D'ALENE RESORT
208/209-5026

Resort Hotel. Rates not provided. **Address:** 115 S 2nd St 83814 **Location:** Waterfront. I-90 exit 11 (Northwest Blvd), 2 mi s. **Facility:** The luxury resort dominates the lake shore. You'll find lavishly decorated guest rooms, admirable service and stunning landscaped grounds. Some rooms have fireplaces and many have patios. 338 units. 18 stories, interior/exterior corridors. **Parking:** on-site (fee) and valet, winter plug-ins. **Terms:** check-in 4 pm. **Amenities:** video games. *Some:* safes. **Dining:** 5 restaurants, also, Beverly's, see separate listing, entertainment. **Pool(s):** heated outdoor, heated indoor. **Activities:** sauna, hot tub, steamroom, marina, fishing, regulation golf, tennis, recreation programs, exercise room, spa. **Guest Services:** valet laundry, area transportation. Affiliated with Preferred Hotels & Resorts.

DAYS INN-COEUR D'ALENE
(208)667-8668

Hotel $65-$200 **Address:** 2200 Northwest Blvd 83814 **Location:** I-90 exit 11 (Northwest Blvd), just se. Located in a business park. **Facility:** 63 units, some efficiencies. 2 stories (no elevator), interior corridors. **Parking:** winter plug-ins. **Amenities:** safes. **Activities:** hot tub, exercise room. **Guest Services:** coin laundry.

FLAMINGO MOTEL
208/664-2159

Motel $110-$180 **Address:** 718 E Sherman Ave 83814 **Location:** I-90 exit 15 (Sherman Ave), 1.1 mi s. Adjacent to city park. **Facility:** 13 units, some two bedrooms and kitchens. 1 story, exterior corridors. **Terms:** cancellation fee imposed.

HAMPTON INN & SUITES COEUR D'ALENE
(208)769-7900

Hotel $129-$229 **Address:** 1500 Riverstone Dr 83814 **Location:** I-90 exit 11 (Northwest Blvd), 0.6 mi sw. **Facility:** 124 units. 5 stories, interior corridors. **Parking:** winter plug-ins. **Terms:** 1-7 night minimum stay, cancellation fee imposed. **Pool(s):** heated indoor. **Activities:** hot tub, exercise room. **Guest Services:** valet and coin laundry.

AAA Benefit: Members save up to 10%!

HOLIDAY INN EXPRESS HOTEL & SUITES COEUR D'ALENE
208/667-3100

Hotel. Rates not provided. **Address:** 2300 W Seltice Way 83814 **Location:** I-90 exit 11 (Northwest Blvd), just s. **Facility:** 101 units. 3 stories, interior/exterior corridors. **Parking:** winter plug-ins. **Pool(s):** heated indoor. **Activities:** hot tub, exercise room. **Guest Services:** valet and coin laundry.

JAPAN HOUSE SUITES
(208)667-0600

Hotel $79-$159 **Address:** 2113 E Sherman Ave 83814 **Location:** I-90 exit 15 (Sherman Ave), just s. **Facility:** 22 units. 2 stories (no elevator), interior corridors. **Parking:** winter plug-ins. **Terms:** cancellation fee imposed, resort fee.

LA QUINTA INN & SUITES COEUR D'ALENE
(208)665-9000

Hotel $86-$383 **Address:** 333 Ironwood Dr 83814 **Location:** I-90 exit 12, just s. **Facility:** 118 units, some efficiencies. 4 stories, interior corridors. **Parking:** winter plug-ins. **Pool(s):** heated indoor. **Activities:** hot tub, exercise room.

QUALITY INN & SUITES COEUR D'ALENE
(208)765-5500

Hotel $69-$199 **Address:** 280 W Appleway Ave 83814 **Location:** I-90 exit 12, just ne. **Facility:** 51 units, some two bedrooms, efficiencies and kitchens. 3 stories (no elevator), interior corridors. **Parking:** winter plug-ins. **Pool(s):** heated indoor. **Activities:** hot tub, playground, exercise room. **Guest Services:** valet and coin laundry.

RAMADA INN COEUR D'ALENE
(208)664-1649

Hotel $69-$197 **Address:** 2303 N 4th St 83814 **Location:** I-90 exit 13 (4th St), just n. **Facility:** 69 units. 3 stories, interior corridors. **Parking:** winter plug-ins. **Pool(s):** heated indoor. **Activities:** hot tub. **Guest Services:** valet and coin laundry.

RESORT CITY INN
(208)676-1225

Motel
$69-$139

Address: 621 Sherman Ave 83814 **Location:** I-90 exit 11 (Northwest Blvd), 2.5 mi e via Northwest Blvd and Sherman Ave; downtown. **Facility:** 18 units, some efficiencies. 2 stories (no elevator), exterior corridors. **Terms:** 3 day cancellation notice-fee imposed.

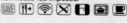

THE ROOSEVELT INN AND SPA
(208)765-5200

Historic Bed & Breakfast $109-$209 **Address:** 105 E Wallace Ave 83814 **Location:** I-90 exit 13 (4th St), 2 mi s, then just w; downtown. **Facility:** Overshadowed by towering pines, The Roosevelt is housed in a converted 1905 red-brick schoolhouse complete with a bell tower. The three-story building hosted classes as recently as the 1960s. 14 units, some two bedrooms. 3 stories, interior corridors. **Terms:** 2 night minimum stay - seasonal and/or weekends, 45 day cancellation notice-fee imposed, resort fee. **Activities:** hot tub, massage.

Keep your focus safely

on the road when driving

SPRINGHILL SUITES BY MARRIOTT COEUR D'ALENE
(208)667-2212

Hotel
$101-$273

SPRINGHILL SUITES Marriott

AAA Benefit: Members save 5% or more!

Address: 2250 W Seltice Way 83814 **Location:** I-90 exit 11 (Northwest Blvd), just s. **Facility:** 118 units. 4 stories, interior corridors. **Parking:** winter plug-ins. **Pool(s):** heated indoor. **Activities:** hot tub, bicycles, exercise room. **Guest Services:** valet and coin laundry. **Featured Amenity: full hot breakfast.**

SAVE CALL 🚲M 🏊 BIZ HS

📶 ✉ 🔌 💻 💳 / SOME UNITS 🛎

WHERE TO EAT

BARDENAY
208/765-1540

American. Gastropub. $9-$20 **AAA Inspector Notes:** The emphasis may be on cocktails and microbrews but a wide variety of menu items such as chicken satay, salmon, and steaks are all tasty. A wall of windows overlooks the pond in Riverstone Village and there is a patio for al fresco dining. There is an age restriction after 10 pm, adults only. **Features:** full bar, patio dining, Sunday brunch, happy hour. **Address:** 1710 W Riverstone Dr 83814 **Location:** I-90 exit 11 (Northwest Blvd), just sw. L D

BEVERLY'S
208/765-4000

Pacific Rim. Fine Dining. $10-$55 **AAA Inspector Notes:** The restaurant serves tantalizing food in a sleek, casually elegant dining room with panoramic views of pristine Lake Coeur d'Alene from its seventh-floor perch. The seasonal menu takes advantage of the freshest Northwest seafood and local produce and complementing the dining experience is one of the finest wine cellars in the world. **Features:** full bar, early bird specials. **Reservations:** suggested. **Address:** 115 S 2nd St 83814 **Location:** I-90 exit 11 (Northwest Blvd), 2 mi s; in The Coeur d'Alene Resort. **Parking:** on-site (fee). L D CALL 🚲M

BONSAI BISTRO
208/765-4321

Asian. Fine Dining. $8-$36 **AAA Inspector Notes:** This stylish Asian-inspired dining room has two levels with the lower level featuring seating around a koi pond as well as outdoor seating amid rockwork and water features. The upper floor takes advantage of the water view with large windows. The wide array of Asian dishes and sushi affords something for every diner. **Features:** full bar, happy hour. **Address:** 101 E Sherman Ave 83814 **Location:** Downtown. L D

THE BREAKFAST NOOK
208/667-1699

American. Family Dining. $5-$12 **AAA Inspector Notes:** Serving up favorites including steak and eggs, eggs Benedict and waffles, this popular breakfast joint is frequented by locals and tourists alike. Burgers and sandwiches are offered during the lunch hour. Expect a wait during peak dining times. **Address:** 1719 N 4th St 83814 **Location:** I-90 exit 13 (4th St), 0.4 mi s on 3rd St, then just e on Poplar Ave. B L CALL 🚲M

THE CEDARS FLOATING RESTAURANT
208/664-2922

Steak Seafood. Casual Dining. $23-$69 **AAA Inspector Notes:** This seafood and steak restaurant floats on Lake Coeur d'Alene. Large windows offer expansive views of the lake and forest. The house specialty is Biergarten steak, a filet mignon basted with beer. **Features:** full bar, patio dining. **Reservations:** suggested. **Address:** 1 Marina Dr 83814 **Location:** I-90 exit 12, 1.5 mi s on US 95. D

CRICKET'S RESTAURANT & OYSTER BAR
208/765-1990

American. Casual Dining. $10-$27 **AAA Inspector Notes:** A model train running on an overhead track contributes to the eclectic décor of this fun and lively establishment. The oyster bar offers up many variations for the oyster lover. Try the Port rib-eye with mushrooms or the homemade pizza. **Features:** full bar, patio dining, happy hour. **Address:** 424 Sherman Ave 83814 **Location:** Downtown. **Parking:** street only. L D CALL 🚲M

JAVA ON SHERMAN
208/667-0010

Coffee/Tea. Quick Serve. $6-$11 **AAA Inspector Notes:** This spot offers only Fair Trade Certified organic coffee and homemade baked goods, soups and entrées. Try the lumpy muffins or apple, Brie and ham panini for lunch. This casual eccentric café is perfect for all types of diners. A happy hour menu is served after 4 pm. **Features:** happy hour. **Address:** 819 Sherman Ave 83814 **Location:** Downtown. **Parking:** street only. B L D

MELTZ EXTREME GRILLED CHEESE
208/664-1717

Sandwiches. Quick Serve. $5-$13 **AAA Inspector Notes:** This unassuming little restaurant takes the tasty grilled cheese sandwich and creates their menu from this foundation. Diners can build their own with a variety of cheeses, vegetables, and meats offered as different choices. They have some signature offerings and a couple of favorites include the oinker and burger bomber. They also feature soup, salad and homemade cookies for dessert. **Address:** 1735 W Kathleen Ave 83815 **Location:** Jct Kathleen Ave and N Ramsey Rd. L D CALL 🚲M

MOON TIME
208/667-2331

American. Casual Dining. $8-$14 **AAA Inspector Notes:** This informal restaurant has the feel of a neighborhood pub, complete with dartboards. With dishes ranging from gumbo and burritos to Bulgogi beef sandwiches and vegetarian Anasazi bean burgers, the food is as eclectic as the restaurant itself. For something light, try a bowl of homemade soup or munch on spicy curried cashews while trying one of the many microbrews. **Features:** beer & wine. **Address:** 1602 Sherman Ave, Suite 116 83814 **Location:** I-90 exit 15 (Sherman Ave), 0.5 mi s. L D

THE OLYMPIA
208/666-9495

Greek. Family Dining. $6-$15 **AAA Inspector Notes:** Diners can enjoy authentic Greek comfort food at this family spot, just a short walk from the lakefront and shopping. The owner's father introduced gyros to the Northwest in 1970, so guests should try the requisite gyro—tender, flavorful and juicy. One of my favorites is the dolmades-grape leaves stuffed with meat and rice, covered with a lemon sauce. I also love the spanakopita (spinach pie made with flaky filo dough). The meal would not be complete without a slice of honey-kissed baklava and a cup of steaming Greek coffee. **Features:** beer & wine. **Address:** 301 E Lakeside Ave 83814 **Location:** Jct N 3rd St; downtown. **Parking:** street only. L D CALL 🚲M

THAI BAMBOO
208/667-5300

Thai. Casual Dining. $10-$20 **AAA Inspector Notes:** Offering a wide variety of traditional Thai dishes, this eatery has a casual, vibrant atmosphere. Guests can enjoy the ever-changing colors of the celestial ceiling while dining. **Features:** full bar. **Address:** 2010 N 4th St 83814 **Location:** I-90 exit 13 (4th St), just se. L D

TOMATO STREET
208/667-5000

Italian. Family Dining. $8-$17 **AAA Inspector Notes:** This family-oriented, Italian market-style restaurant features brick-oven pizza, calzones, salads, sandwiches and traditional items. An attentive and efficient waitstaff cheerfully dons outlandish headgear, which sets this eatery apart from the norm. The canopied tables which occupy the center of the dining room give the feel of a sidewalk café. **Features:** full bar. **Address:** 221 W Appleway Ave 83814 **Location:** I-90 exit 13 (4th St) eastbound, just n, then just w; exit 12 westbound, just n, then just e. L D

TONY'S ON THE LAKE   208/667-9885

▼▼▼ Italian. Casual Dining. $14-$34 **AAA Inspector Notes:** Enjoy views of Lake Coeur d'Alene from this warm and cozy restaurant as you dine on fine Italian cuisine. Select a pasta, veal, chicken or fish dish, then happily dig in. There is a dock available for those arriving by boat. **Features:** full bar, patio dining. **Reservations:** suggested. **Address:** 6823 Coeur d'Alene Lake Dr 83814 **Location:** I-90 exit 15 (Sherman Ave), just s, then 2.6 mi e. D

TOP OF CHINA BUFFET   208/676-8888

▼ Chinese. Family Dining. $7-$12 **AAA Inspector Notes:** All-you-can-eat dining on a near staggering selection of Asian dishes can be had in this comfortable restaurant, including Mongolian grill items. For those who prefer something more familiar there are many American dishes as well as the ever-popular children's favorite, pizza. **Features:** beer & wine. **Address:** 757 W Appleway Ave 83814 **Location:** I-90 exit 12, just n, then just w. L D

THE WINE CELLAR   208/664-9463

▼▼ International. Casual Dining. $10-$25 **AAA Inspector Notes:** The cozy, inviting bistro features unobtrusive live music. Guests can enjoy the varied but predominantly Italian cuisine or just drop in for entertainment and a glass of wine from the extensive list. **Features:** full bar, patio dining, happy hour. **Reservations:** suggested. **Address:** 317 E Sherman Ave 83814 **Location:** Downtown. **Parking:** street only. D

COOLIN (A-1) elev. 2,147'

Coolin is the headquarters for the Priest Lake resort area. Priest Lake, with its 80-mile shoreline, is known for its big Mackinaw trout. The 25-mile-long lake is linked with smaller Upper Priest Lake via a channel called The Thorofare. Of the lake's seven islands, Kalispell, Bartoo, Four Mile and Eight Mile islands are available for camping.

The Roosevelt Grove of Ancient Cedars, a virgin forest, is on the west side of Priest Lake, 13 miles northwest of Nordman via FR 302 in Washington. Priest Lake State Park, on the east shore of Priest Lake, offers trails through cedar-hemlock forests (*see Recreation Areas Chart*).

Priest Lake Chamber of Commerce: P.O. Box 174, Coolin, ID 83821-0174. **Phone:** (208) 443-3191 or (888) 774-3785.

COTTONWOOD (D-1) pop. 900, elev. 3,411'

A way station constructed of cottonwood logs was established here in 1862 amid the rolling uplands of the Camas Prairie. During July 3-5, 1877, the area southeast of Cottonwood was the scene of several skirmishes between the Nez Perce and U.S. Cavalry troops and scouts. State interpretive markers give details of the battles. *See Nez Perce National Historical Park p. 86.*

The Camas Prairie Railroad's 66-mile Second Subdivision passes through Cottonwood. Opened in 1908 to transport the prairie's agricultural bounty, it was known as the "Railroad on Stilts" for its numerous trestles, some of the nation's tallest. Many can be seen from US 95. The line was abandoned in 2000.

Near the northern entrance to the town is a structure shaped like a dog and known as the World's Biggest Beagle.

Cottonwood Chamber of Commerce: P.O. Box 15, Cottonwood, ID 83522. **Phone:** (208) 962-3231.

HISTORICAL MUSEUM AT ST. GERTRUDE is at 465 Keuterville Rd. Mining artifacts, Native American memorabilia, weapons and textiles are among the museum's 70,000-piece permanent collection covering such topics as the Chinese in Idaho, the monastery and local historical figures. A hand-carved wooden high altar in the monastery's chapel was constructed with mortise and glue; not a single nail was used. **Time:** Allow 30 minutes minimum. **Hours:** Tues.-Sat. 9:30-4:30. **Cost:** $6; $3 (ages 7-17). **Phone:** (208) 962-2054.

Weis Rockshelter is in Nez Perce National Historical Park, 8 mi. s. of Cottonwood, 7 miles w. of US 95. It is one of 38 sites in the park. Archeological excavations of this cliff recess have revealed almost continuous human occupation between 5500 B.C. and A.D. 1400. The niche near the Salmon River is thought to be the first shelter for the Nez Perce more than 8,000 years ago. **Hours:** Daily 8-5, Memorial Day weekend-Labor Day; 8-4:30, mid-Mar. through day before Memorial Day weekend and day after Labor Day to mid-Nov.; 9-4, rest of year. Ranger-led programs are offered daily, Memorial Day-Labor Day. **Cost:** Free. **Phone:** (208) 843-7009 for Nez Perce National Historic Park Spalding Visitor Center.

COUNCIL (E-1) pop. 839, elev. 2,940'

COUNCIL VALLEY MUSEUM is at 100 S. Galena St. Area history is depicted through such structures as doctor's and dentist's offices, a jail, a dry goods store and a cowboy's cabin. Also displayed are Native American artifacts, including tools and weapons, and items related to local mining and fruit growing boom periods. **Time:** Allow 30 minutes minimum. **Hours:** Tues.-Sat. 10-4, Sun. 1-4, Memorial Day-Labor Day. **Cost:** Donations. **Phone:** (208) 253-4582.

CRATERS OF THE MOON NATIONAL MONUMENT AND PRESERVE (G-4)

Eighteen miles west of Arco via US 20/26/93, Craters of the Moon National Monument and Preserve is at the base of the Pioneer Mountains.

This 1,100-square-mile area contains more basaltic volcanic features than any other area of its size in the continental United States. Lava rivers once flooded the surrounding countryside, leaving vast lava fields covered by cinder cones with large central vents that were thought by early observers to resemble the craters on the moon. The volcanic activity dates back about 15,000 years, with the last eruptions occurring about 2,000 years ago.

The area's variety of surface patterns and formations is typical of the world's other basaltic lava sites. Visitors should be cautious of sharp lava formations.

A 7-mile loop drive, open from April through November, leads past the monument's main points of interest and takes about 30 minutes to complete. The view from the summit of Inferno Cone takes in the cinder cone chain along the Great Rift, a weakened zone of fissures in the Earth's crust. In winter, when the snow is sufficiently deep, the loop road is closed to vehicular traffic and is groomed for cross-country skiing and snowshoeing.

The cones formed when fountains of molten, gas-charged rock shot into the air. The frothy lava then cooled and hardened into cinders that fell around the vent, producing symmetrical cones. Numerous lava bombs, ejected blobs of less frothy lava that range from an inch to several feet in diameter, are scattered over the slopes. Big Cinder, 700 feet high, is one of the world's largest purely basaltic cinder cones.

Nearby is the Big Craters-Spatter Cone Area. These cones formed when clots of pasty lava stuck together as they fell back to Earth. A trail leads from the drive to the Cave Area, a series of lava tubes that range up to 40 feet in diameter and hundreds of feet in length. The largest is 830-foot Indian Tunnel; Boy Scout Cave has a floor of ice, even in summer. Some of the tubes can be explored; wear sturdy shoes and carry a flashlight. Permits are required and are available at the visitor center.

Other trails lead to Devil's Orchard, cinder fields scattered with fragments of a crater wall, and the Tree Mold Area, where lava slowly enveloped a group of living trees.

More than 700 species of plants and many different species of animals live in this seemingly desolate terrain. In early summer, wildflowers burst into bloom on the cinder fields and slopes of the cones.

Note: Off-road vehicles may be needed on some undeveloped dirt roads. Inquire about road conditions in advance.

A visitor center and campground-picnic area are near the entrance. Guided walks and evening programs are provided during summer months; phone for schedule. The entrance fee is $8 (per private vehicle); $4 (per motorcycle or bicycle).

ROBERT LIMBERT VISITOR CENTER is at the start of the 7-mi. loop drive. Exhibits explain the geology, plants, animals and history of the monument. **Hours:** Daily 8-6, Memorial Day-Labor Day; 8-4:30, rest of year. Closed winter holidays. **Phone:** (208) 527-1335.

DONNELLY (E-2) pop. 152, elev. 4,865'

Donnelly nestles in a scenic 35-mile-long valley with Lake Cascade to the south and Payette Lake on the north. During winter, frozen Lake Cascade is used for ice fishing and cross-country skiing; summer activities include boating, kayaking, sailing and water skiing. The surrounding terrain is ideal for backcountry skiing and snowmobiling.

RECREATIONAL ACTIVITIES
Skiing and Snowboarding
- **Tamarack Resort** is at 311 Village Dr. Other activities, including golf, rafting and mountain biking, are offered seasonally. **Hours:** Open daily 9-4, mid-Dec. to late Mar. (weather permitting). **Phone:** (208) 325-1000, or (208) 325-1111 for snow updates.

DRIGGS (F-6) pop. 1,660, elev. 6,109'
- **Hotels & Restaurants map & index p. 287**
- **Part of Jackson Hole Including Grand Teton National Park area — see map p. 285**

Settled by Mormon pioneers in 1889, Driggs is the main trading center for the Teton Valley. The town center is an eclectic mix of Old West and contemporary, with specialty shops, art galleries, pubs, eateries and outdoor outfitters. Teton Valley Museum, 137 SR 33N, offers a glimpse into the area's history; phone (208) 354-6000.

If you're the outdoorsy type, embark on a horseback riding, hunting, mountain biking or skiing expedition. And if you can handle heights, why not check out the town from a hot air balloon? You can experience the oldest successful human-carrying flight technology during the Teton Valley Summer Festival, a 4-day event held in early July.

Teton Valley Chamber of Commerce: 57 S. Main St., P.O. Box 250, Driggs, ID 83422. **Phone:** (208) 354-2500.

Teton Geotourism Center: 60 S. Main St., P.O. Box 1562, Driggs, ID, 83422. **Phone:** (208) 354-2607.

RECREATIONAL ACTIVITIES
Horseback Riding
- **Dry Ridge Outfitters** departs from the Cabins at Moose Creek at the s. end of Teton Valley. **Hours:** One- to 4-hour trips by reservation, June 1-Sept. 15. Multiday trips by reservation mid-July through Labor Day. **Phone:** (208) 351-1796 or (208) 354-2284.

BEST WESTERN TETON WEST   (208)354-2363

Hotel
$105-$140

AAA Benefit: Save 10% or more every day and earn 10% bonus points!

Address: 476 N Main St 83422 **Location:** 0.7 mi n on SR 33. **Facility:** 38 units. 2 stories (no elevator), interior corridors. **Parking:** winter plug-ins. **Terms:** closed 4/1-5/20. **Pool(s):** heated indoor. **Activities:** hot tub. **Guest Services:** coin laundry.

Discover a wealth of savings
and offers on the AAA/CAA
travel websites

(See map & index p. 287.)

SUPER 8 - TETON WEST   (208)354-8888

Hotel
S65-$182

Address: 1361 N Hwy 33 83422 **Location:** 1.5 mi n on SR 33. **Facility:** 46 units, some efficiencies. 2 stories (no elevator), interior corridors. **Parking:** winter plug-ins. **Pool(s):** heated indoor. **Activities:** hot tub. **Guest Services:** coin laundry. **Featured Amenity: continental breakfast.**

TETON VALLEY CABINS   (208)354-8153 20

Cabin $69-$99 **Address:** 1 Mountain Vista Dr 83422 **Location:** 0.9 mi e of jct SR 33 (Main St) and Little Ave, then just n. Located in a quiet area. **Facility:** 20 cabins, some efficiencies. 1 story, exterior corridors. **Bath:** shower only. **Parking:** winter plug-ins. **Terms:** 7 day cancellation notice-fee imposed. **Activities:** hot tub, lawn sports, picnic facilities.

WHERE TO EAT

AGAVE MEXICAN RESTAURANT   208/354-2003 23

Mexican. Casual Dining. $7-$18 **AAA Inspector Notes:** The décor in this eatery is colorful and festive, while the aroma of the sizzling fajitas will tease appetites. Choose beef, chicken, picadillo or pork with most entrées. The combination appetizer platter includes nachos, quesadillas and chicken taquitos. The dishes for two are ideal for sharing and with twenty-eight lunch specials, guests cannot go wrong. For dessert, the kids can enjoy fried bananas with the cinnamon-coated sopaipillas. **Features:** beer & wine. **Address:** 310 N Main St 83422 **Location:** SR 33, 0.3 mi n of downtown. **Parking:** on-site and street.

BIG HOLE BAGELS & BISTRO   208/354-2245 24

Breakfast Deli. Casual Dining. $6-$10 **AAA Inspector Notes:** When traveling on the road to and from Jackson Hole, or up to Grand Targhee, this cute eatery is the spot to stop for a hearty breakfast bagel, pancakes with lots of blueberries or a hot or cold bagel sandwich. The turkey provolone with pesto and pastrami on rye bagel are local favorites. A kid's menu is available. **Features:** patio dining. **Address:** 285 N Main St 83422 **Location:** North end of town. **Parking:** street only.

FORAGE BISTRO & LOUNGE   208/354-2858 27

Regional American. Casual Dining. $10-$29 **AAA Inspector Notes:** This bistro has a patio worthy of being printed on a postcard. Seasonal small plates, salads, larger plates and desserts are skillfully prepared. I am still craving flavors in the deviled eggs made with mango chutney, jalapeño and tobiko, and the incredible tasting jumbo shrimp set in grits with roasted heirloom tomatoes sprinkled with feta and micro greens. If the lemon mascarpone pie is on the menu, just order it. **Features:** beer & wine, patio dining, happy hour. **Address:** 284 E Little Ave 83422 **Location:** 0.3 mi e of jct SR 33 and Main St. **Parking:** on-site and street.

PENDL'S BAKERY & CAFE   208/354-5623 25

Breads/Pastries Deli. Quick Serve. $7-$9 **AAA Inspector Notes:** Be sure to stop at this quaint bakery to enjoy handmade apple strudel, fruit tarts and danish, a popular cinnamon nut schnecken, quiche and a nice selection of hearty soups such as lentil vegetable and Hungarian gulaschsuppe. Popular sandwich options feature an open-face Reuben with sauerkraut and a tuna melt with tomato and cheddar. Sit out in the garden with an espresso, or by the fire when it is chilly. **Features:** patio dining. **Address:** 40 Depot St 83422 **Location:** Just n of jct SR 33 and Ski Hill Rd, then just w.

PROVISIONS LOCAL KITCHEN   208/354-2333 28

American. Casual Dining. $8-$14 **AAA Inspector Notes:** This restaurant is a favorite in Teton Valley. The Philly cheesesteak with horseradish mayo and meatloaf with caramelized onion are served on a locally-made artisan baguette. The quinoa and kale salad with portobello mushrooms is tossed in a miso-ginger dressing. Guests can customize their burger or salad, and the soup, salad or sandwich combinations are ideal for lunch. Gluten-free menu items are available and children have their own menu. **Features:** patio dining. **Address:** 95 S Main St 83422 **Location:** SR 33, just s of downtown. **Parking:** on-site and street.

SEOUL RESTAURANT - KOREAN CUISINE & SUSHI
208/354-1234 22

Korean Sushi. Casual Dining. $8-$18 **AAA Inspector Notes:** This restaurant features a variety of specialty and house rolls. Well-liked items include the Korean pancake with kimchi, rice noodle soup with mussels and vegetables in a red pepper broth, and the bento box with a little bit of everything. Once you have tried the marinated beef with attractively-cut vegetables topped with a fried egg and served over rice in a hot stone bowl, it just might become your favorite dish. After dinner, order the red bean and mango ice cream—it is delightful. **Features:** beer & wine. **Address:** 528 Valley Center Dr, Suite 4 83422 **Location:** SR 33, 2 mi n of downtown.

TETON THAI   208/787-8424 26

Thai. Casual Dining. $9-$16 **AAA Inspector Notes:** This family-operated restaurant lets guests savor Thai offerings in a contemporary, full-service setting. **Features:** beer & wine, patio dining. **Address:** 18 N Main St 83422 **Location:** Center. **Parking:** street only.

EAGLE pop. 19,908

HILTON GARDEN INN - BOISE/EAGLE   (208)938-9600

Hotel $109-$189 **Address:** 145 E Riverside Dr 83616 **Location:** I-84 exit 46 (Eagle Rd), 6 mi n to Riverside Dr, then just e. **Facility:** 98 units. 3 stories, interior corridors. **Terms:** 1-7 night minimum stay, cancellation fee imposed. **Pool(s):** heated indoor. **Activities:** hot tub, trails, exercise room. **Guest Services:** valet and coin laundry.

AAA Benefit:
Members save up to 10%!

WHERE TO EAT

BARDENAY   208/938-5093

International. Casual Dining. $6-$25 **AAA Inspector Notes:** Perched above the Boise River, this restaurant serves a wide variety of dishes such as cumin and chili-spiced calamari, red bean and chorizo stew and Kobe beef tacos. The pastry chef prepares seasonal desserts daily. Vodka, rum and gin are produced on the premises. Gluten-free items are available. **Features:** full bar, Sunday brunch. **Address:** 155 E Riverside Dr 83616 **Location:** I-84 exit 46 (Eagle Rd), 6.5 mi n, then just e.

THE GRIDDLE   208/939-9070

American. Family Dining. $6-$14 **AAA Inspector Notes:** With made-from-scratch home-style cooking and hefty portions, it is no wonder this restaurant is such a favorite. The menu offers all of the traditional American breakfast favorites and a variety of sandwiches and burgers during the lunch and dinner hour. **Address:** 177 Eagle River St 83616 **Location:** I-84 exit 46 (Eagle Rd), 6.3 mi n, then just ne.

REMBRANDT'S COFFEE HOUSE   208/938-1564

▼▼ ▼▼ Sandwiches Breads/Pastries. Quick Serve. $3-$11 **AAA Inspector Notes:** In a lofty building with a large patio, this local institution always is buzzing both inside and out. The menu lists seasonal soups, specialty sandwiches, gourmet salads and scores of breakfast favorites including delicious omelets and gourmet egg burritos. Local artists' pieces, most available for purchase, can be found throughout. Evening snacks are offered. **Address:** 93 S Eagle Rd 83616 **Location:** I-84 exit 46 (Eagle Rd), 7 mi n; just n of SR 44 and just s of State St. [B] [L] CALL [🖥️M]

SMOKY MOUNTAIN PIZZERIA GRILL   208/939-0212

▼▼ Italian. Casual Dining. $7-$27 **AAA Inspector Notes:** Located in the heart of downtown, this popular Italian eatery serves up a wide variety of pasta, pizzas, calzones and salads. Locals favor the artichoke dip and fettuccine with chicken pesto parmigiana. Gluten-free options and a kids' menu are available. Nothing beats sitting on the patio on a beautiful day. **Features:** full bar, patio dining, happy hour. **Address:** 34 E State St 83616 **Location:** Jct Old State St and Eagle Rd. [L] [D]

ELK RIVER (C-1) pop. 125, elev. 2,854'

Potlatch Lumber Co. built a town for its electrically powered sawmill in 1909. Served by a railroad, Elk River's population peaked at nearly 1,200 in the 1920s. After the mill closed in 1936, the town declined. Relics of Elk River's halcyon days include a 1917 drugstore and an abandoned public school built in 1910. The former mill pond, south of town, is today a recreation area and a habitat for ospreys, bald eagles and otters. On its west shore is the historic Clearwater-Potlatch Timber Protective Association's firefighters camp.

The Morris-Perkins Cedar Grove, 7 miles north on FR 382, then 3 miles west on winding FR 1969, has a 3/4-mile trail looping through an 80-acre stand of old growth western red cedar. The grove is open from mid-March to late October (weather permitting); phone (208) 875-1131. The half-mile Giant Red Cedar National Recreation Trail, 10 mi. n. on CR 382 to FS 4764, leads to Idaho's champion red cedar, a 3,000-year-old giant, measuring 177 feet tall and 18 feet wide.

The Elk River Back Country Byway is a 57-mile scenic route. It follows SR 8 19 miles from Bovill to Elk River, then 39 winding miles south to Orofino. The Elk River to Oroville section includes 17 miles of gravel and crosses Dworshak Reservoir via Dent Bridge, a graceful 1,550-foot suspension bridge.

ELK CREEK FALLS is 2 mi. w. on SR 8, then 2 mi. s. on FR 1452 (gravel road) to trailhead. Elk Creek tumbles over ancient lava flows to form three waterfalls with a collective drop of about 300 feet. The middle and lower falls are the highest at 70 and 50 feet, respectively. Outcrops of columnar basalt enhance the beauty of the canyon. A 1-mile trail, steep in places, leads down through the forest of pine, fir, cedar and larch to a viewpoint of the lower and middle falls. Side trails branch off to other vantage points.

Restrooms and picnic tables are available at the trailhead. Day-use only. **Time:** Allow 1 hour minimum. **Hours:** Daily dawn-dusk, mid-May to late Oct. (weather permitting). Phone ahead to confirm schedule. **Cost:** Free. **Phone:** (208) 875-1131.

EMMETT (F-1) pop. 6,557, elev. 2,362'

Located on the Payette River 30 miles northwest of Boise, Emmett was settled in the mid-1860s. Irrigation works began in the early 1900s and the district became noted for its orchard crops of peaches, apricots, apples and cherries. Freezeout Hill, 7 miles southeast on SR 16, on a ridge separating the Payette and Boise River valleys, offers a grand view of the town and its oasis-like setting.

GEM COUNTY VILLAGE MUSEUM is at 501 E. 1st St. The five-building complex includes a museum with a variety of historical displays as well as a blacksmith shop and a one-room school. A bunkhouse contains early ranching items and a natural history exhibit. The Hunt House showcases the furnishings and personal belongings of Frank W. Hunt, the fifth governor of Idaho. The first weekend in October, the museum features A River Through Time, a hands-on, living-history celebration of the people who settled Payette River Valley, and a Civil War re-enactment. **Time:** Allow 30 minutes minimum. **Hours:** Wed.-Sat. 1-5 or by appointment. Closed Thanksgiving and Christmas. **Cost:** Donations. **Phone:** (208) 365-9530.

FORT HALL (G-5) pop. 3,201, elev. 4,754'

One of the first permanent settlements in Idaho, Fort Hall was established as a trading post on the banks of the Snake River in 1834. Later owned by the Hudson's Bay Co., the trading post was abandoned in 1856 due to increased hostility with Native Americans and a decline in fur trading.

In 1864 a stage station was constructed a short distance southeast of Fort Hall. Built on the banks of Spring Creek with materials from this original fort, this post also was known as Fort Hall. In 1868 a treaty established the Fort Hall Indian Reservation, and agency offices some 20 miles east of the original post also were identified as Fort Hall. Today the Fort Hall Indian Reservation has its headquarters east of the town site on US 91. Guided tours of historic Fort Hall, which must be reserved in advance, can be arranged through the Shoshone-Bannock Tribal Museum *(see attraction listing).*

SHOSHONE-BANNOCK TRIBAL MUSEUM is on Simplot Rd. just w. of I-15 exit 80. Themed displays highlight the history of the Shoshone-Bannock Tribes, the Oregon Trail, the Fort Hall Indian Boarding School and Native American ranchers. Tribal beadwork, artwork, crafts, historical photographs and archeological artifacts are exhibited. **Time:** Allow 30 minutes minimum. **Hours:** Daily 9:30-5, June 1 to mid-Aug.; Mon.-Fri. 9:30-5, rest of year. Closed federal and tribal holidays. **Cost:** $3.50; $2 (ages 6-17); free (ages 0-5 and Native Americans with tribal ID). **Phone:** (208) 237-9791.

GAMBLING ESTABLISHMENTS

• **Fort Hall Casino** is on Simplot Rd. just w. of I-15 exit 80. **Hours:** Daily 24 hours. **Phone:** (208) 237-8778 or (800) 497-4231.

SHOSHONE-BANNOCK HOTEL & EVENT CENTER
208/238-4800

▼▼▼ **Hotel.** Rates not provided. **Address:** 777 Bannock Tr 83203 **Location:** I-15 exit 80, just w. Adjacent to Fort Hall Casino. **Facility:** This hotel offers beautifully appointed public areas and guest rooms with stunning views, including some with a fireplace, balcony or hot tub. 156 units. 5 stories, interior corridors. **Amenities:** safes. **Dining:** 2 restaurants. **Pool(s):** heated indoor. **Activities:** hot tub, exercise room, spa. **Guest Services:** valet and coin laundry.

GLENNS FERRY (G-2) pop. 1,319, elev. 2,560'

Off I-84 on the Snake River, the community traces its beginnings to a ferry crossing established here in 1869. Housed in a former school building built in 1909, the Glenns Ferry Historical Museum exhibits artifacts that depict area history; for more information phone the Glenns Ferry City Hall at (208) 366-7418.

THREE ISLAND CROSSING STATE PARK, 1083 Three Island Park Dr., preserves the site where Oregon Trail wagon trains were forced to ford the Snake River from the early 1840s until 1869, when a ferry began operating. The Oregon Trail History and Education Center features pioneer and Native American exhibits. *See Recreation Areas Chart.*

Time: Allow 1 hour minimum. **Hours:** Grounds daily dawn-dusk. History and education center Tues.-Sun. 9-4. Phone ahead to confirm schedule. **Cost:** $5 (per private vehicle). Camping (includes water and electricity) $30.44-$50.58. Cabins $53. **Phone:** (208) 366-2394, or (888) 922-6743 for camping reservations.

WINERIES

• **Crossings Winery** is off I-84 Glenns Ferry exit at 1289 W. Madison Ave. next to Three Island Crossing State Park, following signs. **Hours:** Mon.-Sat. 8 a.m.-9 p.m., Sun. 10-8. **Phone:** (208) 366-2313.

FUDGE FACTORY GRILL & ICE CREAM   208/366-7687

▼ Sandwiches Desserts. Quick Serve. $5-$9 **AAA Inspector Notes:** Travelers can see the signs for this place on the interstate heading east or west. Do stop by for a great burger, sweet potato fries, barbecue ribs with huckleberry sauce and an old-fashioned chocolate malt. The huckleberry soda from Washington is a must-try. There also is a nice selection of homemade fudge and pies. **Features:** beer only, patio dining. **Address:** 160 S Commercial St 83623 **Location:** I-84 exit 120, 0.4 mi s, 0.3 mi e, then 0.4 mi s; downtown. L D

GRANGEVILLE (D-1) pop. 3,141, elev. 3,323'

A boomtown in gold rush days, Grangeville is a light industry and agricultural center and the largest town on the fertile Camas Prairie, one of the leading wheat-producing areas in the country. The prairie takes its name from *camassia esculenta*, an onion-like bulb common in the area and favored by the Nez Perce Indians. Today it is a site for an archeological excavation for mammoth bones.

A life-size replica of the giant mammoth unearthed in 1995 at nearby Tolo Lake, 6 miles west of town, can be seen in Eimers Park on US 95 at Pine Street. Grangeville also is an outfitting point for wilderness and float trips.

South of Grangeville US 95 descends 3,000 feet to the Salmon River Canyon via the White Bird Grade. This 7-mile section of the highway bypasses the dozens of switchbacks and hairpin curves of the original route, which can be seen to the east. White Bird Battlefield, a designated site of Nez Perce National Historical Park *(see place listing p. 86),* is about 16 miles south on US 95.

Grangeville Chamber of Commerce: US 95 at N. Pine, P.O. Box 212, Grangeville, ID 83530. **Phone:** (208) 983-0460.

Self-guiding tours: A trail guide of White Bird Battlefield is available at the chamber of commerce and at the Nez Perce National Forest office in Grangeville.

RECREATIONAL ACTIVITIES

Horseback Riding

• **White Bird Summit Lodge** is 7 mi. s. on US 95 to mile marker 231, then 1 mi. e. on Old Hwy. 95 to 2141 Old White Bird Hill Rd. Other activities are offered. **Hours:** Trips are offered daily, June-Aug. Departure times vary; phone ahead. **Phone:** (208) 983-1802.

GATEWAY INN   208/983-2500

▼▼▼
Motel
$55-$99

Address: 700 W Main St 83530 **Location:** Jct US 95 and SR 13. **Facility:** 28 units, some efficiencies. 2 stories (no elevator), exterior corridors. **Parking:** winter plug-ins. **Terms:** cancellation fee imposed. **Pool(s):** heated outdoor. **Guest Services:** coin laundry. **Featured Amenity:** continental breakfast.

WHERE TO EAT

HILLTOP CAFE   208/983-1724

▼▼ American. Family Dining. $7-$13 **AAA Inspector Notes:** This is where diners want to go for a hearty breakfast and a good selection of lunch items including a variety of burgers and sandwiches. The atmosphere is cozy and comfortable and be forewarned—the chocolate malt is addictive. **Address:** 500 E Main St 83530 **Location:** At E Main and Florence sts; east end of town. B L CALL M

SEASONS RESTAURANT   208/983-4203

▼▼ American. Casual Dining. $8-$20 **AAA Inspector Notes:** No matter the season, soup, burgers and sandwiches are the main stays for lunch while a nice selection of appetizers, pasta entrées, barbecued ribs and steak is offered in the evening. **Features:** beer & wine. **Address:** 124 W Main St 83530 **Location:** 0.5 mi e of jct US 95 and SR 13. **Parking:** street only. B L D

HAGERMAN (G-3) pop. 872, elev. 2,959'
• Hotels p. 64 • Restaurants p. 64

1000 SPRINGS TOURS, departing from Banbury Hot Springs, 11 mi. s. on US 30, offers 2-hour scenic boat trips through the Snake River Canyon and the

Thousand Springs area. Waterfalls, wildlife and abundant waterfowl can be seen while guides relate area history and geography. Lunch and dinner tours also are available. **Hours:** Two-hour scenic boat tours depart daily. Departure times vary. **Cost:** $25. Reservations are required. **Phone:** (208) 837-9006.

THOUSAND SPRINGS STATE PARK is .2 mi. s. off I-84 exit 147, then .2 mi. w., following signs to the welcome kiosk at Malad Gorge. The highlight of this multi-unit state park are aquifer-fed springs that gush in beautiful cascades from the sides of Snake River Canyon. The springs are believed to be the re-appearance of Lost River, which vanishes into the lava fields near Arco.

Park headquarters is at the Malad Gorge unit, where markers indicate points of interest along a 3.5-mile loop road. From a footbridge visitors can see the bottom of a 250-foot-deep gorge where a waterfall plunges into Devil's Washbowl. Part of the Oregon Trail, volcanic collapse features and under-ground springs also can be viewed.

Wildlife can be seen throughout the state park, which also encompasses the Niagara Springs unit, featuring 350-foot-high sheer basalt cliffs; the his-toric Kelton Trail, boasting pioneer wagon ruts; the Ritter Island unit, host to September's Thousand Springs Festival of the Arts; the Billingsley Creek unit, offering an indoor equestrian arena; and the Earl M. Hardy Box Canyon Springs Nature Pre-serve. *See Recreation Areas Chart.*

Time: Allow 45 minutes minimum. **Hours:** Park open daily 7 a.m.-10 p.m. Ritter Island unit open Fri.-Tues. 10-3, Memorial Day weekend-Labor Day. **Cost:** $5 (per private vehicle). **Phone:** (208) 837-4505. GT ⊠ 🐾 🏕

HAGERMAN VALLEY INN (208)837-6196

◇◇◇
Motel
$68-$108

Address: 661 Frog's Landing 83332 **Location:** South end of town on US 30. **Facility:** 16 units. 2 stories (no elevator), exterior corridors. **Terms:** cancellation fee imposed. **Dining:** Snake River Grill, see separate listing.

SAVE 🍽 🛜 ⊠ 🖥 📺 / SOME UNITS 🛏 📶

WHERE TO EAT

SNAKE RIVER GRILL 208/837-6227

◇◇ American. Casual Dining. $6-$23 **AAA Inspector Notes:** This rustic restaurant is located in a small town near the Snake River and will appeal to the traveling family as well as the undaunted—the menu offers distinct wild game dinners where diners provide the game and the chef/owner prepares it. **Features:** beer & wine. **Address:** 611 Frog's Landing 83332 **Location:** South end of town on US 30; in Hagerman Valley Inn.

B L D

HAGERMAN FOSSIL BEDS NATIONAL MONUMENT (G-2)

The monument is 4 mi. s. on US 30, then 3 mi. w. on Bell Rapids Rd., following signs. The 3.4-million-year-old fossil beds, one of the continent's best Plio-cene freshwater fish and small-mammal fossil sites, have yielded more than 220 plant and animal spe-cies, including complete skeletons of the Hagerman horse. A 10.5-mile auto route provides insights into area geology and geography and access to the Upper Salmon Falls Dam, the Snake River Over-look, the 3-mile trailhead for the Emigrant Trail and the Oregon Trail Overlook.

HAGERMAN FOSSIL BEDS NATIONAL MONU-MENT VISITOR CENTER is at 221 N. State St., di-rectly across US 30 from the high school. With exhibits, fossils, a discovery center, a DVD show, auto tour brochures and trail maps, the center is a good place to stop for information before touring the monument, as access to some trails and overlooks may be restricted. The visitor center also has infor-mation about Minidoka National Historic Site *(see place listing p. 82).* **Note:** The Owsley Bridge is now just a pedestrian bridge. Vehicular traffic has an al-ternate route across U.S. 30. **Hours:** Daily 9-5, late May-late Aug.; Thurs.-Mon. 9-5, rest of year. Closed Jan. 1, Thanksgiving and Christmas. Phone ahead to confirm schedule. **Cost:** Free. **Phone:** (208) 933-4105.

HAILEY (G-3) pop. 7,960, elev. 5,330'

Hailey, laid out in the spring of 1881 by John Hailey, was the center of a rich mining district in its early days. An early Northwest pioneer, Hailey had previously taken part in the Boise Basin Gold Rush in 1862 and had established a name for himself as the owner of a stage and freight line. Fortunes in gold, silver and lead were extracted from mines with such names as Black Cinder, Star, Hope, Climax, Democrat and Big Camas until the mining boom played out in the late 1890s.

On May 7, 1883, Hailey residents witnessed the driving of the last spike of the Wood River branch of the Oregon Short Line. In October of that year the Idaho Territory's first telephone exchange went into use at Hailey. Hailey also was the first to have an electric light plant.

Passing through the community are the Big Wood River and a system of paved recreational trails. Sur-rounded by Sawtooth National Recreation Area *(see place listing p. 98),* Hailey offers a variety of outdoor activities, including hiking, bicycling and cross-country skiing.

Hailey Chamber of Commerce/Welcome Center: 781 Main St. S., P.O. Box 100, Hailey, ID 83333. **Phone:** (208) 788-3484.

Self-guiding tours: Brochures describing a self-guiding walking tour of Hailey's historic area are available at the chamber of commerce.

BLAINE COUNTY HISTORICAL MUSEUM, 218 N. Main St., displays early pioneer relics and memorabilia of local interest, including a replica of a mine tunnel. The American Political Items collection contains memorabilia from political campaigns since the late 1800s. **Time:** Allow 30 minutes minimum. **Hours:** Mon.-Sat. 11-5, Sun. 1-5, Memorial Day weekend-Oct. 31. **Cost:** Donations. **Phone:** (208) 788-1801.

AIRPORT INN (208)788-2477

♦ **Motel** $85-$120 **Address:** 820 S 4th Ave 83333 **Location:** 1 mi s of center to 4th Ave via Main St (SR 75); south end of town. **Facility:** 29 units, some efficiencies. 1-2 stories (no elevator), exterior corridors. **Parking:** winter plug-ins. **Terms:** check-in 4 pm, 3 day cancellation notice. **Activities:** hot tub, picnic facilities. **Guest Services:** coin laundry. 🛜 ▤ ▤ ▥ / SOME UNITS 🐾

AMERICINN LODGE & SUITES - HAILEY/SUN VALLEY
(208)788-7950

♦♦♦ **Hotel** $129-$220 **Address:** 51 Cobblestone Ln 83333 **Location:** 0.5 mi n of center. **Facility:** 64 units. 3 stories, interior corridors. **Parking:** winter plug-ins. **Terms:** cancellation fee imposed. **Pool(s):** heated indoor. **Activities:** hot tub, steamroom, trails, exercise room. **Guest Services:** coin laundry.
🍴 CALL 📶 ⊳⊲ BIZ HS 🛜 ✕ ▤ ▥ / SOME UNITS 🐾 ▤

WOOD RIVER INN (208)578-0600

♦♦♦ **Hotel** $99-$159 **Address:** 601 N Main St 83333 **Location:** 0.3 mi n of center. **Facility:** 56 units, some efficiencies. 3 stories, interior corridors. **Parking:** winter plug-ins. **Terms:** cancellation fee imposed, resort fee. **Pool(s):** heated indoor. **Activities:** hot tub, bicycles, trails, exercise room. **Guest Services:** coin laundry.
🍴 CALL 📶 ⊳⊲ BIZ 🛜 ✕ ▤ ▤ ▥ / SOME UNITS 🐾

WHERE TO EAT

CK'S REAL FOOD 208/788-1223

♦♦♦ Natural/Organic. Fine Dining. $9-$39 **AAA Inspector Notes:** This relaxed, yet upscale, eatery features globally-inspired food with a focus on local, organic and sustainable fare. Seasonal menu items include morel and watercress salad, country pate, grilled chicken over a Greek salad and grilled Idaho trout. Seasonal desserts consist of broccoli pancakes, antioxidant greens and roasted potatoes with smoked pork belly. Colorful desserts are beautifully presented. **Features:** beer & wine. **Reservations:** suggested. **Address:** 320 Main St S 83333 **Location:** On SR 75 at Main and Pine sts, 0.4 mi s of center. **Parking:** street only. D CALL 📶

DIVINE BISTRO & WINE BAR 406/788-4422

♦♦ Small Plates Fondue. Casual Dining. $11-$28 **AAA Inspector Notes:** This darling bistro serves a nice selection of salads such as pear and Cambozola or the caprese. Favorite seasonal sandwiches are served with a mixed green salad or kettle-cooked chips and might include the ham, fontina cheese, apple and Dijon. The cheese fondue, build-your-own cheese plate and chocolate fondue are ideal for sharing. Half and whole options are available for almost everything on the menu. **Features:** beer & wine. **Address:** 400 S Main St 83333 **Location:** Jct S Main and Pine sts. **Parking:** street only. L D CALL 📶

POWER HOUSE PUB & BIKE SHOP 208/788-9184

♦♦ American. Gastropub. $7-$18 **AAA Inspector Notes:** Eating here is like sitting in an upscale bicycle shop where artwork consists of helmets and custom-made bicycles and frames. The motto here is ride, eat and repeat, so stop here to refuel with more than 130 beers, grass-fed burgers, a juicy steak and the best chili around. Diners will not find basketball or football games on these TVs—it is a bike shop so they show bike races. **Features:** beer & wine, patio dining. **Address:** 502 N Main St 83333 **Location:** 0.3 mi n of center. **Parking:** street only. L D

SHORTY'S DINER 208/578-1293

♦ Comfort Food. Casual Dining. $5-$11 **AAA Inspector Notes:** This 1950s-style diner always is bustling with patrons. Serving up traditional American favorites, menu items range from omelets, skillets and pancakes for breakfast to burgers, dogs, sandwiches and chicken-fried steak. **Features:** beer only. **Address:** 126 S Main St 83333 **Location:** On SR 75, at Main and Croy sts. **Parking:** street only. B L D

HAYDEN pop. 13,294

TRIPLE PLAY RESORT HOTEL & SUITES (208)772-7900

♦♦♦ **Hotel** $90-$399 **Address:** 151 W Orchard Ave 83835 **Location:** I-90 exit 12, 4 mi n. **Facility:** 95 units. 4 stories, interior corridors. **Terms:** check-in 4 pm. **Pool(s):** heated indoor. **Activities:** hot tub, miniature golf, game room, exercise room. **Guest Services:** valet and coin laundry.
🍴 CALL 📶 ⊳⊲ BIZ HS 🛜 ✕ ▤ ▤ ▥ / SOME UNITS 🐾

HAYDEN LAKE pop. 574

THE PORCH PUBLIC HOUSE 208/772-7711

♦♦ American. Casual Dining. $9-$18 **AAA Inspector Notes:** This restaurant takes its name from the screened porch that overlooks a golf course and is a favorite spot for seasonal dining. The menu here is fairly eclectic but that means just about every taste can be satisfied. The marinated grilled lamb sandwich and barbecue chicken quesadillas are superb. **Features:** full bar. **Address:** 1658 E Miles Ave 83835 **Location:** I-90 exit 12, 4.1 mi n to Miles Ave, then 1.4 mi e. L D

💎 HELLS CANYON NATIONAL RECREATION AREA (D-1)

Hells Canyon National Recreation Area is reached via SRs 82 and 86 in northeastern Oregon and US 95 in western Idaho. The 652,977-acre area straddles the Snake River Canyon and encompasses parts of national forests in both states.

Confined within steep, eroded black basalt walls, the surging Snake River has carved North America's deepest river gorge, measuring 7,913 feet from He Devil Mountain to Granite Creek below. White-water rapids alternating with deep pools characterize this 72-mile free-flowing portion of the Snake River as it races north to meet the Columbia River.

The varied elevations of Hells Canyon support mixed plant communities sheltering such wildlife as bears, bobcats, bighorn sheep, cougars, elk, mule deer, mountain goats and many smaller birds, mammals and reptiles. Sturgeon, reputedly growing up to 11 feet long, inhabit the Snake River, sharing it with bass, catfish, salmon, steelhead trout and rainbow trout.

From the desertlike canyon floor to the alpine lakes of the Seven Devils region, the area presents a variety of recreational opportunities, including boating, float trips and backpacking. From Pittsburg Landing, the Kirkwood Historic Ranch and Museum, once the home of Idaho governor and U.S. senator Len B. Jordan, is accessible by powerboat, float boat or pack trail.

The Rapid River originates in the Seven Devils Mountains and eventually joins the Little Salmon

River. The forks of the Rapid River provide quality water for raising chinook salmon and, therefore, house the Rapid River Fish Hatchery.

The 214,944-acre Hells Canyon Wilderness, with its extensive trail system, protects a large portion of the canyon along the Oregon-Idaho border. If you plan to fish the lakes and the Snake River shoreline, you must acquire the appropriate state licenses *(see Good Facts To Know)*; both Oregon and Idaho licenses are valid for boat fishing on the river.

Scenic Hells Canyon All American Road/SR 86 is a series of routes to and through the Hells Canyon National Recreation Area. **On the Oregon side** the best route is a two-lane paved loop that originates in Baker City. From Baker City follow SR 86 to Richland for approximately 41 miles. From Richland continue on SR 86 north for 11 miles to Halfway. From Halfway follow SR 86 for 20 miles to Oxbow. Nine miles north off Halfway, SR 86 will intersect with FR 39N. Take FR 39N through the heart of the Wallowa Mountains, high mountain country and through the town of Joseph to Enterprise. One mile west of Enterprise on SR 82 is the Wallowa Mountain Visitor Center. Continue along SR 82 west for approximately 64 miles to arrive back on I-84 at La Grande. The highest elevation portions of FR 39 are closed in winter. The entire loop will take approximately 5 hours.

Another possible route from the Oregon side to the recreation area is via SR 82 to Enterprise and Joseph. From Joseph it is possible to go to Hat Point, a 6,982-foot ridge overlooking Hells Canyon, via Imnaha. The route to Hat Point, open summer through early fall, follows FR 4240, a gravel, narrow road with steep grades.

Another route from Imnaha, FR 3955, parallels the Imnaha River as it meanders through rims and benches similar to those along the Snake River. This route connects with the Wallowa Mountain Loop (FR 39), which leads back to Joseph or Halfway. FR 3955 and FR 39 are maintained for cars and trailers. FR 39 can be followed east to FR 3965, which leads to the Hells Canyon overlook. With an elevation of 6,000 feet, the overlook provides a spectacular view of the Wallowa Mountains in Oregon and Idaho. These roads are closed in winter.

Buckhorn Springs, a scenic area overlooking the Imnaha drainage, can be reached from FR 46 off SR 3, a mostly gravel logging road.

For maps and brochures of different drives contact the Baker County Chamber of Commerce and Visitors Bureau, 490 Campbell St., Baker City, OR 97814; phone (541) 523-5855 or (888) 523-5855.

On the Idaho side there are two routes to the canyon. From Cambridge, SR 71 runs 29 miles northwest to Oxbow, Ore., crossing the Snake River near Brownlee Dam. It crosses back into Idaho at Oxbow, then follows the river north to Hells Canyon Dam. The total distance is about 55 miles. The other access point is Pittsburg Landing, 17 miles west of US 95 at White Bird via gravel FR 493. The drive

from White Bird to Hells Canyon takes about 45 minutes.

Note: The majority of the Idaho side of the canyon is in the Mountain Time Zone; White Bird, Idaho, and the Oregon side of the canyon observe Pacific Time. It is advisable to check with the Hells Canyon National Recreation Area regarding road conditions and construction. Some roads are gravel and caution should be exercised. Phone (541) 426-5546.

More than 30 outfitters provide float and jet boat trips down the Snake River from Hells Canyon Dam and jet boat trips upstream from Lewiston and White Bird, Idaho, and from Asotin and Clarkston, Wash. For a list of local outfitters contact the Supervisor, Hells Canyon National Recreation Area, 2535 Riverside Dr., P.O. Box 699, Clarkston, WA 99403; phone (509) 758-0616, or (509) 758-0270 for powerboat reservations. *See Recreation Areas Chart.*

Visit Lewis Clark Valley: 847 Port Way, Clarkston, WA 99403. **Phone:** (509) 758-7489 or (877) 774-7248.

SAVE **BEAMERS HELLS CANYON TOURS** departs from the Beamers Tour Dock behind the Quality Inn at 700 Port Dr. in Clarkston, Wash. This tour company offers jet boat excursions through Hells Canyon—North America's deepest river gorge. The 1-day Snake River trip provides opportunities to view three mountain ranges, three states and four rivers. Half-day and other excursions also are available. **Hours:** Half- and full-day trips offered daily, May-Sept.; Sat.-Sun. only, Mar.-Apr. and in Oct. Departure times vary; phone ahead. **Cost:** One-day trip $219; free (ages 0-8 with paid adult). Half-day trip $139; free (ages 0-8 with paid adult). A fuel surcharge may apply; phone for details. Reservations are required. **Phone:** (509) 758-4800 or (800) 522-6966. GT TI

HELLS CANYON ADVENTURES is on SR 86 (All American Rd.), 1 mi. n. of Hells Canyon Dam and 23 mi. n. of Oxbow, Ore. Two-hour jet boat tours depart at 10 and at 2. Full-day jet boat tours depart at 10, traveling through the deepest part of Hells Canyon, navigating the largest rapids and visiting the Kirkwood Historical Ranch. Overnight jet boat adventures and fishing charters on the Snake River also are available.

Hours: Tours depart daily May-Sept. Inquire about off-season tours. Departure times vary. **Cost:** Granite Creek Tour $85; $60 (ages 0-11). Wild Sheep Tour $60; $35 (ages 0-11). Kirkwood $177; $88 (ages 0-11). A fuel surcharge may apply; phone ahead for more information. Reservations are recommended. **Phone:** (541) 785-3352 or (800) 422-3568.

HELLS CANYON JET BOAT TRIPS & LODGING checks in guests at its office, 1 mi. s. on Old Hwy. 95 in White Bird, Idaho. The 65-mile, round-trip Wild River Tour through Class II to V rapids on the Snake

River navigates the deepest and most rugged section of Hells Canyon, passing alongside Seven Devils Mountains en route to the dam. Other tours are available.

Time: Allow 6 hours minimum. **Hours:** Departures require a minimum of six people. Trips depart daily, Mar.-Oct. **Cost:** (includes a meal) $175; $110 (ages 0-11). Prices may vary. A shuttle to the departure point at Pittsburgh Landing marina, 17 mi. s.w. on a gravel road, is offered for a fee, or private vehicle parking is available at the marina. Reservations are required. **Phone:** (208) 839-2255 or (800) 469-8757.

HEYBURN pop. 3,089

UPPER CRUST GRILL & BISTRO   208/679-0972

Sandwiches Soup. Quick Serve. $7-$11 **AAA Inspector Notes:** Located above a popular attraction, this casual eatery's menu boasts a nice selection of salads, tasty sandwiches and artisan cheeses. Be sure to finish off the meal with a freshly baked cookie. **Address:** 1360 7th St 83336 **Location:** I-84 exit 211, 1.8 mi sw on US 30 to 7th St; exit 208, 0.5 mi s to 5th St, 1 mi e, then 0.8 mi s to US 30. L D CALL &M

HORSESHOE BEND (F-1) pop. 707, elev. 2,630'

HORSESHOE BEND EXPRESS-THUNDER MOUNTAIN LINE departs from 120 Mill Rd. The nearly 3-hour Horseshoe Bend Miner's Express parallels the Payette River and follows an old wagon trail to Banks, where a short stop is made. Three partially open-air cars and four enclosed cars are available to riders. Dinner, entertainment, holiday and themed excursions also are offered.

Hours: Depot open Sat. 11-6, Sun. noon-4 (also Fri. 4-7, in Oct. and 8-7 in Dec.). Trips depart Apr.-Dec. Train ride schedule varies; phone ahead. **Cost:** $30; $27 (ages 61+); $20 (ages 3-12); $10 (ages 0-2). **Phone:** (208) 331-1184. 🍴

RECREATIONAL ACTIVITIES
White-water Rafting
- SAVE **Cascade Raft and Kayak** is at 7050 SR 55. Other activities are offered. **Hours:** Rafting trips depart daily at 9:30, 1:30 and 5, Apr.-Sept. **Phone:** (208) 793-2221 or (800) 292-7238.

IDAHO CITY (F-2) pop. 485, elev. 4,000'

Soon after gold was discovered in the Boise Basin in 1862, Idaho City became one of the largest cities in the Pacific Northwest. By 1865 it was home to some 7,000 gold seekers; nearly one quarter were Chinese. At its peak the basin was home to 15,000-20,000 miners. The mining district around Idaho City, including nearby Placerville and Centerville, was one of the largest sources of gold ever discovered.

More than 20 pioneer buildings from the 1860s and miles of dredge workings are still visible. The First Masonic Hall, built in 1865 to house Idaho's first Grand Lodge of Masons, displays Masonic items. Idaho City was the site of the territory's first

prison, a portion of which has been restored. Guided town walking tours are available from the Boise Basin Museum (see attraction listing) by appointment; there is a $30 minimum per group.

Boise National Forest (see place listing p. 50) surrounds the town. Idaho City lies on scenic SR 21, also known as the Ponderosa Pine Scenic Route. SR 21 heads northeast through Sawtooth National Forest (see place listing p. 98) and ends in Stanley.

Idaho City Chamber of Commerce: 100 Main St., P.O. Box 507, Idaho City, ID 83631. **Phone:** (208) 392-4159.

BOISE BASIN MUSEUM, Montgomery St. at Wall St., was erected as a post office in 1867 and served as a stage and freight company station before being renovated for its present use. Exhibits, which commemorate the town's origin with memorabilia from its days as a mining boomtown, include a working stamp mill model. A video presentation about basin history is shown.

Hours: Daily 11-4 or by appointment, Memorial Day-Labor Day; Fri.-Sun. 11-4 or by appointment, May 1-day before Memorial Day and day after Labor Day-Oct. 31. Phone ahead to confirm schedule. **Cost:** $2; $1.50 (ages 65+ and students with ID); $5 (family, two adults and two children ages 0-17). **Phone:** (208) 392-4550.

WHERE TO EAT

GOLD MINE EATERY & SPIRITS   208/392-2233

American. Casual Dining. $8-$21 **AAA Inspector Notes:** This is a good stop for a bite to eat when traveling to and from Sun Valley and Boise. Diners can expect a variety of chicken, deli sandwiches, burgers, pizza, flatbreads, battered shrimp and jumbo wings. The chili and granny's tomato bisque are served with grilled sourdough bread. **Address:** 312 SR 21 83631 **Location:** On SR 21. B L D

IDAHO FALLS (G-5) pop. 56,813, elev. 4,742'
• Hotels p. 68 • Restaurants p. 69

Although it lies miles from the silver and gold lodes discovered in the region during the mid-1800s, Idaho Falls owes its formation to these riches. The settlement—originally called Taylor's Crossing—was established about 1860 along one of the few fording points on the upper Snake River. J.M. Taylor's ferry attracted many miners en route to Montana from Salt Lake City.

As the veins of precious metal diminished, transients and disillusioned residents abandoned the area. The few remaining settlers, faced with either adopting a new livelihood or adding the community to the growing list of Western ghost towns, dug channels to irrigate the arid land. Soon the town flourished along with the newly established agriculture. The irrigation system that saved the town now provides water to more than 1 million acres of farmland.

Tautphaus Park has sports facilities, picnic grounds, amusement rides and a zoo (see attraction *listing).* Sandy Downs, 2 miles south of 17th Street on St. Clair Road, is the site of various recreational activities.

Greater Idaho Falls Chamber of Commerce & Visitors Center: 425 N. Capital Ave., Idaho Falls, ID 83402. **Phone:** (208) 523-1010 or (866) 365-6943.

THE ART MUSEUM OF EASTERN IDAHO, 300 S. Capitol Ave., is the only art museum in southeastern Idaho. Changing exhibitions featuring local and regional art are offered. **Time:** Allow 30 minutes minimum. **Hours:** Tues.-Sat. 11-5 (also Thurs. 5-8). Closed major holidays. **Cost:** $4; $2 (ages 6-18 and college students with ID); free (ages 0-5, senior citizens first Tues. of the month and to all first Sat. of the month); $10 (family). **Phone:** (208) 524-7777.

IDAHO FALLS is .5 mi. e. off I-15 Broadway exit 118, then n. on River Pkwy. The low but picturesque and turbulent waterfall in the Snake River is 1,200 feet wide. Next to the scenic falls is a 2.5-mile river walk.

THE IDAHO FALLS ZOO AT TAUTPHAUS PARK is at Rogers St. and Carnival Way. More than 350 creatures reside in Idaho's largest zoo, in regional habitats representing North and South America, Africa, Asia, Australia and New Guinea. Animal encounter shows are scheduled daily in summer. Also popular is the Penguin Interaction Program in which participants meet a zookeeper, interact with the birds and learn about the fascinating lives of penguins. A children's zoo and plant identification gardens are on-site.

　Time: Allow 1 hour minimum. **Hours:** Daily 9-5, Memorial Day weekend-Labor Day; 9-4, mid-Apr. through day before Memorial Day weekend and day after Labor Day-early Oct. Penguin Interaction Program is offered Thurs.-Sun. at 11, late May-early Oct. Phone ahead to confirm schedule. **Cost:** $7.25; $5.75 (ages 62+); $4.25 (ages 4-12). Penguin Interaction Program $20; $10 (ages 4-12). Prices may vary; phone ahead. Reservations for the Penguin Interaction Program are strongly recommended. **Phone:** (208) 612-8552.

　 THE MUSEUM OF IDAHO is off I-15 exit 118 (Broadway) at 200 N. Eastern Ave. It features such exhibits as Race for Atomic Power, which documents important milestones in the history of nuclear energy that occurred in southeastern Idaho; Lewis and Clark in Idaho; a children's discovery room; and Eagle Rock USA, a replica of the 19th-century community that later became Idaho Falls.

　Temporary exhibitions also are offered. **Time:** Allow 1 hour minimum. **Hours:** Mon.-Tues. 9-8, Wed.-Sat. 9-5. Closed Jan. 1, Thanksgiving and Christmas. Phone ahead to confirm schedule. **Cost:** $8; $7 (ages 62+); $6 (ages 4-17); $25 (family); $20 (family, Mon. 5-8 p.m.). Prices may vary. **Phone:** (208) 522-1400.

BEST WESTERN PLUS COTTONTREE INN　　(208)523-6000

Hotel
$95-$200

AAA Benefit: Save 10% or more every day and earn 10% bonus points!

Address: 900 Lindsay Blvd 83402 **Location:** I-15 exit 119, just e. **Facility:** 94 units, some efficiencies. 3 stories, interior corridors. **Parking:** winter plug-ins. **Pool(s):** heated indoor. **Activities:** hot tub, trails, exercise room. **Guest Services:** valet and coin laundry.

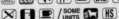

BEST WESTERN PLUS DRIFTWOOD INN　(208)523-2242

Motel
$79-$179

AAA Benefit: Save 10% or more every day and earn 10% bonus points!

Address: 575 River Pkwy 83402 **Location:** I-15 exit 118 (Broadway), 0.5 mi e, then 0.3 mi n. **Facility:** 75 units, some efficiencies and kitchens. 2 stories (no elevator), exterior corridors. **Parking:** winter plug-ins. **Terms:** resort fee. **Pool(s):** heated outdoor. **Activities:** hot tub, bicycles, trails, exercise room. **Guest Services:** valet and coin laundry.

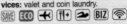

CANDLEWOOD SUITES　　208/525-9800

 Extended Stay Hotel. Rates not provided. **Address:** 665 Pancheri Dr 83402 **Location:** Waterfront. I-15 exit 118 (Broadway), 1 mi e (cross bridge), then 0.5 mi s on S Capital Ave. **Facility:** 81 efficiencies. 4 stories, interior corridors. **Parking:** winter plug-ins. **Activities:** picnic facilities, trails, exercise room. **Guest Services:** complimentary laundry.

FAIRFIELD INN & SUITES BY MARRIOTT　(208)552-7378

Contemporary Hotel
$89-$182

FAIRFIELD INN & SUITES Marriott
AAA Benefit: Members save 5% or more!

Address: 1293 W Broadway St 83402 **Location:** I-15 exit 118 (Broadway), just e. Next to shopping area. **Facility:** 81 units. 3 stories, interior corridors. **Parking:** winter plug-ins. **Pool(s):** heated indoor. **Activities:** hot tub, exercise room. **Guest Services:** valet and coin laundry. **Featured Amenity:** full hot breakfast.

HAMPTON INN IDAHO FALLS
(208)529-9800

 Hotel $109-$250 **Address:** 2500 Channing Way 83404 **Location:** I-15 exit 118 (Broadway), 1 mi e, 0.5 mi s on Yellowstone Hwy, 2.7 mi e on 17th St, then 0.3 mi s. Adjacent to shopping mall. **Facility:** 79 units. 3 stories, interior corridors. **Parking:** winter plug-ins. **Terms:** 1-7 night minimum stay, cancellation fee imposed. **Pool(s):** heated indoor. **Activities:** hot tub, exercise room. **Guest Services:** valet and coin laundry, area transportation.

AAA Benefit: Members save up to 10%!

HAMPTON INN IDAHO FALLS AIRPORT
(208)523-1400

 Contemporary Hotel $89-$229 **Address:** 645 Lindsay Blvd 83402 **Location:** I-15 exit 118 (Broadway), 0.4 mi e, then just n; exit 119, 0.4 mi se. **Facility:** 127 units, some efficiencies. 4 stories, interior corridors. **Terms:** 1-7 night minimum stay, cancellation fee imposed. **Pool(s):** heated indoor. **Activities:** hot tub, trails, exercise room. **Guest Services:** valet and coin laundry, area transportation.

AAA Benefit: Members save up to 10%!

HILTON GARDEN INN IDAHO FALLS
(208)522-9500

 Hotel $109-$189 **Address:** 700 Lindsay Blvd 83402 **Location:** I-15 exit 118 (Broadway), 0.5 mi e, then just n. **Facility:** 119 units. 4 stories, interior corridors. **Parking:** winter plug-ins. **Terms:** 1-7 night minimum stay, cancellation fee imposed. **Pool(s):** heated indoor. **Activities:** hot tub, picnic facilities, trails, exercise room. **Guest Services:** valet and coin laundry, area transportation.

AAA Benefit: Members save up to 10%!

HOLIDAY INN EXPRESS & SUITES
208/542-9800

 Hotel. Rates not provided. **Address:** 2270 Channing Way 83404 **Location:** I-15 exit 118 (Broadway), 1 mi e, 0.5 mi s on Yellowstone Hwy, 2.7 mi e on 17th St, then 0.3 mi s. Adjacent to shopping mall. **Facility:** 79 units. 3 stories, interior corridors. **Parking:** winter plug-ins. **Pool(s):** heated indoor. **Activities:** hot tub, picnic facilities, exercise room. **Guest Services:** valet and coin laundry, area transportation.

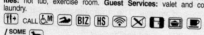

LA QUINTA INN & SUITES IDAHO FALLS
(208)552-2500

Hotel $86-$295 **Address:** 2501 S 25th St E 83406 **Location:** I-15 exit 118 (Broadway), 1 mi e, 0.5 mi s on Yellowstone Hwy, 3.8 mi e on 17th St to Hitt Rd, then just s. Near shopping area. **Facility:** 84 units, some efficiencies and kitchens. 3 stories, interior corridors. **Parking:** winter plug-ins. **Pool(s):** heated indoor. **Activities:** hot tub, exercise room. **Guest Services:** valet and coin laundry.

LE RITZ HOTEL & SUITES
(208)528-0880

 Hotel $69-$189 **Address:** 720 Lindsay Blvd 83402 **Location:** I-15 exit 118 (Broadway), 0.5 mi e, then 0.4 mi n. **Facility:** 116 units. 2 stories, interior corridors. **Terms:** cancellation fee imposed. **Pool(s):** heated indoor. **Activities:** hot tub, trails, exercise room. **Guest Services:** valet and coin laundry.

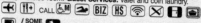

RESIDENCE INN BY MARRIOTT
(208)542-0000

 Extended Stay Hotel $113-$249 **Address:** 635 W Broadway 83402 **Location:** Waterfront. I-15 exit 118 (Broadway), 0.4 mi e. **Facility:** 108 efficiencies, some two bedrooms and kitchens. 5 stories, interior corridors. **Pool(s):** heated indoor. **Activities:** hot tub, picnic facilities, trails, exercise room. **Guest Services:** valet and coin laundry, boarding pass kiosk.

AAA Benefit: Members save 5% or more!

WHERE TO EAT

BLUE HASHI
208/525-2583

Japanese. Casual Dining. $7-$15 **AAA Inspector Notes:** Translated, the name of this casual spot means chopsticks. The chefs here create a few distinctive sushi rolls, and if they are received well, they become a regular menu item. Along with popular sashimi, maki and sushi there are a few yakisoba noodle dishes and fully cooked entrées with rice and vegetables. Diners can expect a wait during peak hours. The lunch combos are varied and quite economical. **Features:** beer & wine. **Address:** 2894 S 25th E 83401 **Location:** I-15 exit 116, 5 mi e on Sunnyside Rd, just n on S Hitt Rd, then just w. L D

Take your imagination to new destinations

with the online AAA/CAA Travel Guides

THE CELT IRISH PUB & GRILL — 208/881-5128

WW WW Irish. Casual Dining. $9-$14 **AAA Inspector Notes:** The architectural details at this friendly pub include stained-glass windows and hand-crafted woodwork on an upscale bar. In addition to local brews and imports, guests can enjoy numerous beers on tap. Locals favor the Reuben, a hearty shepherd's pie, fish and chips made with red snapper and the heart stopper made with a beef patty, bacon, corned beef and pastrami topped with a fried egg. Expect live music on the weekend. **Features:** full bar, happy hour. **Address:** 394 W Broadway St 83402 **Location:** I-15 exit 118, 0.7 mi e, jct Broadway St and Park Ave. **Parking:** street only.

L   D   LATE

CHEF SHANE'S PERSPECTIVE — 208/932-2727

WW WW American. Casual Dining. $14-$19 **AAA Inspector Notes:** Set back in a small strip mall, this simple eatery features cuisine sprinkled with Caribbean and Spanish influences with a strong focus on seasonal preparations. A few popular items are the shrimp piri piri with apple and cucumber slaw, jerk-seasoned chicken and hand-rolled sweet potato gnocchi. A children's menu and gluten-free items are available. Undoubtedly, guests will look forward to returning to another well-prepared meal. **Reservations:** suggested. **Address:** 3192 S 25th E 83404 **Location:** Jct E Sunnyside and S Hitt rds.   D

D'RAILED BAR & GRUB — 208/881-5105

WW WW American. Casual Dining. $9-$28 **AAA Inspector Notes:** A former bunk house for the railroad crew, this charming spot serves a curious selection of menu items using local foods and wine sources. Popular choices include the club car sandwich, seafood-stuffed halibut, juicy steaks and Havana cast-iron shrimp cocktail. **Features:** full bar, patio dining. **Reservations:** suggested, for dinner. **Address:** 468 N Eastern Ave 83402 **Location:** I-15 exit 118 (Broadway), 0.8 mi e to Elm St, then just n.

L   D   CALL &M

JAKERS BAR & GRILL — 208/524-5240

WWWW Steak Seafood. Casual Dining. $11-$67 **AAA Inspector Notes:** This restaurant offers a delectable selection of menu items including a must-see soup and salad bar. Diners cannot go wrong with premium boneless Idaho rainbow trout, Northwest-grown signature melt-in-your mouth filet mignon or boneless beef short ribs. The blackened chicken Alfredo is addictive, as are the little warm rolls served with honey butter. Also, gluten-free, vegetarian and smart light plates are available. For those with friends, try the signature mud pie for four. **Features:** full bar, happy hour. **Address:** 851 Lindsay Blvd 83402 **Location:** I-15 exit 118 (Broadway), 0.3 mi e, then 0.3 mi nw.   L   D   CALL &M

JALISCO'S MEXICAN RESTAURANT — 208/612-0102

WW WW Mexican. Casual Dining. $7-$15 **AAA Inspector Notes:** Across from the falls, this colorful eatery has a varied menu including four choices of soup, traditional beef, chicken and pork entrées and combinations for one, two or three items. All dishes are thoughtfully presented. The background music is festive. **Features:** full bar. **Address:** 325 River Pkwy 83401 **Location:** I-15 exit 118 (Broadway), 0.4 mi e, then just n. **Parking:** on-site and street.

L   D   CALL &M

LA VANILLA BEAN PATISSERIE — 208/680-0572

WW Breads/Pastries Coffee/Tea. Quick Serve. $5-$9 **AAA Inspector Notes:** This downtown corner eatery specializes in sweet and savory European pastries, great coffee, hot chocolate and coconut milk lattes. Patrons can appreciate the laid-back atmosphere. Organic java, piroshkies, quiche and a soup special are featured daily. Also, flourless treats are available. **Address:** 489 Park Ave 83402 **Location:** Corner of Park Ave and B St; downtown. **Parking:** street only.   B   L

Stay connected with #AAA

and #CAA on your favorite

social media sites

REPUBLIC AMERICAN GRILL & TAPAS BAR — 208/523-3355

WW WW Small Plates. Casual Dining. $9-$23 **AAA Inspector Notes:** The décor inside the entrance of this grill is fairly modest, while the long dining room has several comfortable seating nooks and a separate lounge and bar in the back. Food presentations are creative and include bacon-wrapped dates, blackened shrimp and grits and char-grilled chicken breast atop maple-pepper bacon. My favorites include pesto deviled eggs crowned with diced red pepper that look like jewels and the chocolate truffle trio. Vegetarian options and a kids' menu are available. **Features:** beer & wine. **Address:** 355 River Pkwy 83402 **Location:** I-15 exit 18 (Broadway Ave), 0.4 mi e, then just n. **Parking:** street only.

L   D

THE SANDPIPER — 208/524-3344

WW WW American. Casual Dining. $13-$29 **AAA Inspector Notes:** Adjacent to the Snake River, this small-town, locally popular restaurant serves immense amounts of food. For starters, try the tasty pan-fried oysters, then move on to an entrée of hearty barbecued ribs. Seasonal patio dining with views of the river also is available. A kids' menu is available. **Features:** full bar, patio dining. **Address:** 750 Lindsay Blvd 83402 **Location:** I-15 exit 118 (Broadway), 0.5 mi e, then 0.4 mi n.   D

THE SNAKEBITE RESTAURANT — 208/525-2522

WW WW American. Casual Dining. $7-$26 **AAA Inspector Notes:** The comfortable décor and notable food are nice departures from the endless supply of fast food outlets in the area. There is a nice selection of gourmet burgers and salads, sandwiches and pasta. Dinner entrées include bourbon chicken, osso buco and tequila salmon, to name a few. **Features:** beer & wine. **Address:** 401 Park Ave 83402 **Location:** I-15 exit 118 (Broadway), 0.6 mi e, just n on Shoup Ave, then just w; corner of A St and Park Ave; in historic downtown. **Parking:** street only.   L   D

SNOW EAGLE BREWING & GRILL — 208/557-0455

WW WW American. Casual Dining. $9-$18 **AAA Inspector Notes:** Next to the falls, patrons can choose from two dining experiences in one restaurant. Feast on maki, nigiri and sashimi or chow down on burgers, oven-fried sandwiches, juicy steaks, seafood Alfredo, and chicken, shrimp or tofu stir fry with tempura vegetables. There always is a new beer to sample. Whatever you do, try the signature chocolate cake—the pinch of cayenne is delightful. **Features:** full bar. **Address:** 455 River Pkwy 83402 **Location:** I-15 exit 118, 0.5 mi e, just n. **Parking:** on-site and street.

L   D   CALL &M

IDAHO PANHANDLE NATIONAL FORESTS (B-1)

Elevations in the forests range from 2,060 ft. at Lake Pend Oreille to 7,705 ft. at Northwest Peak. Refer to AAA maps for additional elevation information.

In northern Idaho and adjoining parts of Montana and Washington, the many-segmented Idaho Panhandle National Forests have rugged peaks, canyons and valleys. The approximately 2.5-million-acre area includes the former St. Joe, Kaniksu and Coeur d'Alene national forests.

Of particular interest are the stands of old-growth cedars at Hanna Flats and Roosevelt Grove near Priest Lake, the Settlers Grove of Ancient Cedars near Prichard and the Hobo Cedar Grove near Clarkia. Among the nearly 400 species of wildlife are wolves and grizzly bears.

Fishing is available at Priest Lake, Lake Coeur d'Alene and Lake Pend Oreille; nature trails traverse these areas. Float trips are popular on the Coeur d'Alene, St. Joe and Priest rivers. Winter sports areas are off SR 6 between St. Maries and Moscow, at Lookout Pass just off I-90 on the Idaho-Montana border and at 4th of July Pass off I-90.

Information is available at the headquarters in Coeur d'Alene and at ranger stations at Avery, Bonners Ferry, Priest River, St. Maries, Sandpoint and Smelterville. For additional information contact the Forest Supervisor's Office, Idaho Panhandle National Forests, 3815 Schreiber Way, Coeur d'Alene, ID 83815-8363; phone (208) 765-7223. *See Recreation Areas Chart.*

ISLAND PARK (F-6) pop. 286, elev. 6,293'

The scattered settlement of Island Park lies at the northern edge of Henry's Fork Caldera, also known as the Mesa Falls Caldera, an ancient volcanic feature. Millions of years ago, this was an active super volcano. When the volcano collapsed some 1.3 million years ago, it left behind a giant, circular crater with a diameter of 18 to 23 miles. The caldera is known for its beautiful forests, clear streams, waterfalls, springs, lakes, marshes, wildlife and fishing.

HARRIMAN STATE PARK is 9 mi. s. on US 20 to 3489 Green Canyon Rd., following signs. Occupying the site of the 11,000-acre Railroad Ranch owned by Union Pacific Railroad investors from 1902-77, today the park is a wildlife refuge within the greater Yellowstone ecosystem.

More than 20 miles of hiking, mountain biking and equestrian trails traverse the park, which is known for its spectacular summer wildflower displays. Horseback rides are offered in summer and fall, and winter draws Nordic skiers, fat tire snow bikers and snowshoers.

See Recreation Areas Chart.

Note: Pets must be leashed and are allowed in day-use parking lots only. **Time:** Allow 1 hour minimum. **Hours:** Park open daily 7 a.m. to 10 p.m. Visitor center open daily 8-5, June-Oct.; daily 9-5, rest of year. Historic buildings are open for viewing Sat.-Sun. and holidays, Memorial Day-Labor Day (volunteers permitting). Horseback riding on trails is available daily, Memorial Day weekend-Oct. 31 (weather permitting). The Jones House is used as a warming hut during winter. **Cost:** $5 (per private vehicle). **Phone:** (208) 558-7368. ⊠ ⊞

HENRYS LAKE STATE PARK is at 3917 E. 5100 N., about 15 miles west of Yellowstone National Park. With more than 80 camp sites, four miles of biking and walking trails and fields of wildflowers as far as the eye can see, the 585-acre Henrys Lake State Park would be amazing without the lake. But the high mountain lake full of cutthroat, brook and cut-bow hybrid trout is what makes it a jewel for fisherman who flock to this site. Water sports enthusiasts and campers are also fans - but so are the mosquitoes, so bring plenty of bug spray. *See Recreation Areas Chart.* **Hours:** Memorial Day through second Saturday of Oct. **Cost:** Park admission $5 (per private vehicle). Campsite $18-$31 per night.

Cabins $50-$55 per night. **Phone:** (208) 558-7532 Summer, or (208) 558-7368 Winter.

▲ ⊠ 🐾 ⊞

JEROME pop. 10,890

BEST WESTERN SAWTOOTH INN & SUITES
(208)324-9200

Hotel $89-$140

AAA Benefit: Save 10% or more every day and earn 10% bonus points!

Address: 2653 S Lincoln Ave 83338 **Location:** I-84 exit 168, just n. Across from shopping center and next to gas station. **Facility:** 67 units. 2 stories (no elevator), interior corridors. **Terms:** check-in 4 pm. **Pool(s):** heated indoor. **Activities:** hot tub, exercise room. **Guest Services:** valet and coin laundry. **Featured Amenity: full hot breakfast.** *(See ad p. 102.)*

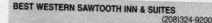

COMFORT INN & SUITES   (208)644-1200

◆◆◆ **Hotel** $89-$129 **Address:** 379 Crossroads Point Blvd 83338 **Location:** I-84 exit 173 (US 93), 0.7 mi n. **Facility:** 103 units. 3 stories, interior corridors. **Amenities:** safes. **Pool(s):** heated indoor. **Activities:** hot tub, exercise room. **Guest Services:** valet and coin laundry.

CALL ⊠M 🏊 BIZ HS 🛜 ✕ 🔌 🖥 ▭
/SOME UNITS 🛏

WHERE TO EAT

BURNT LEMON GRILL   208/324-8800

◆ Sandwiches Burgers. Quick Serve. $5-$9 **AAA Inspector Notes:** This spot serves anything but ordinary fast food. People drive for miles for the lemonade--fresh lemons are burned before they are juiced. The bragging rights burger and crazy bird roll-ups are terrific. However, the chicken wrap with cabbage, rice noodles and sesame Oriental dressing is downright addictive. Kids have their own menu to choose from. **Address:** 306 S Lincoln Ave 83338 **Location:** I-84 exit 168, 2.2 mi n. **Parking:** on-site and street. L D

KAMIAH (D-2) pop. 1,295, elev. 1,196'
• Hotels p. 72 • Restaurants p. 72

Meriwether Lewis and William Clark camped on the north bank of the Clearwater River just north of Kamiah (KAM-ee-eye) in the spring of 1806 on their homeward journey. Today a sawmill occupies the site of their monthlong encampment.

A pasture about a half mile northwest of Kamiah is supposedly the location of the mission that Asa and Sarah Smith started in 1839. They stayed only 2 years, and their work in this area was not resumed until 30 years later.

The 1871 First Presbyterian Church is said to be the oldest Native American church in continuous use in Idaho. The Northwest Passage Scenic Byway (US 12) also passes through town. It's considered one of the top 10 motorcycle roads in the nation.

Kamiah Chamber of Commerce: 518 Main St., P.O. Box 1124, Kamiah, ID 83536. **Phone:** (208) 935-2290.

CLEARWATER 12 MOTEL   208/935-2671
WWW Motel. Rates not provided. **Address:** 108 E 3rd St (Hwy 12) 83536 **Location:** On US 12, just e of center. **Facility:** 29 units, some kitchens. 2 stories (no elevator), exterior corridors. **Parking:** winter plug-ins.

HEARTHSTONE ELEGANT LODGE BY THE RIVER
(208)935-1492

WWWW
Bed & Breakfast
$140-$235

Address: 3250 Hwy 12 at Milepost 64 83536 **Location:** On SR 12, 2.2 mi w of center; MM 64. **Facility:** Spacious, artistically appointed rooms have fine linens on canopied king-size beds with beautiful antique headboards, vaulted ceilings, fireplaces and a covered deck entrance with skylights. 5 units, some cottages. 1-2 stories (no elevator), exterior corridors. **Parking:** winter plug-ins. **Terms:** check-in 4 pm, 3 day cancellation notice-fee imposed. **Activities:** massage. **Guest Services:** area transportation. **Featured Amenity: full hot breakfast.**

WHERE TO EAT

HEARTHSTONE BAKERY & TEA HOUSE   208/935-1912
WW Breakfast Sandwiches. Casual Dining. $5-$16 **AAA Inspector Notes:** *Historic.* This charming restaurant has the feel of a Victorian tea room. Salads, sandwiches and soups are made in-house and taste great with freshly baked breads of several varieties. Desserts abound and range from cookies and cinnamon rolls to fruit and cream pies. **Features:** beer & wine. **Address:** 502 Main St 83536 **Location:** Downtown. **Parking:** on-site and street.

B   L   CALL ⚅M

HUB BAR & GRILL   208/935-2211
WWW American. Casual Dining. $6-$19 **AAA Inspector Notes:** This laid back restaurant serves hot and cold sandwiches, daily soups and chowder and a few basket items with fries. A lot of locals stop in for the egg salad sandwich with fresh made-in-house potato chips. The pecan pie and the apple pie sell out quickly. **Features:** full bar. **Address:** 406 Main St 83536 **Location:** Downtown. **Parking:** street only.
B   L   D

KAMIAH HOTEL BAR AND GRLL   208/935-0545
WW Steak Sandwiches. Casual Dining. $8-$23 **AAA Inspector Notes:** Be sure to stop by this restaurant located in a two-story circa 1902 building for a juicy steak, smoked ribs or shrimp skewer dinner while enjoying an ice cold beer or a classic cocktail. All dinners are served with a salad, baked potato and garlic bread. Friday is prime rib night. **Features:** full bar, senior menu. **Address:** 501 4th St 83536 **Location:** Downtown. **Parking:** street only.
L   D

KELLOGG (B-1) pop. 2,120, elev. 2,305'

Kellogg, the Silver Valley's largest town, celebrates its heritage as a longtime mining community. The Coeur d'Alene mining district has yielded more than a billion dollars in silver, lead, gold and zinc; the Lucky Friday and Galena Mine are a couple of the largest mines that still operate. The Shoshone County Mining and Smelting Museum, also known as The Staff House Museum *(see attraction listing)*, chronicles the colorful history of Silver Valley. The Sunshine Miners Memorial, off I-90 exit 54, commemorates the 1972 mine fire that claimed 91 lives. It was one of the nation's worst metal and nonmetal mine disasters.

The Kellogg area also is known for outdoor recreation, particularly its biking trails, which range from easy to "What was I thinking?" Accessible here is the Trail of the Coeur d'Alenes, a 72-mile paved path that runs from the Montana border to the Washington state line. Hardy cyclists also can take their bikes up the Silver Mountain Gondola *(see attraction listing)* to enjoy 40 miles of trails, including some that descend 3,000 feet.

Historic Silver Valley Chamber of Commerce: 10 Station Ave., Kellogg, ID 83837. **Phone:** (208) 784-0821.

CRYSTAL GOLD MINE is off I-90 exit 54 (Big Creek Rd.) westbound or I-90 exit 51 (N. Division St.) eastbound at 51931 Silver Valley Rd. The guided underground tours conducted by experienced miners provide an interesting glimpse into the hand-labor, hard-rock mining of the late 1800s. Gold, silver and smithsonite are visible inside the mine. The temperature inside the mine is 48 F; visitors should dress appropriately.

Time: Allow 30 minutes minimum. **Hours:** Tours depart every 15 to 30 minutes daily 9-6, May 1-Sept. 15; 10-4, Feb. 1-Apr. 30 and Sept. 16-Dec. 31. Closed Easter, Thanksgiving and Christmas. **Cost:** (includes 1 hour of gold panning Apr.-Sept.) $12; $11 (ages 65+); $8.50 (ages 4-16); $45 (family, two adults and three children, $5 for each additional child). **Phone:** (208) 783-4653. ▲

SILVER MOUNTAIN GONDOLA is .25 mi. e. off I-90 exit 49 to 610 Bunker Ave. Riders travel 3.1 miles in what is said to be North America's longest single-stage gondola. The ride takes 24 minutes to go 3,400 feet from the base to the Mountain House upper terminal. Mountain House features include mountain biking and hiking trails, a children's play area, a nature trail and an amphitheater where concerts are staged.

Time: Allow 2 hours minimum. **Hours:** Sat.-Sun. 9:30-5, Mon.-Tues. 9:30-4, Fri. 9:30-8, July-Aug.; Fri. 9:30-8, Sat.-Sun. 9:30-5, in June; Sat.-Sun. 9:30-5, in Sept. Last departure up the mountain 30 minutes before closing. **Cost:** $18; $14 (ages 4-17); $60 (family, four people, $13 for each additional person). Prices vary on weekends. **Phone:** (208) 783-1111, ext. 8240, or (800) 204-6428.

THE STAFF HOUSE MUSEUM, 820 McKinley Ave., is in a 1906 house built for the Bunker Hill Mine's top executive. The museum has geological, mining, smelting, medical and Boy Scout exhibits. Displays include mineral collections, mine models and photographs. An outdoor display features an 1895 Nordberg compressor once used to pump air underground into mines. **Time:** Allow 30 minutes minimum. **Hours:** Tues.-Sat. 1-5, late May-late Sept. **Cost:** $4; $3 (ages 55+); $1 (ages 6-18); $6 (family). **Phone:** (208) 786-4141.

RECREATIONAL ACTIVITIES
Skiing

- **Silver Mountain Resort** is off I-90 exit 49 at 610 Bunker Ave. Other activities are offered. **Hours:** Winter activities are available Thurs.-Mon. 9-4, late Nov. to mid-Apr. Schedule varies during holiday weeks; phone ahead. **Phone:** (208) 783-1111 or (800) 204-6428.

GUESTHOUSE INN & SUITES   (208)783-1234

◆◆ **Hotel** $84-$319 **Address:** 601 Bunker Ave 83837 **Location:** I-90 exit 49, 0.5 mi se. **Facility:** 60 units. 2 stories (no elevator), interior corridors. **Parking:** winter plug-ins. **Terms:** cancellation fee imposed. **Pool(s):** heated indoor. **Activities:** hot tub, limited exercise equipment. **Guest Services:** coin laundry.

🍴➕ ➤ BIZ 📶 ✕ 📱 🖥 📀 / SOME UNITS 🅂

MORNING STAR LODGE   208/783-0202

◆◆◆ **Resort Condominium** $101-$720 **Address:** 602 Bunker Ave 83837 **Location:** I-90 exit 49, 0.5 mi se. **Facility:** The condos at this ski resort are spacious and feature upscale décor. Included in the room rate is an elaborate onsite water park and nearby is the famous Route of the Hiawatha trail. 215 condominiums. 4-5 stories, interior corridors. **Parking:** winter plug-ins. **Terms:** check-in 4 pm, cancellation fee imposed, resort fee. **Dining:** 3 restaurants. **Activities:** hot tub, regulation golf, downhill skiing, recreation programs in summer, bicycles, trails, exercise room. **Guest Services:** complimentary laundry, area transportation.

🍴 🚗 CALL 🅂 BIZ HS 📶 ✕ 📱 🖥 📀 / SOME UNITS 🅂

KETCHUM (G-3) pop. 2,689, elev. 5,821'
• Hotels p. 74 • Restaurants p. 75

In the late 19th century Ketchum sprang up almost overnight as a shipping and smelting center for the remote mountain mines surrounding the Wood River Valley. Ores and supplies were transported by the giant ore wagons of the Horace Lewis Fast Freight Line. These relics of the area's past are displayed in the Ore Wagon Museum on East Avenue next to City Hall and once again appear on the streets during the Wagon Days Celebration Labor Day weekend. The history and culture of Wood River Valley's sheep industry is spotlighted in October during the Trailing of the Sheep festival. The Ketchum Cemetery includes the grave of Ernest Hemingway.

As the gateway to the Sun Valley *(see place listing p. 100)* resort area and the Sawtooth National Recreation Area *(see place listing p. 98)*, the town offers an abundance of activities year-round. Such outdoor recreational activities as swimming, mountain biking and bicycling, hiking, horseback riding, cross-country skiing, snowshoeing and camping are foremost among Ketchum's attractions. For the spectator Ketchum offers some 30 art galleries and the nexStage Theatre, where local theater companies perform year-round. For theater information phone (208) 726-4857.

Sun Valley Visitors Center: 491 Sun Valley Rd., Ketchum ID 83340. **Phone:** (208) 726-3423 or (800) 634-3347.

Self-guiding tours: The Sun Valley Museum of History, 1st Street and Washington Avenue, has a booklet about the history of Ketchum that includes a walking tour through the downtown area; phone (208) 726-8118.

Shopping: Downtown Ketchum offers more than 70 shops and restaurants offering everything from antiques and books to children's toys and specialty gifts.

RECREATIONAL ACTIVITIES
Horseback Riding

- **Galena Stage Stop Corrals-Trail Rides** is 24 mi. n. on SR 75. Other activities are offered. **Hours:** Horseback riding trips daily 8-5, mid-June through Labor Day. **Phone:** (208) 726-1735.

SAWTOOTH BOTANICAL GARDEN is 5 miles south of Ketchum and Sun Valley off of State Hwy. 75, at 11 Gimlet Rd. Visitors to the 5-acre garden will find a solar greenhouse, native plants from several regions of Idaho and an 800-pound bronze prayer wheel with one million hand-painted prayers that was blessed by the Dalai Lama. After a stroll through the Perennial Garden or the Ellen Long Pavilion, kids can play and families can relax at the Sawtooth Sandbox. Guided tours must be arranged in advance. **Time:** Allow 1 hour minimum. **Hours:** Gardens dawn-dusk year-round. Visitor center 9-5, closed major holidays. **Cost:** Donations. **Phone:** (208) 726-9358. GT 🐾 🍴

BEST WESTERN PLUS KENTWOOD LODGE
(208)726-4114

Hotel
$110-$295

AAA Benefit:
Save 10% or more every day and earn 10% bonus points!

Address: 180 S Main St 83340 **Location:** On SR 75, at Main and Rivers sts. **Facility:** 57 units, some efficiencies. 3 stories, interior corridors. **Parking:** winter plug-ins. **Terms:** 2 night minimum stay - seasonal and/or weekends, 7 day cancellation notice. **Pool(s):** heated indoor. **Activities:** hot tub, trails, exercise room. **Guest Services:** valet and coin laundry.

BEST WESTERN TYROLEAN LODGE
(208)726-5336

Hotel
$110-$180

AAA Benefit:
Save 10% or more every day and earn 10% bonus points!

Address: 260 Cottonwood St 83340 **Location:** Just s of center to Rivers St, w to 2nd Ave, s to Cottonwood St, then just w. **Facility:** 52 units. 3 stories (no elevator), interior corridors. **Parking:** winter plug-ins. **Amenities:** safes. **Pool(s):** heated outdoor. **Activities:** sauna, hot tub, game room, trails, exercise room. **Guest Services:** coin laundry. (See ad this page.)

▼ See AAA listing this page ▼

BEST WESTERN TYROLEAN LODGE

A Beautiful Austrian Style Lodge
Overlooking Majestic Bald
Mountain of Sun Valley

260 Cottonwood St.
P.O. Box 802
Ketchum, ID 83340
208.726.5336

- Free Hot Breakfast
- Outdoor heated pool and hot tub
- 40" LCD TVs with DIRECTV & HBO
- Game room and Fitness Center
- Kids stay free (17 and under)

- Free High Speed Internet Access
- Guest Laundry Facility
- 300 yards to River Run Lodge at Sun Valley Ski Area
- Smoke-free facility

— **Public area renovation completed June 2014** —

For Reservations Call: 208.726.5336
www.bestwestern.com/tyroleanlodge

Dream.
Plan. Go.

Picture yourself on the ideal
road trip. Make it real with
TripTik® Travel Planner.

Online: AAA.com/ttp
On the go:
AAA or CAA Mobile app

WHERE TO EAT

CRISTINA'S RESTAURANT & BAKERY   208/726-4499
WW European. Casual Dining. $10-$19 **AAA Inspector Notes:** This popular eatery is located in a charming salmon-colored house. The seasonally-inspired menu includes an assortment of hot and cold appetizers and entrées, salads, homemade pasta, thin crust pizza and truly mouth-watering desserts, breads and pastries. **Features:** beer & wine, Sunday brunch. **Reservations:** suggested. **Address:** 520 2nd St E 83340 **Location:** Just e on 3rd St, s on East Ave to 2nd St, then just e. B L AC

DESPO'S, MEXICAN WITH ALTITUDE   208/726-3068
WW Mexican. Casual Dining. $8-$15 **AAA Inspector Notes:** This modern Mexican restaurant specializes in sustainable practices when attaining their tasty ingredients. Supporting local and regional farms, the menu is comprised of only the freshest ingredients. **Features:** full bar, patio dining. **Address:** 211 4th St E 83340 **Location:** At 4th St and Washington Ave; downtown. **Parking:** on-site and street. L D CALL &M

GLOBUS   208/726-1301
WWW Asian. Fine Dining. $15-$38 **AAA Inspector Notes:** The ambience is colorful, intimate and inviting. Creative, seasonal and flavorful starters, salads and entrées are meticulously prepared and may include watermelon terrine, steamed clay pot mussels, Korean style pork baby back ribs or pomegranate seared duck breast in celery root purée. The roasted chicken breast in cauliflower-miso purée with glazed carrots, grapefruit and frisée is beautifully presented. An extensive wine list and a nice selection of teas also are offered. **Features:** full bar. **Reservations:** suggested. **Address:** 131 Washington Ave 83340 **Location:** At 6th St and Warm Springs Rd, just w of 6th and Main sts. D

JAVA ON FOURTH   208/726-2882
W American. Quick Serve. $5-$9 **AAA Inspector Notes:** This quaint and eclectic cafe always is bustling with locals and tourists alike. From soup and sandwiches to delicious granola and fresh pastries, the menu offers something for everyone. **Features:** patio dining. **Address:** 191 4th St 83340 **Location:** North end of town; on SR 75 (Main St), just w. **Parking:** on-site and street. B L

KETCHUM GRILL   208/726-4660
WWW American. Fine Dining. $14-$22 **AAA Inspector Notes:** This casual, rustic restaurant located in a converted house offers seasonal appetizers, entrées and desserts, all creatively presented. Desserts are not to be missed, especially the wide array of house ice cream, sorbets and the chocolate chi-chi (just order it). A few smaller portion items are available. **Features:** full bar, patio dining. **Reservations:** suggested. **Address:** 520 East Ave N 83340 **Location:** At East Ave and 5th St; downtown. **Parking:** street only. D

MICHEL'S CHRISTIANIA RESTAURANT & OLYMPIC BAR
208/726-3388
WWW French. Fine Dining. $20-$38 **AAA Inspector Notes:** This casually elegant restaurant serves a variety of fresh dishes in one of the country's premier ski and summer resort communities. The lounge is a local favorite and draws a lively, conversational crowd. Seasonal patio dining also is available. **Features:** full bar. **Reservations:** suggested. **Address:** 303 N Walnut Ave 83340 **Location:** 0.3 mi e on Sun Valley Rd. **Parking:** street only. D

RICKSHAW   208/726-8481
WW Asian. Casual Dining. $11-$15 **AAA Inspector Notes:** The menu here is not expansive, yet it is still hard to make a decision because everything looks good. Diners cannot go wrong with the addictive pork pot stickers, cashew vegetable stir-fry in tamari sauce, KFC (Korean fried chicken) or the mouth-watering pho. As a thoughtful touch, fennel is presented after the meal to cleanse the palate. Lunch is served on Friday only. **Features:** beer & wine, patio dining. **Address:** 460 N Washington Ave 83340 **Location:** On Washington Ave, between 4th and 5th sts. **Parking:** street only. D AC

SAWTOOTH CLUB   208/726-5233
WWW American. Casual Dining. $19-$33 **AAA Inspector Notes:** This rustic and energetic restaurant appeals to the casual après-ski crowd as well as locals and travelers. The distinctive flavor of mesquite grilling infuses the large cuts of beef and the house specialty Idaho rack of lamb. Other menu items may include breast of duck finished with a cherry balsamic reduction and mesquite-grilled Idaho ruby red trout. **Features:** full bar, patio dining. **Reservations:** suggested. **Address:** 231 N Main St 83340 **Location:** At 2nd Ave and SR 75 (Main St); downtown. **Parking:** street only. D AC

SMOKY MOUNTAIN PIZZERIA GRILL   208/622-5625
WW Italian. Casual Dining. $10-$24 **AAA Inspector Notes:** Situated in the Sawtooth Mountains, this local favorite offers the perfect setting for a get-together, with a game room to entertain the kids and a rotating beer tap for the adults. **Features:** beer & wine, patio dining, happy hour. **Address:** 200 Sun Valley Rd 83340 **Location:** North end of town; SR 75 (Main St), just w. **Parking:** street only. L D

VINTAGE RESTAURANT   208/726-9595
WWW American. Fine Dining. $26-$35 **AAA Inspector Notes:** Serving innovative comfort food with a twist, this quaint cabin allows for an intimate dining experience. Tables are elegantly set and include fresh flowers. While menu items can change seasonally, there is a reason the sweet corn and shrimp tamale and pecan-crusted chicken typically remain on the menu—they draw visitors back. Other offerings may include Cajun oysters, rack of lamb in celery root puree and strawberry rhubarb chutney or the chef's old-fashioned crispy-skin duck. **Features:** beer & wine, patio dining. **Reservations:** suggested. **Address:** 231 Leadville Ave N 83340 **Location:** Just ne of SR 75 (Main St) and Sun Valley Rd, then just se. **Parking:** street only. D

WHISKEY JACQUES'   208/726-5297
WW American. Casual Dining. $8-$22 **AAA Inspector Notes:** This favorite watering hole is the place to experience all of the local flavor in the Ketchum and Sun Valley area. With live music multiple evenings per week, the atmosphere is always fun-filled, lively and bustling. The menu offers a variety of pizza, salads, sandwiches, wraps and burgers. **Features:** full bar, patio dining, happy hour. **Address:** 251 N Main St 83340 **Location:** On SR 75 (Main St); downtown. **Parking:** street only. D LATE

KOOSKIA (D-2) pop. 607, elev. 1,261'
• Hotels p. 76 • Restaurants p. 76

Kooskia (KOOS-key), founded in 1895 at the confluence of the Middle and South Forks of the Clearwater River, takes its name from a Nez Perce phrase meaning "where the waters meet."

Kooskia Chamber of Commerce: P.O. Box 310, Kooskia, ID 83539. **Phone:** (208) 926-4362.

KOOSKIA NATIONAL FISH HATCHERY is 2 mi. s.e. on Clear Creek County Rd. Chinook salmon eggs are collected, incubated and hatched, and the young fish are reared. The best times to visit are in early March before the young chinook are set free or during June and July when the adults return to spawn. An interpretive trail passes a historic mill and a Native American village site. **Hours:** Daily 8-3. Closed major holidays. **Cost:** Free. **Phone:** (208) 926-4272.

REFLECTIONS INN 208/926-0855

▼▼▼▼ **Bed & Breakfast** $108-$160 **Address:** 6873 Hwy 12 83539 **Location:** 11 mi e of Kooskia on US 12; between MM 84 and 85. Located in a quiet secluded area. **Facility:** In true ranch style, guest rooms are separate from the main house, dining and indoor common areas. This property is set on 10 wooded acres with surrounding mountain and spectacular river views. 8 units, some kitchens. 2 stories (no elevator), exterior corridors. **Terms:** check-in 4 pm, 7 day cancellation notice. **Activities:** hot tub, picnic facilities, trails. **Guest Services:** complimentary laundry.

CALL 🔽 🛜 ✖ 🅦 ⓩ 🔌 🖃 / 🖥 SOME UNITS 🏠

RIVER DANCE LODGE 208/926-4300

▼▼ ▼▼ **Vacation Rental Cabin.** Rates not provided. **Address:** 7743 Hwy 12 83539 **Location:** On US 12, 16 mi e of Kooskia at MM 89. Located in Syringa. **Facility:** Ideally located for outdoor enthusiasts, this lodge is set back above the banks of the Clearwater River and features hand-crafted custom log cabins, each with a deck and hot tub. 8 cabins. 2 stories (no elevator), exterior corridors. **Terms:** check-in 4 pm. **Dining:** Syringa Cafe, see separate listing. **Activities:** limited beach access, fishing, snorkeling, recreation programs in summer, bicycles.

🍴 🛜 ✖ 🅦 🅦 ⓩ 🔌 🖸 🖥 / SOME UNITS 🛏

WHERE TO EAT

KOOSKIA CAFE 208/926-4351

▼▼ ▼▼ American. Casual Dining. $8-$15 **AAA Inspector Notes:** Diners always can count on a daily special and fresh fruit and cream pies made by grandma at this popular, laid back downtown café. If the chicken fried steak sandwich or Cajun steak and shrimp are on the menu, or served as a special, order it before they run out. **Features:** beer & wine, patio dining. **Address:** 6 N Main St 83539 **Location:** Downtown. **Parking:** street only. B L D

SYRINGA CAFE 208/926-4300

▼▼ ▼▼ Small Plates Sandwiches. Casual Dining. $9-$18 **AAA Inspector Notes:** This darling café and its cozy patio overlook the Clearwater River. Favorite menu items include the hummus platter, prosciutto and blue cheese salad and the fish tacos served with citrus and cilantro slaw and salsa. Be advised they are famous for fresh huckleberry pie—to avoid disappointment, order the pie first before they run out. **Features:** beer & wine, patio dining. **Address:** 7744 Hwy 12 83539 **Location:** On US 12, 16 mi e of Kooskia at MM 89; in River Dance Lodge. L 🅚

KOOTENAI NATIONAL FOREST—See
Montana p. 185

LAPWAI (D-1) pop. 1,137, elev. 891'

Lapwai (LAP-way) is the site of the first military fort in Idaho, built in 1862 to prevent clashes between pioneers and Native Americans in the area. The U.S. Army occupied the fort until 1884. Some of the old buildings around the parade ground are still in use. The Old Fort Lapwai Cemetery is located on the ridge just south of the fort.

NORTHERN IDAHO INDIAN AGENCY, 99 Agency Rd. near Fort Lapwai, is the Bureau of Indian Affairs headquarters of Idaho's Nez Perce, Coeur d'Alene and Kootenai Indians. Established in 1862, the agency is a component of Nez Perce National Historical Park (see place listing p. 86). The 1883 Officer's Quarters is one of the fort's few original buildings. The Nez Perce Tribal Community Building and Bureau of Indian Affairs Office are .25-mile

north of Old Fort Lapwai. **Hours:** Community center Mon.-Sat. 8-4:30. Closed federal holidays. **Phone:** (208) 843-7009.

LAVA HOT SPRINGS (H-5) pop. 407, elev. 5,151'

Lava Hot Springs was named for the mineral springs that boil out of lava rocks at the base of massive cliffs along the Portneuf River. Geologists believe that the pools have remained at the same temperature—110 F—for 50 million years. Lava Hot Springs is a popular health and pleasure resort offering hiking, bicycling, tubing, ziplining and swimming.

For centuries the Shoshone and Bannock Indians regarded the springs as a neutral site. But the tribes camp was disrupted during the 19th century when the springs were discovered by Oregon-bound travelers and Utah pioneers who founded a settlement called Dempsey. By 1902 the Native Americans had ceded their rights to the springs, selling the land to the U.S. government, which in turn gave the area to the state.

Pioneer Country Travel Council: P.O. Box 669, Lava Hot Springs, ID 83246. **Phone:** (208) 776-5221 or (888) 201-1063. *(See ad p. 321.)*

IDAHO WORLD FAMOUS HOT POOLS AND OLYMPIC SWIMMING COMPLEX, on US 30E, is a resort that consists of hot mineral pools on the eastern edge of the village and outdoor Olympic-size swimming pools with tube slides on the western edge. The Sunken Gardens bloom on terraces that cling to the walls of an extinct volcano. Snowmobiling and skiing, subject to local weather conditions, are possible on the surrounding mountains.

Hours: Mineral baths daily 8 a.m.-11 p.m., May-Sept.; Sun.-Thurs. 9 a.m.-10 p.m., Fri.-Sat. 9 a.m.-11 p.m., rest of year. Swimming pool daily noon-8, mid-May through Labor Day. Closed Thanksgiving and Christmas. Phone ahead to confirm schedule.

Cost: Mineral bath Fri.-Sun. and holidays $8; $7.50 (ages 3-11 and 60+); $2 (ages 0-2). Mineral bath Mon.-Thurs. $6; $5.50 (ages 3-11 and 60+); $2 (ages 0-2). Swimming pool Fri.-Sun. and holidays $10; $9 (ages 3-11); $2 (ages 0-2). Swimming pool Mon.-Thurs. $7.50; $7 (ages 3-11); $2 (ages 0-2). A combination mineral bath and swimming pool pass is available, as are discounted family rates and all-day passes some days. **Phone:** (208) 776-5221 or (800) 423-8597.

SOUTH BANNOCK COUNTY HISTORICAL CENTER AND MUSEUM, off US 30 at 110 E. Main St., contains a collection of Native American and pioneer artifacts as well as a permanent exhibit showing the effects of transportation on the area and the six communities of south Bannock County. An interpretive exhibit details the interaction of Native Americans with the natural hot waters. Also featured are A Photographic History of 100 Years of

Southeastern Idaho, exhibited through digital media, and a DVD documenting the history of past influential female residents. Also explored is the history of Charles and Nellie Ball, who were immortalized as characters in Owen Wister's "The Virginian," the first western romantic novel. **Hours:** Daily noon-5. Closed Thanksgiving and Christmas. **Cost:** Donations. **Phone:** (208) 776-5254.

LIONS GATE MANOR BED & BREAKFAST   (208)776-5118
▼▼▼ **Bed & Breakfast** $109-$229 **Address:** 10376 S Dempsey Creek Rd 83246 **Location:** US 30, just s on Center St, just w on Main St, then 0.7 mi s on 4th Ave to Dempsey Creek Rd, follow signs. **Facility:** This property sits on a hillside with a community balcony for enjoying striking views of the mountains and valleys. The culturally themed, modern and spacious guest rooms are well appointed. 8 units. 3 stories (no elevator), interior corridors. **Terms:** check-in 4 pm, cancellation fee imposed. 🛜 ☒

LEWISTON (D-1) pop. 31,894, elev. 738'
• Hotels p. 78 • Restaurants p. 78

At the confluence of the Clearwater and Snake rivers, Lewiston is on a site where Meriwether Lewis and William Clark camped in 1805 and again in 1806. Following the discovery of gold nearby, the settlement became a supply point for mining camps and, subsequently, the state's first territorial capital 1863-65.

Large quantities of grain and other cargo are shipped from Lewiston, known as "Idaho's Seaport," by barge 465 miles down the Snake and Columbia rivers to the Pacific. Boats reach the port by passing through locks at eight dams.

In April the city celebrates the arrival of spring with the 🐦 Dogwood Festival of the Lewis-Clark Valley. Lewiston lies on an especially scenic section of US 95 that extends north to Plummer and south to Banks. North of the city US 95 climbs 2,000 feet to the top of Lewiston Hill, where a viewpoint overlooks the valley. The original road up the hill, known as the Spiral Highway for its 64 curves, opened in 1917. The old road is still open but was replaced in 1979 by the long, easier grade of the new alignment.

Shopping: Lewiston Center Mall, 1 mile south of US 12 via 18th or 21st streets, features JCPenney and Macy's.

HELLS GATE STATE PARK is 4 mi. s. of US 12 off Snake River Ave. This 360-acre riverside park offers fishing, boating, hiking and other outdoor activities. Boat trips to Hells Canyon depart from docks within the park. *See Recreation Areas Chart.* **Time:** Allow 1 hour minimum. **Hours:** Park open daily dawn-dusk. **Cost:** $5 (per private vehicle). **Phone:** (208) 799-5015. ▲ ☒ 🎿 🏕

Jack O'Connor Hunting Heritage and Education Center 4 mi. s. on US 12 to Snake River Ave. then to 5600 Hells Gate Road in Hells Gate State Park. This museum features exhibits about wildlife resource management and the achievements of outdoor writer, magazine editor and sportsman Jack O'Connor. Displays include custom rifles and 65 big

game trophies from three continents. An 8-minute orientation video about Idaho wildlife is available. **Time:** Allow 30 minutes minimum. **Hours:** Mon.-Fri. 10-5, Sat.-Sun. 1-5, Labor Day-Memorial Day; Tues.-Fri. 10-4, Sat.-Sun. 1-4, rest of year. **Cost:** Free. **Phone:** (208) 743-5043.

Lewis and Clark Discovery Center is 4 mi. s. on US 12 to Snake River Ave. to 5100 Hells Gate Rd. in Hells Gate State Park. Exhibits focusing on Meriwether Lewis' and William Clark 's journey through Idaho are complemented by a 32-minute video shown in the auditorium. A 2-acre interpretive plaza overlooks the Snake River. **Time:** Allow 45 minutes minimum. **Hours:** Daily 8-6, June-Aug.; 8-4, rest of year. Closed Jan. 1, Thanksgiving and Christmas. Phone ahead to confirm schedule. **Cost:** Free. **Phone:** (208) 799-5015.

River Quest Excursions departs from the marina in Hells Gate State Park, 4832 Hellsgate Rd., 4 mi. s. on Snake River Ave. Jet boat trips into Hells Canyon include narration about early exploration, mining, wildlife, geology and Native American history. Overnight fishing trips also are available. **Time:** Allow 6 hours minimum. **Hours:** Full-day trips depart daily at 8 a.m., May-Sept. Half-day trips depart daily at 10 a.m., May-Sept. Arrive 30 minutes prior to departure. **Cost:** Full-day trip $175; $87.50 (ages 8-12); free (ages 0-7). Half-day trip $110; $55 (ages 8-12); free (ages 0-7). Reservations are required. **Phone:** (208) 746-8060 or (800) 589-1129.

LEWIS & CLARK INTERPRETIVE CENTER is at the w. end of D St. between 1st St. and US 12 bypass. An open-air pavilion overlooks the confluence of the Snake and Clearwater rivers, where Meriwether Lewis and William Clark camped in 1805, and features interpretive panels about the explorers' expedition, the Nez Perce Indians and the U.S. Army Corps of Engineers' levee system. Exhibits include a replica of a dugout canoe and a sculpture symbolizing the meeting of the waters. **Time:** Allow 30 minutes minimum. **Hours:** Daily dawn-dusk. **Cost:** Free. **Phone:** (509) 751-0240.

LEWIS-CLARK STATE COLLEGE CENTER FOR ARTS AND HISTORY, 415 Main St., features a rotating schedule of exhibitions that showcase the works of local, regional and national artists. Also highlighted are Nez Perce tribal artifacts and an exhibit about Lewiston's Beuk Aie Temple that relates the history of a late 19th-century Chinese community. **Hours:** Tues.-Sat. 11-4. Closed major holidays. **Cost:** Donations. **Phone:** (208) 792-2243.

NEZ PERCE COUNTY HISTORICAL SOCIETY AND MUSEUM is at 3rd and Capital sts. Built in the 1930s, the Art Deco-style building features a chronology of area history with displays of Nez Perce Indian and pioneer artifacts. **Hours:** Tues.-Sat. 10-4, early Mar. to mid-Dec. Closed major holidays. **Cost:** $4; $3 (ages 60+); $2 (ages 7-17). **Phone:** (208) 743-2535.

GAMBLING ESTABLISHMENTS

- **Clearwater River Casino** is 4 mi. e. on US 12 at 17500 Nez Perce Rd. **Hours:** Daily 24 hours. **Phone:** (208) 746-0723 or (877) 678-7423.

CLEARWATER RIVER CASINO & LODGE 208/298-1400

Resort Hotel
$80-$130

Address: 17500 Nez Perce Rd 83501 **Location:** US 12/95, 4 mi e. **Facility:** Near the Snake River, and adjacent to an RV park, the hotel lobby, guestrooms and bathrooms feature beautiful and thoughtfully selected Native American appointments and furnishings. 50 units. 3 stories, interior corridors. **Parking:** winter plug-ins. **Terms:** check-in 4 pm, cancellation fee imposed. **Dining:** 3 restaurants. **Pool(s):** heated indoor. **Activities:** hot tub. **Guest Services:** area transportation.

SAVE 🛆 ➔ 🍴 🍷 CALL 📞M
🛥 🛜 ✕ 🖥 📟 / SOME UNITS 📦

HOLIDAY INN EXPRESS 208/750-1600

Hotel
Rates not provided

Address: 2425 Nez Perce Dr 83501 **Location:** 1.2 mi s on US 12 from jct US 95, 1.2 mi s on 21st St, just e. **Facility:** 100 units. 3 stories, interior corridors. **Pool(s):** heated indoor. **Activities:** hot tub, exercise room. **Guest Services:** valet and coin laundry, area transportation. **Featured Amenity:** breakfast buffet.

SAVE ➔ 🍴 CALL 📞M 🛥 BIZ
HS 🛜 ✕ 📦 🖥 📟 / SOME UNITS 📶

INN AMERICA 208/746-4600

🛎🛎 **Hotel.** Rates not provided. **Address:** 702 21st St 83501 **Location:** 1.2 mi s on US 12 from jct US 95, just s. **Facility:** 61 units. 3 stories, interior corridors. **Pool(s):** heated outdoor. **Guest Services:** coin laundry.

🍴 CALL 📞M 🛥 🛜 📦 🖥 📟 / SOME UNITS 📶

WHERE TO EAT

ANTONIO'S 208/746-6262

🍷🍷 Italian. Casual Dining. $7-$19 **AAA Inspector Notes:** This popular restaurant buzzes with tourists and locals alike. The hearty menu features traditional pasta dishes and pizza, along with steak and seafood preparations. Diners can start off a great meal with a run through the extensive salad bar. **Features:** beer & wine. **Address:** 1407 Main St 83501 **Location:** On US 12. L D

MAIN STREET GRILL 208/746-2440

🍷🍷 American. Casual Dining. $7-$15 **AAA Inspector Notes:** Classic. The walls of this cute diner are decorated with historical photos of the community and baseball players. While the signature basket dishes are chunks of chicken, steak or shrimp battered and fried, they also serve a varied selection of hand-formed burgers, quesadillas, salads, sandwiches and wraps. **Features:** beer & wine, patio dining. **Address:** 625 Main St 83501 **Location:** In historic downtown. **Parking:** on-site and street. L D

Choose real ratings you can trust from professional inspectors who've been there

---

WAFFLES N' MORE 208/743-5189

🍷🍷 Breakfast Sandwiches. Casual Dining. $6-$10 **AAA Inspector Notes:** Servers are energetic and friendly at this favorite breakfast and lunch spot. In addition to excellent waffles, the menu lists a variety of good-value breakfast items, including the iron man or iron woman for hearty appetites. Lighter fare and healthy options also are available. **Features:** Sunday brunch. **Address:** 1421 Main St 83501 **Location:** 1.3 mi e of Snake River. B L

WAYBACK CAFE 208/743-2396

🍷🍷 American. Casual Dining. $8-$19 **AAA Inspector Notes:** Guests can return to the Eisenhower era and dine in a classic 1950s-themed diner, complete with a jukebox, fuzzy dice and servers in poodle skirts. You can't go wrong with a burger, fries and shake. **Features:** beer & wine. **Address:** 2138 13th Ave 83501 **Location:** 1.2 mi s on US 12 from jct US 95, 0.6 mi s on 21st St, just e. B L D CALL 📞M

ZANY GRAZE 208/746-8131

🍷🍷 American. Casual Dining. $6-$19 **AAA Inspector Notes:** Sushi, burgers, sandwiches and steak are featured at this spot accented by a madly eclectic 1950s décor simply chock-full of odd little treasures that are sure to delight the eye. Popular sushi items include smoked salmon, crab and ahi tuna, all hand-rolled in nori sheets and served with wasabi and ginger. Gluten-free and specialty protein meals are available. **Features:** full bar. **Address:** 2004 19th Ave 83501 **Location:** 1.2 mi s on US 12 from jct US 95, 1 mi s on 21st St. L D CALL 📞M

MALAD CITY (H-5) pop. 2,095, elev. 4,550'

The area's name came about in the early 19th century, when French trappers who believed they had become ill after drinking water from the valley's principal stream called it *malade*, meaning "sickly."

In the mid-1850s Brigham Young dispatched 15 families to the upper Malad Valley to establish a Latter-day Saint agricultural outpost. Many other early settlers were Welsh; the community celebrates this heritage during the Malad Valley Welsh Festival in late June.

ONEIDA COUNTY PIONEER MUSEUM is at 27 Bannock St. The ground floor of this 1914 building, which once housed a drugstore, contains artifacts and historical photographs illustrating the history of Malad City and Oneida County. Among the items displayed are a stove, an upright piano, an early telephone switchboard and the drugstore's original safe. The mezzanine features displays of period clothing. **Time:** Allow 30 minutes minimum. **Hours:** Tues.-Sat. 1-5, Sat. before Memorial Day-Sat. after Labor Day and by appointment. **Cost:** Donations. Under 12 must be with an adult. **Phone:** (208) 766-9247, (208) 406-6172 or (208) 766-4847.

MCCALL (E-1) pop. 2,991, elev. 5,025'

At the southern end of beautiful Payette Lake, McCall is a year-round recreational resort with a municipal airport. Fishing, boating, water skiing, horseback riding, white-water rafting, golf, camping and hunting are available. Skiing, snowboarding, snowshoeing and snowmobiling are popular winter sports. Manchester Ice and Event Centre is open year-round for indoor ice-skating and curling.

Firefighting facilities at the Forest Service's Smokejumper Headquarters feature smokejumping equipment, a fire retardant mixing plant and communications services. Tours are offered twice daily; phone (208) 634-0378.

McCall lies on an especially scenic section of SR 55, also called the Payette River Scenic Byway. The highway heads north, merges with US 95 and continues toward Coeur d'Alene. The southern terminus of the route is Boise.

McCall Area Chamber of Commerce and Visitors Bureau: 301 E. Lake St., P.O. Box 350, McCall, ID 83638. **Phone:** (208) 634-7631 or (800) 260-5130.

CENTRAL IDAHO HISTORICAL MUSEUM is at 1001 State St. The 4-acre complex features seven structures erected by the Civilian Conservation Corps (CCC) in 1937 for the Southern Idaho Timber Protective Association (SITPA). A self-guiding tour highlights the buildings, including The Pump House and The Machine Shop, as well as mining equipment, a lookout tower and a statue honoring the CCC.

Guided tours of the seven-bedroom Fire Warden's House, entirely completed using hand tools, also are offered. **Time:** Allow 45 minutes minimum. **Hours:** Wed.-Sat. noon-4, June-Aug. Phone ahead to confirm schedule. **Cost:** Museum free. Fire Warden's House tour $3. **Phone:** (208) 634-4497. 🏛

PONDEROSA STATE PARK is 1.5 mi. n.e. at 1920 N. Davis Ave. Embracing most of a 1,000-acre peninsula on the shores of Payette Lake, the park is named for its old-growth forest of ponderosa pines, some upwards of 150 feet tall. More than 12 miles of trails lead hikers and mountain bikers through the diverse landscape, which ranges from dense woods and sagebrush flats to marsh and lakeside cliffs.

Osprey Cliff, accessible by road and trail, offers stunning views 300 feet above the lake. Along Payette Lake's western bank, the Warren Wagon Road leads to the 500-acre North Beach Unit. A sandy beach and popular canoeing route along 4 miles of the North Fork Payette River is also part of the park, about eight miles north of McCall.

On Saturdays in summer, junior ranger and evening programs are offered. Winter activities include snowshoeing on 3 miles of trails and Nordic skiing on more than 12 miles of groomed trails. Cabins are open year-round. *See Recreation Areas Chart.* **Time:** Allow 1 hour minimum. **Hours:** Park open daily dawn-dusk. Visitor center open daily 9-9, Memorial Day weekend-Labor Day; Tues.-Sat. 10-4, rest of year. **Cost:** Day-use fee $5 (per private vehicle). **Phone:** (208) 634-2164. 🅰 ⊠ 🐾 🏛

RECREATIONAL ACTIVITIES
Skiing

• **Brundage Mountain Resort** is 4 mi. n. on SR 55 to Goose Lake Rd., then 4 mi. n. Other activities, including mountain biking, are offered in summer. **Hours:** Skiing daily 9:30-4:30, early Dec. to mid-Apr. **Phone:** (208) 634-4151.

BEST WESTERN PLUS MCCALL LODGE & SUITES
(208)634-2230

◆◆◆ Hotel $110-$175

AAA Benefit: Save 10% or more every day and earn 10% bonus points!

Address: 211 S 3rd St 83638 **Location:** 1 mi s of center on SR 55. **Facility:** 66 units, some efficiencies. 3 stories, interior corridors. **Terms:** resort fee. **Pool(s):** heated indoor. **Activities:** sauna, hot tub, exercise room. **Guest Services:** coin laundry. **Featured Amenity: full hot breakfast.**

🆓 🍽 CALL 🔊Ⓜ 🔄 BIZ 📶 ⊠ 🛗 🖥 🖨 / SOME UNITS 🐾

THE HUNT LODGE - HOLIDAY INN EXPRESS & SUITES
208/634-4700

◆◆◆ Hotel. Rates not provided. **Address:** 210 N 3rd St 83638 **Location:** 0.7 mi s of center on SR 55. **Facility:** 85 units. 3 stories, interior corridors. **Pool(s):** heated indoor. **Activities:** hot tub, exercise room. **Guest Services:** coin laundry.

🍽 CALL 🔊Ⓜ 🔄 BIZ HS 📶 ⊠ 🛗 🖥 🖨

SHORE LODGE
(208)634-2244

◆◆◆ Resort Hotel $129-$609

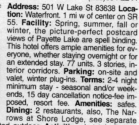

Address: 501 W Lake St 83638 **Location:** Waterfront. 1 mi w of center on SR 55. **Facility:** Spring, summer, fall or winter, the picture-perfect postcard views of Payette Lake are spell binding. This hotel offers ample amenities for everyone, whether staying overnight or for an extended stay. 77 units. 3 stories, interior corridors. **Parking:** on-site and valet, winter plug-ins. **Terms:** 2-4 night minimum stay - seasonal and/or weekends, 15 day cancellation notice-fee imposed, resort fee. **Amenities:** safes. **Dining:** 2 restaurants, also, The Narrows at Shore Lodge, see separate listing. **Pool(s):** heated outdoor. **Activities:** hot tub, limited beach access, marina, regulation golf, tennis, recreation programs in summer, bicycles, game room, exercise room, spa. **Guest Services:** area transportation.

🆓 🎿 🍽 🔄 🍷 CALL 🔊Ⓜ 🔄 BIZ 📶 ⊠ 🛗 🖥 / SOME UNITS 🐾

BEAR CREEK LODGE
208/634-3551

[fyi] Not evaluated. **Address:** 3492 SR 55 83638 **Location:** 4 mi w of downtown; MM 149. Facilities, services, and décor characterize a mid-scale property.

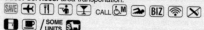
WHERE TO EAT

BISTRO 45 WINE BAR & CAFE
208/634-4515

◆ American. Quick Serve. $6-$13 **AAA Inspector Notes:** This café is frequented by locals and tourists alike. Favorites include the tomato, mozzarella and basil grilled sandwich, quiche, baked Brie topped with roasted garlic, steamed blue mussels or clams and a variety of seasonal bottled beer, drafts and wine offerings. Smaller plates and a children's menu are available. **Features:** beer & wine. **Address:** 1101 N 3rd St 83638 **Location:** Downtown. **Parking:** on-site and street. Ⓑ Ⓛ Ⓓ 🐾

THE MILL STEAKS & SPIRITS
208/634-7683

◆ American. Casual Dining. $15-$45 **AAA Inspector Notes:** Widely known prime rib is served in large portions at this eatery, so bring a healthy appetite when you visit. Surrounded in a casual setting with antiques and nostalgic mining memorabilia, appointments are coordinated with heavy wooden beams and supports, log slab tables in the lounge, and a carnival resort town atmosphere. **Features:** full bar. **Reservations:** suggested. **Address:** 324 N 3rd St 83638 **Location:** 0.3 mi s on SR 55. Ⓓ

MY FATHER'S PLACE   208/634-4401

Burgers. Quick Serve. $4-$10 **AAA Inspector Notes:** Serving up delicious burgers, fries and milkshakes, this local institution is within walking distance from Payette Lake and is always bustling with locals and tourists alike. Expect a wait during peak seasons. Patio dining is available when the weather is nice. **Features:** patio dining. **Address:** 901 N 3rd St 83638 **Location:** Just s on SR 55; downtown. **Parking:** on-site and street. [L] [D] [X]

THE NARROWS AT SHORE LODGE   208/634-2244

American. Fine Dining. $18-$36 **AAA Inspector Notes:** Seasonal menu offerings here feature such starters as hamachi sashimi with pineapple salsa and corn and shrimp chowder, while main courses include Dungeness crab-crusted Alaskan halibut, grilled veal T-bone steak, potato-crusted Idaho trout, dry-aged filet mignon and beef prime rib for two. **Features:** full bar, happy hour. **Reservations:** suggested. **Address:** 501 W Lake St 83638 **Location:** 1 mi w of center on SR 55; in Shore Lodge. [D]

THE PANCAKE & CHRISTMAS HOUSE   208/634-5849

American. Casual Dining. $6-$19 **AAA Inspector Notes:** *Classic.* This warm and inviting restaurant always is loaded with happy and hungry guests that have remained loyal since the restaurant's opening in the 1950s. The themed gift shop sharing the building brings Christmas cheer year round. Menu offerings consist of popular breakfast items, hearty sandwiches, soups, steak and turkey dinners. **Features:** beer & wine. **Address:** 209 N 3rd St 83638 **Location:** 0.8 mi s of center on SR 55. [B] [L] [D]

PUEBLO LINDO MEXICAN RESTAURANT   208/634-2270

Mexican. Casual Dining. $6-$15 **AAA Inspector Notes:** This lovely restaurant offers a charming and vibrant atmosphere. Menu offerings include steak tacos, shredded chicken enchilada with mole sauce, pork tamales, Colorado chili and the best pozole in Idaho. The chips are served with several wonderful salsas. Vegetarian items are available. Bicycle parking is available. **Features:** beer & wine. **Address:** 1007 W Lake St 83638 **Location:** On SR 55, 2 mi w of downtown. [L] [D]

RUPERT'S AT HOTEL MCCALL   208/634-8108

American. Fine Dining. $13-$32 **AAA Inspector Notes:** Across from Payette Lake, the windows in this restaurant frame the postcard picture-perfect views of the lake and mountains. You can expect a seasonal menu with artistic and creative presentations. The ambience is upscale while the service is more casual. A nice selection of appetizers and entrées may include artichoke-Asiago risotto fritters set on pesto, signature bacon-ranch jumbo shrimp scampi or rosemary grilled lamb chops. Decadent desserts are fun to share. **Features:** full bar, patio dining, happy hour. **Address:** 1101 N 3rd St 83638 **Location:** Corner of N 3rd (SR 55) and E Lake sts; downtown. [D]

SALMON RIVER BREWERY   208/634-4772

American. Casual Dining. $9-$14 **AAA Inspector Notes:** While feasting on fried pickle spears, chicken wings, ceviche lettuce wraps, a colorful hummus plate or Thai peanut noodle salad, diners can enjoy craft beer at its best. Gluten-free items and a kids' menu are available. The beer cheese soup is addictive. **Features:** full bar, patio dining, happy hour. **Address:** 411 Railroad Ave 83638 **Location:** Just s of jct SR 55, just e; downtown; in the old train depot. [L] [D]

SI BUENO SOUTHSIDE GRILL & CANTINA   208/634-2128

Mexican. Casual Dining. $8-$25 **AAA Inspector Notes:** This colorful and friendly eatery offers a wide variety of menu items including salads, tostadas, sandwiches, burritos, Baja fish tacos, steaming chile verde, sizzling fajitas, hand-carved rib-eye steak, racks of plump St. Louis ribs, charbroiled chicken seasoned in lemon-pepper and hearty Mexican or combo platters available in one or two servings. Thirst quenching and fun-named margaritas are available slushy or chilled on the rocks and can be enjoyed in the dining room or the spacious cantina. **Features:** full bar. **Address:** 339 Deinhard Ln 83638 **Location:** 1 mi s of center via SR 55; across from McCall Airport. [L] [D]

STEAMERS STEAK & SEAFOOD RESTAURANT   208/634-1411

Steak Seafood. Casual Dining. $19-$32 **AAA Inspector Notes:** This restaurant features a cozy wine bar and offers a wide array of tempting seafood and steak dishes such as steamed clams, pan-fried oysters, a popular walnut and pear salad, poached wild sockeye salmon, filet mignon served with port-cranberry demi-glace and rack of tender lamb. **Features:** full bar, happy hour. **Reservations:** suggested. **Address:** 308 E Lake St 83638 **Location:** Just w of SR 55; downtown. **Parking:** street only. [D]

THE SUSHI BAR   208/634-7874

Asian Sushi. Casual Dining. $8-$14 **AAA Inspector Notes:** Offering awesome views of Payette Lake, this environmentally conscious eatery features specialties such as Kobe beef soba noodle bowls, Korean barbecue and Vietnamese pho soup. Try one of the rotating selections of microbrews or a creative sake such as the Creamsicle, mojito or wasabi Mary. Seating is first come, first served and is worth the wait. **Features:** beer & wine, patio dining, happy hour. **Address:** 414 Railroad Ave 83638 **Location:** Just s of jct SR 55, just e. [D]

MELBA (G-1) pop. 513, elev. 2,667'

CELEBRATION PARK is .7 mi. e. on Baseline Rd., 3 mi. s. on Can Ada Rd., 1.6 mi. w. on Warren Spur Rd., 2.8 mi. s. on Sinker Rd., then just e., following signs to 6530 Hot Spot Ln. Located along the Snake River, this area was once used by the Paiute Indians as wintering grounds. Thousands of petroglyphs, some of which are 12,000 years old, can be seen.

The park affords a variety of recreational activities, such as bird-watching and trails for horseback riding. Visitors also can traverse the historic Guffy Bridge, which is appointed with informational placards. Educational programs, including lectures and guided tours, relate the site's features and history; phone ahead for schedules. *See Recreation Areas Chart.*

Time: Allow 1 hour, 30 minutes minimum. **Hours:** Daily 9-4. Visitor center staffed daily 10-2. Closed Thanksgiving and Christmas. **Cost:** Day-use fee $2. Camping fee $5. Annual pass $15; $5 (senior citizens). Cash only. **Phone:** (208) 455-6022.

MERIDIAN (G-1) pop. 75,092, elev. 2,600'

[SAVE] **ROARING SPRINGS WATERPARK** is off I-84 exit 44, then w. at 400 W. Overland Rd. The water park features more than 20 attractions, including the Corkscrew Cavern, Cliffhanger, two family raft rides, a wave pool, an endless river, tube slides, a bowl slide, a four-lane racing slide and a children's play area. The adjacent Wahooz Family Fun Zone offers miniature golf, laser tag, go-karts, bumper boats, an arcade and a 24-lane bowling center.

Time: Allow 4 hours minimum. **Hours:** Water park daily 11-8, June-Aug.; Sat.-Sun. 11-7, mid-May through May 31 and Sept. 1 to mid-Sept. Wahooz Family Fun Zone daily 10-10, June-Aug.; 11-9, rest of year. Phone ahead to confirm schedule. **Cost:** Water park $29.99; $24.99 (under 48 inches tall). Water park after 3 p.m. $22.99. Wahooz Family Fun Zone prices vary. **Phone:** (208) 884-8842 for water park, or (208) 898-0900 for Wahooz Family Fun Zone. [T]

BEST WESTERN PLUS RAMA INN

(208)887-7888

Hotel
$90-$170

AAA Benefit:
Save 10% or more every day and earn 10% bonus points!

Address: 1019 S Progress Ave 83642 **Location:** I-84 exit 44 (Meridian/Kuna), just ne. **Facility:** 61 units. 2 stories (no elevator), interior corridors. **Pool(s):** heated indoor. **Activities:** hot tub, exercise room. **Guest Services:** valet and coin laundry.

CANDLEWOOD SUITES - BOISE/MERIDIAN

208/888-5121

Extended Stay Hotel. Rates not provided. **Address:** 1855 S Silverstone Way 83642 **Location:** I-84 exit 46 (Eagle Rd), 0.6 mi s, just e on Overland Rd, then just s. **Facility:** 120 efficiencies. 3 stories, interior corridors. **Activities:** hot tub, bicycles, picnic facilities, exercise room. **Guest Services:** complimentary and valet laundry.

COUNTRY INN & SUITES BY CARLSON - BOISE WEST AT MERIDIAN

208/639-3300

Hotel
Rates not provided

Address: 3355 E Pine Ave 83642 **Location:** I-84 exit 46 (Eagle Rd), 0.8 mi n, then just e. **Facility:** 82 units. 4 stories, interior corridors. **Pool(s):** heated indoor. **Activities:** hot tub, exercise room. **Guest Services:** valet and coin laundry. **Featured Amenity:** breakfast buffet.

COURTYARD BY MARRIOTT - BOISE/MERIDIAN

(208)888-0800

Contemporary Hotel
$94-$202 **Address:** 1789 S Eagle Rd 83642 **Location:** I-84 exit 46 (Eagle Rd), just s. **Facility:** 145 units. 4 stories, interior corridors. **Parking:** winter plug-ins. **Pool(s):** heated indoor. **Activities:** exercise room. **Guest Services:** valet and coin laundry.

AAA Benefit:
Members save 5% or more!

HAMPTON INN & SUITES - BOISE/MERIDIAN

(208)887-3600

Hotel $99-$169 **Address:** 875 S Allen St 83642 **Location:** I-84 exit 46 (Eagle Rd), just nw. **Facility:** 128 units. 3 stories, interior corridors. **Terms:** 1-7 night minimum stay, cancellation fee imposed. **Amenities:** video games. **Pool(s):** heated indoor. **Activities:** hot tub, picnic facilities, exercise room. **Guest Services:** valet and coin laundry.

AAA Benefit:
Members save up to 10%!

HOLIDAY INN EXPRESS & SUITES - BOISE WEST/MERIDIAN

208/288-2060

Hotel. Rates not provided. **Address:** 2610 E Freeway Dr 83642 **Location:** I-84 exit 46 (Eagle Rd), just n, then 0.3 mi w. **Facility:** 76 units. 3 stories, interior corridors. **Pool(s):** heated indoor. **Activities:** hot tub, exercise room. **Guest Services:** valet and coin laundry.

LA QUINTA INN & SUITES MERIDIAN BOISE

(208)288-2100

Hotel $86-$262 **Address:** 800 S Allen St 83642 **Location:** I-84 exit 46 (Eagle Rd), just nw. **Facility:** 67 units. 3 stories, interior corridors. **Pool(s):** heated indoor. **Activities:** hot tub, exercise room. **Guest Services:** valet and coin laundry.

TOWNEPLACE SUITES BY MARRIOTT - BOISE/MERIDIAN

(208)884-8550

Extended Stay
Hotel
$101-$181

AAA Benefit:
Members save 5% or more!

Address: 1415 S Eagle Rd 83642 **Location:** I-84 exit 46 (Eagle Rd), just sw. **Facility:** 100 efficiencies, some kitchens. 4 stories, interior corridors. **Terms:** check-in 4 pm. **Pool(s):** heated indoor. **Activities:** hot tub, picnic facilities, exercise room. **Guest Services:** valet and coin laundry. **Featured Amenity:** continental breakfast.

WHERE TO EAT

FLATBREAD NEAPOLITAN PIZZERIA

208/288-0969

Italian. Casual Dining. $7-$17 **AAA Inspector Notes:** This certified Neopolitan pizzeria is always packed with returning fans who favor the pick-any-two-items lunch special. Gluten-free crust is available and diners can choose from a variety of distinctive pizza, pasta and sandwiches while enjoying the bright ambiance the garage door wall and intimate lighting create. **Features:** full bar, patio dining, happy hour. **Address:** 830 N Main St, Suite A 83642 **Location:** I-84 exit 44 (Meridian/Kuna), 1.2 mi n; downtown. **Parking:** on-site and street.

GOODWOOD BARBECUE COMPANY

208/884-1021

Barbecue. Family Dining. $10-$26 **AAA Inspector Notes:** Buzzing with energy, this welcoming restaurant is home to traditional barbecue favorites including prime rib, pulled pork, brisket, and a variety of full and half-racks of beef and pork ribs. **Features:** full bar. **Address:** 1140 N Eagle Rd 83642 **Location:** I-84 exit 46 (Eagle Rd), 1.4 mi n.

THE GRIDDLE

208/288-1848

American. Family Dining. $6-$14 **AAA Inspector Notes:** With made-from-scratch home-style cooking, it is no wonder this diner is such a favorite. The menu offers all of the traditional American breakfast favorites and a variety of sandwiches and burgers during the lunch hour. Popular salads include the Chinese chicken chopped and the roasted beet and quinoa. If the key lime pie is on the menu, order a slice. **Address:** 2310 E Overland Rd, Suite 130 83642 **Location:** I-84 exit 46 (Eagle Rd), 0.5 mi s, then 0.5 mi w.

KAHOOTZ STEAK & ALE HOUSE   208/895-9861
▼▼ ▼▼ American. Casual Dining. $8-$26 **AAA Inspector Notes:** Known for consistently great-tasting food, this brewpub offers a broad selection of draft beers with 43 taps. On the menu are steak sandwiches, pasta and high-grade meat including filet mignon and pork loin. Their bread pudding is an absolute must. In the summer, request a table outside in their unique covered patio. **Features:** beer & wine, patio dining. **Address:** 1603 N Main St 83642 **Location:** I-84 exit 44 (Meridian/Kuna), 1.8 mi n. ⨐L⨑ ⨐D⨑

LOUIE'S PIZZA & ITALIAN RESTAURANT   208/884-5200
▼▼ ▼▼ Italian. Casual Dining. $8-$20 **AAA Inspector Notes:** Murals of the Italian countryside decorate this open dining room, where guests can relax over a meal of Italian food. Browse the menu for an ample selection of pasta favorites, traditional pizza, sandwiches, calzones and salads, each prepared with a distinctive flair. A lunch buffet is an affordable favorite. Gluten free pasta and pizza are available. **Features:** full bar, happy hour. Sunday brunch, happy hour. **Address:** 2500 E Fairview Ave 83642 **Location:** I-84 exit 46 (Eagle Rd), 1.6 mi n, then 0.5 mi w. ⨐L⨑ ⨐D⨑

MISS TAMI'S COTTAGE & TEA ROOM   208/888-6829
▼▼ ▼▼ American. Casual Dining. $6-$14 **AAA Inspector Notes:** This Victorian decorated cottage features full afternoon tea service and offers such favorites as a variety of tea sandwiches, quiche, meatloaf, fish and chips, stuffed salmon and chicken pot pie. A breakfast buffet brunch is offered on Saturday. A children's menu is available. **Features:** beer & wine. **Reservations:** suggested. **Address:** 1031 N Main St 83642 **Location:** I-84 exit 44 (Meridian/Kuna), 1.3 mi n. **Parking:** on-site and street. ⨐L⨑

RAM RESTAURANT AND BREWERY   208/888-0314
▼▼ ▼▼ American. Casual Dining. $11-$24 **AAA Inspector Notes:** The enormous restaurant features high ceilings, huge television screens, large sports-themed banners and a brew pub area. The menu is equally enormous, with steaks, poultry, pasta, seafood, salads, sandwiches and pizza. The on-site brewery turns out a large selection of microbrews. **Features:** full bar, happy hour. **Address:** 3272 E Pine St 83642 **Location:** I-84 exit 46 (Eagle Rd), 1.2 mi n.
⨐L⨑ ⨐D⨑ ⨐LATE⨑

RUDY'S PUB & GRILL   208/884-4453
▼▼ ▼▼ American. Casual Dining. $9-$17 **AAA Inspector Notes:** This casual sports bar can get busy during peak hours. The menu offers up burgers, sandwiches and salads. Locals favor the signature mushroom and Brie soup. **Features:** full bar, patio dining. **Address:** 2310 E Overland Rd, Suite 150 83642 **Location:** I-84 exit 46 (Eagle Rd), 0.5 mi s, then 0.5 mi w. ⨐L⨑ ⨐D⨑ CALL ⨐M⨑

SA-WAD-DEE THAI RESTAURANT   208/884-0701
▼▼ ▼▼ Thai. Casual Dining. $8-$21 **AAA Inspector Notes:** With a name that means hello in Thai, this cute eatery offers guests not only hospitable service, but also many delicious traditional Thai dishes their loyal guests have come to love. Expect the lunch hour to be bustling due to their popular specials. Sushi is offered Monday through Saturday. **Features:** full bar, patio dining, happy hour. **Address:** 1890 E Fairview Ave 83642 **Location:** I-84 exit 46 (Eagle Rd), 1.8 mi n, then 0.8 mi w. ⨐L⨑ ⨐D⨑

SMOKY MOUNTAIN PIZZERIA GRILL   208/884-1067
▼▼ ▼▼ Italian. Casual Dining. $7-$27 **AAA Inspector Notes:** This local favorite, adorned with eclectic décor representing Idaho's history, is a good choice for a family get-together, business luncheon or romantic dinner. The menu offers a wide variety of pastas and grilled meats, all with an Italian flair. **Features:** full bar, patio dining. **Address:** 980 E Fairview Ave 83642 **Location:** I-84 exit 46 (Eagle Rd), 1.6 mi n, then 1.4 mi w.
⨐L⨑ ⨐D⨑ CALL ⨐M⨑

MINIDOKA NATIONAL HISTORIC SITE (G-3)

Minidoka, the site of a relocation camp used for the detainment of Japanese persons living in the United States after the attack on Pearl Harbor, is northeast of Twin Falls via US 93 and SR 25; from the intersection of I-84 and US 93, head 5 miles north on US 93, 9.5 miles east on SR 25 to the Hunt Road exit, then 2.2 miles east on Hunt Road.

President Franklin D. Roosevelt ordered the opening of 10 such facilities in February 1942, displacing more than 120,000 Japanese and Japanese Americans until 1945.

Most of the 600 buildings at the 33,000-acre camp were removed. The current 300-acre site features interpretive signs as well as remains of an entry guard station, a waiting room, a root cellar, an ornamental rock garden and a 1.6-mile crushed rock walking trail. Those who died after leaving the camp to serve in the U.S. military during World War II are commemorated on plaques. More than 900 names of Minidoka residents are listed on the Honor Roll at the entrance to the site.

Note: A visitor center is planned for the site, but until then, exhibits about Minidoka and maps are available at the visitor center for nearby Hagerman Fossil Beds National Monument *(see place listing p. 64)*; phone (208) 933-4100. There is a small gravel parking lot. The historic site is open daily dawn to dusk. Admission is free.

MONTPELIER (H-6) pop. 2,597, elev. 5,934'

Montpelier, one of the state's oldest towns, is at the junction of US 89 and US 30N, the historic Old Oregon Trail. Brigham Young established a Mormon community and named the town for the capital of his home state, Vermont. In 1896 Butch Cassidy relieved the Bank of Montpelier of $7,000. Bear Lake resort is about 17 miles south on US 89.

Bear Lake Convention and Visitors Bureau: 69 N. Paradise Pkwy., Bldg. A, P.O. Box 471, Garden City, UT 84028. **Phone:** (435) 946-2197 or (800) 448-2327.

⨐SAVE⨑ **NATIONAL OREGON/CALIFORNIA TRAIL CENTER** is at jct. US 30 and US 89 at 320 N. 4th St. This living-history center, which sits directly on the site of the historic Clover Creek Encampment on the Oregon Trail, depicts the pioneers' journey across the continent. A wagon master guides visitors through the experience of riding the trail in a covered wagon courtesy of a computer simulation. Displays and artifacts about the history of the Bear Lake valley and the railroad era can be seen in the Rails and Trails Museum. A variety of quilts is on display May to mid-October.

Time: Allow 30 minutes minimum. **Hours:** Mon.-Sat. 9-5; Sun. 9-3, May 15-Oct. 15; Mon.-Thurs. 10-2 by appointment, rest of year. **Cost:** $11; $10 (ages 60+); $8 (ages 8-17); $4 (ages 4-7). **Phone:** (208) 847-3800. ⨐GT⨑

CLOVER CREEK INN
208/847-1782

Motel
$75-$125

Address: 243 N 4th St 83254 **Location:** On US 30, just n of jct US 89. **Facility:** 64 units. 2 stories (no elevator), exterior corridors. **Parking:** winter plug-ins. **Activities:** hot tub, exercise room. **Guest Services:** coin laundry. **Featured Amenity:** full hot breakfast.

SAVE Ⓣ BIZ HS 🛜 🖥 🖨 / SOME UNITS 🍽

MOSCOW (C-1) pop. 23,800, elev. 2,574'
• Hotels p. 84 • Restaurants p. 84

Moscow (MOSS-co) lies on an especially scenic section of US 95, which heads north toward Coeur d'Alene and south to Banks. The area to the west is rolling, fertile Palouse country where black volcanic ash soil, ample rainfall and warm autumn temperatures combine to produce bountiful crops of lentils, dry peas, canola, wheat and barley.

Home to the University of Idaho *(see attraction listing)*, Moscow is a quintessential college town with an emerging arts community. The annual arts scene includes February's ❤ Lionel Hampton Jazz Festival; the Idaho Repertory Theatre; and the Moscow Renaissance Fair, which is held the first weekend in May.

Moscow Chamber of Commerce: 411 S. Main St., Moscow, ID 83843. **Phone:** (208) 882-1800.

Shopping: Macy's anchors Palouse Mall, 1.5 miles west on SR 8.

APPALOOSA MUSEUM AND HERITAGE CENTER, w. on SR 8 in the Appaloosa Horse Club
building at 2720 W. Pullman Rd., contains Nez Perce regalia and artifacts, cowboy tack, photographs and artwork illustrating Appaloosa history. A children's activity area also is available. **Time:** Allow 1 hour minimum. **Hours:** Mon.-Thurs. 11-4, Fri. 10:30-4, Sat. 10-4, or by appointment. Closed major holidays. **Cost:** Donations. **Phone:** (208) 882-5578, ext. 279.

MCCONNELL MANSION, 110 S. Adams St., was built in the late 19th century by Gov. William J. McConnell. Operated by the Latah County Historical Society, the mansion displays relics and Victorian-style furniture from the late 1800s as well as exhibits about area history. A backyard garden and a research library are available. Children's activities are offered. **Time:** Allow 1 hour minimum. **Hours:** Mansion Tues.-Sat. 1-4. Research library Tues.-Fri. 9-5. Closed major holidays. **Cost:** Donations. **Phone:** (208) 882-1004.

PRICHARD ART GALLERY is at 414 S. Main St. Hosting between nine and 11 changing exhibitions each year, the two-level gallery showcases the contemporary works of both professional artists and University of Idaho students. Included are fine arts pieces, photographs, ceramics, computer-generated art, sculpture, folk art and architectural displays.

Time: Allow 30 minutes minimum. **Hours:** Tues.-Sat. 10-8, Sun. 10-6, Sept.-May; Tues.-Thurs. 1-6, Fri. 1-7, Sat. 9-3, rest of year. Closed major holidays. **Cost:** Donations. **Phone:** (208) 885-3586.

UNIVERSITY OF IDAHO is on the s.w. side of town, w. of US 95 via 6th St. Established in 1889, UI sprawls across 1,580 landscaped acres and has around 12,000 students. An 80-foot clock tower atop the Collegiate Gothic-style administration building overlooks a lawn containing the President's Grove and a Spanish-American War statue.

Shattuck Arboretum, on a hill between Rayburn Street and Nez Perce Drive, is a 14-acre tract of trees planted in 1910. Trails loop through groves of mature beech, incense-cedar, maple, hemlock and others. Among these specimens is a giant sequoia. The UI Arboretum and Botanical Garden *(see attraction listing)* is home to a larger collection of trees on the south side of campus.

Guided campus tours depart from the Office of Admissions and Campus Visits at 709 Deakin Ave. **Time:** Allow 1 hour, 30 minutes minimum. **Hours:** Office Mon.-Fri. 7:30-4:30, late May-late Aug.; Mon.-Fri. 8-5, rest of year. Campus tours are offered Mon.-Fri. at 10 and 1:30, Sat. at 9:30. Closed major holidays. **Cost:** Free. **Parking:** $2 (free if tour is registered online). **Phone:** (208) 885-6163 or (888) 884-3246. GT

University of Idaho Arboretum and Botanical Garden is on the s. side of the campus at 1200 W. Palouse River Dr. The 63-acre arboretum features gravel and bark trails leading through plantings grouped into four geographical areas: Asia, Europe, Eastern North America and Western North America. A display garden, showing off irises, daylilies, heather and xeriscape techniques, is at the arboretum's southern end, along with a butterfly garden. Hosta gardens are located at the north end. **Time:** Allow 1 hour minimum. **Hours:** Daily dawn-dusk. **Cost:** Free. **Phone:** (208) 885-5978. 🅿

WINERIES
• **Camas Prairie Winery** is at 110 S. Main St. Free tours are available by request. **Note:** The winery may be moving in 2016; phone ahead to verify hours and location. **Hours:** Mon.-Sat. noon-6:30. Closed Jan. 1, Thanksgiving and Christmas. **Phone:** (208) 882-0214. GT

BEST WESTERN PLUS UNIVERSITY INN (208)882-0550

Hotel
$99-$189

AAA Benefit: Save 10% or more every day and earn 10% bonus points!

Address: 1516 W Pullman Rd 83843 **Location:** Jct US 95, 1 mi w on SR 8. Adjacent to University of Idaho. **Facility:** 173 units. 2 stories, interior corridors. **Parking:** winter plug-ins. **Terms:** check-in 4 pm, resort fee. **Pool(s):** heated indoor. **Activities:** sauna, hot tub, exercise room. **Guest Services:** valet and coin laundry, area transportation.

FAIRFIELD INN & SUITES BY MARRIOTT MOSCOW
(208)882-4600

Hotel
$96-$196

FAIRFIELD INN & SUITES Marriott

AAA Benefit: Members save 5% or more!

Address: 1000 W Pullman Rd 83843 **Location:** Jct US 95, 1 mi w on SR 8. **Facility:** 74 units. 3 stories, interior corridors. **Pool(s):** heated indoor. **Activities:** exercise room. **Guest Services:** valet and coin laundry. **Featured Amenity:** full hot breakfast.

LA QUINTA INN & SUITES MOSCOW PULLMAN
(208)882-5365

Hotel $86-$372 **Address:** 185 Warbonnet Dr 83843 **Location:** 1.6 mi w on SR 8 from jct US 95, just n. **Facility:** 76 units. 3 stories, interior corridors. **Pool(s):** heated indoor. **Activities:** hot tub, exercise room. **Guest Services:** coin laundry.

WHERE TO EAT

SANGRIA GRILLE 208/882-2693

Peruvian. Casual Dining. $9-$26 **AAA Inspector Notes:** The chef/owner pays homage to his varied heritage, Peruvian and Greek. While the menu is extensive and full of specialties like paella, curry, lamb chops and many gluten-free items, a few local favorites include that little green soup and empanadas (go easy on the gringo killer sauce). Seasonal desserts, such as tres leches cake, strawberry shortcake and vanilla bean banana cheesecake, are made in house. **Features:** full bar, happy hour. **Reservations:** suggested. **Address:** 2124 W Pullman Hwy 83843 **Location:** 1.5 mi w on SR 8 from jct US 95; in front of Palouse Mall.

SMOKY MOUNTAIN PIZZERIA GRILL 208/892-8000

Italian. Casual Dining. $7-$27 **AAA Inspector Notes:** Featuring a lunch buffet Monday through Friday, this restaurant is a good spot to meet for a quick lunch, corporate meeting or family dinner. A few local favorites are the brie cheese kisses, grilled chicken or salmon salad, hand-tossed pizza with over 30 toppings to choose from, grilled and baked pastas, and garlic parmesan fries with chipotle dipping sauce. A kid's menu is available. **Features:** beer & wine. **Address:** 1838 W Pullman Rd 83843 **Location:** Jct US 95, 1.1 mi w on SR 8.

MOUNTAIN HOME pop. 14,206

BEST WESTERN FOOTHILLS INN (208)587-8477

Motel
$99-$159

AAA Benefit: Save 10% or more every day and earn 10% bonus points!

Address: 1080 Hwy 20 83647 **Location:** I-84 exit 95, just n. **Facility:** 77 units, some kitchens. 2 stories (no elevator), exterior corridors. **Pool(s):** heated outdoor. **Activities:** hot tub, picnic facilities, exercise room. **Guest Services:** valet and coin laundry. **Featured Amenity:** full hot breakfast.

HAMPTON INN & SUITES (208)587-7300

Contemporary Hotel $109-$189 **Address:** 3175 NE Foothills Ave 83647 **Location:** I-84 exit 95, just n. **Facility:** 74 units. 3 stories, interior corridors. **Terms:** 1-7 night minimum stay, cancellation fee imposed. **Pool(s):** heated indoor. **Activities:** hot tub, exercise room. **Guest Services:** valet and coin laundry.

AAA Benefit: Members save up to 10%!

MOUNTAIN HOME INN (208)587-9743

Hotel $84-$109 **Address:** 1180 Hwy 20 83647 **Location:** I-84 exit 95, just n. **Facility:** 60 units. 2 stories (no elevator), interior corridors. **Terms:** cancellation fee imposed.

MULLAN (B-2) pop. 692, elev. 3,277'

Silver Valley's easternmost mining town was established in 1885 and named for John Mullan, an Army captain credited with blazing a 624-mile road across Montana, Idaho and Washington in the early 1860s. The Lucky Friday Mine, dating back to 1899, still produces silver.

Mullan nestles below Lookout Pass in the Bitterroot Mountains, a popular year-round recreation area for skiing, snowboarding, hiking and mountain biking. The paved Trail of the Coeur d'Alenes follows a former Union Pacific railway path 73 miles west from Mullan to Plummer; phone (208) 682-3814 for additional information. With 10 tunnels and seven trestles, the gravel, 15-mile Route of the Hiawatha runs south of Lookout Pass along another repurposed railroad right-of-way. Shuttles are available at trailheads from late May to late September; phone (208) 744-1301 or (208) 245-2531.

CAPTAIN JOHN MULLAN MUSEUM, 229 Earle St., occupies the 1930 Independent Order of Odd Fellows (I.O.O.F.) Building, which also once served as the town's theater. Historical photos, ladies' wear, school items, work tools and I.O.O.F. regalia are displayed in themed areas, including a drugstore, a nursery and a sitting room. **Time:** Allow 30 minutes minimum. **Hours:** Mon.-Fri. 10-4 or by appointment, June-Aug. **Cost:** Donations. **Phone:** (208) 744-1155.

RECREATIONAL ACTIVITIES
Skiing and Snowboarding

- SAVE **Lookout Pass Ski and Recreation Area** is 6 mi. e. on I-90. Other activities are offered, including mountain biking. **Hours:** Season begins in late Nov. Winter activities are available Thurs.-Mon. 9-4, early-late Dec.; daily 9-4, late Dec.-early Jan.; Wed.-Mon. 9-4, Jan.-Feb. (also Sat.-Sun. from 8:30); Thurs.-Mon. 9-4, Mar.-April (also Sat.-Sun. from 8:30). **Phone:** (208) 744-1301.

NAMPA (G-1) pop. 81,557, elev. 2,492'
• Restaurants p. 86

Col. W.H. Dewey moved his fortune during the 1890s to Nampa, an agricultural hamlet just north of the Great Basin Desert. Dewey brought prosperity to Nampa by attracting several railway branches and constructing the Dewey Palace hotel, which was a town landmark for several decades until it was damaged by fire and torn down. Nampa's name comes from Nampuh, or "Bigfoot," a Shoshone chief who was so large that his feet were supposedly 17 inches long.

Nampa is a central location from which to explore southwestern Idaho's natural wonders and historical sites. Givens Hot Springs is 17 miles south on SR 45, then 8 miles west on SR 78 on the south side of the Snake River. There are steam baths, an indoor natural hot-water pool and a picnic area.

Silver City and DeLamar, high in the Owyhee Mountains, can be reached by taking SR 45 south to Walter's Ferry, then turning east on SR 78 4.5 miles past Murphy. The towns, at one time thriving mining communities in one of the greatest silver-producing areas in the nation, are on a rough gravel and earth road (see Silver City p. 99). DeLamar has been abandoned.

Nampa Chamber of Commerce: 315 11th Ave. S., Nampa, ID 83651. **Phone:** (208) 466-4641.

DEER FLAT NATIONAL WILDLIFE REFUGE is 4 mi. s.w. The refuge consists of two sections: Lake Lowell, an irrigation reservoir, and 104 islands in the Snake River, from Walter's Ferry downstream to Farewell Bend in Oregon. The islands are accessible only by boat.

The refuge harbors waterfowl as well as other birds and mammals. In winter the lake attracts ducks and geese as well as bald eagles that come to feed; in spring and summer, western grebes, great blue herons and black-crowned night herons come to nest.

Boating is permitted mid-April through September. Fishing and hunting are permitted in season in specified portions of the refuge. **Hours:** Refuge daily dawn-dusk. Visitor center Mon.-Fri. 8-4, Sat. 10-4. Closed major holidays. **Cost:** Free. **Phone:** (208) 467-9278.

NAMPA TRAIN DEPOT MUSEUM is at 1200 Front St. The 1903 Baroque Revival-style building, formerly the Oregon Short Line Depot, houses changing exhibits that illustrate Nampa's importance as a railway town. Highlights include Canyon County and Union Pacific Railroad history, model train layouts and a caboose from the 1940s. **Time:** Allow 30 minutes minimum. **Hours:** Thurs.-Sat. 10-3. Closed Jan. 1, July 4, Thanksgiving and Christmas. **Cost:** $3; $2 (ages 13-18 and 65+); $1 (ages 6-12); $7 (family, four people). **Phone:** (208) 467-7611.

SAVE **WARHAWK AIR MUSEUM** is at 201 Municipal Dr. next to Nampa Municipal Airport. The museum features restored and flyable aircraft from World War II, including a Curtiss P-40E Kittyhawk, a P-51 Mustang, a Curtiss P-40N Warhawk and a 1940 Navy N3N biplane trainer. Other World War II items displayed are a restored 1940 DeSoto staff car, period poster art, trench art, uniforms and home-front memorabilia.

Time: Allow 2 hours minimum. **Hours:** Tues.-Sat. 10-5, Sun. 11-4. Closed Jan. 1, Easter, Mother's Day, July 4, Thanksgiving and Christmas. Phone ahead to confirm schedule. **Cost:** $10; $8 (ages 65+ and military with ID); $4 (ages 5-12). **Phone:** (208) 465-6446.

FAIRFIELD INN & SUITES BY MARRIOTT (208)467-5888

Hotel $96-S176

FAIRFIELD INN & SUITES Marriott

AAA Benefit: Members save 5% or more!

Address: 16150 N Midland Blvd 83687 **Location:** I-84 exit 33B westbound; exit 33 eastbound, just e. Located in a commercial area. **Facility:** 88 units. 3 stories, interior corridors. **Pool(s):** heated indoor. **Activities:** hot tub, picnic facilities, exercise room. **Guest Services:** valet and coin laundry. **Featured Amenity:** breakfast buffet.

SAVE 🍴 CALL 🛅M 🉐 BIZ 🛜 ✕ 🛢 🖥 / SOME UNITS HS 🖨

HAMPTON INN & SUITES - NAMPA AT THE IDAHO CENTER
(208)442-0036

Hotel $109-$189 **Address:** 5750 E Franklin Rd 83687 **Location:** I-84 exit 38, 0.5 mi n to Franklin Rd, then just e. **Facility:** 101 units. 4 stories, interior corridors. **Terms:** 1-7 night minimum stay, cancellation fee imposed. **Pool(s):** heated indoor. **Activities:** hot tub, exercise room. **Guest Services:** valet and coin laundry.

AAA Benefit: Members save up to 10%!

🍴 CALL 🛅M 🉐 BIZ HS 🛜 ✕ 🖥 / SOME UNITS 🛢 🖨

HOLIDAY INN EXPRESS & SUITES 208/466-4045

Hotel. Rates not provided. **Address:** 4104 E Flamingo Ave 83687 **Location:** I-84 exit 38, just s, then just w. **Facility:** 74 units. 3 stories, interior corridors. **Pool(s):** heated indoor. **Activities:** hot tub, picnic facilities, exercise room. **Guest Services:** valet and coin laundry.

🍴 CALL 🛅M 🉐 BIZ HS 🛜 ✕ 🛢 🖨 🖥 / SOME UNITS 🛢

SLEEP INN (208)463-6300

Hotel $69-$199 **Address:** 1315 Industrial Rd 83687 **Location:** I-84 exit 36 (Franklin Blvd), just s. Located in a commercial area. **Facility:** 81 units. 3 stories, interior corridors. **Pool(s):** heated indoor. **Activities:** hot tub, picnic facilities. **Guest Services:** valet and coin laundry.

CALL 🛅M 🉐 BIZ 🛜 ✕ 🛢 🖨 🖥 / SOME UNITS 🛢

WHERE TO EAT

BRICK 29 BISTRO   208/468-0029

▼▼▼▼ American. Casual Dining. $7-$33 **AAA Inspector Notes:** By placing an emphasis on ingredients from local farmers and vendors, this eatery offers some of the most flavorful food in the valley. From the all-natural pork chop to the delicious shiitake mushroom soup or tomato bisque, there is something for everyone. Diners will not be disappointed when ordering the brick, the signature dessert. **Features:** full bar, Sunday brunch. **Address:** 320 11th Ave S, Suite 101 83651 **Location:** I-84 exit 36 (Franklin Blvd), 0.9 mi s, 0.8 mi s on 11th Ave N, just e on 3rd St S, 1 mi s on 12th Ave S, then just w. **Parking:** on-site and street. L D CALL ⑤M

THE EGG FACTORY   208/466-2728

▼▼ ▼ Breakfast. Family Dining. $5-$9 **AAA Inspector Notes:** Serving up the home-style cooking your grandma used to make, this quaint and quirky diner offers hearty breakfast favorites, sandwiches, soup, burgers and make-yourself-at-home hospitality. Just look for the gigantic white hen. **Features:** Sunday brunch. **Address:** 820 Caldwell Blvd 83651 **Location:** I-84 exit 35 (Northside Blvd), 1 mi s, then 1.2 mi w. B L

JALAPENO'S BAR & GRILL   208/442-6355

▼▼ ▼▼ Mexican. Casual Dining. $7-$17 **AAA Inspector Notes:** With a vibrant décor, this eatery is a favorite of locals and visitors. A large menu features traditional favorites including burritos, chimichangas, enchiladas, fajitas and tamales. If you are feeling festive, the cantina serves more than 80 types of tequila. **Features:** full bar, patio dining, happy hour. **Address:** 1921 Nampa-Caldwell Blvd 83651 **Location:** I-84 exit 33 eastbound; exit 33A westbound, 0.6 mi sw, then just e. L D

SMOKY MOUNTAIN PIZZERIA GRILL   208/461-7333

▼▼ ▼ Italian. Casual Dining. $7-$27 **AAA Inspector Notes:** Near a movie theater complex, this is a great place to meet for a quick lunch, corporate meeting, family dinner or a bite before the flick. On the menu you will find a good selection of pasta, salads, sandwiches and pizza. Gluten-free menu items are available. **Features:** full bar, patio dining. **Address:** 2007 N Cassia St 83651 **Location:** I-84 exit 33 eastbound; exit 33A westbound, 0.4 mi w, then just s. L D

NEZ PERCE NATIONAL FOREST (D-2)

Elevations in the forest range from 1,350 ft. in Hells Canyon to 9,393 ft. at Devil's Peak. Refer to AAA maps for additional elevation information.

In the north-central part of the state, Nez Perce National Forest was named for the Nez Perce Indians, whose ancestral lands once included this rugged area of 2,223,594 acres. The forest contains the Gospel-Hump Wilderness and portions of the Selway-Bitterroot Wilderness, Frank Church-River of No Return Wilderness, Hells Canyon Wilderness and Hells Canyon National Recreation Area (see place listing p. 65). Portions of the forest are close to parts of Nez Perce National Historical Park (see place listing).

More than 150 miles of the Rapid, Salmon and Selway rivers and the Middle Fork of the Clearwater River are classified as wild and scenic rivers. Elk, moose, deer, cougars, mountain goats, bighorn sheep and bears inhabit the forest, while steelhead trout, white sturgeon and small-mouth bass can be found in the rivers and streams.

The historic Magruder Corridor Road (FR 468) is open to forest visitors July through October. The primitive road, rough but passable to two-wheel-drive, high-clearance vehicles, begins at the Red River Ranger Station and ends in Darby, Mont. The wilderness areas adjoining the route together form the largest tract of roadless land in the U.S. outside Alaska. Other roads, many unpaved, lead to such mining ghost towns as Dixie, Florence and Orogrande.

Ranger stations are located in Elk City, Grangeville, White Bird and near Kooskia. For information contact the Grangeville Office, Nez Perce National Forest, 104 Airport Rd., Grangeville, ID 83530; phone (208) 983-1950. See Recreation Areas Chart.

NEZ PERCE NATIONAL HISTORICAL PARK (C-1)

Encompassing 38 sites scattered across 12,000 square miles of north-central Idaho as well as 10 sites in Oregon, Washington and Montana, each part of Nez Perce National Historical Park reflects a portion of the history and culture of the Nez Perce Indians and their relationships with white explorers, missionaries, miners, settlers and soldiers.

Some sites are scenic views, some are geologic formations and others contain historic places and buildings. They include the Lolo Trail, Native American battlefields and former campsites of Meriwether Lewis and William Clark.

For thousands of years the Nez Perce lived in the valleys of the Clearwater and Snake rivers and their tributaries. Their first documented meeting with white settlers in Nez Perce territory took place in September 1805, when the Lewis and Clark expedition encountered them, and the Indians gave supplies and assistance. In 1855 the Nez Perce reluctantly signed a treaty setting aside their ancestral home as a reservation.

A new treaty was negotiated in 1863 with some of the Nez Perce bands after gold was discovered within the reservation; this treaty reduced the reservation to one-tenth of its original size.

The first major battle of the Nez Perce War was on June 17, 1877, near White Bird (see place listing p. 106). The U.S. Army pursued the bands of Nez Perce who had not signed the 1863 treaty across the Nez Perce Trail to Montana. After many battles the Nez Perce surrendered only 40 miles from the Canadian border. They were exiled for 8 years to Oklahoma Territory; the survivors eventually returned to the Pacific Northwest. Today the Nez Perce National Historic Trail parallels much of the original 1877 route. A brochure for a self-guiding walking tour of White Bird Battlefield is available.

The Weippe (WEE-ipe) Prairie, 18 miles east of US 12 on SR 11, is part of Nez Perce National Historical Park. The Idaho section of the Nez Perce Trail and Pass climbs through 150 miles of rough terrain east of Weippe as it ascends the 5,187-foot Lolo Pass through the Bitterroot Mountains.

The park's headquarters and visitor center are in Spalding *(see place listing p. 99)*. Also see Grangeville, Kamiah, Lapwai, Nez Perce National Forest and Orofino.

Spalding Visitor Center open daily 8-5, Memorial Day weekend-Labor Day; 8-4:30, mid-Mar. through day before Memorial Day weekend and day after Labor Day to mid-Nov.; 9-4, rest of year. Closed Jan. 1, Thanksgiving and Christmas. Free. Phone (208) 843-7009.

Heart of the Monster is 2 mi. e. of Kamiah on US 12. This volcanic rock formation is the place of creation in Nez Perce mythology. Folklore says that in the prehuman years, a monster was devouring the animals. Coyote, the chief animal, slew the monster, cut him into pieces and scattered these bits to the winds. Where each bit landed, a new Native American tribe arose. The Nez Perce tribe came from blood from the monster's heart. East Kamiah is a designated site of Nez Perce National Historical Park *(see place listing p. 86)*. An interpretive display is available. **Hours:** Daily dawn-dusk. **Phone:** (208) 843-7009.

Weis Rockshelter is in Nez Perce National Historical Park, 8 mi. s. of Cottonwood, 7 miles w. of US 95. It is one of 38 sites in the park. Archeological excavations of this cliff recess have revealed almost continuous human occupation between 5500 B.C. and A.D. 1400. The niche near the Salmon River is thought to be the first shelter for the Nez Perce more than 8,000 years ago. **Hours:** Daily 8-5, Memorial Day weekend-Labor Day; 8-4:30, mid-Mar. through day before Memorial Day weekend and day after Labor Day to mid-Nov.; 9-4, rest of year. Ranger-led programs are offered daily, Memorial Day-Labor Day. **Cost:** Free. **Phone:** (208) 843-7009 for Nez Perce National Historic Park Spalding Visitor Center.

is in Nez Perce National Historical Park, 8 mi. s. of Cottonwood, 7 miles w. of US 95. It is one of 38 sites in the park. Archeological excavations of this cliff recess have revealed almost continuous human occupation between 5500 B.C. and A.D. 1400. The niche near the Salmon River is thought to be the first shelter for the Nez Perce more than 8,000 years ago. **Hours:** Daily 8-5, Memorial Day weekend-Labor Day; 8-4:30, mid-Mar. through day before Memorial Day weekend and day after Labor Day to mid-Nov.; 9-4, rest of year. Ranger-led programs are offered daily, Memorial Day-Labor Day. **Cost:** Free. **Phone:** (208) 843-7009 for Nez Perce National Historic Park Spalding Visitor Center.

NORTH FORK (E-3) elev. 3,620'

RECREATIONAL ACTIVITIES
White-water Rafting
- **North Fork Guides** trips meet at the North Fork Store, Motel and Campground at 2046 US 93N. Other activities are offered, including steelhead fishing trips. **Hours:** Rafting trips are offered mid-Apr. through Nov. 30. Schedule varies; phone ahead. **Phone:** (208) 865-2534.

OLDTOWN (B-1) pop. 184, elev. 2,180'

Oldtown is separated from Newport, Wash., by State Avenue and is the site of the original settlement from which the two towns evolved.

Greater Newport Area Chamber of Commerce: 325 W. 4th St., P.O. Box 2006, Newport, WA 99156. **Phone:** (509) 447-5812.

ALBENI FALLS DAM, 2 mi. e. on US 2 on the Pend Oreille River, offers a scenic viewpoint and visitor center. One-hour guided tours to the powerhouse overlook, offered in the summer, provide information about the dam and powerhouse. The films "The Power and Play of the Pend Oreille" and "The Bonneville Power System" are shown in the visitor center, which also has exhibits.

Hours: Visitor center daily 7:30-4, Memorial Day-Labor Day; Mon.-Fri. 7-4:30, rest of year. Tours are available daily at 10, 11, 1 and 2, Memorial Day weekend-Labor Day. **Cost:** Free. **Phone:** (208) 437-4617. ⛺

OROFINO (C-1) pop. 3,142, elev. 1,027'
- **Hotels p. 88** • **Restaurants p. 88**

In 1805 members of Meriwether Lewis' and William Clark's expedition passed near the present site of Orofino on their way west. The first gold miners swarmed into the area 60 years later from California, and soon Idaho's first permanent settlements began to take shape. Orofino is on the Nez Perce Indian Reservation, and the Clearwater River runs through the town's boundaries. The Clearwater National Forest *(see place listing p. 55)* and Nez Perce National Forest *(see place listing p. 86)* are nearby.

Orofino's economy relies on lumbering, farming and government employment. A long growing season, ample precipitation and fertile soil contribute to the prosperity of this agricultural community. Northwest of Orofino, near Ahsahka *(see place listing p. 33)*, is the Dworshak National Fish Hatchery and Dworshak Dam and Reservoir.

Orofino Chamber of Commerce: 217 1st St., P.O. Box 2346, Orofino, ID 83544. **Phone:** (208) 476-4335.

CLEARWATER HISTORICAL MUSEUM is at 315 College Ave. Exhibits describe the Nez Perce culture; the Lewis and Clark expedition; early mining, logging and railroads; achievements of the Civilian Conservation Corps (CCC) in the 1930s; and the construction of the Dworshak Dam. **Time:** Allow 30 minutes minimum. **Hours:** Tues.-Sat. 12:30-5:30, May-Sept.; Tues.-Sat. 1:30-4:30, rest of year. Closed Jan. 1, Thanksgiving and Christmas. **Cost:** Donations. **Phone:** (208) 476-5033.

LEWIS AND CLARK CANOE CAMP, 4 mi. w. on US 12, is part of the Nez Perce National Historical Park *(see place listing p. 86)*. After crossing the Bitterroot Mountains on horseback, Meriwether Lewis' and William Clark's expedition camped here and built five dugout canoes for the remainder of their journey to the Pacific Ocean. **Hours:** Daily dawn-dusk. **Cost:** Free. **Phone:** (208) 843-7009.

BEST WESTERN PLUS LODGE AT RIVER'S EDGE
(208)476-9999

Hotel
$110-$128

AAA Benefit: Save 10% or more every day and earn 10% bonus points!

Address: 615 Main St 83544 **Location:** US 12, 0.3 mi e to Main St, 0.3 mi s. **Facility:** 49 units. 3 stories, interior corridors. **Terms:** check-in 4 pm, resort fee. **Amenities:** *Some:* safes. **Pool(s):** heated indoor. **Activities:** hot tub, fishing, exercise room. **Guest Services:** coin laundry. **Featured Amenity: full hot breakfast!**

    CALL  SOME UNITS

HELGESON PLACE SUITES
208-476-5729

Extended Stay Hotel. Rates not provided. **Address:** 125 Johnson Ave 83544 **Location:** 0.3 mi e; downtown. **Facility:** 20 kitchen units, some two bedrooms. 3 stories, interior corridors. **Parking:** on-site and street. **Activities:** picnic facilities, exercise room.

 CALL    SOME UNITS

KONKOLVILLE MOTEL
(208)476-5584

Motel $60-$90 **Address:** 2600 Michigan Ave 83544 **Location:** 3 mi e of center. **Facility:** 40 units. 2 stories (no elevator), exterior corridors. **Parking:** winter plug-ins. **Terms:** cancellation fee imposed. **Pool(s):** heated outdoor. **Activities:** hot tub, picnic facilities. **Guest Services:** coin laundry.

CALL   SOME UNITS

WHERE TO EAT

AUGIE'S DELI
208/476-5450

Deli Sandwiches. Family Dining. $6-$9 **AAA Inspector Notes:** Serving espresso, sandwiches, panini, homemade potato salad and the best shakes in the county, this casual and friendly deli is family-run by mother and daughter and is the right spot for travelers to sit down a spell, take a break from the road and splurge on some ice cream. **Address:** 202 Johnson Ave 83544 **Location:** Just s of Michigan and Johnson aves; downtown. **Parking:** street only.

B L CALL

DINING ON THE EDGE
208/476-7805

American. Casual Dining. $9-$35 **AAA Inspector Notes:** On the Clearwater River, this restaurant offers guests dining while basking in nature. Be sure to ask for a seat at the deck overlooking the river. They are known for prime rib which comes with fresh-baked rosemary garlic focaccia bread with whipped rosemary butter. Vegetarian items are available. The crème brûlée is a popular dessert. **Features:** full bar, patio dining. **Address:** 625 Main St 83544 **Location:** At Main and 4th sts; downtown. L D CALL

FIESTA EN JALISCO
208/476-7506

Mexican. Casual Dining. $9-$30 **AAA Inspector Notes:** Whether in the mood for charbroiled steak and sautéed shrimp, roasted and stuffed Anaheim chiles or a sizzling chicken fajita, all entrées and combinations at this restaurant are served with rice and beans. This colorful spot features a varied selection of margaritas and cocktails. A kids' menu and vegetarian items are available. **Features:** full bar. **Address:** 207 Johnson Ave 83544 **Location:** Just s of Michigan and Johnson aves. **Parking:** street only. L D

PARIS (H-6) pop. 513, elev. 5,964'

Seat of Bear Lake County, Paris was settled in 1863 by Mormon pioneers who believed they were in Utah until the boundary was surveyed in 1872. The City of Paris Museum, 34 Main St., displays local artifacts, memorabilia and historical photographs; phone (208) 945-9606 from Memorial Day-Labor Day, or (208) 945-2253 rest of year.

The Bear River Range west of town has several remote points of interest. Six miles down the gravel Paris Canyon Road is Paris Springs; Paris Ice Cave is another 6 miles up the canyon. The cave is usually accessible by mid-July; contact the ranger station in Montpelier for more information at (208) 847-0375.

PARIS TABERNACLE, 109 S. Main St., is a Romanesque-style Mormon place of worship dedicated in 1889. Designed by Brigham Young's son Joseph Don Carlos, this impressive sandstone edifice is considered to be one of the pioneer landmarks of the Intermountain Region. The interior, which can hold 1,500 worshipers, features hardwood floors and pine pews. The distinctive ceiling reflects a style common to sailing ships of the time.

Pioneer artifacts and an early 20th-century pipe organ made by Austin Organs Inc., one of the oldest U.S. organ manufacturers still in operation, are displayed. **Time:** Allow 30 minutes minimum. **Hours:** Daily 9:30-5, Memorial Day-Labor Day. **Cost:** Free. **Phone:** (800) 448-2327. GT

PAYETTE NATIONAL FOREST (E-1)

Elevations in the forest range from 1,464 ft. in Hells Canyon to 9,545 ft. at Mormon Mountain. Refer to AAA maps for additional elevation information.

Bounded by the Snake and Salmon rivers and the Middle Fork of the Salmon River in the west-central part of the state, Payette National Forest contains 2,307,897 acres ranging in elevation from 1,400 to 9,000 feet above sea level. More than 1,800 miles of both motorized and non-motorized trails include Lava Ridge National Recreation Trail and Sheep Rock Nature Trail. The forest's remote rivers and mountains offer exceptional fishing, hiking, hunting, climbing and boating opportunities during summer and fall months.

Winter sports include alpine skiing at Brundage Mountain Resort and the smaller Payette Lakes Ski Hill as well as cross-country skiing and snowmobiling in many other areas. Thousands of burned forest acres continue to regenerate as part of the natural cycle after major fires in 1994, 2000 and 2007.

A small portion of the Hells Canyon Wilderness and Hells Canyon National Recreation Area *(see place listing p. 65)* and a large portion of the Frank Church-River of No Return Wilderness are within the forest. These primitive mountainous areas overlap several national forests and contain extensive non-motorized trail networks. For more information, contact Payette National Forest, 501 N. Mission St., McCall, ID 83638; phone (208) 634-0700. *See Recreation Areas Chart.*

PIERCE (C-2) pop. 508, elev. 3,094'

Gold was found here in 1860, triggering a rush of some 6,000 prospectors, many of whom were Chinese. In 1861 the rough mining camp became seat of Shoshone County and the first established town in what was to become Idaho Territory 3 years later. After mining played out in the 1880s, Pierce re-emerged as a forest products center in the 1900s. Its population peaked at over 1,200 in 1970.

Idaho's oldest government building, a courthouse built in 1862, still stands 1 block east of SR 11 on Court Street. It became a private residence after the county seat was moved to Murray in 1885. The J. Howard Bradbury Memorial Logging Museum, 103 S. Main St., has historical photographs, indoor and outdoor displays of mining and logging relics, and a 1920 log cabin; phone (208) 464-2677. An interpretive pavilion, on SR 11 at the north end of town, features 15 panels describing the history of the area.

Pierce is on the Gold Rush Historic Byway, a 43-mile route following SR 11 from Greer up to Weippe *(see place listing p. 106)* and Pierce and ending at Headquarters. Numerous roadside plaques describe points of interest along the byway.

RECREATIONAL ACTIVITIES
Skiing
- **Bald Mountain Ski Area** is 6 mi. n. on SR 11. **Hours:** Sat.-Sun. and holidays 9:30-3:30, mid-Dec. to late Mar. (weather permitting). **Phone:** (208) 464-2311 or (208) 435-4272.

PLUMMER (C-1) pop. 1,044, elev. 2,743'

Plummer is the commercial center of the Coeur d'Alene Indian Reservation and the surrounding farms and timberlands. The town also is the western trailhead of the Trail of the Coeur d'Alenes, a paved walking and bicycling route extending 72 miles east to Mullan.

HEYBURN STATE PARK, 5 mi. e. on SR 5, brackets the south end of Lake Coeur d'Alene. Established in 1908, it is the oldest state park in the Pacific Northwest as well as Idaho's largest state park at 7,825 acres. Heyburn is home to bears, deer, elk and heron and boasts one of the largest concentrations of nesting osprey in North America. A visitor center at Hawleys Landing off SR 5 contains exhibits about area wildlife and tribal history as well as historical photographs documenting the Civilian Conservation Corps' role in the park's development.

Heyburn also offers 40 miles of multiuse trails. A section of the 72-mile, paved Trail of the Coeur d'Alenes passes through the northern part of the park; it is accessible from the Chatcolet Day Use Area 2.5 miles north of the visitor center. You can

hike or bike across the trail's 3,100-foot bridge/trestle, which spans the lake.

Cottonwood Point, 2 miles east of the main park entrance on SR 5, offers an excellent view of the "river flowing through a lake." This unusual feature formed in 1904, when the Post Falls Dam on the Spokane River raised the lake level, drowning the lowlands flanking the lower reaches of the St. Joe River, but leaving its natural, tree-lined levees above the waters. *See Recreation Areas Chart.*

Time: Allow 1 hour minimum. **Hours:** Park open daily 24 hours. Visitor Center open daily 8:30-6, Memorial Day weekend-Labor Day; Mon.-Fri. 7-3:30, rest of year. Phone ahead to confirm schedule. **Cost:** $5 (per private vehicle). **Phone:** (208) 686-1308. 🏕️ 🍴 ⛵ 🏠 🌳

POCATELLO (G-5) pop. 54,255, elev. 4,365'
• Hotels p. 90 • Restaurants p. 91

Originally part of the Fort Hall Indian Reservation, Pocatello is named for a 19th-century Shoshone chief who granted the Utah & Northern a right-of-way for a Salt Lake City-to-Butte railroad line. The subsequent arrival in 1882 of the Union Pacific Railway, which linked the Midwest and Pacific Northwest, spawned a makeshift community—a congregation of tents at the meeting of the two lines—that was first called Pocatello Junction.

Pocatello maintains its position as one of the region's leading industrial, distribution and transportation centers. Education also is a principal concern; Idaho State University, with more than 17,000 students, is one of the state's leading 4-year institutions. The school's state-of-the-art L.E. and Thelma E. Stephens Performing Arts Center, 1002 Sam Nixon Ave., entertains lovers of music, dance and theater; phone (208) 282-3595.

The town is the northern terminus of an especially scenic section of I-15, which heads south into Utah. Just off Main Street visitors can see the exterior of the Union Pacific Depot, a three-story passenger station designed in the late 1800s. Train passengers of the era stayed overnight across the street at the historic Yellowstone Hotel. **Note:** The hotel is undergoing renovations.

Greater Pocatello Visitors Bureau: 2695 S. 5th Ave., Pocatello, ID 83201. **Phone:** (208) 479-7659. *(See ad p. 321.)*

🔻 GEM SAVE **DON ASLETT MUSEUM OF CLEAN** is at 711 S. 2nd Ave. This five-story green building, a renovated 20th-century brick warehouse, is filled with captivating themed displays that relate the history of cleaning. More than 5,000 items are exhibited, including art, appliances, tools and live cleaning plants. How-to videos, such as "How to Clean Your Bathroom in 2-3 Minutes," offer quick and easy cleaning tips to visitors. The three-story Kids' Cleaning World teaches children about cleanliness and responsibility and features mops, buckets and other supplies for wee ones to try out. **Time:**

Allow 1 hour, 30 minutes minimum. **Hours:** Tues.-Sat. 10-5. Closed Jan. 1, Thanksgiving and Christmas. Phone ahead to confirm schedule. **Cost:** $6; $5 (ages 3-11); $20 (family, two adults and three children). **Phone:** (208) 236-6906. GT

SAVE **IDAHO MUSEUM OF NATURAL HISTORY,** affiliated with the Smithsonian Institute, is on the main floor of the museum building at the corner of 5th Ave. and Dillon St. on the Idaho State University campus. Among the permanent exhibits are Giants of the Snake River Plain, which features ice age mammals; the ISU Tree Walk; and a natural history garden. The Discovery Room allows children hands-on encounters with fossils and other specimens.

Time: Allow 30 minutes minimum. **Hours:** Tues.-Sat. 11-5. Closed major holidays. **Cost:** $5; $4 (ages 60+); $2 (college students with ID); $1 (ages 5-18). **Phone:** (208) 282-3317.

ROSS PARK is between 2nd and 5th aves. With such amenities as a skate park and horseshoe and volleyball areas on-site, a variety of recreational activities can be enjoyed. The community park also comprises a museum, a re-created historical trading post and a zoo. In addition its stellar aquatic complex offers a 50-meter swimming pool, a waterslide, a lazy river and an interactive wading area.

Time: Allow 1 hour minimum. **Hours:** Park open daily dawn-dusk. Aquatic complex open daily noon-8, Memorial Day weekend-Labor Day (weather permitting). Phone ahead to confirm schedule. **Cost:** Park admission free. Aquatic complex (excludes waterslide) $6; $5 (ages 7-17); $4 (ages 60+); $2 (ages 1-6). Half-price admission Mon. and Wed. 5-8 p.m. Aquatic complex unlimited waterslide pass $3. **Phone:** (208) 234-0472. 🅷

Bannock County Historical Museum is off I-15 exit 67, then 1 mi. n. on N. 5th Ave. (US 30/91) to 3000 Alvord Loop in Upper Ross Park. The museum contains Native American and railroad displays, a restored stagecoach, a 1915 La France fire truck and a history/donor mural wall. Other displays include a 1900s parlor, Buddhist shrine, a country store, an early dental office and a 1947 Linotype press. **Hours:** Mon.-Sat. 10-6, Sun. 1-5, Memorial Day weekend-Labor Day; Tues.-Sat. 10-4, rest of year. Closed major holidays. **Cost:** Memorial Day weekend-Labor Day (includes Fort Hall Replica) $4; $3 (ages 65+); $2 (ages 6-17). Rest of year (does not include Fort Hall Replica) $2; $1 (ages 6-17). **Phone:** (208) 233-0434.

Fort Hall Replica, off I-15 exit 67, then 1 mi. n. on N. 5th Ave. (US 30/91) to 2990 Avenue of the Chiefs in Upper Ross Park, re-creates the fur-trading post that operated nearby 1834-60. Original Hudson's Bay Co. plans were used to create the full-scale replica. Buffaloes, elk, deer and pronghorn antelopes are kept in a field next to the fort.

Time: Allow 1 hour minimum. **Hours:** Mon.-Sat. 10-6, Sun. 1-5, Sat. before Memorial Day-Labor Day. Phone ahead to confirm schedule. **Cost:** (includes Bannock County Historical Museum) $4; $3 (ages 65+); $2 (ages 6-17). **Phone:** (208) 234-1795.

Pocatello Zoo, 2900 S. 2nd Ave. in the lower level of Ross Park, features native North American wildlife including elk, bison, grizzly and black bears, bighorn sheep, pronghorn, mountain lions and waterfowl in 23 acres of natural habitats. Children can play in a 900-square-foot tree house or a 30-foot tipi. **Time:** Allow 1 hour minimum. **Hours:** Daily 10-5, May 1-31; Mon.-Thurs. 10-5, Fri.-Sun. 10-6, June 1-Labor Day; Sat.-Sun. 10-4, day after Labor Day-last weekend in Oct. and Apr. 1-30. **Cost:** $5.75; $4.50 (ages 60+); $3.75 (ages 3-11). **Phone:** (208) 234-6196 or (208) 234-6264.

AMERITEL INN 208/234-7500

🔻🔻 Hotel. Rates not provided. **Address:** 1440 Bench Rd 83201 **Location:** I-15 exit 71, just e. **Facility:** 148 units, some efficiencies. 3 stories, interior corridors. **Pool(s):** heated indoor. **Activities:** hot tub, exercise room. **Guest Services:** valet and coin laundry.

BEST WESTERN POCATELLO INN (208)237-7650

Hotel
$109-$139

AAA Benefit: Save 10% or more every day and earn 10% bonus points!

Address: 1415 Bench Rd 83201 **Location:** I-15 exit 71, just e. **Facility:** 149 units, some efficiencies. 2-3 stories (no elevator), interior corridors. **Parking:** winter plug-ins. **Amenities:** *Some:* safes. **Pool(s):** heated indoor. **Activities:** hot tub. **Guest Services:** valet and coin laundry, area transportation. **Featured Amenity: full hot breakfast.**

CLARION INN (208)237-1400

Hotel
$89-$159

Address: 1399 Bench Rd 83201 **Location:** I-15 exit 71, just e. **Facility:** 196 units. 2 stories (no elevator), interior/exterior corridors. **Pool(s):** heated indoor. **Activities:** sauna, hot tub, game room, picnic facilities, exercise room. **Guest Services:** valet and coin laundry, area transportation.

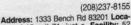

COMFORT INN (208)237-8155

Hotel
$85-$129

Address: 1333 Bench Rd 83201 **Location:** I-15 exit 71, just e. **Facility:** 52 units. 2 stories (no elevator), interior corridors. **Amenities:** safes. **Pool(s):** heated indoor. **Activities:** hot tub. **Guest Services:** valet laundry. **Featured Amenity: continental breakfast.**

HAMPTON INN & SUITES
(208)233-8200

Contemporary Hotel $119-$164 **Address:** 151 Vista Dr 83201 **Location:** just e. **Facility:** 89 units. 4 stories. interior corridors. **Terms:** 1-7 night minimum stay, cancellation fee imposed. **Pool(s):** heated indoor. **Activities:** hot tub, exercise room. **Guest Services:** valet and coin laundry.

AAA Benefit:
Members save up to 10%!

CALL [&M] [⊃] [BIZ] [HS] [☎] [✕] [🎦] [▭]
/ SOME UNITS [🛏] [📷]

HOLIDAY INN EXPRESS & SUITES POCATELLO
(208)478-9800

Hotel $119-$189 **Address:** 200 Venitio 83201 **Location:** I-15 exit 69 (Clark St), 0.6 mi e. **Facility:** 80 units. 3 stories. interior corridors. **Terms:** cancellation fee imposed. **Pool(s):** heated indoor. **Activities:** hot tub, exercise room. **Guest Services:** valet and coin laundry.

CALL [&M] [⊃] [BIZ] [HS] [☎] [✕] [▭] [📷] [▭] [📷]

RED LION HOTEL
208/233-2200

Hotel. Rates not provided. **Address:** 1555 Pocatello Creek Rd 83201 **Location:** I-15 exit 71, just e. **Facility:** 150 units. 2 stories (no elevator), interior corridors. **Pool(s):** heated indoor. **Activities:** hot tub, exercise room. **Guest Services:** valet and coin laundry.

[➕] [🍽] CALL [&M] [⊃] [BIZ] [☎] [✕] [▭]
/ SOME UNITS [🛏] [📷] [📷]

SUPER 8
(208)234-0888

Hotel $60-$90 **Address:** 1330 Bench Rd 83201 **Location:** I-15 exit 71, just e. **Facility:** 80 units. 3 stories, interior corridors. **Guest Services:** valet and coin laundry.

[🍴] [BIZ] [☎] [✕] [▭] / SOME UNITS [🛏] [📷] [📷]

TOWNEPLACE SUITES BY MARRIOTT
(208)478-7000

Extended Stay Hotel $107-$194 **Address:** 2376 Via Caporatti Dr 83201 **Location:** I-15 exit 69 (Clark St), 0.3 mi e. **Facility:** 93 efficiencies, some two bedrooms. 4 stories. interior corridors. **Pool(s):** heated indoor. **Activities:** hot tub, picnic facilities, exercise room. **Guest Services:** valet and coin laundry.

AAA Benefit:
Members save 5% or more!

[🍴] CALL [&M] [⊃] [BIZ] [HS] [☎] [✕] [▭] [📷] [▭]
/ SOME UNITS [🛏]

BLACK SWAN INN
208/233-3051

[fyi] Not evaluated. **Address:** 746 E Center St 83201 **Location:** I-15 exit 69 (Clark St), 1.1 mi w, just s on 7th Ave, then just w; downtown. Facilities, services, and décor characterize a mid-scale property.

WHERE TO EAT

BUDDY'S ITALIAN RESTAUANT
208/233-1172

Italian. Casual Dining. $7-$18 **AAA Inspector Notes:** The locals love the bustling atmosphere and good food at this casual and friendly family-owned restaurant. Italian fare dominates the menu, right up to the handmade ravioli house specialty and the famous salad dressing. Vegetarian marinara sauce is available upon request. **Features:** beer & wine. **Address:** 626 E Lewis St 83201 **Location:** I-15 exit 69 (Clark St), 1 mi w, just s on 7th Ave, then just w. [L] [D]

EL HERRADERO
208/233-6747

Mexican. Casual Dining. $5-$10 **AAA Inspector Notes:** This charming family-run eatery serves an array of combos, appetizers, enchiladas, nachos, burritos and chicken, beef or shrimp fajitas. Visitors appreciate the a la carte menu which features more than eleven items. Vegetarian items are available upon request. **Features:** beer only. **Address:** 123 Jefferson Ave 83201 **Location:** I-15 exit 67 (5th Ave), 2.2 mi n to Center St, 0.5 mi e to 13th Ave, then 0.5 mi n to Oak St; corner of Oak St and Jefferson Ave. [L] [D]

PORTNEUF VALLEY BREWING
970/232-1644

American. Casual Dining. $7-$29 **AAA Inspector Notes:** Some popular favorites served here are the salads and sandwiches, veggie or meat lasagna, teriyaki bowl stir-fry, wacky macaroni and cheese, made-to-order fresh baked pizza and craft-brewed beverages. The Bavarian bun and giant salty pretzel are addictive. Many items are available in smaller portions. **Features:** full bar, patio dining, happy hour. **Address:** 615 S 1st Ave 83201 **Location:** I-15 exit 69 (Clark St), 1.2 mi sw to 4th Ave, 0.3 mi se to Whitman St, 0.3 mi sw to S 1st Ave, then just se. **Parking:** street only.

[L] [D] [LATE]

THE SANDPIPER
208/233-1000

Seafood Steak. Casual Dining. $11-$32 **AAA Inspector Notes:** Good choices are the house salad with shrimp and creamy garlic dressing and the prime rib entrée at this informal, bustling restaurant. Deck dining is available in season. **Features:** full bar. **Reservations:** suggested, weekends. **Address:** 1400 Bench Rd 83201 **Location:** I-15 exit 71, just e, then just n. [D]

PONDERAY pop. 1,137

GUESTHOUSE LODGE-SANDPOINT
(208)263-2210

Hotel $54-$159 **Address:** 476841 Hwy 95 N 83852 **Location:** 0.7 mi n on US 95 from jct SR 200. **Facility:** 59 units. 2 stories (no elevator), interior corridors. **Parking:** winter plug-ins. **Terms:** 3 day cancellation notice-fee imposed, resort fee. **Activities:** hot tub. **Guest Services:** coin laundry.

[🍴] [BIZ] [☎] [✕] [▭] [📷] [▭] / SOME UNITS [🛏]

HOLIDAY INN EXPRESS & SUITES
(208)255-4500

Hotel $110-$220 **Address:** 477326 Hwy 95 N 83852 **Location:** 0.7 mi n on US 95 from jct SR 200. **Facility:** 83 units, some two bedrooms. 3 stories, interior corridors. **Pool(s):** heated indoor. **Activities:** hot tub, exercise room. **Guest Services:** valet and coin laundry.

[🍴] CALL [&M] [⊃] [BIZ] [☎] [✕] [▭] [📷] [▭]
/ SOME UNITS [🛏] [HS]

HOTEL RUBY PONDERAY
(208)263-5383

Hotel $80-$200 **Address:** 477255 Hwy 95 N 83852 **Location:** 1.2 mi n on US 95 from jct SR 200. **Facility:** 70 units. 2 stories (no elevator), interior corridors. **Terms:** cancellation fee imposed. **Amenities:** safes. **Activities:** hot tub. **Guest Services:** coin laundry.

[🍴] [BIZ] [☎] [✕] [▭] / SOME UNITS [🛏] [📷] [▭]

WHERE TO EAT

SWEET LOU'S
208/263-1381

Barbecue. Gastropub. $8-$23 **AAA Inspector Notes:** Sports bar or gastro pub, guests are sure to enjoy the succulent ribs or steak sandwiches along with buckets of beer found here. Hand-cut fries and homemade fry sauce complement the meal. There is a seasonal sister restaurant in the northwestern town of Hope. **Features:** full bar, happy hour. **Address:** 477272 Hwy 95 N 83852 **Location:** 0.7 mi n on US 95 from jct SR 200; adjacent to Holiday Inn Express & Suites. [L] [D] CALL [&M]

POST FALLS (B-1) pop. 27,574, elev. 2,169'
• Hotels p. 92 • Restaurants p. 92

On the Spokane River at the Washington-Idaho state line, Post Falls was founded in the late 1800s by Frederick Post when he harnessed the falls to generate power for his sawmill.

Stateline Speedway, off I-90 exit 2 at 1349 N. Beck Rd., features stock car racing Wednesdays and Saturdays from mid-April through September; phone (208) 773-5019.

Post Falls/Coeur d'Alene Visitor Center: 201 E. Fourth Ave., Post Falls, ID 83854. **Phone:** (208) 773-5016 or (800) 292-2553.

FALLS PARK, off I-90 Spokane St. exit, 2 blks. s. on Spokane St., then 1.5 blks. w. to 305 W. 4th St., offers visitors picturesque views of Post Falls and the gorge. The best viewing is during spring runoff. Children also can fish in a stocked pond. Trails lead to nearby Treaty Rock Historic Site *(see attraction listing)*, which marks the location of Post Falls' founding. **Hours:** Daily dawn-dusk (weather permitting). **Cost:** Free. **Phone:** (208) 773-0539. 🎟

Q'EMILN PARK AND TRAILS is off I-90 exit 5, .9 mi. s. on Spokane St., then .2 mi. w. on Parkway Dr. Twelve connected trails wind along the south bank of the Spokane River. The pathways lead to historic sites, abandoned homesteads, mining camps, logging areas and scenic spots above and below Post Falls Dam. The park is known for its rock climbing, with opportunities that appeal to all skill levels. A boat launch, picnic areas and seasonal community events are offered. Swimming is permitted in designated areas. **Time:** Allow 1 hour minimum. **Hours:** Daily dawn-dusk. **Cost:** Free. **Parking:** Memorial Day weekend-Labor Day $3.50. **Phone:** (208) 773-0539. 🗺 🎟

TREATY ROCK HISTORIC SITE, jct. 7th and Compton sts., commemorates the spot where Coeur d'Alene Indian Chief Andrew Seltice transferred land to Frederick Post, the founder of Post Falls. A trail with interpretive signage features Native American petroglyphs and paintings. **Time:** Allow 30 minutes minimum. **Hours:** Daily dawn-dusk. **Cost:** Free. **Phone:** (208) 773-0539. 🎟

RED LION TEMPLIN'S HOTEL ON THE RIVER - POST FALLS
208/773-1611

◈◈◈◈ **Hotel.** Rates not provided. **Address:** 414 E 1st Ave 83854 **Location:** Waterfront. I-90 exit 5 eastbound, just s to 1st Ave; exit 6 westbound, 0.7 mi w on Seltice Way to Spokane St, 0.5 mi s, then just e. **Facility:** 163 units. 2-3 stories, interior/exterior corridors. **Parking:** winter plug-ins. **Pool(s):** heated indoor. **Activities:** sauna, hot tub, marina, fishing, tennis, exercise room. **Guest Services:** valet and coin laundry.

🅆 🍴 ♿ 🍸 CALL Ⓜ 🏊 BIZ HS 🛜 🗙
🏠 🖼 🖥 / SOME UNITS 🆂

RIVERBEND INN   (208)773-3583

◈◈◈
Hotel
$59-$99

Address: 4100 W Riverbend Ave 83854 **Location:** I-90 exit 2, just s. **Facility:** 71 units, some efficiencies. 2 stories (no elevator), interior corridors. **Parking:** winter plug-ins. **Pool(s):** heated outdoor. **Activities:** hot tub, limited exercise equipment. **Guest Services:** valet and coin laundry. **Featured Amenity:** continental breakfast.

SAVE 🍴 🏊 🛜 🖥
/ SOME UNITS 🏠 🖼

SLEEP INN   (208)777-9394

◈◈◈ **Hotel** $48-$150 **Address:** 157 S Pleasant View Rd 83854 **Location:** I-90 exit 2, just s. **Facility:** 84 units. 2 stories (no elevator), interior corridors. **Parking:** winter plug-ins. **Pool(s):** heated indoor. **Activities:** hot tub. **Guest Services:** valet and coin laundry.

🍴 CALL Ⓜ 🏊 🛜 🗙 🖥
/ SOME UNITS 🆂 🏠 🖼

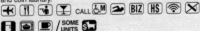

FLEUR DE SEL   208/777-7600

◈◈◈ French. Fine Dining. $9-$24 **AAA Inspector Notes:** Fleur De Sel means flower of salt and not just any salt—the salt on the tables has been hand-raked from the Mediterranean Sea. The chef/owner, Laurent, creates delectable French food that changes seasonally. Many items on the menu are modestly priced, encouraging tasting and sharing. **Features:** full bar, patio dining. **Reservations:** suggested. **Address:** 4365 Inverness Dr 83854 **Location:** I-90 exit 7 (SR 41 N), just e on E Seltice Way, just n on SR 41 N/ Ross Point Rd, just e on E Mullan Rd, then just e on Sterling Rd; in Highlands Day Spa. D CALL Ⓜ

OLD EUROPEAN RESTAURANT   208/777-2017

◈◈ European Breakfast. Family Dining. $6-$12 **AAA Inspector Notes:** Join the crowds who pile into this place at breakfast as well as other times of the day-for European comfort foods. Guests can sample tasty homemade soups and such made-from-scratch baked goods as Swedish cream-filled crepes, Danish aebleskivers (a ball-like pancake), Belgian waffles, German potato pancakes, Hungarian breakfast goulash and Irish shepherd's pie. Plentiful portions ensure that no one will leave hungry. **Address:** 1710 E Schneidmiller Ave 83854 **Location:** I-90 exit 5, just n, 1 mi e on E Seltice Way, then just ne on 5th Ave.

B L CALL Ⓜ

THE WHITE HOUSE GRILL   208/777-9672

◈◈ Mediterranean. Casual Dining. $9-$19 **AAA Inspector Notes:** Not for the faint of heart or those who worry about their breath, the restaurant is a virtual shrine to garlic. The intimate and casual setting incorporates outdoor seating when the weather permits. The primarily Mediterranean menu highlights Chilean sea bass, lamb kabobs as well as desserts that range from sweet baklava to light tiramisu. **Features:** full bar, patio dining. **Reservations:** suggested. **Address:** 712 N Spokane St 83854 **Location:** I-90 exit 5, just n.

L D

PRIEST LAKE—See Coolin p. 59.

PRIEST RIVER (B-1) pop. 1,751, elev. 2,082'

Priest River, at the junction of the Pend Oreille and Priest rivers and 30 miles south of Priest Lake via SR 57, is the gateway to the Idaho Panhandle National Forests *(see place listing p. 70)*. The Priest River Museum and Timber Education Center contains historical displays. The city hosts Priest River Timber Days in July and Oktoberfest in late September.

Priest River Chamber of Commerce: 119 Main St., Suite 102, P.O. Box 929, Priest River, ID 83856. **Phone:** (208) 448-2721.

EAGLE'S NEST MOTEL   (208)448-2000

◈ Motel $70-$149 **Address:** 5678 Hwy 2 83856 **Location:** US 2, 0.5 mi w. **Facility:** 30 units. 1 story, exterior corridors. **Terms:** cancellation fee imposed.

🍴 HS 🛜 🏠 🖼 / SOME UNITS 🆂

REXBURG (F-6) pop. 25,484, elev. 4,861'

In the late 1870s many miners heading into Montana in search of gold stopped along the west side of the Snake River and claimed land under the Homestead Act of 1862. Many of these first homesteaders were Mormons. In 1883 another influx of settlers drove their sleighs to the banks of the Snake River and established the present town site of Rexburg.

In June 1976 the nearby Teton Dam collapsed, sending 8 billion gallons of flood water into the valley below. To see the site, travel 20 miles northeast on SR 33.

Rexburg plays host to the 🐻 Idaho International SummerFest in July. The Centennial Carousel, which took 5 years to restore, is in Porter Park. Located at 2nd West 2nd South in downtown Rexburg, the park offers picnic tables; a playground; and recreational facilities for volleyball, tennis and basketball.

Rexburg Area Chamber of Commerce: 127 E. Main St., Rexburg, ID 83440. **Phone:** (208) 356-5700 or (888) 463-6880.

LEGACY FLIGHT MUSEUM, 400 Airport Rd., features a dozen operational aircraft. A working hanger displays World War II planes, including a rare P-63 Kingcobra, three P-51 Mustangs, a T-6 Texan, a Stearman, a Navy S-2 Tracker and an A-4 Skyhawk, along with aircraft used during the Vietnam and Korean wars. A small museum displays artifacts from the Civil War to present-day conflicts in the Middle East. Orientation flights are available by reservation.

Time: Allow 1 hour minimum. **Hours:** Mon.-Sat. 9-5, Memorial Day-Labor Day; Fri.-Sat. 9-5, day after Labor Day-Oct. 31 and Apr. 1-Memorial Day; Sat. 9-5 Nov. 1-Mar. 31. The Annual Air Show takes place Father's Day weekend on even-numbered years. **Cost:** $6; $5 (students, veterans and active military with ID and senior citizens); $3 (ages 8-18); $15 (family). **Phone:** (208) 359-5905. [GT]

TETON FLOOD MUSEUM is at 51 N. Center St. Photos, exhibits and videos document the 1976 break in the Teton Dam and the subsequent flooding. Other displays include pioneer relics, items related to World Wars I and II, and a children's area with changing exhibits. **Hours:** Mon.-Sat. 10-5 (also Mon. 5-7), May 1-late Sept.; Mon.-Fri. 11-5 (also Mon. 5-7), rest of year. Closed major holidays. **Cost:** $2; $1 (ages 12-18); 50c (ages 2-11). **Phone:** (208) 359-3063.

[SAVE] **YELLOWSTONE BEAR WORLD** is 7 mi. s. on US 20. From the comfort of your automobile, you'll experience up-close encounters with black and grizzly bears at this drive-through wildlife park. Elk, deer and timber wolves also roam the 120-acre grounds.

Guided curator tours and bottle-feeding tours are available. **Time:** Allow 1 hour minimum. **Hours:** Daily 9-6, Memorial Day weekend-Labor Day; 9-5,

early May-day before Memorial Day weekend and day after Labor Day to mid-Oct. **Cost:** $16.95; $15.95 (ages 65+); $10.95 (ages 3-10); $74.95 (family, per private vehicle with up to seven people). Prices may vary; phone ahead. **Phone:** (208) 359-9688. [🍴]

AMERICINN LODGE & SUITES OF REXBURG   208/356-5333

🔷🔷🔷 **Hotel.** Rates not provided. **Address:** 1098 Golden Beauty Dr 83440 **Location:** US 20 exit 332 (S Rexburg). **Facility:** 66 units. 3 stories, interior corridors. **Pool(s):** heated indoor. **Activities:** hot tub, exercise room. **Guest Services:** coin laundry.

CALL [&M] [🏊] [BIZ] [HS] [📶] [✕] [🛗] [🍴] [📺]
/SOME UNITS [🍴]

QUALITY INN   (208)359-1311

🔷🔷🔷
Hotel
$89-$160

Address: 885 W Main St 83440 **Location:** US 20 exit 333 (Salmon), just e. **Facility:** 52 units. 2 stories (no elevator), interior corridors. **Parking:** winter plug-ins. **Pool(s):** heated indoor. **Activities:** hot tub. **Guest Services:** coin laundry. **Featured Amenity:** full hot breakfast.

[SAVE] [🏊] [BIZ] [📶] [✕] [📺]
/SOME UNITS [🐾] [HS] [🛗] [🍴]

SPRINGHILL SUITES BY MARRIOTT REXBURG   (208)356-3003

🔷🔷🔷 **Hotel** $94-$209 **Address:** 1177 S Yellowstone Hwy 83440 **Location:** US 20 exit 332 (S Rexburg). **Facility:** 97 units, some two bedrooms. 4 stories, interior corridors. **Parking:** winter plug-ins. **Pool(s):** heated indoor. **Activities:** hot tub, exercise room. **Guest Services:** valet and coin laundry.

AAA Benefit: Members save 5% or more!

CALL [&M] [🏊] [BIZ] [HS] [📶] [✕] [🛗] [🍴] [📺]

WHERE TO EAT

DA PINEAPPLE GRILL   208/356-4398

🔷🔷 Hawaiian Sushi. Casual Dining. $9-$18 **AAA Inspector Notes:** Diners can see mahi mahi, teriyaki and pulled pork sandwiches along with traditional sushi on the menu at this casual spot. The owner's artistic background not only is reflected in the gorgeous murals of Hawaiian scenes that adorn the walls, but also in the signature sauces and sushi rolls on the menu. **Address:** 383 S 2nd W 83440 **Location:** US 20 exit 333 (Salmon), 1 mi e on SR 33 (Main St), then 0.6 mi s. [L] [D] CALL [&M]

FRONTIER PIES RESTAURANT & BAKERY   208/356-3600

🔷🔷 American. Family Dining. $6-$18 **AAA Inspector Notes:** No matter what you choose from the menu—sandwiches, soup or chicken-fried steak—do not budge before savoring a slice of any one of some 22 varieties of made-from-scratch pie. A recent visit afforded a quite delicious portion of strawberry pie. **Features:** early bird specials, senior menu. **Address:** 460 W 4th S 83440 **Location:** US 20 exit 332 (S Rexburg), 1 mi e. [B] [L] [D]

Trust the recommendations
of AAA/CAA travel experts
to make a good trip great

RIGBY (F-5) pop. 3,945, elev. 4,850'

JEFFERSON COUNTY HISTORICAL SOCIETY AND FARNSWORTH TV PIONEER MUSEUM, 118 West 1st South, highlights Jefferson County history and includes displays about the city's role in the birth of television. Philo Farnsworth, who conceived the world's first all-electronic television, formulated his ideas about the electronic transmission of visual images while a Rigby resident. The museum's varied collection includes vintage TV sets as well as an early barbershop, military memorabilia and a chainsaw barber. Also featured are World War I and World War II uniforms, weapons and mementos.

Time: Allow 30 minutes minimum. **Hours:** Tues.-Sat. 1-5 and by appointment. Closed major holidays. **Cost:** $2; $1 (ages 7-18). **Phone:** (208) 745-8423.

BLUE HERON INN BED & BREAKFAST   208/745-9922

▼▼▼▼ **Bed & Breakfast.** Rates not provided. **Address:** 706 N Yellowstone Hwy 83442 **Location:** US 20 exit 325, just e, then 0.4 mi ne just before railroad tracks; at end of road. **Facility:** Perfect for a romantic visit, this beautiful inn is located in a peaceful country setting with spectacular river views and offers a theater room and cozy nook for puzzles and board and card games. 7 units. 2 stories (no elevator), interior/exterior corridors. **Terms:** age restrictions may apply. **Activities:** hot tub, fishing, game room, picnic facilities, massage.

RIGGINS (E-1) pop. 419, elev. 1,800'

Riggins, where the Little Salmon pours into the main Salmon River, is a starting point for a drive north along US 95 through the scenic gorge of the Salmon River. The town is considered a white-water capital and features opportunities for white-water rafting, boating and fishing.

East of town lies the wilderness of the Payette National Forest *(see place listing p. 88)*. To the west rise the 9,000-foot Seven Devils Mountains, which form a semicircle above the Snake River's chasm, Hells Canyon; some 30 alpine lakes are clustered around the peaks. To the south is the Rapid River Fish Hatchery, one of the Northwest's most successful chinook salmon-breeding operations.

Salmon River Chamber of Commerce: P.O. Box 289, Riggins, ID 83549. **Phone:** (208) 628-3320.

RECREATIONAL ACTIVITIES

Fishing

- **River Adventures Ltd.** trips depart from various locations, including Riggins City Park on US 95. Other activities are offered. **Hours:** Trips are offered daily, Apr.-Sept. Departure times vary; phone ahead. **Phone:** (208) 628-3952 or (800) 524-9710.

White-water Rafting

- **Epley's Whitewater Adventures** is on US 95 at the n. end of town. **Hours:** Trips are offered daily, June-Sept. Departure times vary; phone ahead. **Phone:** (800) 233-1813.
- **Mountain River Outfitters** is at 411 N. Main St. (US 95). Other activities, including drift boat and jet boat fishing excursions, are offered. **Hours:**

Rafting trips are offered daily, May-Sept. Departure times vary; phone ahead. **Phone:** (208) 628-3733 or (888) 547-4837.

- **Northwest Voyageurs** is 9 mi. s. on US 95. Other activities are offered. **Hours:** Rafting trips are offered daily, late Mar. to mid-Oct. Departure times vary; phone ahead. **Phone:** (800) 233-1813.
- **Salmon River Challenge** is on US 95 at Milepost 197. Rafting trips over Class III rapids, inflatable kayaking and fishing trips are offered on the Salmon River near Riggins. **Hours:** Rafting trips available May 15-Oct. 1. Half day trips depart daily 9 and 12:30; Full day trips at 9. Multi-day camping/rafting trips available July 1-Aug. 31. **Cost:** Half-day: Adult, $65; Youth (5-17) $58.50. Full-day: Adult, $95; Youth (5-17) $84.50. Multi-day: $399. **Phone:** (208) 628-3264 or (800) 732-8574.

PINEHURST RESORT CABINS & RV   208/628-3323

▼▼ ◆ **Cabin** $65-$95 **Address:** 5604 Hwy 95 83654 **Location:** Waterfront. 12 mi s of Riggins; MM 182. Located on the Little Salmon River. **Facility:** 7 cabins. 1 story, exterior corridors. **Bath:** shower only. **Terms:** closed 12/15-1/31, cancellation fee imposed. **Activities:** fishing, picnic facilities.

SALMON RAPIDS LODGE   208/628-2743

▼▼▼▼ **Hotel.** Rates not provided. **Address:** 1010 S Main St 83549 **Location:** 0.3 mi s of center. Located on Salmon River. **Facility:** 55 units. 2 stories (no elevator), interior corridors. **Pool(s):** heated indoor. **Activities:** hot tub, fishing, limited exercise equipment. **Guest Services:** coin laundry.

WHERE TO EAT

RIVER ROCK CAFE   208/628-3434

▼▼ **American.** Casual Dining. $8-$24 **AAA Inspector Notes:** Undoubtedly popular with locals, this café is a favorite stop for patrons passing through the area. Varied menu selections include pizza, calzones, burgers, hot and cold sandwiches and a nice selection of salads. The dinner menu features pasta, steak, chicken and seafood. Boxed lunches to go are perfect for those rafting on the river, fishing, hunting or sightseeing. Blackberry cobbler is a great meal-ender. **Features:** beer & wine. **Address:** 1149 S Main St 83549 **Location:** Just s of center. ⓑ ⓛ ⓓ

SEVEN DEVILS STEAK HOUSE & SALOON   208/628-3558

▼▼ ▼▼ **American.** Casual Dining. $9-$24 **AAA Inspector Notes:** Menu items at this restaurant consist primarily of prime rib, steaks, burgers, smoked pork ribs, a popular Cornish game hen and a nice selection of appetizers. Evening specials will hit the spot for sure. Patrons can appreciate the fans on the spacious and lightly shaded outdoor patios. **Features:** full bar, patio dining, happy hour. **Address:** 312 Main St 83549 **Location:** On US 95, just s of center. **Parking:** on-site and street. ⓛ ⓓ

TWO RIVERS COFFEE   208/628-9222

▼ **Coffee/Tea Deli.** Quick Serve. $5-$7 **AAA Inspector Notes:** Whether you traveling north or south, stop here for a good cup of joe and a simple selection of baked goods, breakfast burritos, quiche and a popular chicken ranch pita. Sit a spell out front on the darling patio. **Features:** patio dining. **Address:** 616 S Main St 83549 **Location:** On US 95, just s of center. **Parking:** street only. ⓑ ⓛ

RUPERT (H-4) pop. 5,554, elev. 4,158'

Rupert was platted by the Bureau of Reclamation, which accounts for its business district being built around a square that is now a public park. Irrigation from dam projects on the Snake River has transformed the surrounding area from semiarid land to one of Idaho's principal agricultural areas. Potatoes and sugar beets are important crops.

Camping, picnicking, birding, hiking and other recreational opportunities are available in nearby Lake Walcott State Park. See Recreation Areas Chart.

MINIDOKA NATIONAL WILDLIFE REFUGE extends 20 mi. up the Snake River from Minidoka Dam; refuge headquarters is 12 mi. n.e. via SR 24 and CR 400N. As many as 100,000 waterfowl stop at the refuge as they migrate along the Pacific flyway. Some 200 species of birds plus mule deer, pronghorn antelopes and various predators inhabit the 20,721-acre refuge.

Fishing, boating and picnicking are permitted on the western end of Lake Walcott, though boating is prohibited October through April. A 1.2-mile hiking trail loop with interpretive signs is accessible via Lake Walcott State Park, 11 mi. n.e. of Rupert off SR 24. Roads are primitive. **Hours:** Refuge open daily dawn-dusk. Office open Mon.-Fri. 7-4:30. Closed major holidays. **Phone:** (208) 436-3589.

SAGLE (B-1) elev. 2,149'

BIRD AVIATION MUSEUM AND INVENTION CENTER is 12 mi. e. of US 95 on Sagle Rd., following signs to 500 Bird Ranch Rd. The museum hangar exhibits six mint-condition aircraft (1927-72) and motor vehicles from the same period. Additional displays include military uniforms, models, artwork and items from NASA.

The Imagination Room honors inventors who perfected products ranging from Kitty Litter and Barbie dolls to microprocessors and the artificial heart. An upstairs gallery displays a respiratory ventilator and an Anti-"G" Suit used by high-altitude pilots, both invented by museum co-founder Dr. Forrest Bird.

Time: Allow 1 hour minimum. **Hours:** Mon.-Sat. 8-4, mid-May to mid-Oct.; Mon.-Fri. 8-4, rest of year. Closed Jan. 1, Easter, Thanksgiving, Christmas and Dec. 31. **Cost:** Donations. **Phone:** (208) 255-4321.
🍴

THE LODGE AT SANDPOINT

Hotel
$139-$519

(208)263-2211

Address: 41 Lakeshore Dr 83860 **Location:** Waterfront. 1 mi s of Sandpoint on US 95; just s of Long Bridge. **Facility:** 33 units, some cabins. 4 stories, interior corridors. **Terms:** check-in 4 pm, 2 night minimum stay - seasonal and/or weekends, 14 day cancellation notice-fee imposed. **Dining:** 2 restaurants. **Activities:** hot tub, limited beach access, boat dock, fishing, bicycles, exercise room. **Guest Services:** valet laundry.

SAVE 🍴 🍽 🛜 ✕ 🛗 💻
/ SOME UNITS 🛢 HS 📺

ST. CHARLES (H-6) pop. 131, elev. 5,944'

This small town near the northwest corner of Bear Lake was the birthplace of Gutzon Borglum (1867-1941), the artist and sculptor who carved the Mount Rushmore National Memorial in South Dakota.

Bear Lake straddles the Idaho-Utah border south and east of St. Charles. Known as the "Caribbean of the Rockies" for its turquoise hue, the result of soluble microscopic carbonates suspended in the water, the 120-square-mile lake is popular with fishermen seeking cutthroat trout, sculpin and whitefish. In winter anglers use nets to catch the Bonneville cisco, a species of fish endemic to the lake.

Bear Lake National Wildlife Refuge, a 19,000 acre tract of wetlands north of Bear Lake, provides habitat for migratory birds and small mammals. Bear Lake State Park (see Recreation Areas Chart), just e. of St. Charles at 5637 E. Shore Rd., has two units. The North Beach unit has a boat launch and a 2-mile-long shorefront; the East Beach unit, with its 1.5-mile-long beach, offers a campground. Phone (208) 945-2325.

MINNETONKA CAVE is s.w. via US 89 to St. Charles, then 10 mi. w. to the head of St. Charles Canyon. The cave, 7,700 feet above sea level, contains nine rooms of stalactites, stalagmites and banded travertine originally discovered by grouse hunters. **Note:** The temperature is a constant 40 F; jackets are recommended. The tour involves climbing 444 steps. **Hours:** Guided 1.25-hour tours are given daily on the half-hour 10-5:30, early June-Labor Day (weather permitting). Last tour begins at closing. **Cost:** $8; $6 (ages 6-15); $32 (family). **Phone:** (435) 245-4422.

SALMON (E-4) pop. 3,112, elev. 4,040'
• Hotels p. 96 • Restaurants p. 96

Once the winter campsite of fur trappers, including Jim Bridger and Kit Carson, Salmon is at the fork of the Salmon and Lemhi rivers near the edge of the Salmon Valley, a prosperous livestock and mining area. Permanent settlement of this region began with the discovery of gold in 1866. The town is a favorite starting point for pack trips into the Frank Church-River of No Return Wilderness and for float trips down the Salmon River and its wildest branch, the Middle Fork.

Salmon lies on a scenic section of US 93, which heads north to the Montana border and southwest toward Sawtooth National Forest (see place listing p. 98).

Visit Salmon Valley: 803 Monroe St., Salmon ID, 83467. **Phone:** (208) 756-1505.

LEMHI COUNTY HISTORICAL MUSEUM, 210 Main St., exhibits the largest collection of Lemhi Shoshone (or, Agaideka, the people of Sacagawea) artifacts in the world. Also featured are interpretive exhibits portraying life in the American West, the Ray Edwards Asian Collection and a rotating veterans' photo exhibit. **Hours:** Mon.-Fri. 10-5, Sat. 11-3, May-Oct.; Wed. 11-4, rest of year. Closed major holidays. Phone ahead to confirm schedule. **Cost:** $2; free (ages 0-11). **Phone:** (208) 756-3342.

SACAJAWEA INTERPRETIVE, CULTURAL AND EDUCATIONAL CENTER, 1 mi. e. on SR 28 (Main St.), is in the Lemhi River Valley, the homeland of the Agaidika Shoshone and Sacajawea (Sacagawea). The 71-acre park commemorates Sacajawea's role in the Lewis and Clark expedition and features an interpretive center with exhibits, demonstrations, outdoor art pieces and a 1-mile interpretive trail with a tipi and fishing weir exhibits.

Time: Allow 1 hour minimum. **Hours:** Trails daily dawn-dusk. Interpretive center Mon.-Sat. 9-5, Sun. 12:30-5, Memorial Day-Labor Day. **Cost:** $5; $12 (family). **Phone:** (208) 756-1188. 🎫

RECREATIONAL ACTIVITIES

White-water Rafting

- **Idaho Adventures** trips traverse the Salmon River. Other activities are offered, including steelhead fishing. **Hours:** Rafting trips are offered Mar.-Nov. Schedule varies; phone ahead. **Phone:** (208) 756-2986 or (800) 789-9283.

- **Kookaburra Rafting Trips** is at 1115 US 93S. Other activities are offered, including fishing. **Hours:** One-day rafting trips are offered daily, Apr.-Sept. Three-day rafting trips also are offered May-Sept. Schedules vary; phone ahead. **Phone:** (208) 756-4386 or (888) 654-4386.

- **Rawhide Outfitters** offers day and multi-day trips on the Salmon River. Other activities are offered, including scenic float, fishing and horseback riding excursions. **Hours:** Rafting trips are offered Sun.-Fri., May-Oct. Departure times vary; phone ahead. **Phone:** (208) 756-4276.

STAGECOACH INN   208/756-2919

♦♦ ♦♦ **Hotel.** Rates not provided. **Address:** 201 Riverfront Dr (US 93 N) 83467 **Location:** Waterfront. Jct US 93 and SR 28, just n. **Facility:** 101 units, some kitchens. 2 stories, interior corridors. **Parking:** winter plug-ins. **Pool(s):** heated outdoor. **Activities:** hot tub, fishing, picnic facilities. **Guest Services:** coin laundry, area transportation.

⊞ 🛈 CALL &M 🛬 BIZ 📶 ✉ 💬

/ SOME UNITS 🐾 🛏 📷

WHERE TO EAT

BERTRAM'S BREWERY & RESTAURANT   208/756-3391

♦♦ ♦♦ American. Casual Dining. $9-$25 **AAA Inspector Notes:** After a day of recreational activities, this is an ideal spot for some pub grub and ice cold hand-crafted brews. Food favorites include the drunken mussels marinated in ale, fish tacos and the belly buster double burger. Consider finishing up with a delicious slice of lemon meringue or pecan pie. **Features:** beer & wine, Sunday brunch. **Address:** 101 S Andrews St 83467 **Location:** At Main and S Andrews St. **Parking:** street only. L D CALL &M

JUNKYARD BISTRO   208/756-2466

♦♦ ♦♦ American. Casual Dining. $8-$13 **AAA Inspector Notes:** This funky, off-the-beaten path bistro offers a wide variety of menu selections including a yummy pork and seeds platter, Vietnamese pork sandwich, a popular grilled cheese sandwich with spinach, Asian and chicken fajita salads, create-your-own pasta dishes, habit-forming rice and noodle bowls and creative seasonal soups. **Features:** beer & wine, patio dining. **Address:** 405 Main St 83467 **Location:** Jct Main and S St Charles sts. **Parking:** street only. L D CALL &M

SHADY NOOK RESTAURANT   208/756-4182

American Casual Dining $10-$28

AAA Inspector Notes: Experience the lovely atmosphere at this local landmark restaurant. Menu items include a variety of juicy charbroiled steaks, Alaskan king crab legs, steamer clams and mussels, killer nachos, popular snack baskets and specialty burgers. Enjoy watching the Salmon River while dining on the patio during the summer. Nightly specials and desserts made locally are sure to delight. **Features:** full bar, patio dining, happy hour. **Reservations:** suggested, in summer. **Address:** 501 Riverfront Dr (US 93 N) 83467 **Location:** Jct US 93 and SR 28, just n. D

SALMON-CHALLIS NATIONAL FOREST
(E-3)

Elevations in the forest range from 2,200 ft. in the lower canyon of the Salmon River to 12,662 ft. at Borah Peak. Refer to AAA maps for additional elevation information.

From the headwaters of the Salmon River, down the Lost River, Pahsimeroi and Lemhi Mountain Ranges, to the western slope of the Continental Divide, the Salmon-Challis National Forest covers 4.3 million acres. Over 300,000 acres are in the Frank Church-River of No Return Wilderness (see Payette National Forest p. 88).

The historic Lewis and Clark Trail passes through part of the forest, where several monuments to the explorers have been erected. The Custer Motorway Loop and Salmon River Road provide glimpses of historic mining towns and native wildlife.

Because of swift currents the Salmon River west of Salmon is known as the "River of No Return." Now, however, it is possible to navigate this river upstream via jet boats. Boat trips down the river can be arranged in Salmon (see place listing).

More than 2,800 miles of trail stripe the forest floor. Hiking season is generally between April and October; hunting, fishing, camping and wildlife viewing also are excellent.

The section of the river between Corn Creek and Riggins can be traveled by kayaks, jet boats or rubber rafts. Skiing is available nearby on the Idaho-Montana border at Lost Trail Pass. For more information write the Salmon-Challis National Forest Headquarters, 1206 S. Challis St., Salmon, ID 83467; phone (208) 756-5100. *See Recreation Areas Chart.*

SANDPOINT (B-1) pop. 7,365, elev. 2,086'
• Restaurants p. 98

Sandpoint, at the north end of Lake Pend Oreille, is a year-round resort town and artists' community that offers a wide variety of land- and water-based recreational opportunities. Park facilities at City Beach, west of First Avenue via Bridge Street, include beaches, two marinas, a boat launch and a pedestrian bridge over Sand Creek that links the park with downtown. Lake Pend Oreille Cruises offers a variety of tours; phone (208) 255-5253.

One of the West's great railroad towns, Sandpoint is known as "The Funnel" for the major rail lines that converge here. More than 50 trains a day draw rail fans to the city. A brochure "A Rail Fan's Guide to Sandpoint, Idaho" is available from the chamber of commerce.

Greater Sandpoint Chamber of Commerce: 1202 Fifth Ave., P.O. Box 928, Sandpoint, ID 83864. **Phone:** (208) 263-0887 or (800) 800-2106.

Shopping: One of downtown Sandpoint's focal points is the Cedar Street Bridge Public Market. Formerly a city bridge over Sand Creek, this renovated two-level structure is patterned after the famed Ponte Vecchio bridge in Florence, Italy, and contains two levels of restaurants and shops.

BONNER COUNTY HISTORICAL MUSEUM, 611 S. Ella Ave. in Lakeview Park, uses pioneer relics and other exhibits to chronicle the history of the county, with emphasis on the Kalispel Indians, the local timber industry, and steamboat and railroad transportation. The grounds feature an arboretum with indigenous plants. **Time:** Allow 30 minutes minimum. **Hours:** Tues.-Fri. 10-4, first Sat. of the month 10-2. Closed major holidays. **Cost:** $4; $3 (ages 65+); $1 (ages 6-18); free on first Sat. **Phone:** (208) 263-2344.

INTERNATIONAL SELKIRK LOOP is a 280-mile National Scenic Byway in northern Idaho, northeastern Washington and adjoining British Columbia. Starting at Sandpoint the 89-mile Idaho segment follows US 2 west to the Washington border at Oldtown. North from Sandpoint the byway takes US 2/95 to Bonners Ferry, then US 95 and SR 1 to the Canadian border at Porthill.

West from Sandpoint the loop follows the Pend Oreille (pond-ah-RAY) River, which drains Lake Pend Oreille. Several recreation sites offer access to the river, and there are numerous roadside pullouts. At Priest River, SR 57 runs 30 miles north to jewel-like Priest Lake, a paradise for kayaking, canoeing and fishing set amid cedars and pines in the heart of the Selkirks. Public campgrounds and lodging options are numerous.

North of Sandpoint the route runs along the Purcell Trench, a long, narrow trough between the Selkirk, Cabinet and Purcell Mountains. The trench is a natural funnel for migratory birds. Between Bonners Ferry and Priest Lake, the Selkirks are a rugged wilderness with peaks in excess of 7,000 feet. The Kootenai National Wildlife Refuge, 5 miles west of Bonners Ferry, offers a 4-mile auto-tour route and numerous hiking trails.

Chambers of commerce and visitor centers along the loop provide maps and information. Visitors also can order a free copy of the visitor travel guide online or write to International Selkirk Loop, P.O. Box 920, Bonners Ferry, ID 83805. **Phone:** (208) 267-0822 or (888) 823-2626.

LAKE PEND OREILLE, s. and e. of town, was formed by glaciers and is encircled by lofty mountain peaks. At 43 miles long, Lake Pend Oreille (pond-ah-RAY) is one of the largest freshwater lakes in the Pacific Northwest. Swimming, boating and hiking are popular. Noted for its scenic coves and 1,150-foot depth, the lake is stocked with Kamloops rainbow trout. A special fishing season runs from early May to late November. *See Recreation Areas Chart.*

Facilities for other types of recreation are found at Clark Fork *(see place listing p. 55)*, Athol *(see place listing p. 34)* and numerous lakeside communities. **Time:** Allow a full day. **Phone:** (208) 263-2161 or (800) 800-2106.

RECREATIONAL ACTIVITIES
Horseback Riding
- **Mountain Horse Adventures** is at 10000 Schweitzer Mountain Rd. **Hours:** Horseback riding trips lasting 2.5 hours depart daily at 9 and 1, May 1 to mid-Oct. Under 8 are not permitted. **Cost:** Reservations are recommended. **Phone:** (208) 263-8768.

Skiing
- **Schweitzer Mountain Resort** is 11 mi. n. via US 2/95 at 10000 Schweitzer Mountain Rd. **Hours:** Daily 9-3:30, late Nov.-early Apr. (also Fri.-Sat. 3:30-7, Jan.-early Mar.). **Phone:** (208) 263-9555, (208) 263-9562 for a recorded snow report or (877) 487-4643.

WINERIES
- **Pend d'Oreille Winery** is at 301 Cedar St. Guided tours are available. **Hours:** Daily 11-9. Closed Jan. 1, Thanksgiving and Christmas. **Phone:** (208) 265-8545 or (877) 452-9011.

BEST WESTERN EDGEWATER RESORT (208)263-3194

Hotel
$90-$240

AAA Benefit: Save 10% or more every day and earn 10% bonus points!

Address: 56 Bridge St 83864 **Location:** Just e of US 95; downtown. **Facility:** 54 units. 2-3 stories (no elevator), interior corridors. **Dining:** Trinity at City Beach, see separate listing. **Pool(s):** heated indoor. **Activities:** sauna, hot tub, limited beach access, boat dock, fishing, exercise room.

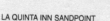

LA QUINTA INN SANDPOINT (208)263-9581

Hotel $64-$317 **Address:** 415 Cedar St 83864 **Location:** Jct US 2 and 95; downtown. **Facility:** 68 units, some efficiencies. 2-3 stories, interior/exterior corridors. **Pool(s):** heated outdoor. **Activities:** hot tub, exercise room. **Guest Services:** coin laundry.

QUALITY INN SANDPOINT (208)263-2111

Hotel $59-$199 **Address:** 807 N 5th Ave 83864 **Location:** US 2 and 95, just s of jct SR 200. **Facility:** 62 units. 2 stories (no elevator), interior corridors. **Pool(s):** heated indoor. **Activities:** hot tub. **Guest Services:** coin laundry.

SELKIRK LODGE AT SCHWEITZER MOUNTAIN RESORT
(208)265-0257

▼▼▼ **Resort Hotel** $117-$605 **Address:** 10000 Schweitzer Mountain Rd 83864 **Location:** 2 mi n on US 95, 10 mi w, follow signs. **Facility:** A combination of European and Northern Idaho influences combine to create a unique décor. This hotel condominium property is ideally located near the ski slopes. 69 units, some condominiums. 4 stories, interior corridors. **Terms:** check-in 4 pm, 14 day cancellation notice, resort fee. **Dining:** 2 restaurants. **Pool(s):** heated outdoor. **Activities:** hot tub, tennis, downhill & cross country skiing, snowmobiling, sledding, recreation programs in season, bicycles, exercise room, massage. **Guest Services:** coin laundry.

🍽 🍸 🏊 BIZ 🛜 ✖ 🖥 / SOME UNITS 🔒 📷

WHITE PINE LODGE AT SCHWEITZER MOUNTAIN RESORT
208/265-0257

▼▼▼ **Condominium** $169-$1078 **Address:** 145 Village Ln 83864 **Location:** 2 mi n on US 95, 10 mi w, follow signs. **Facility:** A modern yet mountain-influenced design creates a warm, inviting ambiance throughout this condo-style hotel. This is a popular resort for ski enthusiasts due to its convenient location to lifts. 25 condominiums. 5 stories, interior corridors. **Terms:** check-in 4 pm, 14 day cancellation notice, resort fee. **Activities:** hot tub, tennis, downhill skiing, snowboarding, recreation programs in season, exercise room. **Guest Services:** complimentary laundry.

🍽 🍸 BIZ 🛜 ✖ 🔒 📷 🖥

WHERE TO EAT

HYDRA STEAKHOUSE   208/263-7123

▼▼ American. Casual Dining. $9-$34 **AAA Inspector Notes:** Dinners feature prime rib, steak, seafood specialties and creative pasta dishes served in a casual atmosphere. This comfortable, intimate eatery boasts a pleasant décor of stained glass, natural wood and greenery. **Features:** full bar, patio dining. **Address:** 115 Lake St 83864 **Location:** Just w of US 95 at 2nd and Lake sts; center.

[L] [D]

IVANO'S RISTORANTE & CAFFE   208/263-0211

▼▼▼ Regional Italian. Fine Dining. $9-$30 **AAA Inspector Notes:** Italian cuisine is served in comfortable, casual surroundings enhanced by distinctive artwork and oak accents. Pasta, veal, chicken, beef and seafood all make a good showing, but it's the chocolate mousse that wins rave reviews. Seasonal outdoor seating is an option at the busy downtown location. **Features:** full bar, patio dining. **Address:** 102 S 1st Ave 83864 **Location:** Downtown.

[L] [D]

JALAPENOS   208/263-2995

▼▼ Mexican. Casual Dining. $10-$15 **AAA Inspector Notes:** Colorful, hand-painted murals and large, potted plants give this restaurant a tropical feel. Friendly service, good food and specialty drinks make it a favorite of tourists and locals alike. Patio seating is available, weather permitting. **Features:** full bar, patio dining, happy hour. **Address:** 314 N 2nd Ave 83864 **Location:** Downtown. **Parking:** street only. [L] [D]

LITTLE OLIVE   208/597-7499

▼▼ Mediterranean. Casual Dining. $12-$32 **AAA Inspector Notes:** The chef here focuses on Mediterranean-influenced delectables including lamb kebabs, gyros and hummus. **Features:** beer & wine, patio dining. **Address:** 124 S 2nd Ave 83864 **Location:** Jct Lake St; center. **Parking:** street only. [L] [D]

PIE HUT SANDWICH SHOP   208/265-2208

▼ American Desserts. Quick Serve. $6-$12 **AAA Inspector Notes:** Two pie cases at this spot are overflowing with cream pies, fruit pies and quiches. Order chicken pot pie or, as the locals do, get a family size one to go. The owner, Heather, offers an ever-changing sandwich menu and daily soups to go with the pie. **Address:** 502 Church St 83864 **Location:** Just w of US 2; downtown.

[L] [D]

TRINITY AT CITY BEACH   208/255-7558

▼▼ American. Family Dining. $8-$35 **AAA Inspector Notes:** Seating at this eatery is available on the patio overlooking Sand Creek or in the quietly elegant dining room. Dinner can be pork tenderloin stuffed with huckleberries or, my favorite, Idaho ruby trout. Lunch is all about sandwiches and tasty soups. **Features:** full bar, patio dining. **Address:** 56 Bridge St 83864 **Location:** Just e of US 95 N; downtown; in BEST WESTERN PLUS Edgewater Resort.

[B] [L] [D]

SAWTOOTH NATIONAL FOREST (F-3)

Elevations in the forest range from 4,514 ft. at Rock Creek Drain to 12,009 ft. at Hyndman Peak. Refer to AAA maps for additional elevation information.

In south-central Idaho, the Sawtooth National Forest embraces approximately 2.1 million acres. Offering a wide range of recreational opportunities and spectacular scenery, the forest consists of a northern division containing the Sawtooth National Recreation Area and a southern division along the Nevada and Utah borders.

Adjacent to Sun Valley *(see place listing p. 100)*, the northern division is bisected by the Sawtooth Scenic Byway (SR 75) and provides hundreds of miles of hiking and horseback-riding trails in the Smoky, Pioneer, Sawtooth, Boulder and White Cloud mountains. The Baumgartner Nature Trail, near Baumgartner Campground in the Fairfield District, is a popular hiking area.

The southern division contains the Rock Creek Canyon, Howell Canyon, Black Pine, Raft River and Sublett areas. Alpine and cross-country skiing as well as snowmobiling are available in areas near Twin Falls *(see place listing p. 101)*, Burley *(see place listing p. 52)*, Fairfield and Sun Valley *(see place listing p. 100)*.

Information about campgrounds and recreational opportunities is available at the forest supervisor's office in Twin Falls and the district ranger stations. For further information write Sawtooth National Forest, 2647 Kimberly Rd. E., Twin Falls, ID 83301; phone (208) 737-3200. *See Recreation Areas Chart.*

SAWTOOTH NATIONAL RECREATION AREA (F-3)

In south-central Idaho, the Sawtooth National Recreation Area comprises 756,000 acres of the northern division of the Sawtooth National Forest. The recreation area features three mountain ranges of peaks exceeding 11,000 feet, deep forests and high mountain lakes. The recreation area includes the Sawtooth Wilderness, the White Cloud-Boulder Mountains, portions of the Smokey Mountains, the Salmon River and five major lakes. The backcountry has 750 miles of hiking trails and more than 300 lakes.

Nature trails in the forest include the Fishhook Creek Nature Trail, adjacent to Redfish Lake Visitor Center, and the Wood River Adventure Trail, bordering the Wood River Campground.

The Stanley Ranger Station is open Mon.-Fri. 8:30-4:30. A visitor center on the northern shore of Redfish Lake, 5 miles south of Stanley on SR 75, is open daily 10-5, mid-June to mid-Sept. The North Fork visitor center and national recreation area headquarters is open Mon.-Fri. 8:30-5 (also Sat., Memorial Day-late Dec.).

A free audio tour explaining the area's history and features can be borrowed at the Sawtooth National Recreation Area headquarters, Stanley Ranger Station or the Ketchum Ranger District. For more information write Sawtooth National Recreation Headquarters, 5 North Fork Canyon Rd., Ketchum, ID 83340; phone (208) 727-5000 for headquarters, (208) 774-3000 for the Stanley Ranger Station or (208) 774-3376 for the Redfish Lake Visitors Center. *See Recreation Areas Chart.*

SHOSHONE (G-3) pop. 1,461, elev. 3,968'

Shoshone, in an irrigated farming belt and sheep-raising area, was settled in 1882. Many buildings, including the Community Methodist Church at Apple and C streets, are made from local dark, porous lava rock.

SHOSHONE INDIAN ICE CAVES, 17 mi. n. on SR 75, are caves of ice that maintain a temperature of 18 to 28 F, while a few feet away on the surface the thermometer might register more than 100. Visitors should wear sturdy shoes and a coat. The 3/4-mile tour includes 100 feet of stairs. A museum features collections of gems, minerals and rocks. **Time:** Allow 1 hour minimum. **Hours:** Tour schedule varies; phone ahead. **Cost:** $10; $8 (ages 62+ and military); $6 (ages 4-12). Prices may vary. **Phone:** (208) 886-2058.

SILVER CITY (G-1) elev. 6,179'

Silver City, high in the Owyhee Mountains of southwestern Idaho, became an important gold and silver mining center after prospectors struck it rich near the headwaters of Jordan Creek in 1862. A 500-pound solid silver crystal from the nearby Poorman mine on War Eagle Mountain won a prize at the 1866 exposition in Paris.

Mining remained a force until 1912, then continued sporadically through the 1930s. In its heyday Silver City boasted a courthouse, hotels, Idaho's first daily newspaper and a population of 3,000. By 1920 its population had fallen to 100.

A walk down Silver City's unpaved streets is a living-history tour. Some 75 buildings remain of this once boisterous mining town. The 1892 schoolhouse and drugstore are now museums. On the knoll near the school is Our Lady of Tears Catholic Church. The 20-bedroom Idaho Hotel, which is also a museum, dominates Main Street and was once the finest in the territory. Several historic cemeteries are in the community.

Note: The 21-mile road leading to Silver City from SR 78 south of Murphy is paved for only the first 8 miles (the rest is graveled) and is not recommended for oversize vehicles. The road is not maintained in winter and is normally closed early October to late May. Phone (208) 583-4104 (Idaho Hotel) or write P.O. Box 75, Murphy, ID 83650-0075, for weather and road conditions.

The first 8 miles of the 25-mile road leading west from Silver City to Jordan Valley, Ore., are rough, winding and narrow. There are no automobile service facilities in the vicinity.

SODA SPRINGS (H-6) pop. 3,058, elev. 5,777'

Since pioneer days Soda Springs has been known for its 30 mineral salt springs. Early trappers called Hooper Spring, a mile north of town, "Beer Spring" because of its natural soda water, which visitors can sample today.

Nearby Captive Geyser is a carbon dioxide geyser controlled to erupt hourly, winds permitting. Foot-deep wagon ruts from the Old Oregon Trail that date from the mid-1800s provide an unusual hazard on the local golf course. The Pioneer Museum downtown displays mementos reflecting area history.

Soda Springs Chamber of Commerce: 9 West 2nd South, City Hall, Soda Springs, ID 83276. **Phone:** (208) 547-2600.

SPALDING (D-1) elev. 840'

Catholic, Protestant and Mormon missionaries occupied much of central Idaho during the mid- and late 1800s in an attempt to convert the Native Americans. Spalding, now within the boundaries of the Nez Perce National Historical Park *(see place listing p. 86)*, is named for the Rev. Henry H. Spalding, who built a mission near the present town of Lapwai *(see place listing p. 76)* in 1836.

Two years later he moved the mission 2 miles north to the Clearwater River, where the headquarters of the Nez Perce National Historical Park is today.

Several geologic formations near Spalding have significance in Nez Perce tradition. Coyote's Fishnet, about 4 miles west, is a formation on the bluffs of the Clearwater River's south shore. A talus slope known as The Bear is high on the north side of the river. Ant and Yellowjacket is a rock arch 1.5 miles west off US 12 just before its junction with US 95.

Idaho's first homestead, the Craig Donation Land Claim, is about 8 miles south along US 95. In 1840 mountain man William Craig settled on 630 acres given to him by the Nez Perce. He is buried in the nearby town of Jacques. St. Joseph's Mission, 4 miles south of Jacques in the village of Slickpoo, was dedicated in 1874 and was the first Catholic church in Nez Perce country.

NEZ PERCE NATIONAL HISTORICAL PARK VISITOR CENTER, on US 95, contains exhibits and audiovisual programs about Nez Perce culture. Area history also is chronicled. A park folder is available for a self-guiding driving tour of the 38 sites included in the park. **Time:** Allow 30 minutes minimum. **Hours:** Daily 8-5, Memorial Day weekend-Labor Day; 8-4:30, mid-Mar. through day before Memorial Day weekend and day after Labor Day to mid-Nov.; 9-4, rest of year. Ranger-led programs are offered daily, Memorial Day-Labor Day. Closed Jan. 1, Thanksgiving and Christmas. **Cost:** Free. **Phone:** (208) 843-7009.

SPALDING SITE, .2 mi. e., is the location of the second mission built by the Rev. Henry H. Spalding and his wife in 1838. The Presbyterian mission included the territory's first printing press, sawmill and gristmill; it was later used as Indian Agency headquarters. The Spaldings and many Nez Perce are buried in the Spalding Mission Cemetery. The Spaldings' first homesite, 2 miles south at Thunder Hill, was built in 1836, the year they arrived in the Northwest. **Time:** Allow 30 minutes minimum.

STANLEY (F-3) pop. 63, elev. 6,260'

On the Salmon River (the "River of No Return"), Stanley is within the Sawtooth National Recreation Area *(see place listing p. 98)*, Sawtooth Valley and the spectacular Sawtooth Basin. Most float trips on the Middle Fork of the Salmon River and the main Salmon River are outfitted at this site. The town lies on two exceptionally scenic highways, SRs 21 and 75.

The Ponderosa Pine Scenic Byway (SR 21) passes through part of the Sawtooth National Forest *(see place listing p. 98)* and ends in Boise; motorists should check for possible temporary closures due to snow. The northeastern segment of SR 75, the Salmon River Scenic Byway, passes through the Sawtooth National Recreation Area and then merges with US 93. The southeastern segment of SR 75, the Sawtooth Scenic Byway, heads south toward Twin Falls and Sun Valley.

Stanley-Sawtooth Chamber of Commerce: P.O. Box 8, Stanley, ID 83278. **Phone:** (208) 774-3411 or (800) 878-7950.

SAWTOOTH FISH HATCHERY, 5 mi. s. on SR 75, is used for trapping and holding spring chinook salmon and steelhead trout. The hatchery produces chinook and collects steelhead eggs for later transport to the Hagerman and Magic Valley hatcheries. The fish trap is emptied daily at 9 a.m. in fall during chinook season, and Monday and Thursday during spring steelhead season. An observation deck is on the premises. **Hours:** Visitor center daily 8-5. Guided 45-minute tours departing from the visitor center are given daily beginning at 1:30, Memorial Day weekend-Labor Day. **Cost:** Free. **Phone:** (208) 774-3684.

RECREATIONAL ACTIVITIES

Horseback Riding

- **Mystic Saddle Ranch** is on SR 75 in the Sawtooth National Recreation Area. **Hours:** Trips are offered daily, June-Sept. Departure times vary; phone ahead. **Phone:** (208) 774-3591.

- **Pioneer Outfitters** is 9 mi. s. on SR 75 at the Idaho Rocky Mountain Ranch. **Hours:** Departure days and times vary; phone ahead. **Phone:** (208) 774-3737 June-Oct., or (208) 308-1770 rest of year.

- **Redfish Lake Corrals-Trail Rides** is off SR 21. **Hours:** Trips are offered daily 9-3, Memorial Day to mid-Sept. **Phone:** (208) 774-3311.

White-water Rafting

- **Middle Fork River Expeditions** offers trips on the Middle Fork of the Salmon River and the main Salmon River near Sun Valley. Other activities are offered. **Hours:** Four-, 6- and 10-day rafting trips are offered June-Sept. Schedule varies; phone ahead. **Phone:** (800) 801-5146.

- **The River Co.** is .7 mi. w. on SR 21. Other activities are offered. **Hours:** Day rafting trips are offered mid-May to early Sept. Schedule varies; phone ahead. **Phone:** (208) 788-5775 or (800) 398-0346.

- **Rocky Mountain River Tours** offers trips on the Salmon River (Middle Fork and main sections). **Hours:** Four- to 6-day trips are offered mid-May to mid-Sept. Schedule varies; phone ahead. **Phone:** (208) 345-2400.

- **ROW Adventures** offers trips on the Middle Fork of the Salmon River. Other activities are offered. **Hours:** One- to 6-day rafting trips are offered mid-May to mid-Sept. Schedule varies; phone ahead. **Phone:** (208) 765-0841 or (800) 451-6034.

- **Sawtooth Adventure Co.** is 1 mi. n. on US 75. Other activities are offered. **Hours:** Trips are offered May 20-Sept. 15. Schedule varies; phone ahead. **Phone:** (866) 774-4644.

- **White Cloud Rafting Adventures** is at jct. US 75 and SR 21. **Hours:** Half- and full-day trips are offered daily, late May-early Sept. Schedule varies; phone ahead. **Phone:** (800) 571-7238.

POT BELLY CAFE   208/774-2202

◆◆◆ American. Casual Dining. $7-$18 **AAA** Inspector **Notes:** Housed in a converted barn, this rustic little eatery serves comfort foods such as barbecue ribs, prime rib, burgers and camp beans made in cast iron. Order the berry blast pie first, before it runs out. **Features:** beer & wine, patio dining. **Address:** 12655 SR 21 83278 **Location:** Jct SR 75, 4.2 mi w; Milepost 126.5.

B L D *AC*

STANLEY BAKING CO. & CAFE   208/774-6573

◆◆ Sandwiches Soup. Casual Dining. $7-$10 **AAA Inspector Notes:** It will only take one visit and travelers always will plan their trip around a mandatory stop here for breakfast or lunch. The creative menu features beautifully presented soups, salads and delicious sandwiches. Scones, cinnamon rolls, sticky buns, croissants, muffins, coffee cake and cookies are baked fresh daily and a full tea and espresso menu is available. **Features:** beer & wine, patio dining, Sunday brunch. **Address:** 250 Wall St 83278 **Location:** 0.3 mi w of jct SR 21 and 75 to Wall St, just s. B L *AC*

SUN VALLEY (F-3) pop. 1,406, elev. 5,926'

Sun Valley got its start in 1935 when Union Pacific Railroad Chairman Averell Harriman hired Austrian Count Felix Shaffgotsch to find the most scenic snow spot in the country for a huge ski resort. Passing up places that would become Aspen,

Jackson Hole and Mount Hood, Shaffgotsch chose Sun Valley. Soon stars from all across the country came to ski down Dollar Mountain (chairlifts were not installed on 9,150-foot-tall Bald Mountain until Sun Valley's fourth operating season) and hobnob in the huge lodge Harriman built. Gary Cooper and Clark Gable were frequent visitors; novelist Ernest Hemingway spent his last years in the area, and a memorial to him stands alongside Trail Creek.

Today nearly a quarter-million persons visit the area, which somehow still manages to maintain an uncrowded, non-tourist atmosphere. Sun Valley, along with the neighboring town of Ketchum (*see place listing p. 73*), offers heated outdoor pools, saunas and indoor and outdoor ice-skating rinks. The list of local summer activities includes golf, tennis, swimming, white-water rafting, camping, bicycling, hiking, horseback riding, skeet shooting, trapshooting, fishing, mountaineering and kayaking. Offering respite from the great outdoors, The Sun Valley Pavilion, 1 Sun Valley Rd., hosts the Sun Valley Summer Symphony for 3 weeks in July and August. Admission is free; phone (208) 622-2135 for the pavilion, (208) 622-5607 for the symphony, or (888) 622-2108 for the schedule.

Winter brings sleigh rides, snowmobiling and ice-skating as well as downhill, cross-country and helicopter skiing. Saturday nights are reserved for hockey games in winter and professional ice shows in summer. Skiing begins on Thanksgiving.

RECREATIONAL ACTIVITIES
Horseback Riding
- **Sun Valley Stables** is off Sun Valley Rd., just n. of the Sun Valley Resort. Other activities are offered. **Hours:** One-hour and 90-minute trips are offered daily 9-4, early June-late Sept. Phone ahead to confirm schedule. **Phone:** (208) 622-2391 for reservations.

Skiing
- **Bald Mountain** is off SR 75; take Serenade Ln. w. to 3rd Ave., then s. to River Run Access. **Hours:** Daily 9-4, Thanksgiving to mid-Apr. (weather permitting). **Phone:** (208) 622-6136.

- **Dollar Mountain** is adjacent to Sun Valley. **Hours:** Daily 9-4, late Nov.-early Apr. (weather permitting). **Phone:** (208) 622-2245 or (208) 622-6136.

SUN VALLEY LODGE & SUN VALLEY INN   208/622-4111

▼▼▼ ▼▼▼ **Resort Hotel.** Rates not provided. **Address:** 1 Sun Valley Rd 83353 **Location:** 1.2 mi ne of Main St (SR 75) and Sun Valley Rd. **Facility:** On manicured grounds with a swan pond at the entrance, this property's lobby overlooks a world-renowned ice skating rink. Elegant guest rooms and spa-quality bathrooms make this a must-see resort. 440 units, some two bedrooms, three bedrooms, kitchens, cottages and condominiums. 1-4 stories, interior corridors. **Parking:** on-site and valet, winter plug-ins. **Terms:** check-in 4 pm. **Amenities:** safes. **Dining:** 4 restaurants, also, Gretchen's, see separate listing, entertainment. **Pool(s):** heated outdoor. **Activities:** sauna, hot tub, fishing, regulation golf, tennis, downhill & cross country skiing, snowmobiling, snowboarding, sledding, ice skating, recreation programs, bicycles, playground, game room, picnic facilities, trails, exercise room, spa. **Guest Services:** valet and coin laundry, area transportation.

[icons]

WHERE TO EAT

GRETCHEN'S   208/622-4111

[fyi] American. Casual Dining. $9-$22 Under major renovation, scheduled to be completed June 2015. **Last rated:** ▼▼▼ AAA **Inspector Notes:** This restaurant features a nice selection of game, pasta dishes, seafood and freshly baked desserts. **Features:** full bar. **Reservations:** suggested. **Address:** 1 Sun Valley Rd 83353 **Location:** 1.2 mi ne of Main St (SR 75) and Sun Valley Rd; in Sun Valley Lodge & Sun Valley Inn. **Parking:** on-site and valet. [B] [L] [D]

SWAN VALLEY pop. 204
- **Part of Jackson Hole Including Grand Teton National Park area — see map p. 285**

SLEEPY J CABINS   208/483-0411

[fyi] Not evaluated. **Address:** 19 Hwy 31 83449 **Location:** Just ne of jct US 26. Facilities, services, and décor characterize a mid-scale property.

SYRINGA (D-2) elev. 1,440'

Syringa is named for Idaho's state flower, a variety of mock orange whose creamy white blooms fill the forest in early summer. The town is nestled along the Middle Fork of the Clearwater River, a designated National Wild & Scenic River.

Lowell/Syringa Chamber of Commerce: 115 Selway Rd., Kooskia, ID 83539. **Phone:** (888) 926-4430.

RECREATIONAL ACTIVITIES
White-water Rafting
- **ROW Adventures** departs from 7743 US 12. Other activities are offered. **Hours:** Rafting trips are offered daily, mid-May to early Sept. Departure times vary; phone ahead. **Phone:** (208) 770-2517 or (866) 836-9340.

TARGHEE NATIONAL FOREST—See
Caribou-Targhee National Forest p. 53

TWIN FALLS (H-3) pop. 44,125, elev. 3,745'
- **Hotels p. 102 • Restaurants p. 103**

Twin Falls is in the center of 500,000 acres of prime farmland irrigated by the waters of the Snake River. Since the turn of the 20th century, the "Magic Valley" area has been known as one of the nation's most prolific crop-producing regions. Twin Falls also is on the edge of the Snake River Canyon, which was gouged out some 30,000 years ago by the Great Bonneville Flood.

From Bliss, the 67.8-mile Thousand Springs Scenic Byway runs southeast, following US 30 through Hagerman (*see place listing p. 63*), Buhl (*see place listing p. 52*) and Twin Falls, and SR 50 north to the junction of I-84; a spur road (US 93) juts due north from Twin Falls to I-84. Cascading from the sides of Snake River Canyon, the lovely natural springs are fed by the Snake River Plain Aquifer, one of the world's largest groundwater systems. The scenic byway affords access to the five units of Thousand Springs State Park (*see attraction listing p. 64)* as well as three hot mineral pools: Banbury Hot Springs, 10 miles west of Buhl, Miracle Hot Springs, 9 miles south of Hagerman, and Thousand Springs Resort, 5 miles south of Hagerman.

Just northeast of Twin Falls, the white waters of the Snake River plunge more than 212 feet at Shoshone Falls, known as the "Niagara of the West." The best time to view the falls is late April through early June, since irrigation waters are retained upstream during the summer months. **Note:** During drought, the falls may be dry; phone the chamber at (208) 733-3974 to check the status.

Twin Falls Area Chamber of Commerce: 2015 Neilsen Point, Twin Falls, ID 83301. **Phone:** (208) 733-3974.

THE HERRETT CENTER FOR ARTS & SCIENCE, on the north side of the College of Southern Idaho campus, contains artifacts from pre-Columbian civilizations of the Western Hemisphere. The center features contemporary art, a mammoth skeleton and changing exhibits. Visitors can see educational and entertainment shows in a planetarium. The observatory has a research-grade 24-inch telescope. A rain forest exhibit is home to live reptiles and features interactive displays.

Time: Allow 30 minutes minimum. **Hours:** Museum Tues.-Fri. 9:30-4:30 (also Tues. and Fri. 4:30-9), Sat. 1-9. Planetarium and observatory show times vary; phone for schedule. Closed major holidays. **Cost:** Museum and galleries free. Planetarium $6; $5 (ages 60+); $4 (ages 3-18). **Phone:** (208) 732-6655.

PERRINE MEMORIAL BRIDGE, on the northern edge of town, spans the Snake River Canyon 486 feet above the water. The four-lane bridge has pedestrian walkways with views of sheer cliffs, the Blue Lakes, waterfalls, a park and two golf courses. A road descends to these areas. The Twin Falls Visitor Center is next to the bridge at the southwest end.

Daredevil Evel Knievel attempted to leap across the Snake River Canyon a mile east of the bridge in 1974; the dirt ramp used to launch his rocket-powered vehicle remains. The bridge is reputedly the only U.S. location where BASE jumping is permitted year-round without a permit. Spectators can view this extreme sport from overlooks. Exhibits highlight the recreational activities and history of the area. **Hours:** Bridge open year-round. Visitor center open daily 8-8, Memorial Day-Labor Day; 8-5, rest of year. Phone ahead to confirm schedule. **Phone:** (208) 733-9458.

BEST WESTERN PLUS TWIN FALLS HOTEL

(208)736-8000

Hotel
$89-$129

AAA Benefit: Save 10% or more every day and earn 10% bonus points!

Address: 1377 Blue Lakes Blvd N 83301 **Location:** I-84 exit 173, 4 mi s on US 93. **Facility:** 120 units. 3 stories, interior corridors. **Parking:** winter plug-ins. **Pool(s):** heated indoor. **Activities:** hot tub, picnic facilities, exercise room. **Guest Services:** valet and coin laundry, area transportation. **Featured Amenity:** full hot breakfast.

▼ *See AAA listing p. 71* ▼

FAIRFIELD INN & SUITES BY MARRIOTT TWIN FALLS
(208)734-8444

Hotel
$80-$158

AAA Benefit: Members save 5% or more!

Address: 1788 Washington St N 83301 **Location:** I-84 exit 173, 3 mi s to Pole Line Rd, 1 mi w, then just n. **Facility:** 92 units. 3 stories, interior corridors. **Pool(s):** heated indoor. **Activities:** hot tub, exercise room. **Guest Services:** valet and coin laundry, boarding pass kiosk. **Featured Amenity: full hot breakfast.**

HAMPTON INN
(208)734-2233

Hotel $99-$179 **Address:** 1658 Fillmore St N 83301 **Location:** I-84 exit 173, 3.5 mi s to Pole Line Rd, then just w. **Facility:** 75 units. 3 stories, interior corridors. **Terms:** 1-7 night minimum stay, cancellation fee imposed. **Pool(s):** heated indoor. **Activities:** hot tub, exercise room. **Guest Services:** valet and coin laundry.

AAA Benefit: Members save up to 10%!

HILTON GARDEN INN
(208)733-8500

Hotel $99-$179 **Address:** 1741 Harrison St N 83301 **Location:** I-84 exit 173, 3 mi s to Pole Line Rd, then 0.3 mi w. **Facility:** 107 units. 4 stories, interior corridors. **Terms:** 1-7 night minimum stay, cancellation fee imposed. **Pool(s):** heated indoor. **Activities:** hot tub, exercise room. **Guest Services:** valet and coin laundry.

AAA Benefit: Members save up to 10%!

HOLIDAY INN EXPRESS & SUITES
(208)732-6001

Hotel $109-$189 **Address:** 1554 Fillmore St N 83301 **Location:** I-84 exit 173, 3.5 mi s to Pole Line Rd, just w, then just s. **Facility:** 91 units. 3 stories, interior corridors. **Terms:** cancellation fee imposed. **Amenities:** safes. **Pool(s):** heated indoor. **Activities:** hot tub, exercise room. **Guest Services:** valet and coin laundry.

LA QUINTA INN & SUITES
(208)736-9600

Hotel $86-$317 **Address:** 539 Pole Line Rd 83301 **Location:** I-84 exit 173, 3 mi s to Pole Line Rd, then 0.3 mi w. **Facility:** 101 units, some two bedrooms. 3 stories, interior corridors. **Pool(s):** heated indoor. **Activities:** hot tub, exercise room. **Guest Services:** valet and coin laundry.

QUALITY INN & SUITES
(208)734-7494

Hotel $79-$169 **Address:** 1910 Fillmore St N 83301 **Location:** I-84 exit 173, 3.3 mi s. **Facility:** 111 units. 3 stories (no elevator), interior corridors. **Parking:** winter plug-ins. **Pool(s):** heated indoor. **Activities:** hot tub, exercise room. **Guest Services:** valet and coin laundry.

WHERE TO EAT

ANCHOR BISTRO & BAR
208/733-6566

American. Casual Dining. $7-$15 **AAA Inspector Notes:** This sports bar features comfortable seating inside and an awesome outdoor patio with televisions. In addition to a decent selection of beer and cocktails, menu favorites include freshly-made Bermuda onion rings, seasonal salads, house beer-battered mahi mahi, sirloin steak sandwich, a variety of burgers and addictive french fries. **Features:** full bar, patio dining, Sunday brunch, happy hour. **Address:** 334 Blue Lakes Blvd N 83301 **Location:** I-84 exit 173, 5 mi s, then just s of Filer Ave. L D CALL

CANYON CREST DINING & EVENT CENTER
208/733-9392

American. Casual Dining. $9-$34 **AAA Inspector Notes:** Overlooking the breathtaking Snake River Canyon, this well-appointed restaurant is home to some of the best views in the Magic Valley. Beautiful wood, stone and glass detail create an exquisite ambience. The open veranda is sure to create an unforgettable experience for diners. **Features:** full bar, patio dining, Sunday brunch, happy hour. **Address:** 330 Canyon Crest Dr 83301 **Location:** I-84 exit 173, 3.9 mi s to Pole Line Rd, 1 mi w, then just n. L D CALL

ELEVATION 486 FOOD & SPIRITS
208/737-0486

American. Casual Dining. $10-$28 **AAA Inspector Notes:** With postcard-picture views, this restaurant is perched on the south rim of the Snake River Canyon, 486 vertical feet above the river. Menu items include fire-grilled artichoke, Northwest steamer clams, hand-cut steaks, tomahawk-cut Idaho pork chops, pan-broiled fresh Alaskan halibut and seared Alaskan scallops. A nice selection of wine is available by the glass. **Features:** full bar, patio dining, Sunday brunch, happy hour. **Address:** 195 River Vista Pl 83301 **Location:** I-84 exit 173, 3.5 mi s to Pole Line Rd, 1 mi w to N 2900 E, 0.3 mi n to Canyon Crest Dr, just e, then just n on Pinnacle Pl; in Magic Valley Arts Complex. L D CALL

IDAHO JOE'S RESTAURANT & BAKERY
208/734-9403

American Casual Dining $5-$14

AAA Inspector Notes: The atmosphere is rustic at this local favorite. In addition to generous portions and satisfying breakfasts, there are many fruit and cream pies. The Navajo taco is one of the house specials. **Features:** beer & wine, Sunday brunch. **Address:** 598 Blue Lakes Blvd N 83301 **Location:** I-84 exit 173, 5 mi s; in Lynwood Shopping Center. B L D

JAKERS BAR & GRILL
208/733-8400

Seafood Steak. Casual Dining. $10-$32 **AAA Inspector Notes:** Expect an impressive selection of land and sea options featuring lobster tail, Alaskan king crab legs, local Idaho trout, filet mignon, Kobe flank steak, miso citrus-glazed salmon and boneless short ribs. Local's favor the blackened chicken Alfredo and almond-crusted chicken. Five soups and an enormous selection of fruit and salads are featured at the buffet. The white chocolate brownie, mud pie and warm apple crisp desserts are meant to be shared. **Features:** full bar, patio dining, Sunday brunch. **Address:** 1598 Blue Lakes Blvd 83301 **Location:** I-84 exit 173, 4 mi s on US 93. L D

JAVA CAFE ON BLUE LAKES
208/733-9555

Breakfast Sandwiches. Quick Serve. $6-$9 **AAA Inspector Notes:** This casual, eccentric café offers Fair Trade Certified organic coffee, homemade muffins and turnovers, seasonal soup and sandwiches made with fresh local ingredients and served with tortilla chips. Favorite menu items include poached eggs, Bill's open-faced grilled cheese sandwich and oatmeal with warm milk, foam, cinnamon and bananas. Their signature coffee known as the "bowl of soul" is highly addictive. **Features:** patio dining. **Address:** 228 Blue Lakes Blvd N 83301 **Location:** I-84 exit 173, 6.2 mi s, then just s of Heyburn Ave. B L

LA CASITA MEXICAN RESTAURANT   208/734-7974

▼▼ ▼▼ Mexican. Casual Dining. $5-$12 **AAA Inspector Notes:** Dine on classic Mexican cuisine featuring a variety of fresh-cooked shredded meat and chicken dishes—all hearty and tasty. This casual, local favorite offers quite a bang for your buck. **Features:** beer & wine. **Address:** 111 S Park Ave W 83301 **Location:** I-84 exit 173, 6.5 mi s on US 93 to Addison Ave, then 1.3 mi sw on Shoshone St.

[L] [D]

LA FIESTA MEXICAN RESTAURANT   208/734-0685

▼▼ ▼▼ Mexican. Casual Dining. $9-$16 **AAA Inspector Notes:** The brightly colored interior and attractive appointments at this restaurant coordinate well with the festive cantina. Guests can expect a nice selection of appetizers, a variety of beef, chicken, shrimp and pork burritos, melt-in-your mouth enchiladas, mouth-watering sizzling fajitas and combination plates in chico, grande and mucho sizes. **Features:** full bar, patio dining, happy hour. **Address:** 1288 Blue Lakes Blvd 83301 **Location:** I-84 exit 173, 3.8 mi s; at Blue Lakes Blvd and College Dr. [L] [D]

SCOOTERS CHILLIN' N GRILLIN' SPORTS BAR   208/969-9940

▼▼ ▼▼ American. Casual Dining. $8-$14 **AAA Inspector Notes:** Those looking for a sports bar with good food and consistently friendly service should try this eatery. Menu offerings include a variety of burgers, sandwiches, tacos, garlic fries, freshly-baked meatballs and more than 16 beers on tap. Desserts are made in house—be sure to try the seasonal strawberry shortcake. **Features:** full bar. **Address:** 137 2nd Ave N 83301 **Location:** Jct Shoshone St and 2nd Ave; downtown. **Parking:** on-site and street. [L] [D] CALL [L M]

TWIN FALLS SANDWICH COMPANY   208/734-8372

▼▼ Deli Coffee/Tea. Quick Serve. $5-$9 **AAA Inspector Notes:** This downtown eatery serves hot and cold sandwiches with a nice selection of sides, such as chips made in house and tasty pasta salad. Menu items are named after local attractions such as Balanced Rock and the Perrine Bridge. Microbrews are available. **Features:** beer & wine, patio dining. **Address:** 128 Main Ave N 83301 **Location:** Just w of Main Ave and Shoshone St; downtown. **Parking:** street only. [B] [L]

WOK'N GRILL RESTAURANT   208/734-6898

▼▼ ▼▼ Chinese. Casual Dining. $8-$22 **AAA Inspector Notes:** This restaurant serves lobster fresh from the lobster tank. Other menu highlights include traditional appetizers, beef, pork, chicken and seafood dishes, as well as sandwiches and steak. Whether visiting or traveling through this area, the popular luncheon specials and family dinners can be enjoyed by everyone. **Features:** beer & wine. **Address:** 1188 Blue Lakes Blvd N 83301 **Location:** I-84 exit 173, 5 mi s. [L] [D]

VICTOR (G-6) pop. 1,928, elev. 6,214'
• Hotels & Restaurants map & index p. 287
• Part of Jackson Hole Including Grand Teton
National Park area — see map p. 285

BAGLEY'S TETON MOUNTAIN RANCH is at 2655 West 8000 South (Cedron Rd.). The ranch offers tours featuring up-close encounters with elk and buffalo herds. Stops are afforded for photos. Horseback riding trips of various lengths from 1 hour to overnight trail rides also are available.

Time: Allow 1 hour, 30 minutes minimum. **Hours:** Tours Mon.-Sat. 9-5, June-Sept. **Cost:** Tour $10; free (ages 0-3). Prices vary for other tours. Reservations are required. **Phone:** (208) 787-9005 or (866) 787-9005.

YELLOWSTONE-GRAND TETON SCENIC LOOP is an approximately 263-mile scenic drive in eastern Idaho, northwestern Wyoming and a small portion of south-central Montana. The route encompasses the Teton and Mesa Falls scenic byways as well as Yellowstone and Grand Teton national parks.

Starting in Victor, Idaho, the 47-mile first segment follows SRs 33 and 32 northwest to Ashton, Idaho *(see place listing p. 34)*, along the Teton Scenic Byway, from which the Teton Mountains can be viewed to the east.

As you take the Mesa Falls Scenic Byway north to Island Park, Idaho *(see place listing p. 71)*, on the 35-mile second segment, you'll pass Upper Mesa Falls *(see Mesa Falls Recreation Area attraction listing p. 34)* and Harriman State Park *(see attraction listing p. 71)*, both to the west.

Following US 20 north on the 28-mile third segment, you'll reach Henry's Lake State Park *(see Recreation Areas Chart)* and then head east through touristy West Yellowstone, Mont. *(see place listing p. 207)*, which is situated at Yellowstone National Park's west entrance (hence the name).

Most of the 98-mile fourth segment traverses the western side of Yellowstone National Park *(see place listing p. 316)*. After exiting the park via the south entrance (which is also the north entrance to Grand Teton National Park), you'll drive over the Continental Divide, through pine and fir forests and past Jackson Lake. Recreational opportunities abound at Jackson Lake and throughout Grand Teton National Park *(see place listing p. 261)*.

The 30-mile fifth segment begins at the Moran junction. US 26/191, with the Tetons on the northern side and pastures with buffalo and elk on the southern side, has numerous pull-offs with informational plaques. The route passes the National Elk Refuge *(see attraction listing p. 270)*, where you can observe elk from boardwalks and decks, and then enters Jackson Hole.

On the 25-mile final segment of the trip, you'll head back to Victor via SR 33, which winds through Caribou-Targhee National Forest *(see place listing p. 53)* over dramatic mountains with hairpin turns.

Note: Mesa Falls Scenic Byway is closed from mid-November to late April; take US 20 toward Island Park as an alternate route. The road between Yellowstone National Park's west and south entrances also is closed from mid-November to late April. **Phone:** (208) 354-2607 (Teton Geotourism Center).

KNOTTY PINE SUPPER CLUB   208/787-2866 (31)

▼▼ ▼▼ American. Casual Dining. $11-$25 **AAA Inspector Notes:** This restaurant also serves as this small community's most popular entertainment venue with a stage located just off the dining floor. The intriguing menu offers a variety of beef, seafood and pork entrées. A large patio allows for al fresco dining. **Features:** full bar, patio dining. **Address:** 58 S Main St 83455 **Location:** South edge of town. **Parking:** street only. [D]

WALLACE (B-2) pop. 784, elev. 2,744'

The center of a great lead- and silver-mining region, Wallace is at the junction of four major canyons, three of which lead to important active mining districts. This region claims several of the world's largest and deepest silver mines; some of the mines founded in the late 1800s have 200 miles of tunnels.

Among the historic buildings still standing in town are the railroad depot with its original Chinese bricks; the Smokehouse Building, which was once the courthouse; and the Rossi Building with its Queen Anne-style turret. The turret is a characteristic architectural feature seen on most of the corner buildings throughout the historic district.

Pulaski Trail, 1 mile south, features interpretive signs describing the 1910 fire that consumed 3 million acres and is said to be one of the largest fires in U.S. history.

At the east end of Wallace, SR 4 leads north from I-90 exit 62 into Burke Canyon, one of the district's historic mining areas. The 7-mile road passes tailings, abandoned mines, derelict buildings and the once bustling towns of Gem and Burke. The latter town, in a narrow canyon, was renowned for the 150-room Tiger Hotel, which was not only built over a creek, but also had a rail line tunneling through its center and a street running under its west end; the hotel was razed in 1964.

Area back roads attract all-terrain vehicle enthusiasts in summer and snowmobilers in winter.

Historic Wallace Chamber of Commerce Visitor Center: 10 River St., Wallace, ID 83873. **Phone:** (208) 753-7151.

Self-guiding tours: A brochure describing driving and walking tours of the mining and historic districts is available at the visitor center.

NORTHERN PACIFIC DEPOT RAILROAD MUSEUM, 219 Sixth St., occupies a restored station that was built in 1901 and operated until 1980. Exhibits include a re-creation of an early 1900s railroad depot as well as photographs and railway relics recalling the history of the Coeur d'Alene mining district. Changing exhibits also are featured. **Time:** Allow 30 minutes minimum. **Hours:** Daily 9-5, Mar.-Oct.; by appointment rest of year. **Cost:** $3; $8 (family). **Phone:** (208) 752-0111.

[SAVE] **SIERRA SILVER MINE TOUR,** at the corner of Fifth and Bank sts., takes visitors into an underground mine where they can view exhibits, equipment in operation and techniques used in hard-rock silver mining. Retired miners conduct the 75-minute guided tour, which includes a ride through town aboard a vintage-style trolley and anecdotes about the mining days. Costumed characters from local history lead a 50-minute tour to Burke, a nearby ghost town.

Time: Allow 1 hour, 30 minutes minimum. **Hours:** Mine tours depart every 30 minutes daily 10-4, June-Aug.; 10-2 in May and Sept. 1 to mid-Oct. Ghost town tours depart Wed.-Sat. on the hour 11-3, July-Aug. **Cost:** Mine tour $15; $13 (ages 60+); $8.50 (ages 4-16); $47 (family, two adults and children). Trolley ride only $6. Ghost town tour $10; $6 (ages 4-16). **Phone:** (208) 752-5151.

SIXTH STREET MELODRAMA is at 212 Sixth St. Audience participation is encouraged each summer during a family-style melodrama that reflects the area's mining background. The play, staged in the 1899 Lux Building, is followed by the Kelly's Alley Revue, during which visitors can enjoy old-fashioned music and humor. Other plays and musicals also are produced during the rest of the year; phone for schedule and rates.

Time: Allow 2 hours minimum. **Hours:** Summer performances are given Wed.-Sat. at 7 p.m., Sun. at 2, early July-late Aug. **Cost:** $18; $16 (ages 55+ and military and students with ID). **Phone:** (208) 752-8871 or (877) 749-8478.

WALLACE DISTRICT MINING MUSEUM, 509 Bank St., displays local mining equipment and photographs. A 30-minute video depicts the life of early miners and the development of one of the richest silver mining districts in the world. Archives are available. **Time:** Allow 1 hour minimum. **Hours:** Daily 9-5, July-Aug.; daily 10-5, May-June and in Sept.; Mon.-Sat. 10-5, in Apr. and Oct.; varies rest of year. Closed Jan. 1, Martin Luther King Jr. Day, Presidents Day, Easter, July 4, Thanksgiving and Christmas. Phone ahead to confirm schedule. **Cost:** $3; $1 (ages 6-15); $7 (family). **Phone:** (208) 556-1592.

RECREATIONAL ACTIVITIES
Ziplines

- **Silver Streak Zipline Tours** departs from 516 Pine St. **Note:** Participants must weigh between 85 and 270 pounds. **Hours:** Open daily June-Sept.; Thurs.-Sun. in May. **Cost:** Reservations are required. **Phone:** (208) 556-1690.

THE WALLACE INN   (208)752-1252

Hotel
$72-$175

Address: 100 Front St 83873 **Location:** I-90 exit 61 (Business Rt 90), just se. **Facility:** 63 units. 2 stories (no elevator), interior corridors. **Parking:** winter plug-ins. **Terms:** check-in 4 pm, cancellation fee imposed. **Dining:** Trailside Restaurant, see separate listing. **Pool(s):** heated indoor. **Activities:** sauna, hot tub, steamroom, exercise room.

WHERE TO EAT

1313 CLUB   208/752-9391

American
Casual Dining
$6-$23

AAA Inspector Notes: The historic mining town's classic old-time bar and grill has an eclectic decor heavy on taxidermists' mounts and collectible items. Try beer-battered french fries with a certified Angus hamburger or steak. **Features:** full bar, patio dining, happy hour.

Address: 608 Bank St 83873 **Location:** Downtown. **Parking:** street only. *Menu on AAA.com*   [B] [L] [D] [🛒]

THE BROOKS RESTAURANT   208/752-8171
◆◆ ◆◆ American. Casual Dining. $8-$16 **AAA Inspector Notes:**
A true local's spot, try the hot roast beef sandwich or fresh Idaho
trout. **Address:** 500 Cedar St 83873 **Location:** I-90 exit 62, just w.

[B] [L] [D]

TRAILSIDE RESTAURANT   208/752-1252
◆◆ ◆◆ American. Casual Dining. $7-$15 **AAA Inspector Notes:**
Patrons can enjoy casual dining in bright and contemporary surroundings with friendly and attentive service. The menu's varied selection includes something for nearly every taste and member of the
family. Dining room hours may vary during the winter months. **Features:** full bar. **Address:** 100 Front St 83873 **Location:** I-90 exit 61
(Business Rt 90), just se; in The Wallace Inn.

[B] [L] [D]

WEIPPE (D-2) pop. 441, elev. 3,015'

Weippe (WEE-ipe) sits on its namesake prairie, a
9-by-20-mile upland area of mixed grassland and
forest, today given over to grain cultivation and forestry. Blue blossoms of camas carpet the expanse
in the spring. The edible bulb was an important food
for the Nez Perce Indians, who had several summer
encampments on the prairie. Just south of Weippe,
members of the Lewis and Clark expedition, nearing
starvation after their arduous crossing of the Bitterroot Mountains, were welcomed and sustained by
the Nez Perce in 1805.

Weippe is on the 43-mile Gold Rush Historic
Byway, which follows SR 11 from Greer to Headquarters. Roadside plaques describe points of interest along the scenic route.

Pierce-Weippe Chamber of Commerce: 204
Wood St., P.O. Box 378, Weippe, ID 83553. **Phone:**
(208) 435-4406.

WEIPPE DISCOVERY CENTER, on SR 11 at Wood
St., features interpretive murals on its exterior walls
that relate the meeting of Meriwether Lewis and William Clark with the Nez Perce Indians in 1805. A trail
loops through the Living Lewis & Clark Landscape,
which showcases local vegetation used by the Nez
Perce and documented by members of the Lewis
and Clark expedition. The center also displays
mounted native animals.

Time: Allow 30 minutes minimum. **Hours:** Outdoor displays and trail open daily dawn-dusk. Center
open Mon.-Fri. 10-5 (also Tues.-Wed. 5-7), Sat.
10-1. Closed major holidays. **Cost:** Free. **Phone:**
(208) 435-4406.

WEISER (F-1) pop. 5,507, elev. 2,114'

Named for Sgt. Peter Weiser (WEE-zer) of the
Lewis and Clark expedition, Weiser is on the Idaho-
Oregon border at the confluence of the Weiser and
Snake rivers. Since 1953, the city has been home to
the ◆ National Oldtime Fiddlers' Contest and Fes-
tival, which takes place the third full week in June.

Scenic views of Hells Canyon are afforded from
viewpoints north of Weiser; open only in summer,
the viewpoints can be reached via US 95 and SR
71. Closer looks at the canyon are made possible by
the float trips and jet boat tours that are available
from Hells Canyon Dam. The minimum age for most
float trips is 6 years; inquire about refund and
weather policies.

The southern trailhead of the Weiser River Trail,
converted from the banks of the former Pacific &
Idaho Northern (PIN) railroad grade, is in Weiser off
Main Street. The 84-mile route also passes through
Midvale, Cambridge and Council. Wildlife including
deer, elk, heron, bear, waterfowl, raptors and wild
turkeys can be seen. While hiking, bicycling or
horseback riding along the trail, visitors view rolling
hills and black lava cliffs in the southern portion of
the canyon; the northern portion is forested. Cross-
country skiing also can be enjoyed in winter.

Fifteen miles northeast of Weiser, just east of the
Snake River, four-wheelers kick up lots of down and
dirty fun at the Weiser Sand Dunes.

Greater Weiser Area Chamber of Commerce:
Vendome Event Center, 309 State St., Weiser, ID
83672. **Phone:** (208) 414-0452.

INDIANHEAD MOTEL & RV   208/549-0331
◆◆ ◆◆ Motel $65-$95 **Address:** 747 Hillcrest Ave 83672 **Location:** 1 mi n of center; jct US 95 and Indianhead Rd. **Facility:** 8 units.
1 story, exterior corridors. **Terms:** cancellation fee imposed. **Activities:** picnic facilities. [🍴] [📶] [✕]

WHITE BIRD (D-1) pop. 91, elev. 1,560'
**See also Hells Canyon National Recreation Area
p. 65**

White Bird, near the Salmon River, provides direct
access to outdoor recreational activities—including
white-water rafting, jet boating and hiking—in the heart
of Hells Canyon National Recreation Area. FR 493, a
gravel road, is the only way in and out of the area. A
boat launch is available, as is a 26-mile trail system
that borders the Snake River. Sturgeon fishing is
popular on both the Snake and Salmon rivers.

White Bird Battlefield, just north on Old Hwy. 95,
was the site of the first confrontation of the Nez
Perce War. It is one of the designated historical sites
of Nez Perce National Historical Park (see place
listing p. 86).

**White Bird Chamber of Commerce Visitor
Center:** 128 White Bird Rd., White Bird, ID 83554.
Phone: (208) 839-2777.

Self-guiding tours: A trail guide of White Bird Battlefield is available at the chamber of commerce. Also
available is a brochure about the town and its history
as well as recreational opportunities in the region.

HELLS CANYON JET BOAT TRIPS & LODGING

(208)839-2255

◆ **Motel** $80-$90 **Address:** 3252 Waterfront Dr 83554 **Location:** Waterfront. US 95 exit White Bird, 1.5 mi s of center. **Facility:** 6 units. 1 story, exterior corridors. **Terms:** 7 day cancellation notice-fee imposed. **Activities:** fishing, recreation programs in summer, picnic facilities.

🛂 📶 ✕ 🆔 🍴 💻 / SOME UNITS 🆔

WINCHESTER (D-1) pop. 340, elev. 3,968'

Early settlers allegedly named this former logging town for the famous firearm. A replica of a Winchester rifle hangs above Main Street. Winchester Lake State Park, just south on US 95 Bus. Rte., occupies the site of the 1910 Craig Mountain Lumber Co., whose 103-acre millpond is today the centerpiece of the park *(see Recreation Areas Chart)*. Remains of the mill can be seen on the hill near the city water tower.

THE WOLF EDUCATION AND RESEARCH CENTER is at 1721 Forest Rd. The center's 300 acres of timberland are home to a pack of gray wolves. Visitors have a chance to observe these animals in their natural habitat, courtesy of a .3-mile trail that comes within 50 yards of the wolves' enclosure, though sightings cannot be guaranteed. A visitor center, built to resemble a Nez Perce tribal long house, has displays about wolves.

Time: Allow 30 minutes minimum. **Hours:** Daily 9-5, Memorial Day weekend-Labor Day; by appointment rest of year. Two-hour guided tours are given daily at 7 a.m. and 7 p.m., Memorial Day-Labor Day. **Cost:** $5; $2 (ages 6-13). Guided tour (includes admission) $10; $4 (ages 6-13). Reservations are required for guided tours and must be made at least 24 hours in advance. **Phone:** (208) 924-6960.

WORLEY (C-1) pop. 257, elev. 2,650'

GAMBLING ESTABLISHMENTS

• **Coeur d'Alene Casino** is just off US 95 at 37914 S. Nukwalqw. **Hours:** Daily 24 hours. **Phone:** (800) 523-2464.

COEUR D'ALENE CASINO RESORT HOTEL

208/769-2600

◆◆◆ **Resort Hotel** **Rates not provided**

Address: 37914 S Nukwalqw Rd 83876 **Location:** On US 95, 3 mi n. **Facility:** Located just outside of Coeur d'Alene, this casino-style property offers guests a variety of entertainment options. Choose between newer 'spa' rooms or more traditional lodge style rooms. 300 units. 3-4 stories, interior corridors. **Parking:** on-site and valet. **Terms:** check-in 4 pm. **Amenities:** *Some:* safes. **Dining:** 5 restaurants, also, Chinook Steak & Pasta, High Mountain Buffet, see separate listings. **Pool(s):** heated indoor. **Activities:** hot tub, regulation golf, exercise room, spa. **Guest Services:** area transportation.

SAVE 🅿️ ✈️ 🍴 🍸 CALL 🆔 🚲 BIZ HS
📶 🎥 💻 / SOME UNITS 🆔 🛂

CHINOOK STEAK & PASTA

208/769-2600

◆◆◆ Regional Steak Seafood. Fine Dining. $16-$35 **AAA Inspector Notes:** With a name meaning stand before the fire, this steakhouse uses that technique to grill its 28-day aged beef. The menu is diverse and the presentation creative. Highlights include local steelhead trout, succulent Alaskan black cod and juicy porterhouse steak for two carved tableside. Most food is homemade, including the butter for the popovers and the custard for the ice cream. The contemporary décor reflects the natural beauty of the Palouse Prairie with the use of natural materials. **Features:** full bar, patio dining, happy hour. **Address:** 37914 S Nukwalqw Rd 83876 **Location:** On US 95, 3 mi n; in Coeur d'Alene Casino Resort Hotel. **Parking:** on-site and valet. D CALL 🆔

HIGH MOUNTAIN BUFFET

208/686-0248

◆◆ American. Casual Dining. $10-$25 **AAA Inspector Notes:** Located inside the casino, this casual restaurant is somewhat remote and specializes in buffet service for the busy gambler, as well as cooked-to-order steak and seafood. **Features:** full bar. **Address:** 37914 S Nukwalqw Rd 83876 **Location:** On US 95, 3 mi n; in Coeur d'Alene Casino Resort Hotel. **Parking:** on-site and valet.

B L D

◆ **YELLOWSTONE NATIONAL PARK**—See Wyoming p. 316

Take Your **Imagination** *to New Destinations*

Use AAA Travel Guides online to explore the possibilities.

Go to AAA.com/travelguide today.

Glacier National Park

Montana

Under a giant sky varying between shades of azure, turquoise and peacock blue, Montana's landscape—encompassing golden wheat fields, timber-covered mountains, flowing trout streams, rocky bluffs and canyon-carved lakes—is a love affair for the eyes.

The state enjoys the best of both worlds. The Continental Divide in western Montana gave rise to the name *montaña,* Spanish for "mountainous." And although the craggy peaks of the northern Rocky Mountains dominate the west, wide-open space is the name of the game in the east: Expansive, dizzying prairie grasslands in this region coined the state's nickname, Big Sky Country.

While there are differences between Montana's agriculture- and ranching-based Great Plains and its lumber-dominated west, residents have one thing in common: appreciation for the beauty of their surroundings. Still,

Virginia City

with a harsh climate and sparse population, no one will argue that living in Montana is a piece of cake. But the view from a ranch window seems to make it worthwhile.

The Treasure State

Vast fortunes were made in Montana, but many would assert they came at the expense of people and land, a notion that doesn't sit well with residents. Many Montanans believe that state resources historically have been exploited in the interests of outsiders.

At Little Bighorn Battlefield National Monument, crooked headstones on a grassy hill attest to the passion that thousands of Lakota, Cheyenne and Arapaho warriors exhibited in an attempt to save their homeland.

And the unearthing of copper ores in Butte began a bitter battle between the "copper kings"—entrepreneurs William A. Clark and Marcus Daly. Today, mining relics are displayed downtown in old mine shafts, cabins and such stately homes as Clark's lavish Copper King Mansion.

Colorful Virginia City sports reminders of its gold mining past with restored buildings. And Helena is home to baroque, Gothic and Italianate mansions recalling the city's golden days.

More recently, locals have exhibited an overwhelming drive to preserve Montana's natural blessings. In the early 1970s, residents amended the state constitution to include strict environmental protection laws, setting a national example.

Spectacular Settings

Take in the snowy peaks, ice-sculpted valleys, and twinkling lakes and waterfalls of Glacier National Park, a majestic region so awe-inspiring the Blackfeet Indians deemed it sacred ground. If the area's resident grizzlies, mountain lions and wolves could talk, they would probably agree.

Your heart will skip a beat on Going-to-the-Sun Road, a mind-boggling scenic byway that snakes around cliffs and climbs 6,646 feet to the summit of Logan Pass.

But save some time for the nation's *first* national park, Yellowstone, which Congress established in 1872. You'll also want to visit the National Bison Range in Moiese, where some 400 buffalo roam the plains.

And, along what is now the Upper Missouri National Wild and Scenic River, you can follow the path of the Lewis and Clark expedition. Journal notes suggest that these explorers were enamored with Montana's scenery as well.

Recreation

What's in the perfect Montana recreation kit? Bear bells. Quick-dry nylon shorts. Ski poles. Maybe some chest waders. Definitely some dry socks. And, of course, a size-2 Sofa Pillow.

The quick-dry shorts will come in handy if you immerse yourself in one of this state's top recreation draws—river rafting. At Glacier National Park you can drift down placid portions of the wild and scenic Flathead River, savoring arching canyon walls and wildflower-filled meadows. Or, you might tackle the bucking, boulder-studded rapids of the Flathead's Middle Fork. And Bear Creek is one of the few runs where mountain goats are regularly sighted, thanks to Goat Lick, a cliff on the waterway's north side that excretes mineral salts irresistible to the horned animals.

As any good fly fisher knows, Montana is trout territory, and that's where the chest waders come in. The best catch must be coaxed out with a deft flick of the wrist and an enticing fly on the end of the line. Such flies can have kind of funny names—hence the Sofa Pillow. For top casting sites, head to Bozeman's outskirts and take your pick of such trout-filled rivers as the Madison, Yellowstone and Gallatin. You'll find plenty of rental boats here, too, complete with guides who will do the rowing for you.

Fly fishing may be out if you hit Bozeman mid-winter, but that doesn't mean you're too late to have fun. Excellent downhill skiing is just around the corner at Big Sky Resort, which averages 400 inches of powder annually. And locals rave about the bowl and chute skiing available at 1,200-acre Bridger Bowl Ski Area. Six cross-country skiing trails rim the region as well, notably the 10-mile Bozeman Creek to Mystic Lake trail and the 4-mile Hyalite Reservoir Ski Loop.

In addition you'll find superb ski venues close to many other Montana towns, including Big Mountain near Whitefish, Red Lodge Mountain near Red Lodge and Snowbowl near Missoula. All make great places to put those ski poles you packed to good use.

Plus, ski poles can often be helpful when hiking Montana's rugged terrain. Such "walking sticks" are especially useful when the only way to follow your trail is to ford a frigid, knee-high creek. The dry socks are for when you get to the other side.

Montana has several great hiking trails, but try not to miss Cinnamon Mountain Lookout Trail in the Gallatin National Forest, or Stoney Indian Pass in Glacier National Park's Belly River Country. Both reward hikers with sudden, stunning vistas of Montana's treasured mountains. One caveat—while such spectacular scenery can be a pleasant surprise, startling an 800-pound grizzly is just plain hazardous. And *that's* why bear bells are number one on any Montana recreational equipment list.

Skiing near Whitefish

Historic Timeline

1805	Meriwether Lewis and William Clark arrive in what is now the state of Montana.
1862	Miners strike gold at Grasshopper Creek and later at Diamond City and Virginia City.
1876	Lt. Col. George Armstrong Custer and troops are defeated at the Battle of the Little Bighorn.
1880	Irish immigrant Marcus Daly purchases the Anaconda, a mine with a rich copper reserve that will make him wealthy.
1916	Montana Republican Jeannette Rankin becomes the first U.S. congresswoman; she later voted against both world wars.
1955	The Anaconda Aluminum Co. opens a $65 million plant in northwestern Montana.
1972	Montana's electorate approves a new state constitution.
1984	Launched in 1967, the Libby Dam hydroelectric project is finally completed.
1988	Forest fires sweep through Montana for nearly 3 months, wiping out trees and wildlife in Yellowstone National Park.
1998	Montana Freemen leaders involved in a 1996 armed standoff with FBI agents are convicted of various charges.
2000	Judy Martz is elected governor and becomes the state's first female chief executive.

What To Pack

Temperature Averages Maximum/Minimum	JANUARY	FEBRUARY	MARCH	APRIL	MAY	JUNE	JULY	AUGUST	SEPTEMBER	OCTOBER	NOVEMBER	DECEMBER
Billings	33/13	36/15	43/23	57/34	68/43	76/51	89/58	86/55	75/46	63/37	46/26	39/19
Great Falls	32/14	34/15	41/21	55/33	66/42	72/49	84/56	81/54	70/46	59/38	44/26	37/20
Havre	26/6	29/8	40/18	57/32	69/43	75/51	86/57	83/54	72/44	60/35	42/21	33/12
Kalispell	26/9	32/12	40/19	55/30	65/39	72/46	83/49	80/46	69/39	55/31	37/21	29/16
Medicine Lake	18/-2	27/7	40/18	56/30	68/42	77/51	83/54	82/53	70/42	58/31	36/16	23/3
Miles City	27/6	32/9	42/19	59/33	71/44	79/53	90/60	88/58	75/47	62/36	44/22	34/12

From the records of The Weather Channel Interactive, Inc.

Good Facts To Know

ABOUT THE STATE

POPULATION: 989,415.

AREA: 147,040 square miles; ranks 4th.

CAPITAL: Helena.

HIGHEST POINT: 12,799 ft., Granite Peak.

LOWEST POINT: 1,862 ft., Kootenai River.

TIME ZONE(S): Mountain. DST.

REGULATIONS

TEEN DRIVING LAWS: No more than one unrelated passenger under 18 for the first 6 months and no more than three unrelated passengers under 18 for the second 6 months. Driving is not permitted 11 p.m.-5 a.m. The minimum age for an unrestricted driver's license is 16. Phone (406) 444-3933 for more information about Montana driver's license regulations.

SEAT BELT/CHILD RESTRAINT LAWS: Seat belts are required for driver and all passengers ages 6 and over and at least 60 pounds. Children under age 6 and less than 60 pounds are required to be in a child restraint. AAA recommends the use of seat belts and appropriate child restraints for the driver and all passengers.

HELMETS FOR MOTORCYCLISTS: Required for riders under 18.

RADAR DETECTORS: Permitted. Prohibited for use by commercial vehicles.

MOVE OVER LAW: Driver is required to slow down and vacate the lane nearest stopped police, fire and rescue vehicles using audible or flashing signals. The law also includes tow trucks. If on a highway with a speed limit of 50 mph or greater, the driver must slow down by at least 20 mph below the posted speed limit.

FIREARMS LAWS: Vary by state and/or county. Contact the Montana Department of Justice, Help Desk, 3013 N. Roberts, Room 470, Helena, MT 59601; phone (406) 444-2800.

HOLIDAYS

HOLIDAYS: Jan. 1 ▪ Martin Luther King Jr. Day, Jan. (3rd Mon.) ▪ Lincoln's and Washington's Birthday/Presidents Day, Feb. (3rd Mon.) ▪ Memorial Day, May (last Mon.) ▪ July 4 ▪ Labor Day, Sept. (1st Mon.) ▪ Columbus Day, Oct. (2nd Mon.) ▪ Election Day, Nov. (1st Tues. following 1st Mon.) ▪ Veterans Day, Nov. 11 ▪ Thanksgiving, Nov. (4th Thurs.) ▪ Christmas, Dec. 25.

MONEY

TAXES: Montana does not have a statewide sales tax. Designated resort communities may enact a resort tax of up to 3 percent for goods and services. There is a 7 percent statewide lodging tax.

VISITOR INFORMATION

INFORMATION CENTERS: State welcome centers are on US 2 just 1 mile east of Culbertson ▪ at jct. Main St. and US 2 in Shelby ▪ off I-94 in Wibaux ▪ on I-90 southbound a half-mile east of Hardin ▪ at jct. US 191 and US 20N in West Yellowstone ▪ and off I-15 southbound in Dillon.

ROAD CONDITIONS: The Montana Department of Transportation provides information about highway conditions and construction; phone (406) 444-6201 or (800) 226-7623.

FURTHER INFORMATION FOR VISITORS:
Montana Office of Tourism
301 S. Park Ave.
Helena, MT 59601
(406) 841-2870
(800) 847-4868

NATIONAL FOREST INFORMATION:
U.S. Forest Service
Lolo National Forest
24 Fort Missoula Rd.
Missoula, MT 59804
(406) 329-3750

FISHING AND HUNTING REGULATIONS:
Montana Department of Fish, Wildlife & Parks
1420 E. 6th Ave.
P.O. Box 200701
Helena, MT 59620
(406) 444-2535

Stay connected with #AAA and #CAA

on your favorite social media sites

Montana Annual Events

Please call ahead to confirm event details.

JANUARY

- Montana PRCA Rodeo Circuit Finals / Great Falls
  406-727-1481
- Seeley Lake Area Winterfest / Seeley Lake
  406-677-2880
- Montana Winter Fair Lewistown
  406-538-2200

FEBRUARY

- Whitefish Winter Carnival Whitefish
  406-862-3501
- Cowtown Beef Breeders Show, Craft Expo and Ag Trade Show / Miles City
  406-234-2890
- Montana Snowkite Rodeo Anaconda
  406-459-6898

MARCH

- West Yellowstone Snowmobile EXPO West Yellowstone
  406-647-7701
- St. Patrick's Day Events Butte
  406-723-3177
- St. Patrick's Day Parade Anaconda
  406-563-2400

APRIL

- Ice Breaker Road Race Great Falls
  406-771-1265
- International Wildlife Film Festival / Missoula
  406-728-9380
- Rendezvous Days / Eureka
  406-889-4636

MAY

- MSU-Billings Wine and Food Festival / Billings
  888-430-6782
- Bigfork Whitewater Festival Bigfork
  406-270-1551
- International Migratory Bird Day / Moiese
  406-644-2211, ext. 207

JUNE

- Montana Mule Days Hamilton
  406-777-2331
- Libby Logger Days / Libby
  406-293-8585
- Lewis and Clark Festival Great Falls
  406-791-7732

JULY

- Wolf Point Wild Horse Stampede / Wolf Point
  406-653-1770
- Montana State Fair Great Falls
  406-727-8900
- Montana Folk Festival Butte
  406-497-6464

AUGUST

- MontanaFair / Billings
  406-256-2400
- Sweet Pea Festival Bozeman
  406-586-4003
- Montana Cowboy Poetry Gathering and Western Music Rendezvous Lewistown
  406-538-4575

SEPTEMBER

- Miner's Union Day Philipsburg
  406-859-5125
- Libby Nordicfest / Libby
  406-293-2253
- Havre Festival Days Havre
  406-265-4383

OCTOBER

- Northern International Livestock Exposition Stock Show, Pro Rodeo and Western Expo / Billings
  406-256-2495
- Humanities Montana Festival of the Book Missoula
  406-243-6022
- McIntosh Apple Day Hamilton
  406-363-3338

NOVEMBER

- Parade of Lights / Forsyth
  406-347-5656
- Holiday Parade / Billings
  406-259-5454
- Seasonal Bazaar & Parade of Lights / Cut Bank
  406-873-4041

DECEMBER

- Montana Ballet Company's Nutcracker / Bozeman
  406-582-8702
- First Night Missoula Missoula
  406-549-4755
- A Montana Country Christmas / Stevensville
  406-777-3773

Miracle of America Museum, Polson

Bitterroot National Forest

Jacobson's Scenic View Cottages, East Glacier Park

Old Trail Museum, Choteau

Wild Goose Island, Glacier National Park

Index: Great Experience for Members

AAA editor's picks of exceptional note

Museum of the Rockies

Cathedral of St. Helena

Yellowstone National Park

C.M. Russell Museum

See Orientation map on p. 126 for corresponding grid coordinates, if applicable.

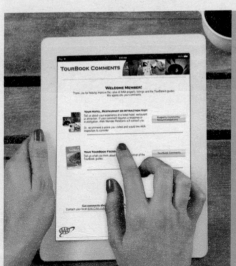

Montana Atlas Section

ROADS/HIGHWAYS

	INTERSTATE
	CONTROLLED ACCESS
	CONTROLLED ACCESS TOLL
	TOLL ROAD
	PRIMARY DIVIDED
	PRIMARY UNDIVIDED
	SECONDARY DIVIDED
	SECONDARY UNDIVIDED
	LOCAL DIVIDED
	LOCAL UNDIVIDED
	UNPAVED ROAD
	UNDER CONSTRUCTION
	TUNNEL
	PEDESTRIAN ONLY
	AUTO FERRY
	PASSENGER FERRY
	SCENIC BYWAY
10	DISTANCE BETWEEN MARKERS
	EXIT NUMBER-FREE/TOLL
	INTERCHANGE FULL/PARTIAL
	WELCOME/INFORMATION CENTER
	REST AREA/ SERVICE CENTER

BOUNDARIES

	INTERNATIONAL
	STATE
	COUNTY
	TIME ZONE
	CONTINENTAL DIVIDE

ROAD SHIELDS

	INTERSTATE/BUSINESS
	U.S./STATE/COUNTY
	FOREST/INDIAN
	TRANS- CANADA
	PROVINCIAL AUTOROUTE/ KING'S HIGHWAY
	MEXICO
	HISTORIC ROUTE 66
VT 41	REFERENCE PAGE INDICATOR

AREAS OF INTEREST

	INDIAN
	MILITARY
	PARK
	FOREST
	GRASSLANDS
	HISTORIC
	INT'L/REGIONAL AIRPORT
	INCORPORATED CITY

POINTS OF INTEREST

	TOWN
	NATIONAL CAPITAL
	STATE/PROVINCIAL CAPITAL
	AAA/CAA CLUB LOCATION
	FEATURE OF INTEREST
	COLLEGE/UNIVERSITY
	CAMPGROUND INFORMATION PROVIDED BY WOODALL'S®
	CUSTOMS STATION
	HISTORIC
	LIGHTHOUSE
	MONUMENT/MEMORIAL
	STATE/PROVINCIAL PARK
	NATIONAL WILDLIFE REFUGE
	SKI AREA
	SPORTS COMPLEX
	DAM

CITIES/TOWNS are color-coded by size, showing where to find AAA Approved and Diamond rated lodgings or restaurants listed in the AAA TourBook guides or on AAA.com:

- Red - major destinations and capitals; many listings
- Black - destinations; some listings
- Grey - no listings

MONTANA

Miles 45 22.5 0 22.5 45 Miles
Kilometers 45 22.5 0 22.5 45 Kilometers
ONE INCH EQUALS APPROXIMATELY 44 MILES OR 70.81 KILOMETERS 1:2,787,840

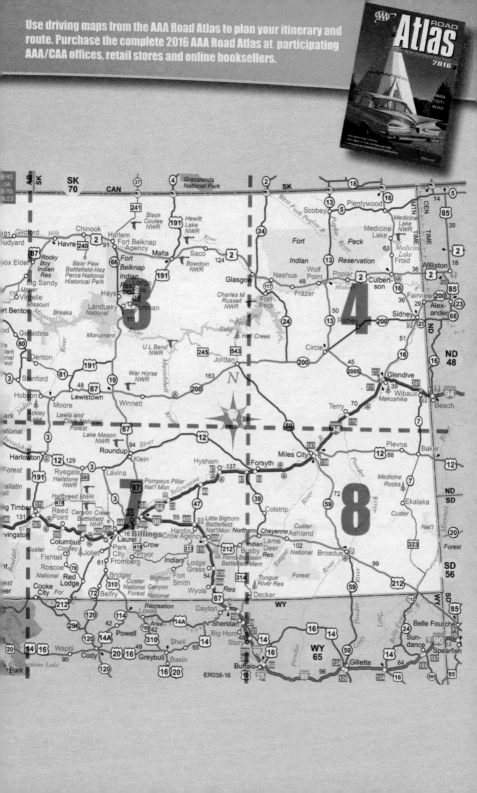

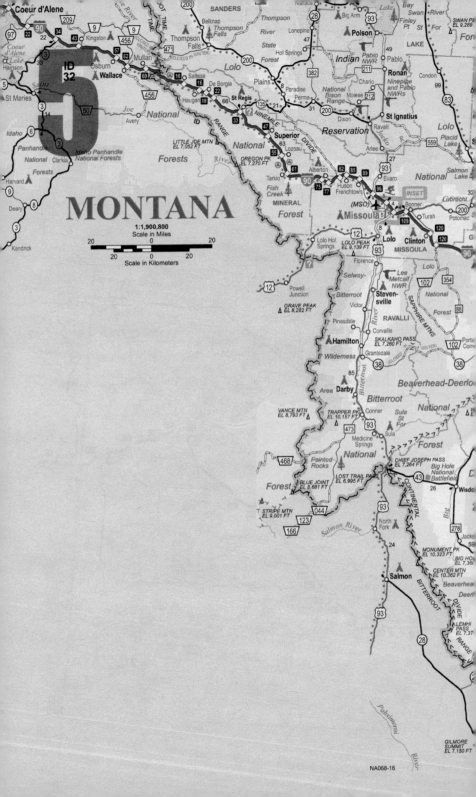

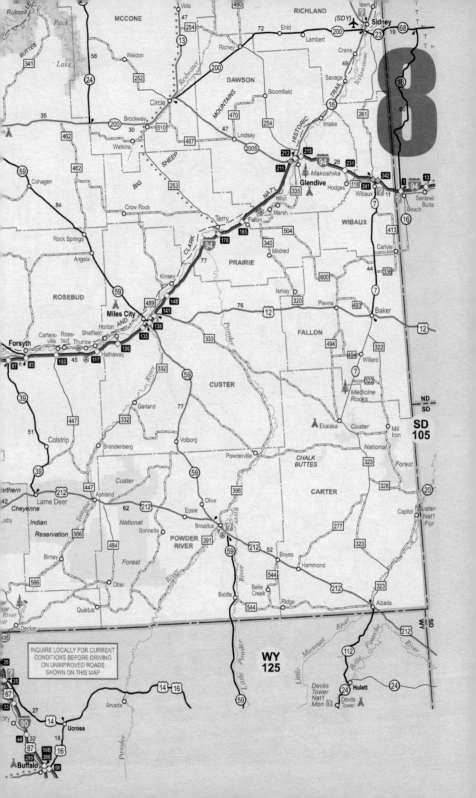

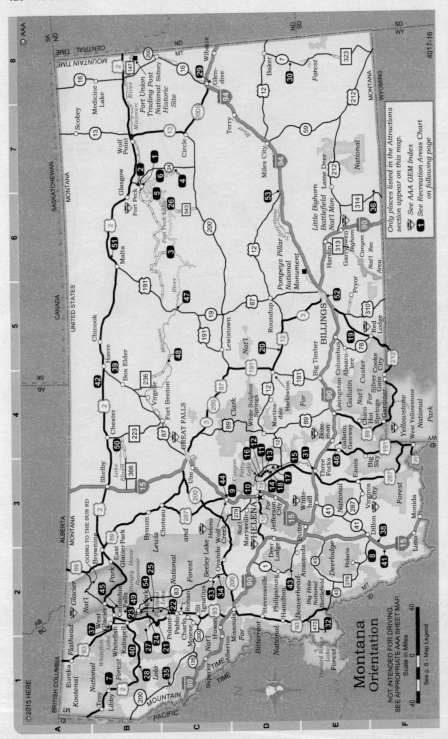

Montana
Orientation

NOT INTENDED FOR DRIVING.
SEE APPROPRIATE AAA SHEET MAP.

Scale in Miles

See p. 6 - Map Legend

Only places listed in the Attractions
section appear on this map.

⬥ See AAA GEM Index
🔲 See Recreation Areas Chart
on following page

©2015 HERE

4017-16

Recreation Areas Chart

The map location numerals in column 2 show an area's location on the preceding map.

	MAP LOCATION	CAMPING	PICNICKING	HIKING TRAILS	BOATING	BOAT RAMP	BOAT RENTAL	FISHING	SWIMMING	PETS ON LEASH	BICYCLE TRAILS	WINTER SPORTS	VISITOR CENTER	LODGE/CABINS	FOOD SERVICE
NATIONAL PARKS *(See place listings.)*															
Glacier (A-2) 1,000,000 acres. Horse rental.		•	•	•	•	•	•	•	•	•		•	•	•	•
NATIONAL FORESTS *(See place listings.)*															
Beaverhead-Deerlodge (E-2) 3,392,930 acres. Southwestern Montana. Horse rental.		•	•	•	•	•		•	•	•	•	•		•	
Bitterroot (D-1) 1,577,883 acres. Western Montana.		•	•	•	•	•		•	•	•	•	•			
Custer (E-4) 1.3 million acres. Southeastern Montana and north-western South Dakota.		•	•	•				•	•	•	•	•		•	
Flathead (A-1) 2,330,029 acres. Northwestern Montana. Horse rental.		•	•	•	•	•		•	•	•	•	•			
Gallatin (E-4) 1,735,239 acres. South-central Montana. Horse rental.		•	•	•	•	•		•	•	•	•	•		•	
Helena (C-3) 976,000 acres. West-central Montana.		•	•	•	•	•		•	•	•	•	•			
Kootenai (A-1) 2.2 million acres. Northwestern Montana. Horse rental.		•	•	•	•	•		•	•	•	•	•			
Lewis and Clark (B-3) 1,843,397 acres. West-central Montana.		•	•	•	•	•		•	•	•	•	•			
Lolo (B-1) 2,100,000 acres. Western Montana. Horse rental.		•	•	•	•	•		•	•	•	•	•			
NATIONAL RECREATION AREAS *(See place listings.)*															
Bighorn Canyon (E-6) 120,000 acres in southern Montana and northern Wyoming.		•	•	•	•	•		•	•	•			•		•
ARMY CORPS OF ENGINEERS															
Fort Peck Lake (B-6) off SR 24 in Fort Peck. Bird-watching, ca-noeing. *(See Fort Peck p. 158.)*		•	•	•	•	•		•	•				•		•
Downstream (B-7) 347 acres 1 mi. e. of Fort Peck off SR 117. Bird-watching; museum, playground.	**1**	•	•	•	•	•		•							
Dredge Cuts (B-7) 650 acres 3 mi. n. of Fort Peck off SR 117.	**2**	•	•	•				•	•						
Fourchette Bay (C-6) 80 acres 60 mi. s.e. of Malta off SR 191. Bird-watching, canoeing, kayaking.	**3**	•	•		•	•		•	•	•					
Nelson Creek (C-7) 468 acres 45 mi. s. of Fort Peck off SR 24. Bird-watching, canoeing, kayaking.	**4**	•	•		•	•		•	•						
The Pines (B-6) 927 acres 4.5 mi. n.w. of Fort Peck on SR 24, 14 mi. s.w. via a gravel road, then 12 mi. s.e. via a gravel road. Bird-watching, canoeing, kayaking; playground.	**5**	•	•		•	•		•	•	•		•			
Rock Creek (C-7) 345 acres 32 mi. s.e. of Fort Peck off SR 24. Bird-watching; beach.	**6**	•	•		•	•		•	•						•
Libby Dam (Lake Koocanusa) (B-1) 46,000 acres 13.5 mi. e. of Libby on SR 37, then 3.5 mi. n. on FR 228, following signs. Disc golf; playground. *(See Libby p. 186.)*	**7**	•	•	•	•	•		•	•	•	•	•	•	•	•
STATE															
Bannack (F-2) 1,529 acres 17 mi. w. of Dillon on SR 278, then 4 mi. s. on Bannack Rd., following signs. Historic. *(See Dillon p. 154.)*	**8**	•	•	•				•			•	•	•		
Beartooth Wildlife Management Area (D-3) 27,000 acres 10 mi. s.e. of Wolf Creek via a gravel road.	**9**	•	•		•	•		•	•	•					
Black Sandy (D-3) 55 acres 14 mi. n.e. of Helena via I-15 and CR 415.	**10**	•	•		•	•		•	•	•				•	
Canyon Ferry Lake (D-3) 5,000 acres 20 mi. e. of Helena off US 287. Hunting.		•	•		•	•	•	•	•	•		•	•		•
Cave Bay (D-4) 19 mi. e. of Helena via US 287 and CR 284.	**11**		•		•	•		•	•						•
Chinaman (D-4) 19 mi. e. of Helena via US 287 and CR 284.	**12**	•	•		•	•		•	•						
Court Sheriff (D-4) 18 mi. e. of Helena via US 287 and CR 284.	**13**	•	•		•			•	•	•					
Hellgate (D-3) 27 mi. e. of Helena via US 287 and CR 284.	**14**	•	•		•	•		•	•	•					
Indian Road (D-3) 1 mi. n. of Townsend on US 287.	**15**	•	•		•			•	•						
Riverside (D-4) 18 mi. e. of Helena via US 287 and CR 284.	**16**	•	•		•	•		•		•					

Recreation Areas Chart

The map location numerals in column 2 show an area's location on the preceding map.

Area	MAP LOCATION	CAMPING	PICNICKING	HIKING TRAILS	BOATING	BOAT RAMP	BOAT RENTAL	FISHING	SWIMMING	PETS ON LEASH	BICYCLE TRAILS	WINTER SPORTS	VISITOR CENTER	LODGE/CABINS	FOOD SERVICE
Silos (D-3) 8 mi. n.w. of Townsend off US 287.	17	•	•		•	•		•		•					•
White Earth (D-3) 5 mi. e. of Winston.	18	•	•		•	•		•		•					
Cooney Reservoir (E-5) 304 acres 5 mi. w. of Boyd via a gravel road.	19	•	•	•	•	•		•	•	•					•
Deadman's Basin (D-5) 500 acres 29 mi. e. of Harlowton off US 12.	20	•	•		•	•		•	•	•					
Flathead Lake (C-2) n. of Polson on US 93.															
Big Arm (C-1) 55 acres 15 mi. n. of Polson on US 93.	21	•	•		•	•		•	•	•					
Finley Point (C-2) 24 acres about 12 mi. n.e. of Polson off SR 35.	22	•	•		•	•		•	•	•					
Wayfarers (B-2) 68 acres 1 mi. s. of Bigfork off SR 35.	23	•	•		•	•		•	•	•					
West Shore (B-1) 146 acres about 20 mi. s. of Kalispell on US 93.	24	•	•	•	•	•		•	•	•					
Yellow Bay (B-2) 10 acres 20 mi. n.e. of Polson off SR 35.	25	•	•		•	•		•	•	•					
Hell Creek (C-6) 172 acres 26 mi. n. of Jordan via a gravel road on Fort Peck Reservoir.	26	•	•		•	•	•	•	•	•				•	•
Lake Mary Ronan (B-1) 76 acres 7 mi. n.w. of Dayton off US 93.	27	•	•		•	•		•	•	•					
Logan (B-1) 18 acres 45 mi. w. of Kalispell off US 2.	28	•	•		•	•		•	•	•					
Makoshika (C-8) 11,531 acres 1 mi. s. of Glendive at 1301 Snyder Ave. *(See Glendive p. 171.)*	29	•	•	•						•			•	•	•
Medicine Rocks (D-8) 320 acres 24 mi. s. of Baker on SR 7. Historic. *(See Baker p. 130.)*	30	•	•	•						•	•				
Missouri Headwaters (E-4) 527 acres 3 mi. e. of Three Forks, then 3 mi. n. of US 10 at 1585 Trident Jct. *(See Three Forks p. 205.)*	31	•	•	•	•			•		•			•		
Painted Rocks (E-2) 263 acres 20 mi. s.w. of Conner off SR 473.	32	•	•		•	•		•	•	•					
Placid Lake (C-2) 32 acres 6 mi. s.w. of Seeley Lake via CR 83.	33	•	•		•	•		•	•	•	•				
Salmon Lake (C-2) 42 acres 5 mi. s. of Seeley Lake on SR 83.	34	•	•	•	•	•		•	•	•					
Thompson Falls (C-1) 36 acres 3 mi. w. of Thompson Falls off SR 200.	35	•	•		•	•		•		•					
Tongue River Reservoir (F-6) 640 acres 6 mi. n. of Decker on CR 314, then 1 mi. e.	36	•	•		•	•		•	•	•					•
Whitefish Lake (A-2) 10 acres 5 mi. w. of Whitefish on US 93.	37	•	•		•	•	•	•	•	•				•	•
OTHER															
Barretts Park (F-3) 38 acres 8 mi. s.w. of Dillon off I-15.	38	•	•					•	•	•					
Beaver Creek (B-5) 10,000 acres 11 mi. s. of Havre on CR 234. Bird-watching. *(See Havre p. 177.)*	39	•	•	•				•		•			•		
Bitterroot Lake (B-1) 36 acres 5 mi. n. of US 2 at Marion.	40	•	•		•	•		•	•				•		
Clark Canyon Reservoir (F-2) 4,131 acres 20 mi. s.w. of Dillon on I-15. Hunting.	41	•	•		•	•	•	•	•	•					
Fresno Reservoir (B-4) 25,668 acres n.w. of Havre. Hunting, water skiing.	42	•	•		•	•		•	•	•					
Georgetown Lake (D-2) 2,850 acres 15 mi. w. of Anaconda on SR 1. Water skiing; playground. *(See Beaverhead-Deerlodge National Forest p. 131.)*	43	•	•	•	•	•		•	•	•		•		•	•
Holter Lake (C-3) 22 acres 2 mi. e. of Wolf Creek on Missouri River Rd., then 3 mi. s. via a gravel road. *(See Wolf Creek p. 214.)*	44	•	•		•	•		•	•	•				•	•
Hungry Horse Reservoir (B-2) 6,836 acres 10 mi. e. of Columbia Falls on SR 40, then s. 5 mi. via a gravel road. Hunting. *(See Glacier National Park p. 165.)*	45	•	•		•	•		•	•				•	•	•
Hyalite Canyon (E-3) 35,000 acres 14 mi. s. of Bozeman on SR 85.	46	•	•	•	•			•	•	•		•			
James Kipp (C-5) 465 acres 65 mi. n.e. of Lewistown off US 191.	47	•	•		•	•		•							
Judith Landing (C-5) 44 mi. s.e. of Big Sandy on CR 236.	48	•			•	•		•							

Recreation Areas Chart

The map location numerals in column 2 show an area's location on the preceding map.

	MAP LOCATION	CAMPING	PICNICKING	HIKING TRAILS	BOATING	BOAT RAMP	BOAT RENTAL	FISHING	SWIMMING	PETS ON LEASH	BICYCLE TRAILS	WINTER SPORTS	VISITOR CENTER	LODGE/CABINS	FOOD SERVICE
Lake Blaine (B-2) 13 acres 7 mi. e. of Kalispell.	49	•		•	•	•		•	•	•	•			•	•
Lake Elwell (B-4) 6,197 acres 18 mi. s.w. of Chester.	50	•	•		•	•		•	•	•					•
Nelson Reservoir (B-6) 7,702 acres 18 mi. n.e. of Malta off US 2.	51	•	•		•	•		•	•	•					
Riverfront Park (E-5) 1 mi. s. of Billings on CR 416.	52		•	•	•			•				•	•		
Rosebud East (D-6) 32 acres e. of Forsyth off I-94. Bird-watching.	53	•	•	•	•	•		•		•		•			
Swan Lake (B-2) 10 acres 14 mi. s.e. of Bigfork on SR 83. Water skiing.	54	•	•		•	•		•	•	•					

ABSAROKEE (E-5) pop. 1,150, elev. 4,039'

RECREATIONAL ACTIVITIES

Horseback Riding

- SAVE **Paintbrush Adventures** is in Stillwater Valley at 86 N. Stillwater Rd. Other activities are offered. **Hours:** Horseback riding trips are offered daily year-round. Departure times vary; phone ahead. **Phone:** (406) 328-4158.

White-water Rafting

- **Absaroka River Adventures** is at 113 Grove St. Other activities are offered. **Hours:** Rafting trips daily 7 a.m.-10 p.m., May-Aug. **Phone:** (406) 328-7440 or (800) 334-7238.

ALBERTON (C-1) pop. 420, elev. 3,029'

RECREATIONAL ACTIVITIES

White-water Rafting

- **Montana River Guides** departs from Missoula and the Alberton Gorge. **Hours:** Full- and half-day white-water rafting trips depart daily at 9 and 2, mid-Apr. to mid-Oct. **Phone:** (406) 722-7238 or (800) 381-7238.

ANACONDA (D-2) elev. 5,288'

Because it had ample water and was surrounded by one of the world's richest copper deposits, Anaconda was chosen for the site of a copper smelter by the originator of Montana's copper industry, Marcus Daly. Daly, an Irish immigrant who was a manager of a mine in Utah, bought the mine when it was thought worthless after the silver lode ran out. Daly saw the mine's potential in its copper reserves—with the invention of the telephone and telegraph, copper wire was in high demand. By the time Daly died in 1900, he was one of the world's richest men.

Daly also founded the nearby town of Hamilton (see place listing p. 176), where he spent summers with his family. Today all that is left of Daly's smelter is the 585-foot smokestack, which can be viewed at Anaconda Smoke Stack State Park on Anaconda Smelter Road.

A number of buildings from the 1800s remain, including the Deer Lodge County Courthouse, 800 S. Main St.; City Hall Center at 401 E. Commercial Ave.; Hearst Free Library at E. Fourth and Main streets; and St. Mark's Episcopal Church, corner of E. Sixth and Main streets. Anaconda's architecture spans Romanesque to Victorian styles. At 305 Main St. is the Art Deco, neoclassical 1936 Washoe Theatre.

A popular scenic highway, SR 1, begins in Anaconda and heads west over Flint Creek Pass.

Anaconda Visitor's Center & Chamber of Commerce: 306 E. Park St., Anaconda, MT 59711. **Phone:** (406) 563-2400.

Self-guiding tours: The visitor's center offers a map describing a walking tour of the historic district; the fee is $2.

COPPER VILLAGE MUSEUM AND ARTS CENTER is at 401 E. Commercial in Anaconda's former city hall. The ornate building houses archives and the Marcus Daly Historical Society Museum, which chronicles the area's heritage through pioneer and smelting relics. Temporary art exhibitions highlight the work of international artists. Regularly scheduled special events and educational activities also are offered.

Time: Allow 30 minutes minimum. **Hours:** Tues.-Fri. 10-4. Closed major holidays. **Cost:** Free. **Phone:** (406) 563-2422. GT 🏕

VINTAGE BUS TOUR departs from the Anaconda Visitor's Center & Chamber of Commerce, 306 E. Park St. Highlights of the sightseeing trip in a 1936 touring bus include the historic business district, several churches, the Washoe Theatre, the smokestack interpretive site, a Jack Nicklaus-designed golf course on reclaimed smelter property and one of the state's oldest fish hatcheries. **Time:** Allow 1 hour minimum. **Hours:** Tours are given Mon.-Sat. at 10 and 2, mid-May to mid-Sept. **Cost:** $8; $4 (ages 0-6). **Phone:** (406) 563-2400. GT

BARCLAY II SUPPER CLUB & LOUNGE   406/563-5541
👙👙 Steak Seafood. Casual Dining. $15-$35 **AAA Inspector Notes:** At this Montana supper club, all meals include a relish tray, salad or soup, a side of spaghetti and a scoop of ice cream for dessert. Patrons dine on large portions, including locally purchased and in-house cut steaks—most notably the tenderloin entrée. In an informal setting just 6 miles from Fairmont Hot Springs, the crowd enjoys good food and pleasant service. **Features:** full bar. **Reservations:** suggested, weekends. **Address:** 1300 E Commercial Ave 59711 **Location:** I-90 exit 208 (Anaconda), 7.5 mi sw on SR 1 (E Commercial Ave). D

MAY PALACE   406/563-3388
👙👙 Chinese. Casual Dining. $8-$12 **AAA Inspector Notes:** This very popular restaurant, with an attached casino, serves tasty, authentic food. The mu shu is quite flavorful and the portion is large. **Features:** full bar. **Address:** 1520 E Commercial Ave 59711 **Location:** I-90 exit 208 (Anaconda), 7 mi sw on SR 1 (E Commercial Ave). L D

BAKER (D-8) pop. 1,741

Named for the superintendent of construction of the Milwaukee Road, Baker is near the middle of vast oil and gas fields. Until 1915 Baker was solely a grazing and farming town. Then, a driller in search of water struck a natural-gas pocket, setting fire to his well, which burned as a natural torch for 6 years. Baker is now a center for local petroleum and agricultural interests.

Baker Chamber of Commerce & Agriculture: 125 S. Main St., P.O. Box 849, Baker, MT 59313. **Phone:** (406) 778-2266.

MEDICINE ROCKS STATE PARK is 24 mi. s. on SR 7. The 320-acre park contains huge sandstone formations once used by Native Americans for ceremonies. An interpretive trail describes the site's history. In summer hiking and bicycling can be enjoyed, and in winter snowshoeing is a popular activity. *See Recreation Areas Chart.* **Cost:** $6 (nonresidents per private vehicle); $4 (nonresidents arriving by other means); free (Montana residents with ID). Camping $24-$28 (nonresidents); $18-$20 (nonresidents with a Montana State Park passport); $14-$18 (Montana residents with ID). **Phone:** (406) 377-6256.

BEAVERHEAD-DEERLODGE NATIONAL FOREST (E-2)

Elevations in the forest range from 4,075 ft. in the valleys to 11,361 ft. on Hilgard Peak. Refer to AAA maps for additional elevation information.

Beaverhead-Deerlodge National Forest is part of the huge complex of national forests occupying most of southwestern Montana. In 1996, Deerlodge National Forest's 1,194,124 acres (nearly 100 square miles) were combined with Beaverhead National Forest to form an outdoor recreation area encompassing more than 3.3 million acres.

Glaciated peaks rise from broad valleys in the area to form some of Montana's most majestic ranges—the Anaconda, Bitterroot, Beaverhead, Flint Creek, Gravelly, Highland, Madison, Tobacco Root and Sapphire. Mountains in these ranges are among the loftiest in the state; more than 40 surpass 10,000 feet. Mount Evans rises to 10,604 feet, and several more, including Hilgard Peak, exceed 11,000 feet.

From the snowpack of these ranges spring the Big Hole, Beaverhead and Ruby rivers, which form three major tributaries of the Jefferson River. The high country also supplies some of the tributaries of the Madison River. The Clark Fork River flows from its headwaters west of the Continental Divide to Idaho's Lake Pend Oreille.

Through this maze of mountains and river valleys Sacagawea led Meriwether Lewis and William Clark in their search for a passage to the Pacific. This was the land of Sacagawea's people, the Shoshones, who re-provisioned and led the expedition over Lemhi Pass in 1805 and north to a final passage to the West. Despite the inroads of progress—lumbering, mining and ranching—much of the forest's lands have changed little since Lewis and Clark's visit.

Within the forest are portions of the Anaconda-Pintler and Lee Metcalf wilderness areas and a large number of roadless tracts. Typical features of roadless areas are glacial lakes, trout streams and rugged mountain vistas.

The Anaconda-Pintler Wilderness straddles 30 miles of the Anaconda Range and the Continental Divide. The land gradually rises from dense stands of lodgepole pine to open parks dotted with lakes, culminating in jagged peaks in the heart of the range. Anglers prize the clear mountain streams and alpine lakes for their abundance and variety of trout.

Another major area is the Taylor-Hilgard portion of the Lee Metcalf Wilderness. This unit is one of the four portions of wilderness along the spine of the Madison Range, which lies just northwest of Yellowstone National Park. Soaring peaks, knife-edged ridges and alpine lakes are characteristics of this popular area. Bird-watchers will find more than 260 species frequenting a variety of habitats in the forest. The region provides winter range for bighorn sheep and mountain goats and a home to grizzly and black bears, mule deer, mountain lions, elk and moose.

The bald eagle nests in the southeastern Gravelly Range and winters along the Red Rock, Ruby, Jefferson, Madison, Big Hole and Beaverhead rivers. Most migration and wintering activities occur in the large river valleys adjoining the forest. The gray wolf is an occasional visitor to parts of the Continental Divide southwest of Dillon. Grizzly bears occupy portions of the Madison Range within the Lee Metcalf Wilderness and are occasional visitors to the Tobacco Root Mountains and the Gravelly Range.

The forest offers fishing streams, hiking trails, groomed snowmobile trails, developed campgrounds and sites for motorized boating. Visitors can explore many old mines near Deer Lodge, plus the ghost town of Elkhorn, near Boulder, an 1880s mining town with a few corporeal residents. Fifteen miles west of Anaconda on SR 1 is Georgetown Lake *(see Recreation Areas Chart),* one of the area's busiest recreation sites, partly due to its excellent fishing. Snowmobiling and cross-country and downhill skiing are available at Discovery Basin, north of Georgetown Lake, and at Maverick Mountain near Dillon.

Detailed information about campgrounds and recreational opportunities is available at the district ranger stations in Butte, Deer Lodge, Dillon, Ennis, Philipsburg, Sheridan, Whitehall, Wisdom and Wise River. For further information contact the Beaverhead-Deerlodge National Forest Supervisor's Office, 420 Barrett St., Dillon, MT 59725; phone (406) 683-3900 or (406) 683-3913 for the park's 24-hour information line. *See Recreation Areas Chart.*

BELGRADE pop. 7,389
• Restaurants p. 132

HOLIDAY INN EXPRESS & SUITES BELGRADE
(406)388-7100

Hotel
$94-$235

Address: 309 W Madison Ave 59714 **Location:** I-90 exit 298, just n on SR 85. **Facility:** 97 units. 3 stories, interior corridors. **Parking:** winter plug-ins. **Terms:** cancellation fee imposed. **Amenities:** safes. **Pool(s):** heated indoor. **Activities:** hot tub, exercise room. **Guest Services:** valet and coin laundry, area transportation. **Featured Amenity:** full hot breakfast.

LA QUINTA INN & SUITES BELGRADE / BOZEMAN
(406)388-2222

 Hotel $64-$273 **Address:** 6445 Jackrabbit Ln 59714 **Location:** I-90 exit 298, just s on SR 85. **Facility:** 65 units, some efficiencies. 3 stories, interior corridors. **Pool(s):** heated indoor. **Activities:** sauna, limited exercise equipment. **Guest Services:** coin laundry.

QUALITY INN
(406)388-0800

Hotel
$59-$139

Address: 6261 Jackrabbit Ln 59714 **Location:** I-90 exit 298, just s on SR 85. **Facility:** 67 units. 3 stories, interior corridors. **Parking:** winter plug-ins. **Activities:** exercise room. **Guest Services:** coin laundry. **Featured Amenity:** continental breakfast.

SUPER 8-BELGRADE/BOZEMAN AIRPORT   (406)388-1493

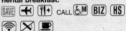 Hotel $70-$99 **Address:** 6450 Jackrabbit Ln 59714 **Location:** I-90 exit 298, just s on SR 85. **Facility:** 72 units. 4 stories, interior corridors. **Parking:** winter plug-ins. **Amenities:** safes. **Pool(s):** heated indoor. **Activities:** hot tub, exercise room. **Guest Services:** coin laundry.

WHERE TO EAT

FIESTA MEXICANA   406/388-8887

Mexican. Casual Dining. $8-$20 **AAA Inspector Notes:** The homemade salsas, sauces, beans and dips will transport you to Mexico. Heat levels are optional and the staff will allow your choice for the sides on the platters. Wood floors, comfy booth seats and Mexican décor add to the appeal. **Features:** beer & wine. **Address:** 6220 Jackrabbit Ln 59714 **Location:** I-90 exit 298, just s.

GALLATIN RIVER GRILL   406/388-0148

Regional American. Casual Dining. $22-$28 **AAA Inspector Notes:** Patrons find quality in the regional meats and fish and in the creative preparations. Views of the surrounding mountains from the casual dining room contribute to a Big Sky adventure. **Features:** full bar, patio dining. **Reservations:** suggested. **Address:** 9105 Thorpe Rd 59718 **Location:** I-90 exit 298, 2.7 mi s on SR 85, 1 mi w on Valley Center Rd (gravel), then 0.5 mi s, follow signs; in Gallatin River Lodge.

MACKENZIE RIVER PIZZA   406/388-0016

Pizza. Casual Dining. $8-$20 **AAA Inspector Notes:** Known for its eclectic Western decor, the restaurant lets patrons choose from several microbrews to accompany a specialty pizza or large, innovative sandwich. Pizza crusts are wonderful and offer the choice of sourdough, natural grain, deep dish or thin crust. **Features:** beer & wine, patio dining. **Address:** 409 W Main St 59714 **Location:** I-90 exit 298, 1 mi s, then just e.

RIO SABINAS SOUTHWESTERN GRILL   406/388-9200

Southwestern. Casual Dining. $10-$20 **AAA Inspector Notes:** This new-concept restaurant is brought to you by the owners of the highly successful Montana/Wyoming Rib & Chop House restaurants. It's in the remodeled Mercantile Building and features Western décor, beautiful reclaimed wood beams and rough-hewn wood accents. In addition to steaks, ribs and a variety of burritos and fajitas, you can expect original sauces, homemade salsas and fresh tortillas. **Features:** full bar, happy hour. **Address:** 11 W Main St 59714 **Location:** Jct Broadway; center; in Belgrade Mercantile Building. **Parking:** street only.

THE WOK   406/388-2838

Chinese. Casual Dining. $9-$22 **AAA Inspector Notes:** The menu offers traditionally prepared cuisine such as beef broccoli, Chinese hot pot and kung pao chicken. Keep in mind that portions are large. **Features:** beer & wine. **Address:** 312 W Main St, Suite B-10 59714 **Location:** I-90 exit 298, 1 mi n, then 0.5 mi w.

BIGFORK (B-2) pop. 4,270, elev. 2,968'

On the bay formed by the Swan River on the northeastern shore of Flathead Lake, Bigfork once was a small fishing village and trade center for nearby orchards and farms. Its reputation as an artists' and writers' colony now makes it a popular cultural retreat. Among recreational pursuits are snowmobiling and skiing in winter and a host of water sports in summer.

Glacially formed Flathead Lake *(see place listing p. 156)* is the largest natural body of fresh water west of the Mississippi River; at points along its 38-mile length the lake stretches 15 miles wide. Jewel Basin, one of the country's most popular hiking areas with 35 miles of trails, is 11 miles north. A Flathead National Forest *(see place listing p. 157)* ranger station provides information about recreational opportunities in the nearby mountains.

Cultural highlights in Bigfork include the Riverbend Concert Series, which stages Sunday performances throughout the summer. From mid-May through Labor Day, Bigfork Summer Playhouse presents a regular repertory of Broadway musicals; phone (406) 837-4886 for ticket information.

Bigfork Area Chamber of Commerce: 8155 Hwy. 35, P.O. Box 237, Bigfork, MT 59911. **Phone:** (406) 837-5888.

QUESTA SAIL BOAT departs from Flathead Lake Lodge, 4150 Flathead Lodge Rd. This 1929 restored 51-foot racing sloop offers 1.5-hour tours on Flathead Lake. A 2-hour sunset cruise also is offered. A sister ship is available in case the *Questa* is filled. **Hours:** Tours depart daily at 1, 3 and 6:30, mid-June to mid-Sept. **Cost:** Fare $45; $40 (ages 0-12 and 65+). Sunset fare $60. Reservations are recommended. **Phone:** (406) 837-5569.

BRIDGE STREET COTTAGES   (406)837-2785

Cottage
$95-$325

Address: 309 Bridge St 59911 **Location:** Downtown. **Facility:** This collection of distinctive cottages is located on the edge of the village among a grove of mature trees next to the Swan River. Enjoy a barbecue meal on the decks. 12 cottages. 1 story, exterior corridors. **Parking:** winter plug-ins. **Terms:** 30 day cancellation notice-fee imposed, resort fee. **Amenities:** safes.

MOUNTAIN LAKE LODGE   406-837-3800

Hotel
Rates not provided

Address: 14735 Sylvan Dr 59911 **Location:** On SR 35, 5 mi s. Located in a quiet area. **Facility:** 30 units, some kitchens. 1-3 stories (no elevator), exterior corridors. **Parking:** winter plug-ins. **Terms:** check-in 4 pm. **Dining:** 2 restaurants. **Pool(s):** heated outdoor. **Activities:** hot tub, exercise room. **Guest Services:** coin laundry.

TIMBERS MOTEL   406-837-6200

🏍 **Motel.** Rates not provided. **Address:** 8540 Hwy 35 59911 **Location:** Just n on SR 35 from jct SR 209. **Facility:** 40 units. 2 stories (no elevator), exterior corridors. **Amenities:** safes. **Pool(s):** heated outdoor. **Activities:** sauna, hot tub.

WHERE TO EAT

ECHO LAKE CAFE   406/837-4252

🍴🍴 Breakfast. Casual Dining. $6-$13 **AAA Inspector Notes:** I tried this café in the foothills of the Mission Mountains and was blown away by the high quality of ingredients. Fresh-squeezed orange juice, wagon-wheel-size pancakes, real maple syrup, fresh fruit, oh, the list goes on and on. The breakfast and lunches are excellent. It's very popular and extremely busy; your wait may be long since they do not accept reservations. **Features:** patio dining. **Address:** 1195 Swan Hwy (SR 83) 59911 **Location:** 2.7 mi w on SR 35, 2.1 mi e. B L

EL TOPO CANTINA   406/837-2114

🍴🍴 Mexican. Casual Dining. $8-$15 **AAA Inspector Notes:** The wildly popular, lively gathering spot serves what many consider to be some of the area's best Mexican food. Fresh ingredients, careful preparation and friendly service are hallmarks. For a true taste treat, don't pass up the fish tacos. **Features:** full bar. **Address:** 7987 SR 35 59911 **Location:** On north end of town. D

SHOWTHYME!   406/837-0707

🍴🍴🍴 American. Fine Dining. $18-$34 **AAA Inspector Notes:** The top-notch staff treats every diner with special enthusiasm at this casual, fun eatery, where imaginative fare is the norm. Seasonal menus feature creative entrees and desserts, such as truffle torte on crème anglaise. Summer deck seating is available. **Features:** full bar, patio dining. **Reservations:** suggested. **Address:** 548 Electric Ave 59911 **Location:** Downtown. **Parking:** street only. D

WHEN IN ROME   406/837-7663

🍴🍴 Mediterranean Pizza. Casual Dining. $7-$23 **AAA Inspector Notes:** Pizza is the specialty, but you'll find some pasta dishes as well, including traditional lasagna. The homemade wholewheat thin crust is topped with fresh meat and veggies, then baked Roman style for a light and crispy result. The chef won a pizza competition in Las Vegas, so the word's out. This is a very popular place and a reservation is a must. **Features:** beer & wine, patio dining. **Reservations:** suggested. **Address:** 8270 Hwy 35 59911 **Location:** 1 mi n on SR 35 from jct SR 209. D

BIG HOLE NATIONAL BATTLEFIELD
(E-2)

Big Hole National Battlefield is 10 miles west of Wisdom on SR 43. Covering 655 acres of Nez Perce National Historical Park (see place listing in Idaho p. 86), the site commemorates the battle fought Aug. 9-10, 1877, when U.S. troops aided by civilian volunteers staged a surprise attack against several bands of Nez Perce Indians. The Nez Perce were attempting to escape confinement to a reservation by fleeing to Idaho Territory.

Although victorious at Big Hole, the Nez Perce sustained severe losses—approximately 90 men, women and children were killed. These losses forced their surrender 2 months later on Oct. 5, 1877, in the Bear Paw Mountains. Some 250 Nez Perce escaped to Canada.

The battlefield became a military reserve in 1883, a national monument in 1910 and a national battlefield in 1963. The visitor center displays Native American and military items and presents an audiovisual program about the battle. An observation deck features scopes for wildlife viewing. Interpretive trails traverse the battlefield to the areas where the soldiers retreated and the Nez Perce camped.

Allow 30 minutes minimum for the visitor center and 1 hour, 30 minutes for the battlefield. Battlefield open daily dawn-dusk. Visitor center open daily 9-5, late Apr.-Sept. 30; 10-5, rest of year. Phone for information about tipi-raising sessions. Guided tours are offered daily, June-Aug. Visitor center closed Jan. 1, Martin Luther King Jr. Day, Presidents Day, Columbus Day, Veterans Day, Thanksgiving and Christmas. Battlefield Road is closed to automobile traffic in winter; skiing and snowshoeing are permitted. Free. Phone (406) 689-3155.

BIGHORN CANYON NATIONAL RECREATION AREA (E-6)

In Montana and northern Wyoming, Bighorn Canyon National Recreation Area centers on a 71-mile-long lake bounded by steep canyon walls. Covering about 120,000 acres, the area features facilities for boat launching, picnicking and camping at Ok-A-Beh Marina, 42 miles southwest of Hardin via SR 313.

Horseshoe Bend in Wyoming, 14 miles north of Lovell, Wyo., via SR 37, and Barry's Landing in Montana, 32 miles south of Yellowtail Dam by boat or north of Lovell via SR 37, have areas for swimming, camping, picnicking and boat launching (personal watercraft are permitted). Hunting and fishing also are available.

Admission to the recreation area is $5 for a daily pass. Yellowtail Dam Visitor Center in Fort Smith offers an orientation film about the area as well as exhibits about wildlife, Native American culture and the construction of Yellowtail Dam, said to be the highest dam in the Missouri River Basin. The center is open daily 8:30-5, Memorial Day to Labor Day. Phone (406) 666-9961.

The Bighorn Canyon Visitor Center, at the junction of US 310 and US 14A in Lovell is open daily 8-6, Memorial Day-Labor Day; 8:30-4:30, rest of year. Closed Jan. 1, Thanksgiving and Christmas. Phone (307) 548-5406.

For further information, contact Bighorn Canyon National Recreation Area, P.O. Box 7458, Fort Smith, MT 59035 or 20 US 14A E., Lovell, WY 82431; to verify schedule phone (406) 666-2412 or (307) 548-5406. See Recreation Areas Chart.

BIG SKY (E-3) pop. 2,308

- Hotels & Restaurants map & index p. 324
- Part of Yellowstone National Park area — see map p. 316

Surrounded by the mountain meadows and forested slopes of Gallatin National Forest *(see place listing p. 160)* and the Spanish Peaks Wilderness, Big Sky is an all-year resort community. Lone Mountain serves as the centerpiece for this village conceived and developed by newsman Chet Huntley.

Skiing and snowmobiling are popular in winter, while summer activity revolves around hiking, horseback riding, white-water rafting and mountain biking.

RECREATIONAL ACTIVITIES

Skiing

- **Big Sky Resort** is at 50 Big Sky Resort Rd. Other activities are offered. **Hours:** Skiing is available daily mid-Nov. to late Apr. Summer activities are available daily June-Sept. Hours vary; phone ahead. **Phone:** (406) 995-5000 or (800) 548-4486.

BUCK'S T-4 LODGE   (406)995-4111 **6**

▼▼▼ Hotel $149-$209 Address: 46625 Gallatin Rd 59716 Location: US 191, 1 mi s of Big Sky entrance. Facility: 72 units, some two bedrooms and efficiencies. 2 stories (no elevator), interior/exterior corridors. Parking: winter plug-ins. Terms: closed 4/16-5/27 & 10/6-11/25, check-in 4 pm, cancellation fee imposed. Dining: Buck's T-4, see separate listing. Activities: hot tub, cross country skiing, snowmobiling, game room.

[icons]

THE LODGE AT BIG SKY   406/995-7858 **5**

▼▼▼▼ Hotel. Rates not provided. Address: 75 Sitting Bull Ln 59716 Location: Jct US 191 and SR 64, 9 mi w on SR 64. Located in Big Sky Mountain Village. Facility: 86 units, some efficiencies. 4 stories, interior corridors. Terms: check-in 4 pm. Pool(s): heated indoor. Activities: hot tub, downhill & cross country skiing, sledding, trails, exercise room. Guest Services: coin laundry, area transportation.

[icons]

RAINBOW RANCH LODGE   406/995-4132 **7**

▼▼▼▼ Resort Hotel. Rates not provided. Address: 42950 Gallatin Rd 59730 Location: 5 mi s on US 191. Facility: In Gallatin National Forest, this property sits in front of the Gallatin River. There is outdoor infinity hot tub and fireplace. Many rooms have decks overlooking a grassy area, waterfall and pond. 21 units, some two bedrooms. 2 stories (no elevator), exterior corridors. Dining: restaurant, see separate listing. Activities: hot tub, fishing, massage.

[icons]

WHERE TO EAT

BUCK'S T-4   406/993-5222 **6**

▼▼▼ Regional American. Fine Dining. $11-$39 AAA Inspector Notes: Such features as a warm, comfy blaze in the stone hearth, game trophies, wildlife pictures and welcoming staff members might make guests feel like lords of a country estate. The chef creates beautiful and delicious meals featuring wild game and other regional delectables. More than 140 wines are on the award-winning list. Features: full bar. Reservations: suggested. Address: 46225 Gallatin Rd 59716 Location: US 191, 1 mi s of Big Sky entrance; in Buck's T-4 Lodge. [D] CALL [M]

THE CABIN BAR & GRILL   406/995-4244 **4**

▼▼ Regional American. Casual Dining. $10-$38 AAA Inspector Notes: After a day on the slopes, snow lovers can stop in for an après-ski snack, but it's well worth the trip to come back for a delicious, creatively prepared dinner. The varied menu focuses on regional cuisine. The Cabin is open only for dinner during the summer months. Features: full bar. Address: Big Sky's Mountain Village 59716 Location: Jct US 191 and SR 64; 9 mi w on SR 64; in Big Sky Resort, 3rd floor of Arrowhead Mall. [L] [D] [M]

THE CORRAL STEAKHOUSE   406/995-4249 **7**

◇◇◇
Steak
Casual Dining
$9-$35

AAA Inspector Notes: Comfort food is served in a Western setting at this local favorite that features a large dining/lounge area. A varied menu offers finger foods to full meals including sandwiches, beef or buffalo burgers, fried chicken, rainbow trout, walleye pike and cod, pork chops, pasta and a selection of steaks. Features: full bar. Address: 42895 Gallatin Rd 59730 Location: 5 mi s on US 191. [B] [L] [D]

LOTUS PAD   406/995-2728 **5**

▼▼ Thai. Casual Dining. $14-$24 AAA Inspector Notes: The owners have really tried to replicate the street foods of Thailand and for the most part have succeeded. There are a few variations of the more well-known dishes. The open kitchen dominates the dining area, which is saying a lot, as the dining room only has six tables. Features: full bar, patio dining. Reservations: required. Address: 3090 Big Pine Dr 59716 Location: Jct US 191 and SR 64 (Lone Mountain Tr), 3 mi w on SR 64, just s. [D] [M]

RAINBOW RANCH LODGE   406/995-4132 **8**

▼▼▼▼ Regional American. Fine Dining. $26-$55 AAA Inspector Notes: Patrons can enjoy the view of the Gallatin River and surrounding mountains of Big Sky while dining on expertly prepared gourmet cuisine. The chef always has special offerings that focus on regional favorites and wild game. Choices on the extensive award-winning wine list will complement a wide selection of meals. Features: full bar, patio dining, happy hour. Reservations: suggested. Address: 42950 Gallatin Rd 59736 Location: 5 mi s on US 191. [D]

BIG TIMBER (E-4) pop. 1,641, elev. 4,075'

CRAZY MOUNTAIN MUSEUM is off I-90 exit 367, s. to Frontage Rd., then e. to Cemetery Rd. Displays relate the history of the Sweet Grass County area. Featured are a one-room schoolhouse; a Norwegian *stabbur* (storehouse); a diorama of the area as it appeared in 1907; a 1915 Ford; paintings by Jessica Zemsky and Jack Hines; photographs; printed history and memorabilia from the 1800s; the Lewis and Clark Montana Native Plant Garden; and displays about the Leo Cremer Rodeo and archeology. Changing exhibits also are offered. **Hours:** Mon.-Sat. 10-4:30, Sun. 1-4:30, Memorial Day-Sept. 30. Phone ahead to confirm schedule. **Cost:** Donations. **Phone:** (406) 932-5126.

BIG TIMBER SUPER 8   (406)932-8888

▼▼ Hotel $84-$109 Address: 20A Big Timber Loop Rd 59011 Location: I-90 exit 367, just s. Facility: 41 units. 2 stories (no elevator), interior corridors. Parking: winter plug-ins. Guest Services: coin laundry.

[icons]

RIVER VALLEY INN   (406)932-4943

▼ Hotel $68-$100 Address: 600 W 2nd St 59011 Location: I-90 exit 367, just n, then 0.6 mi e. Facility: 22 units. 2 stories (no elevator), interior corridors.

[icons]

WHERE TO EAT

THE GRAND 406/932-4459

◆◆◆ Regional American. Casual Dining. $13-$37 **AAA Inspector Notes:** *Historic.* "Offering beautiful accommodations, fine dining and spirits to travelers, fishermen, cowboys and sheepherders since 1890." The motto says it all. Listed on the National Register of Historic Places, The Grand hotel has been restored to her original state, showcasing wood accents that highlight the Western décor. The restaurant serves locally raised beef and lamb and fresh seafood flown in daily. An inexpensive menu is offered in the 1890 saloon. Lunch is not served on Saturday. **Features:** full bar, Sunday brunch. **Address:** 139 McLeod St 59011 **Location:** Jct E 2nd Ave. **Parking:** street only. [L] [D] CALL Ⓔ🄼

BILLINGS (E-5) pop. 104,170, elev. 3,124'
• Hotels p. 136 • Restaurants p. 139

In 1823 at Alkali Creek, the site of present-day Billings, 400 Blackfeet attacked American Fur Co. trappers. Some pelts taken by the Blackfeet were traded to Hudson's Bay Co. and later appeared on the London market. An American recognized the stolen pelts, touching off an international incident.

The Northern Pacific Railroad arrived in 1882, literally putting Billings on the map. Refusing to pay the exorbitant prices the landowners in Coulson were demanding, Northern Pacific Railroad laid out a new city 2 miles upriver and named it in honor of its president, Frederick Billings. In 5 months the town grew from a single building to 250 buildings and 2,000 citizens.

The Rimrocks, Billings' most striking natural feature, rise 500 feet above the Yellowstone Valley, running the length of the city and beyond. Legend has it that Crow warriors once rode over Sacrifice Cliff to appease their gods and to halt the spread of smallpox among their people. At the bottom of Chief Black Otter Trail is Boothill Cemetery. The only vestige of the town of Coulson, the cemetery is the final resting place of two dozen individuals, including peace officers, massacre victims and Muggins Taylor, the scout who brought the world the news of Lt. Col. George Armstrong Custer's last stand.

Pictograph Cave State Park, 7 miles southeast at the I-90 Lockwood exit, features caverns that have sheltered people of many Native American cultures. Pictorial records adorn the walls of one cave.

MontanaFair is a 9-day agricultural celebration beginning the second week in August. Exhibits, music, food, entertainment, a carnival and petting zoo add to the experience. One of the region's largest events, the fair is held annually in MetraPark.

Billings Chamber of Commerce/Convention and Visitors Bureau: 815 S. 27th St., P.O. Box 31177, Billings, MT 59107-1177. **Phone:** (406) 252-4016 or (800) 735-2635.

Self-guiding tours: A map of historic sites can be obtained at the chamber of commerce.

Shopping: Rimrock Mall, at the junction of Central Avenue and 24th Street West, includes Dillard's and JCPenney among its 95 stores.

CHIEF BLACK OTTER TRAIL follows the edge of the Rimrocks north of the city. Swords Park, the area along the Rimrocks from Billings Logan International Airport to Boothill Cemetery, includes the unmarked grave of Crow Indian Chief Black Otter, who was killed in a battle with the Sioux. Yellowstone Kelly, renowned army scout, explorer and frontiersman, also is buried along the route. While the road is difficult to traverse, some of the best views of Sacrifice Cliff can be had here.

Range Rider of the Yellowstone stands at the entrance of Billings Logan International Airport. Cowboy motion picture star William S. Hart posed for this bronze statue of a cowboy and his horse.

MONTANA FUN ADVENTURES TOURS departs the Moss Mansion at 914 Division Ave. for downtown tours, and picks up passengers at area hotels and campgrounds for other tours. Among the trips offered are the 2-hour Historic Billings tour highlighting local landmarks and a narrated 3-hour tour tracing Meriwether Lewis' and William Clark's route along the Yellowstone River to Pompeys Pillar National Monument. A 6-hour trip to Little Bighorn Battlefield also is available. A jeep tour featuring wild mustangs also is offered.

Time: Allow 2 hours minimum. **Hours:** Historic Billings tour departs Mon.-Fri. at 11:30, 2 and 7, Sat.-Sun. at 2, May 1-Labor Day; daily at 2, rest of year. Lewis and Clark tour departs daily at 7:30 and 5:30, Apr.-Sept. Little Bighorn tour departs daily at 8:30 and 5:30, June-Sept.; at 8:30, rest of year. **Cost:** Historic Billings tour $25; $22 (military with ID); $15 (ages 6-15). Historic Billings tour with hotel pickup $40; $25 (ages 6-15). Lewis and Clark tour $65. Little Bighorn tour $155. Reservations are required. **Phone:** (406) 254-7180.

MOSS MANSION is at 914 Division St. An Old World-style house designed by architect H.J. Hardenbergh, this massive red sandstone mansion completed in 1903 features an eclectic decor with original carpet and drapes, ornate ceilings and handmade light fixtures. The Moss family occupied the house until 1984 and left the interior intact. The three-story mansion is an unusually complete example of early 20th-century decorative arts.

Hours: Guided 1-hour tours are given on the hour Tues.-Sat. 10-3, Sun. 1-3, Memorial Day-Labor Day; Tues.-Sun. 1-3, rest of year. Closed Jan. 1, Easter, July 4, second week in Nov., Thanksgiving and Christmas. Last tour begins at closing. **Cost:** $10; $7 (ages 65+ and military with ID); $6 (ages 6-17). **Phone:** (406) 256-5100 to confirm schedule. GT

PETER YEGEN JR. YELLOWSTONE COUNTY MUSEUM is at 1950 Terminal Cir., across from Billings Logan International Airport. Exhibits depict the history of Montana and the northern Plains, including the arrival of Meriwether Lewis and William Clark. More than 20,000 artifacts relate to the military, the railroad, Native Americans and the history of the Yellowstone area. **Time:** Allow 30 minutes minimum. **Hours:** Tues.-Sat. 10:30-5:30. Closed Jan. 1, Thanksgiving and Christmas. **Cost:** Donations. **Phone:** (406) 256-6811.

WESTERN HERITAGE CENTER, at 2822 Montana Ave. in the historic 1901 Parmly Billings Library Building, features changing exhibits about the history and culture of the Yellowstone Valley region. Audiovisual programs are presented regularly. **Time:** Allow 1 hour minimum. **Hours:** Tues.-Sat. 10-5. Closed major holidays. **Cost:** $5; $3 (ages 55+ and students with ID); $1 (ages 6-11). **Phone:** (406) 256-6809.

  YELLOWSTONE ART MUSEUM is at 401 N. 27th St. Housed in the original Yellowstone County jail, the museum offers changing exhibitions of historic and contemporary art. Boundless Visions tells the story of art in Montana with interactive exhibits and works from the museum's permanent collection. **Time:** Allow 30 minutes minimum. **Hours:** Tues.-Sat. 11-5 (also Thurs.-Fri. 5-8), Sun. 11-4. **Cost:** $6; $3 (ages 6-18 and college students with ID). Reservations are required for guided tours. **Phone:** (406) 256-6804. GT

ZOOMONTANA is off I-90 exit 443, 1 mi. w. on Zoo Dr., then just s. to 2100 S. Shiloh Rd. This 72-acre site is home to northern latitude temperate creatures. Eagles, grizzly bears, otters, lynx, red pandas, Siberian tigers, wolves and river otters can be seen. Also featured are various gardens, an amphitheater and a playground.

   Time: Allow 1 hour minimum. **Hours:** Daily 10-4, in summer; 10-2, rest of year. The zoo may be closed due to inclement weather during fall and winter. Closed Jan. 1, Thanksgiving and Christmas. Phone ahead to confirm schedule. **Cost:** $7.95; $5.95 (ages 55+ and military with ID); $4.95 (ages 3-15). **Phone:** (406) 652-8100.

BEST WESTERN PLUS CLOCKTOWER INN
(406)259-5511

Hotel
$95-$175

AAA Benefit: Save 10% or more every day and earn 10% bonus points!

Address: 2511 1st Ave N 59101 **Location:** On I-90 business loop; downtown. **Facility:** 126 units, some kitchens. 1-3 stories, interior/exterior corridors. **Parking:** winter plug-ins. **Terms:** resort fee. **Pool(s):** heated outdoor. **Activities:** sauna, exercise room. **Guest Services:** valet and coin laundry.

BEST WESTERN PLUS KELLY INN & SUITES
(406)256-9400

Hotel
$150-$190

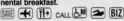

AAA Benefit: Save 10% or more every day and earn 10% bonus points!

Address: 4915 Southgate Dr 59101 **Location:** I-90 exit 447, just w. Across from family fun park. **Facility:** 89 units. 3 stories, interior/exterior corridors. **Parking:** winter plug-ins. **Terms:** check-in 4 pm. **Pool(s):** heated indoor. **Activities:** exercise room. **Guest Services:** valet and coin laundry. **Featured Amenity:** continental breakfast.

BIG HORN RESORT, AN ASCEND HOTEL COLLECTION MEMBER (406)839-9300

Hotel $99-$139 **Address:** 1801 Majestic Ln 59102 **Location:** I-90 exit 443, just n, then just s. Adjacent to Big Horn Resort Water Park. **Facility:** 108 units. 3 stories, interior corridors. **Parking:** winter plug-ins. **Amenities:** safes. **Activities:** hot tub, game room, exercise room, massage. **Guest Services:** valet and coin laundry, area transportation.

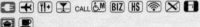

BILLINGS INN BY RIVERSAGE (406)252-6800

Hotel $85-$95 **Address:** 880 N 29th St 59101 **Location:** I-90 exit 450, 2 mi n on 27th St, then just w on 9th Ave. Across from Deaconess Hospital. **Facility:** 59 units. 4 stories, interior corridors. **Parking:** winter plug-ins. **Terms:** cancellation fee imposed. **Activities:** exercise room. **Guest Services:** valet and coin laundry. (See ad p. 137.)

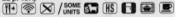

BILLINGS SUPER 8 (406)248-8842

Hotel $79-$94 **Address:** 5400 Southgate Dr 59101 **Location:** I-90 exit 447, just n on S Billings Blvd, 0.8 mi w on King Ave, then just s on Parkway Ln. **Facility:** 106 units. 3 stories, interior corridors. **Parking:** winter plug-ins. **Amenities:** safes. **Activities:** exercise room. **Guest Services:** coin laundry.

BOOTHILL INN & SUITES (406)245-2000

Hotel
$118-$163

Address: 242 E Airport Rd 59105 **Location:** I-90 exit 452, 1.8 mi n on US 87. **Facility:** 69 units. 4 stories, interior corridors. **Parking:** winter plug-ins. **Terms:** cancellation fee imposed. **Pool(s):** heated indoor. **Activities:** hot tub, exercise room. **Guest Services:** coin laundry, area transportation. **Featured Amenity:** breakfast buffet.

C'MON INN

406/655-1100

Hotel
Rates not provided

Address: 2020 Overland Ave 59102 **Location:** I-90 exit 446, 0.5 mi n, then just s. **Facility:** 81 units. 2 stories (no elevator), interior corridors. **Parking:** winter plug-ins. **Pool(s):** heated indoor. **Activities:** hot tub, game room, exercise room. **Guest Services:** valet and coin laundry. **Featured Amenity:** continental breakfast.

COMFORT INN BY CHOICE HOTELS

(406)652-5200

Hotel $109-$149 **Address:** 2030 Overland Ave 59102 **Location:** I-90 exit 446, 0.5 mi n, then just s. **Facility:** 60 units. 2 stories (no elevator), interior corridors. **Pool(s):** heated indoor. **Activities:** hot tub. **Guest Services:** valet and coin laundry.

COUNTRY INN & SUITES BY CARLSON, BILLINGS AT METRA PARK

(406)245-9995

Hotel
$120-$220

Address: 231 Main St 59105 **Location:** I-90 exit 452, 2 mi n, then follow Metra signs. **Facility:** 67 units. 3 stories, interior corridors. **Pool(s):** heated indoor. **Activities:** hot tub, exercise room. **Guest Services:** valet and coin laundry, area transportation. **Featured Amenity:** breakfast buffet.

CROWNE PLAZA

(406)252-7400

Hotel
$119-$499

Address: 27 N 27th St 59101 **Location:** I-90 business loop and SR 3. **Facility:** 289 units. 23 stories, interior corridors. **Terms:** cancellation fee imposed. **Activities:** exercise room. **Guest Services:** valet and coin laundry, luggage security pick-up.

DAYS INN

(406)252-4007

Hotel $73-$125 **Address:** 843 Parkway Ln 59101 **Location:** I-90 exit 447, just n on S Billings Blvd, 0.8 mi w on King Ave, then just s. **Facility:** 61 units. 2 stories (no elevator), interior corridors. **Parking:** winter plug-ins. **Activities:** exercise room. **Guest Services:** coin laundry.

ECONO LODGE

(406)252-2700

Hotel $64-$159 **Address:** 5425 Midland Rd 59101 **Location:** I-90 exit 446, just se. **Facility:** 86 units. 2 stories (no elevator), interior/exterior corridors. **Parking:** winter plug-ins. **Pool(s):** heated outdoor. **Activities:** hot tub. **Guest Services:** coin laundry.

EXTENDED STAY AMERICA-BILLINGS-WEST END

(406)245-3980

Extended Stay Hotel $70-$140 **Address:** 4950 Southgate Dr 59101 **Location:** I-90 exit 447, just w. **Facility:** 104 efficiencies. 3 stories, interior corridors. **Parking:** winter plug-ins. **Guest Services:** coin laundry.

FAIRFIELD INN & SUITES BY MARRIOTT-BILLINGS

(406)652-5330

Hotel $92-$172 **Address:** 2026 Overland Ave 59102 **Location:** I-90 exit 446, 0.5 mi n, then just s. **Facility:** 60 units. 3 stories, interior corridors. **Parking:** winter plug-ins. **Pool(s):** heated indoor. **Activities:** hot tub, exercise room. **Guest Services:** valet and coin laundry.

AAA Benefit:
Members save 5%
or more!

HAMPTON INN

(406)248-4949

Hotel $109-$179 **Address:** 5110 Southgate Dr 59101 **Location:** I-90 exit 447, just w. **Facility:** 120 units, some efficiencies. 4 stories, interior corridors. **Parking:** winter plug-ins. **Terms:** 1-7 night minimum stay, cancellation fee imposed. **Pool(s):** heated indoor. **Activities:** hot tub, exercise room. **Guest Services:** valet and coin laundry.

AAA Benefit:
Members save up to
10%!

Visit the AAA/CAA senior
driver sites for resources
to help you drive safely longer

HAMPTON INN & SUITES — (406)656-7511

▼▼▼ **Hotel** $109-$169 **Address:** 3550 Ember Ln 59102 **Location:** I-90 exit 443 (Zoo Dr), just n. **Facility:** 101 units. 4 stories, interior corridors. **Parking:** winter plug-ins. **Terms:** 1-7 night minimum stay, cancellation fee imposed. **Pool(s):** heated indoor. **Activities:** hot tub, exercise room. **Guest Services:** valet and coin laundry.

AAA Benefit: Members save up to 10%!

[icons]

HILLTOP INN BY RIVERSAGE — (406)245-5000

▼▼ **Hotel** $95-$105 **Address:** 1116 N 28th St 59101 **Location:** I-90 exit 450, 2 mi n on 27th St, just w on 11th Ave, then just n. Adjacent to St. Vincent Hospital. **Facility:** 56 units. 3 stories, interior corridors. **Parking:** winter plug-ins. **Activities:** exercise room. **Guest Services:** valet and coin laundry. *(See ad p. 137.)*

[icons]

HILTON GARDEN INN BILLINGS — (406)655-8800

▼▼▼ Hotel $109-$259

Hilton Garden Inn

AAA Benefit: Members save up to 10%!

Address: 2465 Grant Rd 59102 **Location:** I-90 exit 446, 1.5 mi w, just s on S 24th St W, then just w. **Facility:** 128 units. 5 stories, interior corridors. **Parking:** winter plug-ins. **Terms:** 1-7 night minimum stay, cancellation fee imposed. **Pool(s):** heated indoor. **Activities:** hot tub, exercise room. **Guest Services:** valet and coin laundry.

[icons]

HOLIDAY INN EXPRESS BILLINGS — 406/259-8600

▼▼▼ **Hotel.** Rates not provided. **Address:** 430 Cole St 59101 **Location:** I-90 exit 455, just s, then just e. **Facility:** 66 units. 3 stories, interior corridors. **Parking:** winter plug-ins. **Pool(s):** heated indoor. **Activities:** hot tub, exercise room. **Guest Services:** valet laundry.

[icons]

KELLY INN — 406/248-9800

▼▼ **Hotel.** Rates not provided. **Address:** 5610 S Frontage Rd 59101 **Location:** I-90 exit 446, just s. **Facility:** 80 units. 3 stories, interior/exterior corridors. **Parking:** winter plug-ins. **Pool(s):** heated indoor. **Activities:** hot tub, exercise room. **Guest Services:** coin laundry.

[icons]

LA QUINTA INN AND SUITES — (406)252-1188

▼▼▼ **Hotel** $97-$284 **Address:** 5720 S Frontage Rd 59101 **Location:** I-90 exit 446, just s. **Facility:** 85 units. 4 stories, interior corridors. **Parking:** winter plug-ins. **Pool(s):** heated indoor. **Activities:** hot tub, exercise room. **Guest Services:** valet and coin laundry, boarding pass kiosk.

[icons]

LEXINGTON HOTELS BY VANTAGE — (406)294-9090

▼▼▼ **Hotel** $109-$169 **Address:** 3040 King Ave W 59102 **Location:** I-90 exit 446, 2.5 mi n. **Facility:** 87 units. 4 stories, interior corridors. **Terms:** check-in 4 pm, resort fee. **Pool(s):** heated indoor. **Activities:** hot tub, exercise room. **Guest Services:** valet and coin laundry.

[icons]

MY PLACE HOTEL — 406/259-9970

▼▼▼ Extended Stay Hotel Rates not provided

Address: 4770 King Ave E 59101 **Location:** I-90 exit 447, just e. **Facility:** 64 kitchen units. 3 stories, interior corridors. **Parking:** winter plug-ins. **Guest Services:** coin laundry.

[icons]

QUALITY INN HOMESTEAD — (406)652-1320

▼▼▼ **Hotel** $89-$199 **Address:** 2036 Overland Ave 59102 **Location:** I-90 exit 446, 0.5 mi n, then just s. **Facility:** 118 units. 2 stories (no elevator), interior corridors. **Parking:** winter plug-ins. **Amenities:** safes. **Pool(s):** heated indoor. **Activities:** sauna, hot tub, exercise room. **Guest Services:** valet and coin laundry.

RESIDENCE INN BY MARRIOTT — (406)656-3900

▼▼▼ **Extended Stay Hotel** $116-$254 **Address:** 956 S 25th St W 59102 **Location:** I-90 exit 446, 1.5 mi w, just s on S 24th St, then just s. Located behind Home Depot. **Facility:** 92 kitchen units, some two bedrooms. 4 stories, interior corridors. **Parking:** winter plug-ins. **Pool(s):** heated indoor. **Activities:** hot tub, exercise room. **Guest Services:** valet and coin laundry.

AAA Benefit: Members save 5% or more!

[icons]

RIMVIEW INN — (406)248-2622

▼▼ Motel $74-$84

Address: 1025 N 27th St 59101 **Location:** I-90 exit 450, 2 mi n. **Facility:** 54 units, some efficiencies. 3 stories (no elevator), interior/exterior corridors. **Parking:** winter plug-ins. **Guest Services:** coin laundry, area transportation. **Featured Amenity:** continental breakfast.

[icons]

WESTERN EXECUTIVE INN — 406/294-8888

▼▼▼ Hotel $80-$210

Address: 3121 King Ave W 59102 **Location:** I-90 exit 446, 2.5 mi w. **Facility:** 40 units, some kitchens. 2 stories (no elevator), interior corridors. **Parking:** winter plug-ins. **Terms:** cancellation fee imposed. **Guest Services:** valet laundry. **Featured Amenity:** full hot breakfast.

WHERE TO EAT

THE ATHENIAN RESTAURANT   406/248-5681

♦♦ Greek. Casual Dining. $6-$25 **AAA Inspector Notes:** This family-run restaurant entices guests with the chef-owner's dishes, which combine spices, feta cheese, olives and cooking wines imported from Greece. A variety of desserts are made in house. **Features:** wine only. **Address:** 18 N 29th St 59101 **Location:** Between Montana Ave (I-90 business route) and 1st Ave N; downtown. **Parking:** street only. [L] [D] CALL [&M]

BISTRO ENZO   406/651-0999

♦♦ Mediterranean. Casual Dining. $10-$29 **AAA Inspector Notes:** The menu at this bistro includes an array of delicious pasta, sandwiches and meats prepared with an European flair. Daily specials include appetizer, fish, pork and beef. Try a warm chocolate popover for dessert. **Features:** beer & wine. **Reservations:** suggested. **Address:** 1502 Rehberg Ln 59102 **Location:** West side of town; jct Grand Ave. [D] CALL [&M]

BRUNO'S A TASTE OF ITALY   406/652-4416

♦♦ Italian. Casual Dining. $8-$19 **AAA Inspector Notes:** In the mood for some real Italian? Head to this newly constructed, Italian villa-style eatery for traditional favorites. Enjoy homemade pastas, pizzas, sauces and hand-rolled meatballs. Even the sausage is prepared in house. **Features:** beer & wine. **Address:** 1911 King Ave W 59101 **Location:** I-90 exit 446, after overpass, then just e on Carbon St; in King Ave West Plaza. [L] [D] CALL [&M]

THE BURGER DIVE   406/281-8292

♦ American Burgers. Quick Serve. $5-$10 **AAA Inspector Notes:** Burgers are made with premium, never-frozen Angus beef. With names like "Outlaw" and "Blackened Sabbath," the burgers are large and special. There are also spicy tuna burgers and the "Mazatlan" hot dog on the menu. While waiting for your meal, check out the art-filled walls. **Address:** 114 N 27th St 59101 **Location:** I-90 business loop; downtown. **Parking:** street only. [L]

CHAM THAI CUISINE   406/256-1812

♦ Thai. Casual Dining. $8-$12 **AAA Inspector Notes:** The décor isn't much but the food is classic Thai. The fresh spices make the food "pop!" There are also some Chinese dishes available, and a buffet is offered on Friday. **Address:** 2916 1st Ave N 59101 **Location:** Between 29th and 30th sts; downtown. **Parking:** street only. [L] [D]

CIAO MAMBO   406/325-5100

♦♦ Italian. Casual Dining. $11-$28 **AAA Inspector Notes:** Just like its sister restaurants in Whitefish and Missoula, Mont., this family-owned restaurant serves traditional and inventive dishes in casual and comfortable surroundings. This location is in a converted warehouse. The marinara, with slivers of garlic, is fragrant and delicious. Have a seat at the counter and watch the chefs hand toss your pizza. **Features:** full bar. **Reservations:** required. **Address:** 2301 Montana Ave 59101 **Location:** Jct N 23rd St; downtown; across from historic Billings Depot. **Parking:** street only. [D] CALL [&M]

C J'S BAR & GRILL   406/656-1400

♦ American. Casual Dining. $10-$29 **AAA Inspector Notes:** Diners will enjoy a great selection of ribs, steaks, and seafood cooked over mesquite, oak, or apple wood fires. Try the 18 oz. Montana Cut prime rib if you are really hungry. All this is served in a relaxed, contemporary atmosphere with pleasant and prompt service being the norm. There is also an inviting lounge that features comfortable leather couches and a warm fireplace for your enjoyment. **Features:** full bar. **Reservations:** suggested. **Address:** 2455 Central Ave 59102 **Location:** I-90 exit 446, 1 mi w on King Ave, 1 mi n on 24th St, 0.3 mi w, then just n at light. [L] [D] CALL [&M]

DOS MACHOS RESTAURANT   406/652-2020

♦♦ Mexican. Casual Dining. $9-$19 **AAA Inspector Notes:** In business for 30 years, the popular restaurant is known for its large Mexican/American menu, which lists sizzling fajitas, San Lucas scampi and an 8-ounce top sirloin. **Features:** full bar, Sunday brunch. **Address:** 980 S 24th St W 59102 **Location:** I-90 exit 446, 1.3 mi nw on King Ave, then just s. [L] [D]

GOLDEN PHOENIX RESTAURANT   406/256-0319

♦♦ Chinese. Casual Dining. $9-$28 **AAA Inspector Notes:** The décor is pretty typical of most Chinese restaurants, with large tanks of koi, colorful lanterns and Chinese art in a large dining area. The food is consistently tasty. This family-run restaurant is in a stand-alone building. A lunch buffet is offered on weekdays. **Features:** beer & wine. **Address:** 279 Swords Ln 59105 **Location:** I-90 exit 452, 2 mi n, follow Metra signs; jct Main St and Airport Rd. [L] [D]

INDIA GRILL   406/652-9700

♦♦ Indian. Casual Dining. $10-$18 **AAA Inspector Notes:** Serving mostly Southern Indian comfort foods, this family-run restaurant also has belly dancers for your entertainment. Specialties include entrées cooked in the tandoori oven as well as vegetarian dishes. **Features:** beer & wine. **Address:** 503 N 24th St W 59102 **Location:** Corner of Hewitt Dr. **Parking:** street only. [L] [D]

JAKE'S BAR & GRILL   406/252-9375

♦♦♦ American. Casual Dining. $10-$33 **AAA Inspector Notes:** This is one of the newest additions to the rapidly growing west end of town. Many of this restaurant's downtown-location menu items can be found at this place, too. A 1930s urban-Western ambience complements the informal, contemporary eatery. Locals and tourists flock here for steak, chicken and homemade desserts, along with made-to-order vegetarian dishes. A limited menu is served in the lounge 2-5 and 10-midnight. **Features:** full bar, happy hour. **Address:** 2425 Gabel Rd 59102 **Location:** I-90 exit 446, 0.5 mi nw, then 0.7 mi w on Overland Ave. [L] [D] CALL [&M]

JAKES OF BILLINGS   406/259-9375

♦♦ American. Casual Dining. $9-$33 **AAA Inspector Notes:** A 1930s urban-Western ambience complements the varied menu at this informal, contemporary eatery. Locals and tourists flock here for steak, chicken and homemade desserts, along with made-to-order vegetarian dishes. **Features:** full bar, happy hour. **Reservations:** suggested, weekends. **Address:** 2701 1st Ave N 59101 **Location:** I-90 business loop and SR 3; downtown. **Parking:** on-site (fee). [L] [D] CALL [&M]

MACKENZIE RIVER PIZZA

♦♦ Pizza. Casual Dining. $8-$20 **AAA Inspector Notes:** Known for its eclectic Western decor, the restaurant lets patrons choose from several microbrews to accompany a specialty pizza or large, innovative sandwich. Pizza crusts are wonderful and offer the choice of sourdough, natural grain, deep dish or thin crust. [L] [D]

For additional information, visit AAA.com

LOCATIONS:

Address: 3025 E Grand Ave 59102 **Location:** 4.5 mi w of City Center. **Bar:** beer & wine, patio dining. **Phone:** 406/651-0068
Address: 405 W Main St 59105 **Location:** I-90 exit 452, 1.3 mi w on I-90 business loop, then 0.9 mi e; in Heights Target Complex. **Bar:** full bar, patio dining. **Phone:** 406/254-0066

MCCORMICK CAFE   406/255-9555

♦ American. Casual Dining. $6-$11 **AAA Inspector Notes:** Banana-stuffed French toast, grilled portobello sandwiches and moist, double-layer carrot cake are just a few of the excellent, made-from-scratch dishes at the popular, sunny cafe. Mouthwatering aromas of roasted coffee beans and freshly squeezed fruit and vegetable juices fill the dining area. Breakfast is served until 10 am. **Address:** 2419 Montana Ave 59101 **Location:** I-90 exit 450, 1.5 mi n on 27th St, then just e. [B] [L]

MONTANA'S RIB & CHOP HOUSE   406/839-9200

♦ American. Casual Dining. $9-$39 **AAA Inspector Notes:** Specialties include 24-hour marinated baby back ribs and an 8-ounce Montana tenderloin, hand-cut, beef fillet. Diners also can sink their teeth into a variety of chicken, seafood and other steak entrées. The restaurant serves sushi on select days, so be sure to phone ahead. **Features:** full bar, Sunday brunch, happy hour. **Reservations:** suggested. **Address:** 1849 Majestic Ln 59102 **Location:** I-90 exit 443 (Zoo Dr), just n, just e on Gabel Rd, then just s. [L] [D] CALL [&M]

NA RA RESTAURANT SUSHI BAR 406/245-8866

Asian. Casual Dining. $8-$32 **AAA Inspector Notes:** It may be a bit awkward to find this restaurant, as it's on the point of three streets, Custer, Montana and Division, but please try, because the food is very good. Korean and Japanese dishes are available along with sushi. This is a friendly family-run restaurant. **Features:** beer & wine. **Address:** 3 Custer Ave 59101 **Location:** Jct Montana Ave and Division St; east of downtown. L D CALL M

THE REX 406/245-7477

American. Casual Dining. $14-$40 **AAA Inspector Notes:** Among the choices on the diverse menu are Montana-raised buffalo rib-eye, lobster-stuffed shrimp and the popular blackened prime rib. There are many smoked meats such as baby back ribs, brisket and smoked chicken to try. A patio bar and grill offers lighter fare and outside seating, weather permitting. **Features:** full bar, patio dining. **Address:** 2401 Montana Ave 59101 **Location:** I-90 exit 450, 1.5 mi n on 27th St, then just e. L D

SIAM THAI 406/652-4315

Thai. Casual Dining. $10-$24 **AAA Inspector Notes:** Well-prepared food made with authentic spices is served in an upscale atmosphere at the family-operated eatery. **Address:** 3210 Henesta Dr, Suite G 59102 **Location:** I-90 exit 446, 3.9 mi n on W King St; jct 32nd St; in King's Plaza. L D CALL M

STELLA'S KITCHEN AND BAKERY 406/248-3060

Breakfast Breads/Pastries. Casual Dining. $6-$16 **AAA Inspector Notes:** Hearty breakfasts are served all day. Pick a dessert from the showcase at front—maybe a cinnamon roll, chocolate cookie or caramel roll. Lunch items include burgers and sandwiches. The potato salad is fresh and especially tasty. **Features:** patio dining. **Address:** 2525 1st Ave N 59101 **Location:** On I-90 business loop; downtown. **Parking:** street only. B L

TAO NEW ASIAN 406/655-9898

Asian. Casual Dining. $14-$25 **AAA Inspector Notes:** This restaurant is unassuming on the outside, but the décor inside makes for a welcome surprise. Visit when you're in the mood to ~~variety of tastes.~~ The menu has more than 200 choices fo- ~~China, Japan, Korea and Thailand.~~ On any given day you ~~in the kitchen with his team to~~ provide such favorites as ~~lled Chilean sea bass,~~ wok-grilled halibut, assorted curry ~~aki sushi~~ and sashimi. **Features:** beer & wine. **Address:** 59102 **Location:** I-90 exit 446, 1.3 mi nw on King Ave, then j L D CALL M

WALKER'S GRILL 406/245-9291

Regional American. Fine Dining. $13-$39 **AAA Inspector Notes:** One visit to the restaurant makes it clear why this place is an area institution. Dining in an upscale atmosphere can be found in Billings! With a distinctly Western motif, diners will be pleasantly treated to creative presentations using the freshest ingredients. The eatery employs knowledgeable, friendly servers. A delectable tapas menu is offered starting at 4 pm. **Features:** full bar. **Reservations:** suggested. **Address:** 2700 1st Ave N 59101 **Location:** Jct N 27th St; in Securities Building. **Parking:** on-site and street. D CALL M

THE WINDMILL 406/252-8100

American. Casual Dining. $11-$35 **AAA Inspector Notes:** This place has been an area institution for more than 20 years. The original windmill in front of the building is from an old barn. The inside carries the Western theme throughout with a copper tin-type ceiling, exposed beam rafters, etched-glass accents, large pictures of windmills and a large stone fireplace. A back wall of windows overlooks a large patio dining area and a pond. Dinner only is served on Sunday. **Features:** full bar, happy hour. **Reservations:** suggested, weekends. **Address:** 3429 Trans Tech Way 59102 **Location:** I-90 exit 443 (Zoo Dr), just n, 0.7 mi e on Gabel Rd, then just n. L D CALL M

BITTERROOT NATIONAL FOREST (D-1)

Elevations in the forest range from 3,500 ft. at the Kootenai Creek Trail to 10,175 ft. on Trapper Peak. Refer to AAA maps for additional elevation information.

Bitterroot National Forest is in Montana and Idaho. The Montana section curves around the headwaters of the Bitterroot River, reaching into the Sapphire and Bitterroot ranges. This is a region of strong contrasts, with rolling subalpine woodland, open parks and lakes, and jagged, glaciated peaks and canyons.

The national forest takes its name from the bitterroot plant, whose pink flowers carpet the valleys and foothills from late April to July. Meriwether Lewis, on his journey through the region, added the bitterroot flower to his botanical collection and sampled the meal that the Native Americans ground from its root. A British botanist later honored Lewis' contribution by using his name as the basis of the flower's Latin name, *Lewisia rediviva*.

As one of the first forest reserves, Bitterroot National Forest also is the site of the nation's oldest ~~ranger~~ station, built in Alta in 1899. The forest's Idaho ~~encompasses~~ the headwaters of the Selway River and ~~the Salmon~~ River. Both rivers are components of the Wild and Scenic River system. Portions of the Frank Church-River of No Return Wilderness, the Selway-Bitterroot Wilderness and the Anaconda-Pintler Wilderness occupy about half of the forest's 1.6 million acres. For further information contact Bitterroot National Forest, 1801 N. First St., Hamilton, MT 59840; phone (406) 363-7100. *See Recreation Areas Chart.*

BLACK EAGLE pop. 904

3D INTERNATIONAL
406/453-6561

▼▼▼ International. Casual Dining. $9-$21 **AAA Inspector Notes:** *Classic.* 3D equals "Dine, Drink, Dance," and it has been a Great Falls institution since 1946. While it used to promote big-name acts and dancing, renovations in 1998 transformed it into the setting it is today. The neon lighting and original lounge seating were retained, creating an unique atmosphere in which to enjoy Italian food, Mongolian buffet or Asian cuisine. **Features:** full bar. **Reservations:** suggested. **Address:** 1825 Smelter Ave 59414 **Location:** Jct 9th St and Smelter Ave, 0.5 mi e. **Parking:** on-site and street.

L D

BORRIES
406/761-0300

▼▼▼ American. Casual Dining. $10-$30 **AAA Inspector Notes:** In an older industrial neighborhood of a small mill town, the casual dining establishment prepares simple, hearty food and serves it in generous portions. In addition to steaks, the menu lists Southern Italian pasta dishes, including spaghetti and the signature ravioli. Many pictures and photographs highlight the history of the community when it was a center of the world's copper industry. **Features:** full bar. **Reservations:** suggested, weekends. **Address:** 1800 Smelter Ave 59414 **Location:** Jct 9th St and Smelter Ave, 0.5 mi e. D

BOULDER pop. 1,183

BOULDER HOT SPRINGS INN & SPA
406/225-4339

fyi **Hotel** Did not meet all AAA rating requirements for locking devices in some guest rooms at time of last evaluation on 01/21/2015. **Address:** 31 S Hot Springs Rd 59632 **Location:** I-90 exit 164, 3 mi s on SR 69. Facilities, services, and décor characterize a mid-scale property. This historic building has been an inn since 1863. The property offers a large outdoor hot springs pool and two indoor pools. Sit on one of the rocking chairs on the veranda overlooking Peace Valley.

BOX ELDER (B-4) pop. 87, elev. 2,686'

ROCKY BOY INDIAN RESERVATION is on US 87 in the Bear Paw Mountains. Established in 1916, the Chippewa Cree reservation is named for a Chippewa leader whose Indian name, meaning "Stone Child," later was changed to "Rocky Boy." Tours of historical sites are offered. Fishing is permitted in a number of well-stocked streams and ponds; a tribal license is required. Hiking trails are available. Bear Paw Ski Bowl is on the reservation. **Hours:** Ski area open mid-December to early April. **Cost:** Fishing license (valid for 2 consecutive days) $15 (nonresidents); $5 (Montana residents with ID). A conservation license fee may also apply. Rates may vary; phone ahead. **Phone:** (406) 395-4207.

BOZEMAN (E-4) pop. 37,280, elev. 4,755'
• Hotels p. 142 • Restaurants p. 145

Bozeman was named for John Bozeman, who brought the first wagon train of pioneers to settle the Gallatin Valley. The trail he blazed became not only a highway for settlers and miners but also a flash point between the Native Americans and the settlers. Three years after bringing settlers to the valley, Bozeman was killed by the Sioux, and his trail remained unused for 9 years because of repeated attacks upon wayfarers.

The valley that Bozeman helped settle once was a neutral and sacred hunting ground known to Native Americans as the "Valley of the Flowers." The area has blossomed into one of the state's more agriculturally productive regions.

Bozeman Area Chamber of Commerce: 2000 Commerce Way, Bozeman, MT 59715. **Phone:** (406) 586-5421 or (800) 228-4224.

AMERICAN COMPUTER & ROBOTICS MUSEUM is at 2023 Stadium Dr., Suite 1A. Exhibits chronicle the evolution of the information age, from the abacus to the microchip. **Hours:** Daily 10-4, June-Aug.; Tues.-Sun. noon-4, rest of year. **Cost:** Free. **Phone:** (406) 582-1288. GT

GALLATIN HISTORY MUSEUM is at 317 W. Main St. Housed in a 1911 county jail, the museum contains permanent and rotating exhibits, Native American artifacts, a gun collection, more than 18,000 photographs and a research library. **Hours:** Tues.-Sat. 10-5, Memorial Day-Labor Day; Tues.-Sat. 11-4, rest of year. **Cost:** $5; free (ages 0-12). **Phone:** (406) 522-8122.

MUSEUM OF THE ROCKIES is on the Montana State University campus at 600 W. Kagy Blvd. Home to one of the largest dinosaur fossil collections in the United States, the museum's Siebel Dinosaur Complex features a fully mounted Tyrannosaurus rex skeleton as well as other dinosaur specimens, dinosaur eggs, nests and sculptures. Other exhibits include the Paugh History Hall, which offers an array of regional artifacts; the Enduring Peoples exhibit that examines the life and culture of Native Americans from the Northern Plains and Rockies; the Living History Farm (closed in winter), a historically accurate, late-1800s Montana homestead; and the Martin Children's Discovery Center.

The museum also features the Taylor Planetarium, which presents a breathtaking journey through the cosmos. **Hours:** Daily 8-8, Memorial Day weekend-Labor Day; Mon.-Sat. 9-5, Sun. 12:30-5, rest of year. Planetarium shows are given daily. Closed Jan. 1, Thanksgiving and Christmas. **Cost:** Museum (includes planetarium) $14.50; $13.50 (ages 65+); $9.50 (ages 5-17). **Phone:** (406) 994-2251.

BEST WESTERN PLUS GRANTREE INN   (406)587-5261

Hotel
$129-$249

 AAA Benefit: Save 10% or more every day and earn 10% bonus points!

Address: 1325 N 7th Ave 59715 **Location:** I-90 exit 306, just s. **Facility:** 120 units. 2 stories, interior corridors. **Parking:** winter plug-ins. **Amenities:** safes. **Pool(s):** heated indoor. **Activities:** hot tub, exercise room. **Guest Services:** valet and coin laundry, area transportation.

/ SOME UNITS

BOZEMAN DAYS INN & SUITES   (406)587-5251

Hotel $65-$135 **Address:** 1321 N 7th Ave 59715 **Location:** I-90 exit 306, just s. **Facility:** 113 units. 2-3 stories, interior corridors. **Parking:** winter plug-ins. **Amenities:** safes. **Pool(s):** heated indoor. **Activities:** sauna, hot tub, exercise room. **Guest Services:** valet and coin laundry, area transportation.

/ SOME UNITS

▼ See AAA listing p. 160 ▼

BOZEMAN INN
406-587-3176

▼▼ **Motel.** Rates not provided. **Address:** 1235 N 7th Ave 59715 **Location:** I-90 exit 306, just s. **Facility:** 49 units, some two bedrooms. 2 stories (no elevator), exterior corridors. **Parking:** winter plug-ins. **Guest Services:** coin laundry.

BOZEMAN'S WESTERN HERITAGE INN
(406)586-8534

▼▼ **Hotel** $73-$189 **Address:** 1200 E Main St 59715 **Location:** I-90 exit 309, 0.5 mi w. **Facility:** 37 units, some efficiencies and kitchens. 3 stories (no elevator), interior corridors. **Parking:** winter plug-ins. **Terms:** cancellation fee imposed. **Activities:** hot tub, steamroom, exercise room. **Guest Services:** coin laundry.

CITY CENTER INN
406/587-3158

▼▼ **Hotel.** Rates not provided. **Address:** 507 W Main St 59715 **Location:** Center. **Facility:** 64 units. 3 stories, interior corridors. **Parking:** winter plug-ins. **Amenities:** *Some:* safes. **Pool(s):** heated indoor. **Activities:** hot tub, limited exercise equipment. **Guest Services:** valet parking.

C'MON INN
(406)587-3555

▼▼▼ Hotel $89-$230

Address: 6139 E Valley Center Rd 59718 **Location:** I-90 exit 305, just s on CR 41 (19th St), then just w. **Facility:** 125 units. 3 stories, interior corridors. **Terms:** check-in 4 pm. **Pool(s):** heated indoor. **Activities:** hot tub, exercise room. **Guest Services:** valet and coin laundry. **Featured Amenity: continental breakfast.**

COMFORT INN OF BOZEMAN
(406)587-2322

▼▼ **Hotel** $69-$169 **Address:** 1370 N 7th Ave 59715 **Location:** I-90 exit 306, just s. **Facility:** 122 units, some efficiencies. 3 stories, interior corridors. **Parking:** winter plug-ins. **Pool(s):** heated indoor. **Activities:** hot tub, exercise room. **Guest Services:** valet and coin laundry.

COMFORT SUITES BOZEMAN
(406)587-0800

▼▼▼ **Hotel** $89-$209 **Address:** 2515 Catamount St 59718 **Location:** I-90 exit 305, just s. **Facility:** 80 efficiencies. 3 stories, interior corridors. **Parking:** winter plug-ins. **Pool(s):** heated indoor. **Activities:** hot tub, exercise room. **Guest Services:** valet and coin laundry.

COUNTRY INN & SUITES BY CARLSON - BOZEMAN
406/586-2230

▼▼▼ Hotel
Rates not provided

Address: 5997 E Valley Center Rd 59715 **Location:** I-90 exit 305, 0.3 mi s on 19th Ave. **Facility:** 79 units. 4 stories, interior corridors. **Parking:** winter plug-ins. **Pool(s):** heated indoor. **Activities:** hot tub, exercise room. **Guest Services:** complimentary laundry. **Featured Amenity: breakfast buffet.**

ELEMENT BOZEMAN
406/582-4972

[fyi] **Hotel.** Rates not provided. Too new to rate, opening scheduled for September 2015. **Address:** 25 E Mendenhall St 59715 **Location:** Jct US 191 and SR 86, just w. **Amenities:** 104 units. *(See ad this page.)*

AAA Benefit:
Members save up to 15%, plus Starwood Preferred Guest® benefits!

Stay connected with #AAA and #CAA on your favorite social media sites

▼ *See AAA listing this page* ▼

FAIRFIELD INN BY MARRIOTT (406)587-2222

▼▼▼ **Hotel** $84-$207 **Address:** 828 Wheat Dr 59715 **Location:** I-90 exit 306, just nw. **Facility:** 56 units. 3 stories, interior corridors. **Parking:** winter plug-ins. **Pool(s):** heated indoor. **Guest Services:** valet laundry.

AAA Benefit: Members save 5% or more!

[icons]

FOX HOLLOW BED AND BREAKFAST (406)582-8440

▼▼▼▼ **Bed & Breakfast** $129-$219 **Address:** 545 Mary Rd 59718 **Location:** I-90 exit 305, just s on SR 412 (N 19th St), 3.1 mi w on SR 235 (Valley Center Rd), then 0.6 mi n. **Facility:** This B&B offers gourmet breakfast and spectacular mountain and meadow views. After a day on the hiking trails, sit on the beautiful wraparound porch while sampling fresh baked goods. 5 units, some kitchens. 2 stories (no elevator), interior corridors. **Terms:** 14 day cancellation notice-fee imposed.

[icons]

HAMPTON INN (406)522-8000

▼▼▼ Hotel $99-$209

AAA Benefit: Members save up to 10%!

Address: 75 Baxter Ln 59715 **Location:** I-90 exit 306, just s, then just n. **Facility:** 70 units. 2 stories, interior corridors. **Parking:** winter plug-ins. **Terms:** 1-7 night minimum stay, cancellation fee imposed. **Pool(s):** heated indoor. **Activities:** hot tub, exercise room. **Guest Services:** valet and coin laundry.

[icons]

HILTON GARDEN INN (406)582-9900

▼▼▼ **Hotel** $129-$289 **Address:** 2023 Commerce Way 59715 **Location:** I-90 exit 305, just s, then just e on Baxter Ln. **Facility:** 123 units. 3 stories, interior corridors. **Parking:** winter plug-ins. **Terms:** check-in 4 pm, 1-7 night minimum stay, cancellation fee imposed. **Pool(s):** heated indoor. **Activities:** hot tub, exercise room. **Guest Services:** valet and coin laundry.

AAA Benefit: Members save up to 10%!

[icons]

HOLIDAY INN BOZEMAN 406/587-4561

▼▼▼ **Hotel.** Rates not provided. **Address:** 5 E Baxter Ln 59715 **Location:** I-90 exit 306, just s. **Facility:** 177 units. 2 stories (no elevator), interior corridors. **Parking:** winter plug-ins. **Terms:** check-in 4 pm. **Pool(s):** heated indoor. **Activities:** hot tub, exercise room. **Guest Services:** valet and coin laundry, area transportation.

[icons]

HOLIDAY INN EXPRESS & SUITES 406/582-4995

▼▼▼ **Hotel.** Rates not provided. **Address:** 2305 Catron St 59718 **Location:** I-90 exit 305, just s on CR 41 (19th St), then just w on E Valley Center Rd. **Facility:** 86 units. 3 stories, interior corridors. **Parking:** winter plug-ins. **Terms:** check-in 4 pm. **Amenities:** safes. **Pool(s):** heated indoor. **Activities:** hot tub, exercise room. **Guest Services:** valet and coin laundry.

[icons]

HOMEWOOD SUITES BY HILTON BOZEMAN (406)587-8180

▼▼▼ **Extended Stay Hotel** $119-$279 **Address:** 1023 Baxter Ln 59715 **Location:** I-90 exit 306, just s, then just n. **Facility:** 102 units, some two bedrooms and efficiencies. 4 stories, interior corridors. **Parking:** winter plug-ins. **Terms:** 1-7 night minimum stay, cancellation fee imposed. **Pool(s):** heated indoor. **Activities:** hot tub, exercise room. **Guest Services:** valet and coin laundry.

AAA Benefit: Members save up to 10%!

[icons]

HOWLERS INN BED & BREAKFAST 406/587-5229

▼▼▼ **Bed & Breakfast** $125-$205 **Address:** 3185 Jackson Creek Rd 59715 **Location:** I-90 exit 319 (Jackson Creek Rd), 3.1 mi n, then just e. **Facility:** A wolf sanctuary is on the grounds which offers scenic views plus easy proximity to downtown, ski areas and a national forest. It sits among two mountain ranges and lush, rolling hills. 4 units, some two bedrooms and kitchens. 2-3 stories (no elevator), interior/exterior corridors. **Terms:** check-in 4 pm, 2 night minimum stay - seasonal, 10 day cancellation notice-fee imposed. **Activities:** sauna, hot tub, playground, exercise room. **Guest Services:** valet laundry.

[icons]

LA QUINTA INN & SUITES (406)585-9300

▼▼▼ **Hotel** $64-$273 **Address:** 620 Nikles Dr 59715 **Location:** I-90 exit 306, just ne. **Facility:** 56 units, some two bedrooms. 4 stories, interior corridors. **Parking:** winter plug-ins. **Pool(s):** heated indoor. **Activities:** hot tub, exercise room. **Guest Services:** valet and coin laundry.

[icons]

MICROTEL INN & SUITES BY WYNDHAM BOZEMAN (406)586-3797

▼▼ **Hotel** $60-$140 **Address:** 612 Nikles Dr 59715 **Location:** I-90 exit 306, just ne. **Facility:** 61 units. 3 stories, interior corridors. **Parking:** winter plug-ins. **Pool(s):** heated indoor. **Activities:** hot tub. **Guest Services:** valet laundry.

[icons]

MOTEL 6 BOZEMAN #4818 (406)585-7888

▼▼ **Hotel** $56-$125 **Address:** 817 Wheat Dr 59718 **Location:** I-90 exit 306, just n. **Facility:** 56 units. 2 stories (no elevator), interior corridors. **Bath:** shower only. **Parking:** winter plug-ins. **Pool(s):** heated indoor. **Activities:** sauna, hot tub. **Guest Services:** coin laundry.

[icons]

MOUNTAINVIEW LODGE & SUITES (406)522-8686

▼▼ **Hotel** $89-$179 **Address:** 1121 Reeves Rd W 59718 **Location:** I-90 exit 305, just n. **Facility:** 52 units, some kitchens. 2 stories (no elevator), interior corridors. **Parking:** winter plug-ins. **Pool(s):** heated indoor. **Activities:** sauna, hot tub, game room, exercise room. **Guest Services:** coin laundry.

[icons]

MY PLACE HOTEL (406)586-8228

▼▼ Hotel $82-$119

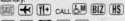

Address: 5889 E Valley Center Rd 59718 **Location:** I-90 exit 305, just s on CR 41 (19th St), then just w. **Facility:** 62 efficiencies. 3 stories, interior corridors. **Parking:** winter plug-ins. **Terms:** cancellation fee imposed, resort fee. **Activities:** hot tub. **Guest Services:** coin laundry.

[icons]

RAINBOW MOTEL

(406)587-4201

Motel
$80-$100

Address: 510 N 7th Ave 59715 **Location:** I-90 exit 306, 0.8 mi s. **Facility:** 42 units, some two bedrooms and efficiencies. 1-2 stories (no elevator), exterior corridors. **Parking:** winter plug-ins. **Terms:** cancellation fee imposed. **Pool(s):** heated outdoor.

SAVE ⬛ 🏊 📶 / SOME UNITS 🐕 🛁 🖥 🖨 ☕

RAMADA LIMITED

(406)585-2626

🏨🏨 **Hotel** $60-$140 **Address:** 2020 Wheat Dr 59715 **Location:** I-90 exit 306, just n, then just w. **Facility:** 50 units. 2 stories (no elevator), interior/exterior corridors. **Parking:** winter plug-ins. **Terms:** 3 day cancellation notice-fee imposed. **Pool(s):** heated indoor. **Activities:** hot tub, exercise room. **Guest Services:** valet and coin laundry.

⬛ CALL 🔓M 🏊 BIZ 📶 ✖ 🛁 🖥 🖨 / SOME UNITS 🐕

SUPER 8

(406)586-1521

🏨🏨 **Hotel** $59-$159 **Address:** 800 Wheat Dr 59715 **Location:** I-90 exit 306, just n, then just w. **Facility:** 107 units. 3 stories (no elevator), interior corridors. **Parking:** winter plug-ins. **Guest Services:** coin laundry.

⬛ BIZ 📶 ✖ 🖨 / SOME UNITS 🐕 🛁 🖥

WHERE TO EAT

CAFE FRANCAIS DES ARTS

406/209-7490

🏆 French. Casual Dining. $5-$10 **AAA Inspector Notes:** Try a little bit of France in Montana. Specialties include scrumptious sweets loaded with real sweet-cream butter, eggs, imported chocolate and even imported flour. Favorite savories include croque-monsieur on homemade bread, French onion soup topped with Gruyere, assorted quiches and crepes. This is a family-run café where you'll find the mother's art decorating the walls and her sons in the kitchen hard at work. **Address:** 24 S Tracy Ave 59715 **Location:** Between Main and Babcock sts; downtown. **Parking:** on-site and street. B L CALL 🔓M 🐕

CAFÉ ZYDECO

406/994-0188

🏆 Cajun. Quick Serve. $6-$14 **AAA Inspector Notes:** Traditionally prepared Cajun goodies are served with a smile at this casual eatery. Beignets are available all day on Saturday and Sunday. **Features:** patio dining. **Address:** 2711 W College St 59715 **Location:** Just e of Huffine Ln/W Main St; in Old Hatchery Winery building. L D

CHINATOWN RESTAURANT

406/587-5168

🏆 Chinese. Casual Dining. $9-$20 **AAA Inspector Notes:** Patrons can choose from more than 100 entrées prepared in the Peking, Hunan, Szechuan and Cantonese styles. The quick lunch menu is popular for those in a hurry and one option is a well stocked buffet. **Address:** 1228 W Main St 59715 **Location:** West of historic downtown; across from Bozeman High School. L D

FERRARO'S

406/587-2555

🏆🏆 Italian. Casual Dining. $11-$60 **AAA Inspector Notes:** Locals frequent this place for its authentic cuisine, daily-made pasta and extensive wine list. The lounge offers exceptional-value choices of wine flights and features overstuffed leather furnishings and a cozy fireplace, wood oven and pizza bar. **Features:** full bar, patio dining. **Reservations:** suggested. **Address:** 726 N 7th Ave 59772 **Location:** I-90 exit 306, 0.6 mi s. D CALL 🔓M

THE GARAGE

406/585-8558

🏆🏆 American. Casual Dining. $8-$19 **AAA Inspector Notes:** First-timers can expect to be pleasantly surprised when they step into the converted retro-era garage. The soup counter allows for a choice between a number of innovative homemade selections with varied toppings. Because sampling before making a final selection is encouraged, the signature clam chowder is a must-try. Contributing to the funky yet casual décor are the restaurant's menus, which are sandwiched between old license plates. Weather permitting, sit on the deck to enjoy downtown. **Features:** beer & wine, patio dining. **Address:** 451 E Main St 59715 **Location:** Jct Church St; center. **Parking:** street only. L D 🚫

I-HO'S KOREAN GRILL

406/522-0949

🏆 Korean. Casual Dining. $7-$15 **AAA Inspector Notes:** You will love the authentic food prepared in a traditional manner. The homey café is a big hit with the local college students and teachers alike. Specials range from Korean teriyaki chicken to daily soups. If you're feeling bold, try the kimchi. Outdoor seating is popular during summer months. **Features:** patio dining. **Address:** 1216 W Lincoln St 59715 **Location:** I-90 exit 306, 1 mi se, 0.5 mi w on W Main St, 1 mi se on 11th St, then just w; adjacent to Montana State University Campus. L D

JOHN BOZEMAN'S BISTRO

406/587-4100

🏆🏆🏆 New American. Casual Dining. $10-$36 **AAA Inspector Notes:** The locals' favorite bistro provides eye-candy décor and a menu with creative international influences. Eclectic choices include bison, fish, tenderloin, poultry and vegetarian dishes including a Super Food menu. Desserts such as mud pie and cheesecake are generous and housemade. Seating in booths and on stools at the counter help provide a casual feel, and the service is attentive and knowledgeable. **Features:** beer & wine, Sunday brunch. **Reservations:** suggested. **Address:** 125 W Main St 59715 **Location:** Center. **Parking:** street only. L D CALL 🔓M

LA PARILLA

406/582-9511

🏆 Fusion. Quick Serve. $7-$12 **AAA Inspector Notes:** The fusion menu includes Cajun, Thai and Indian flavors and features gourmet burritos and fresh salmon. Create your own burrito and taco bowls. **Features:** beer only. **Address:** 1624 W Babcock St 59771 **Location:** Jct N 7th Ave and W Main St, 0.5 mi w, just s on S 11th Ave, then just w. L D

MACKENZIE RIVER PIZZA

406/587-0055

🏆🏆 Pizza. Casual Dining. $8-$20 **AAA Inspector Notes:** Known for its eclectic Western decor, the restaurant lets patrons choose from several microbrews to accompany a specialty pizza or large, innovative sandwich. Pizza crusts are wonderful and offer the choice of sourdough, natural grain, deep dish or thin crust. **Features:** beer & wine. **Address:** 232 E Main St 59715 **Location:** Center. **Parking:** street only. L D

MAIN STREET OVEREASY

406/587-3205

🏆 American. Family Dining. $7-$15 **AAA Inspector Notes:** A hot spot for breakfast, the restaurant prepares homemade biscuits and gravy, home fries, pancakes and gourmet omelets. Excellent coffee and great service are other reasons for its loyal clientele. Save room for a large cinnamon roll. **Address:** 9 E Main St 59715 **Location:** Downtown. **Parking:** street only. B L

THE NAKED NOODLE

406/585-4501

Noodles
Specialty
Quick Serve
$7-$14

AAA Inspector Notes: Diners choose from seven varieties of pasta, including a gluten-free option, then pick one of the many sauces, meats, vegetables, seafoods and toppings in order to create a delicious meal. Can't decide? Choose one of the many tried-and-true combinations or salads posted on the board. The décor is eclectic and for the most part the restaurant is self-serve, but orders are taken by a patient and friendly staff. An extensive healthy children's menu is available. **Address:** 27 S Willson Ave 59715 **Location:** Just s; center. **Parking:** on-site and street. L D

PHO REAL   406/404-1074

Soup. Quick Serve. $7-$12 **AAA Inspector Notes:** The limited menu highlights some of the more popular staples of soup and sandwiches. The cafeteria-style ordering is convenient; you choose your broth and meat, then move on to the vegetables and spices that will top your soup. **Address:** 242 E Main St 59715 **Location:** Between Rouse and Bozeman aves; downtown. **Parking:** street only.

L D CALL M

SANTA FE RED'S   406/587-5838

Mexican. Casual Dining. $8-$18 **AAA Inspector Notes:** The upbeat, bustling and popular Mexican restaurant serves such homemade Southwestern cuisine as fajitas, burritos and tacos. The halibut tacos are very yummy. Guests can top off any meal with the signature dessert: fried ice cream. **Features:** full bar, patio dining. **Address:** 1235 N 7th Ave 59715 **Location:** I-90 exit 306, just s; adjacent to Bozeman Inn. L D

SOLA CAFE   406/922-7652

Deli Breads/Pastries. Quick Serve. $10-$15 **AAA Inspector Notes:** More than a typical deli, you can enjoy made-from-scratch delectable creations using regionally available fresh fruits, veggies, meats and cheeses. Each day brings a new creation for the specials board. Desserts range from cheesecake to peanut butter cookie sandwiches. They offer vegetarian, gluten free or low carb for those with special dietary needs. Drive through is available for those on the go. **Features:** beer & wine, Sunday brunch, happy hour. **Location:** From Main St, 1.3 mi s on S Willson Ave; near Montana State University and Museum of the Rockies. B L D CALL M

SWEET CHILI - ASIAN BISTRO   406/582-1188

Asian. Casual Dining. $9-$25 **AAA Inspector Notes:** The owners/chefs are Chinese but spent quite a few years under the tutelage of the Siam Thai restaurant in Billings. You'll find many classic Thai dishes on the menu, including Pad thai, tom yum soup, basil chicken and fresh rolls. A few classic Chinese dishes also are offered. Along with tables, there is a serious sushi bar. **Features:** full bar. **Reservations:** required. **Address:** 101 E Main St, Unit 1 59715 **Location:** Jct Black St; downtown. **Parking:** street only.

L D

COMMUNITY FOOD CO-OP   406/587-4039

fyi Not evaluated. Located inside a community organic foods market, this deli counter and soup bar offers a wide variety of healthy organic choices. There is another convenient location downtown on Main Street. **Address:** 908 W Main St 59715 **Location:** Between 9th and 10th aves.

LA CHATELAINE CHOCOLAT CO   406/522-5440

fyi Not evaluated. The local chocolate makers specialize in French chocolates with five global regional beans used for production. Selections can change daily and are prepared in small batches on site. There also is a satellite location in the Baxter Hotel (downtown). **Address:** 1516 W Main St 59715 **Location:** Between 15th and 16th aves; behind Café Zydeco.

THE PICKLE BARREL   406/587-2411

fyi Not evaluated. This eatery serves large, fresh deli sandwiches with dill pickles and homemade soups. **Address:** 809 W College St 59715 **Location:** At Montana State University campus.

BROWNING (B-2) pop. 1,016, elev. 4,366'
• Part of Glacier National Park area — see map p. 162

Founded in 1895, Browning is the hub of the Blackfeet Nation and a center for reservation activities. It also is the site of the Blackfeet Tribal Headquarters, which includes a nine-member business council, the governing board of the Blackfeet Tribe. Fifteen miles east on the reservation, a monument marks the northernmost point reached by the Lewis and Clark expedition on July 23, 1806. About 7,000 Native Americans live on the Blackfeet Indian Reservation, which covers 1.5 million acres.

MUSEUM OF THE PLAINS INDIAN is at jct. US 2 and US 89W at 19 Museum Loop. Murals, dioramas, historical and contemporary Native American arts and artifacts of the Northern Plains region are displayed. Changing exhibits also are offered. **Time:** Allow 1 hour minimum. **Hours:** Tues.-Sat. 9-4:45, June-Sept.; Mon.-Fri. 10-4:30, rest of year. Closed major holidays. **Cost:** June-Sept. $5; $4 (ages 65+); $1 (ages 6-16). Rest of year free. **Phone:** (406) 338-2230.

GOING TO THE SUN INN & SUITES   (406)338-7572

Motel **Address:** 121 Central Ave E 59417 **Location:** On US 2; center. **Facility:** 15 $88-$174 units. 1 story, exterior corridors. **Parking:** winter plug-ins. **Terms:** 4 day cancellation notice-fee imposed. **Guest Services:** area transportation. **Featured Amenity:** continental breakfast. SAVE / SOME UNITS

BUTTE (E-3) elev. 5,716'
• Hotels p. 148 • Restaurants p. 148

Silver Bow Creek's gold and silver first brought the mineral wealth of remote Butte to the attention of the world. But it was copper that made Butte's reputation as "the richest hill on Earth," producing more than 20 billion pounds of the metal. "Copper kings" fought for control of Butte's wealth; Marcus Daly's Anaconda Copper Mining Co. eventually gained ownership of every mine in Butte and became the dominant power in Montana.

By 1955, the high-grade copper ore was almost played out and excavation began on Berkeley Open Pit Mine to extract low-grade ore. The mine was one of the larger truck-operated pit mines in the world. The Berkeley Pit Viewing Stand, open daily dawn to dusk from March to mid-November, is $2 for adults and $1 for children and provides an excellent view of the old open mine. As a transportation hub, the city has become one of the nation's larger inland ports, with containerized cargo from the Orient being cleared and routed to points throughout the Midwest.

The Anselmo Mine Yard, uptown at Caledonia and Excelsior streets, is a fine example of surface support facilities that once served the miners. An interpretive center and tours are offered during the summer. The Granite Mountain Mine Memorial, 1308 N. Main St., is dedicated to the 168 men who died in a 1917 mine disaster.

Butte's historic district contains a large concentration of late 19th- and early 20th-century residential and commercial buildings as well as mining relics such as the steel headframes used to lower miners to a network of more than 2,000 miles of tunnels under "the hill."

Butte is surrounded by Beaverhead-Deerlodge National Forest (see place listing p. 131), which offers varied recreational opportunities. Visitors can experience the beauty of the nearby rugged mountains, verdant forests and meadows by driving either north to Helena or south to Monida on I-15.

Butte-Silver Bow Chamber of Commerce and Visitor Center: 1000 George St., Butte, MT 59701. **Phone:** (406) 723-3177 or (800) 735-6814.

Self-guiding tours: Brochures detailing two walking tours of the historic district are available at the chamber of commerce and visitor center.

BUTTE TROLLEY TOUR departs from the Butte-Silver Bow Chamber of Commerce and Visitor Center; take I-90 exit 126 to 1000 George St. These narrated tours relate the city's history. Sites include the Berkeley Pit Viewing Stand and Butte's historic district.

Time: Allow 1 hour, 30 minutes minimum. **Hours:** Tours are given Mon.-Sat. at 10:30, 1 and 3:30, Sun. at 10:30 and 1, June 1-Labor Day; daily at 10:30 and 1, day after Labor Day-Sept. 30. Phone ahead to confirm schedule. **Cost:** $15; $13 (ages 65+); $10 (ages 12-17); $6 (ages 4-11). Fares may vary; phone ahead. **Phone:** (406) 723-3177 or (800) 735-6814.

[SAVE] **CHARLES W. CLARK CHATEAU** is at 321 W. Broadway. Built in 1898, the residence of Charles W. Clark, eldest son of "copper king" William A. Clark, was modeled after a French château. Today the building contains the works of Montana artists. Exhibits change periodically. An antique furniture collection from the University of Montana and the first piano in Montana also are displayed. **Time:** Allow 1 hour minimum. **Hours:** Wed.-Sun. noon-4, June-Sept; phone for schedule, rest of year. **Cost:** General admission $5; $3 (students and military with ID); $15 family (up to five people). Admission with tour $7; $5 (students and military with ID); $15 family (up to five people). **Phone:** (406) 490-6678.

COPPER KING MANSION is at 219 W. Granite St. The 34-room Victorian house was the residence of William A. Clark, a U.S. senator and "copper king." Now a national historic landmark and bed and breakfast, the restored 1884-88 mansion is furnished in period and serves as a showcase for numerous collections. **Time:** Allow 1 hour minimum.

Hours: Guided tours are given daily 9-4, May-Sept.; Sat.-Sun. 9-4, in Apr. **Cost:** $10; $5 (ages 6-14); $30 (family). **Phone:** (406) 782-7580. [GT]

MINERAL MUSEUM, at 1300 W. Park St. in the Museum Building of Montana Tech, exhibits more than 1,500 specimens, including fluorescent minerals, a gold nugget considered to be the largest in Montana and a 400-pound quartz crystal found near Butte. Other features include Montana fossils and information related to the state's geology. **Hours:** Daily 9-5, June 15-Sept. 15; Mon.-Fri. 9-4, rest of year. Closed major holidays. **Cost:** Donations. **Phone:** (406) 496-4414.

OUR LADY OF THE ROCKIES is atop the Continental Divide; tours to the site depart from the Plaza Mall, 3100 Harrison Ave. The 90-foot-high statue of the Virgin Mary—a nondenominational tribute to motherhood—took 6 years to build and was airlifted into place in 1985. Visitors may step inside the metal structure. The road to the statue is not open to public traffic. A chapel observatory is available.

Hours: Bus tours lasting 2.5 hours depart daily at 11 and 2, June-Oct. (weather permitting). Reservations are required. **Cost:** $16; $14 (ages 55+); $12 (ages 13-17); $8 (ages 5-12); $2 (ages 0-4). **Phone:** (406) 782-1221 or (800) 800-5239.

[SAVE] **WORLD MUSEUM OF MINING,** 155 Museum Way, is on the grounds of the Orphan Girl Mine, which operated 1875-1956. The 50-plus structures on the 44-acre site range from a 100-foot-high headframe to the many buildings of Hell Roarin' Gulch, an 1890s mining town. Visitors learn about the evolution of mining technology and about the mining town's culture and ethnic history. A 90-minute underground mine tour is offered.

Time: Allow 2 hours minimum. **Hours:** Complex open daily 9-6, with mine tours at 10:30, 12:30 and 3, Apr.-Oct. Last admission at 4:30. **Cost:** Museum only $8.50; $7.50 (ages 65+); $6 (ages 13-18); $3 (ages 5-12). Museum and underground mine tour $17; $14 (ages 65+); $12 (ages 13-18); $9 (ages 5-12). Space is limited on the mine tour, so reservations are recommended. **Phone:** (406) 723-7211. [GT] [⛎]

AMERICAS BEST VALUE INN
(406)723-5464

Motel
$55-$70

Address: 122001 W Brown's Gulch Rd 59701 **Location:** I-90/15 exit 122 (Rocker Rd), just n. Truck parking on premises. **Facility:** 48 units. 2 stories (no elevator), interior corridors. **Parking:** winter plug-ins. **Terms:** cancellation fee imposed. **Guest Services:** coin laundry.

BEST WESTERN PLUS BUTTE PLAZA INN
(406)494-3500

Hotel
$112-$165

AAA Benefit:
Save 10% or more every day and earn 10% bonus points!

Address: 2900 Harrison Ave 59701 **Location:** I-90/15 exit 127 (Harrison Ave), just s. **Facility:** 133 units. 2 stories, interior corridors. **Parking:** winter plug-ins. **Pool(s):** heated indoor. **Activities:** sauna, hot tub, exercise room. **Guest Services:** valet and coin laundry, area transportation. **Featured Amenity:** full hot breakfast.

A full service hotel, close to Montana Tech, REC Silicon and St. James Hospital.

COMFORT INN OF BUTTE
(406)494-8850

Hotel
$115-$180

Address: 2777 Harrison Ave 59701 **Location:** I-90/15 exit 127 (Harrison Ave), just s. **Facility:** 144 units, some efficiencies. 3 stories, interior corridors. **Parking:** winter plug-ins. **Pool(s):** heated indoor. **Activities:** sauna, hot tub, exercise room. **Guest Services:** coin laundry, area transportation. **Featured Amenity:** full hot breakfast.

Perfect stop between Glacier and Yellowstone Parks. Fresh Hot Breakfast Buffet and Free WiFi.

DAYS INN
(406)494-7000

Hotel $129-$185 **Address:** 2700 Harrison Ave 59701 **Location:** I-90/15 exit 127 (Harrison Ave), just n. **Facility:** 74 units. 3 stories, interior corridors. **Parking:** winter plug-ins. **Pool(s):** heated indoor. **Activities:** hot tub, limited exercise equipment. **Guest Services:** coin laundry.

FINLEN HOTEL
(406)723-5461

Hotel $76-$110 **Address:** 100 E Broadway 59701 **Location:** Jct Wyoming St; in Historic Uptown. **Facility:** 56 units, some two bedrooms. 2-3 stories, interior/exterior corridors.

HAMPTON INN
(406)494-2250

Hotel
$109-$169

AAA Benefit:
Members save up to 10%!

Address: 3499 Harrison Ave 59701 **Location:** I-90/15 exit 127 (Harrison Ave), 0.6 mi s. **Facility:** 91 units. 3 stories, interior corridors. **Parking:** winter plug-ins. **Terms:** 1-7 night minimum stay, cancellation fee imposed. **Pool(s):** heated indoor. **Activities:** hot tub, exercise room. **Guest Services:** valet and coin laundry, area transportation. **Featured Amenity:** breakfast buffet.

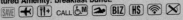

Located 2 mi. from uptown Butte, easy access to Historic District, free shuttle and hot breakfast.

LA QUINTA INN & SUITES
(406)494-6999

Hotel $64-$213 **Address:** 1 Holiday Park Dr 59701 **Location:** I-90/15 exit 127 (Harrison Ave), just n to Cornell St, then just e, follow signs. Across from a park and Greenway Walking Trail. **Facility:** 83 units. 4 stories, interior corridors. **Parking:** winter plug-ins. **Activities:** hot tub, exercise room. **Guest Services:** valet and coin laundry.

SUPER 8 OF BUTTE
(406)494-6000

Hotel
$72-$115

Address: 2929 Harrison Ave 59701 **Location:** I-90/15 exit 127 (Harrison Ave), just s. Opposite a shopping mall. **Facility:** 106 units. 3 stories (no elevator), interior corridors. **Parking:** winter plug-ins. **Guest Services:** coin laundry. **Featured Amenity:** continental breakfast.

WHERE TO EAT

BROADWAY CAFE
406)723-8711

Pizza Natural/Organic. Family Dining. $7-$17 **AAA Inspector Notes:** *Historic.* Gourmet pizzas are served in a converted historic building. Organic ingredients are used in sauces, pizza toppings and salads. Local bands play weekly in the casual eatery. The back room overlooks the city and offers wonderful views of the mountains. **Features:** beer & wine. **Address:** 302 E Broadway 59701 **Location:** I-90/15 exit 126, 1.4 mi n on Montana St, then 2 mi e. **Parking:** street only.

Ask about AAA/CAA Associate membership

to share the benefits you value

CASAGRANDA'S STEAKHOUSE
406/723-4141

▼▼ ◆◆ American. Casual Dining. $15-$32 **AAA Inspector Notes:** In a circa 1900s distribution warehouse, the family-run restaurant has wood floors, beamed ceilings and old paper invoices tacked to the walls. Steak and seafood are served in large portions. Included in the meal price are appetizers and dessert. **Features:** full bar. **Address:** 800 S Utah Ave 59701 **Location:** I-90 exit 126, just n, 1 mi e on Front St, then just n; in Bertoglio Warehouse. D

CHRISTINA'S COCINA CAFE
406/723-8444

▼▼ ▼▼ Tex-Mex. Casual Dining. $8-$19 **AAA Inspector Notes:** The very popular neighborhood restaurant is in a residential district and offers an extensive menu of Tex-Mex cuisine, including slow-cooked beans instead of refried and in-house made taco chips and sauces. **Features:** full bar. **Address:** 2201 Silver Bow Blvd 59701 **Location:** I-90/15 exit Continental Dr, 4 mi w, then 1 mi s on Howard St. L D CALL M

FRED'S MESQUITE GRILL
406/723-4440

▼▼ ▼▼ American. Casual Dining. $11-$26 **AAA Inspector Notes:** The eatery's focal point is the huge wood-fired grill. Those who choose to sit at the counter can watch and smell the kebabs, steaks, chicken, vegetables and seafood sizzling before being served to them piping hot. The chef does it the right way, with homemade onion rings, freshly prepared salads and choice cuts of meat. **Features:** full bar, patio dining. **Address:** 205 S Arizona St 59701 **Location:** Jct Mercury St; in Historic Uptown. L D

MATT'S PLACE DRIVE IN
406/782-8049

▼ American. Family Dining. $6-$12 **AAA Inspector Notes:** *Historic.* This classic diner is on the historic registry. In business since 1930, this place serves classic, made-from-scratch food and homemade ice cream. Thick, rich milkshakes come in a variety of flavors. Distinctive equipment and period furniture are part of the décor. They still have car-hop service. **Address:** 2339 Placer St 59701 **Location:** I-90 exit 126, 0.5 mi s; jct Rowe Rd and Montana Ave. L D

METALS SPORTS BAR & GRILL
406/782-5534

▼▼ ▼▼ American. Casual Dining. $8-$23 **AAA Inspector Notes:** *Historic.* In the historic Metals Bank building, the eatery sports no fewer than 24 TVs. The old vault is used as a wine cave, which offers one intimate table, and the original marble teller counter serves as the bar. The menu features meats from a local butcher. **Features:** full bar. **Address:** 8 W Park St 59701 **Location:** Jct Main St; in Historic Uptown. **Parking:** street only. L D

THE MONTANA CLUB
406/494-1400

▼▼ ▼▼ Regional American. Casual Dining. $12-$30 **AAA Inspector Notes:** Sister restaurants are in Missoula and Kalispell. Fresh Alaskan salmon, halibut and house-cut meats are on the menu. Also a large selection of salads, sandwiches, and pastas available. This family-friendly restaurant has large portions and is next to a casino. **Features:** full bar, senior menu. **Address:** 3540 Harrison Ave 59701 **Location:** I-90/15 exit 127 (Harrison Ave), 0.7 mi s. B L D CALL M

SOHO ASIAN CUISINE
406/221-7288

▼▼ ▼▼ Chinese. Casual Dining. $7-$16 **AAA Inspector Notes:** A few steps up from the Acoma, this restaurant has a wall of windows and a skylight. You'll have lots of light during the day, but at night, the lights of the city sparkle. Drinks may be ordered from the Acoma during the evening. The owners create comfort food and sushi to go along with the comfortable décor. **Features:** full bar, senior menu. **Address:** 60 1/2 E Broadway 59701 **Location:** Jct Wyoming St; in Historic Uptown. **Parking:** street only. L D

TRIMBO'S "OFF THE HOOK" PIZZA
406/782-1700

▼ Eastern Pizza. Family Dining. $9-$30 **AAA Inspector Notes:** *Historic.* "Off the hook" is an expression used by New Yorkers to mean fantastic, super, et cetera. And that's just what this New York-style pizza is. The dough is made from scratch daily, then hand-tossed to stretch it out. And believe me, it needs to be stretched in order for all of those fresh ingredients to fit. The veggies are fresh and the meats and cheeses are imported. But for me, the crust is it—just a bit chewy but mostly crispy with a wonderful fresh taste, just like "back East." **Features:** beer & wine. **Address:** 43 E Park St 59701 **Location:** Just e of jct Main St; in Historic Uptown. **Parking:** street only. L D CALL M

UPTOWN CAFE
406/723-4735

▼▼ ▼▼ Continental Casual Dining $7-$32 **AAA Inspector Notes:** *Historic.* An informal, modern décor and art gallery complement house specials of fresh seafood, steak, poultry and pasta. Gourmet desserts include tortes and cakes, and the homemade bread is excellent. A convenient, upscale luncheon buffet is offered. **Features:** full bar, early bird specials. **Reservations:** suggested, for dinner. **Address:** 47 E Broadway 59701 **Location:** I-90/15 exit 126, 1.5 mi n on Montana St, then just e. **Parking:** street only. L D

BYNUM (B-3) pop. 31, elev. 3,972'

TWO MEDICINE DINOSAUR CENTER, , 120 Second Ave. S., features a variety of exhibits containing fossils and archeological materials. Guided walking tours of an active dinosaur dig site along the front range of the Rocky Mountains are available and include discussions about paleontology. Visitors also have the opportunity to search for fossil specimens during the 3-hour tour. Transportation to the field is provided. Hands-on daylong and multiday paleontology programs also are offered.

Note: The walk may cover up to 2 miles and involve some stooping and bending. Comfortable clothing and shoes are recommended. **Hours:** Center daily 9-6, June 1-Sept. 15; Wed.-Sun. 10-5, in May and Sept. 16-Sept. 30; Mon.-Fri. 10-5 by appointment only, rest of year. Tour departures require a minimum of three people. Tours are given daily at 9 and 1, Memorial Day weekend-Sept. 15; otherwise varies. Closed July 4. Phone ahead to confirm schedule. **Cost:** Center $5; $4 (ages 55+ and military with ID); $3 (ages 4-12). Guided tour $75. Reservations are required. **Phone:** (406) 469-2211 or (800) 238-6873. GT

CARDWELL pop. 50

LAHOOD PARK
406/287-3281

▼▼ ▼▼ American. Casual Dining. $10-$33 **AAA Inspector Notes:** Only 100 yards from where Lewis and Clark camped along the Jefferson River and 4 miles from Lewis and Clark Caverns, this rustic, budget-friendly restaurant offers good cuts of steaks, house-made sauces and homemade sourdough bread, The portions are generous. Popular with the locals, reservations are necessary in summer. **Features:** full bar. **Reservations:** suggested. **Address:** 960 E Hwy 2 59721 **Location:** I-90 exit 256, 2 mi e. L D JC

CHARLO (C-2) pop. 379, elev. 2,936'

NINEPIPES MUSEUM OF EARLY MONTANA is at 40962 US 93. The extensive and in-depth collections include examples of antique and contemporary beadwork and quillwork, photographs dating from the late 1800s, Western artwork by such notables as Charles M. Russell and E.S. Paxson, and period Western and Native American clothing. A large diorama includes mounted specimens. **Time:** Allow 1 hour minimum. **Hours:** Mon.-Sat. 9-5, Apr. 1-late Nov. Phone ahead to confirm schedule. **Cost:** $5; $4.50 (senior citizens); $4 (students with ID); $2.50 (ages 4-12). **Phone:** (406) 644-3435.

CHESTER (B-4) pop. 847

LIBERTY COUNTY MUSEUM is at 230 Second St. E. Housed in a former Methodist church, the museum contains artifacts, photographs and other items depicting the homesteading days on the High Plains. Archives and genealogy records are available for research. **Time:** Allow 30 minutes minimum. **Hours:** Daily 1-5 and 7-9, mid-May through Labor Day. **Cost:** Donations. **Phone:** (406) 759-5256.

CHICO HOT SPRINGS (E-4) elev. 5,274'

RECREATIONAL ACTIVITIES
Dog Sledding
- **Absaroka Dogsled Treks** departs from the Chico Hot Springs Resort and Day Spa at 163 Chico Rd. **Hours:** Trips are offered daily at 9:15, day after Thanksgiving-Mar. 31. **Phone:** (406) 223-6440.

Horseback Riding
- **The Chico Horse Barn** is at the Chico Hot Springs Resort at 1 Old Chico Rd. **Hours:** Horseback riding trips are offered daily year-round (weather permitting). Departure times vary; phone ahead. **Phone:** (406) 333-4933.

CHINOOK (B-5) pop. 1,203, elev. 2,405'

Chinook was named after the Native American word for the winds that often whip through this area during January and February, causing the temperature to rise as much as 70 degrees in a few hours. Melting the snow and exposing the grass, chinooks have saved many cattle herds from disaster. Charles M. Russell captured the significance of these winds to the range cattleman in his picture of a starving cow titled "Waiting for a Chinook."

BEAR PAW BATTLEFIELD-NEZ PERCE NATIONAL HISTORICAL PARK is off US 2, 16 mi. s. on CR 240, following signs. Chief Joseph, leader of the Nez Perce Indians, surrendered to Col. Nelson A. Miles on this site Oct. 5, 1877. A 1.5-mile walking trail is available. Blaine County Museum *(see attraction listing)* serves as the park's visitor center. **Hours:** Daily dawn-dusk. **Cost:** Free. **Phone:** (406) 357-3130, or (406) 357-2590 for the Blaine County Museum. (GT) (🏛)

BLAINE COUNTY MUSEUM is 5 blks. s. of US 2 at 501 Indiana St. In addition to fossil exhibits and Native American and pioneer artifacts, the museum features re-creations of a tar-paper homestead, a schoolroom, medical offices and a church. A multimedia presentation of the Battle of Bear Paw and information about Bear Paw Battlefield-Nez Perce National Historical Park *(see attraction listing)* also are offered.

Time: Allow 1 hour minimum. **Hours:** Mon.-Sat. 8-noon and 1-5, Sun. noon-5, Memorial Day-Labor Day; Mon.-Fri. 8-noon and 1-5, May 1-day before Memorial Day and day after Labor Day-Sept. 30; Mon.-Fri. 1-5, rest of year. Closed Jan. 1, Thanksgiving and Christmas. **Cost:** Free. **Phone:** (406) 357-2590. (GT)

CHOTEAU (C-3) pop. 1,684, elev. 4,000'

Choteau (SHO-toe) was named after French fur trader Pierre Chouteau; the name is spelled with one "u" to distinguish it from the adjoining county, also named after the Frenchman.

Choteau Chamber of Commerce: 815 Main Ave. N., P.O. Box 897, Choteau, MT 59422. **Phone:** (406) 466-5316 or (800) 823-3866.

OLD TRAIL MUSEUM is at 823 N. Main Ave. Set in a Western village, this local history and paleontology museum chronicles the history of the Rocky Mountain Front beginning with the dinosaur era. **Hours:** Daily 9-5, Memorial Day-Labor Day. **Cost:** $2; free (ages 0-3). **Phone:** (406) 466-5332.

CHOTEAU STAGE STOP INN   406/466-5900

Hotel
$104-$140

Address: 1005 N Main Ave 59422 **Location:** On US 89, north of town center. **Facility:** 77 units. 2-3 stories, interior corridors. **Parking:** winter plug-ins. **Terms:** cancellation fee imposed. **Pool(s):** heated indoor. **Activities:** hot tub, exercise room. **Guest Services:** coin laundry. **Featured Amenity:** full hot breakfast. *(See ad p. 170.)*

ELK COUNTRY GRILL   406/466-3311

◆◆ American. Casual Dining. $9-$27 **AAA Inspector Notes:** The roomy dining area has wood accents. Good ribs and chops are offered. Hear the elk bugle when an order is ready in the kitchen. Rib-eye steaks are cut fresh when you order. You will want to try the home-baked breads and desserts. **Features:** beer & wine. **Address:** 925 N Main Ave 59422 **Location:** On US 89, north of town center. (L) (D)

JOHN HENRY'S   406/466-5642

◆◆ American. Casual Dining. $9-$19 **AAA Inspector Notes:** You'll find affordable, tasty pizzas, burgers and family fare served in a casual, friendly atmosphere. **Features:** beer & wine. **Address:** 215 N Main St 59422 **Location:** On US 89; center. **Parking:** street only. (B) (L) (D)

CIRCLE (C-7) pop. 615, elev. 2,424'

Circle takes its name from a cattle ranch that once stood near this site. In the late 19th century the area around Circle was booming cattle country, but the devastation caused by the winter of 1886-87 put many ranchers out of business. Circle remains an agricultural community and the seat of McCone County.

Circle Chamber of Commerce and Agriculture: 300 Main St., P.O. Box 321, Circle, MT 59215. **Phone:** (406) 485-4782.

MCCONE COUNTY MUSEUM is at 801 SR 200S. Featured are a large collection of mounted birds and animals as well as artifacts, farm machinery, tools and guns from the homestead era. Dinosaur bones also are displayed. **Time:** Allow 1 hour minimum. **Hours:** Mon.-Fri. 9-noon and 1-5, May-Sept. **Cost:** $2; free (ages 0-11). **Phone:** (406) 485-2414.

CLINTON pop. 1,052

EKSTROM'S STAGE STATION 406/825-3183
American. Casual Dining. $8-$23 **AAA Inspector Notes:** Dine in what was once the stable of a stagecoach station. Recipes have been handed down from generation to generation in a family that has been in the hospitality business since 1883. Home-baked goods and trout are specialties, served amid rustic décor comprised of antique wood tables and mismatched antique chairs of different styles. The walls are adorned with mounted heads of big-game animals and birds as well as farm tools and century-old objects. It may be open weekends in April. **Features:** beer & wine. **Address:** 81 Rock Creek Rd 59825 **Location:** I-90 exit 126 (Rock Creek Rd), 0.5 mi s. B L D

COLUMBIA FALLS (B-2) pop. 4,688, elev. 3,098'
• Hotels & Restaurants map & index p. 167
• Part of Glacier National Park area — see map p. 162

The union of the North and Middle forks of the Flathead River has carved out Bad Rock Canyon, at the entrance of which lies Columbia Falls. The abundance of water and timber in the area supports Columbia Falls Aluminum Co. and Plum Creek Timber Co., the town's major industries.

Numerous recreational opportunities are available along scenic CR 486, which follows the North Fork of the Flathead River 20 miles north to the Camas Creek entrance to Glacier National Park. Hungry Horse Dam (see Glacier National Park p. 165) and the Great Bear and Bob Marshall wilderness areas also are nearby.

BIG SKY WATERPARK is 2 blks. w. of jct. US 2 and SR 206 at 7211 US 2 E. Among the park's amusements are several waterslides, including a family-friendly tube slide; a miniature golf course; bumper cars; an antique carousel; a rock-climbing wall; a "water wars" balloon game; and a video arcade. **Time:** Allow 2 hours minimum. **Hours:** Daily 11-7, July 1 to mid-Aug.; 11-6, mid-June through June 30 and mid-Aug. through Labor Day. Phone ahead to confirm schedule. **Cost:** Waterpark $24.99; $19.99 (ages 60+ and under 48 inches tall). Waterpark after 3 p.m. $19.99; $14.99 (ages 60+ and under 48 inches tall). Miniature golf $6. **Phone:** (406) 892-5026.

BAD ROCK BED & BREAKFAST (406)892-2829 7

Bed & Breakfast $125-$225 **Address:** 480 Bad Rock Dr 59912 **Location:** Jct US 2 and SR 206, 2.4 mi s on SR 206, 0.9 mi w. Located in a quiet area. **Facility:** 30 acres of manicured grounds offering sweeping mountain views surrounds a large main house built to recreate the grand old farm houses of the turn of the century. 9 units, some cabins. 1-2 stories (no elevator), interior/exterior corridors. **Terms:** 14 day cancellation notice-fee imposed. **Activities:** cross country skiing, bicycles, game room, exercise room, massage. **Guest Services:** complimentary laundry.

MEADOW LAKE RESORT (406)892-8700 5

Vacation Rental Condominium $119-$520

Address: 100 St Andrews Dr 59912 **Location:** Jct US 2 and SR 40, 1.4 mi e on US 2, 1.1 mi n on Meadow Lake Blvd. **Facility:** A destination in itself, the resort is located on a world-class golf course and offers accommodations ranging from hotel rooms to multiple room homes. Patios lead directly onto golf course. 24 units, some condominiums. 1-3 stories, interior/exterior corridors. **Parking:** winter plug-ins. **Terms:** check-in 4 pm, 30 day cancellation notice-fee imposed. **Pool(s):** heated outdoor, heated indoor. **Activities:** sauna, hot tub, steamroom, regulation golf, tennis, cross country skiing, recreation programs, playground, game room, exercise room, spa. **Guest Services:** area transportation.

MEADOW LAKE VIEW BED & BREAKFAST (406)892-0900 4
Bed & Breakfast $110-$229
Address: 180 Meadow Lake Dr 59912 **Location:** Jct US 2 and SR 40, 1.4 mi e on US 2, 1.1 mi n on Meadow Lake Blvd, then just w. **Facility:** 4 units. 2 stories (no elevator), interior corridors. **Parking:** winter plug-ins. **Terms:** check-in 4 pm, 2 night minimum stay - weekends, 7 day cancellation notice-fee imposed. **Featured Amenity:** full hot breakfast.

TRAVEL INN (406)892-0888 6
Hotel $53-$180 **Address:** 7336 US 2 E 59912 **Location:** Jct SR 206, just ne. **Facility:** 32 units. 2 stories (no elevator), interior/exterior corridors. **Parking:** winter plug-ins.

WHERE TO EAT

THE BACK ROOM/NITE OWL RESTAURANTS 406/892-2191 5
American Casual Dining $8-$26
AAA Inspector Notes: Here you're treated to two eateries in one building. The casual Back Room opens at 4 p.m. and features cooked barbecue, steaks and seafood with few frills. Dedicated carnivores can sample any of three styles of ribs served with fry bread. The Nite Owl, open early morning through evening, serves hearty breakfasts all day and comfort foods such as meatloaf and fried chicken. **Features:** full bar, patio dining. **Address:** 522 9th St W 59912 **Location:** Just w of downtown. Menu on AAA.com B L D

CIMARRON CAFE 406/892-9000 4
American. Casual Dining. $6-$14 **AAA Inspector Notes:** The small, unassuming log restaurant serves breakfast and lunch, in addition to dinner four nights a week. On the menu is an array of sandwiches, salads, wraps and a daily quiche special, as well as homemade desserts. **Address:** 700 9th St W 59912 **Location:** Just w of downtown. B L

COLUMBUS (E-5) pop. 1,893, elev. 3,600'
• Hotels p. 152

In 1875, travelers stopped at Countryman stage station on the north bank of the Yellowstone River. The hardy travelers referred to the settlement as Eagle's Nest, or as Sheep Dip, because of its vile whiskey. With the coming of the Northern Pacific Railroad in 1882 the town became a livestock and agricultural center. Initially called Stillwater by the railroad because it lay at the confluence of the Stillwater and Yellowstone rivers, it was renamed Columbus in 1893 to avoid confusion with Stillwater, Minn.

Today the town's economy still rests upon farming and ranching, but the area also is home to the only platinum and palladium mine in the United States. The town manufactures laminated structural wood beams and Western-style buckles, jewelry and saddle trim.

MUSEUM OF THE BEARTOOTHS is off I-90 exit 408, w. on Fourth Ave., then n. on Fifth St. to the corner of Fifth Ave. Displays illustrate the history of Stillwater County, mining and homesteading. The museum also pays tribute to local Congressional Medal of Honor winner Donald J. Ruhl, in whose name SR 78 was designated a Memorial Highway.

An additional building on the grounds displays outdoor machinery. **Time:** Allow 30 minutes minimum. **Hours:** Mon.-Fri. 10-5, Sat. 11-3, Memorial Day-Labor Day; Mon.-Fri. 10-5, early Apr.-day before Memorial Day and day after Labor Day-Dec. 31. **Cost:** Donations. **Phone:** (406) 322-4588.

SUPER 8 OF COLUMBUS   (406)322-4101
Hotel $73-$120 **Address:** 602 8th Ave N 59019 **Location:** I-90 exit 408, just s on SR 78. **Facility:** 72 units, some kitchens. 2 stories (no elevator), interior corridors. **Parking:** winter plug-ins. **Guest Services:** coin laundry.

CONRAD pop. 2,570

SUPER 8   (406)278-7676
Hotel $86-$103 **Address:** 215 N Main St 59425 **Location:** I-15 exit 339, just w. **Facility:** 45 units. 2 stories (no elevator), interior corridors. **Parking:** winter plug-ins. **Guest Services:** coin laundry.

COOKE CITY (F-4) pop. 75, elev. 7,675'
• Hotels & Restaurants map & index p. 324
• Part of Yellowstone National Park area — see map p. 316

Gold miners settled Cooke City in the early 1870s, and by 1880 the town numbered 7,000 fortune-seeking souls. Gold mining continued until the late 1950s, when commercial mining finally ceased. Gold panning in area streams remains popular.

Cooke City is 4 miles from Yellowstone National Park's northeast gate. Beartooth Scenic Highway *(see Red Lodge p. 199)*, the town's eastern access, usually is open Memorial Day through mid-Oct. Cooke City can be reached all year via the road from Gardiner through Yellowstone.

Colter Pass, Cooke City & Silver Gate Chamber of Commerce: 206 W. Main St., P.O. Box 1071, Cooke City, MT 59020. **Phone:** (406) 838-2495.

ELK HORN LODGE   406/838-2332 **24**
Motel $120-$140 **Address:** 103 Main St 59020 **Location:** US 212; center. **Facility:** 8 units, some cabins. 2 stories (no elevator), exterior corridors. **Parking:** winter plug-ins. **Terms:** closed 4/1-4/25 & 10/15-12/1, 14 day cancellation notice. **Activities:** hot tub.

CULBERTSON (B-8) pop. 714, elev. 1,919'

THE KINGS INN   406/787-6277
Motel. Rates not provided. **Address:** 408 E 6th St 59218 **Location:** Jct US 2 and SR 16, 0.3 mi e. **Facility:** 20 units. 1 story, interior corridors. **Parking:** winter plug-ins.

CUSTER NATIONAL FOREST (E-4)

Elevations in the forest range from 1,035 ft. in the grasslands of South Dakota to 12,799 ft. at Granite Peak in Montana. Refer to AAA maps for additional elevation information.

Scattered across counties in Montana and South Dakota, Custer National Forest encompasses nearly 1.3 million acres in three unique districts. The mountainous section, or Beartooth District, includes a portion of the Absaroka-Beartooth Wilderness and Granite Peak, the highest point in Montana. The eastern portions range from the pine-clad hills and rough break country of southeastern Montana to the rolling grassland of northwestern South Dakota and the badlands of western North Dakota.

Beartooth Scenic Highway, usually open Memorial Day through mid-October, traverses the mountain country. Other good routes provide access to campgrounds and trailheads. Guide and pack services are available in nearby towns.

Trail information, which can be obtained from Forest Service offices, should be checked and updated at Beartooth Ranger Station before a trip into Absaroka-Beartooth Wilderness is attempted. The ranger station, south of Red Lodge, Mont., on US 212, is open daily 8-4:30, Memorial Day-Labor Day; Mon.-Fri. 8-4:30, rest of year.

For further information contact the Forest Supervisor, P.O. Box 130, 10 E. Backcock Ave., Bozeman, MT 59771; phone (406) 587-6701 or Beartooth Ranger Station, (406) 446-2103. *See Recreation Areas Chart.*

CUT BANK pop. 2,869

CUT BANK SUPER 8   (406)873-5662

Motel
$95-$215

Address: 609 W Main St 59427 **Location:** On US 2, 0.3 mi w. **Facility:** 61 units. 3 stories (no elevator), interior corridors. **Parking:** winter plug-ins. **Pool(s):** heated indoor. **Activities:** limited exercise equipment. **Guest Services:** coin laundry. **Featured Amenity:** continental breakfast.

DARBY pop. 720

RYE CREEK LODGE   (406)821-3366
 Vacation Rental Cabin $250-$350 Address: 458 Rye Creek Rd 59829 Location: US 93, 4.5 mi s, 1.5 mi e. Located in a quiet, secluded setting. Facility: Spend a weekend relaxing in front of the fire or take an ATV ride. Cabins are spaced to give maximum privacy though you may see elk, moose or deer from your porch. Each cabin has a hot tub. 6 kitchen cabin units, some two bedrooms. 1-2 stories (no elevator), exterior corridors. Parking: winter plug-ins. Terms: check-in 4 pm, 60 day cancellation notice-fee imposed. Activities: fishing, snowmobiling, bicycles. Guest Services: complimentary laundry.

DEER LODGE (D-3) pop. 3,111, elev. 4,519'

The second oldest city in Montana, Deer Lodge is on the Clark Fork River midway between Yellowstone and Glacier national parks. The city was established in 1862 as the result of a nearby gold discovery. With fresh food and a blacksmith as drawing cards, Deer Lodge was a welcome stop for the many settlers and miners who passed through the area.

Southwest Montana: 1105 Main St., Deer Lodge, MT 59722. Phone: (800) 879-1159.

Self-guiding tours: Driving tour maps for the surrounding area are available from the Powell County Chamber of Commerce at 1109 Main St.; phone (406) 846-2094.

GRANT-KOHRS RANCH NATIONAL HISTORIC SITE is off I-90 exit 184 or 187. Established in the early 1860s, the ranch had grown to 27,000 acres by the early 1900s, and the owners controlled more than a million acres of public range in four states and Canada. Though much reduced, the 1,500-acre ranch still has livestock and more than 80 buildings, from bunkhouse row to the 23-room ranch house.

Hours: Daily 9-5:30, Memorial Day-Labor Day; 9-4:30, rest of year. Guided historic house tours are given on the hour in the morning and on the half-hour in the afternoon. Closed Jan. 1, Thanksgiving and Christmas. Phone ahead to confirm schedule. Cost: Free. Phone: (406) 846-2070. GT

OLD MONTANA PRISON is off I-90 exit 184 or 187 at 1106 Main St. Self-guiding tours of the cell house, maximum-security areas, hole, tunnel and walled prison grounds together with an exhibit of photographs provide insight into early prison life and area history. The facility served as a prison 1871-1979.

Time: Allow 30 minutes minimum. Hours: Daily 8-6, mid-May to mid-Sept.; daily 10-4, rest of year. Last admission 50 minutes before closing. Closed for 2 weeks at Christmas. Phone ahead to confirm schedule. Cost: (includes Frontier Montana Museum, Montana Auto Museum and Yesterday's Playthings Doll & Toy Museum) $10; $9 (ages 62+ and military with ID); $6 (ages 10-15). Phone: (406) 846-3111.

Frontier Montana Museum is at 1106 Main St., at the Old Prison Museum complex. An extensive private collection of Western memorabilia from the 1800s is a highlight of this museum. Also featured are Civil War items, a gun collection comprising 250 weapons, Native American artifacts, a railroad saloon diorama, railroad artifacts and a display of "gambler's essentials." Hours: Daily 10-5, mid-May to mid-Sept.; otherwise varies rest of year. Closed for 2 weeks at Christmas. Cost: Entrance included with Old Montana Prison admission of $10; $9 (ages 62+ and military with ID); $6 (ages 10-15). Phone: (406) 846-3111.

Montana Auto Museum is at 1106 Main St., at the Old Prison Museum complex. The museum houses a representative collection of vintage automobiles from the 1800s through the 1970s. Included are a 1903 Model A Ford, a 1914 Detroit Electric Car, 1950s Chevrolets and muscle cars from the late 1960s and early '70s. Interpretive displays and photographs enhance the collection.

Hours: Daily 8-6, mid-May to mid-Sept.; daily 10-4, rest of year. Last admission 30 minutes before closing. Closed for 2 weeks at Christmas. Phone ahead to confirm schedule. Cost: Entrance included with Old Montana Prison admission of $10; $9 (ages 62+ and military with ID); $6 (ages 10-15). Phone: (406) 846-3111.

Powell County Museum is at 1193 Main St., at the Old Prison Museum complex. Permanent and changing exhibits depict the history of Powell County and Deer Lodge Valley. Displays include a woodcarving collection, mining and ranching equipment and household and school items. Hours: Daily noon-5, in summer. Phone ahead to confirm schedule. Cost: Free. Phone: (406) 846-3111.

Yesterday's Playthings Doll & Toy Museum is at 1097 Main St., at the Old Prison Museum complex. The history of children's toys from the 19th century to the present is the focus of this museum. The collection includes an extensive Raggedy Ann and Andy display, dolls from different cultures and dolls made from materials ranging from papier-mâché to china. A model railroad collection also is displayed. Time: Allow 30 minutes minimum. Hours: Daily 10-5, mid-May to mid-Sept. Cost: Entrance included with Old Montana Prison admission of $10; $9 (ages 62+ and military with ID); $6 (ages 10-15). Phone: (406) 846-3111.

TRAVELODGE   (406)846-2370

Motel
$80-$200

Address: 1150 N Main St 59722 Location: I-90 exit 184, 0.3 mi s. Facility: 57 units. 2 stories (no elevator), interior corridors. Parking: winter plug-ins. Featured Amenity: continental breakfast.

WESTERN BIG SKY INN 406/846-2590

 Motel. Rates not provided. Address: 210 N Main St 59722 **Location:** I-90 exit 184, 1 mi w. **Facility:** 20 units, some two bedrooms. 2 stories (no elevator), exterior corridors. **Parking:** winter plug-ins.

DILLON (E-3) pop. 4,134, elev. 5,102'

Dillon was established in 1880 by a group of businessmen who bought out a rancher who refused to give up his land to the railroad. Named for the president of Union Pacific Railroad, Dillon is today a focal point for five rich stock-raising valleys, including Big Hole, Grasshopper and Beaverhead. Beaverhead County is among the top cattle- and hay-producing regions in the state.

West of Dillon is Bannack State Park *(see attraction listing this page)*, on the site of a former mining town. In 1863 Sidney Edgerton, a lawyer from Ohio, arrived in the vicinity and stayed throughout the winter season. When he visited Washington, D.C., in the spring, he advocated the creation of a new territory; President Abraham Lincoln named Edgerton governor and Bannack the temporary capital. The following year the territory's seat was moved to the boomtown of Virginia City.

Fishing is a popular recreational pursuit in the area. Some of Montana's higher mountains can be seen from scenic I-15, which follows the Beaverhead and Red Rock rivers to the Idaho border.

Beaverhead Chamber of Commerce: 10 W. Reeder St., P.O. Box 425, Dillon, MT 59725. **Phone:** (406) 683-5511.

Self-guiding tours: A brochure outlining a walking tour of historic Dillon is available from the chamber of commerce and the Beaverhead County Museum *(see attraction listing this page)*.

BANNACK STATE PARK is 17 mi. w. on SR 278, then 4 mi. s. on Bannack Rd., following signs. Montana's first territorial capital and one of the original gold-rush towns of this area, the park includes weathered remains of the first capitol, jail, hotel and log cabins. The visitor center offers 19th-century photographs of the region and videos about mining and local history. *See Recreation Areas Chart.*

Time: Allow 1 hour minimum. **Hours:** Park daily 8-7, Memorial Day-Labor Day; 8-dusk, May 1-day before Memorial Day; 8-5, rest of year. Visitor center daily 10-7, May-Sept.; Sat.-Sun. 11-6, in Oct. Closed Christmas Eve and Christmas. **Cost:** Park admission $6 (nonresidents per private vehicle); $4 (nonresidents arriving by other means); free (Montana residents with ID). Camping $24-$28 (nonresidents); $18-$20 (nonresidents with a Montana State Park passport); $14-$18 (Montana residents with ID). **Phone:** (406) 834-3413.

BEAVERHEAD COUNTY MUSEUM is at 15 S. Montana St. Included are a native birds exhibit and items pertaining to Native American and pioneer life in Beaverhead County. An outdoor interpretive area features a 1,300-foot boardwalk, an 1885 homesteader's cabin and sheep wagon, and a 1910 one-room schoolhouse. **Hours:** Mon.-Fri. 8-5, Sat. 9-5, June 1-Oct. 1; Mon.-Fri. 8-5, rest of year. Closed major holidays. **Cost:** $3; $2 (ages 12-17 and 55+); $6 (family). **Phone:** (406) 683-5027.

THE UNIVERSITY OF MONTANA WESTERN ART GALLERY/MUSEUM is in Main Hall at 710 S. Atlantic St. Featured are changing art exhibits; a permanent art collection that includes works by Charles M. Russell, Edgar Paxson and Monte Dolack; and the Seidensticker Wildlife Collection, featuring mounted animal trophies from around the world. **Hours:** Mon.-Fri. 9:30-4. **Cost:** Free. **Phone:** (406) 683-7331 or (406) 683-7232.

BEST WESTERN PARADISE INN (406)683-4214

Hotel
$89-$124

 AAA Benefit: Save 10% or more every day and earn 10% bonus points!

Address: 650 N Montana St 59725 **Location:** I-15 exit 63, 0.3 mi s on SR 41. **Facility:** 63 units, some two bedrooms. 2 stories (no elevator), exterior corridors. **Pool(s):** heated indoor. **Activities:** hot tub, exercise room. **Guest Services:** coin laundry, area transportation.

COMFORT INN OF DILLON (406)683-6831

Hotel
$119-$130

Address: 450 N Interchange 59725 **Location:** I-15 exit 63, just e. **Facility:** 48 units. 2 stories (no elevator), interior corridors. **Parking:** winter plug-ins. **Pool(s):** heated indoor. **Guest Services:** coin laundry. **Featured Amenity:** full hot breakfast.

GUESTHOUSE INTERNATIONAL INN & SUITES 406/683-3636

Hotel. Rates not provided. Address: 580 Sinclair St 59725 **Location:** I-15 exit 63, just e. **Facility:** 58 units. 2 stories (no elevator), interior corridors. **Parking:** winter plug-ins. **Pool(s):** indoor. **Activities:** hot tub, exercise room. **Guest Services:** coin laundry.

EAST GLACIER PARK (B-2) elev. 4,795'

• Hotels & Restaurants map & index p. 167
• Part of Glacier National Park area — see map p. 162

In the Two Medicine Valley, East Glacier Park is the recreational center and eastern gateway to Glacier National Park *(see place listing p. 162)*. The community maintains an Old West appearance.

SUN TOURS is at 29 Glacier Ave.; tours depart daily from pick-up points in East Glacier Park, Browning, St. Mary and West Glacier. Knowledgeable guides—residents of the Blackfeet Indian Reservation—discuss Glacier National Park's natural features from a Native

(See map & index p. 167.)

American perspective. The trip, which takes visitors to the top of Logan Pass on Going-to-the-Sun Road, includes stops for photo ops and lunch. **Hours:** Narrated tours depart daily, June-Sept. Departure times vary; phone ahead. **Cost:** $35-$75; $20-$25 (ages 5-12). Reservations are required. **Phone:** (406) 226-9220 or (800) 786-9220. GT

DANCING BEARS INN & SUITES   (406)226-4402 12

Motel
$88-$174

Address: 40 Montana Ave 59434 **Location:** Just off US 2, follow signs; center. **Facility:** 13 units, some efficiencies and cabins. 1 story, interior/exterior corridors. **Parking:** winter plug-ins. **Terms:** 4 day cancellation notice-fee imposed. **Guest Services:** area transportation. **Featured Amenity: continental breakfast.**

JACOBSON'S SCENIC VIEW COTTAGES   406/226-4422 10

Cottage. Rates not provided. **Address:** 1204 Hwy 49 59434 **Location:** On SR 49, 0.8 mi n. Adjacent to Glacier National Park. **Facility:** 12 cottages. 1 story, exterior corridors. **Activities:** playground.

MOUNTAIN PINE MOTEL   406/226-4403 11

Motel $66-$98 **Address:** SR 49 N 59434 **Location:** On SR 49, 0.5 mi n. Adjacent to Glacier National Park. **Facility:** 27 units, some houses and cottages. 1 story, exterior corridors. **Terms:** closed 4/1-4/30 & 10/2-3/31. **Activities:** lawn sports. **Guest Services:** area transportation.

GLACIER PARK LODGE   406/226-5600

fyi Not evaluated. **Address:** SR 49 59434 **Location:** On SR 49, jct US 2; across from Amtrak station. Facilities, services, and décor characterize a mid-scale property. Recently celebrating 100 years, this lodge offers cozy, charming rooms and expansive public areas reflecting the pioneer railroad era of yesteryear.

WHERE TO EAT

SERRANO'S   406/226-9392 8

Mexican. Casual Dining. $9-$18 **AAA Inspector Notes:** This restaurant is inside the historic former Dawson House where the atmosphere is intimate but bustling. Expect a wait. You can't go wrong with the sautéed red snapper or the chile relleno. The Indian taco is always a favorite and so are the margaritas. Patio seating is offered weather permitting. **Features:** full bar, patio dining. **Address:** 29 Dawson Ave 59434 **Location:** Center. **Parking:** street only.

EMIGRANT   pop. 488

• **Part of Yellowstone National Park area — see map p. 316**

JOHNSTAD'S BED & BREAKFAST & LOG CABIN
406/333-9003

Bed & Breakfast $125-$180 **Address:** 03 Paradise Ln 59027 **Location:** I-90 exit 333 (US 89), 18 mi s; between MM 36 and 37. **Facility:** Surrounded by views of the Paradise Valley and the Beartooth/Absaroka mountain ranges, the B&B offers private access to Yellowstone River. Rooms are full family history and long collected antiques. 4 units, some three bedrooms and cabins. 1 story, exterior corridors. **Terms:** check-in 4 pm, 2 night minimum stay - seasonal and/or weekends, 30 day cancellation notice-fee imposed. **Activities:** fishing.

PARADISE GATEWAY BED & BREAKFAST & GUEST CABIN
406/333-4063

Bed & Breakfast $85-$600 **Address:** 2644 Hwy 89 S 59027 **Location:** I-90 exit 333 (US 89), 4.5 mi s of town; between MM 26 and 27, 0.3 mi e on gravel road. **Facility:** Nestled in the majestic Absaroka Mountains along the banks of the pristine Yellowstone River, the B&B is just minutes away from scenic Yellowstone National Park. It's a great spot for avid fishermen. 3 units, some two bedrooms and cabins. 1-2 stories (no elevator), interior/exterior corridors. **Parking:** winter plug-ins. **Terms:** check-in 4 pm, 2 night minimum stay - weekends, 14 day cancellation notice-fee imposed. **Activities:** fishing, limited exercise equipment.

MOUNTAIN SKY GUEST RANCH   406/333-4911

fyi Hotel Did not meet all AAA rating requirements for locking devices in some guest rooms at time of last evaluation on 08/27/2015. **Address:** Big Creek Rd 59027 **Location:** I-90 exit 333 (US 89), 27 mi s; 6 mi s of town, 4.5 mi w. Facilities, services, and décor characterize an upscale property. Nestled in the Gallatin Mountain Range, the ranch offers modern guest rooms and one- to three-bedroom rustic cabins. All are supplied with baskets of fruit, coffee and tea.

ENNIS   (E-3) pop. 838, elev. 4,939'
• **Hotels p. 156 • Restaurants p. 156**

Ennis is in the broad, rolling Madison Valley, flanked on both sides by mountain ranges. Built along the Madison River, the town is convenient to the historic gold-mining towns of Virginia City and Nevada City as well as to the trout-filled lakes and streams of the Beaverhead-Deerlodge and Gallatin national forests *(see place listings p. 131 and p. 160)*.

Ennis Chamber of Commerce: 201 E. Main St., P.O. Box 291, Ennis, MT 59729. **Phone:** (406) 682-4388.

FAN MOUNTAIN INN
406/682-5200

Motel
$65-$90

Address: 204 N Main St 59729 **Location:** US 287, just nw of City Center. **Facility:** 27 units. 2 stories (no elevator), exterior corridors. **Parking:** winter plug-ins. **Terms:** 10 day cancellation notice-fee imposed.

(SAVE) 🛏️ 📶 ✕ 🧳 🖥️ / SOME UNITS 🛏️

WHERE TO EAT

CONTINENTAL DIVIDE
406/682-7600

Regional Continental. Fine Dining. $18-$39 **AAA Inspector Notes:** The chef/owner of this little gem of a bistro splits his creative talents seasonally. In the winter, his creative bent is jazz trombone, and for our eating pleasure in the summer, his artistry shines through in dishes such as sautéed Manila clams in an Asian-style broth or lobster cannelloni. His warm and approachable manner is also evident during his visits with patrons. While the dining room in the cabin is intimate and comfortable, dining al fresco is available. **Features:** beer & wine, patio dining. **Reservations:** suggested. **Address:** 47 Geyser St 59729 **Location:** 1.3 mi n on US 287, just e.

D CALL 🅜

ESSEX
- **Hotels & Restaurants map & index p. 167**
- **Part of Glacier National Park area — see map p. 162**

GLACIER HAVEN INN
(406)888-5720 ㉙

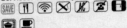
Motel
$79-$159

Address: 14305 US Hwy 2 E 59916 **Location:** Between MM 173 and 174; 20 mi e of West Glacier; 35 mi w of East Glacier. **Facility:** 8 units. 1 story, exterior corridors. **Terms:** 31 day cancellation notice-fee imposed. **Dining:** Healthy Haven Cafe, see separate listing. **Guest Services:** coin laundry.

(SAVE) 🛏️ 📶 ✕ 🧳 🖥️ 🖥️ 🖥️

IZAAK WALTON INN
406/888-5700 ㉚

Historic Country Inn. Rates not provided. **Address:** 290 Izaak Walton Inn Rd 59916 **Location:** On US 2; between MM 179 and 180. **Facility:** This is one of the original hotels built by railroad magnate J.J. Hill to provide lodging for turn-of-the-century visitors from the East wishing to explore the park. It still serves that purpose. 49 units, some two bedrooms, kitchens, cabins and cottages. 1-3 stories (no elevator), interior/exterior corridors. **Parking:** winter plug-ins. **Dining:** The Dining Car, see separate listing. **Activities:** sauna, hot tub, cross country skiing, game room, lawn sports, picnic facilities, trails. **Guest Services:** coin laundry, rental car service.

🛏️ 🍴 📶 ✕ 🧳 / SOME UNITS 🖥️ 🖥️ 🖥️

WHERE TO EAT

THE DINING CAR
406/888-5700 ㉖

American. Casual Dining. $10-$33 **AAA Inspector Notes:** This restaurant is set up like you're on a train — complete with observation windows overlooking the train line, while a model train circles the room overhead. The seasonal menu features fresh seafood, regional meats and veggies. For dessert try the heavenly cake — a flour-less chocolate cake topped with huckleberry ice cream and surrounded by meringue. **Features:** full bar, patio dining. **Address:** 290 Izaak Walton Inn Rd 59916 **Location:** On US 2; between MM 179 and 180; in Izaak Walton Inn.

B L D LATE

HEALTHY HAVEN CAFE
406/888-5720 ㉕

American. Casual Dining. $10-$26 **AAA Inspector Notes:** This is a family run operation. A limited menu of healthy choices such as steak and tilapia is offered in the evening, while an extensive breakfast buffet is available in the morning. **Address:** 14305 US 2 E 59916 **Location:** Between MM 173 and 174; 20 mi e of West Glacier; 35 mi w of East Glacier; in Glacier Haven Inn.

B D CALL 🅜 🍴

EUREKA (A-1) pop. 1,037

Located in the Tobacco River Valley 7 miles south of the Canadian border, Eureka was settled in the 1880s. Fur trader and explorer David Thompson passed through the valley in the early 1880s, an event commemorated each April during Rendezvous Days. Recreational activities, including fishing, kayaking, swimming, water skiing and ice-skating, are available on 90-mile-long Lake Koocanusa *(see Libby p. 186)*, 4 miles west of town, as well as on numerous smaller lakes in the vicinity. Huckleberries abound in the clearings of area forests.

Seven-mile Flathead Tunnel, the second longest railroad tunnel in the country, is 16 miles south of US 93 on Fortine Creek Road (FR 36). The tunnel was built in 1970 when the rising waters of Lake Koocanusa behind Libby Dam forced the railroad to relocate.

Eureka Area Chamber of Commerce and Visitors Center: 2 Dewey Ave., P.O. Box 186, Eureka, MT 59917. **Phone:** (406) 889-4636.

TOBACCO VALLEY HISTORICAL VILLAGE, 4 Dewey Ave., features a collection of late 19th- and early 20th-century buildings, each of which contains historical displays and artifacts. Among the structures assembled in this parklike setting are a general store; a log house; a church; a railroad depot; a one-room school; a library; a fire tower; and Eureka's first log cabin, built in 1891. Also on the grounds are a covered wagon, antique farm equipment and a Great Northern caboose.

Walking trails lead visitors along the banks of the Tobacco River. **Time:** Allow 1 hour minimum. **Hours:** Grounds daily dawn-dusk. Buildings daily 1-5, Memorial Day-Labor Day. **Cost:** Donations. **Phone:** (406) 297-7654. 🎫

FLATHEAD LAKE (B-2)

A recreational mecca, Flathead Lake appeals to those who enjoy a wide array of activities ranging from water skiing and fishing to sailing and sightseeing. The 28-mile-long, 15-mile-wide lake boasts several islands; sheep, deer, bears, eagles and ospreys inhabit Wild Horse. Nearby communities include Bigfork, Kalispell, Lakeside and Polson *(see individual place listings).*

Turn your road trip dreams into reality

with the TripTik® Travel Planner

FLATHEAD NATIONAL FOREST (A-1)

Elevations in the forest range from 3,500 ft.
at the valley floor to 9,289 ft. on Swan Peak
in the Swan Valley. Refer to AAA maps for
additional elevation information.

Flathead National Forest stretches along the
spine of the Rocky Mountains south from the Canadian border for more than 120 miles. With parts of its
eastern and northern boundaries bordering Glacier
National Park *(see place listing p. 162)*, the forest
shares much of the park's spectacular scenery of
high ridges and mountains. Its principal rivers are
the Swan, Stillwater and the three forks of the
Flathead—the North Fork, Middle Fork and South
Fork, all in the National Wild and Scenic River
system. This is augmented by 3,400 miles of
streams and many small lakes.

Almost half the national forest's approximately 2.3
million acres lies within the Bob Marshall Wilderness
complex, which includes the Bob Marshall, Great
Bear and Scapegoat wilderness areas. The combined 1.5 million acres attracts those who seek out
a challenging recreation experience in a natural setting where mechanized travel and equipment are
prohibited.

Popularly known as the "Bob," the Bob Marshall
Wilderness straddles the Continental Divide. There
are many rugged peaks, alpine lakes, mountain valleys, meandering streams, wildflower-strewn
meadows and waterfalls. Sunsets often are highlighted by long streamers of wave-shaped clouds, a
phenomenon created partly by strong winds blowing
perpendicular to a mountain range.

For those seeking utter solitude, winter use of the
"Bob" is almost nil. This vast reserve, appropriately
named for the man who helped preserve millions of
acres of the wilderness system, shelters one of the
country's largest wildlife populations, including elk,
bighorn sheep, black bears and several hundred
grizzly bears. About 50 outfitting and guiding businesses serve the area.

Other areas of interest in the forest are Mission
Mountain Wilderness and Hungry Horse Reservoir
*(see Recreation Areas Chart and Hungry Horse
Dam in Glacier National Park p. 165)*, along the
shores of which are almost half of the forest's
camping and picnic areas. The 15,000-acre Jewel
Basin Hiking Area, reached by forest roads from
SRs 83 or 35, is a scenic area of rushing waterways,
open meadows and subalpine forests; mechanized
vehicles and pack animals are not permitted. Hiking,
fishing and floating the three forks of the Flathead
River are popular activities.

Information about the forest's 31 campgrounds
and recreational opportunities is available at the
forest headquarters in Kalispell and at district ranger
stations. For further information contact the Supervisor's Office, Flathead National Forest, 650 Wolfpack
Way, Kalispell, MT 59901; phone (406) 758-5204.
See Recreation Areas Chart.

FORSYTH pop. 1,777

MAGNUSON HOTELS SUNDOWNER INN (406)346-2115

Motel
$95-$130

Address: 1018 Front St 59327 **Location:** I-94 exit 95, 0.5 mi nw. **Facility:** 40
units. 2 stories (no elevator), exterior
corridors. **Parking:** winter plug-ins.
Guest Services: coin laundry. **Featured
Amenity: continental breakfast.**

RAILS INN MOTEL 406/346-2242

Hotel
$69-$96

Address: 290 Front St 59327 **Location:**
I-94 exit 93, just n, then 0.5 mi e. **Facility:** 50 units. 2 stories (no elevator),
interior corridors. **Parking:** winter plug-
ins. **Terms:** 3 day cancellation notice-fee
imposed. **Featured Amenity: breakfast
buffet.**

RESTWEL MOTEL 406/346-2771

Motel
$75-$95

Address: 810 Front St 59327 **Location:**
I-94 exit 95, 0.8 mi nw. **Facility:** 20 units,
some efficiencies. 1 story, exterior corridors. **Parking:** winter plug-ins. **Terms:**
cancellation fee imposed.

WESTWIND MOTOR INN 406/346-2038

Motel
$69-$96

Address: 225 Westwind Ln 59327 **Location:** I-94 exit 93, 0.3 mi n. **Facility:**
32 units, some two bedrooms. 2 stories
(no elevator), interior corridors. **Parking:**
winter plug-ins. **Terms:** 3 day cancellation notice-fee imposed. **Featured Amenity: breakfast buffet.**

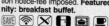

FORT BENTON (C-4) pop. 1,464, elev. 2,632'
• Hotels p. 158 • Restaurants p. 158

At the head of navigation on the Missouri River,
Fort Benton is one of Montana's oldest communities
and was the link between east and west. Thousands
of immigrants and miners marked this landing as the
beginning of the way west along Mullan Road or
north along WhoopUp Trail. Fort Benton also was
their chief means of supply, as all goods were
brought by steamboat from St. Louis. In 1868, 39
steamboats unloaded 8,000 tons of freight and

10,000 passengers; one steamboat returned to St. Louis with $1.5 million in gold.

The Lewis and Clark Memorial overlooks the Missouri River from the levee not far from the old fort; the memorial stands as a reminder of the explorers' stay in the area and the role they and Fort Benton played in opening the West. A statue of Lt. John Mullan, the first white man to pave the way west from Fort Benton to Walla Walla, Wash., and for whom the Mullan Trail is named, also stands on the levee.

Fort Benton is on the western fringe of the Upper Missouri River Breaks National Monument, and its corridor traces the Upper Missouri River 149 miles east into the Charles M. Russell National Wildlife Refuge. Recreation information can be obtained from the Upper Missouri River Breaks National Monument Interpretive Center *(see attraction listing this page)*.

Fort Benton Chamber of Commerce: 1421 Front St., P.O. Box 12, Fort Benton, MT 59442. **Phone:** (406) 622-3864.

Self-guiding tours: A brochure outlining a walking and driving tour of Fort Benton is available from the Museum of the Upper Missouri *(see attraction listing this page)* and from the visitor information center on Front Street.

MUSEUM OF THE NORTHERN GREAT PLAINS is at 1205 20th St. This museum contains the mounted remains of the Hornaday bull, the bovine model for the buffalo nickel; a 1920s village exhibit; and displays relating to agriculture. **Time:** Allow 1 hour minimum. **Hours:** Mon.-Sat. 10:30-4:30, Sun. noon-4, Memorial Day weekend-Sept. 30; by appointment rest of year. **Cost:** (includes Museum of the Upper Missouri and Upper Missouri River Breaks National Monument Interpretive Center) $10; $1 (children). **Phone:** (406) 622-5316.

MUSEUM OF THE UPPER MISSOURI is in Old Fort Park at 1900 River St. Dioramas and exhibits about early trading and river steamers are offered, and visitors can take a self-guiding tour of Old Fort Benton. **Hours:** Mon.-Sat. 10:30-4:30, Sun. noon-4, Memorial Day weekend-Sept. 30; by appointment rest of year. **Cost:** (includes Museum of the Northern Great Plains and Upper Missouri River Breaks National Monument Interpretive Center) $10; $1 (children). **Phone:** (406) 622-5316.

UPPER MISSOURI RIVER BREAKS NATIONAL MONUMENT INTERPRETIVE CENTER is at 701 7th St. Through displays highlighting the region's resources and a 20-minute overview about the national monument, the center documents the cultural and natural history of the Fort Benton area. Planning assistance with self-guiding river trips is available. **Time:** Allow 30 minutes minimum. **Hours:** Daily 8-5, Memorial Day weekend-Sept. 30; Mon.-Fri. 8-5, rest

of year. **Cost:** (includes Museum of the Northern Great Plains and Museum of the Upper Missouri) $10; $1 (children). **Phone:** (406) 622-4000.

GRAND UNION HOTEL   (406)622-1882

Historic Hotel
$108-$198

Address: 1 Grand Union 59442 **Location:** Center. **Facility:** This fully restored 1882 hotel commands picturesque views of the Missouri River. With an eye to maintaining its historic ambience, guest rooms are tastefully appointed with modern conveniences. 26 units. 3 stories, interior corridors. **Parking:** street only, winter plug-ins. **Terms:** check-in 4 pm, 7 day cancellation notice, 14 day in season-fee imposed. **Dining:** Union Grille Restaurant, see separate listing. **Activities:** trails. **Featured Amenity:** continental breakfast.

SAVE ▯¶ BIZ 🛜 ☒

/ SOME UNITS ▯▯

WHERE TO EAT

UNION GRILLE RESTAURANT   406/622-1882

Regional American Fine Dining
$16-$34

AAA Inspector Notes: *Historic.* Traditional and innovative cuisine will give your taste buds something to sing about. Inside this historic hotel dining room is cozy wood accent décor, which sets the stage for an intimate and impressive evening. The chef expertly chooses and prepares the freshest locally available ingredients, utilizing a farm-to-table philosophy. Menu items include cioppino, Thai spiced duck and rack of lamb. **Features:** beer & wine, patio dining. **Reservations:** suggested. **Address:** 1 Grand Union 59442 **Location:** Center; in Grand Union Hotel. **Parking:** street only. *Menu on AAA.com* ▯D▯

FORT PECK (B-7) pop. 233, elev. 2,100'

The federal government developed Fort Peck in the early 1930s as a support community for the construction of Fort Peck Dam. Built by the U.S. Army Corps of Engineers, the dam harnesses the Missouri River, providing electric power, irrigation and recreation.

Fort Peck Summer Theatre, 201 Missouri Ave., presents contemporary productions from mid-June to early September; phone the box office at (406) 526-9943.

FORT PECK DAM & LAKE is on SR 24. The construction of the largest hydraulic earth-filled dam in the world created Fort Peck Lake *(see Recreation Areas Chart)*, which offers excellent fishing, camping, boating, hiking, bird-watching and other recreation along its 130-mile length.

A testament to the human spirit, the dam was originally authorized in 1933 by President Franklin D. Roosevelt, who believed it would provide jobs for thousands of Depression-era people and serve as flood protection-a concern since the 1860s. Today, a hard-surfaced highway follows the crest of the dam 250 feet above the tunnel outlets. **Phone:** (406) 526-3411. GT ▮▲▮ ☒ 🗷

Fort Peck Dam Interpretive Center & Museum, on SR 24, adjacent to the powerhouses, offers exhibits depicting the fauna of the Charles M. Russell National Wildlife Refuge, along with information about the history of the Fort Peck Dam & Lake. A cast of Peck's Rex, a Tyrannosaurus rex specimen found in the area, is on display. A cretaceous sea exhibit features several ocean species hanging from the ceiling; other exhibits spotlight a struthiomimus and an edmontosaur. Two large aquariums housing native and game fish of Fort Peck Lake and the Missouri River can be seen.

A children's discovery area offers hands-on displays for kids. Interpretive programs and theater presentations are available in summer. **Time:** Allow 2 hours minimum. **Hours:** Daily 9-5, May-Sept. Hours vary rest of year; phone for schedule. Closed major holidays, except Memorial Day, July 4 and Labor Day. **Cost:** Free. **Phone:** (406) 526-3493.

Powerhouse Tour departs from the Fort Peck Dam Interpretive Center & Museum adjacent to the dam powerhouses. The tour describes how the power plants at Fort Peck Dam transform flowing water into electricity. Generators, surge tanks and turbines are displayed.

Note: Adult visitors must present a valid, government-issued photo ID. **Time:** Allow 1 hour minimum. **Hours:** Tours depart Mon.-Fri. at 9:30, 11:30, 1:30 and 3:30, Sat.-Sun. and holidays on the hour 9-4, Memorial Day-Labor Day; by appointment, rest of year. Visitors must sign up at least 15 minutes prior to the tour. **Cost:** Free. **Phone:** (406) 526-3493. GT

FORT UNION TRADING POST NATIONAL HISTORIC SITE (B-8)

Fort Union Trading Post National Historic Site, reached via US 2 and SR 1804, is 25 miles southwest of Williston, N.D., and 24 miles northeast of Sidney, Mont. Founded by John Jacob Astor for his American Fur Co. in 1828, the trading post became the center for the fur trade on the Upper Missouri River. The fort was 1,800 miles by river from St. Louis, the nearest supply point.

Excavators unearthed the foundations of the Bourgeois House, palisades, bastions, a Native American trade house, an icehouse and other structures. The trade house has been rebuilt and furnished as it might have appeared in the early 1850s. The fort's walls and bastions also have been reconstructed. A visitor center in the reconstructed Bourgeois House features exhibits about the fort and the fur trade.

Allow 1 hour minimum. Daily 8-6:30 CST, Memorial Day weekend-Labor Day; 9-5:30 CST, rest of year. Closed Jan. 1, Thanksgiving and Christmas. Trade house open 10-5:45 CST, Memorial Day weekend-Labor Day. Free. Phone (701) 572-9083.

GALLATIN GATEWAY (E-4) pop. 856, elev. 4,941'

RECREATIONAL ACTIVITIES
White-water Rafting

- **Geyser Whitewater Expeditions** is on US 191 1 mi. s. of the entrance to Big Sky Resort at 46651 Gallatin Rd. **Hours:** Trips are offered daily, early May to mid-Sept. Departure times vary; phone ahead. **Phone:** (406) 995-4989 or (800) 914-9031.
- **Montana Whitewater Rafting and ZipLine Co.** is on US 191 at Milepost 64. Other activities are offered. **Hours:** Trips are offered daily, May-Sept. Departure times vary; phone ahead. **Phone:** (406) 995-4613 or (800) 799-4465.

GALLATIN NATIONAL FOREST (E-4)

Elevations in the forest range from 4,300 ft. at Derby Gulch to 12,799 ft. on Granite Peak. Refer to AAA maps for additional elevation information.

Gallatin National Forest is in south-central Montana. Some of the most rugged mountains in the state can be found in the 1,735,239-acre forest. On the western side are the Madison and Gallatin ranges; to the east, the Absaroka and Beartooth; and to the north, the Bridger Mountains and the isolated block encompassing the Crazy Mountains.

To some, such as the Crow Indians who sought their visions in the Crazies, these mountains inspire a mystical reverence; to others, such as the mountain men who thought the Beartooth Range resembled the teeth of a familiar predator, they inspire a sense of awe. Much of this region remains unchanged, protected in the forest's two wilderness units, the Lee Metcalf and the Absaroka-Beartooth.

Absaroka-Beartooth Wilderness is named for its two very different mountain ranges. Rugged mountains, broad forested valleys and a variety of plant life characterize the Absaroka Range, which receives precipitation that is unusually abundant for this region. In contrast, the Beartooths present a jagged silhouette of monumental walls and spires soaring to heights of more than 12,000 feet. Forming the roof of these massive peaks are broad plateaus of alpine tundra carpeted with summer wildflowers and hundreds of lakes. The ranges are an integral part of the Yellowstone ecosystem, offering shelter to grizzlies, moose, deer, eagles and turkeys.

The Yellowstone, Gallatin, Madison and Boulder, which are the principal rivers, are renowned for excellent fishing. Natural Bridge State Monument, 28 miles south of Big Timber via SR 289, features a 100-foot waterfall at the mouth of Boulder River Canyon. Several short trails lead from the parking area to observation sites of the falls.

Hikers favor Lee Metcalf Wilderness (see Beaverhead-Deerlodge National Forest p. 131) and the Hyalite area of the Gallatin Range. Also scenic are the trails in the Bridger Mountains near Bozeman. To experience the region's beauty by car travel Beartooth Scenic Highway (see Red Lodge p. 199) or US 191 from West Yellowstone to Gallatin Gateway; or take a self-guiding tour of the Madison River Canyon Earthquake Area.

Information about the forest's numerous campgrounds and picnic areas is available at district ranger stations. For further information, contact the Bozeman Ranger District, 3710 Fallon St., Ste. C, Bozeman, MT 59718; phone (406) 522-2520. See Recreation Areas Chart.

MADISON RIVER CANYON EARTHQUAKE AREA—see West Yellowstone p. 207.

GARDINER (F-4) pop. 875, elev. 5,267'
- Hotels & Restaurants map & index p. 324
- Part of Yellowstone National Park area — see map p. 316

The northern entrance to Yellowstone National Park (see place listing p. 316), Gardiner is the only approach open all year. The Devil's Slide, an unusual rock formation 5 miles northwest on US 89, is visible from the highway. A mile north of town by gravel road is a travertine rock quarry. Theodore Roosevelt dedicated Roosevelt Arch in 1903.

Gardiner Chamber of Commerce: 222 Park St., P.O. Box 81, Gardiner, MT 59030. **Phone:** (406) 848-7971.

[SAVE] **WILD WEST RAFTING** departs from 906 W. Scott St. in the Yellowstone Outpost Mall. Passengers may view and photograph Montana wildlife on a leisurely 5-mile float trip on the Yellowstone River. A guide rows the vessel through Paradise Valley. Other activities as well as white-water rafting excursions also are available.

Time: Allow 2 hours minimum. **Hours:** Scenic float trips depart daily at 9:30, 1 and 4, May 1-Sept. 7. Half-day white-water rafting trips depart daily at 9, 10, 12:30, 3:30 and 5:30, May 1-Sept. 7. **Cost:** Scenic float trip or half-day white-water rafting trip $41; $31 (ages 3-12). **Phone:** (406) 848-2252 or (800) 862-0557.

RECREATIONAL ACTIVITIES
White-water Rafting

- **Montana Whitewater Rafting and ZipLine Co.** is at 603 Scott St. Other activities are offered. **Hours:** Trips are offered daily, May-Sept. Departure times vary; phone ahead. **Phone:** (406) 848-7398 or (800) 799-4465. **(See ad p. 142.)**
- **Yellowstone Raft Co.** is .5 mi. s. of Yellowstone River bridge on US 89. **Hours:** Trips are offered daily, mid-May to late Sept. Departure times vary; phone ahead. **Phone:** (406) 848-7777 or (800) 858-7781.

(See map & index p. 324.)

BEST WESTERN BY MAMMOTH HOT SPRINGS
(406)848-7311

Motel
$94-$239

AAA Benefit:
Save 10% or more every day and earn 10% bonus points!

Address: 905 Scott St W 59030 **Location:** 0.5 mi n. **Facility:** 86 units, some two bedrooms and kitchens. 2 stories (no elevator), interior/exterior corridors. **Parking:** winter plug-ins. **Terms:** check-in 4 pm, 3 day cancellation notice. **Dining:** Yellowstone Mine Restaurant, see separate listing. **Pool(s):** heated indoor. **Activities:** sauna, hot tub. **Guest Services:** coin laundry.

COMFORT INN YELLOWSTONE NORTH
(406)848-7536

Hotel $125-$275 **Address:** 107 Hellroaring St 59030 **Location:** North entrance, just s on US 89. **Facility:** 77 units, some two bedrooms. 3 stories, interior corridors. **Parking:** winter plug-ins. **Terms:** closed 10/31-4/13, check-in 4 pm, 3 day cancellation notice. **Dining:** The Antler Pub & Grill, see separate listing. **Activities:** game room, limited exercise equipment. **Guest Services:** coin laundry.

YELLOWSTONE BASIN INN
(406)848-7080 ⓾

Motel $205-$450 **Address:** 4 Maiden Basin Dr 59030 **Location:** 5 mi n on US 89 at MM 5. **Facility:** 14 units, some two bedrooms, three bedrooms and kitchens. 2 stories (no elevator), exterior corridors. **Terms:** check-in 4 pm, 30 day cancellation notice-fee imposed. **Activities:** hot tub.

YELLOWSTONE RIVER MOTEL
(406)848-7303 ⓯

Motel
$65-$134

Address: 14 E Park St 59030 **Location:** Just e of US 89. **Facility:** 38 units, some two bedrooms and kitchens. 1-2 stories (no elevator), exterior corridors. **Terms:** closed 11/1-4/15, cancellation fee imposed, resort fee.

YELLOWSTONE SUPER 8-GARDINER
(406)848-7401 ⓮

Hotel $50-$210 **Address:** Hwy 89 S 59030 **Location:** 0.4 mi n. **Facility:** 66 units, some two bedrooms and kitchens. 2-3 stories (no elevator), interior corridors. **Parking:** winter plug-ins. **Pool(s):** heated indoor. **Guest Services:** coin laundry.

YELLOWSTONE VILLAGE INN
406/848-7417 ⑪

Hotel. Rates not provided. **Address:** Yellowstone Park North Entrance 59030 **Location:** 0.8 mi n on US 89. **Facility:** 45 units, some two bedrooms and kitchens. 1-2 stories (no elevator), interior/exterior corridors. **Terms:** check-in 3:30 pm. **Pool(s):** heated indoor. **Guest Services:** coin laundry.

THE ANTLER PUB & GRILL
406/848-7536 ⑪

American. Casual Dining. $9-$28 **AAA Inspector Notes:** Located atop the hotel on the second floor, this family-friendly pub offers views of the town and mountains. As the name implies, the décor has a hunting lodge motif with wild game trophy mounts covering the walls. While the menu features pub fare like wings, burgers, sandwiches, tacos, chicken and fish, you may want to try something a little more exotic like bison or elk. Irregular hours in the off-season demand a call ahead to avoid disappointment. **Features:** full bar. **Address:** 107 Hellroaring St 59030 **Location:** North entrance, just s on US 89; in Comfort Inn Yellowstone North.

THE RAVEN GRILL
406/848-7600 ⑭

American. Casual Dining. $9-$26 **AAA Inspector Notes:** Favorites are rib-eye, salmon and pastas. The chef/owner makes a delicious fennel and lemon preserve slaw as an accompaniment to some seafood dishes. The decadent chocolate cake is worth the extra calories. They are closed for lunch Saturday and Sunday. **Features:** beer & wine, patio dining. **Address:** 220 W Park St 59030 **Location:** Center. **Parking:** street only.

TEDDY'S YELLOWSTONE CAFE
406/318-1200 ⑬

Italian. Casual Dining. $8-$16 **AAA Inspector Notes:** Share your day's experiences in nearby Yellowstone Park with other patrons while enjoying fresh pasta and house-made desserts. This small eatery has nightly specials such as pork chops or maybe Italian meatloaf. Lunch has a number of inventive sandwiches and salads. **Address:** 220 Park St 59030 **Location:** Center; on US 89. **Parking:** street only.

YELLOWSTONE MINE RESTAURANT
406/848-7336 ⑫

American
Casual Dining
$9-$22

AAA Inspector Notes: Entering this eatery is like walking into an Old West mine, chock-full of Old West artifacts on the walls. Chicken, steak and seafood are all good menu choices. **Features:** full bar, happy hour. **Address:** 905 Scott St W 59030 **Location:** 0.5 mi n; in BEST WESTERN By Mammoth Hot Springs.

GARRYOWEN (E-6) elev. 3,114'

CUSTER BATTLEFIELD MUSEUM is at 4185 Garryowen Road, on the site of the Battle of the Little Bighorn, which pitted the U.S. Army's seventh cavalry against Lakota, Cheyenne and Arapaho Indians in 1876. The tomb of an unknown soldier killed in the battle as well as photographs and artifacts pertaining to Plains Indian culture and the seventh cavalry are displayed. Personal effects of Lt. Col. George Armstrong Custer and Lakota leaders Crazy Horse and Sitting Bull may be seen.

Time: Allow 1 hour minimum. **Hours:** Daily 8-6, May-Sept.; 8-4:30, rest of year. Closed major holidays. **Cost:** $7.50; free (ages 0-12). **Phone:** (406) 638-1876.

GLACIER NATIONAL PARK (A-2)
- Hotels p. 170 • Restaurants p. 170
- Attractions map p. 164
- Hotels & Restaurants map & index p. 167

Elevations in the park range from a low of 3,100 ft. in the West Glacier Area to 10,466 ft. on Mt. Cleveland. Refer to AAA maps for additional elevation information.

Glacier National Park is in northwestern Montana. Geologic processes formed and sculpted the peaks, leaving about 25 glaciers and 750 lakes. The mountains are a result of an overthrust of the Earth's crust. Rock layers about a billion years old lie above layers millions of years younger. Some of the finest mountain scenery in America is within this million-acre national park.

The U-shaped valleys, as well as most of the lakes, are the legacy of the last ice age. Most glaciers are accessible only by trail; a few can be viewed from the road. Glacier National Park and Waterton Lakes National Park, in Alberta, together form Waterton-Glacier International Peace Park, although each is administered separately. Scenic Going-to-the-Sun Road (see attraction listing p. 165) connects the east and west sections of Glacier National Park.

Though Glacier is a refuge for many large mammals, most of the animals seek the undisturbed areas, and few are seen along the roads during the travel season. The park also is a haven for more than 260 species of birds.

The brilliance and diversity of its floral life is one of Glacier's outstanding features; July marks the height of bloom for many of the alpine species of vascular plants. In the valleys on the east side are dense stands of Engelmann spruce, subalpine fir and lodgepole pine. The western valleys present a different picture with their many dense stands of western red cedars, hemlocks and other conifers.

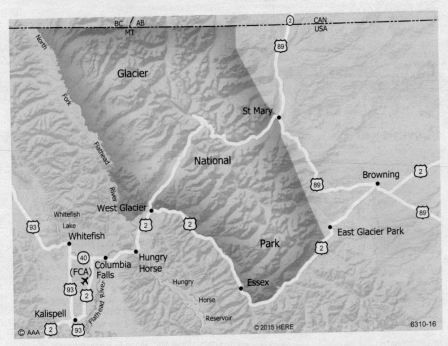

This map shows cities in Glacier National Park where you will find attractions, hotels and restaurants. Cities are listed alphabetically in this book on the following pages.

(See map & index p. 167.)

General Information and Activities

The park's peak travel season is roughly from mid-June to mid-September; however, the park is open year-round. Visitors can use the park's shuttle system for unlimited one-way or round-trip travel to various park locations from 7:30-7, early July through Labor Day. The last shuttle buses leave Logan Pass at 7 p.m. for both Apgar Transit Center and St. Mary Visitor Center. Check the shuttle schedule upon arrival. The shuttle is free with park admission. Canoe and motor boat rentals are available at the Apgar dock; phone (406) 257-2426. Additional docks and rentals are at Lake McDonald Lodge, Two Medicine and Rising Sun.

Note: Vehicles and vehicle combinations longer than 21 feet or wider than 8 feet (including mirrors) are prohibited from traveling the section of the Going-to-the-Sun Road between the Avalanche Creek picnic area and Sun Point parking areas, where they may park.

More than 700 miles of trails penetrate the park, and many points of interest are within easy walking distance of the hotels and chalets. Swan Mountain Outfitter offers guided horseback rides through the park. Tours depart from Lake McDonald Corral near Lake McDonald Lodge, Apgar Corral and Many Glacier Corral; phone (406) 387-4405 or (877) 888-5557.

There are more than 60 campsites for backpackers; backcountry camping permits are required ($5 per person per night, May 1-Nov. 1) and can be obtained at Apgar backcountry office, St. Mary Visitor Center and the Two Medicine, Many Glacier or Polebridge ranger stations. For more information about permits phone (406) 888-7857. Topographic maps can be purchased at the park visitor centers.

Mountain whitefish and cutthroat trout are the most common fish. Lake trout are taken from the larger lakes, principally McDonald, St. Mary and Waterton lakes. Grayling thrive in Elizabeth Lake. A fishing license is not required inside the park; regulations are available at the visitor centers. When fishing or participating in any activity in or near park water, watch for slippery rocks at the water's edge.

Several concessionaires within the park provide tours. Glacier Guides arranges guided backpacking trips. Glacier Park Boat Co. *(see attraction listing this page)* operates guided lake cruises on McDonald, St. Mary, Two Medicine, Swiftcurrent and Josephine lakes. Boats and canoes can be rented at Two Medicine, Swiftcurrent and McDonald lakes and at the Many Glacier Hotel on Swiftcurrent Lake. Shuttle services are available at Upper Waterton Lake.

CCInc. Auto Tape Tours of the park are available at Glacier Gift Shop in West Glacier or St. Mary's Lodge in St. Mary; phone (201) 236-1666.

Trail rides ranging from 1 hour to all day depart from Lake McDonald Lodge and Many Glacier Hotel. Daily schedules of ranger-led hikes, junior ranger activities, boat trips and campfire programs are printed as a supplement to the *Waterton-Glacier Guide,* the park's newspaper, which is handed out at the visitor centers. *See Recreation Areas Chart.*

Note: Although the animals in the park might appear tame, they are wild and potentially dangerous. Do not approach, feed, molest or tease them in any manner. Bears and mountain lions especially should be avoided; if one approaches, stay in your closed vehicle. Sightings should be reported to park rangers.

ADMISSION May-Oct. is $30 (per private vehicle); $12 (per motorcyclist or person arriving by other means). Admission rest of year is $20 (per private vehicle); $10 (per motorcyclist or person arriving by other means). The above fees permit entrance to the park for 7 calendar days from date of purchase.

PETS are permitted in the park only if they are leashed, crated or otherwise physically restrained at all times. They are not allowed on park trails or in the water.

ADDRESS inquiries to the Superintendent, Glacier National Park, P.O. Box 128, West Glacier, MT 59936; phone (406) 888-7800.

AVALANCHE CREEK is on Going-to-the-Sun Rd. A deep, narrow gorge cut through brilliant red mudstone is filled with potholes scoured out by stones swirled in the foaming torrent. From the gorge a 2-mile trail travels to Avalanche Basin and Lake, a semicircular amphitheater with walls more than 2,000 feet high, over which plunge a half-dozen waterfalls. A nature trail with a boardwalk for physically impaired visitors leads to the gorge. **Time:** Allow 30 minutes minimum. **Phone:** (406) 888-7800.

BELLY RIVER COUNTRY is accessible by trail from Many Glacier through Ptarmigan Tunnel, from Waterton Lake over Stoney Indian Pass, or from Chief Mountain customs station on Chief Mountain International Rd. Spurs are available to Helen, Cosley, Glenns, Mokowanis and Elizabeth lakes and Gros Ventre and Dawn Mist falls. The region is wild and heavily forested in some places.

A 33-mile drive through the Chief Mountain area to Waterton Lakes National Park of Canada offers scenic views. Waterton Inter-Nation Shoreline Cruise Co. operates a launch on Waterton Lake early May to mid-October (weather permitting). **Time:** Allow 2 hours minimum. **Cost:** Round-trip launch fare (in Canadian dollars) $46; $23 (ages 13-17); $15 (ages 4-12).

CUT BANK, at the s.e. portion of Glacier National Park off US 89, is a primitive, densely wooded valley. At the head of the valley is 8,020-foot Triple Divide Peak.

GLACIER PARK BOAT CO. departs from Lake McDonald, Many Glacier, Rising Sun and Two Medicine. The company offers scenic cruises aboard classic wooden boats that have plied the lakes here

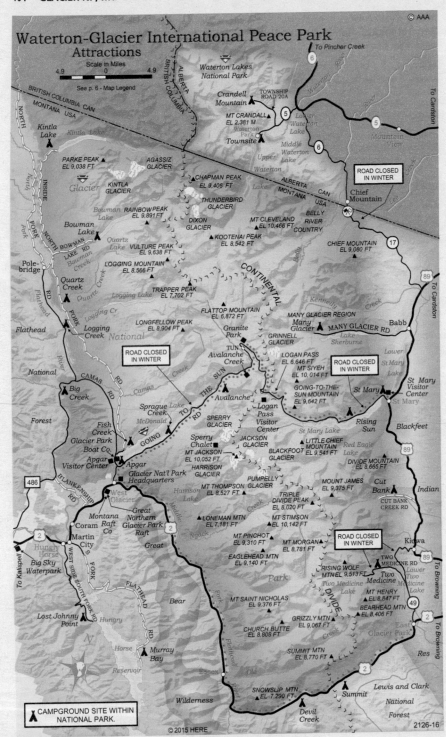

© AAA

Waterton-Glacier International Peace Park
Attractions

Scale in Miles
4.9　0　4.9

See p. 6 - Map Legend

To Pincher Creek

Waterton Lakes National Park

Crandell Mountain

TOWNSHIP ROAD 20A

MT CRANDALL EL 2,381 M

Waterton Park Townsite

Townsite

Lower Waterton Lake

Middle Waterton Lake

Upper Waterton Lake

Mountain View

ROAD CLOSED IN WINTER

Chief Mountain

PARKE PEAK EL 9,038 FT

AGASSIZ GLACIER

CHAPMAN PEAK EL 9,406 FT

KINTLA GLACIER

THUNDERBIRD GLACIER

CHIEF MOUNTAIN EL 9,080 FT

Kintla Lake

Glacier

RAINBOW PEAK EL 9,891 FT

DIXON GLACIER

MT CLEVELAND EL 10,466 FT

BELLY RIVER COUNTRY

Bowman Lake

VULTURE PEAK EL 9,638 FT

KOOTENAI PEAK EL 8,542 FT

Quartz Lake

LOGGING MOUNTAIN EL 8,566 FT

CONTINENTAL

Pole-bridge

Quartz Creek

Logging Creek

TRAPPER PEAK EL 7,702 FT

FLATTOP MOUNTAIN EL 6,872 FT

MANY GLACIER REGION

Many Glacier

MANY GLACIER RD

Babb

LONGFELLOW PEAK EL 8,904 FT

Granite Park

GRINNELL GLACIER

Lake Sherburne

Lower St Mary Lake

National

Avalanche Creek

TO THE SUN

LOGAN PASS EL 6,646 FT

ROAD CLOSED IN WINTER

St Mary Visitor Center

ROAD CLOSED IN WINTER

Big Creek

Avalanche

MT SIYEH EL 10,014 FT

GOING-TO-THE-SUN MOUNTAIN EL 9,642 FT

St Mary

Sprague Creek

Lake McDonald

Logan Pass Visitor Center

Rising Sun

Blackfeet

Fish Creek

SPERRY GLACIER

Sperry Chalet

JACKSON GLACIER

LITTLE CHIEF MOUNTAIN EL 9,541 FT

Red Eagle Lake

Glacier Park Boat Co.

MT JACKSON EL 10,052 FT

BLACKFOOT GLACIER

DIVIDE MOUNTAIN EL 8,665 FT

Apgar Visitor Center

Apgar

Glacier Nat'l Park Headquarters

HARRISON GLACIER

PUMPELLY GLACIER

MT THOMPSON EL 8,527 FT

MOUNT JAMES EL 9,375 FT

Cut Bank

Indian

West Glacier

Montana Great Northern Glacier Park Raft

Raft Co.

Harrison Lake

TRIPLE DIVIDE PEAK EL 8,020 FT

CUT BANK CREEK RD

LONEMAN MTN EL 7,181 FT

MT STIMSON EL 10,142 FT

Coram

Martin City

Great

MT PINCHOT EL 9,310 FT

MT MORGAN EL 8,781 FT

ROAD CLOSED IN WINTER

Kiowa

Big Sky Waterpark

EAGLEHEAD MTN EL 9,140 FT

TWO MEDICINE RD

To Kalispell

WEST SIDE SOUTH FORK RD

RISING WOLF MTN EL 9,513 FT

Two Medicine

Lower Two Medicine Lake

FLATHEAD

Two Medicine Lake

MT HENRY EL 8,847 FT

Lost Johnny Point

Hungry

MT SAINT NICHOLAS EL 9,376 FT

BEARHEAD MTN EL 8,406 FT

East Glacier Park

To Browning

Murray Bay

Bear

GRIZZLY MTN EL 9,067 FT

DIVIDE

Res

Horse

Reservoir

CHURCH BUTTE EL 8,808 FT

SUMMIT MTN EL 8,770 FT

Lewis and Clark National Forest

Wilderness

SNOWSLIP MTN EL 7,290 FT

Devil Creek

Summit

© 2015 HERE

2126-16

CAMPGROUND SITE WITHIN NATIONAL PARK.

BRITISH COLUMBIA CAN / MONTANA USA

ALBERTA / BRITISH COLUMBIA

ALBERTA CAN / MONTANA USA

(See map & index p. 167.)

since the park's early days. Narrated trips offer views of wilderness areas, glacial formations, waterfalls and rugged cliffs. Tours last between 45 minutes and 1.5 hours. Guided hikes also are available. Canoes, rowboats, kayaks, paddleboards and motorboats can be rented at Apgar late May through Aug. 31. Rowboats and motorboats can be rented at Lake MacDonald Lodge late May through late September. Rowboats, kayaks and canoes can be rented at Two Medicine early June through Labor Day and at Many Glacier early June through late September.

Hours: Tours depart from Lake McDonald Lodge daily at 11, 1:30, 3, 5:30 and 7, late May-Labor Day; at 1:30, 3 and 5:30, day after Labor Day-late Sept. Tours depart from Many Glacier daily at 8:30, 9, 11, 2 and 4:30, mid-June to mid-Sept. (also at 1 and 3, July 1-Labor Day). Tours depart from Rising Sun daily at 10, noon, 2, 4 and 6:30, mid-June to early Sept. Tours depart from Two Medicine daily at 10:30, 1, 3 and 5, early June-early Sept. (also at 9 a.m., July 1-Labor Day). Phone ahead to confirm schedule. **Cost:** Fares $12.50-$25.45; $6.25-$12.50 (ages 4-12). Rates may vary. Reservations are recommended. **Phone:** (406) 257-2426.

GOING-TO-THE-SUN ROAD joins US 89 at St. Mary and US 2 at West Glacier. Acclaimed as one of the outstanding scenic roadways of the world, the 50-mile route traverses the width of the park, crossing the Continental Divide through Logan Pass at an elevation of 6,646 feet while affording magnificent views of some of the park's loveliest scenery. Several miles of the two-lane highway had to be cut out of steep mountainsides and consequently it took more than a decade to complete.

At its official dedication on July 15, 1933, the road was given its current whimsical name, which comes from a mountain looming over the route east of Logan Pass. The source of the mountain's name is open to debate. It may have originated in a Blackfeet Indian legend or simply been made up by a white explorer with an active imagination.

You could drive Going-to-the-Sun Road from one end to the other in around 2 hours without stopping, but take your time because pulling over at one or more of the road's many scenic overlooks is an essential Glacier National Park experience. Some of the classic photo ops you should look for, from east to west: tiny Wild Goose Island in the midst of St. Mary Lake; Jackson Glacier, one of the few glaciers visible from the road; Bird Woman Falls, a silver ribbon of water falling hundreds of feet down the face of Mount Oberlin; the Weeping Wall, a waterfall that actually splashes onto the roadway; and McDonald Creek, a picturesque boulder-strewn stream.

Several trailheads are just off Going-to-the-Sun Road. Some paths go for miles into the backcountry while others offer short hikes to beauty spots. At Avalanche Creek (see attraction listing p. 163), the Trail of the Cedars offers a pleasant .7-mile boardwalk loop among moisture-loving cedars and hemlocks. At Logan Pass, the Hidden Lake Overlook Trail is a 3-mile roundtrip journey through alpine meadows filled with wildlife and ending with a spectacular view high above a mountain lake.

Note: Logan Pass closes for the season no later than November 1 and reopens in mid-June (weather permitting). *For vehicle restrictions, see General Information and Activities p. 163.* The park's optional, free Going-to-the-Sun Road shuttle stops at various points along the road July through Labor Day. **Road Closures:** Due to an ongoing, multiyear maintenance project, construction delays along sections of Going-to-the-Sun Road are likely. Portions may be entirely closed before and after the main season (roughly mid-June to mid-September, weather permitting) to accelerate the project. **Phone:** (406) 888-7800 for road closure information.

GRANITE PARK is reached from Waterton by the northern portion of the Highline Trail, from Logan Pass along the Highline Trail and from Many Glacier over Swiftcurrent Pass Trail. Exposed is a great mass of lava that once spread over the region. Trails radiate into the surrounding mountains. Granite Park Chalet, operated by a concessioner, is open July 1 through mid-Sept.; reservations are required. **Phone:** (888) 345-2649 for chalet information.

HUNGRY HORSE DAM is 15 mi. s.e. of Glacier National Park. One of the world's largest concrete dams, Hungry Horse's 2,115-foot crest is crossed by a 39-foot-wide roadway. A visitor center 4 miles east of US 2 has interactive displays and a video. *See Recreation Areas Chart.* **Hours:** Visitor center daily 8:30-5. Phone ahead to confirm schedule. **Cost:** Free. **Phone:** (406) 387-5241, ext. 361.

LAKE MCDONALD is reached via Going-to-the-Sun Road, which runs along the eastern shore. Ten miles long and 1 mile wide, the lake is the largest in the park. Its shores are heavily forested, and impressive rocky summits rise 6,000 feet above. Lake McDonald Lodge, near the upper end of the lake, is the focal point for trails to Sperry Chalet, Gunsight Pass, Sperry Glacier, Upper McDonald Valley and the summit of Mount Brown. A cruise boat operates from the lodge Memorial Day weekend through Labor Day. Boat rentals and naturalist programs are available at the lodge and at Apgar.

LOGAN PASS lies between the headwaters of Logan and Reynolds creeks. At an elevation of 6,646 feet, it straddles the Continental Divide and carries Going-to-the-Sun Road from St. Mary to West Glacier. Though there are no overnight stopping places, other than campgrounds along the road, easy access by automobile makes it a favorite starting point for several walks, including the trail to

(See map & index p. 167.)

Hidden Lake Overlook. Naturalist-led day trips and orientation talks are offered. **Note:** Parking is limited during peak visiting hours, generally mid-morning to late afternoon.

MANY GLACIER REGION is in the n.e. sector of the park. The area encompasses Swiftcurrent Lake, from which branch many deep, glaciated valleys. It can be reached by road 13 miles from US 89 at Babb or by trail from Siyeh Bend, Granite Park, Belly River and Waterton Lake. Launch trips on Swiftcurrent and Josephine lakes depart daily, late July-late Sept.

RED EAGLE LAKE is in Red Eagle Valley. Access to the valley is by trail from the St. Mary park entrance, from Sun Point via Red Eagle Trail and from Cut Bank over Triple Divide Pass.

ST. MARY LAKE lies at the foot of the Lewis Range. Peaks of the front barrier of the Rockies soar a mile above lake waters. A trail radiating from Sun Point is the shortest and best trail to Baring Falls. Red Eagle Trail along the south shore leads to Red Eagle Lake. Programs are presented nightly in summer at the visitor center and at Rising Sun campground. Launch trips and boat tours are available at the boat landing at Rising Sun from mid-June to late August.

SPERRY CHALET can be reached only by foot or on horseback from Lake McDonald and by foot from the St. Mary Valley via Gunsight and Lincoln passes. In a high, steep hollow at the upper end of a mountain valley, the chalet is hemmed in on three sides by precipitous peaks. Hiking and exploring the Sperry Glacier and fishing in nearby Lake Ellen Wilson are the chief diversions. Mountain goats frequently are seen on the cirque walls, usually during the late afternoon. **Hours:** Open mid-July to mid-Sept. **Phone:** (888) 345-2649.

TWO MEDICINE VALLEY is 11 mi. from East Glacier and 7 mi. off SR 49. Features include a lake surrounded by majestic peaks separated by deep, glaciated valleys. Trails for hikers and saddle horse parties radiate to adjacent points of interest; one short trail leads through dense evergreen forest to the foot of Twin Falls. Launch trips across Two Medicine Lake depart daily, early July to early September.

A readily accessible .3-mile scenic trail is at Running Eagle Falls, 2 miles below the lake near the road bridge across Two Medicine Creek. A portion of the falls' waters flows from a cave beneath the brink of the main falls. Early in the year it appears to be an ordinary waterfall, but late in the season water issues from the cave alone, and the waterfall above it is dry.

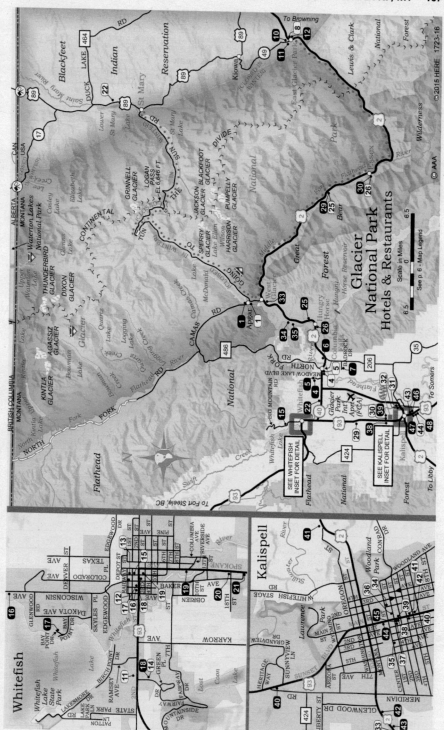

Glacier
National Park
Hotels & Restaurants

See p. 6 - Map Legend

Scale in Miles

©2015 HERE 1723-16

Glacier National Park

This index helps you "spot" where approved hotels and restaurants are located on the corresponding detailed maps. Hotel daily rate range is for comparison only. Restaurant price range is a combination of lunch and/or dinner. Turn to the listing page for more detailed rate and price information and consult display ads for special promotions.

GLACIER NATIONAL PARK

Map Page	Hotel	Diamond Rated	Rate Range	Page
1 p. 167	Apgar Village Lodge	◆	Rates not provided	170

Map Page	Restaurant	Diamond Rated	Cuisine	Price Range	Page
① p. 167	Eddie's Restaurant	◆	American	$9-$16	170

COLUMBIA FALLS

Map Page	Hotels	Diamond Rated	Rate Range	Page
4 p. 167	**Meadow Lake View Bed & Breakfast**	◆◆	$110-$229 SAVE	151
5 p. 167	**Meadow Lake Resort**	◆◆◆	$119-$520 SAVE	151
6 p. 167	Travel Inn	◆◆	$53-$180	151
7 p. 167	Bad Rock Bed & Breakfast	◆◆◆	$125-$225	151

Map Page	Restaurants	Diamond Rated	Cuisine	Price Range	Page
④ p. 167	Cimarron Cafe	◆◆	American	$6-$14	151
⑤ p. 167	**The Back Room/Nite Owl Restaurants**	◆◆	American	$8-$26	151

EAST GLACIER PARK

Map Page	Hotels	Diamond Rated	Rate Range	Page
10 p. 167	Jacobson's Scenic View Cottages	◆	Rates not provided	155
11 p. 167	Mountain Pine Motel	◆	$66-$98	155
12 p. 167	**Dancing Bears Inn & Suites**	◆	$88-$174 SAVE	155

Map Page	Restaurant	Diamond Rated	Cuisine	Price Range	Page
⑧ p. 167	Serrano's	◆◆	Mexican	$9-$18	155

WHITEFISH

Map Page	Hotels	Diamond Rated	Rate Range	Page
15 p. 167	Whitefish Mountain Resort	◆◆	$85-$1245	213
16 p. 167	**The Lodge at Whitefish Lake**	◆◆◆◆	$109-$299 SAVE	212
17 p. 167	Bay Point on the Lake	◆◆	Rates not provided	212
18 p. 167	**Grouse Mountain Lodge**	◆◆◆	Rates not provided SAVE	212
19 p. 167	**Pine Lodge**	◆◆	$89-$199 SAVE	212
20 p. 167	**BEST WESTERN Rocky Mountain Lodge**	◆◆	$99-$325 SAVE	212
21 p. 167	**Chalet Motel**	◆◆	$60-$145 SAVE	212
22 p. 167	North Forty Resort	◆◆	$119-$309	212

Map Page	Restaurants	Diamond Rated	Cuisine	Price Range	Page
⑪ p. 167	**Whitefish Lake Restaurant**	◆◆◆	American	$12-$46	213
⑫ p. 167	The Naked Noodle	◆	Noodles	$8-$15	213
⑬ p. 167	**Tupelo Grille and Wine Bar**	◆◆◆	Continental	$16-$42	213
⑭ p. 167	Logan's Grill	◆◆◆	American	$9-$38	213
⑮ p. 167	Amazing Crêpes & Catering	◆	Specialty	$6-$11	213
⑯ p. 167	Ciao Mambo	◆◆◆	Italian	$10-$25	213

Map Page	Restaurants (cont'd)	Diamond Rated	Cuisine	Price Range	Page
⑰ p. 167	Loula's	◇◇	American	$9-$24	213
⑱ p. 167	**Wasabi Sushi Bar & The Ginger Grill**	◇◇◇	Asian	$8-$45	213
⑲ p. 167	Buffalo Cafe	◇◇	American	$8-$25	213

HUNGRY HORSE

Map Page	Hotels	Diamond Rated	Rate Range	Page
㉕ p. 167	**Historic Tamarack Lodge & Cabins**	◇	$63-$320 SAVE	182
㉖ p. 167	**Mini Golden Inns Motel**	◇	$86-$160 SAVE	182

ESSEX

Map Page	Hotels	Diamond Rated	Rate Range	Page
㉙ p. 167	**Glacier Haven Inn**	◇	$79-$159 SAVE	156
㉚ p. 167	Izaak Walton Inn	◇◇	Rates not provided	156

Map Page	Restaurants	Diamond Rated	Cuisine	Price Range	Page
㉕ p. 167	Healthy Haven Cafe	◇	American	$10-$26	156
㉖ p. 167	The Dining Car	◇◇◇	American	$10-$33	156

WEST GLACIER

Map Page	Hotels	Diamond Rated	Rate Range	Page
㉝ p. 167	**Glacier Raft Company Cabins at Glacier Outdoor Center**	◇◇	$150-$649 SAVE	207
㉞ p. 167	Glaciers' Mountain Resort, LLC	◇◇	$129-$265	207
㉟ p. 167	**Silverwolf Log Chalets**	◇◇	Rates not provided SAVE	207

KALISPELL

Map Page	Hotels	Diamond Rated	Rate Range	Page
㊳ p. 167	Holiday Inn Express & Suites	◇◇◇	Rates not provided	184
㊴ p. 167	Homewood Suites by Hilton	◇◇◇	$119-$309	184
㊵ p. 167	Americas Best Value Inn	◇◇	$70-$150	183
㊶ p. 167	La Quinta Inn & Suites Kalispell	◇◇◇	$83-$372	184
㊷ p. 167	**Hampton Inn Kalispell**	◇◇◇	$99-$399 SAVE	183
㊸ p. 167	Comfort Inn	◇◇	$79-$279	183
㊹ p. 167	Red Lion Hotel Kalispell	◇◇	Rates not provided	184
㊺ p. 167	Kalispell Grand Hotel	◇◇	$91-$165	184
㊻ p. 167	Kalispell/Glacier Int'l Airport area Super 8	◇◇	$53-$120	184
㊼ p. 167	**Aero Inn**	◇	Rates not provided SAVE	183
㊽ p. 167	**Hilton Garden Inn Kalispell**	◇◇◇	$129-$299 SAVE	183

Map Page	Restaurants	Diamond Rated	Cuisine	Price Range	Page
㉙ p. 167	Spencer & Co	◇◇	Steak	$14-$30	185
㉚ p. 167	Bullman's Wood Fired Pizza	◇◇	Pizza	$8-$19	184
㉛ p. 167	Cislo's	◇◇	American	$8-$16	184
㉜ p. 167	Nickel Charlie's Casino & Eatery	◇◇	American	$8-$24	185
㉝ p. 167	Bojangles' Diner	◇◇	American	$4-$13	184

Map Page	Restaurants (cont'd)	Diamond Rated	Cuisine	Price Range	Page
34 p. 167	Julie's Center Street Cafe	▼▼	American	$6-$10	184
35 p. 167	Montana Coffee Traders	▼	Coffee/Tea	$6-$10	185
36 p. 167	Bonelli's Bistro	▼▼	Mediterranean	$6-$12	184
37 p. 167	The Alley Connection	▼▼	Chinese	$6-$18	184
38 p. 167	ScottiBelli's Ristorante Italiano	▼▼	Italian	$15-$32	185
39 p. 167	Hops Downtown Grill	▼▼▼	Western Burgers	$10-$25	184
40 p. 167	Genki	▼▼	Asian Sushi	$8-$19	184
41 p. 167	Thai Palace Restaurant	▼▼	Thai	$12-$22	185
42 p. 167	Wheat Montana Bakery & Deli	▼	Breads/Pastries Deli	$5-$10	185
43 p. 167	The Montana Club	▼▼	Western Steak Seafood	$8-$24	185
44 p. 167	Blue Canyon Kitchen & Tavern	▼▼▼	American	$12-$34	184

ST. MARY

Map Page	Restaurant	Diamond Rated	Cuisine	Price Range	Page
22 p. 167	Two Sisters Cafe	▼▼	American	$15-$25	201

APGAR VILLAGE LODGE   406/888-5484   1

▼ **Cabin.** Rates not provided. **Address:** 200 Going to the Sun Rd 59936 **Location:** 2 mi nw of West Glacier from jct US 2; in park at Apgar Village. **Facility:** 48 units, some cabins. 1 story, exterior corridors. *Bath:* shower only. **Activities:** fishing.

[icons] / SOME UNITS

MANY GLACIER HOTEL   406/892-2525

[fyi] Not evaluated. **Address:** Swiftcurrent Lake 59434 **Location:** East side of Glacier National Park; 12 mi e of Babb Jct. Facilities, services, and décor characterize an economy property. Swiss chalet-style buildings are set among the backdrop of stunning glacial peaks and a mountain lake. Find boat rentals on site, as well as numerous trail heads into the backcountry wilderness.

WHERE TO EAT

EDDIE'S RESTAURANT   406/888-5361   1

▼ American. Family Dining. $9-$16 **AAA Inspector Notes:** A friendly staff serves sandwiches, salad, soup and several dinner entrées such as pan-fried trout and broasted chicken. Named for one of the earliest settlers, this is one of a handful of eateries inside the park. **Features:** beer & wine. **Address:** 1 Fish Creek Rd 59936 **Location:** 2 mi nw of West Glacier from jct US 2; in park at Apgar Village.

[B] [L] [D]

▼ See AAA listing p. 150 ▼

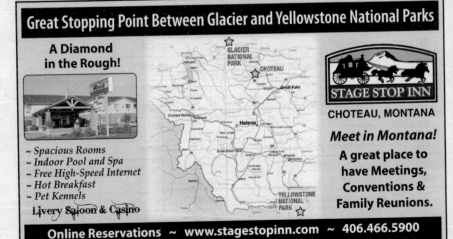

GLASGOW (B-6) pop. 3,250, elev. 2,090'

In the midst of the Milk and Missouri River valleys, Glasgow began as a railroad station. It is now an agricultural and commercial center for northeastern Montana, and the surrounding area is known for its hunting, fishing and outdoor recreation.

Glasgow Area Chamber of Commerce and Agriculture: 313 Klein Ave., P.O. Box 832, Glasgow, MT 59230. **Phone:** (406) 228-2222.

VALLEY COUNTY PIONEER MUSEUM is at 816 US 2. Displays include 19th-century Native American and pioneer artifacts, Lewis and Clark expedition memorabilia, paleontology specimens, photographs and agricultural tools. Mounted wildlife and a historic barroom exhibit also are featured. **Time:** Allow 1 hour minimum. **Hours:** Mon.-Sat. 9-5, June 1-Labor Day; Tues.-Sat. 9-5, in May; Tues.-Sat. 1-4, day after Labor Day-Oct. 31; Tues. 1-4, rest of year. Closed major holidays. Phone ahead to confirm schedule. **Cost:** $3; $2 (ages 7-21). **Phone:** (406) 228-8692.

COTTONWOOD INN   406/228-8213
◆◆◆ **Hotel** $90-$115 **Address:** 45 1st Ave NE 59230 **Location:** 0.5 mi e on US 2. **Facility:** 145 units. 2 stories (no elevator), interior corridors. **Parking:** winter plug-ins. **Pool(s):** heated indoor. **Activities:** hot tub, exercise room. **Guest Services:** valet and coin laundry, area transportation.

✈ ⑪ ⑦ ⚤ BIZ 🛜 🔲 🍴 ☕ / SOME UNITS 🐾 HS

WHERE TO EAT

DURUM RESTAURANT   406/228-2236
◆◆ American. Casual Dining. $6-$33 **AAA Inspector Notes:** This restaurant specializes in steak and pasta. Casual but also a little upmarket, they also offer grilled entrées of pork, chicken and fish and some more simple things like burgers. Lunch is more basic with a range of salads, burgers and sandwiches. **Features:** full bar. **Reservations:** suggested, for dinner. **Address:** 803 US Hwy 2 59230 **Location:** Just w on US 2; across from Pamida.

L D CALL 👪M

GLENDIVE (C-8) pop. 4,935, elev. 2,070'

Once a center for cattle ranches, Glendive is now a distribution point for diverse agricultural products. The surrounding area is rich in petroleum, natural gas and coal. Another natural resource, the boneless paddlefish, roams the bottom of the Yellowstone River in such numbers that Glendive has assumed the title of "Paddlefish Capital." Paddlefish season is mid-May to late June. Besides anglers, Glendive attracts rock hounds in search of moss agates and fossils, which are plentiful in the area.

Glendive Area Chamber of Commerce and Agriculture: 808 N. Merrill Ave., Glendive, MT 59330. **Phone:** (406) 377-5601.

Self-guiding tours: Brochures of a walking tour of the downtown historic district are available from the chamber of commerce and agriculture.

FRONTIER GATEWAY MUSEUM is 1 mi. e. off I-94 exit 215 on Belle Prairie Rd. This museum contains dinosaur fossils, Native American artifacts, farm machinery and other items depicting eastern Montana from prehistoric times to the present. Among buildings on the grounds are a rural schoolhouse, log cabin and smithy. **Hours:** Mon.-Sat. 9-noon and 1-5, Sun. and holidays 1-5, Memorial Day-Labor Day. Phone ahead to confirm schedule. **Cost:** Donations. **Phone:** (406) 377-8168.

MAKOSHIKA STATE PARK is 1 mi. s. at 1301 Snyder Ave. Makoshika comes from the Lakota word meaning "bad earth" or "badlands." The area encompasses 11,531 acres of eroded and vividly colored buttes and gullies, which can be viewed along the Kinney Coulee, Cap Rock and Diane Gabriel nature trails. A visitor center displays fossils and a triceratops skull. *See Recreation Areas Chart.*

Time: Allow 2 hours minimum. **Hours:** Park open daily 24 hours (weather permitting). Visitor center open daily 10-5, third Fri. in May-third Sun. in Sept; Wed.-Sun. 10-5, rest of year. **Cost:** Park admission $6 (nonresidents per private vehicle); $4 (nonresidents arriving by other means); free (Montana residents with ID). Camping $24-$28 (nonresidents); $18-$20 (nonresidents with a Montana State Park passport); $14-$18 (Montana residents with ID). **Phone:** (406) 377-6256. 🏞 🏕 🎣

ASTORIA HOTEL & SUITES   (406)377-6000
◆◆◆ **Hotel** $89-$119 **Address:** 201 California St 59330 **Location:** I-94 exit 215, just n. **Facility:** 89 units. 4 stories, interior corridors. **Parking:** winter plug-ins. **Terms:** cancellation fee imposed. **Pool(s):** heated indoor. **Activities:** hot tub, picnic facilities, exercise room. **Guest Services:** coin laundry.

⑪ CALL 👪M ⚤ BIZ HS 🛜 ✕ 🔲 🍴 🍽 / SOME UNITS 🐾

GREAT FALLS (C-4) pop. 58,505, elev. 3,312'
• Hotels p. 173 • Restaurants p. 175

Meriwether Lewis and William Clark visited the Great Falls of the Missouri River in 1805. Clark mapped the area while the other expedition members portaged around a series of five falls. The party returned to this site on its trip from the Pacific coast a year later. In 1882 Paris Gibson visited the site; he returned in the spring of 1883 with a surveyor and an attorney, and a townsite soon was plotted and named Great Falls. Important contributors to the economy are Malmstrom Air Force Base, agriculture and tourism.

Symbolizing the importance of the railroad in the city's development are two former railroad stations, both of which are located downtown near the east bank of the Missouri River. Built in 1909, the Great Northern Depot, now an office building, is just south of First Avenue. North of First Avenue, the impressive Milwaukee Road Depot was erected in 1915 and sports a handsome "flash" brick facade. Its 135-foot tower is emblazoned with the railroad's name, which is spelled out in red, yellow and white tiles.

River's Edge Trail, which begins north of US 89 on River Drive and stretches along the Missouri River, is popular with pedestrians and bicyclists. The trail's 40-plus miles include both paved and graveled sections.

A large American flag marks the visitor center on the Broadwater Overlook; follow directional signs on the approach and throughout the city. The center can provide information about guided tours; phone (406) 771-0885. An audio tour tracing 34 miles of the Lewis and Clark National Historic Trail is available from The History Museum, 422 Second St. S.; phone (406) 452-3462.

The ▽ Lewis and Clark Festival features historic re-enactments, foods that were typically eaten on the expedition, tours, exhibits and demonstrations. Other events also include outdoor art, a dinner gala, and live and silent auctions. The 3-day celebration in late June takes place at various locations, including the Lewis and Clark National Historic Trail Interpretive Center *(see attraction listing p. 173)* and Giant Springs State Park.

Great Falls Area Convention and Visitors Bureau: 1106 9th St. S., Great Falls, MT 59405. **Phone:** (406) 770-3078 or (800) 735-8535.

Shopping: Holiday Village Mall, 2.5 miles east of US 15 at 1200 10th Ave. S., houses 95 stores including Herberger's, JCPenney and SCHEELS.

CHILDREN'S MUSEUM OF MONTANA is at 22 Railroad Sq. The museum's hands-on exhibits are designed to encourage a lifetime interest in math, science and culture. **Time:** Allow 1 hour minimum. **Hours:** Mon.-Sat. 9:30-5. Closed Jan. 1, July 4, Thanksgiving, Christmas Eve and Christmas. **Cost:** $4; $3 (ages 65+); free (ages 0-1). **Phone:** (406) 452-6661.

▽ SAVE **C.M. RUSSELL MUSEUM,** 400 13th St. N., pays homage to the cowboy artist Charles Marion Russell. The complex contains a museum, Russell's home and log studio, and a sculpture garden. Russell's observation of life, personal philosophy and love of Montana greatly influenced his paintings and sculpture. Though Russell was an established artist at the time of his death in 1926, creating art was not always his ambition. Rather, he was attracted to the exciting life of a cowboy.

Just days after celebrating his 16th birthday, Russell moved from St. Louis to Judith Basin in Montana where he tended sheep for a brief stint. He spent 2 years learning from a hunter and trapper. His experience led him to become a night wrangler and he seized the time and opportunity to closely observe and sketch all the daily and nightly activities of the camp. After 11 years of being a ranch hand, he retired to pursue his life as a full-time artist.

Russell's great admiration of Native Americans, especially those of the Northern Plains, is quite evident in his detailed works on the subject. The cowboy's life is romanticized in many works. In addition,

images of bison, wolves, elk and other wild animals also feature in his paintings and reflect his life in Montana.

A visit to the museum reveals several galleries of Russell's watercolors, sculptures, oil paintings and illustrated cards and letters. Also featured are historical photographs of the Old West; a collection of Browning firearms; and the permanent exhibition, The Bison: American Icon, Heart of Plains Indian Culture. Changing temporary exhibitions showcase contemporary Western artists and historic artists, including O.C. Seltzer, Winold Reiss, Henry Farny and J.H. Sharp.

Time: Allow 2 hours minimum. **Hours:** Tues.-Sun. 10-5, mid-May to early Nov.; Wed.-Sun. 10-5, rest of year. Closed Jan. 1, Easter, Thanksgiving and Christmas. Phone ahead to confirm schedule. **Cost:** (includes C.M. Russell Home and Log Studio of C.M. Russell) $9; $7 (ages 60+ and retired military with ID); $4 (students with ID); free (ages 0-5 and active military with ID and their family members). Additional fees may be charged for special exhibitions. Reservations are required for guided tours. **Phone:** (406) 727-8787. GT

C.M. Russell Home is at the C.M. Russell Museum complex, 400 13th St. N. Russell's permanent residence was built in 1900 and is furnished in period. **Hours:** Tues.-Sun. 11-4, mid-May to early Nov. Phone ahead to confirm schedule. **Cost:** Included in C.M. Russell Museum admission of $9; $7 (ages 60+ and retired military with ID); $4 (students with ID); free (ages 0-5 and active military with ID and their family members). Additional fees may be charged for special exhibitions. **Phone:** (406) 727-8787.

Log Studio of C.M. Russell is at the C.M. Russell Museum complex, 400 13th St. N. Built in 1903, the studio contains Russell's pallet and brushes, cowboy memorabilia and Native American artifacts he used as models. **Hours:** Tues.-Sun. 10-4:45, mid-May to early Nov.; Wed.-Sun. 10-4:45, rest of year. Phone ahead to confirm schedule. **Cost:** Included in C.M. Russell Museum admission of $9; $7 (ages 60+ and retired military with ID); $4 (students with ID); free (ages 0-5 and active military with ID and their family members). Additional fees may be charged for special exhibitions. **Phone:** (406) 727-8787.

GIANT SPRINGS FISH, WILDLIFE AND PARKS VISITOR CENTER AND FISH HATCHERY is 2.5 mi. n.e. off US 87 on 4600 Giant Springs Rd. The regional headquarters visitor center has wildlife displays, photographs about park history and film presentations. Across the street is the hatchery for six strains of rainbow trout and two species of salmon; a visitor center explains fish raising. The park preserves one of the largest freshwater springs in the world. Scenic overlooks are available from two dams within 2 miles of the site.

Time: Allow 1 hour minimum. **Hours:** Park daily 8 a.m.-dusk. Park visitor center Mon.-Fri. 8-5.

Hatchery visitor center daily 8-4:30. **Cost:** Park admission $6 (nonresidents per private vehicle); $4 (nonresidents arriving by other means); free (Montana residents with ID). Visitor centers free. **Phone:** (406) 454-5840 for the regional headquarters visitor center, or (406) 452-5734 for the hatchery.

GREAT FALLS HISTORIC TROLLEY departs from the Paris Gibson Square Museum of Art at 1400 1st Ave. N. Highlights of the 1-hour Urban Adventure Tour are the historic downtown business district, the railroad area, the historic home district, a waterfall, parks, museums and churches. The 2-hour Historic Tour includes Lewis and Clark Trail sites, four waterfalls, Giant Springs, museums, historic homes and downtown districts, saloons, churches, the railroad area and parks.

Tours are available on a first come, first serve basis. **Hours:** Urban Adventure Tour departs Mon.-Thurs. at 4:30, Fri.-Sat. at 1:30 and 4:30, Sun. at 1:30, June-Aug.; by appointment rest of year. Historic Tour departs Mon.-Sat. at 10:30, June-Aug.; by appointment rest of year. Phone ahead to confirm schedule. **Cost:** Urban Adventure Tour $15; $5 (ages 6-17). Historic Tour $22; $5 (ages 6-17). **Phone:** (406) 564-0539.

LEWIS AND CLARK NATIONAL HISTORIC TRAIL INTERPRETIVE CENTER is at 4201 Giant Springs Rd. Exhibits detail the 1804-06 Lewis and Clark expedition, particularly the portion that took place in what is now Montana. Highlighted are the Indian tribes of the Plains and Pacific Northwest who aided the explorers. Rangers demonstrate skills used on the journey. A 30-minute introductory film by Ken Burns sets the stage for the visitor's own discovery journey. A second 20-minute movie depicts the arduous journey around the Great Falls of the Missouri River.

The interpretive center, managed by the USDA Forest Service, overlooks the Missouri River. On-site features include walking trails, scenic overlooks and grounds landscaped with plants described in the explorers' journals. Outdoor living-history programs are presented in the summer. Audio tours are available in several languages.

Time: Allow 2 hours minimum. **Hours:** Daily 9-6, Memorial Day weekend-Sept. 30; Tues.-Sat. 9-5, Sun. noon-5, rest of year. Closed Jan. 1, Thanksgiving and Christmas. **Cost:** $8; free (ages 0-15). **Phone:** (406) 727-8733.

MALMSTROM AIR FORCE BASE MUSEUM AND AIR PARK is on Malmstrom Air Force Base, just inside the base's main gate at the east end of Second Ave. N. The museum displays uniforms, Minuteman Missile Launch equipment and photographs relating to base history. An outdoor air park contains aircraft that date from the mid-20th century. **Note:** Adult visitors must present a valid, government-issued photo ID. Travelers with passports should notify the museum of their intent to visit 48 to 72 hours in advance. **Time:** Allow 1 hour minimum. **Hours:** Mon.-Fri. 10-4. Closed major holidays. **Cost:** Free.

Phone: (406) 731-2705 for museum information, or (406) 731-4050 for Malmstrom AFB Public Affairs.

PARIS GIBSON SQUARE MUSEUM OF ART is at jct. 14th St. and First Ave. N. in the Norman Architectural Building. The museum contains contemporary art exhibits. **Time:** Allow 1 hour, 30 minutes minimum. **Hours:** Mon.-Fri. 10-5 (also Tues. 5-9 and first Fri. of the month 5-8), Sat. noon-5. Closed major holidays. **Cost:** Free. **Phone:** (406) 727-8255.

TOUR DE GREAT FALLS picks up passengers at area hotels for guided bus tours or shuttle service to museums, parks and natural scenic sites in town via pre-packaged or custom tours. Tours and shuttle service to Glacier National Park and attractions in north-central Montana also are offered. **Time:** Allow 2 hours minimum. **Hours:** Trips are offered year-round by appointment. **Cost:** Great Falls tour $22; $20 (ages 65+ and active military with ID); $12 (ages 2-12). Attraction admissions are not included in fare. Phone for other tour prices. Reservations are required. **Phone:** (406) 771-1100. GT

RECREATIONAL ACTIVITIES
Canoeing
- **ROW Adventures** departs from local lodgings. **Hours:** Canoe trips are offered early June to mid-Sept. Departure days and times vary; phone ahead. **Phone:** (208) 765-0841 or (800) 451-6034.

BEST WESTERN PLUS HERITAGE INN   (406)761-1900

Hotel
$104-$159

Best Western PLUS
AAA Benefit: Save 10% or more every day and earn 10% bonus points!

Address: 1700 Fox Farm Rd 59404 **Location:** I-15 exit 278, 0.8 mi e on 10th Ave S, US 87/89 and SR 3/200. **Facility:** 231 units, some kitchens. 2 stories, interior corridors. **Parking:** winter plug-ins. **Amenities:** video games. **Pool(s):** heated indoor. **Activities:** sauna, hot tub, exercise room. **Guest Services:** valet and coin laundry, area transportation.

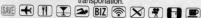

CENTRAL MOTEL   (406)453-0161

Motel
$65-$125

Address: 715 Central Ave W 59404 **Location:** I-15 exit 280 (Central Ave), 0.7 mi e. **Facility:** 29 units, some two bedrooms, efficiencies and kitchens. 1 story, exterior corridors. **Parking:** winter plug-ins. **Terms:** 3 day cancellation notice-fee imposed.

COMFORT INN & SUITES   (406)455-1000

Hotel $109-$189 **Address:** 1801 Market Place Dr 59404 **Location:** I-15 exit 278, just sw. **Facility:** 88 units, some two bedrooms. 4 stories, interior corridors. **Parking:** winter plug-ins. **Activities:** exercise room. **Guest Services:** valet and coin laundry.

COMFORT INN BY CHOICE HOTELS (406)454-2727

◆◆ Hotel
$87-$117

Address: 1120 9th St S 59405 **Location:** I-15 exit 278, 3 mi e on 10th Ave S, US 87/89 and SR 3/200, then just s. Next to a mall. **Facility:** 64 units. 3 stories, interior corridors. **Parking:** winter plug-ins. **Amenities:** safes. **Pool(s):** heated indoor. **Guest Services:** valet and coin laundry. **Featured Amenity: breakfast buffet.**

DAYS INN OF GREAT FALLS (406)727-6565

◆◆ Hotel $78-$93 **Address:** 101 14th Ave NW 59404 **Location:** I-15 exit 280 (Central Ave), 1.3 mi e on Central Ave/Business Rt I-15, 0.8 mi n on 3rd St NW, then just w. Adjacent to a high school. **Facility:** 60 units. 2 stories (no elevator), interior corridors. **Parking:** winter plug-ins. **Activities:** exercise room. **Guest Services:** coin laundry.

EXTENDED STAY AMERICA-GREAT FALLS-MISSOURI RIVER
(406)761-7524

◆◆ Extended Stay Hotel $70-$140 **Address:** 800 River Dr S 59405 **Location:** I-15 exit 278, 1.7 mi e on 10th Ave S, then 0.7 mi n. Located along the river. **Facility:** 104 kitchen units. 3 stories, interior corridors. **Parking:** winter plug-ins. **Activities:** fishing. **Guest Services:** coin laundry.

FAIRFIELD INN BY MARRIOTT (406)454-3000

◆◆ Hotel
$84-$155

FAIRFIELD INN & SUITES Marriott

AAA Benefit: Members save 5% or more!

Address: 1000 9th Ave S 59405 **Location:** I-15 exit 278, 3 mi e on 10th Ave S, US 87/89 and SR 3/200, then just n. Across from a mall. **Facility:** 62 units. 3 stories, interior corridors. **Parking:** winter plug-ins. **Pool(s):** heated indoor. **Guest Services:** valet and coin laundry. **Featured Amenity: continental breakfast.**

THE GREAT FALLS INN BY RIVERSAGE 406/453-6000

◆◆ Hotel. Rates not provided. **Address:** 1400 28th St S 59405 **Location:** I-15 exit 278, 1.7 mi e on 10th Ave S, 0.3 mi s on 26th St S, then just e on 15th Ave S. Next to a medical facility. **Facility:** 60 units. 4 stories, interior corridors. **Parking:** winter plug-ins. **Activities:** limited exercise equipment. **Guest Services:** valet and coin laundry.

HAMPTON INN (406)453-2675

◆◆◆ Hotel $129-$209 **Address:** 2301 14th St SW 59404 **Location:** I-15 exit 278, just sw. **Facility:** 97 units. 4 stories, interior corridors. **Parking:** winter plug-ins. **Terms:** 1-7 night minimum stay, cancellation fee imposed. **Pool(s):** heated indoor. **Activities:** hot tub, exercise room. **Guest Services:** valet and coin laundry, area transportation.

AAA Benefit: Members save up to 10%!

HILTON GARDEN INN (406)452-1000

◆◆◆ Hotel $99-$199 **Address:** 2520 14th St SW 59404 **Location:** I-15 exit 278, just sw. **Facility:** 118 units. 4 stories, interior corridors. **Terms:** 1-7 night minimum stay, cancellation fee imposed. **Amenities:** Some: safes. **Pool(s):** indoor. **Activities:** hot tub, exercise room. **Guest Services:** valet and coin laundry, area transportation.

AAA Benefit: Members save up to 10%!

HOLIDAY INN (406)727-7200

◆◆◆ Hotel
$89-$169

Address: 1100 5th St S 59405 **Location:** I-15 exit 278, 2 mi e on 10th Ave S, then just s. Located in a commercial area. **Facility:** 168 units, some two bedrooms. 7 stories, interior corridors. **Parking:** winter plug-ins. **Terms:** check-in 4 pm. **Pool(s):** heated indoor. **Activities:** hot tub, bicycles, exercise room. **Guest Services:** valet and coin laundry, area transportation. **Featured Amenity: full hot breakfast.**

HOLIDAY INN EXPRESS & SUITES (406)453-4000

◆◆◆ Hotel $109-$189 **Address:** 1625 Market Place Dr 59404 **Location:** I-15 exit 278, just sw. **Facility:** 85 units. 4 stories, interior corridors. **Parking:** winter plug-ins. **Terms:** cancellation fee imposed, resort fee. **Pool(s):** heated indoor. **Activities:** hot tub, exercise room. **Guest Services:** valet and coin laundry.

LA QUINTA INN & SUITES GREAT FALLS (406)761-2600

◆◆◆ Hotel $81-$301 **Address:** 600 River Dr S 59405 **Location:** I-15 exit 278, 1.7 mi e on 10th Ave S, then 0.8 mi n. Located along the river. **Facility:** 92 units, some kitchens. 3 stories, interior corridors. **Parking:** winter plug-ins. **Pool(s):** heated indoor. **Activities:** hot tub, bicycles, trails, exercise room. **Guest Services:** valet and coin laundry.

MOTEL 6 #4238 (406)453-1602

◆ Motel
$67-$95

Address: 2 Treasure State Dr 59404 **Location:** I-15 exit 278, 0.8 mi e on 10th Ave S and US 87/89 and SR 3/200. **Facility:** 59 units. 2 stories (no elevator), interior corridors. **Parking:** winter plug-ins. **Guest Services:** area transportation. **Featured Amenity: continental breakfast.**

O'HAIRE MOTOR INN 406/454-2141

◆◆ Motel. Rates not provided. **Address:** 17 7th St S 59401 **Location:** Center of downtown. **Facility:** 67 units, some two bedrooms. 3 stories, interior/exterior corridors. **Parking:** winter plug-ins. **Pool(s):** heated indoor. **Activities:** limited exercise equipment. **Guest Services:** valet laundry.

STAYBRIDGE SUITES

(406)761-4903

▼▼▼▼ **Extended Stay Hotel** $109-$199 **Address:** 201 3rd St NW (US 87) 59404 **Location:** I-15 exit 280 (Central Ave), 1 mi w, then just n. Located along the river. **Facility:** 113 kitchen units, some two bedrooms. 4 stories, interior corridors. **Parking:** winter plug-ins. **Terms:** check-in 4 pm, cancellation fee imposed. **Pool(s):** heated indoor. **Activities:** hot tub, exercise room. **Guest Services:** complimentary and valet laundry.

[icons]

TOWNHOUSE INN OF GREAT FALLS

406/761-4600

Motel
Rates not provided

Address: 1411 10th Ave S 59404 **Location:** I-15 exit 278, 2.6 mi e on 10th Ave S, US 87/89 and SR 3/200. **Facility:** 108 units. 2 stories (no elevator), interior corridors. **Parking:** winter plug-ins. **Pool(s):** heated indoor. **Activities:** sauna, hot tub, game room. **Guest Services:** valet and coin laundry. **Featured Amenity: full hot breakfast.**

[icons]

TownHouse INNS

Spacious rooms, Free Hot Breakfast, a Fantastic location near the mall and great dining.

WHERE TO EAT

BERT & ERNIE'S

406/453-0601

▼▼ American. Casual Dining. $8-$30 **AAA Inspector Notes:** Fresh ingredients, locally procured Montana beef and a pleasantly relaxed atmosphere are all waiting for you at this local favorite. Try out some of the fresh seafood, pasta dishes, or one of their famous burgers. You will also find a good selection of wine and local microbrews. **Reservations:** suggested. **Address:** 300 1st Ave S 59401 **Location:** Jct 3rd St S and 1st Ave S; downtown.

L D CALL M

THE CATTLEMEN'S CUT SUPPER CLUB BAR & CASINO

406/452-0702

▼▼ Steak Seafood. Casual Dining. $12-$46 **AAA Inspector Notes:** This seems like an unlikely place to find quality prepared steaks, but here it is! Not only does the meat cut like butter, but the taste is exquisite. The owner does it right, offering a bottomless salad bar and the entrées for one price. A limited lunch menu is served in the lounge. **Features:** full bar. **Reservations:** suggested. **Address:** 369 Vaughn Frontage Rd 59404 **Location:** I-15 exit 286, just w, then just n. D CALL M

THE CELTIC COWBOY

406/952-0393

▼▼ Irish. Gastropub. $8-$30 **AAA Inspector Notes:** *Historic.* Locally owned, this pub and restaurant offers more than just delicious Irish fare such as Jameson-glazed salmon or chicken roulade Mornay. Come by any Sunday for a wonderful jazz brunch and stay through the afternoon to enjoy a traditional Irish seisun featuring various musicians playing classical Irish music. Be sure to ask for a tour of the wine snug downstairs, which is the first of its kind in the city. **Features:** full bar, Sunday brunch, happy hour. **Address:** 116 1st Ave S 59401 **Location:** Downtown. **Parking:** on-site and street.

L D CALL M

DANTE'S CREATIVE CUISINE

406/453-9599

▼▼ Italian. Casual Dining. $10-$29 **AAA Inspector Notes:** In an imposing red-brick structure that was built in 1908 as an ironworks, this casual restaurant offers a variety of dishes. The menu lists many traditional pasta dishes, as well as Mexican and Southwestern dishes, steaks, prime rib and seafood. Signature dishes include the Gorgonzola salad and sourdough bread served with olive oil and roasted garlic. The dining room has extensive oak woodwork and a pressed-tin ceiling. **Features:** full bar. **Reservations:** suggested, weekends. **Address:** 1325 8th Ave N 59401 **Location:** Jct 14th St and 8th Ave N. L D CALL M

DIMITRI'S

406/452-5774

▼▼ Greek. Casual Dining. $9-$23 **AAA Inspector Notes:** A family-run restaurant with delicious traditional favorites such as homemade salad dressings, tzatziki sauce, Aegean shrimp and baklava. Not open for dinner on Sunday. Be sure to check when the belly dancers are scheduled to entertain. Opa! **Features:** beer & wine. **Address:** 1919 3rd St NW 59404 **Location:** I-15 exit 280 (Central Ave), 1.3 mi e on Central Ave/Business Rt I-15, then 1 mi n.

L D CALL M

FASTER BASSET COFFEE & CREPE HAUS

406/727-3947

▼ Coffee/Tea. Quick Serve. $5-$12 **AAA Inspector Notes:** Mostly American-influenced versions of the French crepe can be enjoyed with your favorite form of coffee. Dessert crepes are on the menu also. Burgers and beers are offered, too. **Address:** 215 3rd St NW (US 87) 59404 **Location:** I-15 exit 280 (Central Ave), 1.2 mi w, then just n. B L D CALL M

KOBE SEAFOOD & STEAK

406/315-3775

▼▼ Japanese. Casual Dining. $9-$37 **AAA Inspector Notes:** Step into this delight and enjoy your choice of teppanyaki-style cooking or fresh-made sushi. There are two different sections here that allow for different dining experiences. For a real treat, choose the teppanyaki side of the restaurant where your food is prepared on a flat grill right in front of you in an entertaining and dramatic way. **Features:** beer & wine. **Address:** 115 3rd St NW 59404 **Location:** I-15 exit 280 (Central Ave), 1 mi w, then just n. L D CALL M

LITTLE ATHENS

406/453-1430

▼ Greek. Quick Serve. $6-$12 **AAA Inspector Notes:** This is not typical mall fast food. The owner and his family prepare true Greek food with authentic ingredients. A splurge on the baklava (or two) is a must. **Address:** 1200 10th Ave S 59404 **Location:** I-15 exit 278, 2.5 mi e; in Holiday Village Mall, lower level.

L D CALL M

MACKENZIE RIVER PIZZA

406/761-0085

▼▼ Pizza. Casual Dining. $8-$20 **AAA Inspector Notes:** Known for its eclectic Western decor, the restaurant lets patrons choose from several microbrews to accompany a specialty pizza or large, innovative sandwich. Pizza crusts are wonderful and offer the choice of sourdough, natural grain, deep dish or thin crust. **Features:** beer & wine, patio dining. **Address:** 500 River Dr S 59405 **Location:** I-15 exit 278, 1.7 mi e on 10th Ave S, then 0.8 mi n. L D

RIKKI'S PIZZA & PASTA

406/761-8052

▼▼ American. Casual Dining. $10-$16 **AAA Inspector Notes:** Ask anyone around town where to eat and Rikki's is at the top of the list. They make their own salad dressings and pasta sauces. Thai street noodles with spicy sauce and loads of vegetables is one of the favorites. Save room for gooey butter cake—the name says it all. **Features:** beer & wine. **Address:** 1220 9th St S 59405 **Location:** I-15 exit 278, 3 mi e on 10th Ave S, US 87/89 and SR 3/200, then just s; next to mall. L D CALL M

SUKI CAFE

406/770-3038

▼▼ Thai Sushi. Casual Dining. $9-$17 **AAA Inspector Notes:** She's from Thailand, he's from Japan. A married couple share their respective cuisines in this unique café. The Thai dishes stray a bit from the traditional, but the flavors mesh. The sushi is traditional, very fresh and displayed creatively. **Features:** wine only, patio dining. **Address:** 1229 10th Ave S 59405 **Location:** Jct 12th St.

L D

WHEAT MONTANA BAKERY AND DELI   406/771-7456

◈ Breads/Pastries Deli. Family Dining. $6-$12 **AAA Inspector Notes:** Choose from a number of sweets in the display case at this deli—large cinnamon rolls, cookies and muffins. Sandwiches are made from fresh Montana wheat bread and go great with the variety of espresso drinks offered. **Features:** patio dining. **Address:** 1116 9th St S 59405 **Location:** I-15 exit 278, 3 mi e on 10th Ave S, US 87/89 and SR 3/200, then just S. [B] [L] [D]

HAMILTON (D-2) pop. 4,348, elev. 3,572'

The seat of Ravalli County and headquarters of Bitterroot National Forest, Hamilton was founded by 19th-century copper magnate Marcus Daly.

Bitterroot Valley Chamber of Commerce: 105 E. Main St., Hamilton, MT 59840. **Phone:** (406) 363-2400.

[SAVE] **DALY MANSION** is at 251 Eastside Hwy. (CR 269). The riverside estate of Montana copper baron Marcus Daly contains original furniture and Italian marble fireplaces. The Georgian Revival house is on the grounds of the 27-acre Margaret Daly Memorial Arboretum and is surrounded by a 22,000-acre stock farm where Daly raised Thoroughbred racehorses. **Time:** Allow 1 hour minimum. **Hours:** Guided mansion tours depart daily on the hour 10-3, mid-May to mid-Oct.; by appointment rest of year. Phone ahead to confirm schedule. **Cost:** $9; $8 (ages 60+); $6 (ages 6-17). Grounds free. **Phone:** (406) 363-6004. [GT]

RAVALLI COUNTY MUSEUM, 205 Bedford St., is in the original Ravalli County Courthouse, which once served as the meeting spot for social and political activity in the Bitter Root Valley. The museum includes a collection of Native American artifacts, a miner and trapper exhibit, a display about the Lewis and Clark Expedition, a natural history room, and historical photographs and newspapers. A Walk Through Bitter Root is a period room that depicts life in the valley during the late 1800s; rotating exhibits, events and educational programs are offered throughout the year.

Time: Allow 1 hour minimum. **Hours:** Tues.-Fri. 10-4 (also Thurs. 4-8), Sat. 9-1. Closed major holidays. Phone ahead to confirm schedule. **Cost:** $3; $1 (ages 55+ and students with ID); $6 (family); free (Thurs.). **Phone:** (406) 363-3338.

BITTERROOT RIVER INN & CONFERENCE CENTER
(406)375-2525

◈◈ Hotel $79-$159 **Address:** 139 Bitterroot Plaza Dr 59840 **Location:** US 93, 1 mi n, then just w. Adjacent to city park, bird sanctuary and river. **Facility:** 65 units. 3 stories, interior/exterior corridors. **Parking:** winter plug-ins. **Terms:** cancellation fee imposed, resort fee. **Pool(s):** heated indoor. **Activities:** sauna, hot tub, exercise room. **Guest Services:** coin laundry.
[ⓘ+] CALL [⅘M] [▣] [BIZ] [◌] [✕] [▤] [▥] [▦]
/ SOME UNITS [▦]

MOTEL 6 HAMILTON BLACK BEAR INN   406/363-2142

◈◈ Motel. Rates not provided. **Address:** 409 S 1st St (US 93) 59840 **Location:** On US 93, s of City Center, jct Madison St. **Facility:** 37 units. 1-2 stories (no elevator), exterior corridors. **Parking:** winter plug-ins. [ⓘ+] [◌] [✕] [▤] [▥] / SOME UNITS [▦] [HS]

TOWN HOUSE INNS   (406)363-6600

◈◈◈ Hotel $65-$140

Address: 1113 N 1st St 59840 **Location:** On US 93, n of City Center. **Facility:** 62 units. 2 stories (no elevator), interior corridors. **Parking:** winter plug-ins. **Activities:** sauna, exercise room. **Guest Services:** coin laundry. **Featured Amenity: full hot breakfast.**
[SAVE] [ⓘ+] [BIZ] [◌] [✕] [▤] [▦]
[▣] / SOME UNITS [▥] [HS]

WHERE TO EAT

2ND STREET SUSHI & ASIAN GRILL   406/363-0600

◈◈◈ Asian Sushi. Casual Dining. $10-$29 **AAA Inspector Notes:** This quaint grill flies in seafood from Seattle. Fresh choices range from the yokisoba noodle bowl to the maki rolls. **Features:** beer & wine, happy hour. **Address:** 322 S 2nd St 59840 **Location:** On US 93, s of City Center, just w on Madison St; in shared building with American Legion. **Parking:** on-site and street.
[L] [D] CALL [⅘M]

SPICE OF LIFE   406/363-4433

◈◈ American. Casual Dining. $14-$28 **AAA Inspector Notes:** The café's eclectic menu runs from Jamaican to Italian to Thai, and also includes good old American burgers. Organic greens and vegetables, as well as locally produced meats and handcrafted breads, are used when available. Dinner is served Wednesday through Saturday only. **Features:** beer & wine. **Reservations:** suggested. **Address:** 163 S 2nd St 59840 **Location:** Just s of Main St; downtown. **Parking:** street only. [L] [D] [Ⓐ]

HARDIN (E-6) pop. 3,505, elev. 2,902'

Hardin borders Crow Indian Reservation and serves as a trading center for its people. The town was named after Samuel Hardin, a rancher from Wyoming who leased land on the reservation. Nearby is the former site of Fort Custer, a military garrison said to have been one of the finest cavalry posts in the world. It was established in 1877, just after Lt. Col. George Armstrong Custer's defeat at the Battle of the Little Bighorn.

The 5-day Little Big Horn Days celebration takes place in June. Festivities include a grand ball with period music, costumes and dances; ◈ Custer's Last Stand Re-enactment; a powwow; arts and crafts shows; and dancing.

Hardin Area Chamber of Commerce: 10 E. Railway St., P.O. Box 446, Hardin, MT 59034. **Phone:** (406) 665-1672.

BIG HORN COUNTY HISTORICAL MUSEUM AND STATE VISITOR CENTER is 1 mi. e. off I-90 exit 497 to 1163 3rd St. E. The 35-acre complex features 26 historic buildings, including a 1911 farmhouse and barn, a Native American log cabin, a railroad depot, a doctor's building, the Will James studio and a church. Exhibits about Fort Custer, Plains Indians, and restored tractors and automobiles also are on display. The main building contains a library, educational rooms, a gallery and a state visitor center. **Hours:** Museum open daily 8-6, Memorial Day-Labor Day; Mon.-Fri. 9-5, rest of year. Outbuildings open Memorial Day-Labor Day only. **Cost:** $6; $5 (ages 60+); free (ages 0-6). **Phone:** (406) 665-1671.

LITTLE BIGHORN BATTLEFIELD NATIONAL MONUMENT—see place listing p. 187.

HARLOWTON (D-4) pop. 997

UPPER MUSSELSHELL MUSEUM is in two buildings at 11 and 36 S. Central Ave. Life in the early 1900s is depicted through replicas of a general store, schoolroom, kitchen and living room. Supplementing these exhibits are displays of period clothing, farm tools and other artifacts. Also displayed is a replica of an avaceratops lammersi dinosaur whose remains were found north of town on Careless Creek. The museum is one of several stops along the Montana Dinosaur Trail. **Time:** Allow 30 minutes minimum. **Hours:** Mon.-Sat. 10-5, Memorial Day-Labor Day; by appointment rest of year. **Cost:** $5; $2.50 (ages 55+); free (ages 0-16). **Phone:** (406) 632-5519.

COUNTRYSIDE INN   406/632-4119

Motel $55-$65 **Address:** 309 3rd St NE 59036 **Location:** US 12 E. **Facility:** 19 units. 1 story, exterior corridors. **Parking:** winter plug-ins. **Terms:** cancellation fee imposed.

HAVRE (B-5) pop. 9,310, elev. 2,493'
• Restaurants p. 178

Havre's beginnings as a transportation hub were forged by the railroad, which brought supplies to trappers, miners and the military at nearby Fort Assinniboine. The town was named by railroad officials after the French city Le Havre, but its citizens gave it a different pronunciation: HAV-er.

Guided tours of Fort Assinniboine, 8 miles southwest off US 87, are offered for a fee daily (weather permitting), June 1-Labor Day. High Line Heritage Resources Walking Tours offers 1-hour tours of the downtown area departing from 132 Third St. A separate hour-long walking tour leaving from the corner of Third Avenue and Main Street explores a 36-block residential historic district. High Line's tours are available by appointment Memorial Day weekend through the last weekend in December (weather permitting); phone (406) 265-6233.

Area geography can best be described as dichotomous. Here, rolling plains meet the Bear Paw Mountains, providing unlimited summer and winter recreation opportunities. Beaver Creek Park, a 17-mile-long, 1-mile-wide strip park 11 miles south on CR 234, encases Beaver Creek and two lakes and offers a variety of activities including camping, fishing, hiking, cross-country skiing and snowshoeing *(see Recreation Areas Chart).*

Havre Chamber of Commerce: 130 Fifth Ave., P.O. Box 308, Havre, MT 59501. **Phone:** (406) 265-4383.

Self-guiding tours: Brochures for self-guiding walking tours of the 36-block historic district are available from the chamber of commerce.

HAVRE BENEATH THE STREETS is at 120 Third Ave. This guided walking tour takes visitors through the city's historical underground. Many of the original buildings built in 1904 are now beneath the city streets. Included are a Chinese laundry, post office, bordello, meat market, bakery, opium den, barbershop and saloon. **Time:** Allow 1 hour minimum. **Hours:** Tours depart daily 9:30-3:30, Memorial Day-Sept. 30; Mon.-Sat. 10:30-2:30, rest of year. Closed major holidays. **Cost:** $14; $12 (ages 65+); $8 (ages 6-12). Prices may vary; phone ahead. Reservations are recommended. **Phone:** (406) 265-8888. GT

H. EARL CLACK MUSEUM is at 1753 US 2 N.W., #30, in the Holiday Village Mall. Local history is chronicled through artifacts, dioramas and exhibits. **Time:** Allow 1 hour minimum. **Hours:** Mon.-Sat. 11-5, Sun. noon-5, Memorial Day-Labor Day; Tues.-Sat. 1-5, rest of year. Phone ahead to confirm schedule. **Cost:** Donations. **Phone:** (406) 265-4000.

Wahkpa Chu'gn Buffalo Jump is on US 2 behind the Holiday Village Mall. Pronounced "walk-paw chew-gun," an Assiniboine name for the Milk River, this prehistoric buffalo jump site was occupied by three separate cultures from 355 to 2,000 years ago. A 45-minute guided walking tour features exposed campsites and buffalo bone deposits as deep as 20 feet below the surface. An off-road vehicle transports visitors from the Interpretive Center into the handicapped-accessible site area.

Hours: Guided tours daily 9-4, June 1-Labor Day; by appointment rest of year (weather permitting). **Cost:** $9; $8 (ages 65+); $5 (ages 6-17). **Phone:** (406) 265-6417 or (406) 945-3503. GT

AMERICINN LODGE & SUITES OF HAVRE   (406)395-5000

Hotel $83-$152 **Address:** 2520 Hwy 2 W 59501 **Location:** On US 2, west side of town. **Facility:** 52 units. 2 stories (no elevator), interior corridors. **Parking:** winter plug-ins. **Terms:** cancellation fee imposed. **Pool(s):** heated indoor. **Activities:** hot tub, limited exercise equipment. **Guest Services:** coin laundry.

BEST WESTERN PLUS GREAT NORTHERN INN
                                    (406)265-4200

Hotel
$90-$125

AAA Benefit: Save 10% or more every day and earn 10% bonus points!

Address: 1345 1st St 59501 **Location:** On US 2, 0.7 mi e of town center. **Facility:** 74 units. 3 stories, interior corridors. **Parking:** winter plug-ins. **Terms:** resort fee. **Pool(s):** heated indoor. **Activities:** hot tub, steamroom, exercise room. **Guest Services:** valet laundry.

BEST WESTERN PLUS HAVRE INN & SUITES
(406)265-2888

Hotel
$130-$166

AAA Benefit: Save 10% or more every day and earn 10% bonus points!

Address: 1425 2 Hwy NW 59501 **Location:** On US 2, 1 mi w of town. **Facility:** 68 units. 3 stories, interior corridors. **Pool(s):** heated indoor. **Activities:** hot tub, exercise room. **Guest Services:** valet and coin laundry, area transportation.

TOWNHOUSE INN OF HAVRE
406/265-6711

Hotel
Rates not provided

Address: 601 1st St W 59501 **Location:** Just w of town center on US 2. **Facility:** 100 units, some kitchens. 2 stories (no elevator), interior corridors. **Parking:** winter plug-ins. **Pool(s):** heated indoor. **Activities:** sauna, hot tub. **Guest Services:** coin laundry, area transportation. **Featured Amenity:** full hot breakfast.

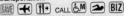

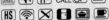

WHERE TO EAT

WOLFER'S DINER
406/265-2111

American. Casual Dining. $8-$11 **AAA Inspector Notes:** You will feel like you took a step back in time when you enter this cute little 1950s-style diner. Try one of their delicious handmade ice cream floats or shakes that come in a variety of flavors, including blueberry, caramel, butterscotch and marshmallow, to name a few. The menu also has a variety of salads, sandwiches and burgers to satisfy your appetite. **Address:** 126 3rd Ave 59501 **Location:** Just w of city center on US 2, then just s. **Parking:** street only. L D

HELENA (D-3) pop. 28,190, elev. 4,047'
• Restaurants p. 180

Helena succeeded the other gold camps of Bannack and Virginia City as the territorial capital in 1875. It became the state capital in 1889 after a hotly contested fight between "copper kings" William A. Clark and Marcus Daly. The city owes its existence to "The Georgians," four weary and discouraged Southern prospectors, who in 1864 stumbled down a gulch and grimly dubbed it "Last Chance Gulch," only to find gold where the city's main street now runs.

Later a more suitable name, Helena (He-LAY-na), was put to a vote. But the miners and the bullwhackers did not like the name's feminine ring. Consequently the emphasis was shifted to the first syllable, with the second "e" almost silent, and HEL-e-na became the accepted pronunciation. The gold rush faded quickly, and Helena settled down to become a trade center for the surrounding goldfields.

Reminders of the early days can be found in the architecture of the buildings that line Reeder's Alley off the 200 block of South Park Avenue in southwest Helena. Said to be the oldest structure in Helena,

the 1864 Pioneer Cabin, 210 Park Ave., is furnished with pioneer artifacts.

The Mount Helena Music Festival provides 2 days of blues, rock, reggae and zydeco. Held late June in downtown, the event also includes crafts, food and children's activities.

Helena Tourism Alliance: 105 Reeder's Alley, Helena, MT 59601. **Phone:** (406) 449-1270.

Self-guiding tours: The Helena Montana Geocaching Tour, available through the tourism alliance, highlights 38 historic, scenic and cultural sites located in the city and in the surrounding area. The GPS-directed treasure hunt includes the Mansion District, landmark structures such as the Capitol building and the "Guardian of the Gulch" Fire Tower, and Centennial Park.

Shopping: Once the quarters of miners, muleskinners and Chinese laborers during the gold rush, the buildings along Reeder's Alley, 100 S. Park Ave., now contain specialty shops as well as an 1864 cabin furnished with pioneer artifacts.

ARCHIE BRAY FOUNDATION FOR THE CE-RAMIC ARTS is at 2915 Country Club Ave. Supporting artists who work in ceramics, the foundation was established in 1951 in a former brickyard by Western Clay Manufacturing Co. president and art patron Archie Bray. The 26-acre grounds, set among the Rocky Mountain foothills, feature hundreds of whimsical sculptures created by resident artists over the years. The North Gallery is open year-round with rotating exhibitions. In summer, current residents exhibit their work in the Warehouse Gallery. **Time:** Allow 1 hour minimum. **Hours:** Mon.-Sat. 10-5, Sun. 1-5, June-Aug.; Mon.-Sat. 10-5, rest of year. Closed major holidays. **Cost:** Free. **Phone:** (406) 443-3502.

CATHEDRAL OF ST. HELENA is at 530 N. Ewing St. This handsome Victorian Gothic structure was modeled after the Votive Church of the Sacred Heart in Vienna, Austria, and completed in 1914. Interior finishings are of Carrara marble, and the stained-glass windows were made in Munich, Germany, by F.X. Zettler Co. An open-air sculpture gallery contains 29 statues of historical persons from the arts, sciences and religion.

Time: Allow 30 minutes minimum. **Hours:** Mon.-Fri. 6:30-6, Sat. 8-6, Sun. -1. Guided tours are given Tues.-Thurs. 1-3, late May-Labor Day; by reservation rest of year. **Cost:** Donations. **Phone:** (406) 442-5825. GT

HOLTER MUSEUM OF ART is at 12 E. Lawrence St. The museum hosts contemporary exhibitions and has a permanent collection of regional and national prominence. **Hours:** Tues.-Sat. 10-5:30, Sun. noon-4. Closed Jan. 1, Thanksgiving and Christmas. **Cost:** Donations. **Phone:** (406) 442-6400.

LAST CHANCE TOUR TRAIN departs from the Montana Historical Society Museum, Library and Archives at 225 N. Roberts St. This 1-hour jaunt makes a circuit through Helena's present and past on an automotive tour train. Passengers view such whimsical downtown architectural features as giant lizards, thumbprints and gargoyles; the Cathedral of St. Helena's splendid 230-foot-tall spires; Reeder's Alley; and the city's mansion district.

Hours: Tours depart Mon.-Sat. at 11, 1, 3 and 5:30, July-Aug.; at 11, 1 and 3, in June; at 11 and 3, Sept. 1-14. **Cost:** $8; $7.50 (ages 60+); $6.50 (ages 4-12). **Phone:** (406) 442-1023.

MONTANA HISTORICAL SOCIETY MUSEUM, LIBRARY AND ARCHIVES is across from the state Capitol at 225 N. Roberts St. The history of Montana and the West is recounted through an extensive collection of Charles M. Russell's paintings and sculpture in addition to frequently changing exhibits. The Montana Homeland exhibition uses more than 2,000 artifacts, photographs and documents to trace Montana history from the end of the most recent ice age through World War II. A highlight is the display of "Big Medicine," a rare white bison with blue eyes and tan hooves born in 1933.

Hours: Mon.-Sat. 9-5 (also Thurs. 5-8). Closed major holidays. **Cost:** $5; $1 (ages 5-18); $12 (family, two adults and children ages 0-18). **Phone:** (406) 444-2694.

ORIGINAL GOVERNOR'S MANSION is at 304 N. Ewing St. Built in 1888, the Victorian mansion was the home of nine Montana governors 1913-59. The house is furnished in period. **Time:** Allow 30 minutes minimum. **Hours:** Guided tours are given Tues.-Sat. on the hour noon-3, May-Sept.; Sat. on the hour noon-3, rest of year. Closed major holidays. **Cost:** $4; $1 (ages 5-12); $10 (family, up to five people). **Phone:** (406) 442-3115 Apr.-Dec., or (406) 444-4789 rest of year for tour reservations. [GT]

STATE CAPITOL is at 1301 Sixth St. Faced with sandstone and Montana granite, the capitol is topped by a dome of Montana copper. The cornerstone was laid July 4, 1899, and the building was dedicated July 4, 1902. Historical paintings and statues decorate the interior; prominent among these is Charles M. Russell's largest painting, the 12-by-25-foot "Lewis and Clark Meeting Indians at Ross' Hole," in the House of Representatives.

Time: Allow 45 minutes minimum. **Hours:** Mon.-Fri. 8-5, Sat.-Sun. and holidays 9-3. Guided tours are given on the hour Mon.-Sat. 10-2, May-Sept.; Sat. 10-2, Oct.-Dec. The Jan.-Apr. tour schedule in even-numbered years is Sat. 10-2; Mon.-Sat. 10-2 in odd-numbered years. Closed Jan. 1, Thanksgiving and Christmas. Phone ahead to confirm schedule. **Cost:** Free. **Phone:** (406) 444-4789. [GT]

BARRISTER BED & BREAKFAST   406/443-7330

▼▼▼ **Historic Bed & Breakfast** $122-$137 **Address:** 416 N Ewing St 59601 **Location:** I-15 exit 192 (Prospect Ave), 1.5 mi sw via Prospect and Montana aves to 9th Ave, 0.8 mi w, then just s. Across from St. Helena Cathedral. **Facility:** The bedrooms in this 1874 Victorian mansion have ornate fireplaces. Common areas include a parlor, library, den and enclosed sun porch with antiques galore. 5 units. 3 stories (no elevator), interior corridors. **Parking:** winter plug-ins. **Terms:** check-in 4 pm, 3 day cancellation notice-fee imposed. **Guest Services:** complimentary laundry.

BEST WESTERN PREMIER HELENA GREAT NORTHERN HOTEL   (406)457-5500

Hotel
$153-$189

AAA Benefit: Save 10% or more every day and earn 10% bonus points!

Address: 835 Great Northern Blvd 59601 **Location:** I-15 exit 193 (Cedar St), 2 mi w, just w on Lyndale Ave, then just s on Getchell St; downtown. **Facility:** 100 units. 4 stories, interior corridors. **Parking:** winter plug-ins. **Amenities:** safes. **Dining:** Silver Star Steak Company, see separate listing. **Pool(s):** heated indoor. **Activities:** hot tub, exercise room. **Guest Services:** valet and coin laundry. **Featured Amenity:** full hot breakfast.

COMFORT SUITES   (406)495-0505

Hotel
$92-$140

Address: 3180 N Washington St 59602 **Location:** I-15 exit 194 (Custer Ave), just e. **Facility:** 90 units, some efficiencies. 3 stories, interior corridors. **Parking:** winter plug-ins. **Amenities:** safes. **Pool(s):** heated indoor. **Activities:** hot tub, exercise room. **Guest Services:** valet and coin laundry, area transportation. **Featured Amenity:** full hot breakfast.

DAYS INN HELENA   (406)442-3280

▼▼ **Hotel** $80-$250 **Address:** 2001 Prospect Ave 59601 **Location:** I-15 exit 192 (Prospect Ave), just w. **Facility:** 89 units. 2 stories (no elevator), interior corridors. **Parking:** winter plug-ins. **Amenities:** safes. **Activities:** hot tub, limited exercise equipment. **Guest Services:** valet and coin laundry.

FAIRFIELD INN & SUITES BY MARRIOTT (406)449-9944

Hotel
$82-$167

FAIRFIELD INN & SUITES Marriott

AAA Benefit: Members save 5% or more!

Address: 2150 11th Ave 59601 **Location:** I-15 exit 192 (Prospect Ave), just sw. **Facility:** 58 units. 3 stories, interior corridors. **Parking:** winter plug-ins. **Terms:** check-in 4 pm. **Pool(s):** heated indoor. **Activities:** hot tub, exercise room. **Guest Services:** valet and coin laundry. **Featured Amenity:** breakfast buffet.

HAMPTON INN-HELENA (406)443-5800

Hotel $109-$169 **Address:** 725 Carter Dr 59601 **Location:** I-15 exit 192 (Prospect Ave), just e. **Facility:** 81 units. 3 stories, interior corridors. **Parking:** winter plug-ins. **Terms:** 1-7 night minimum stay, cancellation fee imposed. **Pool(s):** heated indoor. **Activities:** hot tub, exercise room. **Guest Services:** valet and coin laundry, area transportation.

AAA Benefit: Members save up to 10%!

HOLIDAY INN CONFERENCE CENTER DOWNTOWN
406/443-2200

Hotel. Rates not provided. **Address:** 22 N Last Chance Gulch 59601 **Location:** Jct Park Ave and Broadway St. **Facility:** 71 units. 7 stories, interior corridors. **Pool(s):** heated indoor. **Activities:** hot tub, exercise room. **Guest Services:** valet and coin laundry.

HOLIDAY INN EXPRESS HOTEL & SUITES 406/442-7500

Hotel. Rates not provided. **Address:** 3170 N Sanders St 59602 **Location:** I-15 exit 194 (Custer Ave), just w, then just n. **Facility:** 87 units. 3 stories, interior corridors. **Parking:** winter plug-ins. **Pool(s):** heated indoor. **Activities:** hot tub, exercise room. **Guest Services:** valet and coin laundry.

JORGENSON'S INN & SUITES (406)442-1770

Hotel $80-$129 **Address:** 1714 11th Ave 59601 **Location:** I-15 exit 192 (Prospect Ave), just w of I-15 and US 287/12. **Facility:** 113 units. 1-3 stories, interior/exterior corridors. **Parking:** winter plug-ins. **Terms:** cancellation fee imposed. **Dining:** Jorgenson's Restaurant & Lounge, see separate listing. **Pool(s):** indoor. **Activities:** hot tub. **Guest Services:** valet and coin laundry, area transportation.

LA QUINTA INN & SUITES HELENA (406)449-4000

Hotel $68-$185 **Address:** 701 Washington St 59601 **Location:** I-15 exit 192 (Prospect Ave), just w. **Facility:** 74 units. 4 stories, interior corridors. **Parking:** winter plug-ins. **Pool(s):** heated outdoor. **Activities:** exercise room. **Guest Services:** valet and coin laundry.

RED LION COLONIAL HOTEL 406/443-2100

Hotel. Rates not provided. **Address:** 2301 Colonial Dr 59601 **Location:** I-15 exit 192 (Prospect Ave) southbound; exit 192B northbound. **Facility:** 149 units. 2 stories, interior corridors. **Parking:** winter plug-ins. **Pool(s):** heated indoor. **Activities:** hot tub, exercise room. **Guest Services:** valet and coin laundry, area transportation.

RESIDENCE INN BY MARRIOTT (406)443-8010

Extended Stay Hotel $123-$209 **Address:** 2500 E Custer Ave 59602 **Location:** I-15 exit 192 (Custer Ave), just e. **Facility:** 91 kitchen units. 3 stories, interior corridors. **Parking:** winter plug-ins. **Pool(s):** indoor. **Activities:** hot tub, exercise room. **Guest Services:** valet and coin laundry, area transportation.

AAA Benefit: Members save 5% or more!

THE SANDERS-HELENA'S BED & BREAKFAST 406/442-3309

Historic Bed & Breakfast $145-$175 **Address:** 328 N Ewing St 59601 **Location:** 0.3 mi from Last Chance Gulch, 0.8 mi w of state capitol on 6th Ave, then just n. **Facility:** This restored 1875 home, located one block from the original Governor's Mansion, features period furnishings and many little extras. The owners have much to share about Helena and its history. 7 units. 3 stories (no elevator), interior corridors. **Parking:** on-site and street, winter plug-ins. **Terms:** check-in 4 pm. **Guest Services:** complimentary laundry.

WINGATE BY WYNDHAM (406)449-3000

Hotel
$99-$225

Address: 2007 N Oakes St 59601 **Location:** I-15 exit 193 (Cedar St), just sw. **Facility:** 100 units. 3 stories, interior corridors. **Parking:** winter plug-ins. **Amenities:** safes. **Pool(s):** heated indoor. **Activities:** hot tub, exercise room. **Guest Services:** valet and coin laundry, area transportation. **Featured Amenity:** full hot breakfast.

In the foothills of the Rocky Mountains, close to the Capitol and minutes from downtown Helena.

WHERE TO EAT

BENNY'S BISTRO 406/443-010█

American Casual Dining
$9-$27

AAA Inspector Notes: Whether you choose to dine here at lunch or at dinner you'll always be served fresh, delicious innovative cuisine. The focaccia bread is wonderful for any sandwich creation or as an accompaniment to an entrée. Tapas are served daily. Be sure to ask about the soup du jour and the chef's choice for cheesecake. **Features:** beer & wine. **Address:** 108 E 6th Ave 59601 **Location:** Center; in historic downtown; across from Chamber of Commerce. **Parking:** street only. L D

JADE GARDEN
406/443-8899

▼▼▼ Chinese. Casual Dining. $10-$33 **AAA Inspector Notes:** The traditional Chinese menu features Cantonese cooking and a wide selection of traditional favorites. The atmosphere is inviting and contemporary, and the service prompt and pleasant. **Features:** beer & wine. **Address:** 3128 N Montana Ave 59602 **Location:** I-15 exit 194 (Custer Ave), 0.5 mi w. [L] [D]

JORGENSON'S RESTAURANT & LOUNGE
406/442-6380

▼▼▼
American
Casual Dining
$9-$25

AAA Inspector Notes: This family restaurant serves a variety of menu items, including seafood, beef and chicken entrees. Service is pleasant, casual and efficient. **Features:** full bar, patio dining, senior menu, happy hour. **Address:** 1720 11th Ave 59601 **Location:** I-15 exit 192 (Prospect Ave), just w of I-15 and US 287/12; in Jorgenson's Inn & Suites. [B] [L] [D]

LUCCA'S
406/457-8311

▼▼▼▼ Italian. Casual Dining. $22-$34 **AAA Inspector Notes:** Contemporary Italian fare in a relaxed atmosphere. Seafood risotto is just one of the specialties featured. Homemade desserts such as tiramisu and panna cotta are extremely popular. **Features:** full bar. **Reservations:** suggested. **Address:** 56 N Last Chance Gulch 59601 **Location:** Downtown; north end of Walking Mall. **Parking:** street only. [D] CALL &M

MACKENZIE RIVER PIZZA
406/443-0033

▼▼ Pizza. Casual Dining. $8-$20 **AAA Inspector Notes:** Known for its eclectic Western decor, the restaurant lets patrons choose from several microbrews to accompany a specialty pizza or large, innovative sandwich. Pizza crusts are wonderful and offer the choice of sourdough, natural grain, deep dish or thin crust. **Features:** beer & wine. **Address:** 1110 Road Runner Dr 59602 **Location:** Just w of jct N Montana and E Custer aves. [L] [D] CALL &M

MEDITERRANEAN GRILL
406/495-1212

▼▼ Mediterranean. Casual Dining. $9-$27 **AAA Inspector Notes:** Patrons experience the tastes of the Mediterranean in the restaurant's large dining area, which is decorated in a villa style. Pizza dough is made in house. The large stone, gas-fired oven is a focal point. **Features:** beer & wine, patio dining, Sunday brunch. **Address:** 42 S Park Ave 59601 **Location:** From Montana State Capitol; 0.8 mi w on E 6th Ave, just s on N Jackson St, just w on Broadway St, then just s. **Parking:** street only. [L] [D]

ON BROADWAY
406/443-1929

▼▼ Italian. Casual Dining. $17-$43 **AAA Inspector Notes:** Guests may sit in the loft, overlooking the music stage, or in the intimate dining room. Either way, friendly, knowledgeable service is the norm. The menu changes seasonally, and the chef's creative and well-prepared offerings delight. On Thursdays, a jazz ensemble performs. **Features:** full bar. **Address:** 106 Broadway St 59601 **Location:** Jct Cruse St; center; in historic downtown. **Parking:** street only. [D]

SILVER STAR STEAK COMPANY
406/495-0677

▼▼ Steak. Casual Dining. $15-$69 **AAA Inspector Notes:** This downtown location offers a diverse menu with regional favorites such as bison steaks. The steaks are tender and enhanced with a number of sauces, including bacon-bleu-cheese cream and Jack Daniels peppercorn. King crab legs, pasta and sandwiches are just a few of the other choices. **Features:** full bar. **Reservations:** suggested. **Address:** 833 Great Northern Blvd 59601 **Location:** I-15 exit 193 (Cedar St), 2 mi w, just w on Lyndale Ave, then just s on Getchell St; downtown; in BEST WESTERN PREMIER Helena Great Northern Hotel. **Parking:** street only. [L] [D] CALL &M

STEVE'S CAFE
406/449-6666

▼▼ American. Casual Dining. $8-$13 **AAA Inspector Notes:** Stuffed huckleberry French toast, slow-roasted corned beef hash and large slices of ham are just a sampling of what you can expect at this popular breakfast spot. Daily specials are always a treat. Soups are hot and tasty, and the Italian sausages and meatballs are homemade. **Address:** 630 N Montana Ave 59601 **Location:** I-15 exit 192, 0.7 mi w. [B] [L]

STEVE'S CAFE
406/444-5010

▼▼ American Breakfast. Casual Dining. $8-$13 **AAA Inspector Notes:** If you feel like breakfast any time of day, this is the spot to have huckleberry pancakes, biscuits and gravy or even a breakfast burrito. Lunch selections include sandwiches, salads and homemade chili. The Italian meatball sandwich is spicy and filled with homemade meatballs. Daily dessert specials such as bread pudding and chocolate cake round out your meal. **Address:** 1225 E Custer Ave 59601 **Location:** I-15 exit 194, 0.3 mi w. [B] [L] CALL &M

TOI'S THAI CUISINE
406/443-6656

▼▼ Thai. Casual Dining. $13-$21 **AAA Inspector Notes:** What big flavors are created in this small kitchen. The spices are bold and heat levels can be adjusted to your liking. Be sure to make a reservation, as this place has very limited seating and is very popular. **Reservations:** suggested. **Address:** 423 N Last Chance Gulch St 59601 **Location:** Center; in historic downtown. **Parking:** street only. [D]

WINDBAG SALOON
406/443-9669

▼▼ American. Casual Dining. $10-$32 **AAA Inspector Notes:** Bustling at lunch and dinner, you'll be served comfort foods in a casual atmosphere. The old-time décor in this historic building is rustic and the ambiance is charming. **Features:** full bar. **Address:** 19 S Last Chance Gulch 59601 **Location:** Jct Broadway St; center; in Walking Mall. **Parking:** street only. [L] [D] CALL &M

HELENA NATIONAL FOREST (C-3)

> Elevations in the forest range from 3,600 ft. at the gates of the Missouri River to 9,411 ft. on Red Mountain in the Lincoln district. Refer to AAA maps for additional elevation information.

In west-central Montana, Helena National Forest encompasses 976,000 acres. The forest straddles the Continental Divide and embraces the Big Belt and the Elkhorn mountains. The Missouri River passes through the Helena Valley near the center of the forest. Vegetation ranges from sagebrush and bunchgrass to Douglas fir, lodgepole pine and spruce.

There are more than 1,000 miles of trails and 1,600 miles of forest roads. Continental Divide National Scenic Trail passes through the forest. Ten campgrounds, picnic grounds, good hunting and fishing, historic sites, wilderness areas and several ghost towns are among the forest's attractions. For further information contact the Forest Supervisor, Helena National Forest, 2880 Skyway Dr., Helena, MT 59602; phone (406) 449-5201. *See Recreation Areas Chart.*

▼ **THE GATES OF THE MOUNTAINS RECREATION AREA** is 20 mi. n. of Helena via I-15 exit 209 to Gates of the Mountains Landing and is reached by boat or trails. In 1805, the members of the Lewis and Clark expedition were fortunate to gaze upon the majestic natural wonder that lay before them. Limestone walls towering 1,200 feet stood like rock sentries within the canyon where the Missouri River pushes through the Big Belt Range. Named by Meriwether Lewis as "gates of the mountains," the name stuck and today visitors continue to marvel at the splendor of the rock formations.

Wildlife that call the canyon home include bighorn sheep, mountain goats, deer, mountain lions, black bears, ospreys and falcons. The recreation area provides swimming, hiking, fishing and narrated boat trip opportunities. A dinner cruise also is available.

Hours: Narrated 2-hour boat trips, with stopovers at Meriwether picnic area, depart Mon.-Fri. at 9, 11, 1 and 3, Sat.-Sun. and holidays on the hour 10-4, in July; Mon.-Fri. at 11, 1 and 3, Sat.-Sun. on the hour 10-4, Aug. 1-Labor Day; Mon.-Fri. at 11 and 2, Sat.-Sun. and holidays at 10, noon, 2 and 4, Memorial Day-June 30; Wed.-Fri. at 11 and 2, Sat.-Sun. and holidays at 11, 1 and 3, day after Labor Day-Sept. 30. Dinner cruises Fri. at 6, mid-July to mid-Aug.; reservations are required. **Cost:** Narrated boat trip $16; $14 (ages 60+ and military with ID); $10 (ages 4-17). Dinner cruise $44. **Phone:** (406) 458-5241.

HUNGRY HORSE pop. 826
- Hotels & Restaurants map & index p. 167
- Part of Glacier National Park area — see map p. 162

HISTORIC TAMARACK LODGE & CABINS
(406)387-4420 **25**

Cabin
$63-$320

Address: 9549 US 2 E 59919 **Location:** 1.6 mi n. **Facility:** 26 units, some cabins. 1 story, exterior corridors. **Terms:** cancellation fee imposed, resort fee. **Activities:** fishing, cross country skiing, snowmobiling, bicycles.

MINI GOLDEN INNS MOTEL
(406)387-4313 **26**

Motel
$86-$160

Address: 8955 US 2 E 59919 **Location:** East end of town. **Facility:** 38 units, some two bedrooms and efficiencies. 1 story, exterior corridors. **Parking:** winter plug-ins. **Terms:** 30 day cancellation notice-fee imposed. **Guest Services:** coin laundry. **Featured Amenity:** continental breakfast.

HUSON (C-2) pop. 210, elev. 3,015'

THE NINEMILE REMOUNT DEPOT AND RANGER STATION is off I-90 to exit 82, then 4 mi. n. on Remount Rd. A working ranger station on a 5,000-acre ranch features Cape Cod-style buildings. A self-guiding tour through the historic site reveals the daily life of the firefighting rangers 1930-53. Grand Menard Discovery Trail, 1.5 miles north of the station, features two .7-mile self-guiding tours through a pine forest. Tour and trail brochures are available.

Time: Allow 1 hour minimum. **Hours:** Site daily dawn-dusk. Ranger station Mon.-Fri. 8-4:30. Visitor

center daily 9-5, Memorial Day-Labor Day. **Cost:** Donations. **Phone:** (406) 626-5201.

JEFFERSON CITY (D-3) pop. 472

TIZER BOTANIC GARDEN & ARBORETUM, 38 Tizer Lake Rd., is a test site for high altitude-, cold weather- and drought-tolerant plants for the Denver Botanic Gardens and Colorado State University. Sheltering numerous rare specimens, the nearly 7-acre site intersected by Prickly Pear Creek comprises themed flower gardens, vegetable and herb patches, and a children's garden. Visitors can stroll along a walking trail traversed by several wooden bridges as they take in the beauty of 550 varieties of specialty conifers, 450 varieties of deciduous trees and shrubs, about 100 types of roses and 100 varieties of clematis.

Special events, including high tea, concerts, guided walks and family-friendly festivals, are offered regularly. **Time:** Allow 30 minutes minimum. **Hours:** Daily 10-6, May-Sept. **Cost:** $7; free (ages 0-5). **Phone:** (406) 933-8789 or (866) 933-8789.

KALISPELL (B-2) pop. 19,927, elev. 2,956'
- Restaurants p. 184
- Hotels & Restaurants map & index p. 167
- Part of Glacier National Park area — see map p. 162

Kalispell (KAL-is-pell) is in the Flathead Valley between Glacier National Park (see place listing p. 162) and Flathead Lake, a region noted for the production of sweet cherries. The area was known only to the Salish, who called it "the land between the mountains," until 1891 when the Great Northern Railroad laid track to this point. The nearby settlements of Demersville and Ashley were moved to create Kalispell.

Kalispell is circled by dense forests, lakes, rivers and mountains. To the east is the Swan Range of the Rocky Mountains, and to the west, the Kootenai Range. Flathead National Forest (see place listing p. 157) has its headquarters in the city.

Local parks include Woodland Park, with lagoons, formal gardens and picnicking. Three forks of the Flathead River drain into Flathead Lake, making the area an ideal place for fly fishing, white-water rafting, kayaking and sailing.

Flathead Convention & Visitor Bureau: 15 Depot Park, Kalispell, MT 59901-4008. **Phone:** (406) 756-9091 or (800) 543-3105.

Self-guiding tours: Information about walking tours of the historic district is available from the Kalispell Chamber of Commerce; phone (406) 758-2800. For information about the greater northwestern Montana area contact Glacier Country at (800) 338-5072.

Shopping: The Kalispell Farmers Market, in the Flathead Valley Community College parking lot, offers more than 100 vendors selling homemade and

(See map & index p. 167.)

homegrown products Saturdays 9-12:30 from spring through fall.

 CONRAD MANSION MUSEUM is 6 blks. e. of Main St. at 330 Woodland Ave. Built in 1895 for Kalispell's founder, Charles E. Conrad, who traded and freighted on the Missouri River, the 26-room mansion has been restored to its Victorian splendor and contains original furnishings. Visitors can take guided tours of the mansion and self-guiding tours of the 3-acre site's gardens.

Time: Allow 1 hour minimum. **Hours:** Guided tours are given Tues.-Sun. on the hour 10-4, mid-June to mid-Oct.; Wed.-Sun. 10-4, mid-May to mid-June. Holiday tours are offered Thanksgiving weekend-late Dec. Phone ahead to confirm schedule. **Cost:** $12; $10 (ages 65+); $8 (ages 12-17); $6 (ages 0-11). **Phone:** (406) 755-2166. GT

 HOCKADAY MUSEUM OF ART is at 302 Second Ave. E. Permanent and rotating exhibits showcase the art and culture of Montana, with special focus on Glacier National Park and the Northern Plains and Blackfeet Indians. **Time:** Allow 1 hour minimum. **Hours:** Tues.-Sat. 10-5. **Cost:** $5; $4 (ages 60+); $2 (college students with ID); free (ages 0-18). **Phone:** (406) 755-5268.

NORTHWEST MONTANA HISTORICAL SOCIETY'S MUSEUM AT CENTRAL SCHOOL is at 124 Second Ave. E. Exhibits housed in a renovated 1894 school building cover such topics as Native American culture, the history of the Flathead Valley and the timber industry. Noteworthy is an exhibit about pioneer trapper-turned-legislator Frank Bird Linderman, who documented northwest Montana's Native American culture through sculpture and writings.

Time: Allow 1 hour minimum. **Hours:** Mon.-Fri. 10-5. Closed major holidays. **Cost:** $5; $4 (ages 63+); free (ages 0-11 and students with ID). **Phone:** (406) 756-8381.

RECREATIONAL ACTIVITIES
Hot Air Ballooning

• **Fantasy Flights** departs from various locations in Flathead Valley. **Hours:** Hot air balloon trips depart daily at dawn and 2 hours before sunset, June-Sept. (weather permitting). **Phone:** (406) 755-4172.

AERO INN   406/755-3798   47

Hotel
Rates not provided

Address: 1830 US 93 S 59901 **Location:** 1.3 mi s on US 93 from jct US 2. **Facility:** 62 units. 2 stories (no elevator), interior corridors. **Parking:** winter plug-ins. **Pool(s):** heated indoor. **Activities:** sauna, hot tub. **Featured Amenity:** continental breakfast.

AMERICAS BEST VALUE INN   (406)756-3222   40

Hotel $70-$150 **Address:** 1550 Hwy 93 N 59901 **Location:** 1.3 mi n on US 93 from jct US 2. **Facility:** 53 units. 2 stories (no elevator), interior corridors. **Parking:** winter plug-ins. **Terms:** cancellation fee imposed, resort fee.

BEST WESTERN PLUS FLATHEAD LAKE INN & SUITES
(406)857-2400

Hotel
$89-$269

AAA Benefit: Save 10% or more every day and earn 10% bonus points!

Address: 4824 Hwy 93 S 59901 **Location:** 7 mi s; jct SR 82. **Facility:** 59 units. 3 stories, interior corridors. **Parking:** winter plug-ins. **Terms:** 2-3 night minimum stay - seasonal and/or weekends, resort fee. **Pool(s):** heated indoor. **Activities:** hot tub, exercise room. **Guest Services:** coin laundry. **Featured Amenity:** breakfast buffet.

COMFORT INN   (406)755-6700   43

Hotel $79-$279 **Address:** 1330 Hwy 2 W 59901 **Location:** 1 mi w on US 2 from jct US 93. **Facility:** 63 units, some two bedrooms. 2 stories (no elevator), interior corridors. **Parking:** winter plug-ins. **Pool(s):** heated outdoor. **Activities:** hot tub, exercise room. **Guest Services:** valet and coin laundry.

HAMPTON INN KALISPELL   (406)755-7900   42

Hotel
$99-$399

 AAA Benefit: Members save up to 10%!

Address: 1140 US 2 W 59901 **Location:** 0.9 mi w on US 2 from jct US 93. **Facility:** 120 units. 3 stories, interior corridors. **Parking:** winter plug-ins. **Terms:** check-in 4 pm, 1-7 night minimum stay, cancellation fee imposed. **Pool(s):** heated indoor. **Activities:** hot tub, exercise room. **Guest Services:** valet and coin laundry, area transportation. **Featured Amenity:** full hot breakfast.

HILTON GARDEN INN KALISPELL   (406)756-4500   48

Hotel
$129-$299

 AAA Benefit: Members save up to 10%!

Address: 1840 US 93 S 59901 **Location:** 1.4 mi s on US 93 from jct US 2. **Facility:** 144 units. 4 stories, interior corridors. **Parking:** winter plug-ins. **Terms:** 1-7 night minimum stay, cancellation fee imposed. **Dining:** Blue Canyon Kitchen & Tavern, see separate listing. **Pool(s):** heated indoor. **Activities:** hot tub, exercise room. **Guest Services:** valet and coin laundry, area transportation.

(See map & index p. 167.)

HOLIDAY INN EXPRESS & SUITES
406/755-7405 **38**

◇◇◇◇ **Hotel.** Rates not provided. **Address:** 275 Treeline Rd 59901 **Location:** 3 mi n on US 93 from jct US 2, just w. **Facility:** 111 units. 3 stories, interior corridors. **Parking:** winter plug-ins. **Pool(s):** heated indoor. **Activities:** hot tub, exercise room. **Guest Services:** valet and coin laundry.

HOMEWOOD SUITES BY HILTON
(406)755-8080 **39**

◇◇◇◇ **Extended Stay Hotel** $119-$309 **Address:** 195 Hutton Ranch Rd 59901 **Location:** US 93 N, just e. **Facility:** 100 kitchen units, some two bedrooms. 4 stories, interior corridors. **Parking:** winter plug-ins. **Terms:** check-in 4 pm, 1-7 night minimum stay, cancellation fee imposed. **Amenities:** *Some:* safes. **Pool(s):** heated indoor. **Activities:** hot tub, exercise room. **Guest Services:** valet and coin laundry, area transportation.

AAA Benefit: Members save up to 10%!

KALISPELL/GLACIER INT'L AIRPORT AREA SUPER 8
(406)755-1888 **46**

◇◇ **Hotel** $53-$120 **Address:** 1341 1st Ave E 59901 **Location:** 1.2 mi s on US 93 from jct US 2. **Facility:** 74 units. 3 stories, interior corridors. **Parking:** winter plug-ins.

KALISPELL GRAND HOTEL
(406)755-8100 **45**

◇◇ **Historic Hotel** $91-$165 **Address:** 100 Main St 59901 **Location:** On US 93; jct 1st St; downtown. **Facility:** This historic property was one of the first modern hotels built in the area. After being allowed to deteriorate for years, it has been lovingly restored and anchors a corner of the downtown area. 40 units. 3 stories, interior corridors. **Parking:** on-site and street. **Activities:** massage. **Guest Services:** valet laundry.

LA QUINTA INN & SUITES KALISPELL
(406)257-5255 **41**

◇◇◇◇ **Hotel** $83-$372 **Address:** 255 Montclair Dr 59901 **Location:** Jct US 93 and 2, 1 mi e. **Facility:** 71 units, some efficiencies. 3 stories, interior corridors. **Pool(s):** heated indoor. **Activities:** hot tub, exercise room. **Guest Services:** valet and coin laundry.

RED LION HOTEL KALISPELL
406/751-5050 **44**

◇◇ **Hotel.** Rates not provided. **Address:** 20 N Main St 59901 **Location:** Just s on US 93 from jct US 2; connected to Kalispell Center Mall. Adjacent to casino. **Facility:** 170 units, some efficiencies. 3 stories, interior corridors. **Parking:** winter plug-ins. **Terms:** check-in 4 pm. **Pool(s):** heated indoor. **Activities:** sauna, hot tub, exercise room. **Guest Services:** valet laundry.

WHERE TO EAT

THE ALLEY CONNECTION
406/752-7077 **37**

◇◇ **Chinese. Casual Dining.** $6-$18 **AAA Inspector Notes:** Guests dine on a variety of dishes with foundations of steak, seafood and poultry. Asian beef, a lemon grass-marinated filet served with rice and stir-fried vegetables, proves to be a good choice. You can't go wrong no matter what you order at this restaurant that's been an institution in Kalispell since 1977. A personal favorite is the wonton soup, chock-full of wontons, roasted pork and vegetables. It's a meal in itself. **Features:** beer & wine. **Address:** 22 1st St W 59901 **Location:** On US 93; jct 1st St; downtown. L D

BLUE CANYON KITCHEN & TAVERN
406/758-2583 **44**

◇◇◇ **American. Casual Dining.** $12-$34 **AAA Inspector Notes:** This casual restaurant constructed of large peeled log beams and braces is definitely upscale cowboy chic. The walls are decorated with the ubiquitous Montana stuffed elk heads and antler chandeliers light the dining room. The chairs are unpeeled, small log frames with upholstered seats and backs and the booths and benches are all finely upholstered. Ninety-eight percent of all the food coming out of the kitchen is made from scratch and the in-house pastry chef produces all of their desserts. **Features:** full bar. **Reservations:** suggested. **Address:** 1840 US 93 59901 **Location:** 1.4 mi s on US 93 from jct US 2; in Hilton Garden Inn Kalispell. D CALL

BOJANGLES' DINER
406/755-3222 **33**

◇◇ **American. Family Dining.** $4-$13 **AAA Inspector Notes:** The 1950s are fondly remembered via memorabilia that covers nearly every available space. Home-style choices include all-day breakfast items and soups and pies prepared in house. Don't pass up huckleberry sour cream pie, which is made from berries collected in the nearby mountains. **Address:** 1319 US 2 59901 **Location:** 1.1 mi w from jct US 93. B L CALL

BONELLI'S BISTRO
406/257-8669 **36**

◇◇◇ **Mediterranean. Casual Dining.** $6-$12 **AAA Inspector Notes:** Through the use of fresh organic and local farmers' products, the kitchen creates the essence of Mediterranean cuisine. A nice touch is offering seasonal specials of soups, panini or Mediterranean wraps. Italian groceries line the display shelves and the pastry case spotlights tiramisu or limoncello cake. **Features:** patio dining. **Address:** 38 1st Ave E 59901 **Location:** Between E Center and 1st sts; downtown. **Features:** street only. B L CALL

BULLMAN'S WOOD FIRED PIZZA
406/257-3473 **30**

◇◇ **Pizza. Casual Dining.** $8-$19 **AAA Inspector Notes:** If you like thin-crust pizza, this is your spot. With names like Sawtooth, Bear Tooth and Crazy Mountain, you can't go wrong. My favorite is the Bitterroot with pistachios, onions and rosemary. Salads and sandwiches such as Beef N Cheddar and BlackFoot round out the menu. **Features:** beer & wine. **Address:** 175 Hutton Ranch Rd 59901 **Location:** US 93 N, just e. L D

CISLO'S
406/756-7330 **31**

◇◇ **American. Family Dining.** $8-$16 **AAA Inspector Notes:** As it has for generations, this longtime family-owned favorite serves no-nonsense home-style food to local families. The relaxed atmosphere evokes the feel of a home kitchen. Daily specials and homemade pies keep locals coming back. **Address:** 2046 US 2 E 59901 **Location:** Just n of jct US 2 and SR 82. B L D

GENKI
406/257-8889 **40**

◇◇ **Asian Sushi. Casual Dining.** $8-$19 **AAA Inspector Notes:** The menu has a definite focus on sushi and sashimi. However, those who prefer their fish cooked can choose from a full array of traditional Asian dishes. Two large fish tanks provide focal points of interest at this attractive eatery. **Features:** beer & wine. **Address:** 302 Main St 59901 **Location:** Downtown. L D

HOPS DOWNTOWN GRILL
406/755-7687 **39**

◇◇◇ **Western Burgers. Gastropub.** $10-$25 **AAA Inspector Notes:** This place is known for its burgers, but fish tacos and calamari also are worth trying. A large selection of beer and wine is offered. **Features:** beer & wine. **Reservations:** suggested. **Address:** 121 Main St 59903 **Location:** Downtown. **Parking:** street only. D

JULIE'S CENTER STREET CAFE
406/755-7171 **34**

◇◇ **American. Family Dining.** $6-$10 **AAA Inspector Notes:** This cozy family restaurant serves breakfast all day in addition to a variety of burgers, sandwiches, soups and salads. Made from a family recipe, the homemade sauerkraut, with or without a sandwich, is delicious. The biscuits and gravy are a local favorite. **Features:** senior menu. **Address:** 200 E Center St 59901 **Location:** Downtown. B L

(See map & index p. 167.)

THE MONTANA CLUB
406/260-4401 **43**

▼▼ ▼▼ Western Steak Seafood. Casual Dining. $8-$24 **AAA Inspector Notes:** This family-friendly spot with an adjacent casino has sister restaurants in Missoula and Butte. The building sports a wood interior with numerous historical pictures and menu items that include fresh Alaskan salmon, halibut and meats cut in house. Portions are plentiful. **Features:** full bar, happy hour. **Address:** 1301 S Main St 59901 **Location:** 1.3 mi s on US 93 from jct US 2.

B L D CALL ⬩M

MONTANA COFFEE TRADERS
406/756-2326 **35**

▼ Coffee/Tea. Quick Serve. $6-$10 **AAA Inspector Notes:** This eclectic, popular restaurant roasts its own coffee beans for sale and specializes in espresso drinks. Service is limited, but the soups, salads and sandwiches are generous and well prepared. The in-house bakery produces some of the best dessert bars, muffins, scones and brownies in town. **Address:** 328 W Center St 59901 **Location:** Downtown. B L

NICKEL CHARLIE'S CASINO & EATERY
406/257-7756 **32**

▼▼ ▼▼ American. Casual Dining. $8-$24 **AAA Inspector Notes:** The food is served in large portions and attracts locals and tourists alike. Try the peppercorn steak or mesquite pork chops with apple compote and candied pecans. There's something for everyone. The staff provides service with a smile. Be sure to check out the vintage children's riding toys on the ceiling. **Features:** beer & wine. **Address:** 1275 US 2 E 59901 **Location:** 1.3 mi e of jct US 93.

B L D

SCOTTIBELLI'S RISTORANTE ITALIANO
406/890-7800 **38**

▼▼ ▼▼ Italian. Casual Dining. $15-$32 **AAA Inspector Notes:** Using recipes handed down from their Mama from Italy, this multi-generational family restaurant cooks up traditional favorites: pasta e fagioli soup, pasta carbonara, Margherita pizza and veal marsala are sure to please. For family-style dinners, large portion entrées are offered. One of the more popular dishes is the vongole pomodoro; clams sautéed in a garlic and olive oil. **Features:** full bar. **Address:** 110 Main St 59901 **Location:** On US 93; jct 1st St; downtown. **Parking:** on-site and street. D CALL ⬩M

SPENCER & CO
406/756-8941 **29**

▼▼ ▼▼ Steak. Casual Dining. $14-$30 **AAA Inspector Notes:** The classic steakhouse serves large, succulent cuts of beef on a sizzling platter. Although beef occupies the spotlight, chicken, seafood and pasta also have a place on the menu. **Features:** full bar. **Address:** 4010 US 93 N 59901 **Location:** 7.3 mi n from jct US 2. D

THAI PALACE RESTAURANT
406/756-7956 **41**

▼▼ ▼▼ Thai. Casual Dining. $12-$22 **AAA Inspector Notes:** This casual storefront main street restaurant serves a variety of traditional Thai food as well as other Asian dishes. If you like mangos, the mango salad and mango sweet rice are excellent. **Features:** beer & wine. **Address:** 319 Main St 59901 **Location:** Between 3rd and 4th sts; center. **Parking:** street only. L D

WHEAT MONTANA BAKERY & DELI
406/257-6530 **42**

▼ Breads/Pastries Deli. Family Dining. $5-$10 **AAA Inspector Notes:** Stop by for early-morning coffee and huge cinnamon rolls. Order sandwiches made with fresh baked breads to enjoy later. Breads and bagels are made with chemical-free flour freshly ground from Montana wheat. **Address:** 405 Main St 59901 **Location:** Downtown. B L

Trust the recommendations
of AAA/CAA travel experts
to make a good trip great

KOOTENAI NATIONAL FOREST (A-1)

> Elevations in the forest range from 1,862 ft. where the Kootenai River crosses into Idaho to 8,736 ft. on Snowshoe Peak. Refer to AAA maps for additional elevation information.

Kootenai National Forest is in the northwest corner of Montana, with a small section extending into Idaho. High, craggy peaks characterize the 2.2 million-acre region; portions of the Cabinet, Whitefish and Purcell mountains are the main ranges, attaining elevations as high as 8,700 feet. The area's climate is modified Pacific Maritime, and as a result Kootenai has an abundance of plant species more common to the Pacific Coast than to other parts of Montana.

There are diverse wildlife species, including bear, elk, deer, mountain goats, bighorn sheep and wolves. The forest also is home to many non-game species. Throughout the year bald eagles can be seen along the Kootenai River north of Libby; 205 species of birds have been recorded in the forest. Cabinet Mountains Wilderness has 85 small lakes; many are scenic, stocked with fish and reached by trail. Ski facilities are available northwest of Libby. The area has more than 50 campgrounds and 1,500 miles of hiking trails.

Ross Creek Cedars Scenic Area, off SR 56 southwest of Libby, and Ten Lakes Scenic Area, on the Canadian border northeast of Eureka, are reached by local and forest roads. Lake Koocanusa also is a popular recreational spot *(see Libby p. 186)*.

For further information, contact the Forest Supervisor, Kootenai National Forest, 31374 US 2, Libby, MT 59923; phone (406) 293-6211. *See Recreation Areas Chart.*

LAME DEER (E-7) pop. 2,052, elev. 3,380'

A popular destination for winter recreation, Lame Deer also is the headquarters for the Northern Cheyenne Indian Reservation. Activities on the reservation include the Sun Dance (dates vary) and a powwow in July. Cheyenne crafts, including moccasins, belts and jewelry, are available at the Northern Cheyenne Arts and Crafts Center at US 212 and Old Cemetery Rd.

LAUREL pop. 6,718

BEST WESTERN YELLOWSTONE CROSSING
(406)628-6888

▼▼ ▼▼
Hotel
$80-S86

AAA Benefit: Save 10% or more every day and earn 10% bonus points!

Address: 205 SE 4th St 59044 **Location:** I-90 exit 434, just n, then just e. **Facility:** 60 units. 3 stories, interior corridors. **Parking:** winter plug-ins. **Amenities:** *Some:* safes. **Pool(s):** heated indoor. **Activities:** hot tub, limited exercise equipment. **Guest Services:** coin laundry.

SAVE 🍴 CALL ⬩M 🏊 BIZ 📶
✕ 🖥 / SOME UNITS 🛏 🚪 🖼

LEWIS AND CLARK NATIONAL FOREST (B-3)

Elevations in the forest range from 4,000 ft. in the valley bottoms to 9,204 ft. on Scapegoat Mountain. Refer to AAA maps for additional elevation information.

Lewis and Clark National Forest is in west-central Montana. Consisting of 1,843,397 acres, the forest has two units. The Rocky Mountain Unit, which embraces about half of the acreage, lies along the eastern slope of the Continental Divide south of Glacier National Park. It includes portions of the Bob Marshall *(see Flathead National Forest p. 157)* and Scapegoat wildernesses.

The Rocky Mountain Unit rises sharply from grasslands to peaks between 7,000 and 8,000 feet in elevation. Access to the area is by a number of gravel roads off US 89 that connect with forest roads and trailheads and serve several campgrounds.

Southeast of Great Falls is the Jefferson Unit, scattered inland mountain ranges dotting the prairie, including the Little Belt, Castle, Highwoods, Big Snowy and Little Snowy mountain ranges and the north end of the Crazy Mountains. The Jefferson Division has short, dome-like mountains rather than jagged peaks.

The mountains are forest-covered and have moderate slopes that present less demanding hiking and riding trails than those found in the Rocky Mountain Unit. There are many streams but no large rivers or lakes.

Winter sports are available near Kings Hill Summit, some 40 miles north of White Sulphur Springs *(see place listing p. 214)*, Monarch and Neihart. For further information contact the Forest Supervisor, Lewis and Clark National Forest, 1101 15th St. N., Great Falls, MT 59405; phone (406) 791-7700. *See Recreation Areas Chart.*

LEWISTOWN (C-5) pop. 5,901, elev. 3,963'

Lewistown originally was a trading post on the Carroll Trail between Helena and Carroll. First called Reed's Fort, it later was renamed Lewistown after the military officer who established a fort nearby in 1876. Trading, only on a larger scale, continues to support the town, which is a market for the large cattle ranches and wheat farms of central Montana.

Lewistown Area Chamber of Commerce: 408 N.E. Main St., Lewistown, MT 59457. **Phone:** (406) 535-5436.

CENTRAL MONTANA MUSEUM is at 408 N.E. Main St. Area history is documented through collections of minerals, guns and Native American and Western artifacts. **Time:** Allow 30 minutes minimum. **Hours:** Daily 10-4, Memorial Day-Labor Day. **Cost:** Donations. **Phone:** (406) 535-3642.

B & B MOTEL 406/535-5496

Ⓦ **Motel.** Rates not provided. **Address:** 520 E Main St 59457 **Location:** Downtown. **Facility:** 36 units, some efficiencies. 2 stories (no elevator), exterior corridors. **Parking:** winter plug-ins.

LEWISTOWN SUPER 8 (406)538-2581

ⓌⓌ **Hotel** $72-$125 **Address:** 102 Wendell Ave 59457 **Location:** West side of town, on US 87; near airport. **Facility:** 45 units. 2 stories (no elevator), interior corridors. **Parking:** winter plug-ins. **Guest Services:** coin laundry.

LIBBY (B-1) pop. 2,628, elev. 2,086'

Natural resources have been the mainstay of Libby's economy since its settlement in the 1860s. Drawn by stories of gold in the north, prospectors first gathered in this region and named the town after the daughter of one of the men who discovered gold in a nearby creek. Mining, timber and tourism are the town's leading businesses.

Libby's environs contribute to the town's popularity as a recreational center. The nearby Kootenai National Forest *(see place listing p. 185)* provides extensive lands for public use, and anglers enjoy fishing in the Kootenai River and its tributaries.

Libby Area Chamber of Commerce: 905 W. 9th St., P.O. Box 704, Libby, MT 59923. **Phone:** (406) 293-4167.

HERITAGE MUSEUM is at 34067 US 2. A 12-sided log building contains exhibits about mining and forestry along with historical information about the Kootenai Indians, explorer David Thompson, local participation in World War II and the Civilian Conservation Corps (CCC). Wildlife displays, as well as rotating art, quilt and photography exhibits in the Tower Gallery, also can be seen. Outbuildings include an 1800s log cabin, a miner's cabin and the cookhouse from the Sylvanite Ranger Station. Archives are available by appointment. **Hours:** Mon.-Sat. 10-5, Sun. 1-5, late May-Aug. 31; by appointment rest of year. Phone ahead to confirm schedule. **Cost:** Donations. **Phone:** (406) 293-7521.

LIBBY DAM is 13.5 mi. e. on SR 37, then 3.5 mi. n. on FR 228, following signs. Built 1966-72 to generate power and control flooding on the Kootenai River, the straight-axis dam is 422 feet high and 3,055 feet long. Its reservoir, Lake Koocanusa, extends 90 miles upstream and into British Columbia.

The Libby Dam Visitor Center, off FR 228, has interpretive displays and interactive exhibits about natural history, river navigation, flood control and electricity generation. A theater screens a 9-minute video describing the construction of the dam as well as a 10-minute video about Army Corps of Engineers dams on the Columbia River system.

Free ranger-led, 1-hour tours are available. Following the Kootenai River and Lake Koocanusa via SR 37, the 67-mile-long Lake Koocanusa Scenic Byway stretches between Libby and Eureka. *See*

Recreation Areas Chart. **Hours:** Grounds daily dawn-dusk. Visitor center daily 9:30-6, Memorial Day-Labor Day; open by appointment rest of year. Tours are given daily at 10, noon, 2 and 4, Memorial Day-Labor Day, when staff is available; by appointment rest of year. Phone ahead to confirm schedule. **Cost:** Free. **Phone:** (406) 293-5577 or (406) 293-7751. 🅰 🍴 ⊠ 🏕 🏕

SANDMAN MOTEL (406)293-8831

◈ Motel $55-$95 **Address:** 31901 US 2 59923 **Location:** Just w on US 2 from jct SR 37. Located in a quiet area. **Facility:** 16 units. 2 stories (no elevator), exterior corridors. **Parking:** winter plug-ins. **Terms:** cancellation fee imposed.

🛅 📶 ⊠ 🖥 🖨 / SOME UNITS 🔲

VENTURE MOTOR INN 406/293-7711

◈◈ Hotel. Rates not provided. **Address:** 1015 W 9th St (US 2) 59923 **Location:** Just w on US 2 from jct SR 37. **Facility:** 71 units. 3 stories, interior corridors. **Parking:** winter plug-ins. **Dining:** Venture Inn Restaurant, see separate listing. **Pool(s):** heated indoor. **Activities:** hot tub. **Guest Services:** coin laundry.

🍴 🏊 📶 ⊠ 🖥 🖨 🖥 / SOME UNITS 🔲 (HS)

WHERE TO EAT

HENRY'S 406/293-7911

◈ American. Family Dining. $10-$17 **AAA Inspector Notes:** Traditional homemade fare is served at this informal coffee shop and adjoining dining room that sport antique-accented décor and some Western-themed items. The service staff's friendly demeanor adds a comfortably homey touch to the dining experience. The prices are good, too. **Address:** 405 W 9th St 59923 **Location:** Just w on US 2 from jct SR 37. [B] [L] [D]

THE LAST STRAW CAFE 406/293-4000

◈◈ American. Family Dining. $7-$17 **AAA Inspector Notes:** Serving breakfast all day, this restaurant also features emu and buffalo burgers along with awesome salads and more traditional meals. Try the extra-large hot biscuits and the brownie sundaes. **Address:** 30890 US Hwy 2 59923 **Location:** 1 mi w of downtown; adjacent to Homesteader's Ranch & Feed store. [B] [L] CALL 🄼

VENTURE INN RESTAURANT 406/293-7711

◈◈ American. Casual Dining. $11-$24 **AAA Inspector Notes:** Ask anyone in Libby where to find a good salad bar and they'll tell you Venture Motor Inn. The potato and pasta salads are made in house as is the soup. The night I was here, I had a huge bowl of the rich and flavorful beef barley soup. I usually try to just taste the soup, as I don't want to fill up before my meal, but I couldn't help myself, it was that good. The salad bar has the requisite orange and green vegetables, all replenished regularly and kept clean of any stray drips or crumbs. **Address:** 1015 W 9th St (US 2) 59923 **Location:** Just w on US 2 from jct SR 37; in Venture Motor Inn. [B] [L] [D] CALL 🄼

LIMA (F-3) pop. 221, elev. 6,256'

RED ROCKS LAKES NATIONAL WILDLIFE REFUGE is off I-15 exit 0, then 28 mi. e. on a gravel road. Established as a refuge in 1935, this sanctuary with lakes, marshes, creeks and the isolation of the Centennial Valley has become one of North America's more important nesting areas for trumpeter swans and other wildlife. The prime viewing season is May through September. Primitive camping facilities are available. Inquire locally about road conditions. **Hours:** Refuge headquarters Mon.-Fri. 8-4:30. **Cost:** Free. **Phone:** (406) 276-3536.

🅰

◆ LITTLE BIGHORN BATTLEFIELD NATIONAL MONUMENT (E-6)

The main entrance to Little Bighorn Battlefield National Monument is 15 miles southeast of Hardin via exit 510 off I-90, then a half-mile east via US 212. In the Valley of the Little Bighorn River in June 1876, Lt. Col. George Armstrong Custer and the 210 men of the 7th Cavalry Regiment under his command made their last stand against several thousand Lakota, Arapaho and Northern Cheyenne, many of whom were fleeing the restrictions of the reservation. Covering 1.2 square miles, the monument commemorates the dramatic climax of the Indian Wars by preserving the site of this Native American victory.

The monument embraces a national cemetery established in 1879, various monuments and memorials, and a historical museum with maps, photographs and dioramas depicting the battle. Just inside the entrance is a visitor center where park rangers provide tour information and self-guiding tour brochures.

Auto tours with maps are available at the center and from Big Horn County Historical Museum and State Visitor Center *(see Hardin p. 176)* and other local outlets; phone (406) 665-1671.

Monument 8-8, Memorial Day-Labor Day; 8-6, Apr. 1-day before Memorial Day and day after Labor Day-Sept. 30; 8-4:30, rest of year. Closed Jan. 1, Thanksgiving and Christmas. Admission $15 (per private vehicle); $10 (per person arriving by other means). Cemetery free. Phone (406) 638-2621.

APSAALOOKE TOURS departs from the Little Bighorn Battlefield National Monument Visitor Center. Narrated van tours of the site of the Battle of the Little Bighorn are given by Native American guides. **Time:** Allow 1 hour minimum. **Hours:** Tours are given daily on the hour 10-3, Memorial Day-Labor Day; other times by appointment. **Cost:** $10; $8 (ages 65+); $5 (ages 4-12). **Phone:** (406) 638-2621. (GT)

LIVINGSTON (E-4) pop. 7,044, elev. 4,501'
• Hotels p. 188 • Restaurants p. 188
• Part of Yellowstone National Park area — see map p. 316

The lush grasses of Paradise Valley were ideal for raising cattle, and the valley's warm Chinook winds protected the area from bitter Montana winters. When the Northern Pacific Railroad laid tracks in 1882, both the cattle industry and Livingston flourished. Among the town's more memorable residents was Calamity Jane.

Livingston is at the head of Paradise Valley, through which flows the Yellowstone River and around which range the Crazy Mountains and the Absaroka and Gallatin ranges of the Rockies. The area offers opportunities for wildlife viewing, hunting, fishing, rafting, backpacking, camping, skiing and snowmobiling.

A scenic drive, US 89, connects Livingston to Gardiner and the northern entrance to Yellowstone National Park *(see place listing p. 316)*. Livingston was the original entrance to Yellowstone.

Livingston Area Chamber of Commerce: 303 E. Park St., Livingston, MT 59047. **Phone:** (406) 222-0850.

Self-guiding tours: A brochure outlining a walking tour of the historic business district is available at Yellowstone Gateway Museum *(see attraction listing this page)* and the chamber of commerce.

LIVINGSTON DEPOT CENTER is at 200 W. Park St. Built in 1902, the restored Northern Pacific Railroad station was designed in the Italian Renaissance style by the original architects of New York's Grand Central Station. An exhibit of the railroad photography of Warren McGee is featured. Special events are scheduled throughout the year. **Hours:** Mon.-Sat. 10-5, Sun. 1-5, Memorial Day-Labor Day. **Cost:** $5; $4 (ages 7-12 and 62+). **Phone:** (406) 222-2300.

SAVE **YELLOWSTONE GATEWAY MUSEUM** is off I-90 exit 333 at 118 W. Chinook St. Housed in a three-story, 1907 schoolhouse, the museum features a variety of local history exhibits, including Yellowstone National Park memorabilia and stagecoaches once used within the park. Historic vehicles include a turn-of-the-20th-century Northern Pacific Railway caboose.

A map traces William Clark's route through the area. Rounding out the museum's offerings are exhibits about military, fire and transportation history; American Indian artifacts; local Yellowstone art; and household items from area pioneers. **Time:** Allow 30 minutes minimum. **Hours:** Daily 10-5, Memorial Day-Sept. 30; Thurs.-Sat. 10-5, rest of year. **Cost:** $5; $4 (ages 55+); free (ages 0-18). **Phone:** (406) 222-4184.

LIVINGSTON COMFORT INN (406)222-4400
Hotel $95-$215 **Address:** 114 Loves Ln 59047 **Location:** I-90 exit 333, just s on US 89, then just w. **Facility:** 49 units. 2 stories (no elevator), interior corridors. **Parking:** winter plug-ins. **Amenities:** safes. **Pool(s):** heated indoor. **Activities:** hot tub. **Guest Services:** coin laundry.

LIVINGSTON RODEWAY INN (406)222-6320
Motel $66-$140 **Address:** 102 Rogers Ln 59047 **Location:** I-90 exit 333, just n on US 89, then just w. **Facility:** 44 units. 1 story, interior/exterior corridors. **Parking:** winter plug-ins. **Amenities:** safes. **Pool(s):** heated indoor. **Guest Services:** coin laundry.

SUPER 8 LIVINGSTON (406)222-7711
Motel $70-$150 **Address:** 105 Centennial Dr 59047 **Location:** I-90 exit 333, just s on US 89. **Facility:** 37 units, some kitchens. 2 stories (no elevator), interior corridors. **Parking:** winter plug-ins. **Amenities:** safes. **Guest Services:** coin laundry.

YELLOWSTONE PIONEER LODGE 406/222-6110

Hotel
Rates not provided

Address: 1515 W Park St 59047 **Location:** I-90 exit 333, just n. **Facility:** 99 units, some kitchens. 3 stories, interior corridors. **Parking:** winter plug-ins. **Pool(s):** heated indoor. **Guest Services:** coin laundry, area transportation. **Featured Amenity:** breakfast buffet.

YELLOWSTONE VALLEY LODGE, AN ASCEND HOTEL COLLECTION MEMBER 406/333-4787

Resort Cabin
Rates not provided

Address: 3840 US Hwy 89 S 59047 **Location:** I-90 exit 333, 15 mi s on US 89 S; between MM 38 and 39. **Facility:** There are two outside fire pits for fun evening gatherings. Each cabin offers a deck overlooking the river. Choose a cabin with basic accommodations or a newer upscale room. 23 cabins, some two bedrooms and kitchens. 1 story, interior corridors. **Activities:** fishing. **Featured Amenity: continental breakfast.** Affiliated with Ascend Hotel Collection Member.

WHERE TO EAT

2ND STREET BISTRO 406/222-9463
Regional American. Casual Dining. $22-$45 **AAA Inspector Notes:** In a historic building, this bistro has antique oak chairs in the dining room and original art on the walls. Varying menu items are prepared with creative twists. Diners will find dishes prepared from only organic and specially purchased seafood, poultry, meats and game from local farms. A wide variety of house-specialty drinks, libations and wines from a wine cave complements meals. Homemade desserts change daily. **Features:** full bar, patio dining. **Reservations:** suggested. **Address:** 123 N 2nd St 59047 **Location:** Jct E Park St; downtown; in Murray Hotel. **Parking:** on-site and street.

GIL'S GOODS 406/222-9463
Pizza Breads/Pastries. Casual Dining. $6-$14 **AAA Inspector Notes:** Brought to you by the same owner as the 2nd Street Bistro, this eatery's concept is based on the European café, with a simple menu made from great ingredients. Try a specialty pizza with homemade dough topped with homemade sausage and fired in a brick oven, organic salad greens, homemade bakery items and sandwiches. **Features:** full bar, patio dining. **Address:** 207 W Park St 59047 **Location:** Jct N 2nd St; downtown; in Murray Hotel. **Parking:** street only.

MONTANA'S RIB & CHOP HOUSE 406/222-9200
American. Casual Dining. $9-$29 **AAA Inspector Notes:** This restaurant's specialties include 24-hour marinated baby back ribs and an 8-ounce Montana tenderloin, hand-cut beef fillet. Diners also can sink their teeth into a variety of chicken, seafood and other steak entrées. Reservations are suggested at this bustling eatery. **Features:** full bar, patio dining, happy hour. **Reservations:** suggested. **Address:** 305 E Park Rd 59047 **Location:** Downtown; adjacent to Chamber of Commerce.

LOLO NATIONAL FOREST (B-1)

Lolo National Forest is in western Montana. With boundaries stretching from the Swan Range in the northeast to the Idaho border, an area 120 miles long and 40 to 80 miles wide, the forest embraces about 2,100,000 acres. Although the Lolo is an important timber producer, many of its south-facing slopes are open and grassy. It also is one of the principal elk areas in western Montana.

Wilderness areas within the forest include the 33,000-acre Rattlesnake National Recreation Area and Wilderness as well as Welcome Creek and portions of Scapegoat.

Recreational opportunities abound on 3,500 miles of streams, including Rock Creek, a haven for trout-fishing enthusiasts. Approximately 485 species of fish and wildlife inhabit the forest, which has numerous camping and/or picnic sites and 1,780 miles of hiking trails; winter activities include downhill and cross-country skiing, snowmobiling along 360 miles of designated trails and ice fishing. Some recreation facilities are designed for handicapped access; inquire at a ranger station.

The forest has five offices: the Ninemile Ranger Station in Huson *(see Huson p. 182)*; the Missoula Ranger Station at Fort Missoula; and stations in the outlying districts of Seeley Lake, Superior and Plains/Thompson Falls.

For further information, contact Lolo National Forest, 24 Fort Missoula Rd., Missoula, MT 59804; phone (406) 329-3750. *See Recreation Areas Chart.*

MALTA (B-6) pop. 1,997, elev. 2,248'

Named for the island in the Mediterranean, Malta was the center of a cattle empire that reached from Glasgow to Havre and from the Missouri River to Canada during the late 19th century. Wheat and alfalfa have joined cattle as the area's leading products.

A large boulder at the intersection of US 2 and Sleeping Buffalo Resort looks like a sleeping buffalo. The Assiniboine Indians revered it, and the markings on it had a part in their tribal rituals.

The Little Rocky Mountains, called "island mountains" by early Native Americans, are 40 miles southwest on US 191. Gold was discovered in the mountains in 1884, and the historic remains set the scene for the mountain communities of Zortman and Landusky.

Notable Wild Bunch outlaws Butch Cassidy and Landusky resident Harvey "Kid Curry" Logan hid out in the area in 1901 after robbing a Great Northern passenger train, making off with around $60,000.

The Charles M. Russell National Wildlife Refuge, 60 miles south of Malta via US 191, sprawls across 1,100,000 acres around Fort Peck Reservoir. Drivers can access a scenic, 19-mile, self-guiding automobile tour route from two points along US 191. Signs along the way describe the area's history, geology and wildlife. Phone (406) 538-8706.

Malta Area Chamber of Commerce: 10½ S. 4th St. E., P.O. Box 1420, Malta, MT 59538. **Phone:** (406) 654-1776.

BOWDOIN NATIONAL WILDLIFE REFUGE is 7 mi. e. on CR 2 following signs to 194 Bowdoin Auto Tour Rd. This 15,500-acre breeding and feeding area for migratory waterfowl, shorebirds and other wildlife, including deer, is one of the few northwestern nesting areas of the white pelican. The refuge can be seen via a 15-mile, self-guiding automobile tour (weather permitting); ideal viewing times are early fall and late spring. **Time:** Allow 1 hour minimum. **Hours:** Refuge open daily dawn-dusk. Headquarters open Mon.-Fri. 7:30-4. **Cost:** Free. **Phone:** (406) 654-2863.

GREAT PLAINS DINOSAUR MUSEUM & FIELD STATION is at 405 E. US 2. Guided tours offer visitors a glimpse into the world of dinosaurs and reveal fossil preparation techniques as well as the latest in dinosaur discoveries. **Time:** Allow 1 hour minimum. **Hours:** Mon.-Sat. 10-5, Sun. 12:30-5, June-Aug.; Tues.-Sat. 10-5, in May; by appointment rest of year. Closed major holidays. **Cost:** $5; $3 (ages 6-12). **Phone:** (406) 654-5300. GT

PHILLIPS COUNTY MUSEUM is at 431 E. US 2. Visitors are greeted by Elvis, a 33-foot brachylophosaurus, and meet the Outlaw Kid Curry, ranchers and homesteaders inside the museum. A collection of Native American beadwork and numerous fossils are on display. The refurbished, historic H.G. Robinson House and Gardens are next door. **Time:** Allow 1 hour minimum. **Hours:** Mon.-Sat. 10-5, Apr.-Dec. **Cost:** $5; $3 (ages 5-18); $12 (family). **Phone:** (406) 654-1037.

EDGEWATER INN & RV PARK   406/654-1302

Motel $79 **Address:** 101 Hwy 2 W 59538 **Location:** Jct US 2 and 191 N. **Facility:** 32 units. 1 story, exterior corridors. **Parking:** winter plug-ins. **Pool(s):** heated indoor. **Activities:** sauna, hot tub, limited exercise equipment. **Guest Services:** valet and coin laundry, area transportation.

MALTANA MOTEL   406/654-2610

Motel. Rates not provided. **Address:** 138 S 1st Ave W 59538 **Location:** Just s of US 2 via US 191, just w; downtown. **Facility:** 19 units. 1 story, exterior corridors. **Parking:** winter plug-ins. **Guest Services:** complimentary laundry, area transportation.

WHERE TO EAT

GREAT NORTHERN HOTEL   406/654-2100

American. Casual Dining. $18-$45 **AAA Inspector Notes:** For breakfast or lunch, visit the retro coffee shop setting in this hotel lobby. At dinner, you'll eat in a more formal, yet not stuffy, dining room. A separate lounge area invites relaxation. **Features:** full bar. **Address:** 2 S 1st Ave E 59538 **Location:** US 2, just s on US 191. **Parking:** on-site and street. B L D CALL M

MANHATTAN pop. 1,520

LAND OF MAGIC   406/284-3794

American. Casual Dining. $18-$40 **AAA Inspector Notes:** The large dining room, where locals and travelers alike gather, features Western-themed décor. Choose from more than eight cuts of steak or maybe try the Kansas ribs. A relish tray and dessert are included in the price. **Features:** full bar. **Address:** 11060 Front St 59741 **Location:** I-90 exit 283 (Logan Frontage Rd), just n, then 1 mi e. D CALL M

SIR SCOTT'S OASIS   406/284-6929

♦♦♦ 💎 Steak Seafood. Casual Dining. $12-$67 **AAA Inspector Notes:** This is a true Montana steakhouse known for serving large, quality cuts of Montana beef. Other choices include seafood and fried chicken. All meals come with a vegetable tray, soup, salad and ice cream. **Features:** full bar. **Reservations:** suggested. **Address:** 204 W Main St 59741 **Location:** I-90 exit 288, 1 mi n. **Parking:** on-site and street. Ⓓ 🎦

MARTINSDALE (D-4) pop. 64, elev. 4,819'

BAIR FAMILY MUSEUM is at 2751 SR 294. Charles M. Bair moved to Montana in 1883. He went into ranching and made his fortune in the Alaskan Gold Rush. The circa 1890s Bair ranch comprises antiques and paintings. Highlights include a collection of Paul Storr silver and an 18th-century British sideboard. **Time:** Allow 1 hour minimum. **Hours:** Daily 10-5, Memorial Day-Labor Day.; Wed.-Sun. 10-5, day after Labor Day-Oct. 31. Last tour begins 1 hour before closing. **Cost:** $5; $3 (ages 62+); $2 (ages 6-16). **Phone:** (406) 572-3314. 🎫

MARYSVILLE (D-3) pop. 80

Marysville, accessible by a 6-mile paved road branching off SR 279 northwest of Helena, is a semi-ghost town. Today scattered buildings on a grid of mostly unpaved streets offer faint echoes of the town's halcyon days. Located at the head of a ravine below the Continental Divide, gold was discovered here in 1870, and in the 1880s and early 1890s, this was Montana's richest gold mining district. The camp was named for Mary Ralston, the area's first pioneer woman.

At its peak the community boasted 4,000 residents, two railroad lines, 60 business establishments and two newspapers, but by the mid-1890s, the town began to decline. Fire devastated the commercial district in 1910, and the Northern Pacific Railroad abandoned its branch line in 1925.

RECREATIONAL ACTIVITIES

Skiing

- **Great Divide Ski Area** is at 7385 Belmont Dr. **Hours:** Downhill skiing Wed.-Sun., late Nov.-early Apr. (weather permitting). **Phone:** (406) 449-3746 or (406) 447-1310.

THE MARYSVILLE HOUSE   406/443-6677

♦♦♦ Steak. Casual Dining. $9-$60 **AAA Inspector Notes:** This very rustic, distinctive eatery serves up Porterhouse steak, shrimp, oysters, grilled chicken, crab legs and lobster. If you still have room, there is homemade cheesecake for dessert. A lively bar and down-home service staff round out the experience in this old ghost town. **Features:** full bar. **Address:** 153 Main St 59640 **Location:** I-15 exit 200 (SR 279), 9.2 mi w, 6 mi s on Marysville Rd (from sign), then just n. **Parking:** on-site and street. Ⓓ 🎦

MEDICINE LAKE (B-8) pop. 225, elev. 1,951'

MEDICINE LAKE NATIONAL WILDLIFE REFUGE is 24 mi. n. on SR 16 to 223 N. Shore Rd. A nesting place for waterfowl and shorebirds, the 31,702-acre refuge houses about 230 species of birds at various times of the year. Fishing and hunting for waterfowl, upland game birds and deer are permitted in season; obtain maps and information at refuge headquarters, 1 mile south and 2 miles east of Medicine Lake. An automobile tour route runs from SR 16 along the northern boundary of the refuge to East Lake Highway.

The condition of the gravel roads throughout the refuge is usually good but temporary closures may occur if rain or snow cause the roads to become hazardous. During hunting season (September 1 through late December), a portion of the wildlife drive is closed to protect migratory birds, although you may still access the east section of the wildlife drive via East Lake Highway. **Hours:** Refuge open daily dawn-dusk. Headquarters open Mon.-Fri. 7-3:30. **Cost:** Free. **Phone:** (406) 789-2305. 🎫

MILES CITY (D-7) pop. 8,410, elev. 2,364'

Miles City developed on the bottomland at the confluence of the Tongue and Yellowstone rivers. Gen. Nelson A. Miles arrived at the mouth of the Tongue River in August 1876 to force the Cheyenne and Sioux to return to the reservations. Miles built Fort Keogh at the site in 1877 and used it as a base for controlling the local tribes.

Main Street in times past was a block of saloons, gambling dens and brothels on the south, and banks, businesses and pawn shops on the north. Miles City has become a growing retail and service hub for eastern Montana and a center for cattle, sheep and crop farms.

Miles City Area Chamber of Commerce: 511 Pleasant St., Miles City, MT 59301. **Phone:** (406) 234-2890.

RANGE RIDERS MUSEUM AND BERT CLARK GUN COLLECTION is 1 mi. w. on US 10/I-94 Bus. Loop, across the Tongue River Bridge to 435 LP Anderson Rd. This 12-building complex features Western antiques and artifacts, archeological and geological specimens, and one of the Fort Keogh officer's quarters.

A detailed miniature replica of Fort Keogh is in the coach house. The Bert Clark gun collection comprises more than 400 pieces, including an elephant gun and a set of Belgian dueling pistols. **Time:** Allow 1 hour minimum. **Hours:** Daily 8-5, Apr.-Oct. **Cost:** $7.50; $5 (ages 62+); $3 (students in high school or college); $1 (students in grade school or junior high school). **Phone:** (406) 232-6146.

WATERWORKS ART MUSEUM is at 85 Water Plant Rd. Housed in a 1910 former water-treatment plant in a park overlooking the Yellowstone River, the center has two galleries featuring changing exhibits of Western, historical and contemporary art. **Hours:** Tues.-Sun. 9-5, May-Sept.; 1-5, rest of year. Closed major holidays. **Cost:** Free. **Phone:** (406) 234-0635.

BEST WESTERN WAR BONNET INN (406)234-4560

Motel
$110-$200

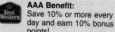

AAA Benefit: Save 10% or more every day and earn 10% bonus points!

Address: 1015 S Haynes Ave 59301 **Location:** I-94 exit 138 (Broadus), 0.3 mi n. **Facility:** 53 units. 2 stories (no elevator), exterior corridors. **Parking:** winter plug-ins. **Pool(s):** heated indoor. **Activities:** sauna, hot tub, exercise room. **Featured Amenity: breakfast buffet.**

COMFORT INN MILES CITY (406)234-3141

Hotel $100-$119 **Address:** 1615 S Haynes Ave 59301 **Location:** I-94 exit 138 (Broadus), just s. **Facility:** 49 units. 2 stories (no elevator), interior corridors. **Parking:** winter plug-ins. **Pool(s):** heated indoor. **Activities:** hot tub. **Guest Services:** coin laundry.

GUESTHOUSE INTERNATIONAL INN & SUITES 406/232-3661

Hotel. Rates not provided. **Address:** 3111 Steel St 59301 **Location:** I-94 exit 138 (Broadus), just s. **Facility:** 61 units, some two bedrooms and efficiencies. 2 stories (no elevator), interior corridors. **Parking:** winter plug-ins. **Pool(s):** heated indoor. **Activities:** hot tub, exercise room. **Guest Services:** coin laundry.

MILES CITY HOTEL & SUITES (406)234-1000

Hotel
$109-$169

Address: 1720 S Haynes Ave 59301 **Location:** I-94 exit 138 (Broadus), just s. **Facility:** 52 units. 2 stories (no elevator), interior corridors. **Parking:** winter plug-ins. **Pool(s):** heated indoor. **Activities:** hot tub. **Guest Services:** coin laundry. **Featured Amenity: full hot breakfast.**

SLEEP INN & SUITES MILES CITY (406)232-3000

Hotel
$104-$239

Address: 1006 S Haynes Ave 59301 **Location:** I-94 exit 138 (Broadus), 0.3 mi n. **Facility:** 90 units, some efficiencies. 3 stories, interior corridors. **Parking:** winter plug-ins. **Amenities:** safes. **Pool(s):** heated indoor. **Activities:** exercise room. **Guest Services:** coin laundry. **Featured Amenity: full hot breakfast.**

WHERE TO EAT

MONTANA'S RIB & CHOP HOUSE 406/234-9200

Regional American. Casual Dining. $8-$30 **AAA Inspector Notes:** Steaks, ribs, lamb and seafood are all served in a friendly atmosphere at an affordable price. **Features:** full bar, patio dining, happy hour. **Address:** 3020 Stower St 59301 **Location:** I-94 exit 138 (Broadus), 1 mi n; jct Haynes Ave. L D

MISSOULA (D-2) pop. 66,788, elev. 3,223'

• Hotels p. 192 • Restaurants p. 194

Missoula lies astride the Clark Fork River, a tributary of the Columbia River named for William Clark. The town also occupies a valley that was once part of Glacial Lake Missoula, a prehistoric lake.

At the mouth of Hell Gate Canyon, Missoula straddles the route the Salish Indians traveled to reach the Great Plains hunting buffalo. Meriwether Lewis and William Clark later followed the same route through the canyon and camped approximately 9 miles southwest at Travellers Rest, near present-day Lolo. Many Native Americans died in the canyon, as the Blackfoot regularly ambushed the Salish, which prompted French-Canadian trappers to christen the site Porte de L'Enfer, "Gate of Hell."

One of the first lumber mills in the region began in Missoula. Lumber remains not only a major industry but also a major concern. The U.S. Forest Service maintains in Missoula its Region No. 1 headquarters, a research station devoted to forest fire research and the smokejumpers' training center. The University of Montana supports these studies with a 22,000-acre experimental forest in addition to conservation and wildlife research stations.

A short drive in any direction will lead into a national forest or a wilderness area. The Rattlesnake National Recreation Area and Wilderness, 6 miles north of downtown, has many small lakes, streams and trails.

A Carousel for Missoula near Caras Park is a hand-carved 1918 merry-go-round created by volunteers. Rides are offered year-round; phone (406) 549-8382.

The International Wildlife Film Festival provides an opportunity for wildlife and conservation filmmakers, broadcasters, scientists, educators and students to network and share ideas relating to projects. The 8-day event takes place in spring.

The 3-day Montana Book Festival takes place in September. It is a literary celebration that features some 50 events showcasing more than 70 writers in a variety of demonstrations, exhibits, readings, receptions, signings and workshops.

Missoula Convention & Visitors Bureau: 101 E. Main St., Missoula, MT 59802. **Phone:** (406) 532-3250 or (800) 526-3465.

Self-guiding tours: Brochures outlining walking tours of public art and historical buildings in the downtown district are available from the convention and visitors bureau.

Shopping: Southgate Mall, US 93 and South Avenue, counts Dillard's, Herberger's and JCPenney among its 105 stores. The restored historic downtown, with a lighted riverfront nearby, also offers distinctive shopping opportunities. Montana Antique Mall, 331 W. Railroad St., has four floors of dealers in the red-bricked Hotel Montana building, which was built in 1890.

GARNET GHOST TOWN, I-90 e. to exit 109 (Bonner), then 23 mi. e. on SR 200, after mile marker 22 turn s. on Garnet Range Rd. and proceed 11 mi. on gravel road to parking lot. Lost in time, this intact mining town still reflects life as the community knew it at the end of the 19th century. Different from typical mining towns of the era, gold miners were encouraged to bring their families. After the 1930s, the town fell into disrepair and the last resident died in 1947. The remaining buildings, including the Wells Hotel, Davey Store and Kelly Saloon, have been preserved.

Time: Allow 2 hours minimum. **Hours:** Daily 9:30-4:30, Memorial Day-Sept. 30. Phone for schedule rest of year. Although the site is open year-round the roads are generally closed due to snow mid-Dec. to early May. **Cost:** $3; free (ages 0-15). **Phone:** (406) 329-3914. 🏕️

HISTORICAL MUSEUM AT FORT MISSOULA, 3400 Captain Rawn Way, is at the center of what was Fort Missoula, established in 1877 at the height of the conflict with the Nez Perce under Chief Joseph. Galleries and exhibits depict the roles of the timber industry, forest management, the fort and early settlement in Missoula County history. Of the 21 historic structures and several original fort buildings that remain, 10 have been restored.

Time: Allow 1 hour minimum. **Hours:** Mon.-Sat. 10-5, Sun. noon-5, Memorial Day weekend-Labor Day; Tues.-Sun. noon-5, rest of year. Closed major holidays except Memorial Day, July 4 and Labor Day. **Cost:** $3; $2 (ages 62+); $1 (students with ID); $10 (family). Guided tours are available by appointment. **Phone:** (406) 728-3476. GT

MISSOULA ART MUSEUM, 335 N. Pattee St., is housed in the old public library and hosts more than 25 rotating exhibitions from local and international artists each year. Artworks reflect the culture of the American West with a focus on contemporary Montana artists. Free 20-minute guided tours are offered on Saturdays. **Time:** Allow 1 hour minimum. **Hours:** Tues.-Sat. 10-5. Closed major holidays. **Cost:** Free. **Phone:** (406) 728-0447. GT

SAVE **ROCKY MOUNTAIN ELK FOUNDATION/ELK COUNTRY VISITOR CENTER** is off I-90 exit 101, then .25 mile n. to 5705 Grant Creek Rd. The visitor center features conservation and hunting heritage exhibits and wildlife displays that include world-record elk. **Hours:** Mon.-Fri. 8-6, Sat.-Sun. 9-6, May-Dec.; Mon.-Fri. 8-5, Sat. 10-5, rest of year. Closed Jan. 1, Thanksgiving and Christmas. **Cost:** Donations. **Phone:** (406) 523-4545.

ST. FRANCIS XAVIER CHURCH is at 420 W. Pine St. Built in 1889, the church is noted for its 144-foot steeple, stained-glass windows and paintings by Brother Joseph Carignano. Visitors may watch a 10-minute video explaining the paintings. **Time:** Allow 30 minutes minimum. **Hours:** Mon.-Sat. 8:30-5. **Cost:** Free. **Phone:** (406) 542-0321.

SMOKEJUMPERS BASE AERIAL FIRE DEPOT is 7 mi. w. to 5765 W. Broadway, next to Johnson-Bell Airport. Displays include dioramas, artifacts, videos, photographs and exhibits about U.S. Forest Service firefighting and the history of smokejumping.

Tour guides lead tours of the smokejumper base and the visitor center and describe in detail the training, preparation and practice of smokejumping as well as challenges in wildland firefighting. Visitors may have a chance to speak with smokejumpers or see them suiting up to go out on a fire. **Hours:** Daily 8:30-5, Memorial Day-Labor Day; by appointment rest of year. Tours are given at 10, 11, 1, 2, 3 and 4. **Cost:** Donations. **Phone:** (406) 329-4934. GT

RECREATIONAL ACTIVITIES
Skiing
- **Montana Snowbowl** is at I-90 Reserve St. exit. Other activities are offered in summer. **Hours:** Skiing available daily, late Dec.-Feb. 28. Hours vary early to late Dec. and Mar.-Apr. (weather permitting); phone ahead to confirm schedule. Closed Christmas. **Phone:** (406) 549-9777.

White-water Rafting
- **10,000 Waves Raft and Kayak Adventures** is at 131 E. Main St. Other activities are offered. **Hours:** Rafting trips are offered daily, mid-Apr. to mid-Oct. Departure times vary; phone ahead. **Phone:** (406) 549-6670 or (800) 537-8315.

CAMPUS INN 406/549-5134

◆◆ **Motel. Rates not provided. Address:** 744 E Broadway 59802 **Location:** I-90 exit 105 (Van Buren St), just s to Broadway, then just w. **Facility:** 78 units, some kitchens. 2 stories (no elevator), interior/exterior corridors. **Parking:** winter plug-ins. **Pool(s):** heated indoor. **Activities:** hot tub, limited exercise equipment. **Guest Services:** coin laundry.

C'MON INN (406)543-4600

◆◆◆ **Hotel** $109-$149 **Address:** 2775 Expo Pkwy 59808 **Location:** I-90 exit 101 (Reserve St), just n. **Facility:** 118 units, some kitchens. 3 stories, interior corridors. **Parking:** winter plug-ins. **Pool(s):** heated indoor. **Activities:** hot tub, game room, exercise room. **Guest Services:** valet and coin laundry.

COMFORT INN - UNIVERSITY (406)549-7600

◆◆◆ **Hotel** $129-$175 **Address:** 1021 E Broadway 59802 **Location:** I-90 exit 105 (Van Buren St), just s, then just e. **Facility:** 95 units. 4 stories, interior corridors. **Parking:** winter plug-ins. **Terms:** check-in 4 pm. **Activities:** exercise room. **Guest Services:** valet and coin laundry, area transportation.

DAYS INN/MISSOULA AIRPORT (406)721-9776

◆◆ **Hotel** $64-$104 **Address:** 8600 Truck Stop Rd 59808 **Location:** I-90 exit 96, just n. Adjacent to truck parking. **Facility:** 70 units, some kitchens. 2 stories (no elevator), interior corridors. **Parking:** winter plug-ins. **Activities:** playground, exercise room. **Guest Services:** coin laundry.

DOUBLETREE BY HILTON HOTEL MISSOULA - EDGEWATER
(406)728-3100

Hotel
$89-$209

AAA Benefit: Members save 5% or more!

Address: 100 Madison St 59802 **Location:** I-90 exit 105 (Van Buren St), just s, then just w on Front St. **Facility:** 171 units. 2-3 stories, interior corridors. **Parking:** winter plug-ins. **Terms:** 1-7 night minimum stay, cancellation fee imposed. **Dining:** Finn & Porter, see separate listing. **Pool(s):** heated outdoor. **Activities:** hot tub, exercise room. **Guest Services:** valet laundry.

ECONO LODGE (406)542-7550

◆◆ **Hotel** $65-$95 **Address:** 4953 N Reserve St 59808 **Location:** I-90 exit 101 (Reserve St), just s. **Facility:** 67 units. 3 stories, interior corridors. **Parking:** winter plug-ins. **Activities:** hot tub. **Guest Services:** coin laundry.

GUESTHOUSE INN & SUITES - MISSOULA 406/251-2665

◆◆ **Hotel. Rates not provided. Address:** 3803 Brooks St 59804 **Location:** I-90 exit 101 (Reserve St), 5 mi s to Brooks St, then just w. **Facility:** 80 units. 3 stories, interior corridors. **Parking:** winter plug-ins. **Activities:** limited exercise equipment. **Guest Services:** valet and coin laundry.

HAMPTON INN (406)549-1800

Hotel
$99-$189

AAA Benefit: Members save up to 10%!

Address: 4805 N Reserve St 59808 **Location:** I-90 exit 101 (Reserve St), just s. **Facility:** 61 units. 4 stories, interior corridors. **Parking:** winter plug-ins. **Terms:** 1-7 night minimum stay, cancellation fee imposed. **Pool(s):** heated indoor. **Activities:** hot tub, exercise room. **Guest Services:** valet and coin laundry, area transportation. **Featured Amenity:** continental breakfast.

HILTON GARDEN INN MISSOULA AND MISSOULA CONFERENCE CENTER (406)532-5300

◆◆◆ **Hotel** $109-$259 **Address:** 3720 N Reserve St 59808 **Location:** I-90 exit 101 (Reserve St), just s. **Facility:** 146 units. 6 stories, interior corridors. **Parking:** winter plug-ins. **Terms:**

AAA Benefit: Members save up to 10%!

1-7 night minimum stay, cancellation fee imposed. **Dining:** Blue Canyon Kitchen & Tavern, see separate listing. **Pool(s):** heated indoor. **Activities:** hot tub, exercise room. **Guest Services:** valet and coin laundry.

HOLIDAY INN EXPRESS & SUITES 406/830-3100

◆◆◆ **Hotel. Rates not provided. Address:** 150 Expressway Blvd 59808 **Location:** I-90 exit 101 (Reserve St), just s. **Facility:** 82 units. 4 stories, interior corridors. **Parking:** winter plug-ins. **Amenities:** *Some:* video games. **Pool(s):** heated indoor. **Activities:** hot tub, game room, exercise room. **Guest Services:** valet and coin laundry.

HOLIDAY INN MISSOULA-DOWNTOWN AT THE PARK
(406)721-8550

Hotel
$99-$209

Address: 200 S Pattee St 59802 **Location:** I-90 exit 104 (Orange St), 0.5 mi s to Broadway, just e to Pattee St, then just s. **Facility:** 200 units. 3 stories, interior corridors. **Parking:** winter plug-ins. **Terms:** check-in 4 pm, cancellation fee imposed. **Pool(s):** heated indoor. **Activities:** sauna, hot tub, exercise room. **Guest Services:** valet laundry, area transportation.

LA QUINTA INN MISSOULA (406)549-9000

◆◆ **Hotel** $75-$295 **Address:** 5059 N Reserve St 59808 **Location:** I-90 exit 101 (Reserve St), just s. **Facility:** 80 units. 3 stories, interior corridors. **Parking:** winter plug-ins. **Pool(s):** heated indoor. **Activities:** hot tub, exercise room. **Guest Services:** valet and coin laundry.

MY PLACE HOTEL (406)926-1001

◆◆ **Hotel** $65-$130 **Address:** 2952 Expo Pkwy 59808 **Location:** I-90 exit 101 (Reserve St), just n. **Facility:** 64 efficiencies. 3 stories, interior corridors. **Parking:** winter plug-ins. **Guest Services:** valet and coin laundry.

QUALITY INN & SUITES-MISSOULA   (406)542-0888

WWWW **Hotel** $80-$190 **Address:** 4545 N Reserve St 59808 **Location:** I-90 exit 101 (Reserve St), 0.7 mi s. **Facility:** 52 units. 2 stories (no elevator), interior corridors. **Parking:** winter plug-ins. **Amenities:** safes. **Pool(s):** heated indoor. **Activities:** hot tub. **Guest Services:** complimentary laundry.

RED LION INN   (406)728-3300

WWW **Motel** $89-$199 **Address:** 700 W Broadway 59802 **Location:** I-90 exit 104 (Orange St), just s, then just w. **Facility:** 76 units. 2 stories (no elevator), exterior corridors. **Parking:** winter plug-ins. **Terms:** cancellation fee imposed. **Pool(s):** heated outdoor. **Activities:** hot tub, exercise room. **Guest Services:** valet and coin laundry.

RUBY'S INN & CONVENTION CENTER   (406)721-0990

WWW
Hotel
$79-$125

Address: 4825 N Reserve St 59808 **Location:** I-90 exit 101 (Reserve St), just s. **Facility:** 124 units, some kitchens. 2 stories, interior/exterior corridors. **Parking:** winter plug-ins. **Terms:** 7 day cancellation notice-fee imposed. **Pool(s):** heated outdoor. **Activities:** sauna, hot tub, exercise room. **Guest Services:** valet and coin laundry. **Featured Amenity:** full hot breakfast.

SLEEP INN BY CHOICE HOTELS   (406)543-5883

WW **Hotel** $79-$169 **Address:** 3425 Dore Ln 59801 **Location:** I-90 exit 101 (Reserve St), 5 mi s, then just e on Brooks St. **Facility:** 59 units. 3 stories, interior corridors. **Parking:** winter plug-ins. **Pool(s):** heated indoor. **Activities:** hot tub.

STAYBRIDGE SUITES   (406)830-3900

WWW **Extended Stay Hotel** $99-$299 **Address:** 120 Expressway Blvd 59808 **Location:** I-90 exit 101 (Reserve St), just s. **Facility:** 101 units, some two bedrooms, efficiencies and kitchens. 4 stories, interior corridors. **Terms:** check-in 4 pm. **Pool(s):** heated indoor. **Activities:** hot tub, exercise room. **Guest Services:** complimentary and valet laundry.

STONECREEK LODGE   (406)541-3600

WWW **Extended Stay Hotel** $91-$189 **Address:** 5145 Airway Blvd 59808 **Location:** I-90 exit 99 (Airway Blvd), just s. **Facility:** 101 units, some efficiencies. 3 stories, interior corridors. **Parking:** winter plug-ins. **Terms:** cancellation fee imposed, resort fee. **Pool(s):** heated indoor. **Activities:** hot tub, exercise room. **Guest Services:** valet and coin laundry, area transportation.

SUPER 8-BROOKS ST   (406)251-2255

WW **Hotel** $78-$87 **Address:** 3901 Brooks St 59804 **Location:** I-90 exit 101 (Reserve St), 5 mi s to Brooks St, then just w. **Facility:** 103 units. 3 stories (no elevator), interior corridors. **Parking:** winter plug-ins. **Guest Services:** coin laundry.

SUPER 8-RESERVE ST   (406)549-1199

WW **Hotel** $73-$137 **Address:** 4703 N Reserve St 59808 **Location:** I-90 exit 101 (Reserve St), 0.4 mi s. **Facility:** 58 units. 3 stories, interior corridors. **Parking:** winter plug-ins. **Terms:** cancellation fee imposed. **Guest Services:** coin laundry.

TOWNEPLACE SUITES BY MARRIOTT MISSOULA   (406)721-6000

WWW **Extended Stay Hotel** $88-$193

AAA Benefit: Members save 5% or more!

Address: 3055 Stockyard Rd 59808 **Location:** I-90 exit 101, 0.3 mi s on N Reserve St, then 0.3 mi e. **Facility:** 90 units, some two bedrooms, efficiencies and kitchens. 4 stories, interior corridors. **Terms:** check-in 4 pm. **Pool(s):** heated outdoor. **Activities:** hot tub, exercise room. **Guest Services:** valet and coin laundry.

WINGATE BY WYNDHAM   (406)541-8000

WWW
Hotel
$99-$195

Address: 5252 Airway Blvd 59808 **Location:** I-90 exit 99 (Airway Blvd), just s to E Harrier Dr. **Facility:** 100 units. 3 stories, interior corridors. **Parking:** winter plug-ins. **Terms:** check-in 4 pm. **Amenities:** safes. **Pool(s):** heated indoor. **Activities:** hot tub, exercise room. **Guest Services:** valet and coin laundry, area transportation. **Featured Amenity:** breakfast buffet.

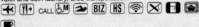

WHERE TO EAT

BAGELS ON BROADWAY   406/728-8900

W Deli. Quick Serve. $3-$9 **AAA Inspector Notes:** Authentic New York-style bagels and other baked goods are offered. Eat in or take out. Great coffee beverages also are available. **Address:** 223 W Broadway 59802 **Location:** I-90 exit 104 (Orange St), just s, then just e; downtown; across from courthouse. **Parking:** street only.

BIGA PIZZA   406/728-2579

WW Pizza Natural/Organic. Casual Dining. $5-$19 **AAA Inspector Notes:** Here's a recipe for success: Jersey-born, bakes in a brick oven, uses organic/local ingredients and loves to eat. What do you get? A man who conjures up awesome pizza with signature combos such as house-made fennel marmalade, local bacon, Gouda cheese, mozzarella, garlic and olive oil. Sandwiches on homemade bread, salads and calzones also are offered and are just as creative. **Features:** beer & wine, patio dining. **Address:** 241 W Main St 59802 **Location:** Between Ryman and Woody sts; downtown. **Parking:** street only.

BLUE CANYON KITCHEN & TAVERN   406/541-2583

WWW American. Casual Dining. $12-$50 **AAA Inspector Notes:** This casual restaurant is definitely upscale "cowboy chic," constructed of large peeled log beams and braces. The walls are decorated with the ubiquitous Montana elk head mounts, and antler chandeliers light the dining room. The chairs are unpeeled, small log frames with upholstered seats and backs, and the booths and benches are all finely upholstered. Ninety-eight percent of all the food coming out of the kitchen is made from scratch, and the in-house pastry chef produces all desserts. **Features:** full bar, patio dining, happy hour. **Address:** 32720 N Reserve St 59808 **Location:** I-90 exit 101 (Reserve St), just s; in Hilton Garden Inn Missoula and Missoula Conference Center.

THE BROADWAY BAR, GRILL & CASINO
406/543-5678

WWW American. Casual Dining. $9-$18 **AAA Inspector Notes:** Alongside the Inn on Broadway, this restaurant has a large TV screen as well as smaller TVs positioned to enable diners in any seat to have a view. Sports is the watchword here. There is a large choice of snack foods, appetizers and finger foods, as well as full meals. Patrons meet, eat and cheer for their favorite teams. **Features:** full bar, patio dining, happy hour. **Address:** 1609 W Broadway 59808 **Location:** I-90 exit 104 (Orange St), 0.5 mi w, then 1 mi w; in Broadway Inn Conference Center. D CALL &M

CATALYST
406/542-1337

WW American. Casual Dining. $6-$11 **AAA Inspector Notes:** The menu choices change practically daily and utilize local produce when available. Fresh, creatively prepared homemade soups, sandwiches and salads are among the options, as are made-from-scratch cookies for dessert. You may want to visit the espresso bar. **Address:** 111 N Higgins Ave 59802 **Location:** Between Front and Main sts; downtown. **Parking:** street only. B L

CHINA GARDEN
406/721-1785

WWW Chinese. Casual Dining. $9-$20 **AAA Inspector Notes:** In a small strip shopping center, this established, family-run restaurant serves authentic traditional Cantonese dishes and some Szechuan menu items. **Features:** beer & wine. **Address:** 2100 Stephens Ave 59801 **Location:** I-90 exit 104 (Orange St), 2.5 mi s to Stephens Ave; in Stephens Center. **Parking:** on-site and street. L D

CIAO MAMBO
406/543-0377

WWW Italian. Casual Dining. $9-$30 **AAA Inspector Notes:** Just like its sister restaurants, this family-owned location serves traditional and inventive dishes with a mambo twist. The marinara, with slivers of garlic, is fragrant and delicious. Have a seat at the counter and watch the chefs hand toss your pizza. Modern and contemporary décor surrounds guests adjacent to the open kitchen. **Features:** beer & wine. **Reservations:** suggested. **Address:** 541 S Higgins Ave 59801 **Location:** Jct S 4th St W, s of bridge; downtown. **Parking:** street only. D

THE DEPOT
406/728-7007

WW American. Casual Dining. $12-$39 **AAA Inspector Notes:** Historic. This historic railroad hotel offers casual dining either in the pub or the dining room and features fresh seafood, hand-cut steak, pasta and choice prime rib. The atmosphere is bustling and busy and the service prompt. Patio seating is available in season. The restaurant is just off the downtown area and is close to the railroad tracks. Seafood selections such as lobster and crab legs offer some variety. **Features:** full bar, patio dining. **Reservations:** suggested. **Address:** 201 W Railroad St 59802 **Location:** I-90 exit 104 (Orange St), just s, e on Spruce St, then n on Ryman St. D CALL &M

EL CAZADOR
406/728-3657

WWW Mexican. Casual Dining. $7-$15 **AAA Inspector Notes:** Brightly lit with colorful art-glass light shades, this convenient family-owned downtown restaurant has big windows perfect for people-watching. The freshly made salsa comes in a small glass pitcher to go with the hot chips. The wide variety of Mexican dishes is served by a very friendly staff. **Features:** beer & wine. **Address:** 101 S Higgins Ave 59801 **Location:** Downtown. **Parking:** street only. L D CALL &M

FINN & PORTER
406/542-4660

WWW American. Fine Dining. $8-$40 **AAA Inspector Notes:** Guests can dine on prime beef, fresh seafood and daily specials in the sleek, modern dining room, which overlooks the Clark Fork River. Those in the mood for a lighter meal might try a specialty pizza from the wood-fired oven. **Features:** full bar, patio dining, Sunday brunch, happy hour. **Reservations:** suggested. **Address:** 100 Madison St 59802 **Location:** I-90 exit 105 (Van Buren St), just s, then just w on Front St; in DoubleTree by Hilton Hotel Missoula - Edgewater. B L D CALL &M

IRON HORSE BREW PUB
406/728-8866

WW American. Casual Dining. $10-$18 **AAA Inspector Notes:** This popular, lively watering hole serves a large selection of snacks, finger food and sandwiches. Enjoy their many specialty drinks, premium liquors and wide array of bottled and draft beers. During summer months, the deck is the place to be. **Features:** full bar, patio dining, happy hour. **Address:** 501 N Higgins Ave 59802 **Location:** Downtown. L D CALL &M

IZA ASIAN RESTAURANT
406/830-3237

WWW Asian. Casual Dining. $9-$17 **AAA Inspector Notes:** Authentic dishes from Korea, India, Malaysia, Japan, Indonesia and Thailand are offered. For the uninitiated, the staff will explain all ingredients and recommend various condiments for each plate. The Asian theme of the restaurant is carried through to the clean lines of the décor; bamboo floors, wall accents and live plants complete the look. There's even traditional Japanese seating with footwells. Lunch values include bento boxes. **Features:** beer & wine, happy hour. **Address:** 529 S Higgins Ave 59801 **Location:** Jct S 4th St W, s of bridge; downtown. **Parking:** street only. L D

THE KEEP
406/728-5132

WWW American. Fine Dining. $27-$40 **AAA Inspector Notes:** Located in a quiet residential area, this restaurant sits high on a hill overlooking the city. The building's design features include a faux castle turret, heavy stone/masonry construction and attractively landscaped grounds. A favorite with the locals, this landmark restaurant is often busy, so consider making reservations. Dine in the elegant dining room or on the terrace (open seasonally). Steaks, seafood and salads are made with flair. **Features:** full bar, patio dining. **Reservations:** suggested. **Address:** 102 Ben Hogan Dr 59803 **Location:** I-90 exit 101 (Reserve St), 5.4 mi s to 39th St, 1.2 mi e to High Park Way, 0.6 mi s to Whitaker Dr, 0.5 mi w to Ben Hogan Dr, then just s. D CALL &M

THE MONTANA CLUB
406/543-3200

WW Regional American. Casual Dining. $8-$30 **AAA Inspector Notes:** Inside a timbered building, this family-friendly eatery serves large portions of regional, house-cut meats and fresh Alaskan seafood. With the large menu, everyone will be happy. The restaurant has an adjacent casino, as well as sister locations in Kalispell, Great Falls and Butte. **Features:** full bar. **Address:** 2620 Brooks St 59801 **Location:** I-90 exit 101 (Reserve St), 5 mi s, then 1 mi e. B L D

THE MONTANA CLUB
406/541-8141

WW Regional American. Casual Dining. $8-$28 **AAA Inspector Notes:** This family-friendly spot with an adjacent casino has sister restaurants in Kalispell, Butte and another in Missoula. The building sports a wood interior, and menu items include fresh Alaskan salmon, halibut and meats cut in house. Portions are plentiful. **Features:** full bar, senior menu, happy hour. **Address:** 4561 N Reserve St 59808 **Location:** I-90 exit 101 (Reserve St), just s. B L D

THE MUSTARD SEED ASIAN CAFE
406/542-7333

WW Asian. Casual Dining. $8-$18 **AAA Inspector Notes:** Located in Southgate Mall with a convenient private entrance, this restaurant serves a blend of Pacific Rim cuisines geared to American tastes. Enjoy a spicy noodle bowl, Thai curry or even an Asian taco. Pick a dessert from the wide selection. **Features:** full bar. **Address:** 2901 Brooks St 59801 **Location:** I-90 exit 101 (Reserve St), 5 mi s, 0.7 mi e, then just n; in Southgate Mall. L D CALL &M

NARA KOREAN BAR-B-QUE & SUSHI
406/327-0731

WW Asian Sushi. Casual Dining. $6-$25 **AAA Inspector Notes:** In a strip mall near major shopping and with easy freeway access, the lively restaurant presents an extensive menu of sushi and tempura, as well as a wide array of Korean specialties. **Features:** beer & wine. **Address:** 3075 N Reserve St, Suite K 59808 **Location:** I-90 exit 101 (Reserve St), 1.4 mi s; in Grant Creek Town Center. L D

PARADISE FALLS RESTAURANT, LOUNGE & CASINO
406/728-3228

♦♦ American. Casual Dining. $8-$20 **AAA Inspector Notes:** A lively sports bar, casino and restaurant featuring a wide array of appetizers, sandwiches and burgers as well as build-your-own pizzas and traditional entrées. **Features:** full bar, patio dining, Sunday brunch, happy hour. **Address:** 3621 Brooks St 59801 **Location:** I-90 exit 101 (Reserve St), 5 mi s, then just e.

B L D

THE PEARL CAFE
406/541-0231

♦♦♦ Regional American. Fine Dining. $20-$38 **AAA Inspector Notes:** *Historic.* Self-described as country-French fare with a city flair, the owner-chef creates such sumptuous savories as rabbit with red-wine-mushroom sauce and Idaho trout. The courses are served in a relaxed manner and the staff is very knowledgeable about the various ingredients that go into each dish. This place started life as a café and bakery, and thank goodness the kitchen never stopped baking its own bread when the bakery in the name was dropped. **Features:** beer & wine. **Address:** 231 E Front St 59802 **Location:** I-90 exit 104 (Orange St), 0.5 mi s, 0.3 mi e on W Broadway, just s on N Pattee St, then just e. **Parking:** street only. D

RED BIRD
406/549-2906

♦♦ American. Fine Dining. $25-$41 **AAA Inspector Notes:** This chef-owned intimate hideaway is known for inventive seasonal cuisine served in quiet, architecturally dramatic surroundings adorned with Art Deco chandeliers. The menu consists of beef, chicken, bison and seafood along with appetizers such as Thai quail satay. Patrons enter through a well-lit alley just off the main downtown street. **Features:** beer & wine. **Reservations:** suggested. **Address:** 111 N Higgins Ave, Suite 100 59802 **Location:** I-90 exit 104 (Orange St), s to Broadway, e to Higgins Ave, then just s; in Florence Building. **Parking:** street only. D CALL &M

SA-WAD-DEE
406/543-9966

♦♦ Thai. Casual Dining. $8-$14 **AAA Inspector Notes:** Popular with locals, this family-run eatery serves authentic cuisine. The posted menu changes daily. **Features:** beer & wine. **Address:** 221 W Broadway St 59802 **Location:** I-90 exit 104 (Orange St), just s, then just e; downtown; across from courthouse. **Parking:** street only. L D

SCOTTY'S TABLE
406/549-2790

♦♦♦ International. Fine Dining. $14-$33 **AAA Inspector Notes:** This stylish bistro serves a mix of Mediterranean, French and shades of rustic Italian dishes. Choices the day I dined here included fried fennel pasta, Moroccan chicken soup, braised short ribs and vegetable polenta. The chef uses local and regional ingredients to make sure each dish is as fresh as possible. **Features:** beer & wine, patio dining, Sunday brunch. **Reservations:** suggested. **Address:** 131 S Higgins Ave, Unit P3 59802 **Location:** Just n of Higgins Ave Bridge; downtown. **Parking:** street only. L D

SEAN KELLY'S, A PUBLIC HOUSE
406/542-1471

♦♦ Irish. Gastropub. $8-$20 **AAA Inspector Notes:** Where the Gaelic and garlic mix, this restaurant has the clubby atmosphere of a traditional Irish pub and food that transcends corned beef and cabbage (although that dish does make it onto the menu). Leave room for the house-made desserts. **Features:** full bar, Sunday brunch. **Address:** 130 W Pine St 59802 **Location:** Downtown; near jct Higgins Ave. **Parking:** street only.

L D CALL &M

SEAN KELLY'S, THE STONE OF ACCORD
406/830-3210

♦♦ Irish. Gastropub. $10-$24 **AAA Inspector Notes:** Where the Gaelic and garlic mix, this restaurant has the clubby atmosphere of a traditional Irish pub and food that transcends corned beef and cabbage (although that dish does make it onto the menu). The menu is the same as at their sister location downtown. Brunch is served on Saturday and Sunday. **Features:** full bar, Sunday brunch. **Address:** 4951 N Reserve St 59801 **Location:** I-90 exit 101 (Reserve St), just s. B L D CALL &M

THE SHACK CAFÉ
406/549-9903

♦♦♦ American. Casual Dining. $7-$22 **AAA Inspector Notes:** Innovative, freshly prepared foods, a multitude of vegetarian dishes, and exceptional breakfast items are hallmarks of this slightly eclectic eatery. You might want to try the burritos at lunchtime or the trout with lemon caper sauce at dinner. Patio seating is available in summer and dinner is only offered Friday through Sunday. **Features:** beer & wine, patio dining, happy hour. **Address:** 222 W Main St 59802 **Location:** Downtown. **Parking:** street only.

B L D 🅐

THE SILK ROAD
406/541-0752

♦♦♦ International Small Plates. Casual Dining. $4-$11 **AAA Inspector Notes:** Just the name of this restaurant conjures up exotic smells and sounds. The owner harkens to a time when friends sat down to an array of appetizers and everyone shared in good food and conversation. The menu is truly global and specializes in using its own global spice blends. The knowledgeable staff expertly recommends wine flights and pairings. **Features:** beer & wine, Sunday brunch. **Address:** 515 S Higgins Ave 59801 **Location:** Jct S 4th St W, s of bridge; downtown. **Parking:** street only. D

SUSHI HANA
406/549-7979

♦ Japanese. Casual Dining. $6-$33 **AAA Inspector Notes:** This casual but stylish restaurant serves sushi, sashimi and teriyaki in a dining room infused with traditional Japanese koto music. Daily lunch and happy hour specials always are a delight to your taste buds. **Features:** beer & wine, happy hour. **Address:** 403 N Higgins Ave 59802 **Location:** Downtown. **Parking:** street only.

L D CALL &M

VIETNAM GRILL
406/721-3410

♦♦ Vietnamese. Casual Dining. $8-$11 **AAA Inspector Notes:** This family-run place has a menu full of homemade street food. I call it tasty comfort food, especially the steaming bowl of fragrant pho (soup) and grilled pork sandwiches. **Address:** 420 N Higgins Ave 59802 **Location:** Jct Pine St; downtown. **Parking:** street only. L D

VIETNAM NOODLE RESTAURANT
406/542-8299

♦♦ Vietnamese. Casual Dining. $8-$15 **AAA Inspector Notes:** In a small strip shopping center, this casual restaurant presents an extensive menu that includes a few Thai choices that are very popular with locals. The restaurant also has a small selection of Asian groceries for sale. **Address:** 2100 Stephens Ave, Suite 103 59801 **Location:** I-90 exit 104 (Orange St), 2.5 mi s to Stephens Ave; in Stephens Center. L D

WHEAT MONTANA BAKERY & DELI
406/327-0900

♦ Breads/Pastries Deli. Family Dining. $6-$12 **AAA Inspector Notes:** Create your own deli sandwich or choose from the favorites. While you're at the counter the many baked goods are sure to tempt. The cinnamon rolls are large; try the caramel or strawberry. **Address:** 2520 S 3rd St W 59804 **Location:** I-90 exit 101 (Reserve St), 3.5 mi s to US 93. B L D

MOIESE (C-2) elev. 2,600'

NATIONAL BISON RANGE is s.w. via SR 212. Up to 400 bison as well as herds of elk, pronghorn antelope, deer and bighorn sheep live on the 18,700-acre range. From mid-May to mid-October the refuge can be explored via a 19-mile self-guiding driving tour on a one-way gravel road. The tour takes about 2 hours. Only portions of the site are open the rest of the year.

Note: Two-wheeled vehicles are not allowed off the paved roads. Trailers and larger motor homes are restricted to the West Loop Drive; check at the visitor center. The gravel and dirt roads present some long climbs and steep downgrades. Visitors must keep their vehicles on the tour road and must remain in or near them. **Hours:** Range open daily dawn-dusk. Visitor center open daily 9-5, mid-May to early Oct.; Mon.-Thurs. 10-2, rest of year. Closed holidays Oct.-May. **Cost:** $5 (per private vehicle). **Phone:** (406) 644-2211.

MONIDA (F-3)

Monida is a former railroad town at the foot of Monida Pass and the Continental Divide. Scenic highway I-15 passes near town, offering views of the Centennial Mountains to the east and the Italian Peaks to the west. The name Monida is derived from the combination of Montana and Idaho.

MONTANA CITY pop. 2,715

ELKHORN MOUNTAIN INN   (406)442-6625
▼ **Hotel** $70-$90 **Address:** 1 Jackson Creek Rd 59634 **Location:** I-15 exit 187 (Montana City), just w. **Facility:** 22 units. 2 stories (no elevator), interior corridors. **Parking:** winter plug-ins. **Guest Services:** valet laundry.

[†↑] CALL [&M] [HS] 🛜 ✕ 🛢 💻 /SOME UNITS 🔊 🖼

WHERE TO EAT

MONTANA CITY GRILL AND SALOON   406/449-8890
▼ ▼ American. Casual Dining. $12-$30 **AAA Inspector Notes:** Specialties of the house include slow-roasted prime rib, fresh seafood, homemade soup, chicken, pasta, charbroiled steak and huckleberry barbecued pork ribs. The atmosphere is casual with some booth seating; service is friendly and prompt. A good selection of microbrews and wines is offered. Breakfast is available on Sundays. **Features:** full bar, senior menu, Sunday brunch, happy hour. **Reservations:** suggested. **Address:** 4 Hwy 518 59634 **Location:** I-15 exit 187 (Montana City), just w. [L] [D]

NEVADA CITY—See Virginia City p. 206.

OVANDO (C-2) pop. 81, elev. 4,100'

RECREATIONAL ACTIVITIES
Hunting
- **Murphy's WTR Outfitters** is at 477 Green Meadow Ln. **Hours:** Hunting trips are offered in fall. Other activities are offered in summer. **Phone:** (406) 824-2471 or (406) 754-2471.

PABLO (C-2) pop. 2,254, elev. 3,085'

Pablo is home to the 1,317,000-acre Flathead Indian Reservation and the headquarters of the Confederated Salish and Kootenai Indian tribes. Approximately 5,000 tribal members live on or near the reservation and manage wildlife and natural resources.

THE PEOPLE'S CENTER is 1 mi. n. of the tribal complex at 56633 US 93. Exhibits focus on the history and culture of the Salish, Kootenai and Pend d'Oreille tribes. Art, photographs, oral histories and crafts are included in the collection. **Hours:** Mon.-Fri. 9-5 (also Sat. 9-5, June-Sept.). Closed major holidays. Phone ahead to confirm schedule. **Cost:** $5; $3 (ages 55+ and students with ID); $10 (family). **Phone:** (406) 675-0160.

PHILIPSBURG (D-2) pop. 820, elev. 5,270'

In the heart of mineral-rich Flint Creek Valley, the town of Philipsburg emerged at the height of a silver-mining boom in 1867 and was named for Philip Deidesheimer, a former Comstock engineer who built the area's first ore processing mill. The mill closed in 1869, marking the first of several mining busts and subsequent booms. The demand for manganese in steel production during World War I fueled a final ore producing period that lasted until the Great Depression.

The historic district, centered on Broadway, contains numerous late 19th- and early 20th-century structures. Outlying abandoned mines and ghost towns also attest to Philipsburg's mining legacy, although very few are still accessible. The surrounding Sapphire and Flint Creek mountain ranges attract a new breed of prospector, the rock hound, in search of gems and minerals.

Philipsburg is midway between Drummond and Anaconda on the Pintler Scenic Highway (SR 1). Broad views of Flint Creek Valley are available near mile markers 28 and 42.

Visit Philipsburg: 204 W. Broadway St., P.O. Box 825, Philipsburg, MT 59858. **Phone:** (406) 859-6726.

GRANITE COUNTY MUSEUM & CULTURAL CENTER is at 135 S. Sansome St. An overview of a miner's life includes a mural depicting above-ground activities, an assay office and a reconstructed cabin. Exhibits include a sample of a real vein as well as tools, an ore car and mining memorabilia. **Hours:** Daily noon-4, Memorial Day-Sept. 30; by appointment rest of year. **Cost:** $4; free (ages 0-11). **Phone:** (406) 859-3020.

THE RANCH AT ROCK CREEK   406/859-6027
[fyi] Not evaluated. **Address:** 79 Carriage House Ln 59858 **Location:** 14 mi w on Rock Creek Rd (SR 348); 5.5 mi s on CR 102 (dirt road). Facilities, services, and décor characterize an upscale property. Find luxury accommodations in a Western setting. The all-inclusive ranch resort set on 6,000 acres offers horseback riding, bowling, a spa and a gourmet restaurant. The fly fishing is worth the trip.

WHERE TO EAT

DOE BROTHERS RESTAURANT   406/859-6676
▼ American. Casual Dining. $6-$13 **AAA Inspector Notes:** Historic. Take a step back and enjoy this historic building dating from 1887. The soda fountain was built in 1920 and is still in use. There is an Italian marble front and other memorabilia from bygone eras. Try a vanilla phosphate or other ice cream treat. **Features:** beer & wine. **Address:** 120 E Broadway 59858 **Location:** Downtown. **Parking:** street only. [L] [D] CALL [&M] [🎵]

POLARIS (E-2) elev. 6,355'

Polaris is the beginning point of the Pioneer Scenic Byway, which stretches for 32 miles to the Wise River and affords glimpses of such wildlife as antelope, deer and hawks. The route passes Crystal Park, a natural crystal mountain where visitors can dig for various crystals. Another stop along the drive is Elkhorn Hot Springs, a hot springs pool. This picturesque road is open until the first snowfall.

POLSON (C-2) pop. 4,488, elev. 2,931'

Polson is in a natural amphitheater at the foot of Flathead Lake. During May and June water pours through the 200- to 500-foot perpendicular walls of the Flathead River Gorge at the rate of 500,000 gallons per second. Legend has it that Paul Bunyan dug the channel connecting the river and the lake.

Polson Area Chamber of Commerce: 418 Main St., Polson, MT 59860. **Phone:** (406) 883-5969.

MIRACLE OF AMERICA MUSEUM is 2 mi. s. on US 93 to 36094 Memory Ln. This potpourri of Americana includes vintage automobiles, motorcycles, bicycles, jets, trains, tractors, steam engines and a 65-foot logging boat. Visitors also can see dolls and toys, historic logging and pioneer items, Native American artifacts, antique musical instruments and sheet music, and military collectibles. A pioneer village with more than 40 walk-in buildings and the Montana Fiddlers Hall of Fame also are on the grounds. Live History Days are held over 2 days in July.

Hours: Daily 8-8, June-Aug.; Mon.-Sat. 8-5, Sun. 1:30-5, rest of year. Closed Easter and Christmas. **Cost:** $6; $3 (ages 3-12). **Phone:** (406) 883-6804.

POLSON-FLATHEAD HISTORICAL MUSEUM is at 708 Main St. Exhibits preserve the Native American and pioneer heritage of the surrounding area. Included are farm machinery, Native American artifacts, a chuck wagon, a stagecoach and a restored 1881 trading post. Marionettes created by puppeteer Blanche Harding are featured in an exhibit about the Lewis and Clark expedition. A model railroad is displayed. **Hours:** Mon.-Sat. 10-4, June-Sept. **Cost:** $5; free (ages 0-12). **Phone:** (406) 883-3049.

THE SHADOW LAKE CRUISES is on US 93E. Ninety-minute narrated tours of scenic Flathead Lake, the largest natural freshwater lake west of the Mississippi, are offered. Passengers enjoy views of the majestic Mission Mountains as well as 2,163-acre Wild Horse Island, inhabited by such wildlife as bighorn sheep, mule deer and wild horses Two-hour dinner cruises, 2- and 4-hour brunch cruises, 2-hour wine-tasting cruises and fireworks cruises also are offered.

Hours: Ninety-minute tour requires a minimum of six people and departs Fri.-Sun. at 4, mid-June to mid-Sept. Dinner cruises depart Thurs. and Sun. at 7. Phone for information about brunch, wine-tasting

and fireworks tours. **Cost:** Ninety-minute tour $15; free (ages 0-5). Dinner cruise $30. Reservations are recommended. **Phone:** (406) 883-3636.

RECREATIONAL ACTIVITIES

White-water Rafting

- **Flathead Raft Co.** is at 50362 S. US 93. Other activities are available. **Hours:** Rafting trips are offered daily, Memorial Day-early Sept. Departure times vary; phone ahead. **Phone:** (406) 883-5838 or (800) 654-4359.

AMERICAS BEST VALUE PORT POLSON INN   (406)883-5385

WWWW **Motel** $69-$160 **Address:** 49825 US Hwy 93 E 59860 **Location:** Just s of downtown. **Facility:** 43 units, some efficiencies and kitchens. 2 stories (no elevator), interior/exterior corridors. **Parking:** winter plug-ins. **Terms:** cancellation fee imposed. **Guest Services:** coin laundry.

KWATAQNUK RESORT AND CASINO   (406)883-3636

WWWW
Hotel
$95-$186

Address: 49708 US Hwy 93 E 59860 **Location:** Waterfront. Just s of downtown. **Facility:** 106 units. 2-3 stories, interior corridors. **Terms:** 3 day cancellation notice-fee imposed. resort fee. **Pool(s):** heated indoor. **Activities:** hot tub, marina. **Guest Services:** valet laundry. **Featured Amenity:** continental breakfast.

WHERE TO EAT

CHERRIES BBQ PIT   406/571-2227

W Barbecue. Quick Serve. $8-$25 **AAA Inspector Notes:** This is a small operator-owned joint without high-brow attitude or pretension. But it does have plenty of local patrons and a strong reputation for its slow-smoked meats. Pork ribs, chicken, pulled pork and beef brisket are served up with sides like coleslaw, baked beans, spiral-cut potato chips and potato salad, all made fresh daily. There are a variety of sauces to choose from such as jalapeño honey, classic mild or bold sweet sauces, Carolina mustard, Jack Daniel's, Buffalo and Sriracha. **Features:** patio dining. **Address:** 105 2nd St E 59860 **Location:** Just s; downtown. **Parking:** on-site and street.

HOT SPOT THAI CAFE   406/883-4444

W Thai. Casual Dining. $7-$18 **AAA Inspector Notes:** The casual restaurant serves Americanized dishes, though with authentic spices. A climb up the stairs to the second floor leads to dining with views of Flathead Lake. **Address:** 50440 US Hwy 93 E 59860 **Location:** Just s of downtown.

POMPEYS PILLAR NATIONAL MONUMENT (D-6)

Pompeys Pillar National Monument is 1 mi. n. of Pompeys Pillar off I-94 exit 23. William Clark carved his name on this huge sandstone formation in 1806; it is the only physical evidence of the Lewis and Clark expedition through the area. Clark named the rock after guides Charbonneau and Sacagawea's son, Baptiste, whom he nicknamed Pomp. The pillar also bears Native American pictographs and the names of early trappers, soldiers and settlers. Interpretive tours are available upon request at the visitor center.

Daily 9-6, early May-Sept. 30. The site is accessible the rest of the year only by a half-mile walk from a parking area. Admission $7 (per private vehicle). Phone (406) 875-2400 for the visitor center, or (406) 896-5013 for the Bureau of Land Management.

PRAY pop. 681

CHICO HOT SPRINGS LODGE   406/333-4933

[fyi] **Hotel** Did not meet all AAA rating requirements for locking devices in some guest rooms at time of last evaluation on 05/19/2015. **Address:** 1 Old Chico Rd 59065 **Location:** I-90 exit 333, 23 mi s on US 89, 1.2 mi e on Murphy Ln (flashing yellow light), 0.5 mi n on E River Rd, then 1 mi e. Facilities, services, and décor characterize an economy property.

WHERE TO EAT

CHICO HOT SPRINGS RESTAURANT   406/333-4933

▼▼▼ American. Fine Dining. $9-$55 **AAA Inspector Notes:** Historic. The kitchen consistently delivers on quality and creativity with dishes like wild Alaskan king salmon or tender, local rack of lamb with homemade basil jelly while retaining signature dishes such as the beef Wellington and the orange flambé dessert. The setting, in the historic Chico Hot Springs Lodge, is a relaxing throwback to a time without TVs and smart phones. A breakfast buffet also is offered. **Features:** full bar. **Reservations:** suggested. **Address:** 1 Old Chico Rd 59065 **Location:** I-90 exit 333, 23 mi s on US 89, 1.2 mi e on Murphy Ln (flashing yellow light), 0.5 mi n on E River Rd, then 1 mi e; in Chico Hot Springs Lodge. [B] [D]

PRYOR (E-5) pop. 618, elev. 4,065'

CHIEF PLENTY COUPS STATE PARK is 1 mi. w. off SR 416 following signs to 1 Edgar/Pryor Rd. A museum features relics and interpretive displays that describe Crow Indian culture and Chief Plenty Coups, the tribe's last traditional chief. The Crow leader is buried near his home at nearby Medicine Spring.

Fishing opportunities are available. Day of Honor, an event featuring speakers and cultural activities, takes place Labor Day weekend. **Time:** Allow 1 hour minimum. **Hours:** Park open daily 8-8, mid-May to late Sept.; Wed.-Sun. 8-5, rest of year. Visitor center open daily 10-5, mid-May to late Sept.; Wed.-Sun. 10-5, rest of year. Phone ahead to confirm schedule. **Cost:** $6 (nonresidents per private vehicle); $4 (nonresidents arriving by other means); free (Montana residents with ID). **Phone:** (406) 252-1289.

RED LODGE (F-5) pop. 2,125, elev. 5,548'
• Hotels p. 200 • Restaurants p. 200
• Hotels & Restaurants map & index p. 324
• Part of Yellowstone National Park area — see map p. 316

At the base of the Beartooth Mountains, Red Lodge is an all-year resort town. Winter sports include downhill and cross-country skiing, while summer pursuits range from trout fishing and boating to water skiing on Cooney Reservoir (see Recreation Areas Chart).

Local legend attributes the town's name to a tribe of Crow Indians called the Red Lodge Clan, who covered their tepees with the local red clay. Coal-mining operations later drew many Europeans to the area.

The Carbon County Arts Guild & Depot Gallery, 11 W. Eighth St., displays the works of local and regional artists in the 1889 Northern Pacific Depot building; phone (406) 446-1370. A red Northern Pacific caboose sits on a section of restored track adjacent to the depot.

Red Lodge Area Chamber of Commerce and Visitors Center: 701 N. Broadway, P.O. Box 988, Red Lodge, MT 59068. **Phone:** (406) 446-1718.

Self-guiding tours: A guide distributed by the chamber of commerce features a walking tour of the historic district and includes buildings that once served as schools, jails, courthouses, banks and hospitals.

▼GEM **BEARTOOTH SCENIC HIGHWAY** is US 212 from Red Lodge to the northeastern entrance of Yellowstone National Park via Cooke City. The Native Americans called the original Beartooth Pass the "trail above the eagles." This 64-mile road begins at 5,650 feet and rises to the Beartooth Plateau via a series of switchbacks.

After cresting the plateau at an elevation of almost 11,000 feet, where an unobstructed view of more than 75 miles is possible, the road winds past snowfields, small lakes and fields of flowers. Finally it descends into a dense pine forest, passing tumbling waterfalls and streams interspersed with occasional jagged peaks.

Many scenic overlooks have been constructed. Even in mid-summer, cool temperatures can be expected at higher elevations; a jacket or sweater is recommended. **Time:** Allow 3 hours minimum. **Hours:** The two-lane highway is usually open Memorial Day to mid-Oct. Phone ahead to confirm schedule. **Phone:** (800) 226-7623.

CARBON COUNTY HISTORICAL SOCIETY & MUSEUM is at 224 N. Broadway Ave. This local history museum occupies two floors of the 1909 Labor Temple, a three-story red brick building in Red Lodge's historic business district. Among the exhibits on the museum's main floor are rodeo memorabilia, guns, Native American artifacts and a stagecoach.

Simulated coal and hard rock mines on the lower level help visitors imagine what working in the area's coal mines was like at the turn of the 20th century. **Time:** Allow 1 hour minimum. **Hours:** Mon.-Sat. 10-5, Sun. 11-3, Memorial Day-late Sept.; Thurs.-Sat. 11-4, rest of year. **Cost:** $5; $3 (ages 6-17); $12 (family, two adults and children ages 6-17 in the same household). **Phone:** (406) 446-3667.

(See map & index p. 324.)

RECREATIONAL ACTIVITIES

Fishing

- **Fly Fishing Only Adventures** offers fishing trips on the Yellowstone River. **Hours:** Trips are available daily year-round. Departure times vary; phone ahead. **Phone:** (406) 446-3819 or (406) 425-1761.

Skiing

- **Red Lodge Mountain Resort** is 6 mi. w. to 305 Ski Run Rd. **Hours:** Skiing available daily 9-4, late Nov.-early Apr. **Phone:** (406) 446-2610 or (800) 444-8977.

White-water Rafting

- SAVE **Adventure Whitewater Inc.** meets passengers on SR 78 at the red barn 1 mi. n. of Absarokee. Other activities are offered. **Hours:** Rafting trips daily at 10, 2 and 5:30, Memorial Day weekend-Labor Day. **Phone:** (406) 446-3061 or (800) 897-3061.

COMFORT INN OF RED LODGE (406)446-4469 **18**

Hotel $104-$220 **Address:** 612 N Broadway Ave 59068 **Location:** Jct US 212 and SR 78, north entrance. **Facility:** 55 units. 2 stories (no elevator), interior corridors. **Parking:** winter plug-ins. **Terms:** resort fee. **Pool(s):** heated indoor. **Activities:** hot tub, limited exercise equipment. **Guest Services:** coin laundry.

CALL 🛗 🏊 BIZ 🛜 ✕ 🛏 🖥 🖨 / SOME UNITS 🔒🛏

THE POLLARD 406/446-0001 **19**

Historic Hotel. Rates not provided. **Address:** 2 N Broadway Ave 59068 **Location:** US 212; downtown. **Facility:** A history room is among the common spaces at this 1893 inn. All guest rooms are supplied with robes and some overlook the courtyard area. If you like antiques and old photos, this is the spot for you. 39 units. 3 stories, interior corridors. **Terms:** check-in 4 pm. **Dining:** The Dining Room at The Pollard, The Pub at the Pollard, see separate listings. **Activities:** sauna, exercise room.

🍴 CALL 🛗 BIZ 🛜 ✕ / SOME UNITS 🖨

ROCK CREEK RESORT (406)446-1111 **21**

Resort Hotel
$130-$390

Address: 6380 US Hwy 212 S 59068 **Location:** 5.8 mi s. Adjacent to a wilderness area. **Facility:** This hotel offers townhouse, condominium and standard lodgings. Only the main hotel building has an elevator. Most units have balconies and many overlook the rushing waters of Rock Creek. 87 units, some three bedrooms, efficiencies, kitchens, cabins and condominiums. 1-3 stories, interior/exterior corridors. **Terms:** 15 day cancellation notice-fee imposed, resort fee. **Amenities:** Some: safes. **Dining:** Old Piney Dell, see separate listing. **Pool(s):** heated indoor. **Activities:** sauna, hot tub, fishing, bicycles, playground, exercise room. **Guest Services:** coin laundry. **Featured Amenity:** continental breakfast.

SAVE 🍴 CALL 🛗 🏊 BIZ 🛜 ✕ 🅰🄲 🖨 / SOME UNITS 🔒🛏 🛏 🖨

YODELER MOTEL (406)446-1435 **20**

Historic Motel $72-$165 **Address:** 601 S Broadway Ave 59068 **Location:** Just s on US 212. **Facility:** Scandinavian-style décor enhances this motel. Steam baths are in 18 rooms. Lower and upper levels are accessible by short flights of stairs. No two rooms are the same. Ski wax rooms are available. 23 units, some two bedrooms and kitchens. 2 stories (no elevator), exterior corridors. **Parking:** winter plug-ins. **Terms:** cancellation fee imposed, resort fee. **Activities:** hot tub.

📶 HS 🛜 ✕ 🛏 🖥 🖨 / SOME UNITS 🔒🛏 🅰🄲

BOGART'S 406-1784 **19**

American. Casual Dining. $9-$24 **AAA Inspector Notes:** This local favorite offers large portions of specialty pizza, Mexican dishes, charbroiled burgers and standard American cuisine amid Humphrey Bogart memorabilia, wild-animal busts and varied antiques. **Features:** full bar, happy hour. **Address:** 11 S Broadway Ave 59068 **Location:** City Center. **Parking:** street only. L D

BRIDGE CREEK BACKCOUNTRY KITCHEN & WINE BAR 406/446-9900 **21**

American. Casual Dining. $10-$34 **AAA Inspector Notes:** The restaurant is a 'must-go' spot for visitors to the town. Extensive, award-winning wine choices complement the chef's creative preparations. A menu staple is the 'famous for 17 years' clam chowder. There is something for everyone - pizza, burgers, salads, steak, seafood. All are made fresh using local ingredients. **Reservations:** suggested. **Address:** 116 S Broadway Ave 59068 **Location:** Center. **Parking:** street only. L D CALL 🛗

CARBON COUNTY STEAKHOUSE 406/446-4025 **20**

Steak. Casual Dining. $12-$36 **AAA Inspector Notes:** The in-house-cut organic steaks are the star attraction. The comfortable setting offers some al fresco dining in season. Lunch is served from Memorial Day to Labor Day. **Features:** full bar, patio dining, Sunday brunch. **Reservations:** suggested. **Address:** 121 S Broadway Ave 59068 **Location:** Center; in historic district. **Parking:** on-site and street. D

CHINA GARDEN 406/446-9909 **23**

Chinese. Casual Dining. $8-$17 **AAA Inspector Notes:** Tasty food is served in a casual setting. The décor is contemporary rather than traditional. **Address:** 202 S Broadway Ave 59068 **Location:** Center. **Parking:** street only. L D

THE DINING ROOM AT THE POLLARD 406/446-0001 **17**

Regional American. Casual Dining. $10-$36 **AAA Inspector Notes:** *Historic.* You may find ribs or salmon on the menu. The intimate dining room is in a historic hotel. The décor includes Western art on the walls, wood accents and seats upholstered in leather. It's open weekends only in the winter. **Features:** full bar, patio dining. **Address:** 2 N Broadway Ave 59068 **Location:** US 212; downtown; in The Pollard. **Parking:** on-site and street.

B D CALL 🛗

OLD PINEY DELL 406/446-1196 **24**

American. Casual Dining. $16-$32 **AAA Inspector Notes:** Steak, seafood, veal and pasta entrées head up the list of eclectic selections served in this rustic 1920s log cabin next to Rock Creek. Try the house-smoked trout for starters. **Features:** full bar, Sunday brunch. **Reservations:** suggested. **Address:** 6380 US Hwy 212 S 59068 **Location:** 5.8 mi s; in Rock Creek Resort.

D 🅰🄲

THE PUB AT THE POLLARD 406/446-0001 **18**

American. Gastropub. $7-$20 **AAA Inspector Notes:** *Historic.* This local pub is known to have a variety of musicians play. The menu includes Gouda and bacon mac 'n cheese, a lobster BLT and elk nachos. **Features:** full bar, happy hour. **Address:** 2 N Broadway Ave 59068 **Location:** US 212; downtown; in The Pollard. **Parking:** on-site and street. D CALL 🛗

RED LODGE PIZZA CO. 406/446-3333 **22**

Pizza. Family Dining. $9-$25 **AAA Inspector Notes:** Fresh ingredients line the nightly salad bar, and varied items go into creative pizzas or calzones made with homemade dough. Diners can get single slices or whole pies. A pizza bar is set up Monday and Tuesday. **Features:** full bar. **Address:** 115 S Broadway Ave 59068 **Location:** Center; in historic district. **Parking:** on-site and street.

L D CALL 🛗

(See map & index p. 324.)

RED BOX CAR DRIVE-IN
406/446-2152

fyi Not evaluated. Popular with the locals, the summer drive-in is known for its burgers, hot dogs and shakes. I suggest an order of onion rings, they are large and sweet. Guests can relax on the patio next to Rock Creek. **Address:** 1300 S Broadway Ave 59068 **Location:** S on US 212.

RONAN (C-2) pop. 1,871

NINEPIPE AND PABLO NATIONAL WILDLIFE REFUGES are 4 mi. s. of Ronan off US 93, and 3 mi. n. of Pablo off US 93 then 1 mi. w. on Reservoir Rd., respectively. Each refuge covers more than 2,000 acres. Primarily of interest to bird-watchers, these areas are inhabited by ducks, geese and other water birds. A cooperative state, federal and tribal wildlife-viewing area is at Ninepipe National Wildlife Refuge.

Hours: Refuges are open daily dawn-dusk. Portions of Ninepipe are closed during hunting season (late Sept.-early Jan.) and nesting season (Mar. 1-July 15). The south and west sides of Pablo are closed to public use; the entire refuge is closed during hunting season. **Cost:** Free. **Phone:** (406) 644-2211.

STARLITE MOTEL
406/676-7000

Motel. Rates not provided. **Address:** 18 Main St SW 59864 **Location:** Just w of jct US 93 and Main St. **Facility:** 15 units. 2 stories (no elevator), exterior corridors. **Parking:** winter plug-ins.

ROUNDUP (D-5) pop. 1,788, elev. 3,226'

Renowned for the natural geographical design that made it ideal for herding livestock, Roundup features mountainous scenery and tree-lined streets. Fishing opportunities abound in the Musselshell River and at nearby Fort Peck Reservoir and Deadman's Basin.

MUSSELSHELL VALLEY HISTORICAL MUSEUM, 524 First St. W., houses a variety of items detailing Roundup's history, including fossils, Native American artifacts and paintings. Changing exhibits are featured in summer. On the grounds are a smithy, a print shop, a restored 1932 Pietenpol airplane and the 1884 NF Ranch house. **Hours:** Daily 1-5, May-Sept. **Cost:** Donations. **Phone:** (406) 323-1525 or (406) 323-1662.

BUSY BEE RESTAURANT & GIFT SHOP
406/323-2204

American
Casual Dining
$7-$23

AAA Inspector Notes: Both the Honeycomb and Fireside dining rooms at this restaurant are well suited to family dining. Selections include crisp chicken, tender beer-battered shrimp and homemade pie. Prime rib is offered weekend evenings. The 1950s-style diner area also is a fun place to dine. **Features:** beer & wine. **Address:** 317 1st Ave W 59072 **Location:** South edge of city on US 12 and 87.

Ⓑ Ⓛ Ⓓ

ST. IGNATIUS (C-2) pop. 842, elev. 2,940'

ST. IGNATIUS MISSION is .2 mi. s. on US 93 to sign, then .2 mi. e. to 300 Beartrack Ave. Established in 1854 by the Jesuit Fathers and Brothers, the 1891 brick church is decorated with 58 dry-fresco paintings executed about 1900 by Brother Joseph Carignano, the mission cook.

The missionaries' log cabin residence and chapel feature Native American and religious items. The first residence of the Sisters of Providence also is on the grounds. **Hours:** Mission daily 9-7, June-Aug.; 9-5, rest of year. Museum daily 10-4, Memorial Day-Labor Day. **Cost:** Donations. **Phone:** (406) 745-2768.

SUNSET MOTEL
406/745-3900

Motel $60-$80 **Address:** 333 Mountain View 59865 **Location:** Just s of downtown, exit 59 US 93. **Facility:** 8 units. 2 stories (no elevator), exterior corridors. **Terms:** resort fee.

ST. MARY

- **Hotels & Restaurants map & index p. 167**
- **Part of Glacier National Park area — see map p. 162**

TWO SISTERS CAFE
406/732-5535 (22)

American. Casual Dining. $15-$25 AAA Inspector Notes: Driving down the road from Glacier National Park, you can't miss the bright, multicolored café. This eatery, with its funky décor, serves up tasty twists on traditional favorites in a casual family-friendly setting. **Features:** full bar. **Address:** US 89 59411 **Location:** On US 89, 4.5 mi n. Ⓛ Ⓓ

ST. REGIS pop. 319

LITTLE RIVER MOTEL
(406)649-2713

Motel
$50-$85

Address: 424 Little River Ln 59866 **Location:** I-90 exit 33, just n to flashing light, just w, then just sw. **Facility:** 11 units, some cottages. 1 story, exterior corridors. **Parking:** winter plug-ins. **Featured Amenity: continental breakfast.**

SUPER 8-ST. REGIS
406/649-2422

Hotel
$59-$93

Address: 9 Old Hwy 10 E 59866 **Location:** I-90 exit 33, just w. **Facility:** 53 units, some kitchens. 2 stories (no elevator), interior/exterior corridors. **Parking:** winter plug-ins. **Activities:** hot tub. **Guest Services:** coin laundry. **Featured Amenity: continental breakfast.**

Ask about on-the-spot
vehicle battery testing and replacement

SCOBEY (A-7) pop. 1,017, elev. 2,507'

 DANIELS COUNTY MUSEUM AND PIONEER TOWN is at 7 W. County Rd. Some 40 buildings in this restored pioneer town portray early 20th-century homestead life. A collection of period antiques includes vintage vehicles. **Time:** Allow 1 hour, 30 minutes minimum. **Hours:** Daily 12:30-4:30, Memorial Day-Labor Day; by appointment, rest of year. **Cost:** $7; $4 (ages 5-12). **Phone:** (406) 487-5965. GT

SEELEY LAKE (C-2) pop. 1,659, elev. 4,028'

Seeley Lake is a year-round recreation area tucked between the Mission Mountains and Swan Range on scenic SR 83. In summer visitors can indulge in camping, hiking, golf, fishing, swimming, boating, backpacking and horseback riding. Fewer than 10 miles from town are Placid Lake and Salmon Lake state parks *(see Recreation Areas Chart)*; Seeley Lake itself has three Forest Service campgrounds, and at the north end of the lake is the 3.5-mile-long Clearwater Canoe Trail. Northeast of Seeley Lake is the 2.5-mile-long Morrell Falls National Recreation Trail, rated as "easy." Just east of the Morrell Falls trailhead access road is the Pyramid Pass Trail into Bob Marshall Wilderness. Head north to enjoy the 1.6-mile-long Holland Falls National Recreation Trail.

In the winter the average snow on the ground is about 3 feet. With a Nordic ski trail system for cross-country skiing and more than 300 miles of groomed snowmobile trails, the Seeley-Swan area provides good opportunities for winter recreation. Contact the Seeley Lake Ranger District office, 3 miles north of town on SR 83, for maps and brochures about access to trails and wildlife in the area; phone (406) 677-2233. Other local wintertime diversions include cultural presentations, ice fishing and dog sledding.

Seeley Lake Area Chamber of Commerce: 2920 SR 83 N., P.O. Box 516, Seeley Lake, MT 59868. **Phone:** (406) 677-2880.

LINDEY'S PRIME STEAK HOUSE   406/677-9229

Steak
Casual Dining
$22-$32

AAA Inspector Notes: Diners should be craving beef, because this menu features only flavorful, aged Prime sirloin and beef. Sharing is allowed. As a highlight during the summer, guests can enjoy thick "bayburgers," as they sit outside and overlook Seeley Lake. **Features:** full bar. **Address:** 3129 SR 83 59868 **Location:** Just s.
L D

SHELBY (B-3) pop. 3,376, elev. 3,276'

Shelby was one of the towns that the Great Northern Railroad left in its path as it pushed across the prairie. In its heyday, the town was paradise to cowboys after months on the range. A Saturday night might include carousing, horse racing, or—as once happened—holding up a passing opera troupe and making the train conductor do a clog dance to the rhythm of bullets.

Ranching, farming and the railroad supported the town until the 1922 discovery of oil in the Kevin-Sunburst fields. The area retains a few working oil pumps. Shelby's location on major transportation corridors established its right as an inland port for truck and rail shipping via the Northwest Express Transportation Authority.

Shelby Area Chamber of Commerce Office and Visitor Information Center: 100 Montana Ave., P.O. Box 865, Shelby, MT 59474. **Phone:** (406) 434-7184.

MARIAS MUSEUM OF HISTORY AND ART is at 1129 1st St. N. Exhibits depicting highlights of Toole County history focus on the oil industry, homesteading, the 1923 Dempsey-Gibbons prize fight (which nearly bankrupted the community), barbed wire, and dinosaur and other fossil discoveries. **Time:** Allow 1 hour minimum. **Hours:** Mon.-Fri. 1-7, Sat. 1-4, June-Aug.; Tues. noon-4 or by appointment, rest of year. Closed major holidays. **Cost:** Donations. **Phone:** (406) 424-2551.

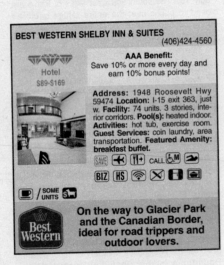

COMFORT INN OF SHELBY
(406)434-2212

Hotel
$98-$145

Address: 455 McKinley Ave 59474 **Location:** I-15 exit 363, just e, then just s. **Facility:** 128 units, some efficiencies. 3 stories, interior corridors. **Parking:** winter plug-ins. **Amenities:** *Some:* safes. **Pool(s):** heated indoor. **Activities:** sauna, hot tub, exercise room. **Guest Services:** coin laundry, area transportation. **Featured Amenity:** full hot breakfast.

Comfort INN
CHOICE

Perfect stop on the way to Canada and Glacier Park. Casino in hotel. Near fuel, snacks and dining.

BEST WESTERN GOLDEN PRAIRIE INN & SUITES
(406)433-4560

Hotel
$104-$159

AAA Benefit: Save 10% or more every day and earn 10% bonus points!

Address: 820 S Central Ave 59270 **Location:** 1.8 mi n of jct SR 16 and 200. **Facility:** 72 units. 4 stories, interior corridors. **Terms:** cancellation fee imposed. **Pool(s):** heated indoor. **Activities:** hot tub, exercise room. **Guest Services:** coin laundry, area transportation.

Best Western

Business friendly, well appointed, comfortable rooms, minutes from local attractions.

WHERE TO EAT

KOW LOON RESTAURANT
406/434-2030

Chinese. Casual Dining. $8-$14 **AAA Inspector Notes:** Large portions and a weekday lunch buffet draw folks from all around. The décor is minimal at this downtown location. **Features:** full bar. **Address:** 220 Main St 59474 **Location:** Center. **Parking:** street only. L | D | CALL

SHERIDAN pop. 642

IN-BACK STEAKHOUSE
406/842-7632

American. Casual Dining. $8-$27 **AAA Inspector Notes:** Diners can expect huge portions of hand-cut fries, big juicy burgers, well-prepared steaks and fish entrées at this casual eatery. **Features:** full bar. **Address:** 102 Mill St 59749 **Location:** Center.

B | L | D

SIDNEY (B-8) pop. 5,191, elev. 1,950'

Sidney is a marketing center for sugar beets and wheat and serves an active oil drilling and coal mining region. One of the larger auction houses in Montana, the Sidney Livestock Market Center on E. Main Street conducts cattle auctions on Wednesdays.

Sidney Area Chamber of Commerce and Agriculture: 909 S. Central Ave., Sidney, MT 59270. **Phone:** (406) 433-1916.

MONDAK HERITAGE CENTER is at 120 3rd Ave. S.E. The museum's lower level houses a re-created pioneer town. Upper-level galleries feature local and national traveling art exhibits. **Time:** Allow 1 hour minimum. **Hours:** Tues.-Fri. 10-4, Sat. 1-4. Closed major holidays. **Cost:** Free. **Phone:** (406) 433-3500.

Pick up colorful, top-quality travel guides and atlases at AAA/CAA offices

---

CANDLEWOOD SUITES SIDNEY
406/482-9692

Extended Stay Hotel. Rates not provided. **Address:** 201 6th St NW 59270 **Location:** Just n of jct SR 16 and 200. **Facility:** 114 efficiencies. 4 stories, interior corridors. **Parking:** winter plug-ins. **Terms:** check-in 4 pm. **Activities:** picnic facilities, exercise room. **Guest Services:** complimentary laundry.

HOLIDAY INN EXPRESS & SUITES
406/433-3200

Hotel. Rates not provided. **Address:** 251 W Holly St 59270 **Location:** Just nw of jct SR 16 and 200. **Facility:** 75 units. 4 stories, interior corridors. **Pool(s):** heated indoor. **Activities:** hot tub, exercise room. **Guest Services:** valet and coin laundry.

MICROTEL INN & SUITES BY WYNDHAM SIDNEY
(406)482-9011

Hotel $116-$179 **Address:** 1500 S Central Ave 59270 **Location:** 1.3 mi n of jct SR 16 and 200. **Facility:** 76 units. 4 stories, interior corridors. **Parking:** winter plug-ins. **Pool(s):** heated indoor. **Activities:** hot tub, exercise room. **Guest Services:** valet and coin laundry.

RICHLAND INN & SUITES
406/433-6400

Motel. Rates not provided. **Address:** 1200 S Central Ave 59270 **Location:** 1.5 mi n of jct SR 16 and 200. **Facility:** 86 units. 2 stories, interior corridors. **Parking:** winter plug-ins. **Activities:** exercise room. **Guest Services:** coin laundry.

SILVER GATE (F-4) pop. 20, elev. 7,389'

Resembling an alpine village, Silver Gate is said to be the only municipality in the nation whose building codes mandate that all structures be made of logs and other materials native to the area.

The town is at the northeast entrance to Yellowstone National Park *(see place listing p. 316)*; nearby Cooke City *(see place listing p. 152)* also has access to the park. Silver Gate is an outfitting center for both cross-country skiing and snowmobiling. Fly fishing is excellent in nearby lakes and streams.

 **BEARTOOTH SCENIC HIGHWAY**—see Red Lodge p. 199.

STEVENSVILLE (D-2) pop. 1,809, elev. 3,524'

HISTORIC ST. MARY'S MISSION is at the w. end of Fourth St. at 315 Charlos St. The mission was established in 1841 by Father Pierre DeSmet. The present complex includes the 1880s-style restored chapel and a study, dining room and kitchen. Also restored is Father Anthony Ravalli's log house, which contains a pharmacy with a "ride-up" window. Chief Victor's cabin is a small museum that displays original furnishings and Native American and missionary artifacts.

Time: Allow 30 minutes minimum. **Hours:** Guided 1-hour tours are given Tues.-Sat. 10-4, Apr. 15-Oct. 15. **Cost:** $8; $7 (ages 60+); $6 (ages 6-18). **Phone:** (406) 777-5734. GT A

BITTERROOT RIVER BED AND BREAKFAST   406/777-5205
♥♥ ♥♥ **Bed & Breakfast.** Rates not provided. **Address:** 501 South Ave 59870 **Location:** 1 mi s on Main St (SR 269), just w. **Facility:** 4 units. 2 stories (no elevator), interior corridors. **Activities:** fishing, bicycles. ⊠ ☎ / SOME UNITS Ⓦ

SUPERIOR (C-1) pop. 812

RECREATIONAL ACTIVITIES
White-water Rafting

• SAVE **Pangaea River Rafting** departs from 11111 Mullan Rd. E. Other activities are available. **Hours:** Rafting trips are offered daily at 10:30, 12:30 and 4, Apr.-Sept. Phone ahead to confirm schedule. **Phone:** (406) 239-2392, or (877) 239-2392 for reservations.

• **ROW Adventures** departs from 62 Lynch Ranch Ln. **Hours:** White-water rafting trips depart daily at 9, mid-July to early Sept. **Phone:** (208) 770-2517 or (866) 836-9340.

• **Wiley E. Waters-Clark Fork** trips depart from 201 William Lloyd Ln. **Hours:** Full- and half-day rafting trips generally depart daily at 9 (PST), July 1-early Sept. Phone ahead to confirm schedule. **Phone:** (509) 998-1120 or (888) 502-1900.

BIG SKY MOTEL   (406)822-4831
◆ **Motel** $86-$96 **Address:** 103 4th Ave E 59872 **Location:** I-90 exit 47, just n. **Facility:** 24 units, some two bedrooms. 2 stories, exterior corridors. **Terms:** cancellation fee imposed. **Guest Services:** coin laundry. 📶 CALL M BIZ ⊠ / SOME UNITS

TERRY (D-7) pop. 605, elev. 2,253'

In the heart of agate country, Terry was the home of acclaimed photographer Evelyn Cameron. Many of the pictures she took 1894-1928 to chronicle the lives of Terry's early settlers were compiled in a book more than 50 years later, "Photographing Montana" by Donna Lucey.

PRAIRIE COUNTY MUSEUM is at 101 Logan Ave. at jct. Laundre Ave. Housed in the Old State Bank of Terry building, the museum displays local memorabilia. A dentist's office, a barbershop, a schoolroom and hospital rooms are among the highlights. Area fossils also are featured.

Visitors also can see an unusual outhouse, a homestead shack, a depot and a caboose. The Evelyn Cameron Gallery features a collection of photographs that Cameron took of the area in the early 20th century. **Hours:** Mon. and Wed.-Fri. 9-3, Sat.-Sun. 1-4, Memorial Day weekend-Labor Day; other times by appointment. **Cost:** Donations. **Phone:** (406) 635-4040.

THREE FORKS (E-3) pop. 1,869, elev. 4,061'

Three Forks was a favorite Native American hunting ground near the headwaters of the Missouri River. In 1805 Meriwether Lewis and William Clark documented their exploration of the beginning of the world's longest river system. Sacajawea (Sacagawea), the wife of one of their guides, was kidnapped and raised by the Minnetaree. A plaque in Sacajawea Park downtown commemorates her contribution to the success of the Lewis and Clark expedition. A statue, commissioned by the Three Forks Area Historical Society in 2005, depicts Sacajawea with her baby.

A trading post was established by fur trappers in 1810. The first permanent non-native settlement was established nearby in 1862. As railroads and highways provided access to the area, settlers arrived, and Three Forks was founded in 1908. Excellent hunting and fishing opportunities continue to attract visitors today.

Three Forks Chamber of Commerce: 110 N. Main St., P.O. Box 1103, Three Forks, MT 59752. **Phone:** (406) 285-4753 or (406) 595-4755.

HEADWATERS HERITAGE MUSEUM is at 202 S. Main St. Life in the early 1900s is depicted through replicas that include a village blacksmith shop, railroad dispatcher's office, schoolhouse and millinery shop. Other rooms include a dental office, military display, kitchen and beauty shop. An American-made anvil, possibly the oldest of its kind in the United States, and the largest brown trout caught in Montana are displayed. Another exhibit features 571 types of barbed wire. Artifacts from the surrounding towns in the Missouri Headwaters area also are exhibited. **Hours:** Mon.-Sat. 9-5, Sun. 11-3, June-Sept.; by appointment rest of year. **Cost:** Donations. **Phone:** (406) 285-4778 in season, or (406) 285-3644 for appointments rest of year.

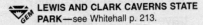 **LEWIS AND CLARK CAVERNS STATE PARK**—see Whitehall p. 213.

MADISON BUFFALO JUMP STATE PARK is 5 mi. e. on I-90, then 7 mi. s. to 6990 Buffalo Jump Rd. As long as 2,000 years ago Native Americans hunted by driving buffalo off a cliff on this 618-acre site. Interpretive displays and hiking trails are offered. **Note:** Approach road is gravel; trailers are not recommended. **Time:** Allow 30 minutes minimum. **Hours:** Park open daily dawn-dusk. **Cost:** $6 (nonresidents per private vehicle); $4 (nonresidents arriving by other means); free (Montana residents with ID). **Phone:** (406) 285-3610. 🍽

MISSOURI HEADWATERS STATE PARK is 3 mi. e., then 3 mi. n. of US 10 to 1585 Trident Rd. Discovered July 27, 1805, by the Lewis and Clark expedition, the headwaters in this 527-acre park are formed by the joining of the Madison, Gallatin and Jefferson rivers. A scenic overlook and a campground are nearby. *See Recreation Areas Chart.* **Hours:** Park open daily dawn-dusk. **Cost:** Park admission $6 (nonresidents per private vehicle); $4 (nonresidents arriving by other means); free (Montana residents with ID). Camping $24-$28 (nonresidents); $18-$20 (nonresidents with a Montana State Park passport); $14-$18 (Montana residents with ID). **Phone:** (406) 285-3610. 🏕 ✖ 🐾 🍽

BROKEN SPUR MOTEL 406/285-3237

Motel
$69-$130

Address: 124 W Elm (Hwy 2) 59752 **Location:** I-90 exit 278 westbound, 1.3 mi sw; exit 274 eastbound, 1 mi s on SR 287 to jct SR 2, then 3 mi se. **Facility:** 24 units, some efficiencies. 2 stories (no elevator), exterior corridors. **Parking:** winter plug-ins. **Terms:** cancellation fee imposed. **Featured Amenity:** continental breakfast.

[SAVE] 🍴 🛜 🗄
/ SOME UNITS 🔲 🖼

FORT THREE FORKS MOTEL & RV PARK 406/285-3233
🛏 **Motel.** Rates not provided. **Address:** 10776 Hwy 287 59752 **Location:** I-90 exit 274, just n. **Facility:** 24 units. 2 stories (no elevator), exterior corridors. **Parking:** winter plug-ins. **Guest Services:** coin laundry. 🍴 🛜 🖳 / SOME UNITS 🔲 🖬 🖼

SACAJAWEA HOTEL 406/285-6515
[fyi] **Hotel** Did not meet all AAA rating requirements for locking devices in some guest rooms at time of last evaluation on 06/03/2015. **Address:** 5 N Main St 59752 **Location:** I-90 exit 278, 0.5 mi s. Facilities, services, and décor characterize a mid-scale property. Founded in 1910 by a purchasing agent for the Milwaukee Railroad, this historic railroad hotel has been restored in a Western theme with wood accents and floors in rich hues.

WHERE TO EAT

POMPEY'S GRILL 406/285-6515
🍷🍷🍷 Western American. Casual Dining. $18-$43 **AAA Inspector Notes:** *Historic.* Hand-cut Certified Angus steaks and specialty seafood are prepared to perfection. Pasta dishes and a Montana farm rack of lamb also are offered. The bar boasts reclaimed wood from the Lucin Cutoff railroad trestle, which once spanned the Great Salt Lake. Pompey was the name of Sacajawea's son. **Features:** full bar, Sunday brunch. **Reservations:** suggested. **Address:** 5 N Main St 59752 **Location:** I-90 exit 278, 0.5 mi s; in Sacajawea Hotel. **Parking:** street only. [D] CALL Ⓜ 🅰

TROY (B-1) pop. 938

Nestled between forested mountains on the banks of the Kootenai River, Troy is Montana's lowest-elevation town. Pioneers called the region Montana's Wilds, for its deep valleys, steep mountains and dense forests. Gold prospectors camped in the area in the mid-1880s, but the town wasn't permanently settled until the Great Northern established a freight yard here in 1892.

Ross Creek Cedars Scenic Area, 21 miles south on SR 56 then 4 miles west on Ross Creek Road, has a .9-mile interpretive nature trail that leads visitors through a 100-acre stand of old growth western red cedar. The lush woodland, with trees upward of 8 feet thick and 175 feet tall, is a modified temperate rain forest.

KOOTENAI FALLS is 5 mi. e. on US 2. The Kootenai River foams through a narrow, rocky gorge, forming a cataract that drops 300 feet over a distance of several hundred yards. Sacred to the Kootenai Indians, the area can be traversed via a network of trails.

Bridging the Burlington Northern Santa Fe mainline, a trail—the uppermost portion of which is paved and features an interpretive display and a picnic area—leads down through the forest to the edge of the gorge. Visitors can continue east to the falls or west to a swinging suspension bridge that connects to trails on the north side of the river. **Note:** A portion of the trail system lacks guardrails, is uneven and can be muddy in wet weather. **Time:** Allow 1 hour minimum. **Hours:** Daily dawn-dusk. **Cost:** Free.

ULM (C-3) pop. 738, elev. 3,346'

FIRST PEOPLES BUFFALO JUMP STATE PARK is off I-15 exit 270, then 3.5 mi. w. on Ulm-Vaughn Rd. The park preserves one of the largest known buffalo jump sites and interprets the buffalo culture. Exhibits depict how Native Americans hunted bison by stampeding them over the cliffs. Featured are several mounted buffalo, implements fashioned from buffalo remains and a furnished tepee made of buffalo hides. Interpretive trails to the cliffs and grasslands are available.

Time: Allow 1 hour minimum. **Hours:** Daily 8-6, Apr.-Sept.; Wed.-Sat. 10-4, Sun. noon-4, rest of year. **Cost:** $6 (per private motorized vehicle); $4 (per person arriving by other means). **Phone:** (406) 866-2217.

VIRGINIA CITY (E-3) pop. 190, elev. 5,822'

After fruitless panning along the Yellowstone River, six prospectors stumbled onto Alder Creek in May 1863, and their discovery of gold led to the establishment of a town. The settlement attracted thousands of miners and a band of renegades said to have committed more than 190 murders in 6 months. The miners formed a secret group called The Vigilantes, who captured and hanged 21 of the criminals, including the outlaws' leader, the sheriff.

One of the older cities in the state, Virginia City served as territorial capital 1865-75. More than 130 early buildings have been preserved; others have been reconstructed and can be visited. Among these are the state's first newspaper office, an equipped pharmacy of the period, the Wells Fargo Express Office, the Bale of Hay Saloon and general stores carrying 1860-80 merchandise. Boot Hill Cemetery contains the graves of road agents hanged by vigilantes in 1864.

Gold panning, hunting and fishing opportunities are available. A 1935 gold dredge can be seen at the River of Gold Mining Museum. All facilities are open Memorial Day through Labor Day.

Virginia City Visitor Information Center: 300 W. Wallace St., P.O. Box 338, Virginia City, MT 59755. **Phone:** (406) 843-5247 or (800) 829-2969.

GILBERT BREWERY is at Hamilton and Cover sts. Featured is "The Brewery Follies," a contemporary comedy variety show by the Brewery Players. Performances take place in a renovated 1860s brewery. **Note:** According to the attraction, "Due to mature content, parental guidance is suggested." **Hours:** Brewery Follies performances are given daily at 4 and 8 p.m., late May-late Sept. **Cost:** Brewery Follies $20. Reservations are recommended. **Phone:** (406) 843-5218 or (800) 829-2969, ext. 3.

NEVADA CITY is 1.5 mi. w. on SR 287. The city sprang up with the discovery of gold in 1863. Some of Montana Territory's original buildings have been moved to this site and restored to form the Nevada City Museum. The Music Hall contains a collection of mechanical musical machines.

Time: Allow 1 hour minimum. **Hours:** Daily 10-6, mid-May to mid-Sept. **Cost:** Museum Sat.-Sun. and holidays $10; $8 (ages 5-16 and 55+). Museum Mon.-Fri. $8; $6 (ages 5-16 and 55+). Gold panning experience $8. Combination tickets are available. **Phone:** (406) 843-5247 or (800) 829-2969.

Alder Gulch Shortline Railroad runs between Virginia City and Nevada City. The small, narrow-gauge train is pulled by a gasoline-powered engine.

Time: Allow 1 hour minimum. **Hours:** Daily 10-5, May-Sept. **Cost:** Round-trip fare $10; $8 (ages 5-16 and 55+). Combination tickets are available. **Phone:** (406) 843-5247.

THOMPSON-HICKMAN MEMORIAL MUSEUM, 220 E. Wallace St., offers state and local memorabilia interpreting the history, geology and culture of 19th-century Virginia City. **Time:** Allow 30 minutes minimum. **Hours:** Daily 10-5, Memorial Day-Labor Day. **Cost:** Donations. **Phone:** (406) 843-5238 or (406) 843-5833.

VIRGINIA CITY OPERA HOUSE is at 338 W. Wallace St. Vaudeville and melodramas are performed in the style of the 19th-century touring companies that regularly stopped in this town. Three shows are performed during the season. **Time:** Shows Wed. and Sat. at 2 and 7, Thurs. and Sun. at 2, Tues. and Fri. at 7, late May-late Sept. **Cost:** $20; $17 (ages 60+, students with ID and military with ID); $10 (ages 0-17). Reservations are required. **Phone:** (800) 829-2969 for reservations.

WEST GLACIER (B-2) pop. 227, elev. 3,215'
• Hotels & Restaurants map & index p. 167
• Part of Glacier National Park area — see map p. 162

West Glacier is the western rail and highway entrance to Glacier National Park (see place listing p. 162). White-water rafting, skiing, hiking and year-round camping are the area's most popular recreational activities. Fishing and golf also draw visitors in pursuit of outdoor fun. One golf course has rules that include: "do not throw clubs or balls at tame deer" and "players may move balls without penalty to avoid elk tracks."

KRUGER HELICOP-TOURS is 1 mi. w. of Glacier National Park on SR 2. Narrated 30-minute and 1-hour tours reveal breathtaking bird's-eye views of glaciers as you fly over Glacier National Park. Waterfalls and lakes rarely seen by park visitors are some additional highlights providing photographic opportunities. **Time:** Allow 30 minutes minimum. **Hours:** Departures require a minimum of four people. Daily 8-5, June-Sept. A 24-hour notice is required to cancel a tour reservation. **Cost:** Fares $125-$975 per person. **Phone:** (406) 387-4565 in the Flathead Valley in season, (406) 857-3893 in the Flathead Valley in the off-season, or (800) 220-6565 in season.

RECREATIONAL ACTIVITIES
Backpacking
• **Glacier Guides** is 1.5 mi. w. on US 2. Other activities are offered. **Hours:** Backpacking trips are offered daily, May-Sept. Departure times vary; phone ahead. **Phone:** (406) 387-5555 or (800) 521-7238.

White-water Rafting
• **Glacier Raft Co.** is on Going-to-the-Sun Rd. at the west entrance to Glacier National Park. Other activities are offered. **Hours:** Rafting trips are offered daily, late May to mid-Sept. Departure times vary; phone ahead. **Phone:** (406) 888-5454 or (800) 235-6781.

(See map & index p. 167.)

- **Great Northern Glacier Park Raft** is 1 mi. w. to 12127 US 2 E. Other activities are offered. **Hours:** Rafting trips are offered daily, mid-May to late Sept. Departure times vary; phone ahead. **Phone:** (406) 387-5340 or (800) 735-7897.

- **Montana Raft Co.** is 1.5 mi. w. on US 2. Other activities are offered. **Hours:** Rafting trips are offered daily, May-Sept. Departure times vary; phone ahead. **Phone:** (406) 387-5555 or (800) 521-7238.

- **Wild River Adventures** is 1 mi. w. on US 2. Other activities are offered. **Hours:** Rafting trips are offered daily, late May to mid-Sept. Departure times vary; phone ahead. **Phone:** (406) 387-9453 or (800) 700-7056.

GLACIER RAFT COMPANY CABINS AT GLACIER OUTDOOR CENTER 406/888-5454 **33**

Cabin
$150-$649

Address: 12400 US Hwy 2 E 59936 **Location:** On US 2, 0.5 mi w. **Facility:** 13 cabins, some two bedrooms. 1-2 stories (no elevator), exterior corridors. **Terms:** closed 10/16-4/14, check-in 4 pm, 45 day cancellation notice-fee imposed. **Activities:** fishing.

GLACIERS' MOUNTAIN RESORT, LLC (406)387-5712 **34**

Cabin $129-$265 **Address:** 1385 Old Hwy 2 E 59936 **Location:** 6 mi sw on US 2, between MM 147 and 148, on west side of road to Old US 2, then just w. **Facility:** 5 cabins. 1 story, exterior corridors. **Terms:** check-in 4 pm, 2 night minimum stay - seasonal, 30 day cancellation notice-fee imposed.

SILVERWOLF LOG CHALETS 406/387-4448 **35**

Cabin
Rates not provided

Address: 160 Gladys Glen Rd 59936 **Location:** 6 mi sw on US 2; close to Coram, outside of park. Located in a quiet rural area. **Facility:** 10 cabins. 1 story, exterior corridors. *Bath:* shower only. **Featured Amenity:** continental breakfast.

BELTON CHALET 406/888-5000

[fyi] Not evaluated. **Address:** 12575 US 2 E 59936 **Location:** US 2 E, at west entrance to Glacier National Park, just outside the park. Facilities, services, and décor characterize a mid-scale property.

WEST YELLOWSTONE (F-4) pop. 1,271, elev. 6,667'

As its name suggests, West Yellowstone is at the west entrance to Yellowstone National Park (see place listing p. 316). Due to this strategic location, the town's major industry is tourism. Numerous outfitters and rental operations supply visitors with various sports equipment, particularly snowmobiles and cross-country skis, for use in the park and in bordering national forest areas. Fly fishing, hiking and horseback riding can be enjoyed during summer.

Two miles north of West Yellowstone on US 287, the Interagency Aerial Fire Control Center provides tours explaining firefighting techniques in summer, when staff is available; phone (406) 646-7691.

For evening entertainment The Playmill Theatre at 29 Madison Ave. presents 2-hour musical comedy performances Monday through Saturday nights, with occasional Saturday matinees, mid-May through early September. Reservations are recommended. For more information and schedules contact the theater; phone (406) 646-7757.

West Yellowstone Chamber of Commerce: 30 Yellowstone Ave., P.O. Box 458, W. Yellowstone, MT 59758. **Phone:** (406) 646-7701.

[SAVE] **GRIZZLY & WOLF DISCOVERY CENTER** is 1 blk. s. of the Yellowstone National Park west entrance at 201 S. Canyon St. in Grizzly Park. Grizzly bears and two separate gray wolf packs can be viewed in naturalistic habitats. Also offered are educational presentations, Yellowstone ranger talks, live birds of prey exhibits, safety in bear country demonstrations, films, an interactive bear museum, and wolf enrichment and children's programs. **Time:** Allow 1 hour minimum. **Hours:** Daily 8:30-dusk. **Cost:** (valid for 2 consecutive days) $11.50; $10.75 (ages 62+); $6.50 (ages 5-12). **Phone:** (406) 646-7001 or (800) 257-2570.

MADISON RIVER CANYON EARTHQUAKE AREA is on US 287, 17 mi. n. of jct. US 191, in the Hebgen Lake Area. This 37,800-acre tract embraces Hebgen and Earthquake lakes. Traces remain of the 1959 earthquake, which blocked a river, moved huge boulders and tilted a lake bed. An observation room features a DVD presentation telling the story of the quake. The visitor center contains a working seismograph. **Time:** Allow 30 minutes minimum. **Hours:** Visitor center daily 10-6, Memorial Day-Labor Day. **Cost:** Free. **Phone:** (406) 682-7620 or (406) 823-6961.

YELLOWSTONE HISTORIC CENTER MUSEUM is at 104 Yellowstone Ave. Housed in a 1909 Union Pacific Railroad depot, the museum highlights the Yellowstone experience, from early tourism and railroad history to the 1988 fires and the rejuvenation of the park's ecosystems. Exhibits include early park stage coaches, a 1940s snow plane and a variety of films. Old Snaggletooth, a legendary grizzly bear, is prominently displayed among the wildlife specimens.

Time: Allow 1 hour minimum. **Hours:** Daily 9-9, late May-Labor Day; 9-6, mid to late May and day after

(See map & index p. 324.)

Labor Day to mid-Oct. **Cost:** $6; $5 (ages 60+ and active military with ID); $3 (ages 13-18 and students with ID); $2 (ages 4-12). **Phone:** (406) 646-1100.

YELLOWSTONE GIANT SCREEN THEATRE is at 101 S. Canyon St., adjacent to Yellowstone National Park's west entrance. IMAX films about the history, wildlife, geothermal activity and grandeur of America's first national park is shown on a six-story screen with stereo surround sound. **Hours:** Shows daily 9-7, June-Aug.; schedule varies rest of year. **Cost:** $9; $8.50 (ages 60+); $6.50 (ages 4-12). **Phone:** (406) 646-4100 or (888) 854-5862.

ALPINE MOTEL　　　406/646-7544 [39]

Motel
$95-$175

Address: 120 Madison Ave 59758 **Location:** Just w of US 191 (Canyon St) and Madison Ave; 0.3 mi nw of park entrance. **Facility:** 15 units, some kitchens. 1-2 stories (no elevator), exterior corridors. **Terms:** 7 day cancellation notice-fee imposed. **Activities:** picnic facilities.

BEST WESTERN DESERT INN　　(406)646-7376 [34]

Hotel
$90-$290

AAA Benefit: Save 10% or more every day and earn 10% bonus points!

Address: 133 Canyon St 59758 **Location:** Jct US 191 (Canyon St) and Firehole Ave; 0.3 mi n of park entrance. **Facility:** 76 units. 3 stories, interior corridors. **Parking:** winter plug-ins. **Terms:** cancellation fee imposed, resort fee. **Pool(s):** heated indoor. **Activities:** hot tub. **Guest Services:** coin laundry.

BEST WESTERN WESTON INN　　(406)646-7373 [28]

Motel
$149-$319

AAA Benefit: Save 10% or more every day and earn 10% bonus points!

Address: 103 Gibbon Ave 59758 **Location:** Jct US 191 (Canyon St) and Gibbon Ave; 0.5 mi n of park entrance. Across from Pioneer Park. **Facility:** 66 units, some kitchens. 2-3 stories (no elevator), interior/exterior corridors. **Terms:** closed 11/1-4/30, 3 day cancellation notice-fee imposed. **Pool(s):** heated outdoor. **Activities:** hot tub. **Guest Services:** coin laundry.

BRANDIN' IRON INN　　　406/646-9411 [33]

Motel
Rates not provided

Address: 201 Canyon St 59758 **Location:** Jct US 20 (Firehole Ave) and 191 (Canyon St); 0.3 mi n of park entrance. **Facility:** 80 units, some kitchens. 2 stories (no elevator), exterior corridors. **Parking:** winter plug-ins. **Activities:** hot tub, snowmobiling. **Guest Services:** coin laundry. **Featured Amenity:** breakfast buffet.

　Free expanded continental breakfast and hi-speed Internet

---

CLUBHOUSE INN　　　(406)646-4892 [42]

Hotel $129-$299 **Address:** 105 S Electric St 59758 **Location:** Just sw of jct US 20/191/287; 0.4 mi w of park entrance. **Facility:** 77 units. 3 stories, interior corridors. **Parking:** winter plug-ins. **Terms:** cancellation fee imposed. **Pool(s):** heated indoor. **Activities:** hot tub, exercise room. **Guest Services:** valet and coin laundry.

CROSSWINDS INN　　　(406)646-9557 [32]

Motel
$85-$234

Address: 201 Firehole Ave 59758 **Location:** At US 20 (Firehole Ave) and Dunraven St; 0.5 mi n of park entrance. Across from West Yellowstone Town Park. **Facility:** 70 units. 2 stories (no elevator), exterior corridors. **Terms:** closed 11/1-4/15, check-in 4 pm, cancellation fee imposed, resort fee. **Pool(s):** heated indoor. **Activities:** hot tub, playground. **Guest Services:** coin laundry. **Featured Amenity:** continental breakfast.

DAYS INN WEST YELLOWSTONE　　(406)646-7656 [36]

Hotel
$100-$219

Address: 301 Madison Ave 59758 **Location:** At Madison Ave and Electric St; 0.5 mi nw of park entrance. **Facility:** 116 units. 3 stories, interior/exterior corridors. **Parking:** winter plug-ins. **Amenities:** *Some:* safes. **Pool(s):** heated indoor. **Activities:** hot tub. **Guest Services:** coin laundry.

EVERGREEN MOTEL　　　406/646-7655 [30]

Motel. Rates not provided. **Address:** 229 Firehole Ave 59758 **Location:** At US 20 (Firehole Ave) and Electric St; 0.6 mi nw of park entrance. **Facility:** 17 units. 1 story, exterior corridors. **Guest Services:** coin laundry.

Recommend places you'd like us to inspect
at AAA.com/TourBookComments

(See map & index p. 324.)

EXPLORER CABINS AT YELLOWSTONE

(406)646-7075 **44**

Cabin
$109-$479

Address: 201 Grizzly Ave 59758 **Location:** 0.4 mi w of park entrance. **Facility:** These very nice cabins have a front porch with seating, are beautifully furnished and come with lots of convenient amenities including a smore's kit to use at the firepit. 50 efficiency cabin units, some two bedrooms. 1 story, exterior corridors. *Bath:* shower only. **Terms:** off-site registration, 3 day cancellation notice-fee imposed, resort fee. **Amenities:** safes. **Activities:** cross country skiing, snowmobiling.

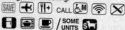

GRAY WOLF INN AND SUITES

(406)646-0000 **46**

Hotel
$89-$279

Address: 250 S Canyon St 59758 **Location:** Just w of park entrance, just s. Across from Grizzly Discovery Center. **Facility:** 103 units, some two bedrooms and kitchens. 3 stories, interior corridors. **Terms:** check-in 4 pm, 3 day cancellation notice-fee imposed, resort fee. **Pool(s):** heated indoor. **Activities:** sauna, hot tub. **Guest Services:** coin laundry. **Featured Amenity:** continental breakfast.

HOLIDAY INN WEST YELLOWSTONE CONFERENCE HOTEL

(406)646-7365 **40**

Hotel
$119-$319

Address: 315 Yellowstone Ave 59758 **Location:** 0.4 mi w of park entrance. **Facility:** 123 units. 3 stories, interior corridors. **Parking:** winter plug-ins. **Terms:** check-in 4 pm, 5 day cancellation notice-fee imposed, resort fee. **Pool(s):** heated indoor. **Activities:** sauna, hot tub, exercise room. **Guest Services:** coin laundry.

LAZY G MOTEL

406/646-7586 **31**

Motel
$89-$120

Address: 123 Hayden St 59758 **Location:** Jct US 20 (Firehole Ave) and Hayden St, just s; 0.8 mi w of park entrance. **Facility:** 15 units, some two bedrooms and efficiencies. 1-2 stories (no elevator), exterior corridors. **Parking:** winter plug-ins. **Terms:** closed 4/1-5/1 & 10/16-11/20, 2 night minimum stay - seasonal and/or weekends, 5 day cancellation notice-fee imposed. **Activities:** picnic facilities.

ONE HORSE MOTEL

406/646-7677 **29**

Motel
$79-$161

Address: 216 Dunraven St 59758 **Location:** Jct US 20 (Firehole Ave) and Dunraven St, just n; 0.6 mi nw of park entrance. Across from West Yellowstone Town Park. **Facility:** 19 units. 1 story, exterior corridors. **Terms:** closed 10/19-5/10, 7 day cancellation notice-fee imposed. **Activities:** playground. **Guest Services:** coin laundry.

STAGE COACH INN

(406)646-7381 **37**

Hotel
$49-$329

Address: 209 Madison Ave 59758 **Location:** At Dunraven St and Madison Ave; 0.4 mi nw of park entrance. **Facility:** 84 units. 2 stories, interior corridors. **Terms:** cancellation fee imposed. **Pool(s):** heated indoor. **Activities:** sauna, exercise room. **Guest Services:** coin laundry. **Featured Amenity:** continental breakfast.

SUPER 8 - WEST YELLOWSTONE

(406)646-9584 **27**

Hotel
$82-$186

Address: 1545 Targhee Pass Hwy (US 20) 59758 **Location:** 7 mi w of downtown. Adjacent to Gallatin National Forest. **Facility:** 44 units. 2 stories (no elevator), interior corridors. **Terms:** closed 10/16-5/14. **Activities:** fishing, playground, lawn sports, trails. **Guest Services:** coin laundry. **Featured Amenity:** continental breakfast.

THREE BEAR LODGE

(406)646-7353 **41**

Hotel
$99-$259

Address: 217 Yellowstone Ave 59758 **Location:** Just w of park entrance. **Facility:** 70 units. 1-2 stories (no elevator), interior/exterior corridors. **Terms:** check-in 4 pm, cancellation fee imposed, resort fee. **Dining:** Three Bear Restaurant, see separate listing. **Pool(s):** heated outdoor. **Activities:** hot tub, snowmobiling, recreation programs in winter, limited exercise equipment. **Guest Services:** valet and coin laundry. **Featured Amenity:** full hot breakfast.

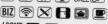

Take your imagination to new destinations

with the online AAA/CAA Travel Guides

(See map & index p. 324.)

WEST YELLOWSTONE CITY CENTER MOTEL
406/646-7337 **38**

Motel
Rates not provided

Address: 214 Madison Ave 59758 **Location:** Jct Madison Ave and Dunraven St; 0.4 mi nw of park entrance. **Facility:** 25 units. 1-2 stories (no elevator), exterior corridors.

Game room, communal kitchen and free Wi-Fi.

YELLOWSTONE LODGE
406/646-0020 **45**

Hotel $89-$269 **Address:** 251 S Electric St 59758 **Location:** Just s of Yellowstone Ave and Electric St; 0.6 mi sw of park entrance. **Facility:** 80 units. 3 stories, interior corridors. **Parking:** winter plug-ins. **Terms:** cancellation fee imposed. **Pool(s):** heated indoor. **Activities:** hot tub. **Guest Services:** coin laundry.

YELLOWSTONE PARK HOTEL
(406/646-0255 **43**

Hotel
$99-$299

Address: 201 Grizzly Ave 59758 **Location:** 0.4 mi sw of park entrance. **Facility:** 66 units. 3 stories, interior corridors. **Terms:** 3 day cancellation notice-fee imposed, resort fee. **Pool(s):** heated indoor. **Activities:** hot tub, trails, limited exercise equipment. **Guest Services:** valet and coin laundry, area transportation. **Featured Amenity: continental breakfast.**

YELLOWSTONE WEST GATE HOTEL
(406/646-4212 **35**

Hotel $180-$300 **Address:** 638 Madison Ave 59758 **Location:** At Iris St and Madison Ave; 1 mi nw of park entrance. **Facility:** 79 units, some kitchens. 3 stories, interior corridors. **Parking:** winter plug-ins. **Terms:** closed 4/1-5/7 & 10/20-3/31, check-in 4 pm, cancellation fee imposed. **Pool(s):** heated indoor. **Activities:** hot tub, snowmobiling, trails. **Guest Services:** coin laundry.

WHERE TO EAT

ARROWLEAF ICE CREAM PARLOR & GRILL
406/646-9776 **38**

Burgers. Quick Serve. $6-$9 **AAA Inspector Notes:** If you are craving a burger, chicken basket or fish tacos, stop by this family-run diner. Or go straight to the ice cream-making machine for a cone, malt, shake or sundae. The most talked about flavor is huckleberry, but the available flavor combinations are endless. **Address:** 27 N Canyon St 59758 **Location:** Just s of Madison Ave; downtown. **Parking:** street only. L D

BEARTOOTH BBQ
406/646-0227 **33**

Barbecue. Family Dining. $8-$15 **AAA Inspector Notes:** In-house-smoked meats and poultry make up the casual restaurant's menu. Those having a hard time deciding might consider a platter with any of a combination of ribs, brisket, chopped or sliced meats and smoked chicken with sauces made on site. **Features:** beer & wine. **Address:** 111 Canyon St 59758 **Location:** Center. **Parking:** street only. L D

BULLWINKLE'S SALOON & EATERY
406/646-7974 **31**

American. Casual Dining. $9-$29 **AAA Inspector Notes:** Even though the dining room is a large one, during the summer months you may find a wait for a table at this extremely popular place. The menu is varied and includes tasty seasonal soup and buffalo chili, steaks, a decent salad bar, and a nice selection of pasta and chicken. **Features:** full bar. **Address:** 115 N Canyon St 59758 **Location:** Just n of park entrance. **Parking:** on-site and street. L D

CAFE MADRIZ
406/646-9245 **27**

Spanish Small Plates. Casual Dining. $8-$30 **AAA Inspector Notes:** This is traditional Spanish comfort food such as meatballs in a savory broth, a fluffy potato and onion omelet and cold, cured meats and cheeses. The servings are a bit larger than tapas, so three dishes shared with two people should be enough. Seafood and chicken paella for two or four is on the menu, but allow 30 minutes, as it is cooked to order. **Features:** beer & wine, patio dining. **Address:** 311 N Canyon St 59758 **Location:** 1 mi n from park entrance. **Parking:** street only. L D

CANYON STREET GRILL
406/646-7548 **39**

Burgers Sandwiches. Casual Dining. $8-$15 **AAA Inspector Notes:** Take a trip down memory lane to experience what music was like in the '50s. Salads and entrées are named for people, places and stars of the past. Sandwiches are served with fries or apple slices. The chicken, fish and shrimp baskets are served with potato wedges or another side dish. Locals favor the Peggy Sue burger on pumpernickel, the Maybelene made with green chile peppers, and the Bo Diddley layered with bacon, fried egg and ham. Chicago and Coney Island hot dogs are offered. **Address:** 22 Canyon St 59758 **Location:** Just n of Alley A; downtown. **Parking:** street only. L D CALL M

ERNIE'S BAKERY, SANDWICH SHOP & DELI
406/646-9467 **28**

Breakfast Sandwiches. Quick Serve. $7-$14 **AAA Inspector Notes:** The chicken and fish and chip baskets are popular here, as are the tomato pie, quiche, specialty burgers, hot and cold deli sandwiches, meatballs, Mama's meatloaf and chicken-fried steak sandwich. Tip: The pastries sell out quickly. **Address:** 406 Hwy 20 59758 **Location:** 0.5 mi w of US 287 (N Canyon St). **Parking:** on-site and street. B L CALL M

EURO CAFE
406/646-1170 **29**

Breakfast Sandwiches. Casual Dining. $9-$12 **AAA Inspector Notes:** The décor is stylish and inviting and the menu features a nice selection of crepes, omelets, salads and sandwiches. Locals favor the spicy sriracha chicken sandwich and themed burgers named after European countries such as Italy and Spain. The hummus plate is perfect for one or two people and the colors used in the Greek salad are vibrant. My favorite spot to sit for a meal is on a stool at the espresso bar. **Features:** patio dining. **Address:** 237 Firehole Ave W 59758 **Location:** Jct US 20 (Canyon St) and Firehole Ave. B L

THE GUSHER PIZZA AND SANDWICH SHOPPE
406/646-9050 **36**

American. Casual Dining. $8-$16 **AAA Inspector Notes:** This popular restaurant features a wide variety of toppings for their pizzas, sandwiches, burgers and steaks. Takeout and delivery are available. **Features:** beer & wine. **Address:** 40 Dunraven St 59758 **Location:** Corner of Madison and Dunraven sts. L D

(See map & index p. 324.)

MADISON CROSSING LOUNGE
406/646-7621 (34)

◆◆ American. Casual Dining. $13-$25 **AAA Inspector Notes:** This restaurant serves an array of items such as steamed mussels in garlic-tomato broth; Mediterranean bison sliders with mint, almonds and raisins finished with saffron yogurt sauce; lemon-herb-crusted Idaho rainbow trout; and Montana-raised Angus beef topped with chipotle huckleberry spread. You might get a kick out of the fact that the lounge in this former school is positioned in the first-grade classroom. **Features:** full bar. **Address:** 121 Madison Ave 59758 **Location:** Jct US 191 (Canyon St) and Madison Ave, just e. **Parking:** street only. [D]

PETE'S ROCKY MOUNTAIN PIZZA & PASTA
406/646-7820 (32)

◆◆ Pizza Sandwiches. Casual Dining. $8-$22 **AAA Inspector Notes:** This casual eatery offers a good selection of specialty pasta and pizza, including a build-your-own pizza. The breast of chicken and summer seafood salads are popular. Dinner is served only during the winter months. Vegetarian items and a children's menu are available. **Features:** beer & wine. **Address:** 112 Canyon St 59758 **Location:** Center; in Canyon Square. **Parking:** street only. [L] [D]

RED LOTUS
406/646-7002 (35)

◆◆ Chinese. Casual Dining. $9-$28 **AAA Inspector Notes:** You will be pleasantly surprised when you walk into this eatery, which has vibrant décor in various shades of red, pretty bamboo accents and a variety of lovely lighting fixtures. You simply can't beat the lunch specials or the dinner combination plates. On a cold night, a steaming bowl of the supreme corn or fragrant hot and sour soup will hit the spot. **Address:** 19 Madison Ave 59758 **Location:** Just nw of park entrance. **Parking:** street only. [L] [D]

RUNNING BEAR PANCAKE HOUSE   406/646-7703 (30)

◆◆
Breakfast
Sandwiches
Family Dining
$7-$15

AAA Inspector Notes: The focal point at this restaurant is a hanging bear named "Running Bear." Feast on an assortment of pancakes, but also try the strawberry crepes, build-your-own omelet, steak and eggs, yummy cinnamon roll and their seasonal muffins. It will be tough deciding which sandwich to order; the hot homemade meatloaf, pulled pork, Southwest chicken and three mini burgers are just a few of the options. Locals favor the beer-battered walleye fingers and the citrus avocado salmon salad. **Address:** 538 Madison Ave 59758 **Location:** 0.6 mi w of park entrance at Madison Ave and Hayden St. **Parking:** on-site and street. *Menu on AAA.com* [B] [L] [D]

SERENITY BISTRO
406/646-7660 (40)

◆◆ New French. Casual Dining. $12-$38 **AAA Inspector Notes:** This intimate little bistro serves creative dishes that incorporate local and regional ingredients and is a nice alternative in a town full of pizza and burger joints. Open for breakfast during the summer months. **Features:** beer & wine. **Reservations:** suggested. **Address:** 38 N Canyon St 59758 **Location:** Just n of park entrance. **Parking:** street only. [L] [D] [XC]

THREE BEAR RESTAURANT
406/646-7811 (41)

◆◆
American
Casual Dining
$8-$25

AAA Inspector Notes: Varied dishes ranging from beef and fish entrées to sandwiches, soups and salads are likely to please just about anyone at this family restaurant. Home-baked pastries are mouth-watering treats. The décor is certainly Northwestern with a feel reminiscent of what it was like in Yellowstone's early days. The staff here makes you feel like a welcome guest. **Features:** full bar. **Address:** 205 Yellowstone Ave 59758 **Location:** Just w of park entrance; next to Three Bear Lodge. **Parking:** street only. [B] [D]

TIMBERLINE CAFE
406/646-9349 (42)

◆◆ American. Casual Dining. $8-$19 **AAA Inspector Notes:** This casual down-home café offers a nice selection of menu items, including sandwiches, wraps, steak, daily specials, a soup and a salad bar. Pies are made in house, and the coconut cream goes fast. Vegetarian items are available. **Features:** beer & wine. **Address:** 135 Yellowstone Ave 59758 **Location:** Just w of park entrance. **Parking:** street only. [B] [L] [D]

WILD WEST PIZZERIA & SALOON
406/646-4400 (37)

◆◆ Pizza Sandwiches. Casual Dining. $9-$25 **AAA Inspector Notes:** Calzones and pizzas are prepared from dough that's made here and then tossed by hand in the open kitchen. The finest cheese Wisconsin offers is brought in and grated in house. The most popular specialty pizza is the "Butch Cassidy" made with barbecue sauce, baked beans, red onions and pulled pork. Live bands play on the weekends and a DJ is scheduled each Wednesday night. **Features:** full bar. **Address:** 14 Madison Ave 59758 **Location:** Just n of park entrance. **Parking:** street only. [L] [D] CALL [&M] [XC]

WHITEFISH (B-2) pop. 6,357, elev. 3,033'

- Hotels & Restaurants map & index p. 167
- Part of Glacier National Park area — see map p. 162

Whitefish Lake borders Whitefish and extends 7 miles north. The area offers scenic vistas, fishing, swimming, boating and beach activities.

Restored to its 1927 chalet-like appearance, the Great Northern Railway Depot houses railroad artifacts and area memorabilia. On the grounds is the Great Northern Locomotive #181, one of only seven ever built.

Offering spectacular views of the Flathead Valley and Glacier National Park, the Whitefish Mountain Resort Scenic Lift carries passengers to the 7,000-foot summit; phone (406) 862-2900.

RECREATIONAL ACTIVITIES
Skiing

- **Whitefish Mountain Resort** is at 3840 Big Mountain Rd. Skiing and other activities are offered. **Hours:** Winter sports are available daily, early Dec. to mid-Apr. Summer activities are offered mid-June through Sept. 30. Hours vary; phone ahead. **Phone:** (406) 862-2900 or (877) 754-3474.

BAY POINT ON THE LAKE   406/862-2331   **17**

WWW Condominium. Rates not provided. **Address:** 300 Bay Point Dr 59937 **Location:** Jct US 93 and SR 487, 0.6 mi n on SR 487 to Skyles Pl, 0.3 mi w to Dakota Ave, 0.3 mi n, then just w. **Facility:** 16 condominiums, some two and three bedrooms. 2 stories (no elevator), exterior corridors. **Parking:** winter plug-ins. **Terms:** check-in 5 pm. **Pool(s):** heated indoor. **Activities:** sauna, hot tub, marina, fishing, playground. **Guest Services:** coin laundry.

BEST WESTERN ROCKY MOUNTAIN LODGE
(406)862-2569   **20**

Hotel
$99-$325

AAA Benefit: Save 10% or more every day and earn 10% bonus points!	

Address: 6510 Hwy 93 S 59937 **Location:** 1.3 mi s on US 93 from jct SR 487. **Facility:** 79 units. 2-3 stories, interior/exterior corridors. **Parking:** winter plug-ins. **Pool(s):** heated outdoor. **Activities:** hot tub, exercise room. **Guest Services:** complimentary laundry, area transportation.

CHALET MOTEL   (406)862-5581   **21**

Motel
$60-$145

Address: 6430 US 93 S 59937 **Location:** 1 mi n on US 93 from jct SR 40. **Facility:** 34 units. 2 stories (no elevator), exterior corridors. **Parking:** winter plug-ins. **Terms:** cancellation fee imposed, resort fee. **Pool(s):** heated indoor. **Guest Services:** coin laundry.

GROUSE MOUNTAIN LODGE   406/862-3000   **18**

Hotel
Rates not provided

Address: 2 Fairway Dr 59937 **Location:** 1 mi w on US 93. **Facility:** 142 units. 3 stories, interior corridors. **Parking:** winter plug-ins. **Terms:** check-in 4 pm. **Dining:** Logan's Grill, see separate listing. **Pool(s):** heated indoor. **Activities:** sauna, hot tub, cross country skiing, exercise room, spa. **Guest Services:** valet and coin laundry, area transportation.

THE LODGE AT WHITEFISH LAKE   (406)863-4000   **16**

Hotel
$109-$299

Address: 1380 Wisconsin Ave 59937 **Location:** Waterfront. Jct US 93 and SR 487, 1.5 mi n on SR 487. **Facility:** Surrounded by mountains and a wildlife preserve, this lodge offers amenities for all seasons. Public areas have wrought iron chandeliers and animal mounts. All rooms are luxurious with western decor. 117 units, some kitchens. 3 stories, interior/exterior corridors. **Parking:** on-site and valet, winter plug-ins. **Terms:** check-in 4 pm, 3 day cancellation notice, 14 day 6/1-9/30-fee imposed. **Amenities:** safes. *Some:* video games. **Dining:** 2 restaurants. **Pool(s):** heated outdoor. **Activities:** sauna, hot tub, steamroom, limited beach access, motor boats, self-propelled boats, marina, bicycles, exercise room, spa. **Guest Services:** valet and coin laundry, area transportation.

NORTH FORTY RESORT   (406)862-7740   **22**

WW Cabin $119-$309 **Address:** 3765 Hwy 40 W 59912 **Location:** 2.5 mi e on SR 40 from jct US 93. Located in a quiet secluded area. **Facility:** 22 kitchen cabin units. 1 story, exterior corridors. **Parking:** winter plug-ins. **Terms:** check-in 4 pm, 2 night minimum stay - seasonal, 14 day cancellation notice-fee imposed. **Activities:** sauna, hot tub.

PINE LODGE   (406)862-7600   **19**

Hotel
$89-$199

Address: 920 Spokane Ave 59937 **Location:** 1 mi s on US 93 from jct SR 487. **Facility:** 76 units, some kitchens. 3 stories, interior corridors. **Parking:** winter plug-ins. **Terms:** check-in 4 pm, cancellation fee imposed, resort fee. **Pool(s):** heated outdoor. **Activities:** hot tub, exercise room. **Guest Services:** valet and coin laundry, area transportation. **Featured Amenity:** continental breakfast.

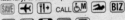

(See map & index p. 167.)

WHITEFISH MOUNTAIN RESORT
(406)862-1960 **15**

Vacation Rental Condominium $85-$1245 **Address:** 3889 Big Mountain Rd 59937 **Location:** Jct US 93 and SR 487, 2.4 mi n on SR 487, 5.2 mi n at flashing light. **Facility:** With multiple buildings and styles, all of the property's rooms are spacious with fireplaces, ski lockers, and ceiling fans. 147 units, some two bedrooms, three bedrooms, kitchens, houses and condominiums. 2-4 stories, interior/exterior corridors. **Parking:** winter plug-ins. **Terms:** check-in 4 pm, 1-5 night minimum stay, 30 day cancellation notice-fee imposed. **Pool(s):** heated indoor. **Activities:** hot tub, downhill & cross country skiing, snowmobiling, recreation programs, bicycles. **Guest Services:** valet and coin laundry, area transportation.

WHERE TO EAT

AMAZING CRÊPES & CATERING
406/862-6002 **15**

Specialty. Quick Serve. $6-$11 **AAA Inspector Notes:** Starting out as a humble food cart, the owners brought their savory and sweet creations to a more permanent location. The creative buckwheat crepes are a treat for gluten-wary diners. **Address:** 123 Central Ave 59937 **Location:** Center. **Parking:** street only. B L

BUFFALO CAFE
406/862-2833 **19**

American. Casual Dining. $8-$25 **AAA Inspector Notes:** A longtime favorite with locals and skiers on their way to Big Mountain, this café serves hearty breakfasts, including breakfast pies and Mexican specialties. Also on the menu are a variety of salads, burgers and sandwiches. Milkshakes are made with local ice cream. **Features:** beer & wine. **Address:** 514 3rd St E 59937 **Location:** Downtown. **Parking:** street only. B L D

CIAO MAMBO
406/863-9600 **16**

Italian. Casual Dining. $10-$25 **AAA Inspector Notes:** With the feel of an Italian villa, patrons enjoy dishes like Papa Biagio's Bolognese and linguine alla carbonara. The brick-fired pizzas and desserts are not to be missed. **Features:** full bar. **Address:** 234 E 2nd St E 59937 **Location:** Center. D

LOGAN'S GRILL
406/862-3000 **14**

American. Fine Dining. $9-$38 **AAA Inspector Notes:** Fine dining is the mode in this mountain resort atmosphere, which features a river rock fireplace and mounted big game heads. The menu supports wide-ranging taste temptations, including inventive burgers and sandwiches, all well prepared and made to order. Side dishes are varied and similarly tasty. **Features:** full bar, patio dining, happy hour. **Reservations:** suggested. **Address:** 2 Fairway Dr 59937 **Location:** 1 mi w on US 93 from jct SR 487; in Grouse Mountain Lodge. B L D CALL M

LOULA'S
406/862-5614 **17**

American. Casual Dining. $9-$24 **AAA Inspector Notes:** This very popular, open and bright restaurant serves a full breakfast menu until 2 pm. Save room for the pies and other delicious desserts, all made in house in a dining room surrounded by dramatic landscape photos of the area. Handicap access is through the Lupfer Street entrance. **Features:** beer & wine. **Address:** 300 2nd St E 59937 **Location:** Jct Lupfer St; downtown. **Parking:** street only. B L D

THE NAKED NOODLE
406/862-6253 **12**

Noodles. Quick Serve. $8-$15 **AAA Inspector Notes:** Diners choose pasta, soba, rice or spinach noodles, then decide from the many sauces, meats, vegetables, seafood and toppings in order to create a scrumptious meal. Can't decide? Choose one of the tried-and-true combinations posted on the board. For the most part, the restaurant is self-serve, but orders are taken by a patient and friendly staff. **Address:** 10 Baker Ave 59937 **Location:** Jct Railway St; downtown. L D CALL M

TUPELO GRILLE AND WINE BAR
406/862-6136 **13**

Continental Casual Dining $16-$42

AAA Inspector Notes: In keeping with the experience of the owners, who hail from the South, the menu's Continental dishes show hints of Southern Creole and Cajun influences. **Features:** beer & wine. **Address:** 17 Central Ave 59937 **Location:** Downtown. **Parking:** street only. D

WASABI SUSHI BAR & THE GINGER GRILL
406/863-9283 **18**

Asian Casual Dining $8-$45

AAA Inspector Notes: The menu centers on sushi and Asia-influenced dishes grilled with a contemporary flair. The lively, colorful dining room displays original artwork in oils, acrylics and fiber. **Features:** beer & wine. **Reservations:** suggested. **Address:** 419 E 2nd St 59937 **Location:** Downtown. **Parking:** street only. D

WHITEFISH LAKE RESTAURANT
406/862-5285 **11**

American Casual Dining $12-$46

AAA Inspector Notes: On one of the area's finest golf courses, the restaurant is housed in a structure made of logs from the surrounding forests. Guests dine on steak and seafood as well as inventive specials created nightly. **Features:** full bar, patio dining. **Reservations:** suggested. **Address:** 1200 US Hwy 93 N 59937 **Location:** 1 mi w on US 93 from jct SR 487. L D

WHITEHALL (E-3) pop. 1,038, elev. 4,351'

GEM **LEWIS AND CLARK CAVERNS STATE PARK** is 7.3 mi. e. on SR 2 to 25 Lewis and Clark Rd. Dedicated in 1941, Montana's first state park includes a limestone cavern of vaulted chambers, intricate passageways and delicate, varicolored formations that make this one of the most beautiful caverns in the country. On the surface, 10 miles of hiking trails showcase the rugged site's 3,000 acres.

Note: The 2-hour guided cavern tours involve walking a total of 2 miles and require visitors to negotiate 600 (mostly descending) steps; full mobility is required and rubber-soled shoes are advised. Because the cavern temperature remains around 50 F, a jacket is recommended. Pets are not permitted in the cavern.

Hours: Park open daily 9-9, mid-June. to mid-Aug.; 9-5, rest of year. Cavern tours are given daily 9-6:30, mid-June to mid-Aug.; 9-4:30, May 1 to mid-June and mid-Aug. through Sept. 30. Candlelight cave tours are offered are offered in late December; reservations are required. **Cost:** Park admission $6 (nonresidents per private vehicle); $4 (nonresidents arriving by other means); free (Montana residents with ID). Two-hour, 2-mile guided cavern tour $12; $5 (ages 6-11). **Phone:** (406) 287-3541. GT

WHITE SULPHUR SPRINGS (D-4)
pop. 939, elev. 5,100'

Nestled in the Smith River valley between the Little Belt Mountains in Lewis and Clark National Forest *(see place listing p. 186)* on the east and the Big Belt Mountains on the west, White Sulphur Springs offers numerous outdoor summer and winter recreational opportunities, including hunting, cross-country skiing, downhill skiing, snowmobiling, hiking and mountain biking. The Smith River and nearby Lake Sutherlin, Newlan Reservoir and several other lakes and reservoirs invite fishing, camping and water sports.

CASTLE MUSEUM CARRIAGE HOUSE is 4 blks. n.e. off US 12/89 to 310 Second Ave. N.E., entered from the carriage house behind the castle. This restored Victorian house built in 1892 by B.R. Sherman, a cattleman and mine owner, sits on a hilltop overlooking the town. The gray stone structure, furnished in period, houses the Meagher County Historical Association Museum, which explores county history. **Time:** Allow 30 minutes minimum. **Hours:** Daily 10-5, Memorial Day-Labor Day; Fri.-Sun. 10-5, May 15-day before Memorial Day and day after Labor Day-Sept. 15. Last tour begins 1 hour before closing. **Cost:** $5; $3 (ages 4-12 and 60+). **Phone:** (406) 547-2324 in season.

WIBAUX (C-8) pop. 589, elev. 2,634'

Wibaux has the distinction of being the first town to greet visitors entering Montana westbound on I-94. A statue of Frenchman Pierre Wibaux (WEE-bo), for whom the town is named, stands on the western edge of town.

Self-guiding tours: Brochures of a walking tour are available at the information center in The Pierre Wibaux Museum Complex.

THE PIERRE WIBAUX MUSEUM COMPLEX is at 112 E. Orgain Ave. It features the restored Pierre Wibaux office and house, built in 1892, and an adjoining barbershop with antique furnishings. A livery stable and a 1964 Montana Centennial Train railroad car are on the grounds. Displays include dinosaur fossils and homestead artifacts. **Hours:** Mon.-Sat. 9-5, Sun. 1-5, Memorial Day-Labor Day. **Cost:** Donations. **Phone:** (406) 796-9969.

WILLOW CREEK pop. 210

WILLOW CREEK CAFE AND SALOON   406/285-3698
♥♥ Western American. Casual Dining. $10-$30 **AAA Inspector Notes:** *Historic.* In a historic building, this restaurant is well known for its fall-off-the-bone ribs and homemade desserts. Guests come from all around the region for dinner and drinks at the saloon. **Features:** full bar. **Reservations:** suggested. **Address:** 21 Main St 59760 **Location:** I-90 exit 278, 6 mi s of Three Forks, follow signs.
D

WISDOM pop. 98

THE CROSSING BAR & GRILL   406/689-3260
♥♥ American. Family Dining. $12-$29 **AAA Inspector Notes:** There's a lot to see around town, including Bighole National Battlefield 10 miles to the west, Beaverhead Deerlodge National Forest, Chief Joseph Pass to Idaho and skiing. Abundant wildlife and incredible scenery can be seen. After a day of fishing, camping, hunting or sightseeing, thank goodness this place is serving up the best chow in the county. Huge burgers, perfectly cooked steaks, homemade soups, healthy salads and homemade desserts are offered. Prime rib is served on Saturday night. **Features:** beer & wine. **Address:** 327 Hwy 43 59761 **Location:** Center. B L D ✗

WOLF CREEK (C-3) elev. 3,560'

Wolf Creek is a popular point for sports enthusiasts bound for Holter Lake *(see Recreation Areas Chart)*, 5 miles southeast of town. The result of one of a series of dams on the Upper Missouri River, the lake is bordered by the Sleeping Giant Wilderness, Beartooth Wildlife Management Area and Helena National Forest *(see place listing p. 181).*

Almost all of the lake's recreational facilities are on its eastern shore. A particularly scenic drive begins at the junction of US 287 and SR 200 north of Wolf Creek, proceeds south on US 287 to the junction with I-15, then on to Helena, Butte and the Idaho border, passing some of Montana's most impressive mountains.

WOLF POINT (B-7) pop. 2,621, elev. 2,001'

While sustained mostly by agriculture, Wolf Point's economy also benefits from small manufacturing firms and Honeyland Inc., which maintains more than 4,000 bee colonies and produces about a half-million pounds of honey annually. Wolf Point also is the home of many Sioux and Assiniboine, who perform dances and observe celebrations June through August. The Wolf Point Wild Horse Stampede, said to be the state's oldest rodeo, takes place during the second week in July.

Wolf Point Chamber of Commerce & Agriculture: 218 Third Ave. S., Suite B, Wolf Point, MT 59201. **Phone:** (406) 653-2012.

WOLF POINT AREA MUSEUM is at 202 US 2. The museum exhibits clothing, arrowheads and other items used by the area's Native American residents and pioneer settlers. Early radios and phonographs, military items, and sculptures and paintings by local artists also are on display. **Hours:** Tues.-Sat. 9-5, mid-May to mid-Sept. Closed major holidays. **Cost:** Donations. **Phone:** (406) 653-1912.

▼ YELLOWSTONE NATIONAL PARK—See Wyoming p. 316

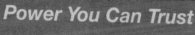

Grand Teton National Park

Wyoming

You could say that Wyoming is *Mecheweami-ing* to the max. The Delaware Native American word meaning "at the great plains" or "on the great plain"—helpfully simplified to the present state name—is certainly geographically apt. But Wyoming's mountains, grasslands, canyons, deserts and other natural attributes also are worthy of greatness.

The Continental Divide cuts a diagonal swath across this almost precisely rectangular state, bisecting it into the Missouri and Columbia and Colorado river basins. The divide winds northwest to southeast along the curved, jagged spine of the Rocky Mountains, and some of Wyoming's most scenic jewels can be found in this formidably mountainous territory.

Grand Teton National Park fully deserves gushing adjectives like "breathtaking" and "magnificent"; it was first photographed way back in 1872, and ever since shutterbugs

Buffalo Bill Center of the West, Cody

have commemorated for posterity the region's sparkling blue lakes, impressive glaciers, mammoth snowfields and lush green stands of fir, pine and spruce. This awesome natural setting begat Jackson Hole, an outdoor recreation paradise offering thrill seekers a range of temptations from mountain climbing and windsurfing to skiing and whitewater rafting.

Yellowstone is the nation's first national park, and one of its most beloved. It's also a hot spot for geyser activity, the result of a volcanic eruption some 600,000 years ago. The thermal theatrics of Old Faithful receive top billing; this cone geyser shoots up to 8,000 gallons of boiling water some 150 feet in the air every 90 or so minutes, providing a spectacular show. But Yellowstone offers everything from the terrace-like formations of Mammoth Hot Springs and colorful hot clay bubbling from vivid paint pots to photographic encounters with the likes of grizzlies, black bears, elk, bison and bighorn sheep.

In Bighorn Canyon National Recreation Area, shared with neighboring Montana, canyon walls of sculpted rock rise up and encircle a 55-mile stretch of serene Bighorn Lake. Imposing Shell and Crazy Woman canyons punctuate the terrain of Bighorn National Forest. The Green River carved the backdrop of appropriately named Flaming Gorge National Recreation Area; as Creedence Clearwater Revival once observed in a song, you can kick your feet way down in shallow water and skip a flat rock across Green River.

Like a bad haircut, sagebrush crowns the massive monolith that is the centerpiece of Devils Tower National Monument. The remarkably well-preserved remains of fish, insects, reptiles, plants and birds at Fossil Butte National Monument provide compelling evidence that the region basked in a sub-tropical environment some 50 million years ago.

Rolling Westward

Wyoming's topographic highlights must have been eye-popping to the 19th-century pioneers who rumbled along the Oregon Trail in a series of wagon train processions, heading to a new life in California and the Pacific Northwest. Western lore is well documented at places like Fort Laramie National Historic Site, a fur-trading post established in 1834 that witnessed the unfolding drama of westward expansion as well as its varied cast: trappers, traders, missionaries, treasure seekers, homesteaders, cowboys and the Native American tribes that fiercely resisted the encroachments on their land.

Museums like The Nelson Museum of the West in Cheyenne, the Buffalo Bill Center of the West in Cody, the Wyoming Pioneer Memorial Museum in Douglas and the Wyoming Territorial Prison State Historic Site in Laramie all are repositories for this rich heritage. Cody not only pays tribute to its founder, Col. William "Buffalo Bill" F. Cody, but to Harry Longabaugh—or the Sundance Kid—who adopted his better-known moniker from the Wyoming town in which he once served time. And as fans of Paul Newman and Robert Redford know, that particular Wyoming legend was made into a pretty darn good movie.

Recreation

Wyoming lets you experience Wild West life without having to put up with Wild West hardships. Mount a trusty horse at the crack of dawn and head into the mountains, experience breathtakingly unspoiled wilderness and end the day relaxing around an open campfire. Outfitters offer everything from cattle herding adventures to overnight chuck wagon trips.

Yellowstone has more than 1,000 miles of hiking trails ranging from easy loops to strenuous treks; many visitors opt for a trail that ventures past at least one of the park's bubbling geysers. Yellowstone Lake is tops for boating; Shoshone Lake is a favorite for canoeing. If you're in the mood for a less demanding activity, the Togwotee Trail (US 26/287 through Fremont and Teton counties) offers scenery that is magnificent viewed from the passenger seat of a car.

A short skip south is Wyoming's *other* national park, Grand Teton. Extreme adventure enthusiasts will relish the challenge of climbing one of the park's four principal mountains—Grand Teton, Middle Teton, Buck Mountain and Mount Moran. Allow 2 days for a summertime ascent of Grand Teton; the Owen-Spaulding route, a 7-mile trek, is the most popular scramble to the top of this 13,770-foot peak.

There's another natural landmark in the state's opposite (northeastern) corner. Devils Tower, the nation's first national monument, soars 1,267 feet above the Belle Fourche River. Climbing the formation's fluted, nearly perpendicular heights is permitted, but most folks are content to hike the popular 1.3-mile Tower Trail that circles it.

White-water rafting in the vicinity of Jackson Hole has the bonus of spectacular mountain backdrops. The upper Snake River's relatively gentle water is well-suited for novices, but the lower Snake's white water will take you for a wild ride. And winter in Wyoming brings lots of snow and plenty of terrain for cross-country and downhill skiing; the packed powder typical of Snow King Mountain in Jackson Hole makes it a good spot for beginners.

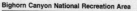

Bighorn Canyon National Recreation Area

Historic Timeline

1807	John Colter, a member of the Lewis and Clark Expedition, spends months alone in a wilderness of mountains and geysers.
1834	Fur traders William Sublette and Robert Campbell establish a trading post at Fort Laramie.
1849	The United States buys Fort Laramie to use as a base to protect and supply travelers along the Oregon Trail.
1863	The Wyoming Territory's first newspaper, *The Daily Telegraph*, begins printing in Fort Bridger.
1869	Wyoming women become the first in the nation to obtain the right to vote.
1890	Wyoming becomes the 44th state.
1872	The wilderness area John Colter described as "Colter's Hell" is designated Yellowstone, the country's first national park.
1925	Nellie Tayloe Ross is sworn in as Wyoming's—and the nation's—first woman governor.
1958	The 4320th Strategic Missile Wing is established at F.E. Warren Air Force Base in Cheyenne.
1988	Wildfires in Yellowstone National Park scorch more than 1 million acres.
2010	Yellowstone receives nearly 1 million visitors in July, the most people ever to visit the park in a single month.

What To Pack

Temperature Averages Maximum/Minimum

	JANUARY	FEBRUARY	MARCH	APRIL	MAY	JUNE	JULY	AUGUST	SEPTEMBER	OCTOBER	NOVEMBER	DECEMBER
Casper	33/14	37/16	43/21	56/31	66/40	77/49	87/56	85/55	74/45	61/36	44/23	37/18
Cheyenne	38/14	40/15	44/20	55/29	64/39	76/48	84/54	82/53	73/43	62/33	47/22	42/18
Evanston	29/10	34/12	42/19	52/26	61/33	72/40	79/46	78/45	68/37	57/28	40/18	32/10
Lander	31/8	36/12	45/20	56/31	66/40	76/48	86/55	84/54	73/45	60/34	43/19	35/12
Sheridan	34/9	36/11	43/19	56/31	67/40	75/48	87/56	86/53	74/43	62/33	46/21	39/14
Yellowstone NP	26/10	30/11	37/17	48/26	57/33	67/41	76/47	74/45	64/37	52/29	38/20	28/12

From the records of The Weather Channel Interactive, Inc.

Good Facts To Know

ABOUT THE STATE

POPULATION: 563,626.

AREA: 97,914 square miles; ranks 9th.

CAPITAL: Cheyenne.

HIGHEST POINT: 13,804 ft., Gannett Peak.

LOWEST POINT: 3,100 ft., Belle Fourche River Valley.

TIME ZONE(S): Mountain. DST.

GAMBLING

MINIMUM AGE FOR GAMBLING: 18.

REGULATIONS

TEEN DRIVING LAWS: No more than one passenger under the age of 18 is permitted (family members are exempt). Driving is not permitted 11 p.m.-5 a.m. The minimum age for an unrestricted driver's license is 16 and 6 months with driver's education course and 17 without driver's education course. Phone (307) 777-4800 for more information about Wyoming driver's license regulations.

SEAT BELT/CHILD RESTRAINT LAWS: Seat belts are required for driver and all passengers ages 9 and over. Children under age 9 are required to be in a child restraint in the rear seat, if possible. AAA recommends the use of seat belts and appropriate child restraints for the driver and all passengers.

CELLPHONE RESTRICTIONS: All drivers are banned from text messaging.

HELMETS FOR MOTORCYCLISTS: Required for riders under 18.

RADAR DETECTORS: Permitted. Prohibited for use by commercial vehicles.

MOVE OVER LAW: Driver is required to slow down to 20 mph under the posted speed limit and vacate the lane nearest stopped police, fire and rescue vehicles, including tow trucks, using audible or flashing signals.

FIREARMS LAWS: Vary by state and/or county. Contact the Wyoming Highway Patrol, 5300 Bishop Blvd., P.O. Box 1708, Cheyenne, WY 82009-3340; phone (307) 777-4301.

HOLIDAYS

HOLIDAYS: Jan. 1 ▪ Martin Luther King Jr. Day, Jan. (3rd Mon.) ▪ Washington's Birthday/Presidents Day, Feb. (3rd Mon.) ▪ Memorial Day, May (last Mon.) ▪ July 4 ▪ Labor Day, Sept. (1st Mon.) ▪ Veterans Day, Nov. 11 ▪ Thanksgiving, Nov. (4th Thurs.) ▪ Christmas, Dec. 25.

MONEY

TAXES: Wyoming's statewide sales tax is 4 percent, with local options for an additional increment up to 2 percent. Localities may also impose a lodging tax of up to 4 percent.

VISITOR INFORMATION

INFORMATION CENTERS: State welcome centers are on I-90 at E. 5th Street interchange east of Sheridan ▪ on I-90 exit 187 at Sundance ▪ on US 26/89/187 on north edge of Jackson ▪ 1 mile south of Cheyenne on I-25 at W. College Drive interchange ▪ on I-80 on east edge of Evanston ▪ on I-80 exit 401 south of Pine Bluffs ▪ and on I-80, 10 miles east of Laramie at Sherman Hill exit. The centers are open daily 8-6, Memorial Day-Labor Day, and daily 8-5, rest of year.

FURTHER INFORMATION FOR VISITORS:
Wyoming Travel and Tourism
5611 High Plains Rd.
Cheyenne, WY 82007
(307) 777-7777
(800) 225-5996

NATIONAL FOREST INFORMATION:
U.S. Forest Service, Rocky Mountain Region
740 Simms St.
Golden, CO 80401
(303) 275-5350

USDA Forest Service, Ogden Ranger District
507 25th St.
Ogden, UT 84401
(801) 625-5112
(877) 444-6777 (reservations)

FISHING AND HUNTING REGULATIONS:
Wyoming Game and Fish Department
5400 Bishop Blvd.
Cheyenne, WY 82006
(307) 777-4600

RECREATION INFORMATION:
Wyoming State Parks and Cultural Resources
Barrett Building
2301 Capitol Ave.
Cheyenne, WY 82002
(307) 777-6323

STATE PARK INFORMATION:
Division of State Parks and Historic Sites
Barrett Building
2301 Central Ave., 4th Floor
Cheyenne, WY 82002
(307) 777-6323

Wyoming Annual Events

Please call ahead to confirm event details.

JANUARY	FEBRUARY	MARCH
■ Sierra Madre Winter Carnival / Encampment 307-327-5501 ■ Wild West Winter Carnival Riverton 307-856-4801 ■ Ice Fishing Derby Saratoga 307-326-8855	■ Donald E. Erickson Memorial Chariot Races Saratoga 307-326-8855 ■ Buffalo Bill's Birthday Celebration / Cody 307-527-5626 ■ Glass Art Celebration Cheyenne 307-637-6458	■ Jackson Hole Rendezvous Teton Village 307-733-2292 ■ World Championship Snowmobile Hill Climb Jackson 307-734-9653 ■ Ceili at the Roundhouse Celtic Festival / Evanston 307-679-2348

APRIL	MAY	JUNE
■ Society of Petroleum Engineers Crawfish Boil Gillette 307-680-6789 ■ Western Spirit Art Show and Sale / Cheyenne 307-778-7290 ■ Big Wyoming Horse Expo Douglas 307-244-4922	■ ElkFest and Antler Auction Jackson 307-733-3316 ■ Old West Days / Jackson 307-733-3316 ■ Cody's Wild West Days Cody 307-587-4221	■ Woodchopper's Jamboree and Rodeo / Encampment 307-710-5558 ■ Cody Nite Rodeo / Cody 800-207-0744 ■ Flaming Gorge Days Green River 307-778-3133

JULY	AUGUST	SEPTEMBER
■ Cheyenne Frontier Days Cheyenne 307-778-7222 ■ Green River Rendezvous Pinedale 307-367-4101 ■ Sheridan-Wyo-Rodeo Sheridan 307-672-9715	■ Wyoming State Fair and Rodeo / Douglas 307-358-2398 ■ Texas Trail Days in Pine Bluffs / Pine Bluffs 307-245-3746 ■ Gift of the Waters Indian Pageant and Powwow Thermopolis 800-786-6772	■ Fort Bridger Rendezvous Fort Bridger 435-213-5133 ■ Rendezvous Royale / Cody 307-587-5002 ■ Jackson Hole Fall Arts Festival / Jackson 307-733-3316

OCTOBER	NOVEMBER	DECEMBER
■ Chili Cook-Off / Gillette 307-687-5213 ■ Oktoberfest / Rock Springs 307-352-6789 ■ Moonlight Madness Thermopolis 877-864-3192	■ Cheyenne Christmas Parade, Concert and Craft Show / Cheyenne 307-637-3376 ■ Parade of Lights / Worland 307-347-3226 ■ Christmas Stroll / Sheridan 307-672-2485	■ Powell Country Christmas Powell 307-754-3494 ■ Lighted Christmas Parade Buffalo 307-684-5544 ■ Mountain Man Christmas Pinedale 307-367-2242

Spring at Grand Teton National Park

West Thumb Geyser Basin, Yellowstone National Park

Chief Washakie statue, State Capitol, Cheyenne

Jim Gatchell Memorial Museum, Buffalo

Fort Laramie National Historic Site

Index: Great Experience for Members

AAA editor's picks of exceptional note

Cheyenne Frontier Days Old West Museum

Devils Tower National Monument

Wyoming Territorial Prison State Historic Site

Yellowstone National Park

See Orientation map on p. 232 for corresponding grid coordinates, if applicable.

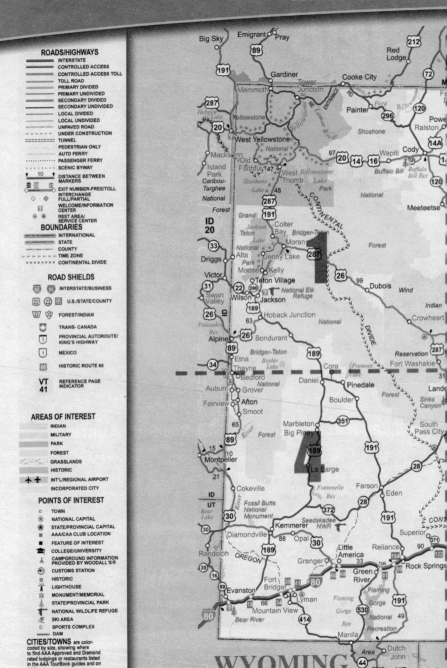

ROADS/HIGHWAYS
- INTERSTATE
- CONTROLLED ACCESS
- CONTROLLED ACCESS TOLL
- TOLL ROAD
- PRIMARY DIVIDED
- PRIMARY UNDIVIDED
- SECONDARY DIVIDED
- SECONDARY UNDIVIDED
- LOCAL DIVIDED
- LOCAL UNDIVIDED
- UNPAVED ROAD
- UNDER CONSTRUCTION
- TUNNEL
- PEDESTRIAN ONLY
- AUTO FERRY
- PASSENGER FERRY
- SCENIC BYWAY
- DISTANCE BETWEEN MARKERS
- EXIT NUMBER-FREE/TOLL
- INTERCHANGE FULL/PARTIAL
- WELCOME/INFORMATION CENTER
- REST AREA/ SERVICE CENTER

BOUNDARIES
- INTERNATIONAL
- STATE
- COUNTY
- TIME ZONE
- CONTINENTAL DIVIDE

ROAD SHIELDS
- INTERSTATE/BUSINESS
- U.S./STATE/COUNTY
- FOREST/INDIAN
- TRANS- CANADA
- PROVINCIAL AUTOROUTE/ KING'S HIGHWAY
- MEXICO
- HISTORIC ROUTE 66
- VT 41 REFERENCE PAGE INDICATOR

AREAS OF INTEREST
- INDIAN
- MILITARY
- PARK
- FOREST
- GRASSLANDS
- HISTORIC
- INTL/REGIONAL AIRPORT
- INCORPORATED CITY

POINTS OF INTEREST
- c TOWN
- NATIONAL CAPITAL
- STATE/PROVINCIAL CAPITAL
- AAA/CAA CLUB LOCATION
- FEATURE OF INTEREST
- COLLEGE/UNIVERSITY
- CAMPGROUND INFORMATION PROVIDED BY WOODALL'S®
- CUSTOMS STATION
- HISTORIC
- LIGHTHOUSE
- MONUMENT/MEMORIAL
- STATE/PROVINCIAL PARK
- NATIONAL WILDLIFE REFUGE
- SKI AREA
- SPORTS COMPLEX
- DAM

CITIES/TOWNS
CITIES/TOWNS are color-coded by size, showing where to find AAA Approved and Diamond rated lodgings or restaurants listed in the AAA TourBook guides and on AAA.com:

- ● Red - major destinations and capitals; many listings
- ● Black - destinations; some listings
- ● Grey - no listings

WYOMING

Miles 20 10 0 10 20 Miles
Kilometers 20 10 0 10 20 Kilometers
ONE INCH EQUALS APPROXIMATELY 33 MILES OR 53.11 KILOMETERS 1:2,090,580

Use driving maps from the AAA Road Atlas to plan your itinerary and route. Purchase the complete 2016 AAA Road Atlas at participating AAA/CAA offices, retail stores and online booksellers.

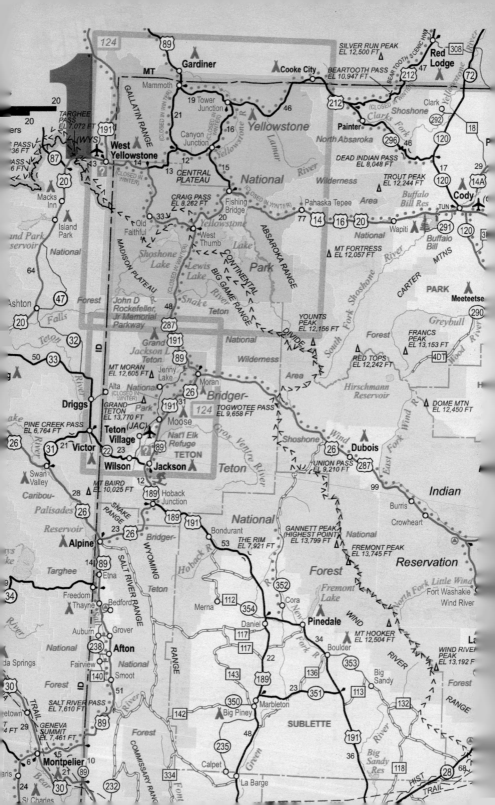

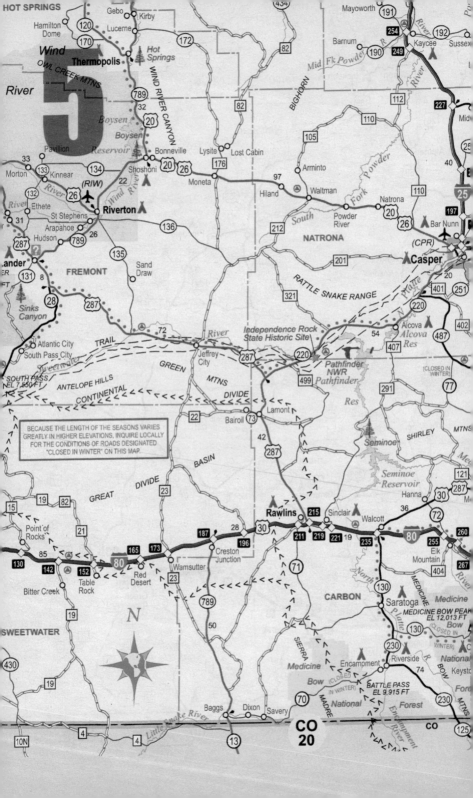

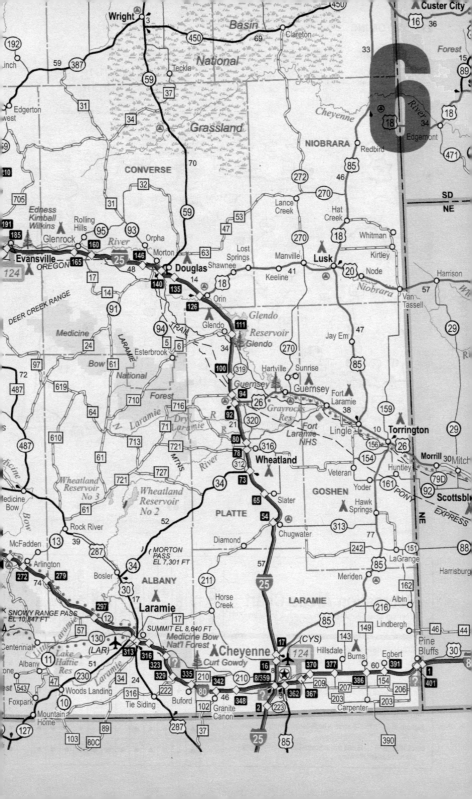

Recreation Areas Chart

The map location numerals in column 2 show an area's location on the preceding map.

	MAP LOCATION	CAMPING	PICNICKING	HIKING TRAILS	BOATING	BOAT RAMP	BOAT RENTAL	FISHING	SWIMMING	PETS ON LEASH	BICYCLE TRAILS	WINTER SPORTS	VISITOR CENTER	LODGE/CABINS	FOOD SERVICE
NATIONAL PARKS (See place listings.)															
Grand Teton (B-1) 485 square miles in northwest Wyoming. Horse rental.		•	•	•	•	•	•	•	•	•	•	•	•	•	•
Yellowstone (B-1) 3,472 square miles in mostly northwest Wyoming and small portions of eastern Idaho and southwest Montana. Horse rental.		•	•	•	•	•	•	•		•		•	•	•	•
NATIONAL FORESTS (See place listings.)															
Bighorn (B-3) 1,115,073 acres in north-central Wyoming. Horse rental.		•	•	•	•	•		•		•	•	•	•		•
Black Hills (B-6) 1,246,660 acres. Southwestern South Dakota and northeastern Wyoming.		•	•	•	•	•		•	•	•	•		•		•

Recreation Areas Chart

The map location numerals in column 2 show an area's location on the preceding map.

	MAP LOCATION	CAMPING	PICNICKING	HIKING TRAILS	BOATING	BOAT RAMP	BOAT RENTAL	FISHING	SWIMMING	PETS ON LEASH	BICYCLE TRAILS	WINTER SPORTS	VISITOR CENTER	LODGE/CABINS	FOOD SERVICE
Bridger-Teton (C-2) 3,439,809 acres in western Wyoming. Horse rental.		•	•	•	•	•	•	•	•	•	•	•	•	•	•
Medicine Bow (D-5) 1,093,618 acres in eastern Wyoming. Horse rental.		•	•	•	•			•	•	•	•	•	•	•	•
Shoshone (C-2) 2,466,586 acres in northwestern Wyoming.		•	•	•				•		•					
NATIONAL MONUMENTS *(See place listings.)*															
Devils Tower (B-6) 1,347 acres in northeast Wyoming.		•	•	•						•			•		
NATIONAL RECREATION AREAS *(See place listings.)*															
Bighorn Canyon (A-3) 120,000 acres in southern Montana and northern Wyoming.		•	•	•	•			•		•			•		•
Flaming Gorge (E-2) 207,363 acres in northeast Utah and southwest Wyoming. Cross-country skiing, horseback riding, hunting, ice fishing, parasailing, rafting, snowmobiling, water skiing.		•	•	•	•	•	•	•	•	•	•	•	•	•	•
STATE															
Bear River (E-1) 320 acres on I-80 near Evanston. Captive bison herd. *(See Evanston p. 256.)*	❶		•	•				•		•	•		•		
Big Sandy (D-2) 6,190 acres 6 mi. n. of Farson on US 191.	❷	•	•	•	•	•		•		•					
Boysen (C-3) 39,545 acres 14 mi. n.w. of Shoshoni off US 20. *(See Thermopolis p. 311.)*	❸	•	•		•	•	•	•	•	•					•
Buffalo Bill (B-2) 12,000 acres 9 mi. w. of Cody on US 14/16/20.	❹	•	•	•	•	•		•		•	•		•		
Curt Gowdy (E-5) 1,960 acres 26 mi. w. of Cheyenne off SR 210.	❺	•	•	•	•	•		•		•	•		•		
Edness Kimball Wilkins (C-5) 315 acres 6 mi. e. of Casper off I-25.	❻		•	•				•		•	•		•		
Glendo (D-5) 22,430 acres 4 mi. e. of Glendo off US 87.	❼	•	•	•	•	•	•	•	•	•					
Guernsey (D-6) 8,638 acres 3 mi. w. of Guernsey off US 26.	❽	•	•	•	•	•		•	•	•	•		•		
Hawk Springs (E-6) 2,000 acres 39 mi. s. of Torrington off US 85.	❾	•	•		•	•		•		•	•				
Hot Springs (C-3) 1,034 acres in n.e. Thermopolis on SR 789 and US 20. *(See Thermopolis p. 311.)*	❿		•	•				•	•	•	•		•		
Keyhole (B-6) 15,674 acres 7 mi. n. of I-90 between Moorcroft and Sundance.	⓫	•	•	•	•	•		•		•				•	•
Seminoe (D-4) 10,381 acres 35 mi. n. of Sinclair off I-80.	⓬	•	•	•	•	•		•	•	•					
Sinks Canyon (D-2) 600 acres 7.5 mi. s.w. of Lander on SR 131. *(See Lander p. 291.)*	⓭	•	•	•				•		•			•		
OTHER															
Alcova Reservoir (D-4) 2,470 acres 4 mi. s. of Alcova off SR 220.	⓮	•	•	•	•	•	•	•	•	•					•
Casper Mountain Park (D-4) 3,315 acres 7 mi. s. of Casper on SR 251. Cross-country and downhill skiing, snowmobiling; archery range, braille nature trail, bridle trails.	⓯	•	•	•								•	•	•	•
Fontenelle Reservoir (D-2) 8,000 acres 35 mi. n. of Kemmerer via US 189.	⓰	•	•	•	•			•		•					
Fremont Lake (D-2) 5,000-acre lake 3.5 mi. n.e. of Pinedale off Fremont Lake Rd. Ice fishing, cross-country skiing, skating, snowmobiling. *(See Pinedale p. 298.)*	⓱	•	•	•	•	•		•		•				•	•
Lake Viva Naughton (D-1) 1,375 acres 12 mi. n. of Kemmerer via SR 233.	⓲	•			•	•		•							
Saratoga Lake (E-4) 270-acre lake 1.5 mi. n. of Saratoga off SR 130.	⓳	•	•	•	•	•		•		•	•	•	•		

Ask about AAA/CAA Associate membership
to share the benefits you value

AFTON (D-1) pop. 1,911, elev. 6,267'

Mormon emigrants surveyed the already-settled site of Afton in 1896, using a carpenter's square, a rope and an almanac and taking their bearings from the North Star and the sun. An official survey made years later found the plot only about 5 feet off.

In addition to the arch of 3,011 elk antlers that spans Washington Street at the center of town, Afton is noted for Periodic Spring, a natural cold-water geyser. The spring is 5 miles east in Bridger-Teton National Forest *(see place listing p. 236).*

Afton lies in Star Valley along the scenic portion of US 89, which runs 255 miles between Mammoth Hot Springs in Yellowstone National Park *(see place listing p. 323)* and Geneva on the Idaho border.

Star Valley Chamber of Commerce: 150 S. Washington St., P.O. Box 190, Afton, WY 83110. **Phone:** (800) 426-8833.

LINCOLN COUNTY DAUGHTERS OF UTAH PIONEER MUSEUM is at 150 S. Washington St. (US 89). The museum displays artifacts chronicling Mormon history in southwestern Wyoming. **Hours:** Mon.-Fri. 1-5, June-Aug. **Cost:** Free. **Phone:** (800) 426-8833 for information.

LAZY B MOTEL   307/885-3187

 Motel $82-$110 **Address:** 219 S Washington St (US 89) 83110 **Location:** US 89; downtown. **Facility:** 25 units. 1 story, exterior corridors. **Parking:** winter plug-ins. **Pool(s):** heated outdoor. **Guest Services:** coin laundry.

ALCOVA (D-4) pop. 76, elev. 5,364'

Alcova lies in a small valley rimmed by rocky hills. In 1891 a group of Easterners bought a nearby site where hot springs flowed from the walls of a canyon. An analysis of the water showed a high concentration of minerals, but the $250,000 the syndicate planned to spend on improvements never materialized.

The water that finally proved important to the town is that impounded by Alcova Dam, 4 miles south of town off SR 220. The dam stretches 700 feet in length and rises 800 feet from the canyon riverbed. Reservoirs created by Alcova and nearby Pathfinder dams provide popular recreation sites for residents of Casper and other communities. *See Recreation Areas Chart.*

One of the more colorful local legends involves Ella "Cattle Kate" Watson, unpopular with townsfolk because of her freewheeling lifestyle and skill at raising cattle. She secretly married rancher Jim Averill so they could double their herd while she retained her homestead in her own name. Other ranchers demanded that both leave town, but before they could make their getaway the two were hanged unceremoniously from a scrub pine. Cattle Kate's 1889 lynching made her the only woman to suffer this fate in Wyoming.

INDEPENDENCE ROCK STATE HISTORIC SITE is 25 mi. w. on SR 220. Called "The Great Register of the Desert," this well-known landmark is a 136-foot-high granite boulder with a base that covers more than 24 acres. Members of an expedition led by Robert Stuart, credited with the discovery of the Oregon Trail, first visited the rock in 1812. Since then more than 5,000 explorers, adventurers, missionaries and soldiers have carved their names on it.

Independence Rock was named during a celebration held July 4, 1830, by a party of fur trappers led by William Sublette. **Hours:** Daily dawn-dusk. **Cost:** Free.

ALPINE pop. 828
- **Part of Jackson Hole Including Grand Teton National Park area — see map p. 285**

FLYING SADDLE RESORT RESTAURANT   307/654-4422

 American. Casual Dining. $9-$38 **AAA Inspector Notes:** This casual eatery serves traditional American fare both in its dining room and on the summer patio. The chef takes care to buy seafood from Seattle, and the Kobe strip steak is butter-tender. **Features:** full bar, patio dining, happy hour. **Address:** 118878 Jct US 26 & 89 83128 **Location:** 0.5 mi e of jct US 26 and 89; in Flying Saddle Resort. [D]

ALTA (C-1) pop. 394, elev. 6,440'
- **Part of Jackson Hole Including Grand Teton National Park area — see map p. 285**

RECREATIONAL ACTIVITIES

Skiing
- **Grand Targhee Resort** is 12 mi. e. at 3300 E. Ski Hill Rd. Other activities are offered. **Hours:** Daily 9-4, Thanksgiving-early Apr. Scenic lift rides daily 10-5, late June-Sept. 30. **Phone:** (307) 353-2300 or (800) 827-4433.

BEULAH

BUFFALO JUMP SALOON & STEAKHOUSE   307/643-7173

Steak Casual Dining $11-$29 **AAA Inspector Notes:** Step into the Wild West with a visit to this family-owned restaurant. Housed in an original building from the 1890s, the décor features wagon wheel chandeliers, taxidermy animals and cowboy-themed artwork. The menu consists of flavorful cowboy rib-eye, elk, salmon, chicken and pork ribs. **Features:** full bar. **Address:** 5877 Old Hwy 14 82712 **Location:** I-90 exit 205, just n, then 0.5 mi w. [D]

BIG HORN (B-4) pop. 490, elev. 4,081'

THE BRINTON MUSEUM, 239 Brinton Rd., interprets the atmosphere of Western ranch life. The main house was built in 1892; businessman Bradford Brinton bought the property in 1923 and built several additions 1927-28. A large collection of Western art includes paintings, sculpture and etchings by John James Audubon, Edward Borein, Frank Tenney Johnson, Frederic Remington and Charles M. Russell.

Extensive collections of equipment, Plains Native American crafts, rare books and documents (including letters and manuscripts by William Penn, George Washington and Abraham Lincoln), and items pertaining to the history of the ranch are displayed in their original setting in the fully furnished ranch house and outbuildings. The Forrest E. Mars, Jr., Building features four galleries of Western and Native American art and artifacts, including changing exhibits of living artists' works and items on loan from other institutions.

Time: Allow 1 hour minimum. **Hours:** Mon.-Sat. 9:30-5, Sun. noon-5. **Cost:** $10; $8 (ages 62+ and students with ID); free (ages 0-12). **Phone:** (307) 672-3173.

BIGHORN CANYON NATIONAL RECREATION AREA—See Montana p. 133

BIGHORN NATIONAL FOREST (B-3)

Elevations in the forest range from 4,600 ft. in the northern section to 13,165 ft. at Cloud Peak. Refer to AAA maps for additional elevation information.

In the Bighorn Mountains of north-central Wyoming, the Bighorn National Forest encompasses 1,115,073 acres. The forest is traversed by US 14 (Bighorn Scenic Byway), which crosses 8,950-foot Granite Pass and winds through scenic Shell Canyon and Falls; US 14A (Medicine Wheel Passage), which passes by Medicine Mountain near the enigmatic Medicine Wheel; and US 16 (Cloud Peak Skyway), which crosses 9,677-foot Powder River Pass and threads through beautiful Ten Sleep Canyon.

Cloud Peak is the highest peak within the forest. Motorists pulling trailers should use caution on US 14/14A.

Backpacking and saddle and pack trips can be taken into 189,039-acre Cloud Peak Wilderness; horse and foot trails begin at trail heads accessible via gravel roads off US 14 and US 16. This scenic area has miles of streams and more than 200 lakes

containing brook, cutthroat, golden and rainbow trout. Hunters come in search of deer and elk.

Throughout the forest are 30 campgrounds, 10 picnic grounds and a good trail network, including the Bucking Mule Falls National Recreation Trail. Downhill skiing is available east of Worland (west of Buffalo); cross-country skiing can be pursued in all sections of the forest. Mountain climbing and snowmobiling also are popular.

Maps of the forest are available at the District Ranger's office in Sheridan at 2013 Eastside Second St., (307) 674-2600; in Greybull at 95 US 16/20, (307) 548-5300 or (307) 765-4435; and in Buffalo at 1415 Fort St., (307) 684-7806.

Shell Falls Wayside Visitor Center is on US 14, 5 miles west of Burgess Junction. The Center offers nature trails, exhibits, maps and other information about the forest, recreational activities and nearby communities; open daily 9-5, Memorial Day weekend through Labor Day. For additional information contact the Forest Supervisor's Office, 2013 Eastside Second St., Sheridan, WY 82801; phone (307) 674-2600. *See Recreation Areas Chart.*

MEDICINE WHEEL is off US 14A on Medicine Mountain, about 27 mi. e. of Lovell. The pre-Columbian structure, a circular arrangement of stones 245 feet in circumference with 28 spokes extending from a central cairn, is believed to have been used for religious ceremonies or celestial observations. **Note:** The road to Medicine Wheel is closed to vehicular traffic. Visitors are required to walk 1.5 miles to the site. Exceptions can be made for elderly or physically impaired visitors.

SHELL CANYON AND FALLS is 22 mi. e. of Greybull on US 14. The site can be seen from the Shell Falls overlook on US 14. An interpretive trail provides views of the imposing limestone cliffs and deep granite gorge cut by Shell Creek. **Phone:** (307) 548-6541.

BLACK HILLS NATIONAL FOREST (B-6)

Elevations in the forest range from 3,300 ft. south of Hot Springs to 7,242 ft. at Harney Peak. Refer to AAA maps for additional elevation information.

In the scenic Black Hills of South Dakota and extending westward into Wyoming, the Black Hills National Forest covers more than 1.2 million acres. It was established in 1897. Stands of ponderosa pine, spruce and aspen are home to mountain lions, white-tailed and mule deer, elk and turkeys. Mountain goats and bighorn sheep are sometimes seen throughout the hills. Visitors should note that while summer days are warm, the nights can be quite cool.

Various routes make for a scenic drive. Peter Norbeck Scenic Byway creates a 70-mile loop via the Needles Highway, Iron Mountain Road—with its views of Mount Rushmore framed by tunnels—and the pigtail bridges. Norbeck Overlook, on Iron Mountain Road (US 16A south from Keystone, S.D.), offers a view of the Black Elk Wilderness area.

The 20-mile Spearfish Canyon Scenic Byway along US 14A follows the pine- and spruce-covered banks of Spearfish Creek. Hiking trails to the canyon rims offer views of canyon walls and forests. Beautiful fall colors may be seen along this route in late September and early October.

The 111-mile Centennial Trail runs the length of the Black Hills from Bear Butte State Park to Wind Cave National Park. With more than 30 access points, portions of the route are open to motorized vehicles, horseback riders and mountain bicycles.

The forest's visitor center at Pactola Reservoir, on US 385 west of Rapid City, S.D., provides information about the history and management of the forest, including wildlife, scenery and recreation areas. Maps and information also are available at the forest supervisor's office in Custer City, S.D., and at district rangers' offices in Custer City, Rapid City and Spearfish, S.D., and in Sundance and Newcastle, Wyo. Allow 30 minutes minimum. Visitor center open daily 8-7, Memorial Day weekend-Labor Day. Free.

Most of the forest's developed recreational facilities are in South Dakota, but the Wyoming segment does have four campgrounds with 76 sites. Entrance to the forest is free, but there are fees for day-use areas and camping. For further information contact the Forest Supervisor's Office, 1019 N. 5th St., Custer City, SD 57730; phone (605) 673-9200. *See Recreation Areas Chart.*

BRIDGER-TETON NATIONAL FOREST
(C-2)

Elevations in the forest range from 5,660 ft. near Alpine to 13,804 ft. at Gannett Peak. Refer to AAA maps for additional elevation information.

Bordering Grand Teton *(see place listing p. 261)* and Yellowstone *(see place listing p. 316)* national parks, Bridger-Teton National Forest covers 3,439,809 acres in the Gros Ventre, Salt River, Teton, Wind River and Wyoming ranges. Within the forest are several live glaciers, an outstanding example of a geologic landslide and the state's highest mountain, Gannett Peak, shared by Shoshone National Forest *(see place listing p. 307)*. Fishing, hunting, white-water rafting and winter sports attract visitors to the area.

The forest has three wilderness areas, all accessible only on foot or horseback. The Bridger Wilderness, 428,169 acres of scenic mountain country, lies on the west slope of the Continental Divide in the Wind River Range. More than 1,300 lakes, Gannett Peak and many glaciers highlight this rugged landscape, which is traversed by more than 500 miles of hiking and snowmobiling trails.

The Green River, beginning at the base of Gannett Peak, races through the Wind River Mountains before turning southward to join the Colorado River.

The Teton Wilderness preserves 585,468 acres in the northern section of the forest. Snow sometimes stays on the ground until early July in this barren alpine country of broad meadows, lakes, steep canyons, streams and waterfalls.

At Two Ocean Pass, Two Ocean Creek divides and sends one stream to the Pacific Ocean and another to the Atlantic; this geographic phenomenon supposedly exists nowhere else on the continent. The 287,000-acre Gros Ventre Wilderness, immediately east of Jackson, also is rugged, mountainous country ideally suited to backpacking, fishing and hunting.

Gros Ventre Slide is 5 miles east of Kelly on Gros Ventre Road. When the landslide occurred on the morning of June 23, 1925, this large earth movement dammed up the Gros Ventre (Big Belly) River. In a matter of minutes, trees and land fell from an elevation of 9,000 feet. Two years later part of the slide gave way, and the resulting wall of water, mud and rock destroyed the town of Kelly.

Scenic drives include Centennial National Scenic Byway from Dubois to Pinedale, the Green River Road from Pinedale north to the Green River Lakes, and the Skyline Drive from Pinedale northeast to Elkhart Park. Greys River Road leaves US 89 near Alpine and follows the river on its southward run; from its headwaters roads lead to US 89 near Geneva and to US 189 at Big Piney or Fontenelle reservoirs.

Pinedale *(see place listing p. 298)* and the resort town of Jackson *(see place listing p. 269)* are recreational activity centers. Near these two towns are the forest's three ski areas; trails for cross-country skiing also are available. Nearby hot springs include Granite Hot Springs, 35 miles southeast of Jackson on US 189, then 9 miles north. The Jackson Visitor Center, 532 N. Cache St., is open daily 8-7, June-Sept.; 9-5, rest of year.

For additional information contact the Forest Supervisor's Office, P.O. Box 1888, Jackson, WY; phone (307) 739-5500. *See Recreation Areas Chart.*

INSIDER INFO:
High-Altitude Health

Temples throbbing, gasping for breath and nauseated, you barely notice the scudding clouds or the spectacular view.

You might be suffering from Acute Mountain Sickness (AMS). Usually striking at around 8,000 feet (2,450 m) in altitude, AMS is your body's way of coping with the reduced oxygen and humidity of high altitudes. Among the symptoms are headaches, shortness of breath, loss of appetite, insomnia and lethargy. Some people complain of temporary weight gain or swelling in the face, hands and feet.

You can reduce the effect of high altitude by being in top condition. If you smoke or suffer from heart or lung ailments, consult your physician before your trip. Certain drugs will intensify the symptoms. To avoid Acute Mountain Sickness, adjust to elevations slowly; a gradual ascent with a couple days of acclimatization is best if you have time. For example, if you are planning a trip to the Rocky Mountains of Colorado, you might want to spend the first night in a lower altitude city such as Denver as opposed to heading directly to an environment with extreme elevations.

On the way up, eat light, nutritious meals and stay hydrated by drinking a large amount of water, taking care to avoid caffeine, alcohol and salt. In addition, your doctor may be able to prescribe medication that can offset the effects of high-altitude.

If you develop AMS, you should stop ascending; you will recover in a few days. If the AMS is mild, a quick descent will end the suffering immediately.

Other high-altitude health problems include sunburn and hypothermia. Dress in layers to protect yourself from the intense sun and wide fluctuations in temperature.

Finally, after you lounge in the sauna or hot tub at your lodgings, remember to stand up carefully, for the heat has relaxed your blood vessels and lowered your blood pressure.

PERIODIC SPRING is about 5 mi. e. of Afton on FR 10211 (Swift Creek Rd.). In late summer the spring ceases to flow every 18 minutes, then gradually builds to a thundering, ice-cold torrent. This cycle occurs regularly for 9 months and fluctuates during the period of highest snow melt, from about mid-May to mid-August. A narrow dirt road leads to within half a mile of the spring; the last 200 yards of the hike are very steep. The road, not recommended for trailers, is closed during winter.

BUFFALO (B-4) pop. 4,585, elev. 4,645'
• Hotels p. 239 • Restaurants p. 239

Retaining the atmosphere and hospitality of the Old West, Buffalo is a ranching town on the eastern slope of the Bighorn Mountains. Many Native American battles took place in this area 1866-77, triggered by the presence of the Bozeman Trail and the forts built to protect it.

After the area was opened to settlement, Buffalo was founded in 1879. Buffalo became known as the "Rustlers' Capital," and by 1892 the tensions between the region's big cattlemen and farmers, or "nesters," had erupted into the Johnson County War. It took the U.S. Army to restore order.

The growth of sheep ranching in the late 1890s brought Basque herders, who were drawn to Buffalo because of the Bighorn Mountains' resemblance to their homeland in the Pyrenees. Basque descendants continue to practice their time-honored traditions.

Guided saddle trips and jeep tours of nearby scenic and historical attractions can be arranged through local operators. Sightseeing is most rewarding along the Cloud Peak Scenic Byway portion of US 16 that runs between Buffalo and Ten Sleep.

Hunters can visit the Hunters Information Station in the chamber of commerce building.

Buffalo Chamber of Commerce: 55 N. Main St., Buffalo, WY 82834. **Phone:** (307) 684-5544 or (800) 227-5122. *(See ad p. 238.)*

Self-guiding tours: Information about walking and driving tours is available from the chamber of commerce.

JIM GATCHELL MEMORIAL MUSEUM is at 100 Fort St. The museum, which honors a frontier pharmacist known for his friendship with and knowledge of the Plains Native Americans, houses more than 30,000 artifacts. Included in the displays are a variety of firearms, historical photographs depicting the early days of the West, Native American artifacts and pioneer items. **Hours:** Mon.-Sat. 8-6, Sun. noon-6, Memorial Day weekend-Labor Day; Mon.-Fri. 8-4, Sat. 10-5, day after Labor Day-Sept. 30; Mon.-Fri. 8-4, rest of the year. Closed Jan. 1, Thanksgiving and Christmas. Phone ahead to confirm schedule. **Cost:** $5; $3 (ages 6-16). **Phone:** (307) 684-9331. *(See ad p. 238.)*

MUSEUM OF THE OCCIDENTAL HOTEL is at 10 N. Main St. Founded in a tent in 1879, the Occidental quickly became one of the state's most renowned hotels. Guests included Buffalo Bill Cody, Teddy Roosevelt and Calamity Jane. Reputedly the only fully restored frontier hotel in Wyoming, antique furnishings and Old World ambience reflect its original grandeur. The lobby's embossed ceilings and the 1908 saloon's original back bar are particularly noteworthy. **Hours:** Daily 8-8. **Cost:** Donations. **Phone:** (307) 684-0451. ⟦🍴⟧

BUFFALO INN
307/684-7000

Hotel. Rates not provided. Address: 100 Flatiron Dr 82834 Location: On US 16, between I-25 and 90. Facility: 43 units. 2 stories, interior corridors. Parking: winter plug-ins. Guest Services: coin laundry.

COMFORT INN
(307)684-9564

Hotel
$95-$205

Address: 65 US Hwy 16 E 82834 Location: I-25 exit 299 (US 16), just e; I-90 exit 58, 1.3 mi w. Facility: 63 units. 2 stories, interior/exterior corridors. Parking: winter plug-ins. Pool(s): heated indoor. Activities: hot tub. Guest Services: coin laundry.

HAMPTON INN & SUITES
(307)684-8899

Hotel $89-$309 Address: 85 US Hwy 16 E 82834 Location: I-90 exit 58, 1.6 mi w. Facility: 75 units. 3 stories, interior corridors. Parking: winter plug-ins. Terms: 1-7 night minimum stay, cancellation fee imposed. Pool(s): heated indoor. Activities: hot tub, exercise room. Guest Services: coin laundry.

AAA Benefit: Members save up to 10%!

HISTORIC MANSION HOUSE INN
307/684-2218

Historic Bed & Breakfast. Rates not provided. Address: 313 N Main St 82834 Location: US 16; downtown. Facility: An original structure, built in 1903, houses the property's inn-style accommodations. Guests can relax or read in the second-floor sunroom. 7 units. 2 stories (no elevator), interior corridors. Parking: winter plug-ins.

HOLIDAY INN EXPRESS HOTEL & SUITES
307/684-9900

Hotel. Rates not provided. Address: 106 US Hwy 16 E 82834 Location: I-25 exit 299 (US 16), 0.5 mi e; I-90 exit 58, 1 mi w. Facility: 69 units. 3 stories, interior corridors. Pool(s): heated indoor. Activities: hot tub, exercise room. Guest Services: coin laundry.

THE OCCIDENTAL HOTEL
307/684-0451

Historic Hotel
$75-$285

Address: 10 N Main St 82834 Location: Center. Facility: This historic property--consisting of a hotel, restaurant and bar--spans one city block. Most rooms are themed after Western characters, and the décor includes antiques and period pieces. 18 units, some two and three bedrooms. 2 stories (no elevator), interior corridors. Parking: street only. Terms: 14 day cancellation notice. Dining: The Virginian Restaurant, see separate listing. Guest Services: valet laundry. (See ad p. 238.)

RODEWAY INN
(307)684-5505

Motel
$49-$152

Address: 610 E Hart St 82834 Location: I-25 exit 299 (US 16), just w; I-90 exit 58, 1.3 mi w. Facility: 27 units, some efficiencies. 1 story, exterior corridors. Parking: winter plug-ins. Pool(s): heated outdoor. Activities: picnic facilities. Guest Services: coin laundry.

WHERE TO EAT

BOZEMAN'S TRAIL STEAKHOUSE
307/684-5555

American
Casual Dining
$8-$28

AAA Inspector Notes: The steakhouse's varied menu lists not only burgers, buffalo steak and the house specialty baby back ribs but also shrimp dinners and a few Mexican items. The décor contributes to a Western and Plains Indian atmosphere. Features: full bar. Address: 675 E Hart St 82834 Location: I-25 exit 299 (US 16), just w. Menu on AAA.com   L   D

CHINA GARDENS
307/684-9208

Chinese. Casual Dining. $8-$20 AAA Inspector Notes: The chef concentrates on Americanized Cantonese-style cooking at this spot using less oil and more flavorful spices in the sauces. There is a nice sampling of Thai dishes also available. Address: 386 N Main St 82834 Location: US 16; downtown.   L   D

CLEAR CREEK CANTINA
307/278-0043

Tex-Mex. Casual Dining. $8-$24 AAA Inspector Notes: Stopping at this cantina is a must. It's colorful, cheerful and has great food. Menu items include a to-die-for green chili, terrific Tex-Mex cobb salad, Baja fish tacos, a variety of wraps and big burgers, slow-roasted and marinated pork tips, several selections of rib-eye dinners and their popular Two, Two n' Two lunch specials. I'd go back just for their refreshing margarita pie. Yum! Features: full bar. Address: 4 S Main St 82834 Location: I-25 exit 298 northbound; exit 299 southbound; downtown. Parking: street only.   L   D

THE VIRGINIAN RESTAURANT
307/684-5976

Steak Seafood. Fine Dining. $18-$33 AAA Inspector Notes: Historic. The authentic, Old West décor is reminiscent of the 1890s. The specialty is locally grown, organic Buffalo steak but the menu also features seafood, chicken and pasta. Table settings and the ambiance are delightful. Request a seat in the cozy alcove. Features: full bar. Address: 10 N Main St 82834 Location: Center; in The Occidental Hotel. Parking: street only.   D

WINCHESTER STEAK HOUSE
307/684-8636

Steak
Casual Dining
$15-$38

AAA Inspector Notes: Voted as having the city's best steak and seafood, this family-run restaurant attracts folks from miles around for a casual dinner at a location convenient to both interstates and downtown. Features: full bar. Address: 117 US Hwy 16 E 82834 Location: I-25 exit 299 (US 16), 0.5 mi e; I-90 exit 58, just e.   D

CARIBOU-TARGHEE NATIONAL FOREST—See Idaho p. 53

CASPER (D-4) pop. 55,316, elev. 5,123'
• Hotels p. 241 • Restaurants p. 241

Casper's roots are buried in commerce. The town began as a ferry site on the Oregon Trail in 1847, when a group of Mormon immigrants who were camping realized that there was money to be made by boating travelers across the North Platte River. The idea caught on, and in the early 1850s a toll bridge was built; soon a military post was established to protect the span and its traffic.

The town's real asset, however, was not discovered until 1889, when the first well in the Salt Creek oil field was tapped; by 1915 the town was in an oil boom that matched the frenzy of the California, Colorado and Montana gold rushes.

The boom brought not only prosperity but also a national scandal over the nearby Teapot Dome oil field. In 1927 the U.S. Supreme Court handed down verdicts in the case, which included sentencing Secretary of the Interior Albert Fall to prison for secretly leasing the rich field to Mammoth Crude Oil Co. without taking competitive bids.

Casper is a major service and supply center for mineral, oil, natural gas, uranium and coal industries, as well as a center for many medical and financial services.

Stargazers can view astronomy-related programs throughout the year at Casper Planetarium, a half-mile north of I-25 exit 188B at 904 N. Poplar, phone (307) 577-0310. Along SRs 20/26 and 220, markers identify the California, Mormon, Oregon and Pony Express trails.

Casper Area Convention and Visitors Bureau: 139 W. Second St., Suite 1B, Casper, WY 82601. **Phone:** (307) 234-5362 or (800) 852-1889.

DAN SPEAS FISH HATCHERY is 10 mi. w. on SR 220, then 4.5 mi. w. on CR 308, following signs. The station is one of Wyoming's most productive fish hatcheries. Its use of a nearby spring, which promotes rapid fish growth, enables it to produce a 4-inch fish in 120 days. About 1.35 million fish are stocked annually. **Hours:** Daily 8-5. **Cost:** Free. **Phone:** (307) 473-8890.

FORT CASPAR MUSEUM AND HISTORIC SITE is .5 mi. n. of SR 220 off Wyoming Blvd. at 4001 Fort Caspar Rd. This site on the Oregon, California, Mormon, and Pony Express trails includes reconstructions of an 1847 Mormon Trail ferry, an 1859 Guinard bridge and an 1865 frontier Army fort. Museum exhibits recount the history of central Wyoming, from prehistory to the present.

Hours: Museum daily 8-6, June-Aug.; daily 8-5 in May and Sept.; Tues.-Sat. 8-5, rest of year. Reconstructed buildings daily 8:30-5:30, June-Aug.; 8:30-4:30 in May and Sept. **Cost:** $3; $2 (ages 13-18). **Phone:** (307) 235-8462.

HISTORIC TRAILS INTERPRETIVE CENTER is off I-25 exit 189, then 1 mi. n. to 1501 N. Poplar St. Seven galleries represent Western trail history through interactive and multimedia exhibits and dioramas. Visitors can sit in a covered wagon and experience a simulated crossing of the North Platte River. A five-screen theater features an audio-visual presentation illustrating pioneer and Native American life. During the summer months, encampment reenactments take place and interpreters in period costume perform demonstrations.

Time: Allow 2 hours minimum. **Hours:** Tues.-Sun. 8-5, June-Aug.; Tues.-Sat. 9-4:30, rest of year. Closed federal holidays. **Cost:** $6; $5 (ages 62+); $4 (students ages 16+ with ID). **Phone:** (307) 261-7700.

HISTORIC TRAILS WEST departs from Fort Caspar Museum and Historic Site, off Wyoming Blvd.; and from the Historic Trails Interpretive Center, 1501 N. Poplar St. The tour features a wagon train that travels along the actual ruts of the California, Mormon and Oregon trails. Visitors also can take an excursion where they ride horses as Pony Express riders did alongside the wagons. Historical accounts are given. Three- and 5-day expeditions also are available.

Hours: Daily, May-Oct. (weather permitting). **Cost:** Trips lasting 2 hours to overnight $45-$255. Trips lasting 3 to 5 days $795-$1,295. Reservations are recommended. **Phone:** (307) 266-4868. GT

INDEPENDENCE ROCK STATE HISTORIC SITE—see Alcova p. 234.

NICOLAYSEN ART MUSEUM AND DISCOVERY CENTER is at 400 E. Collins Dr. The center presents changing exhibits by national and regional artists. The Discovery Center offers informal hands-on and supervised programs, including a painting center, an image-rubbing table, a library and an art gallery. **Hours:** Tues.-Sat. 10-5, Sun. noon-4. Closed major holidays. **Cost:** $5; $3 (ages 5-17 and students with ID); free (on Sun.). **Phone:** (307) 235-5247.

PAINTED PAST LIVING HISTORY TOURS, 330 S. Center, Suite 414, offers three tours. The 1890s tour features Casper characters from the era; the Sand Bar murder mystery tour takes visitors back to the 1920s during Prohibition. The Casper the Friendly Ghost tour travels along the back alleys of downtown, where visitors will learn about historic buildings and past inhabitants. **Time:** Allow 1 hour, 30 minutes minimum. **Hours:** Tours offered June-Sept. Phone ahead to confirm schedule. **Cost:** $25. **Phone:** (307) 258-2585. GT

PLATTE RIVER RAFT N' REEL is at 1775 W. 1st St. Visitors can view wildlife during scenic float trips on the North Platte River. Fly-fishing trips on the river's Grey Reef stretch and white-water rafting trips also are offered. **Time:** Allow 1 hour minimum. **Hours:** Float trips daily, June-Aug. Phone ahead to confirm schedule. **Cost:** Float trips $40-$70. Reservations are recommended. **Phone:** (307) 267-0170. GT

TATE GEOLOGICAL MUSEUM is on the Casper College campus at 125 College Dr.; take Wolcott St./Casper Mountain Rd. s. Almost 3,000 fossil and mineral specimens are on display.

You can tour a fossil preparation lab and meet "Dee," said to be one of the world's largest mounted Columbian mammoths. **Time:** Allow 1 hour minimum. **Hours:** Mon.-Fri. 9-5, Sat. 10-4. Closed major holidays. **Cost:** Donations. **Phone:** (307) 268-2447.

WERNER WILDLIFE MUSEUM is s. via Wolcott St. to 405 E. 15th St. The museum houses a pronghorn antelope diorama, a collection of Western birds and mounted specimens of wildlife native to Wyoming and other parts of North America. The Werner Trophy Room exhibits specimens from around the world. **Hours:** Mon.-Fri. 9-5. Closed Jan. 1, Thanksgiving and Christmas. Phone ahead to confirm schedule. **Cost:** Free. **Phone:** (307) 235-2108.

WYOMING VETERANS MEMORIAL MUSEUM is at 3740 Jourgensen Ave. at the Natrona County International Airport. Veterans are honored by displays of uniforms, military artifacts, historical documents and other memorabilia. The facility also creates oral and video recordings depicting the experiences of local and visiting veterans. **Time:** Allow 1 hour minimum. **Hours:** Tues.-Sat. 9-4. **Cost:** Free. **Phone:** (307) 472-1857.

COURTYARD BY MARRIOTT CASPER   (307)473-2600

Hotel $101-$233 **Address:** 4260 Hospitality Ln 82601 **Location:** I-25 exit 185, just s, then just w. **Facility:** 100 units. 4 stories, interior corridors. **Pool(s):** heated indoor. **Activities:** hot tub, exercise room. **Guest Services:** valet and coin laundry, boarding pass kiosk.

AAA Benefit: Members save 5% or more!

DAYS INN CASPER   (307)234-1159

Hotel $90-$175 **Address:** 301 E 'E' St 82601 **Location:** I-25 exit 188A (Center St), just s, then just e. **Facility:** 121 units. 2 stories (no elevator), interior corridors. **Parking:** winter plug-ins. **Terms:** 3 day cancellation notice-fee imposed. **Pool(s):** heated outdoor. **Activities:** exercise room. **Guest Services:** valet and coin laundry.

HAMPTON INN & SUITES CASPER   (307)235-6668

Hotel $89-$189 **Address:** 1100 N Poplar St 82601 **Location:** I-25 exit 188B (N Poplar St), just e. **Facility:** 100 units. 4 stories, interior corridors. **Parking:** winter plug-ins. **Terms:** 1-7 night minimum stay, cancellation fee imposed. **Pool(s):** heated indoor. **Activities:** hot tub, exercise room. **Guest Services:** valet and coin laundry, area transportation.

AAA Benefit: Members save up to 10%!

HILTON GARDEN INN CASPER   (307)266-1300

Hotel $99-$199 **Address:** 1150 N Poplar St 82601 **Location:** I-25 exit 188B (N Poplar St), just e. **Facility:** 121 units. 4 stories, interior corridors. **Parking:** winter plug-ins. **Terms:** 1-7 night minimum stay, cancellation fee imposed. **Pool(s):** heated indoor. **Activities:** hot tub, exercise room. **Guest Services:** valet and coin laundry.

AAA Benefit: Members save up to 10%!

HOLIDAY INN CASPER EAST AT MCMURRY PARK   307/577-5000

Hotel. Rates not provided. **Address:** 721 Granite Peak Dr 82609 **Location:** I-25 exit 182 (Hat Six Rd), just s, then just w. **Facility:** 119 units. 4 stories, interior corridors. **Pool(s):** heated indoor. **Activities:** hot tub, exercise room. **Guest Services:** valet and coin laundry, area transportation.

MAINSTAY SUITES CASPER   (307)472-7829

Extended Stay Hotel $69-$155 **Address:** 551 Granite Peak Dr 82609 **Location:** I-25 exit 182 (Hat Six Rd), just s, then just w. **Facility:** 93 efficiencies, some two bedrooms. 4 stories, interior corridors. **Amenities:** safes. **Pool(s):** heated indoor. **Activities:** hot tub, exercise room. **Guest Services:** valet and coin laundry.

QUALITY INN & SUITES CASPER   (307)266-2400

Hotel $135-$195 **Address:** 821 N Poplar St 82601 **Location:** I-25 exit 188B (N Poplar St), just e. **Facility:** 92 units. 2 stories (no elevator), interior corridors. **Parking:** winter plug-ins. **Amenities:** safes. **Activities:** exercise room. **Guest Services:** valet and coin laundry.

RAMKOTA HOTEL & CONFERENCE CENTER   307/266-6000

Hotel
Rates not provided

Address: 800 N Poplar St 82601 **Location:** I-25 exit 188B (N Poplar St), just ne. **Facility:** 230 units. 6 stories, interior corridors. **Parking:** winter plug-ins. **Pool(s):** heated indoor. **Activities:** hot tub, exercise room. **Guest Services:** valet and coin laundry, area transportation. **Featured Amenity:** breakfast buffet.

SUPER 8 CASPER WEST   (307)266-3480

Hotel $95-$145 **Address:** 3838 CY Ave 82604 **Location:** I-25 exit 188B (N Poplar St), 1.5 mi s to CY Ave, then 1.7 mi w. **Facility:** 66 units. 3 stories (no elevator), interior corridors. **Parking:** winter plug-ins. **Activities:** picnic facilities. **Guest Services:** coin laundry.

WHERE TO EAT

BOSCO'S ITALIAN RESTAURANTE   307/265-9658

Italian. Casual Dining. $6-$24 **AAA Inspector Notes:** This casual, child-friendly restaurant is worth seeking out for create-your-own Alfredo dishes and traditional veal, chicken, shrimp and gnocchi preparations. Also on the menu are gluten-free items. **Features:** full bar, patio dining. **Reservations:** suggested, for dinner. **Address:** 847 E 'A' St 82601 **Location:** I-25 exit 188A (Center St), 0.4 mi s to E 'A' St, then 0.5 mi e. **Parking:** street only.

COTTAGE CAFE   307/234-1157

Deli. Casual Dining. $9-$10 **AAA Inspector Notes:** This quaint little cottage serves healthy and delicious grilled panini and specialty sandwiches, wicked wraps, a popular tequila-lime chicken soup and a variety of fresh salads, including the Chinese chicken, grilled steak, Santa Fe, cucumber dill and more. The mild green chili quiche is served daily, as are the homemade breads. Sun porch dining is available. **Address:** 116 S Lincoln St 82601 **Location:** I-25 exit 187, 0.4 mi s, just w, then just s. **Parking:** street only.

DSASUMO ASIAN BISTRO 307/237-7874

▼▼▼ Thai. Casual Dining. $11-$25 **AAA Inspector Notes:** This contemporary restaurant serves authentic Thai cuisine and features an extensive sushi menu. **Features:** full bar, patio dining. **Address:** 320 W 1st St 82601 **Location:** I-25 exit 188A (Center St), just s, then just w. **Parking:** on-site and street. L D CALL M

EGGINGTON'S RESTAURANT 307/265-8700

▼▼▼ Breakfast Comfort Food. Family Dining. $6-$15 **AAA Inspector Notes:** This downtown eatery offers the best comfort food around. Highlights include freshly-squeezed orange juice, an array of coffees, daily homemade soups, burgers, sandwiches, wraps and the specialty eggs with everything that goes with them. I highly recommend the Florentine Benedict—the hollandaise sauce is spectacular. **Address:** 229 E 2nd St 82602 **Location:** City center; between Wolcott and Durbin. **Parking:** street only. B L CALL M

FIRE ROCK STEAK HOUSE 307/234-2333

▼▼▼ Steak Seafood. Casual Dining. $9-$39 **AAA Inspector Notes:** While this restaurant serves chicken, fish, pasta and a nice selection of sandwiches, the real reason to come here is for the beef. The fine Mid-Western steaks are aged for 21 days, resulting in a great dining experience. **Features:** full bar, patio dining. **Reservations:** suggested. **Address:** 6100 E 2nd St 82609 **Location:** I-25 exit 185, 0.5 mi s on Wyoming Blvd, then 1 mi e; in McMurry Business Park. L D CALL M

J'S PUB & GRILL 307/472-3100

▼▼▼ New American. Casual Dining. $9-$29 **AAA Inspector Notes:** This nice atmosphere and fun eatery on the other side of town. Presentations are artistic and whimsical. Menu items are creative, such as tacoshimi with house-made kimchee and whiskey piggy pork chops topped with whiskey-glazed apples. The house-made Irish stew with slow-simmered beef tips is a must try. **Features:** full bar, patio dining, happy hour. **Address:** 3201 SW Wyoming Blvd 82604 **Location:** I-25 exit 188B (N Poplar St), 1.5 mi s to CY Ave, then 1.8 mi w to SR 228. L D CALL M

LA COCINA 307/266-1414

▼▼▼ Mexican. Casual Dining. $9-$16 **AAA Inspector Notes:** This cozy eatery features popular daily specials, appetizers, sizzling fajitas and traditional Mexican fare. Favorites include pork chili soup, a variety of quesadillas, chicken or steak fajita salad, Santa Fe stir-fry and the ultimate combo plate. There may be a wait, but it's worth it. **Features:** full bar. **Address:** 321 E 'E' St 82601 **Location:** I-25 exit 188A (Center St), just s, then just e. L D

LIME LEAF ASIAN BISTRO 307/315-6888

▼▼▼ Asian. Casual Dining. $12-$20 **AAA Inspector Notes:** This cute building features attractive décor accents of wood, bamboo and live plants. The menu is lined with Chinese and Vietnamese specialties, and the daily lunch special is popular with locals and travelers. **Features:** beer & wine. **Address:** 845 E 2nd St 82601 **Location:** I-25 exit 188A (Center St), 0.5 mi s, just e on E 1st St, just s on S Kimball St, then just e. L D

POOR BOYS STEAKHOUSE 307/237-8325

▼▼ Steak. Casual Dining. $9-$30 **AAA Inspector Notes:** This Western-themed eatery offers hearty steaks and monthly dinner specials that include a relish boat, bucket of salad, homemade bread and an entrée with a vegetable and potato—all topped off with a dessert. Guests will not leave here hungry. **Address:** 756 N Center St 82602 **Location:** I-25 exit 188A (Center St), just n. **Parking:** on-site and street. L D CALL M

SILVER FOX STEAKHOUSE 307/235-3000

▼▼ American. Casual Dining. $10-$40 **AAA Inspector Notes:** Well-prepared dishes of prime rib and aged steaks are served in this relaxing setting that affords a nice mountain view in the main dining room. The filet mignon, fried green tomatoes and chicken pot pie are popular. Intimate booths also are available for a quieter dining experience. **Features:** full bar. **Reservations:** suggested. **Address:** 3422 S Energy Ln 82604 **Location:** I-25 exit 188B (N Poplar St), 4.2 mi sw on S Poplar St (SR 220). L D CALL M

CHEYENNE (E-6) pop. 59,466, elev. 6,060'
• Hotels p. 244 • Restaurants p. 246

Cheyenne was named for the tribe of Plains Native Americans that once roamed southeastern Wyoming. In 1867 Union Pacific Railroad chief engineer Maj. Gen. Grenville M. Dodge built a depot on the site, situated at the junction of several roads leading to military camps.

Before the track even reached town, it was overrun by gamblers, cowboys, speculators, shopkeepers and real estate salesmen, thus earning Cheyenne the nickname "Hell on Wheels." The town's reputation was so widespread that in 1868 a resident received a letter from Pennsylvania addressed simply "Cheyenne."

By 1869 Cheyenne had outgrown some of its cow-town adolescence to assume the more mature stature of territorial capital, an honor it retained when Wyoming became the 44th state in 1890.

Noted town residents include Nellie Tayloe Ross, the first woman governor in the United States; and Esther Morris, a pioneer for women's suffrage in Wyoming and former justice of the peace of South Pass City *(see place listing p. 308)*. A statue honoring Morris is on Capitol Avenue. The Cowgirls of the West Museum, 205 W. 17th St., preserves the role of women in Western culture with exhibits of rodeo and ranching memorabilia including saddles, photographs and clothing; phone (307) 638-4994.

"Big Boy," one of the world's largest steam locomotives, is on permanent display in Holliday Park.

Since it was established in 1867 as a headquarters for the cavalry troops protecting pioneers and railroad construction workers, F.E. Warren Air Force Base has served various branches of the military, including the nation's first intercontinental ballistic missile group.

Happy Jack Road (SR 210) is a 38-mile scenic byway to Laramie that runs from rolling grasslands to the rocky foothills of the Pole Mountain Division of Medicine Bow National Forest. Equally interesting is a trip to Snowy Range, a region of fishing streams and mountain lakes.

In July ▷ Cheyenne Frontier Days recaptures the city's Wild West heritage with horse races, parades, nightly entertainment and what is claimed to be the world's largest outdoor rodeo.

Visit Cheyenne: 1 Depot Sq., 121 W. 15th St., Suite 202, Cheyenne, WY 82001. **Phone:** (307) 778-3133 or (800) 426-5009. *(See ad on inside front cover, p. 243.)*

Shopping: Frontier Mall, 1400 Dell Range Blvd., has more than 75 stores including Dillard's, JCPenney and Sears.

Self-guiding tours: A pamphlet describing a self-guiding walking tour of Cheyenne's historic downtown area is available at Visit Cheyenne.

CHEYENNE BOTANIC GARDENS, 710 S. Lions Park Dr., has a variety of themed gardens, including annual and perennial displays, xeriscape, rose and herb gardens. A 6,800-square-foot solar-heated greenhouse conservatory houses tropical foliage, cacti, herbs and roses as well as a waterfall and a pond. Visitors can walk through a seven-circuit labyrinth; for blind and physically impaired visitors there are four stone benches inscribed with "finger labyrinths." Wyoming's oldest steam locomotive is on the grounds.

Kids learn about sustainability as they explore Paul Smith Children's Village. This LEED-certified site has a solar-powered discovery lab, a solar-heated and solar-powered greenhouse, a wetlands area, a tepee village, a secret garden and an amphitheater where kids can put on puppet shows. Special activities and events are offered.

Time: Allow 1 hour, 30 minutes minimum. **Hours:** Grounds daily dawn-dusk. Conservatory Mon.-Fri. 8-4:30, Sat. 11-3:30. Paul Smith Children's Village Tues.-Sat. 9-5, Sun. 10-4. Conservatory and Children's Village closed major holidays. **Cost:** Free. **Phone:** (307) 637-6458. *(See ad on inside front cover.)*

CHEYENNE DEPOT MUSEUM is housed in the restored Union Pacific Railroad Depot at 121 W. 15th St. Regional railroad history is depicted through photographs, narratives, artifacts and a brief film presentation. Exhibits focus on the impact that Union Pacific Railroad operations had on the town and its residents. The second floor baggage room houses The Union Central and Northern Model Railroad layout created by Harry S. Brunk. He spent more than 30 years handcrafting everything from the scenery to the rolling stock for this HO scale of the narrow gauge Clear Creek Lines, which includes the Colorado and Southern Railway.

Hours: Mon.-Fri. 9-6, Sat. 9-5, Sun. 11-5, May-Sept.; Mon.-Sat. 9-5, Sun. 11-3, rest of year. Closed major holidays. **Cost:** $8; $7 (ages 60+ and military with ID); free (ages 0-12). **Phone:** (307) 632-3905. *(See ad on inside front cover.)*

CHEYENNE FRONTIER DAYS OLD WEST MUSEUM is in Frontier Park at 4610 N. Carey Ave. The museum has some 60,000 artifacts, including a collection of more than 150 horse-drawn carriages and wagons, and classic Western and folk art. Also included is authentic clothing dating from the 1850s and an interactive children's gallery.

Hours: Daily 9-5, with extended hours during Cheyenne Frontier Days, June-Aug.; 10-5, rest of year. Closed Jan. 1, Thanksgiving and Christmas. **Cost:** $10; $8 (ages 65+ and military with ID); $5 (ages 13-18); free (ages 0-12 with adult). **Phone:** (307) 778-7290. *(See ad on inside front cover.)*

CHEYENNE STREET RAILWAY TROLLEY departs the Cheyenne Depot Square at 121 W. 15th St. Highlights of the 90-minute sightseeing tour include the Cheyenne Frontier Days Old West Museum, State Capitol and Wyoming State Museum. **Hours:** Tours depart Mon.-Fri. at 10, 11:30, 1, 2:30 and 4, Sat. at 10, noon and 2, Sun. at noon and 2, early May-late Sept. **Cost:** $10; $5 (ages 2-12). **Phone:** (307) 778-3133 or (800) 426-5009. *(See ad on inside front cover.)* GT

HISTORIC GOVERNORS' MANSION STATE HISTORIC SITE is at 300 E. 21st St. From 1905 to 1976 the site was the home of Wyoming's chief executives. Touch screens provide information about former governors and first ladies as well as the mansion's architecture. **Time:** Allow 1 hour minimum. **Hours:** Mon.-Sat. 9-5, Sun. 1-5, June-Sept.; Wed.-Sat. 9-5, Dec.-May. **Cost:** Free. **Phone:** (307) 777-7878.

THE NELSON MUSEUM OF THE WEST is at 1714 Carey Ave. The museum celebrates the American West through exhibits of antique weapons, cowboy saddles, spurs, chaps, Native American beadwork, pottery, baskets and weavings. Cowgirl, outlaw and lawmen memorabilia is featured in addition to the "Cavalry in the West" exhibit. Mounted taxidermy from all continents also is highlighted. **Time:** Allow 1 hour minimum. **Hours:** Mon.-Sat. 9-4:30, June-Aug.; Mon.-Fri. 9-4:30, May and Sept.-Oct. Closed major holidays. **Cost:** Donations. **Phone:** (307) 635-7670. *(See ad on inside front cover.)*

▼ *See AAA listing p. 242* ▼

STATE CAPITOL is on Capitol Ave. between 24th and 25th sts. This neoclassic sandstone building, with a golden dome 50 feet in diameter, is architecturally uncommon for the region. Within the building are murals, woodwork, marble floors and displays of native wildlife. **Note:** The interior of the capitol is closed. Renovations are scheduled to be complete in 2018. **Phone:** (307) 777-7220. *(See ad on inside front cover.)*

TERRY BISON RANCH is accessed by taking I-80 to I-25S, then taking exit 2 off I-25S, then s. on Terry Ranch Rd. to ranch entrance. The historic working bison ranch has more than 3,000 bison. Fishing (no state license required), horseback rides, ATV tours and train tours are offered.

Hours: Bison tours daily dawn-dusk (weather permitting). **Cost:** Bison tours $12; $6 (ages 4-12). Horseback rides $40 per hour; $8 pony ride. Ages 0-7 are not permitted on horseback rides, but 15-minute pony rides are available for ages 0-9. ATV tour $40 (driver); $30 (passenger). **Phone:** (307) 634-4171 or (800) 319-4171. *(See ad on inside front cover.)*

 WYOMING STATE MUSEUM, in the Capitol complex at 2301 Central Ave., features a variety of permanent and changing exhibits that allow visitors to delve into Wyoming's history.

The Drawn to This Land gallery catalogs the reasons people and businesses chose Wyoming as a place to flourish, and Swamped with Coal traces the development of the mining industry. Social history is the theme of the Living in Wyoming exhibition.

Visitors encounter a skeletal replica of a camptosaur—one of Wyoming's earliest inhabitants—in the R.I.P.-Rex in Pieces gallery; Wild Bunch focuses on other animals that have called the state home.

An interactive map pinpointing historical sites is the highlight of the Wyoming's Story collection; guns, a cowboy diorama and Native American baskets and jewelry are just some of the items on display in the Barber Gallery. Designed for the little ones, the Hands-on History Room has a kid-size tepee, a chuck wagon and a curiosity cabinet.

Time: Allow 2 hours minimum. **Hours:** Mon.-Sat. 9-4:30. Closed major holidays. **Cost:** Free. **Phone:** (307) 777-7022. *(See ad on inside front cover.)*

BEST WESTERN PLUS FRONTIER INN   (307)638-8891

Hotel
$109-$199

AAA Benefit: Save 10% or more every day and earn 10% bonus points!

Address: 8101 Hutchins Dr 82007 **Location:** I-80 exit 367, just n. **Facility:** 74 units. 3 stories, interior corridors. **Parking:** winter plug-ins. **Amenities:** safes. **Pool(s):** heated indoor. **Activities:** hot tub, exercise room. **Guest Services:** valet and coin laundry. **Featured Amenity: breakfast buffet.**

CANDLEWOOD SUITES   307/634-6622

Extended Stay Hotel. Rates not provided. **Address:** 2335 Tura Pkwy 82001 **Location:** I-25 exit 9, just e on I-80 business loop/US 30, then just n. **Facility:** 86 efficiencies. 3 stories, interior corridors. **Parking:** winter plug-ins. **Activities:** picnic facilities, exercise room. **Guest Services:** complimentary and valet laundry.

CHEYENNE MY PLACE HOTEL   307/634-1400

Hotel. Rates not provided. **Address:** 1920 W Lincolnway 82001 **Location:** I-25 exit 9, 0.6 mi e. **Facility:** 64 efficiencies. 3 stories, interior corridors. **Parking:** winter plug-ins. **Activities:** picnic facilities. **Guest Services:** coin laundry.

DAYS INN CHEYENNE   (307)778-8877

Hotel $90-$160 **Address:** 2360 W Lincolnway 82001 **Location:** I-25 exit 9, just e. **Facility:** 108 units. 2-4 stories, interior corridors. **Pool(s):** heated indoor. **Activities:** hot tub, exercise room. **Guest Services:** coin laundry.

FAIRFIELD INN & SUITES BY MARRIOTT CHEYENNE   (307)637-4070

Hotel $106-$205 **Address:** 1415 Stillwater Ave 82001 **Location:** 1.2 mi e of jct Dell Range Blvd and Yellowstone Rd. Located on north side of airport. **Facility:** 60 units. 3 stories, interior corridors. **Parking:** winter plug-ins. **Pool(s):** heated indoor. **Activities:** hot tub, exercise room. **Guest Services:** valet and coin laundry.

AAA Benefit: Members save 5% or more!

HAMPTON INN CHEYENNE   (307)632-2747

Hotel
$114-$315

AAA Benefit: Members save up to 10%!

Address: 1781 Fleischli Pkwy 82001 **Location:** I-25 exit 9, just e on I-80 business loop/US 30, then just n. **Facility:** 64 units. 3 stories, interior corridors. **Terms:** 1-7 night minimum stay, cancellation fee imposed. **Pool(s):** heated indoor. **Activities:** hot tub, exercise room. **Guest Services:** valet and coin laundry.

HOLIDAY INN CHEYENNE   (307)638-4466

Hotel
$109-$399

Address: 204 W Fox Farm Rd 82007 **Location:** I-80 exit 362, just s. **Facility:** 244 units. 6 stories, interior corridors. **Terms:** 3 day cancellation notice-fee imposed. **Pool(s):** heated indoor. **Activities:** exercise room. **Guest Services:** valet and coin laundry, area transportation. **Featured Amenity:** breakfast buffet.

[SAVE] [symbols] CALL [&][M]
[symbols] [BIZ] [symbols] [X] [symbols]
/ SOME UNITS [symbols]

HOLIDAY INN EXPRESS HOTEL & SUITES   307/433-0751

[symbols] **Hotel.** Rates not provided. **Address:** 1741 Fleischli Pkwy 82001 **Location:** I-25 exit 9, just e. **Facility:** 76 units. 4 stories, interior corridors. **Amenities:** Some: safes. **Pool(s):** heated indoor. **Activities:** hot tub, exercise room. **Guest Services:** valet and coin laundry.

[symbols] CALL [&][M] [symbols] [BIZ] [HS] [symbols] [X] [symbols] [symbols]
[symbols]

LA QUINTA INN CHEYENNE   (307)632-7117

[symbols] **Hotel** $75-$424 **Address:** 2410 W Lincolnway 82009 **Location:** I-25 exit 9, just e. **Facility:** 105 units. 3 stories, interior corridors. **Parking:** winter plug-ins. **Pool(s):** heated outdoor. **Guest Services:** coin laundry.

[symbols] [symbols] [symbols] [symbols] / SOME UNITS [symbols] [symbols] [symbols]

LITTLE AMERICA HOTEL 307/775-8400

Hotel
Rates not provided

Address: 2800 W Lincolnway 82009 **Location:** I-25 exit 9, just w on US 30. Located in a quiet secluded area. **Facility:** 188 units. 1-3 stories (no elevator), interior/exterior corridors. **Amenities:** safes. **Dining:** 2 restaurants, also, Hathaway's Restaurant & Lounge, see separate listing. **Pool(s):** heated outdoor. **Activities:** regulation golf, playground, exercise room. **Guest Services:** valet and coin laundry. *(See ad p. 245.)*

SAVE ⊀ ⟵ ❙❘ ◻ ▣ Y CALL &M 🛌 BIZ HS 🛜 ✕ ❙ 🖻 ▣

MICROTEL INN & SUITES BY WYNDHAM CHEYENNE (307)634-3200

▽▽ Hotel $90-$140 **Address:** 1400 W Lincolnway 82001 **Location:** I-25 exit 9, 1.1 mi e. **Facility:** 56 units. 3 stories, interior corridors. **Parking:** winter plug-ins. **Activities:** exercise room. **Guest Services:** coin laundry.

❙❘ CALL &M BIZ 🛜 ✕ ▣ / SOME UNITS ❙ 🖻

NAGLE WARREN MANSION B & B (307)637-3333

Historic Bed
& Breakfast
$158-$192

Address: 222 E 17th St 82001 **Location:** I-80 exit 362, 1.2 mi n on I-25 business loop/US 85/87 business route, then just e; jct House St; downtown. **Facility:** Handmade tiles adorn the fireplaces in most guest rooms at this Romanesque-style 1888 building. Furnishings include a variety of period antiques, and fabulous architectural features throughout. 12 units. 3 stories (no elevator), interior corridors. **Parking:** on-site and street. **Terms:** 3 day cancellation notice-fee imposed. **Activities:** hot tub, bicycles, exercise room, massage. **Guest Services:** valet laundry. **Featured Amenity:** full hot breakfast. *(See ad p. 245.)*

SAVE ❙❘ BIZ 🛜 ✕ / SOME UNITS ❙

OAK TREE INN CHEYENNE 307/778-6620

▽ Hotel. Rates not provided. **Address:** 1625 Stillwater Ave 82009 **Location:** I-25 exit 12, 0.8 mi se to Yellowstone Rd, 0.3 mi n to Dell Range Blvd, 1.2 mi e, then just se. Located on north side of airport. **Facility:** 30 units. 2 stories (no elevator), interior/exterior corridors. **Activities:** exercise room. **Guest Services:** coin laundry.

❙❘ 🛜 ✕ ❙ 🖻 / SOME UNITS 🛒 ▣

QUALITY INN OF CHEYENNE (307)638-7202

▽▽ Hotel $99-$249 **Address:** 2245 Etchepare Dr 82007 **Location:** I-25 exit 7, just w. **Facility:** 77 units. 2 stories, interior corridors. **Parking:** winter plug-ins. **Pool(s):** heated outdoor. **Activities:** exercise room. **Guest Services:** valet and coin laundry.

⊀ ❙❘ CALL &M 🛌 BIZ 🛜 ✕ ❙ 🖻 ▣ / SOME UNITS ❙

SPRINGHILL SUITES BY MARRIOTT (307)635-0006

▽▽ **Hotel** $98-$184 **Address:** 416 W Fox Farm Rd 82007 **Location:** I-80 exit 362, just s, then just w. **Facility:** 92 units. 3 stories, interior corridors. **Pool(s):** heated indoor. **Activities:** hot tub, exercise room. **Guest Services:** valet and coin laundry.

> **AAA Benefit:** Members save 5% or more!

❙❘ CALL &M 🛌 BIZ HS 🛜 ✕ ❙ 🖻 ▣

SUPER 8 CHEYENNE (307)635-8741

▽▽ Motel $69-$179 **Address:** 1900 W Lincolnway 82001 **Location:** I-25 exit 9, 0.7 mi e. **Facility:** 60 units. 3 stories (no elevator), interior corridors. **Amenities:** safes. **Guest Services:** coin laundry.

BIZ 🛜 ❙ 🖻 ▣ / SOME UNITS ❙

TOWNEPLACE SUITES BY MARRIOTT CHEYENNE WY (307)634-0400

Extended Stay
Hotel
$116-$233

TownePlace SUITES Marriott

> **AAA Benefit:** Members save 5% or more!

Address: 1710 W Lincolnway 82001 **Location:** I-25 exit 9, 0.3 mi se, then 0.8 mi ne. **Facility:** 88 units, some two bedrooms, efficiencies and kitchens. 4 stories, interior corridors. **Parking:** winter plug-ins. **Pool(s):** heated indoor. **Activities:** picnic facilities, exercise room. **Guest Services:** valet and coin laundry. **Featured Amenity:** breakfast buffet.

SAVE ❙❘ CALL &M 🛌 BIZ HS 🛜 ✕ ❙ 🖻 ▣ / SOME UNITS ❙

WINDY HILLS GUEST HOUSE 307/632-6423

▽▽ Bed & Breakfast $179-$250 **Address:** 393 Happy Jack Rd 82009 **Location:** I-25 exit 10B, 22 mi w on SR 210 (Happy Jack Rd), then 1 mi s on private gravel road. Located in a rural area. **Facility:** Adjacent to Curt Gowdy State Park, this beautiful property offers a B&B experience in the main house and well-thought-out options for vacation rentals and extended stays. Open weather permitting. 8 units, some efficiencies, kitchens, cabins and condominiums. 1-2 stories (no elevator), exterior corridors. **Terms:** check-in 4 pm, 3 day cancellation notice. **Activities:** sauna, hot tub, steamhouse, boat dock, fishing, cross country skiing, lawn sports, picnic facilities. **Guest Services:** coin laundry.

❙❘ BIZ 🛜 ✕ 🎿 🐾 ▣ / SOME UNITS ❙ 🖻

WHERE TO EAT

2 DOORS DOWN 307/634-6008

▽ Burgers. Quick Serve. $8-$14 **AAA Inspector Notes:** Many locals claim this casual eatery offers the best burger in town. The juicy burgers, made from fresh ground beef, come straight up or topped with everything from pineapple and teriyaki sauce to bacon and cheddar. Other options include a salmon burger, grilled tuna burger, pot roast burger and a Philly cheesesteak. Entrée salads, a variety of soups and the heartier platters add some diversity to the menu. There are even vegetarian options. **Address:** 118 E 17th St 82001 **Location:** Jct Warren Ave and US 30, just n; downtown. **Parking:** street only. L D

THE ALBANY 307/638-3507

♦♦♦ American Casual Dining $8-$24

AAA Inspector Notes: *Classic Historic.* In business since 1942, this restaurant is in a large brick building and features high-back booths, wood floors and casual, friendly service. Serving steaks, seafood and chicken, the eatery is a good value at lunch and a bit more upscale at dinner. **Features:** full bar. **Address:** 1506 Capitol Ave 82001 **Location:** Jct Lincolnway, just s; downtown. L D

ANONG'S THAI CUISINE 307/638-8597

▽▽ Thai. Casual Dining. $10-$20 **AAA Inspector Notes:** Great homemade tortilla chips and zesty fresh salsa accompany meals, which pair well with the varied beers and margaritas. Typical fare includes tacos, burritos and enchiladas. Enhancing the look of this small and popular restaurant are a wall mural and Mexican blankets. Casually dressed staffers offer friendly, quick service in the festive, bustling setting. **Features:** beer & wine. **Address:** 620 Central Ave 82007 **Location:** I-80 exit 362, just nw on I-180/US-85 N, then just sw on e 5th St. L D CALL &M

BREAD BASKET BAKERY & SANDWICH SHOPPE
307/432-2525

Breads/Pastries Sandwiches. Quick Serve. $4-$8 **AAA Inspector Notes:** The unassuming building of this bakery doesn't do justice to the delightful treasures waiting inside. The smell of freshly baked bread wafts through the air as patrons browse the bakery. Order a sandwich to go, or eat a meal at one of the small tables. Friendly staff members clearly enjoy their jobs. **Features:** patio dining. **Address:** 1819 Maxwell Ave 82001 **Location:** Between 18th and 19th sts; downtown. **Parking:** street only. B L

HATHAWAY'S RESTAURANT & LOUNGE
307/775-8400

American. Casual Dining. $9-$25 **AAA Inspector Notes:** This restaurant features an elegantly-styled interior with friendly staff and casual service. Menu items include burgers, pasta, salads, sandwiches and steaks. A lunch buffet is offered Monday through Friday. **Features:** full bar, patio dining, Sunday brunch. **Address:** 2800 W Lincolnway 82009 **Location:** I-25 exit 9, just w on US 30; in Little America Hotel. B L D CALL M

J'S TACO BISTRO
307/433-0202

Mexican. Quick Serve. $10-$25 **AAA Inspector Notes:** Inventive presentations, expanded variety and bold fresh flavors are waiting for diners at this downtown eatery. A special treat is the homemade tomato-watermelon salsa. **Features:** full bar. **Address:** 112 E 17th St 82001 **Location:** Jct Warren Ave and US 30, just n, then just w; downtown. **Parking:** street only. L D

KOREAN HOUSE RESTAURANT
307/638-7938

Korean. Casual Dining. $6-$11 **AAA Inspector Notes:** Guests are sure to be delighted by this unassuming restaurant. It is the type of place where the adage, do not judge a book by its cover, is useful. The gracious and attentive staff prepares food to order. Highlights include bulgogi, fried mondoo and yukkae jung. Parking is limited and credit cards are not accepted. **Address:** 3219 Snyder Ave 82001 **Location:** Just s of W Pershing Blvd. **Parking:** street only. L D CALL M

L'OSTERIA MONDELLO
307/778-6068

Italian. Casual Dining. $9-$20 **AAA Inspector Notes:** Upon entering this restaurant, patrons can see a fast food pizzeria. Offering a sit-down restaurant in the back, a full Italian menu features such entrées as pizza and pasta dishes including veal, chicken and scallops. **Features:** beer & wine. **Address:** 1507 Stillwater Ave 82009 **Location:** 1.2 mi e of jct Dell Range Blvd and Yellowstone Rd. L D

LUXURY DINER
307/638-8971

Breakfast. Casual Dining. $5-$14 **AAA Inspector Notes:** This is the place for breakfast in Cheyenne. The biscuits rate high and are either used for breakfast sandwiches or served with gravy. Omelets, French toast with almonds and huevos rancheros hint at some of the diversity on the menu. Lunch includes burgers, sandwiches, and hearty platters as well as homemade pie. Locals fill up the tables, but visitors are made to feel welcome. According to oral tradition, the main building used to be an operating trolley before becoming a diner in 1926. **Address:** 1401 W Lincolnway 82001 **Location:** I-25 exit 9, 1.1 mi e. B L

MITCHELL'S BBQ & CATERING
307/635-9960

Barbecue. Quick Serve. $7-$20 **AAA Inspector Notes:** Serving up some of the best barbecue in town, this no-frills eatery does not mess around. Expect large servings at an affordable price and friendly service. **Address:** 1720 Capitol Ave 82001 **Location:** Jct Central Ave and E 18th St, just w; downtown. **Parking:** street only. L D CALL M

MORRIS HOUSE BISTRO
307/369-1378

Southern American. Fine Dining. $18-$31 **AAA Inspector Notes:** Located in a historic landmark, the former home of suffragette Esther Hobart Morris, the Victorian inspired décor creates a warm, inviting atmosphere. Inspired by South Carolina's Low-country, the seasonal menu features Southern cuisine virtually unknown in this area of the country. Examples include hushpuppies stuffed with crab, shrimp with grits and Carolina fried flounder. Duck also makes an appearance on the menu and it wouldn't be Wyoming without a Cowboy rib-eye or other steak option. **Features:** full bar, patio dining, Sunday brunch. **Reservations:** suggested. **Address:** 2114 Warren Ave 82001 **Location:** Between 21st and 22nd sts; downtown. **Parking:** street only. D

MORT'S BAGELS
307/637-5400

Breads/Pastries. Quick Serve. $4-$7 **AAA Inspector Notes:** Freshly made and baked bagels are served here. The Pershing bagel sandwich is not to be missed—crunchy peanut butter, sliced bananas and honey served on a bagel of your choice. Come early for the best selection. **Address:** 1815 Carey Ave 82001 **Location:** Center, 0.6 mi n. **Parking:** street only. B L CALL M

POOR RICHARD'S
307/635-5114

American. Casual Dining. $10-$28 **AAA Inspector Notes:** This eatery takes its name from Benjamin Franklin's Almanac, which he wrote under the pseudonym Poor Richard. The tasteful décor features antiques, replicas and general Americana from the Colonial era. The salad bar offers an impressive array of fresh vegetables. Entrées include steaks, veal, chicken, lobster, king crab legs, salmon and shrimp. **Features:** full bar. **Address:** 2233 E Lincolnway 82001 **Location:** I-80 exit 364, just n on N College Dr (SR 212); 1.5 mi w on I-80 business loop/US 30. L D

R & B BREAKFAST CLUB
307/433-0023

American. Casual Dining. $7-$11 **AAA Inspector Notes:** Calling all Elvis lovers—this cozy diner has a nice collection of Elvis memorabilia. Well known by locals for its massive breakfast burritos, the diverse menu consists of typical breakfast fare, hamburgers, German sausage, tacos and fajitas. **Address:** 2102 E Lincolnway 82001 **Location:** I-80 exit 364, just n on N College Dr (SR 212); 1.6 mi w on I-80 business loop/US 30. B L

RIB & CHOP HOUSE
307/514-0271

American. Casual Dining. $8-$40 **AAA Inspector Notes:** This downtown eatery offers a wide selection ranging from buffalo rib-eye steak and fresh grilled fish to a fried green tomato burger for the lighter appetite. A parking garage is located across the street. **Features:** full bar. **Reservations:** suggested. **Address:** 400 W Lincolnway 82001 **Location:** Jct Lincolnway and Pioneer Ave. **Parking:** on-site and street. L D CALL M

RUBYJUICE
307/634-3022

Deli. Quick Serve. $4-$10 **AAA Inspector Notes:** Here they aim to serve fresh, healthy and wholesome food. Guess what? It tastes good too. This place will get diners in and out in no time at all. They specialize in making smoothies, offer freshly pressed wheat grass and a variety of salads, sandwiches and soups. Head on in for your daily dose of goodness. **Address:** 113 E 17th St 82001 **Location:** Jct Warren Ave and US 30, just n; downtown. **Parking:** street only. B L

SANFORD'S GRUB & PUB
307/634-3381

American. Casual Dining. $10-$25 **AAA Inspector Notes:** This casual, busily decorated restaurant presents a varied menu, which includes Cajun chicken, catfish and finger foods, as well as numerous beers. The Monte Cristo sandwich is a favorite. **Features:** full bar. **Address:** 115 E 17th St 82001 **Location:** I-80 exit 362, 1.2 mi n on I-25 business loop/US 85/87 business route, then just w. **Parking:** street only. L D

SENATOR'S RESTAURANT & BRASS BUFFALO SALOON
307/634-4171

◇◇◇◇

Steak
Casual Dining
$8-$40

AAA Inspector Notes: Resembling an old Western barn, this rustic pine dining room at this working ranch has dark wood walls and floors, basic tables with metal chairs and casual décor. For those that do not opt for the specialty, barbecued and grilled bison, there are other choices and a salad bar. The more basic lunch menu lists just sandwiches. This place is in a rural area along the interstate frontage road and is surrounded by various buildings. The casually dressed staff carries out friendly service. **Features:** full bar, patio dining. **Address:** 51 I-25 Service Rd E 82007 **Location:** I-25 exit 2, just e, then 2.6 mi se on Terry Ranch Rd; in Terry Bison Ranch Resort. L D ▧

SHADOWS PUB & GRILL
307/634-7625

◇◇ ◇◇ American. Casual Dining. $8-$20 **AAA Inspector Notes:** Popular with locals and tourists alike, this pub is located inside a train depot and offers a variety of burgers, sandwiches, pizzas, steaks and traditional pub fare. Sports games are shown on 12 flat-screen TVs. **Features:** full bar. **Address:** 115 W 15th St, Suite 1 82001 **Location:** Jct Lincolnway and Central Ave, just se; downtown; in historic train depot. **Parking:** street only. L D

STEAMBOAT'S STEAK & SMOKEHOUSE
307/514-5939

◇◇ ◇◇ Steak Barbecue. Family Dining. $10-$30 **AAA Inspector Notes:** This Western-themed restaurant offers a variety of dishes ranging from dinner salads, sandwiches, pasta and burgers to seafood, chicken, ribs and steaks. I know it will be hard, but guests might want to save room for such homemade dessert as delicious lemon squares. **Features:** full bar. **Address:** 1947 Dell Range Blvd 82009 **Location:** I-25 exit 12 (US 85), 0.8 mi e, just n, then 1.9 mi e. L D CALL ⛟ⓂⒷ

TWIN DRAGON
307/637-6622

◇◇ ◇◇ Chinese. Casual Dining. $9-$16 **AAA Inspector Notes:** In a convenient downtown location, this restaurant is known for authentic food and friendly service from its staff, some of whom have been here for many years. **Features:** full bar. **Address:** 1809 Carey Ave 82001 **Location:** From center, 0.5 mi n. L D

CODY (B-2) pop. 9,520, elev. 5,095'
- Hotels p. 251 • Restaurants p. 253
- Hotels & Restaurants map & index p. 324
- Part of Yellowstone National Park area — see map p. 316

Founded by Col. William "Buffalo Bill" F. Cody in 1896, Cody is near the east and northeast entrances to Yellowstone National Park (see place listing p. 316). Some of the state's most scenic areas, including Shoshone National Forest (see place listing p. 307), Sunlight Basin, the Absaroka and Beartooth mountains and the Bighorn Canyon National Recreation Area (see place listing p. 133), are nearby.

US 14/16/20, alternately known as the Buffalo Bill Cody Scenic Byway, has been called the most scenic 52 miles in America. Along the route are many unusual rock formations as well as the State of Wyoming Veterans Memorial Park (near Yellowstone Regional Airport), which honors those who served in World War II, the Korean and Vietnam wars and the Iraq and Afghanistan wars. The highway runs 182 miles between Ranchester and Yellowstone National Park. Cody also is the northern terminus of the scenic section of SR 120 that travels 83 miles southeast to Thermopolis (see place listing p. 311). Scenic US 14A heads 107 miles northeast to Burgess Junction.

Outfitters offer fishing, hayrides, horseback riding, hunting and pack trips and river float trips. Scenic flights overlooking the Bighorn Mountains and Grand Teton and Yellowstone national parks can be arranged through Choice Aviation, (307) 587-9262.

Of interest downtown are historic buildings dating from the beginning of the 20th century. Irma Hotel, 12th Street and Sheridan Avenue, has been a meeting place for local cattlemen, oilmen and shepherds since the early 1900s. Its $100,000 bar was a gift from Queen Victoria to Buffalo Bill in appreciation of his Wild West Show. Pahaska Tepee, Buffalo Bill's first hunting lodge, is at the east entrance to Yellowstone National Park.

Cody Chamber of Commerce: 836 Sheridan Ave., Cody, WY 82414. **Phone:** (307) 587-2297. *(See ad p. 249, p. 320.)*

◆GEM SAVE **BUFFALO BILL CENTER OF THE WEST** is at 720 Sheridan Ave. The five museums that comprise the center are dedicated to the art, artifacts, crafts, cultures, traditions and history of the American West. In addition, a research library contains book and manuscript collections and thousands of historic photographs.

Time: Allow 4 hours minimum. **Hours:** Daily 8-6, May 1 to mid-Sept.; daily 8-5, mid-Sept. through Oct. 31; daily 10-5, Mar.-Apr. and in Nov.; Thurs.-Sun. 10-5, rest of year. Closed Jan. 1, Thanksgiving and Christmas. **Cost:** (Valid for 2 consecutive days for all five museums) $19; $17 (ages 65+); $15 (students ages 18+ with ID); $11 (ages 6-17). **Phone:** (307) 587-4771. *(See ad p. 249.)* ⛾

Buffalo Bill Museum is at 720 Sheridan Ave. at Buffalo Bill Center of the West. The museum displays belongings of the showman and scout, one of the most famous men of his time, along with possessions of Annie Oakley and artifacts of the early West. Exhibits provide insight into the history of the American cowboy, conservation and dude ranching.

Hours: Daily 8-6, May 1 to mid-Sept.; daily 8-5, mid-Sept. through Oct. 31; daily 10-5, Mar.-Apr. and in Nov.; Thurs.-Sun. 10-5, rest of year. **Cost:** Included with Buffalo Bill Center of the West admission of $19; $17 (ages 65+); $15 (students ages 18+ with ID); $11 (ages 6-17). **Phone:** (307) 587-4771. *(See ad p. 249.)*

Cody Firearms Museum is at 720 Sheridan Ave. at Buffalo Bill Center of the West. The museum is noted for its exhibits of American firearms, including the Winchester collection. The museum, featuring some 3,000 items, traces the development of firearms from the early 16th century. Examples range from centuries-old projectile arms to flintlocks and Gatling guns to modern sport rifles.

Hours: Daily 8-6, May 1 to mid-Sept.; daily 8-5, mid-Sept. through Oct. 31; daily 10-5, Mar.-Apr. and in Nov.; Thurs.-Sun. 10-5, rest of year. **Cost:** Included with Buffalo Bill Center of the West admission of $19; $17 (ages 65+); $15 (students ages 18+

WILDLIFE ELK PHOTO
MEETEETSE POWELL MUSIC WILD
YELLOWSTONE
OLD FAITHFUL HORSES
COWBOYS
CABINS BUFFALO BILL
HIKE BEARS
DUDE GEYSERS MUSEUMS SCENIC FISH
RANCH RODEO FOOD HEART
CATTLE CODY HISTORY MOUNTAIN LAKES
WYOMING ART WEST TRAIL
DRIVES RIVER RIDE
BISON RAFTING
SHOWS

FULL OF SPIRIT.

There's plenty to see and do. Start planning your Cody, Wyoming winter fun today.
1-800-393-2639 or yellowstonecountry.org

Buffalo Bill's CODY/YELLOWSTONE COUNTRY

THE WILDEST WAY INTO YELLOWSTONE

(See map & index p. 324.)

with ID); $11 (ages 6-17). **Phone:** (307) 587-4771. *(See ad p. 249.)*

Draper Natural History Museum is at 720 Sheridan Ave. at Buffalo Bill Center of the West. The museum features exhibits about the Yellowstone region's natural history and human influence from early explorers to ranchers. A highlight is a virtual expedition through mountain forests and valleys.

Hours: Daily 8-6, May 1 to mid-Sept.; daily 8-5, mid-Sept. through Oct. 31; daily 10-5, Mar.-Apr. and in Nov.; Thurs.-Sun. 10-5, rest of year. **Cost:** Included with Buffalo Bill Center of the West admission of $19; $17 (ages 65+); $15 (students ages 18+ with ID); $11 (ages 6-17). **Phone:** (307) 587-4771. *(See ad p. 249.)*

The Plains Indian Museum is at 720 Sheridan Ave. at Buffalo Bill Center of the West. The museum has an extensive collection of art, artifacts, ceremonial items and beadwork as well as dress and weaponry of the Arapaho, Blackfeet, Cheyenne, Crow, Shoshone and Sioux tribes. Exhibits depict the everyday existence of these Plains tribes.

Hours: Daily 8-6, May 1 to mid-Sept.; daily 8-5, mid-Sept. through Oct. 31; daily 10-5, Mar.-Apr. and in Nov.; Thurs.-Sun. 10-5, rest of year. **Cost:** Included with Buffalo Bill Center of the West admission of $19; $17 (ages 65+); $15 (students ages 18+ with ID); $11 (ages 6-17). **Phone:** (307) 587-4771. *(See ad p. 249.)*

Whitney Western Art Museum is at 720 Sheridan Ave. at Buffalo Bill Center of the West. The gallery houses a comprehensive collection of paintings, sculpture and prints depicting the West. Artists represented include Albert Bierstadt, George Catlin, Thomas Moran, Frederic Remington, Charles M. Russell and Joseph Henry Sharp. Reconstructed studios enable visitors to view artists' work areas.

Hours: Daily 8-6, May 1 to mid-Sept.; daily 8-5, mid-Sept. through Oct. 31; daily 10-5, Mar.-Apr. and in Nov.; Thurs.-Sun. 10-5, rest of year. **Cost:** Included with Buffalo Bill Center of the West admission of $19; $17 (ages 65+); $15 (students ages 18+ with ID); $11 (ages 6-17). **Phone:** (307) 587-4771. *(See ad p. 249.)*

BUFFALO BILL DAM VISITOR CENTER is 6 mi. w. on US 14/16/20. In addition to a dam overlook, the visitor center has views of Shoshone Canyon, area wildlife displays, dinosaur and fossil exhibits and a short movie. Self-guiding historical audio tours are available. **Time:** Allow 30 minutes minimum. **Hours:** Mon.-Fri. 8-7, Sat.-Sun. 9-5, June-Aug.; Mon.-Fri. 8-6, Sat.-Sun. 9-5 in May and Sept. **Cost:** Free. **Phone:** (307) 527-6076.

BUFFALO BILL-THE SCOUT STATUE is at the w. end of Sheridan Ave. The statue, by Gertrude Vanderbilt Whitney, represents young William F. Cody as a mounted Army scout signaling the discovery of enemy tracks.

THE CODY CATTLE COMPANY, 2.9 mi. w. on US 14/16/20, then .4 mi. n.w. to 1910 Demaris St., offers a chuck wagon supper and a live Western musical show. Dinner guests have the option of eating before or during the hour-long performance. Seating is in a large mess hall with a stage in front; special lighting and a backdrop create the illusion of being outdoors.

Time: Allow 1 hour minimum. **Hours:** Supper daily 5:30-8, June-Sept. Show daily at 6:30, June-Sept. **Cost:** Show only $14; $7 (ages 3-12). Dinner and show $28; $14 (ages 3-12). A combination ticket for the dinner, the show and admission to Cody Nite Rodeo *(see attraction listing this page)* is available most days June-Aug. and costs $45; $24 (ages 7-12); $14 (ages 3-6). Reservations are recommended. **Phone:** (307) 272-5770. ⓣ

CODY CHAPEL MURALS INFORMATION CENTER is in Cody Chapel at Wyoming Ave. and 18th St. The center displays exhibits, artifacts, murals, paintings and sculpture relating to the Mormon colonization of the Big Horn Basin. Film presentations are given. **Hours:** Mon.-Sat. 9-7, Sun. 3-7, June 1-Sept. 15; by appointment rest of year. **Cost:** Free. **Phone:** (307) 587-3290. GT

CODY DUG UP GUN MUSEUM, 1020 12th St., has an extensive collection of guns and other weapons used during the American Revolutionary War, the Gold Rush era, the Civil War, the Indian Wars era, World War I, the 1920s and World War II. **Time:** Allow 1 hour minimum. **Hours:** Daily 9-9, May-Oct. **Cost:** Donations. **Phone:** (307) 587-3344.

CODY NITE RODEO is 2 mi. w. on US 14/16/20. The 2-hour rodeo features events like bronc riding, bull riding, team roping and barrel racing. Little ones can participate in the kids' calf scramble. **Hours:** Daily at 8 p.m., June-Aug. Special performances are held July 1-4 during Stampede Days. **Cost:** $20; $10 (ages 7-12). A combination ticket with the dinner and the show at The Cody Cattle Company *(see attraction listing this page)* is available most days June-Aug. and costs $45; $24 (ages 7-12); $14 (ages 3-6). **Phone:** (307) 587-5155 or (800) 207-0744.

TRAIL TOWN is 3 mi. w. on US 14/16/20. Featured is a group of historic buildings with indoor exhibits reassembled on the first site of the frontier town of Old Cody. Highlights include the grave of John "Jeremiah" Johnson and a log cabin used as a hideout by Butch Cassidy, the Sundance Kid and other members of the Wild Bunch.

The Museum of the Old West houses guns, carriages, clothing and many prehistoric and historic Plains Native American relics. **Hours:** Daily 8-7, May 15-Sept. 30. **Cost:** $9; $8 (ages 65+); $5 (ages 6-12). **Phone:** (307) 587-5302.

(See map & index p. 324.)

WILD SHEEP FOUNDATION is at 720 Allen Ave. The den-like educational area features audio and visual presentations, paintings, prints and mounted exhibits pertaining to wild sheep. A variety of bronzed bighorn sheep stand outside. **Time:** Allow 1 hour minimum. **Hours:** Mon.-Fri. 8-5. Closed major holidays. **Cost:** Donations. **Phone:** (307) 527-6261.

RECREATIONAL ACTIVITIES

White-water Rafting

- **Red Canyon River Trips** is at 1119 12th St. **Hours:** Trips depart daily at 9, 1 and 3, May 1 to mid-Sept. **Phone:** (307) 587-6988. GT

- **River Runners of Wyoming** is at 1491 Sheridan Ave. **Hours:** Two-hour and half-day trips run late May-late Sept. **Phone:** (307) 527-7238 or (800) 535-7238. GT

- **Wyoming River Trips** depart from 233 Yellowstone Ave. **Hours:** Trips offered several times daily, May-Sept. **Phone:** (307) 587-6661 or (800) 586-6661. GT

AMERICINN LODGE & SUITES OF CODY

(307)587-7716 **62**

Hotel $99-$219

Address: 508 Yellowstone Ave 82414 **Location:** 1.9 mi w on US 14/16/20. **Facility:** 67 units. 2 stories (no elevator), interior corridors. **Parking:** winter plug-ins. **Terms:** cancellation fee imposed. **Amenities:** safes. **Pool(s):** heated indoor. **Activities:** sauna, hot tub. **Guest Services:** coin laundry. **Featured Amenity: continental breakfast.**

A WESTERN ROSE

307/587-4258 **57**

Motel. Rates not provided. **Address:** 1807 Sheridan Ave 82414 **Location:** 0.4 mi e. Located in a quiet area close to downtown. **Facility:** 24 units. 1 story, exterior corridors. **Guest Services:** coin laundry.

BEARTOOTH INN OF CODY

307/527-5505 **65**

Hotel
Rates not provided

Address: 2513 Greybull Hwy 82414 **Location:** 1.5 mi e on US 14/16/20. Located in a quiet area. **Facility:** 49 units. 2 stories (no elevator), interior/exterior corridors. **Parking:** winter plug-ins. **Activities:** sauna, hot tub, limited exercise equipment. **Guest Services:** coin laundry. **Featured Amenity: continental breakfast.**

BEARTOOTH INN

Adjacent to Yellowstone Regional Airport, minutes to Buffalo Bill Historical Ctr & Cody Night Rodeo.

BEST WESTERN PREMIER IVY INN & SUITES

(307)587-2572 **61**

Hotel $139-$300

 PREMIER

AAA Benefit: Save 10% or more every day and earn 10% bonus points!

Address: 1800 8th St 82414 **Location:** 1 mi w on US 14/16/20. **Facility:** 70 units. 3 stories, interior corridors. **Parking:** winter plug-ins. **Amenities:** safes. **Dining:** 8th Street at the Ivy, see separate listing. **Pool(s):** heated indoor. **Activities:** hot tub, exercise room. **Guest Services:** complimentary and valet laundry, boarding pass kiosk.

BEST WESTERN SUNSET MOTOR INN

(307)587-4265 **60**

Motel $155-$185

AAA Benefit: Save 10% or more every day and earn 10% bonus points!

Address: 1601 8th St 82414 **Location:** 0.8 mi w on US 14/16/20. **Facility:** 120 units. 1-2 stories (no elevator), exterior corridors. **Terms:** closed 10/12-4/30. **Pool(s):** heated outdoor, heated indoor. **Activities:** hot tub, playground, exercise room. **Guest Services:** coin laundry. **Featured Amenity: full hot breakfast.**

BUFFALO BILL'S ANTLERS INN

(307)587-2084 **58**

Hotel $80-$165 **Address:** 1213 17th St 82414 **Location:** Just e of jct US 14/16/20. **Facility:** 39 units. 2 stories (no elevator), interior corridors. **Terms:** closed 5/5-9/30, cancellation fee imposed.

BUFFALO BILL VILLAGE

307/587-5544 **56**

Historic Cabin $100-$199 **Address:** 1701 Sheridan Ave 82414 **Location:** On US 14/16/20 and SR 120, just e of jct US 14 and SR 120; center. **Facility:** Despite being built between 1920 and 1923, this complex of closely-spaced log cabins offers today's modern conveniences. Check-in is handled at the extensive gift shop. 83 cabins. 1 story, exterior corridors. **Terms:** closed 10/1-3/31, 3 day cancellation notice-fee imposed.

THE CODY

307/587-5915 **63**

Hotel. Rates not provided. **Address:** 232 W Yellowstone Ave 82414 **Location:** 2 mi w on US 14/16/20. **Facility:** 75 units. 3 stories, interior corridors. **Parking:** winter plug-ins. **Terms:** check-in 4 pm. **Amenities:** Some: safes. **Pool(s):** heated indoor. **Activities:** sauna, hot tub, bicycles, exercise room. **Guest Services:** coin laundry, area transportation.

(See map & index p. 324.)

CODY MOTOR LODGE   307/527-6291   **53**

Motel
Rates not provided

Address: 1455 Sheridan Ave 82414 **Location:** Just w on US 14/16/20 and SR 120. **Facility:** 30 units. 2 stories (no elevator), interior corridors. **Guest Services:** coin laundry. **Featured Amenity:** continental breakfast.

 / SOME UNITS

COMFORT INN AT BUFFALO BILL VILLAGE RESORT   (307)587-5556   **54**

Hotel $123-$278 **Address:** 1601 Sheridan Ave 82414 **Location:** US 14/16/20 and SR 120. **Facility:** 74 units. 2 stories, interior corridors. **Terms:** 3 day cancellation notice. **Guest Services:** valet and coin laundry.

CALL M BIZ HS / SOME UNITS

HOLIDAY INN AT BUFFALO BILL VILLAGE RESORT   307/587-5555   **55**

Hotel. Rates not provided. **Address:** 1701 Sheridan Ave 82414 **Location:** US 14/16/20 and SR 120. **Facility:** 189 units. 2 stories (no elevator), interior corridors. **Parking:** winter plug-ins. **Pool(s):** heated outdoor. **Activities:** exercise room. **Guest Services:** valet and coin laundry.

CALL M BIZ

MOOSE CREEK LODGE & SUITES   307/587-2221   **52**

Hotel
Rates not provided

Address: 1015 Sheridan Ave 82414 **Location:** On US 14/16/20; downtown. **Facility:** 56 units. 1-2 stories (no elevator), interior/exterior corridors. **Pool(s):** heated indoor. **Activities:** limited exercise equipment. **Guest Services:** coin laundry. **Featured Amenity:** continental breakfast. *(See ad this page.)*

 / SOME UNITS

RODEWAY INN   (307)587-4201   **64**

Motel
$54-$250

Address: 1919 17th St 82414 **Location:** 0.8 mi e on US 14/16/20 and SR 120. **Facility:** 46 units. 1-2 stories (no elevator), exterior corridors. **Activities:** playground. **Featured Amenity:** continental breakfast.

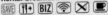

 / SOME UNITS

SUNRISE MOTOR INN   307/587-5566   **59**

Motel. Rates not provided. **Address:** 1407 8th St 82414 **Location:** 0.8 mi w on US 14/16/20. Next to Buffalo Bill Historical Center. **Facility:** 40 units. 1 story, exterior corridors. **Pool(s):** heated outdoor. **Guest Services:** coin laundry.

/ SOME UNITS

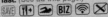
▼ See AAA listing this page ▼

Pick up colorful, top-quality travel guides and atlases at AAA/CAA offices

(See map & index p. 324.)

WHERE TO EAT

8TH STREET AT THE IVY   307/587-2572   50

Western American Casual Dining $13-S29

AAA Inspector Notes: This upscale dining experience features a Western-style décor with stone, wood and leather accents. Regionally available ingredients include lamb, steaks, elk and trout. **Features:** full bar, patio dining, happy hour. **Address:** 1800 8th St 82414 **Location:** 1 mi w on US 14/16/20; in BEST WESTERN PREMIER Ivy Inn & Suites.

B L D CALL &M

Upscale Casual Dining with Bar & Mtn View Patio Seating

ADRIANO'S ITALIAN RESTAURANT   307/527-7320   46
Italian. Casual Dining. $9-$26 **AAA Inspector Notes:** The smells of authentic Italian pizza are what hit your nose as you enter Adriano's. Partake of the pizza or enjoy some of their other Italian entrees at this family style restaurant. **Features:** full bar. **Address:** 1244 Sheridan Ave 82414 **Location:** On US 14/16/20; downtown. **Parking:** street only. L D

THE BREADBOARD   307/527-5788   52
Sandwiches. Quick Serve. $4-$15 **AAA Inspector Notes:** Sub sandwiches are made at this spot with fresh baked breads including sunflower and sourdough. Soups are filling and come in fresh bread bowls. **Features:** patio dining. **Address:** 1725 17th St 82414 **Location:** On US 14/16/20 and SR 120; center. B L

BUBBA'S BAR-B-QUE RESTAURANT   307/587-7427   51
Barbecue. Family Dining. $7-$25 **AAA Inspector Notes:** Texas meats are slow-smoked over a hickory fire at this restaurant. Although spare ribs are the house specialty, guests also can try salmon, pulled pork, charbroiled steak and the popular sloppy Bubba sandwich. **Features:** beer & wine. **Address:** 512 Yellowstone Ave 82414 **Location:** US 14/16/20, 1.9 mi w. L D CALL &M

HERITAGE BAKERY & BISTRO   307/587-2622   45
American. Casual Dining. $9-$14 **AAA Inspector Notes:** This cute little bistro is in a converted house. The owners take the time to do it right with a homey touch, from baking the bread for sandwiches to using local and fresh ingredients. The quiches and soups change daily. Fresh-baked pie, cakes, and cookies are just some of the yummy desserts. **Address:** 1532 Wyoming Ave 82414 **Location:** From Sheridan Ave, just n on 16th St, just w. **Parking:** street only. L

LA COMIDA   307/587-9556   48
Mexican. Casual Dining. $8-$18 **AAA Inspector Notes:** This family-owned restaurant is popular and provides a relaxed, attractive setting. Good sized, attractively presented courses are offered. Expect pleasant, expedient service. Patio dining is available during the summer. **Features:** full bar. **Reservations:** suggested, weekends. **Address:** 1385 Sheridan Ave 82414 **Location:** On US 14/16/20; center. **Parking:** street only. L D

WYOMING'S RIB & CHOP HOUSE   307/527-7731   47
American. Casual Dining. $8-$32 **AAA Inspector Notes:** This spot is popular, so reservations are a must. Famous for the ribs, the meat falls off the bone. Most dinners include an appetizer and a starch. Delicious steaks and burgers also are an option. The setting is cowboy casual and includes a lounge area. **Features:** full bar, happy hour. **Address:** 1367 Sheridan Ave 82414 **Location:** On US 14/16/20. **Parking:** street only. L D CALL &M

ZAPATA'S   307/527-7181   49
Mexican. Casual Dining. $9-$18 **AAA Inspector Notes:** Spices in the made-in-house sauces of New Mexican dishes are a bit more defined than those found in standard Tex-Mex fare. The mood is casual and the decor Mexican in style. **Features:** full bar, patio dining. **Address:** 1362 Sheridan Ave 82414 **Location:** On US 14/16/20; center. **Parking:** street only.

L D &

◆GEM DEVILS TOWER NATIONAL MONUMENT (B-6)

Devils Tower National Monument is accessible from SR 24, north off I-90 via US 14 or west from Belle Fourche, S.D.; from Alzada, Mont., SR 112 runs southwest off US 212. Occupying 1,347 acres in the area between Sundance and Hulett, the monument contains Devils Tower, the most conspicuous landmark in northeastern Wyoming.

The tower, a huge monolith resembling a colossal stone tree stump, rises 867 feet from its base and 1,267 feet above the Belle Fourche River. The 1.5-acre top has a growth of sagebrush and grass, and the almost perpendicular sides are fluted columns. The tower was formed when numerous sedimentary layers eroded from around a volcanic intrusion that had cooled in a teardrop formation.

About a half-mile from the entrance is a prairie dog colony. Near the monument's campground is an outdoor amphitheater. Ranger-naturalists conduct summer interpretive walks, talks and campfire programs.

The Tower Trail encircles Devils Tower. Climbing on the tower is permitted, but climbers must sign in before and after expeditions. **Note:** During the month of June, the National Park Service asks climbers to voluntarily refrain from climbing on the tower and hikers to voluntarily refrain from scrambling within the interior of the Tower Trail Loop out of respect for the Native American tribes that consider the tower a sacred site.

A visitor center about 3 miles from the park entrance contains geological specimens, artifacts and exhibits. Dogs, which must be leashed, are not permitted on the trails.

Allow 2 hours, 30 minutes minimum. The monument is open daily 24 hours. The visitor center is open daily 9-4 (weather permitting). Admission $10 per private vehicle; $5 per person arriving on foot, bicycle or motorcycle; free (ages 0-15). Phone (307) 467-5283 Mon.-Fri. 8-4. *See Recreation Areas Chart.*

DOUGLAS (D-5) pop. 6,120, elev. 4,815'
• Hotels p. 254 • Restaurants p. 254

Known as Tent Town at its founding in 1886, Douglas served as a supply post for cattlemen and a distribution point for railroad consignments. The town's history is typical of the colorful, brawling days when cavalrymen, cowboys and railroad crews were opening the West, but in contrast to many other towns, few killings were recorded.

One of the town's rowdiest characters was George Pike, a cowhand whose rustling habits were so well-known that the cattle companies decided to hire him so he would at least benefit his current employer. One company thought so highly of Pike that at his death it erected an expensive tombstone with the following inscription:

Underneath this stone in eternal rest, Sleeps the wildest one of the wayward west. He was a gambler and sport and cowboy, too, And he led the pace in an outlaw crew. He was sure on the trigger and staid to the end, But was never known to quit on a friend. In the relations of death all mankind's alike, But in life there was only one George Pike.

Douglas also is said to be the original home of the "jackalope," a fanciful creation of Wyoming's taxidermists. Doubters are confronted with dozens of convincing mounted specimens of this animal—best described as a jackrabbit sporting antlers—displayed throughout the state. A 10-foot replica of the "hybrid" stands downtown in Centennial Jackalope Square at 3rd and Center streets and at the Douglas Area Chamber of Commerce, which is housed in a historic train depot.

Scenic River Path, running along the bank of the North Platte River in downtown, offers 2.5 miles of trails for walking, bicycling and observing nature. The river also provides opportunities for trout fishing, canoeing and float trips. Washington Park contains the burial monument of racehorse Sir Barton, the first triple crown winner in the United States.

The Wyoming State Fair, off I-25 adjacent to the town's business district, occurs for 8 days in mid-August. Visitors can enjoy livestock and horticultural exhibits as well as a demolition derby and rodeos; for information phone (307) 358-2398.

Douglas Area Chamber of Commerce: 121 Brownfield Rd., Douglas, WY 82633. **Phone:** (307) 358-2950.

AYRES NATURAL BRIDGE is in Ayres Park, 12 mi. w. on I-25, then 5 mi. s. on Natural Bridge Rd. La Prele Creek has worn a passageway through thick stone, leaving an arch 30 feet high and 50 feet wide surrounded by an amphitheater of red rock. **Hours:** Daily 8-8, Apr.-Oct. **Cost:** Free. 🅰 🎁

FORT FETTERMAN STATE HISTORIC SITE is 7 mi. n.w. via SR 93 off the North Douglas exit of I-25. The site preserves the fort's restored officers' quarters and an ordnance warehouse. Built in 1867, the fort was once a major Army supply post for the troops sent to subdue Native American uprisings. A museum contains exhibits depicting the history of the military and Fetterman City. Period rooms, weapons, artifacts and clothing are displayed.

Time: Allow 2 hours minimum. **Hours:** Daily 9-5, Memorial Day weekend-Labor Day. **Cost:** $4; $2 (Wyoming residents); free (ages 0-17). **Phone:** (307) 358-2864.

WYOMING PIONEER MEMORIAL MUSEUM is on the state fairgrounds at 400 W. Center St. The museum began as a log structure in 1925 and has since enlarged to accommodate one of the largest displays of historic artifacts in the state. The museum contains an extensive collection of Wyoming pioneer items, military relics, Native American artifacts, maps, charts, newspapers and photographs from the late 1800s.

The Johnson Gallery houses the museum's Native American collection that includes such highlights as a 1864 Sioux-style teepee used in the movie "Dances with Wolves," numerous examples of decorative arts and multiple displays of Native American sculpture. Other museum highlights include clothing worn during Wyoming's territorial period, an art display with changing exhibits, a research library about Wyoming history and two 1885 one-room schoolhouses. **Hours:** Mon.-Fri. 8-5 (also Sat. 1-5, June-Sept.). **Cost:** Free. **Phone:** (307) 358-9288.

HOLIDAY INN EXPRESS & SUITES　　(307)358-4500

🔻🔻🔻
Hotel
$159-$209

Address: 900 W Yellowstone Hwy 82633 **Location:** I-25 exit 140, 1 mi e. **Facility:** 76 units. 3 stories, interior corridors. **Parking:** winter plug-ins. **Amenities:** video games. **Pool(s):** heated indoor. **Activities:** hot tub, picnic facilities, exercise room. **Guest Services:** valet and coin laundry. **Featured Amenity: continental breakfast.**

SLEEP INN & SUITES　　(307)358-2777

🔻🔻🔻
Hotel
$129-$189

Address: 508 Cortez Dr 82633 **Location:** I-25 exit 140, 0.5 mi e. **Facility:** 63 units. 3 stories, interior corridors. **Parking:** winter plug-ins. **Pool(s):** heated indoor. **Activities:** hot tub, exercise room. **Guest Services:** valet and coin laundry. **Featured Amenity: continental breakfast.**

WHERE TO EAT

THE DEPOT RESTAURANT　　307/358-9999

🔻🔻🔻 American. Casual Dining. $9-$22 **AAA Inspector Notes:** This modern eatery offers a variety of appetizers, burgers, wraps and entrées including beef tenderloin, baby back pork ribs and some traditional Italian dishes. Call in advance for a boxed lunch to take on the road. **Features:** full bar, patio dining. **Address:** 100 E Walnut St 82633 **Location:** I-25 exit 140, 2 mi e to 2nd St, just n, then just w; downtown. Ⓛ Ⓓ CALL 📶Ⓜ

DUBOIS (C-2) pop. 971, elev. 6,917'

Dubois grew from a rendezvous point for French, American and Native American trappers at the head of the Wind River Valley into a headquarters for cattle outfits, tie hack crews and river tie drives. From 1914 to 1946, stacked decks of railroad ties were floated down the Wind River from tie camps west of town to the railhead at Riverton. Dubois now is bordered by extensive cattle and dude ranching operations.

Northwest of Dubois is Union Pass, said to be the only place in the United States from which three rivers flow in different directions: Fish Creek is the source of the Columbia River, Jakeys Fork flows to the Mississippi, and Roaring Fork is part of the Colorado River drainage system.

Pack trips leave Dubois for Gannett Peak, Wyoming's highest peak, and the Fitzpatrick Wilderness, where there are 44 active glaciers.

Snowmobiling, dog sledding and cross-country skiing are popular at Union Pass and Togwotee Pass; both cross the Continental Divide west of Dubois.

Dubois Chamber of Commerce: 616 W. Ramshorn St., P.O. Box 632, Dubois, WY 82513. **Phone:** (307) 455-2556.

DUBOIS FISH HATCHERY is 3 mi. e. on US 26/287, then 1.5 mi. s. at 5 Fish Hatchery Ct. Supplied by well and spring water, the station incubates and ships to other hatcheries nationwide up to 7 million eggs; it also rears nearly a half million fish yearly for stocking. Varieties include cutthroat, rainbow, grayling, brown and brook trout. **Hours:** Daily 8-5. **Cost:** Free. **Phone:** (307) 455-2431.

DUBOIS MUSEUM is at 909 W. Ramshorn St. The museum contains local artifacts depicting the industry, history, cultures and geology of Dubois and the Upper Wind River Valley. **Hours:** Mon.-Sat. 9-6, June-Aug.; Mon.-Sat. 10-4, rest of year. Hours may be extended during peak season. **Cost:** Free. **Phone:** (307) 455-2284.

NATIONAL BIGHORN SHEEP INTERPRETIVE CENTER is at 10 Bighorn Ln. Through the use of dioramas, mounted animals, hands-on exhibits and DVDs visitors can learn about the history and biology of the bighorn sheep. "Sheep Mountain" replicates the bighorn's natural habitat. It focuses on predator-prey relationships, seasonal changes in habitat conditions, and plant and animal life with which bighorns interact.

Guided tours are available by reservation Nov.-Mar. **Time:** Allow 1 hour minimum. **Hours:** Daily 9-6, Memorial Day weekend-Labor Day; Mon.-Sat. 10-4, rest of year. Closed Jan. 1, Thanksgiving and Christmas. Phone ahead to confirm schedule. **Cost:** $4; $2 (ages 8-17); $8 (family). **Phone:** (307) 455-3429 or (888) 209-2795. GT

THE LONGHORN RANCH LODGE AND RV RESORT
(307)455-2337

Motel
$89-$169

Address: 5810 US Hwy 26 82513 **Location:** Jct US 26 and 287, 3 mi e. Next to a river. **Facility:** 24 units, some two bedrooms, kitchens and cabins. 1 story, exterior corridors. **Terms:** closed 11/1-5/1, 3 day cancellation notice-fee imposed. **Activities:** fishing, playground, lawn sports, picnic facilities. **Guest Services:** coin laundry. **Featured Amenity:** continental breakfast.

ROCKY MOUNTAIN LODGE
(307)455-2444

Motel $60-$100 **Address:** 1349 W Ramshorn St 82513 **Location:** Waterfront. 1.6 mi w on US 26 and 287. **Facility:** 15 units, some kitchens. 2 stories (no elevator), exterior corridors. **Terms:** cancellation fee imposed. **Activities:** fishing, picnic facilities.

STAGECOACH MOTOR INN
(307)455-2303

Motel
$69-$129

Address: 103 Ramshorn St 82513 **Location:** On US 26 and 287; downtown. **Facility:** 44 units, some kitchens. 1-2 stories (no elevator), exterior corridors. **Parking:** winter plug-ins. **Terms:** cancellation fee imposed. **Pool(s):** heated outdoor. **Activities:** hot tub, fishing, playground, lawn sports. **Guest Services:** coin laundry.

WHERE TO EAT

COWBOY CAFE
307/455-2595

American. Casual Dining. $6-$21 **AAA Inspector Notes:** This café dishes up home-style cooking in hearty portions. Coffee is always brewing and at least six to eight fruit and cream pies are on hand daily, until they run out. Buffalo burgers and the cranberry chicken sandwich are just a few favorites. **Features:** beer & wine, patio dining. **Address:** 115 E Ramshorn St 82513 **Location:** On US 26 and 287; center. **Parking:** street only. B L D

NOSTALGIA BISTRO
307/455-3528

American. Casual Dining. $9-$30 **AAA Inspector Notes:** Turn-of-the-19th-century décor will lure guests in, but the creative and expertly prepared food will keep them coming back. The chef uses regional ingredients and turns them into world-class cuisine with Asian and European bents. Breads and desserts are made in-house and a coffee shop adjoins the restaurant. **Features:** full bar, patio dining, happy hour. **Address:** 202 E Ramshorn St 82513 **Location:** Jct 1st St; downtown. **Parking:** on-site and street. L D CALL

PAYA DELI & PIZZA
307/455-3331

Deli Pizza. Quick Serve. $6-$19 **AAA Inspector Notes:** Gluten-free pizza, hand stretched and cooked in a wood oven are among the choices at this spot that also serves simple deli favorites, homemade soups and sausages. Baked goods end the meal on the right note. Guests can eat inside or sit on the covered deck. **Features:** beer & wine. **Address:** 112 E Ramshorn St 82513 **Location:** Center. **Parking:** street only. L D CALL

RUSTIC PINE GRILL
307/455-2772

American. Casual Dining. $8-$22 **AAA Inspector Notes:** This restaurant has a casually rustic feel and serves a wide variety of burgers, pasta and nice selection of specialty salads. **Features:** full bar, patio dining. **Address:** 123 E Ramshorn St 82513 **Location:** Jct US 26 and 287; center. L D

ELK MOUNTAIN (E-4) pop. 191, elev. 7,240'

Originally known as "The Crossing" by pioneers who traversed the Overland Trail, Elk Mountain is noted for the wild game that take shelter on the nearby refuge in the shadow of 11,156-foot Elk Mountain. Both Elk Mountain Hotel and Garden Spot Pavilion Dance Hall, next to the hotel, are on the National Register of Historic Places.

Carbon County Visitors Council: 215 S. SR 70, Riverside, WY 82325. **Phone:** (307) 324-3020 or (800) 228-3547. *(See ad p. 300.)*

ENCAMPMENT (E-4) pop. 450, elev. 7,323'

Encampment takes its name from a Native American camp where tribes gathered to hunt big game between the Medicine Bow and Sierra Madre ranges. It was a copper mining town from 1897 until the vein was exhausted in 1908; a gold strike was reported as late as 1937. Stock raising and lumbering are now the principal industries.

Legend has it that Thomas Edison conceived of the light bulb filament while looking at a frayed line during a fishing trip near Encampment.

GRAND ENCAMPMENT MUSEUM is 2 blks. e. of the post office, then 1 blk. s. to 807 Barnett Ave. The museum houses memorabilia recalling the area's copper mining days. The museum complex also encompasses a pioneer village whose 18 buildings include a two-story outhouse and a forest service lookout tower. A park next to the museum has picnic facilities and a playground. **Time:** Allow 2 hours minimum. **Hours:** Daily 9-5, late May to mid-Oct.; by appointment rest of year. **Cost:** Donations. **Phone:** (307) 327-5308. GT

ETHETE (C-3) pop. 1,553, elev. 5,354'

GAMBLING ESTABLISHMENTS
- **Little Wind Casino** is at 800 Blue Sky Hwy. **Hours:** Daily 24 hours. **Phone:** (307) 438-7000.

EVANSTON (E-1) pop. 12,359, elev. 6,743'

Designated the seat of Uinta County in 1870, Evanston lies in the center of the energy-rich Overthrust Belt. It also is a departure point for trips into the Uinta Mountains to the south. Depot Square Park is the center of such summer activities as band concerts and barbecues. Other recreational opportunities include water sports at Woodruff Narrows Reservoir, north via US 89, and cross-country skiing at Bear River State Park *(see Recreation Areas Chart)*.

Bear River Information Center: 601 Bear River Dr., Evanston, WY 82930. **Phone:** (307) 789-6540.

Evanston Wyoming Chamber of Commerce: 1020 Front St., Evanston, WY 82930. **Phone:** (307) 783-0370. *(See ad this page.)*

UINTA COUNTY MUSEUM is at 1020 Front St., in the historic Carnegie Library building. The museum features permanent and changing exhibits about railroads, ranching and other aspects of the county's history. **Hours:** Mon.-Fri. 9-5, Sat. 11-3 by appointment. **Cost:** Free. **Phone:** (307) 789-8248.

▼ See AAA listing this page ▼

Say YES to ERS text updates to stay

posted when your tow truck is on the way

Chinese Joss House Museum, at 920 Front St. adjacent to the Uinta County Museum, pays tribute to Chinese immigrants who resided in the area circa 1870-1930. The building is a replica of an 1874 Chinese temple that burned down in 1922. Exhibits include archeological artifacts; historic photographs; and items from the late 19th to early 20th centuries, including pottery, paintings and other *objets d'art.* **Time:** Allow 45 minutes minimum. **Hours:** Mon.-Fri. 9-5, Sat. 11-3 by appointment. Closed major holidays. **Cost:** Free. **Phone:** (307) 783-6320.

HOLIDAY INN EXPRESS HOTEL & SUITES

(307)789-7999

Hotel
$99-$169

Address: 1965 Harrison Dr 82930 **Location:** I-80 exit 3 (Harrison Dr), just n. **Facility:** 62 units. 3 stories, interior corridors. **Terms:** cancellation fee imposed. **Amenities:** video games. **Pool(s):** heated indoor. **Activities:** hot tub, exercise room. **Guest Services:** valet and coin laundry. **Featured Amenity:** full hot breakfast.

BEST WESTERN DUNMAR INN

(307)789-3770

Hotel
$120-$130

AAA Benefit: Save 10% or more every day and earn 10% bonus points!

Address: 1601 Harrison Dr 82930 **Location:** I-80 exit 3 (Harrison Dr), 0.3 mi n. **Facility:** 165 units. 1 story, exterior corridors. **Parking:** winter plug-ins. **Dining:** Legal Tender Restaurant & Lounge, see separate listing. **Pool(s):** heated outdoor. **Activities:** sauna, hot tub, exercise room. **Guest Services:** valet laundry, area transportation. *(See ad this page.)*

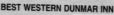

LEGAL TENDER RESTAURANT & LOUNGE

307/789-3770

American
Casual Dining
$8-$29

AAA Inspector Notes: You can expect friendly service in a relaxed atmosphere. Walls are adorned with some memorabilia of the original owner's career as a FBI agent. The steaks and salad bar beckons locals as well as being favorites with guests. **Features:** full bar, early bird specials, senior menu. **Address:** 1601 Harrison Dr 82930 **Location:** I-80 exit 3 (Harrison Dr), just n; in BEST WESTERN Dunmar Inn. *Menu on AAA.com (See ad this page.)*

HAMPTON INN

(307)789-5678

Hotel $112-$189 **Address:** 101 Wasatch Rd 82930 **Location:** I-80 exit 3 (Harrison Dr), just n. **Facility:** 73 units. 4 stories, interior corridors. **Terms:** 1-7 night minimum stay, cancellation fee imposed. **Pool(s):** heated indoor. **Activities:** hot tub, exercise room. **Guest Services:** valet and coin laundry.

AAA Benefit: Members save up to 10%!

SUDS BROTHERS BREWERY

307/444-7837

American. Casual Dining. $8-$13 **AAA Inspector Notes:** This lively pub serves good food and plays loud music. Diners cannot go wrong with award-winning beer, grande nachos, chicken tenders, fish and chips, chicken Alfredo and burgers. The daily house soups are good and hearty. **Features:** full bar, happy hour. **Address:** 1012 Main St 82930 **Location:** I-80 exit 3 (Harrison Dr), 0.3 mi n, then 1.2 mi e to Main St; downtown. **Parking:** street only.

▼ See AAA listing this page ▼

EVANSVILLE pop. 2,544

CASPER C'MON INN
307/472-6300

▼▼▼▼ **Hotel.** Rates not provided. **Address:** 301 E Lathrop Rd 82636 **Location:** I-25 exit 185, just n to Lathrop Rd, then 0.5 mi e. **Facility:** 125 units, some kitchens. 3 stories, interior corridors. **Parking:** winter plug-ins. **Pool(s):** heated indoor. **Activities:** hot tub, exercise room. **Guest Services:** valet and coin laundry.

〒➕ CALL 🄼 ➣ BIZ HS 🛜 ✕ 🖥 🖳 🖵

COMFORT INN
(307)237-8100

▼▼▼ **Hotel** $109-$199 **Address:** 269 Miracle St 82636 **Location:** I-25 exit 185, just n to Lathrop Rd, then just e. **Facility:** 57 units. 3 stories, interior corridors. **Parking:** winter plug-ins. **Pool(s):** heated indoor. **Activities:** hot tub, exercise room. **Guest Services:** valet and coin laundry.

〒➕ CALL 🄼 ➣ BIZ 🛜 ✕ 🖥 🖳 🖵

/SOME /UNITS 🛏

SLEEP INN & SUITES CASPER EAST
(307)235-3100

▼▼▼ **Hotel** $84-$159 **Address:** 6733 Bonanza Rd 82636 **Location:** I-25 exit 182, just n on Hat Six Rd. **Facility:** 80 units. 3 stories, interior corridors. **Parking:** winter plug-ins. **Pool(s):** heated indoor. **Activities:** hot tub, exercise room. **Guest Services:** valet and coin laundry.

〒➕ ➣ BIZ HS 🛜 ✕ 🖥 🖳 🖵

/SOME /UNITS 🛏

FLAMING GORGE NATIONAL RECREATION AREA (E-2)

Reached by SR 530 or US 191 from I-80 in Wyoming or US 191 from Utah, Flaming Gorge National Recreation Area straddles the border between Wyoming and Utah. The area includes a 91-mile-long reservoir and the Flaming Gorge and Red canyons, which were carved through the Uinta Mountains by the Green River.

Lake Flaming Gorge is bounded primarily by Red Canyon to the south and by rolling hills and occasional abrupt cliffs and promontories to the north. Of geologic interest are the exposed strata in Firehole Canyon and the Sheep Creek Geological Loop.

Once belonging to Mexico, Wyoming's portion of the Flaming Gorge region was annexed to the United States after the Mexican War. John Wesley Powell, a one-armed Army major and professor, mapped the area on his way down the Green River in the late 1860s and early 1870s, naming Flaming Gorge and many other prominent landmarks.

I-80 is connected to SR 530 and US 191. In Utah, US 191 joins with SRs 43 and 44, which then link with SR 530 again, to form a complete 160-mile loop around the recreation area. Along the route are the Flaming Gorge Dam and Visitor Center, off US 191 adjacent to the Bureau of Reclamation offices; the Red Canyon Visitor Center and Overlook, which offers a spectacular view from 1,400 feet above Red Canyon and Flaming Gorge Reservoir off SR 44; the Sheep Creek Geological Loop; and Flaming Gorge.

Known for its bountiful fishing waters, Lake Flaming Gorge also is a popular setting for swimming, boating and water skiing. Large boat ramps are found near campgrounds at convenient access points along the western and eastern sides of the lake.

The western shore, accessible from Buckboard, Wyo., and Lucerne Valley, Utah, has campsites and two marinas that provide boat rentals and supplies. Cedar Springs to the southeast is similarly equipped; the latter has a dock and marina. Other campgrounds are scattered throughout the Utah and Wyoming sections.

The reservoir contains a broad sampling of fish, including German brown, lake, rainbow and cutthroat trout; small-mouth bass; and kokanee salmon. Fishing is permitted all year. A license from either Utah or Wyoming is required.

Seasonal hunting is permitted except near public-use facilities. Cross-country skiing, snowmobiling and ice fishing are popular winter activities. For further information, contact the Flaming Gorge Ranger District, Flaming Gorge National Recreation Area, P.O. Box 279, Manila, UT 84046.

The recreation area is open all year, but most developed facilities are closed during the winter. The Red Canyon Visitor Center is open Mon.-Thurs. 10-5, Fri.-Sun. 9-6, mid-May to mid-Sept.; phone for schedule, rest of year. The Flaming Gorge Dam Visitor Center is open daily 8-6, Memorial Day-Labor Day; daily 9-5, Apr. 1-day before Memorial Day and day after Labor Day to mid-Oct.; Fri.-Mon. 10-4, rest of year. Guided tours of the dam depart from the visitor center daily every 20 minutes 9:10-3:50, mid-Mar. to mid-Oct.; phone ahead to confirm schedule.

A use fee pass is required for all facilities. Passes are $5 (1 day), $15 (16 days) and $35 (annual), beginning from the date of purchase. America the Beautiful–National Parks and Federal Recreational Lands Pass holders enter free. Phone (435) 784-3445 for the ranger district, (435) 889-3713 for the Red Canyon Visitor Center, or (435) 885-3135 for the Flaming Gorge Dam and Visitor Center. *See Recreation Areas Chart.*

FLAMING GORGE DAM is off US 191 near Dutch John, Utah. The dam is a concrete arch structure rising 502 feet above bedrock. **Note:** Pets are allowed only in the parking lot, not on the dam. **Hours:** Guided 1-hour tours are offered every 20 minutes daily 9:10-3:50, mid-Mar. to mid-Oct. Phone ahead to confirm schedule. **Cost:** Free. **Phone:** (435) 885-3135. GT

JOHN JARVIE HISTORIC RANCH is about 8 mi. n.w. of Dutch John, Utah, on US 191, then 22 mi. e. on a gravel road, following signs to Browns Park. A haven for outlaws around the turn of the 20th century, Browns Park formerly was the site of a successful ranching operation started by Scottish immigrant John Jarvie in the 1880s. The ranch today includes a replica of the general store originally built in 1881, a blacksmith shop, a corral and a two-room dugout that was once Jarvie's residence.

A 15-minute orientation video is shown in a historical stone house that now serves as a museum.

Time: Allow 1 hour minimum. **Hours:** Daily 10-4:30, Memorial Day-Labor Day; Tues.-Sat. 10-4:30, rest of year when staff is available. Phone ahead to confirm schedule. **Cost:** Donations. **Phone:** (435) 885-3307 or (435) 781-4400. GT A

FORT BRIDGER (E-1) pop. 345, elev. 6,670'

One of Fort Bridger's early residents was the renowned mountain man and scout Jim Bridger. Bridger, who hired himself out as a wilderness guide, was known for telling tall tales. According to popular lore, one of Bridger's most repeated stories was the one in which he tried to jump across a gorge in a petrified forest. The gorge turned out to be wider than he expected, but Bridger managed to escape death by remaining aloft on the gorge's petrified air.

Self-guiding tours: A driving tour atop an original hand-built roadbed of the Union Pacific begins 9 miles west of Fort Bridger at Leroy; from I-80 exit 24, follow CR 173 and SR 150. Utilize caution, as 22 miles of the route are unpaved. The tour continues past the abandoned town of Piedmont, several beehive-shaped charcoal kilns and the Uinta Mountains before entering Evanston (see place listing p. 256).

FORT BRIDGER STATE HISTORIC SITE is 3 mi. s. of I-80 exit 34. The fort was established in 1843 by Jim Bridger and Louis Vasquez. Visitors can see original buildings from the Army occupation 1858-90 and restored Lincoln Highway Motel cabins dating from 1842. Recent excavations have revealed the site of the original trading post, which has been reconstructed nearby. A museum offers exhibits tracing different periods of occupation.

Time: Allow 2 hours minimum. **Hours:** Grounds daily 8-dusk. Museum daily 9-5, May-Sept.; schedule varies rest of year based on staff availability. Phone ahead to confirm schedule. **Cost:** $4; $2 (Wyoming residents); free (ages 0-17). **Phone:** (307) 782-3842. A

FORT LARAMIE NATIONAL HISTORIC SITE (D-6)

Fort Laramie National Historic Site is off US 26, 3 miles southwest of the town of Fort Laramie. Near the confluence of the Laramie and North Platte rivers, the site covers 832 acres. From its founding as Fort William in 1834 and until 1849, the fort was an important fur-trading post. Purchased by the U.S. government in 1849 and renamed Fort Laramie, the fort served to aid in the migrations to Oregon and California. By 1890 the fort had outlived its usefulness and was abandoned, its land and buildings sold at public auction.

Eleven structures, including the 1874 cavalry barracks, have been restored and refurnished to recall the flavor of daily life at this post. A visitor center museum displays artifacts relating to civilian, military

and Native American history on the northern Plains. From June to mid-August, staff members in period clothing demonstrate aspects of both military and civilian life in the 1870s. A vehicle for the physically impaired is available when the number of staff permits. An 1875 iron Army bridge that spans the North Platte River is 2 miles above the fort.

Grounds open daily dawn-dusk. Visitor center open daily 8-6, Memorial Day weekend-Labor Day; 8-4:30, rest of year. Visitor center closed Jan. 1, Thanksgiving and Christmas. Free. Phone (307) 837-2221.

FOSSIL BUTTE NATIONAL MONUMENT (E-1)

Fourteen miles west of Kemmerer on US 30, Fossil Butte National Monument rises nearly 1,000 feet above the Twin Creek Valley. The buff-to-white beds of the Green River Formation contain one of the world's largest deposits of the fossils of freshwater fish that lived 50 million years ago. Fossils of mammals, reptiles, fish, insects and plants can be seen at the visitor center; a video presentation also is available.

A self-guiding hiking trail, 2.5 miles long, leads to the site of a historic fossil quarry, and a 1.5-mile trail takes visitors through an aspen tree grove. Interpretive programs are offered June through August.

Allow 2 hours, 30 minutes minimum. Grounds open all year but may be snow-covered Oct.-Apr. Visitor center daily 9-5:30, May-Sept.; 8-4:30, rest of year. Closed winter holidays. Free. Phone (307) 877-4455.

GILLETTE (B-5) pop. 29,087, elev. 4,538'
• Hotels p. 260 • Restaurants p. 260

Gillette lies on a high plateau between the Black Hills and the Bighorn Mountains. The town's livestock industry dates from the early 1800s. Mule deer, pronghorns and buffalo graze on unspoiled land nearby.

Named for railroad surveyor Edward Gillette, the town was developed as a ranching area and became a hub for transporting livestock to market. Now coal and oil industries fuel Gillette's economy. During summer, coal mine tours can be arranged through the convention and visitors bureau. The bureau also offers an assistance program for hunters interested in the mule deer, pronghorn antelopes and elk populations in the area.

Campbell County Convention and Visitors Bureau: 1810 S. Douglas Hwy., Suite A, Gillette, WY 82718. **Phone:** (307) 686-0040.

ROCKPILE MUSEUM is 1 mi. from I-90 exit 124 at 900 W. Second St. (US 14/16E). The museum takes its name from a nearby rock formation. Local history is depicted through extensive displays that include firearms, pioneer and Native American artifacts and a restored sheep wagon. Next to the museum are two furnished rural schoolhouses. **Hours:** Mon.-Sat. 9-5. **Cost:** Free. **Phone:** (307) 682-5723.

ARBUCKLE LODGE
307/685-6363

 Hotel. Rates not provided. **Address:** 1400 S Garner Lake Rd 82718 **Location:** I-90 exit 129, just e. **Facility:** 86 units, some two bedrooms and efficiencies. 3 stories, interior corridors. **Parking:** winter plug-ins. **Terms:** check-in 4 pm. **Pool(s):** heated indoor. **Activities:** hot tub, limited exercise equipment. **Guest Services:** valet and coin laundry.

CALL 🍽️M 🏊 BIZ 🛜 ✕ 🖥️ 🖨️ 💻 / SOME UNITS 🐾

CANDLEWOOD SUITES
307/682-6100

 Extended Stay Hotel. Rates not provided. **Address:** 904 Country Club Rd 82718 **Location:** I-90 exit 126, 0.5 mi s, then just e. **Facility:** 83 efficiencies. 3 stories, interior corridors. **Activities:** picnic facilities, exercise room. **Guest Services:** complimentary and valet laundry.

[↑] BIZ HS 🛜 🖥️ 🖨️ 💻 / SOME UNITS 🐾

COMFORT INN & SUITES OF GILLETTE
(307)685-2223

Hotel
$110-$220

Address: 1607 W 2nd St 82716 **Location:** I-90 exit 124, 0.3 mi ne, then just se. **Facility:** 60 units. 3 stories, interior corridors. **Parking:** winter plug-ins. **Pool(s):** heated indoor. **Activities:** hot tub, exercise room. **Guest Services:** valet and coin laundry. **Featured Amenity:** full hot breakfast.

SAVE [↔] [↑] CALL 🍽️M 🏊 BIZ HS 🛜 ✕ 💻 / SOME UNITS 🐾 🖥️ 🖨️

COUNTRY INN & SUITES BY CARLSON
307/682-0505

Hotel
Rates not provided

Address: 2597 S Douglas Hwy 82718 **Location:** I-90 exit 126, 0.6 mi s, then just e. **Facility:** 80 units. 3 stories, interior corridors. **Parking:** winter plug-ins. **Pool(s):** heated indoor. **Activities:** hot tub, exercise room. **Guest Services:** valet and coin laundry. **Featured Amenity:** full hot breakfast.

SAVE [↔] [↑] CALL 🍽️M 🏊 BIZ HS 🛜 ✕ 🖥️ 🖨️ 💻

FAIRFIELD INN & SUITES BY MARRIOTT
(307)682-1717

 **Hotel** $116-$244 **Address:** 2577 S Douglas Hwy 82718 **Location:** I-90 exit 126, 0.6 mi s, then ne. **Facility:** 80 units. 3 stories, interior corridors. **Pool(s):** heated indoor. **Activities:** hot tub, exercise room. **Guest Services:** valet and coin laundry.

AAA Benefit: Members save 5% or more!

[↔] [↑] CALL 🍽️M 🏊 BIZ HS 🛜 ✕ 💻 / SOME UNITS 🖥️ 🖨️

HAMPTON INN
(307)686-2000

 Hotel $109-$329 **Address:** 211 Decker Ct 82716 **Location:** I-90 exit 124, just ne. **Facility:** 57 units. 3 stories, interior corridors. **Terms:** 1-7 night minimum stay, cancellation fee imposed.

AAA Benefit: Members save up to 10%!

Pool(s): heated indoor. **Activities:** hot tub, exercise room. **Guest Services:** valet and coin laundry.

[↔] [↑] CALL 🍽️M 🏊 BIZ HS 🛜 ✕ 💻 / SOME UNITS 🖥️ 🖨️

HOLIDAY INN EXPRESS & SUITES
307/686-9576

 **Hotel.** Rates not provided. **Address:** 1908 Cliff Davis Dr 82718 **Location:** I-90 exit 126, just s to Boxelder Rd, then just e to Cliff Davis Dr. **Facility:** 83 units. 3 stories, interior corridors. **Amenities:** video games. **Pool(s):** heated indoor. **Activities:** hot tub, exercise room. **Guest Services:** valet and coin laundry.

[↑] 🏊 BIZ HS 🛜 ✕ 📷 🖥️ 🖨️ 💻 / SOME UNITS 🐾

WINGATE BY WYNDHAM
(307)685-2700

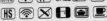 **Hotel** $99-$209 **Address:** 1801 Cliff Davis Dr 82718 **Location:** I-90 exit 126, just s to Boxelder Rd, then just e. **Facility:** 84 units. 3 stories, interior corridors. **Amenities:** video games, safes. **Pool(s):** heated indoor. **Activities:** hot tub, exercise room. **Guest Services:** valet and coin laundry, area transportation.

[↔] [↑] CALL 🍽️M 🏊 BIZ HS 🛜 ✕ 📷 🖥️ 🖨️ 💻

RAMADA PLAZA GILLETTE
307/686-3000

[fyi] Not evaluated. **Address:** 2009 S Douglas Hwy 82718 **Location:** I-90 exit 126, just s, then e. Facilities, services, and décor characterize a mid-scale property.

WHERE TO EAT

311 LOUNGE
307/685-8055

 American. Casual Dining. $12-$22 **AAA Inspector Notes:** Good food, mojitos, margaritas and martinis are creatively prepared at this lounge where the philosophy is eat, drink and unwind. Menu items include Mediterranean and Asian salads, baked Brie with honey and pecans, rosemary-infused and prosciutto-wrapped stuffed cherry peppers, salmon burger with lemon caper aioli, chicken satay sandwiches and a few tasty desserts. Watch out, the two mini burger sliders are addictive. **Features:** full bar, Sunday brunch, happy hour. **Address:** 311 S Gillette Ave 82716 **Location:** Downtown. **Parking:** street only. [L] [D]

THE CHOPHOUSE RESTAURANT
307/682-6805

American. Casual Dining. $6-$30 **AAA Inspector Notes:** Prime beef cuts are cooked to the diner's liking in this upscale restaurant. The warm and inviting dining room's menu also is laden with made-to-order fresh fish and shellfish specialties and interesting interpretations of classic dishes. Gluten-free items are available. **Features:** full bar, early bird specials, happy hour. **Address:** 113 S Gillette Ave 82716 **Location:** I-90 exit 124, 0.3 mi n, then 1.5 mi e; at W 2nd St (US 16) and Gillette Ave. **Parking:** on-site and street. [L] [D] CALL 🍽️M

LOS COMPADRES
307/682-1101

Mexican. Casual Dining. $6-$15 **AAA Inspector Notes:** This little eatery offers great food, friendly service and a colorful atmosphere. **Features:** full bar. **Address:** 1700 W 2nd St 82716 **Location:** I-90 exit 124, just ne, then just se. [L] [D]

THE MAIN BAGEL COMPANY
307/687-1616

Deli Coffee/Tea. Quick Serve. $6-$7 **AAA Inspector Notes:** At this family-owned and -operated eatery, bagels are boiled first, then baked, resulting in a chewy center and crunchy crust. Croissants, pizza, salads, sandwiches and wraps make up the menu. Daily soups are made in house. **Features:** patio dining. **Address:** 2610 S Douglas Hwy 82718 **Location:** I-90 exit 126, 0.5 mi s; in Power Basin Mall. [B] [L]

MUFA CAFE
307/257-2469

Breakfast Deli. Casual Dining. $4-$17 **AAA Inspector Notes:** MUFA means Melanie's Unadulterated Food Acquisition, a place where you'll find healthy options for breakfast and lunch. Melanie (the owner) takes great care to ensure foods are freshly prepared and proves that food good for you can taste great, too. **Features:** Sunday brunch. **Address:** 500 O-R Dr 82718 **Location:** I-90 exit 126, just s on SR 59 S (S Douglas Hwy), 0.8 mi w on E Boxelder Rd, then just n. [B] [L] CALL 🍽️M

THE PRIME RIB RESTAURANT & WINE CELLAR
307/682-2944

American
Casual Dining
$9-$34

AAA Inspector Notes: This bustling upscale restaurant offers patrons many variations of well-prepared steaks, prime rib and seafood. An extensive selection of wine is kept in a state-of-the-art, glass-enclosed wine case. **Features:** full bar, happy hour. **Reservations:** suggested. **Address:** 1205 S Douglas Hwy 82717 **Location:** I-90 exit 126, 0.5 mi n. *Menu on AAA.com*

Ⓛ Ⓓ CALL Ⓜ

SMILING MOOSE DELI   307/363-4104

Deli. Quick Serve. $4-$10 **AAA Inspector Notes:** This not-so-typical fast food restaurant offers breakfast all day in addition to a variety of hot and cold sandwiches, wraps, soups and salads. Diners can create their own signature sandwich with the abundance of ingredients available. Do not forget a sweet treat to finish off the meal. **Address:** 2711 Douglas Hwy 82718 **Location:** I-90 exit 129, 0.7 mi s.

Ⓑ Ⓛ Ⓓ CALL Ⓜ

GLENROCK (D-5) pop. 2,576, elev. 5,102'

Glenrock's hunting, fishing, hiking and mountain-climbing opportunities make it a hot spot for outdoor enthusiasts. Originally called Deer Creek Station, Glenrock was a stop along the Oregon Trail and the Pony Express National Historic Trail. The more than 350,000 settlers traversing the area from 1841 to 1869 would break at a certain rock situated in a nearby glen—hence the name that later was adopted by the town. The large, domelike Rock in the Glen, located just west of town off I-25, is inscribed with the names of some of the settlers.

Glenrock Area Chamber of Commerce: 506 W. Birch St., Glenrock, WY 82637. **Phone:** (307) 436-5652.

GLENROCK PALEONTOLOGICAL MUSEUM is at 506 W. Birch St. On display are a Triceratops skull, Oligocene mammal fossils and Tyrannosaurus rex teeth. Permanent exhibits include Sea Life in Wyoming: Devonian to Cretaceous Ages. **Time:** Allow 1 hour minimum. **Hours:** Tues.-Sat. 11-4, June-Aug.; Tues., Thurs. and Sat. 11-4, rest of year. Closed major holidays. Phone ahead to confirm schedule. **Cost:** Donations. **Phone:** (307) 436-2667.

GRAND TETON NATIONAL PARK
(B-1)

• Hotels p. 266 • Restaurants p. 266
• Attractions map p. 262
• Hotels & Restaurants map & index p. 287
• Part of Jackson Hole Including Grand Teton National Park area — see map p. 285

Elevations in the park range from 6,800 ft. at the valley floor to 13,770 ft. at Grand Teton Peak. Refer to AAA maps for additional elevation information.

Grand Teton National Park's southern entrance is north of Jackson on US 26/89/191; an eastern entrance is at Moran Junction on US 26/287. From this point US 89/191/287 heads north through the park into Yellowstone National Park *(see place listing p. 316)*. The park's 485 square miles include the major portion of Wyoming's Teton Range and the valley of Jackson Hole. Together the mountain range and valley frame a majestic landscape of eight large lakes and many smaller ones, glaciers, numerous snowfields and extensive pine, fir and spruce forests.

The Tetons are among the youngest mountains on the continent. The elevations established by the U.S. Geological Survey for the major peaks are Grand Teton, 13,770 feet; Mount Owen, 12,928 feet; Middle Teton, 12,804 feet; Mount Moran, 12,605 feet; South Teton, 12,514 feet; Teewinot Mountain, 12,325 feet; Thor Peak, 12,028 feet; Buck Mountain, 11,938 feet; Nez Perce Peak, 11,901 feet; Mount Wister, 11,490 feet; and Mount St. John, 11,430 feet.

Few mountain ranges have a greater variety of glaciated canyons than the Tetons. The fault-block mountains of this alpine park are rare in this country. Part of the park area lies above the tree line, which is at about 10,000 feet.

The Tetons were first photographed by William H. Jackson, a member of the Hayden Expedition sent by the government to survey the area in 1872.

General Information and Activities

The park is open all year, although most park facilities operate only from mid-May to mid-October. Visitor information is available at Colter Bay and Jenny Lake visitor centers and the Craig Thomas Discovery & Visitor Center in Moose. Free ranger-led activities in summer include hikes. Entrance stations and visitor centers distribute a park newspaper listing the schedule of activities.

More than 250 miles of trails afford short walks, strenuous hikes and overnight backcountry trips. Trail booklets can be found at some trail heads and at the visitor centers. Campsites along backcountry trails require a camping permit, available at the visitor centers and the Jenny Lake Ranger Station.

Game fish include brook, brown, cutthroat, Mackinaw, and rainbow trout, as well as whitefish. Fish can be taken with artificial flies and lures during most of the summer and autumn, but the Mackinaw trout in Jackson and Jenny lakes are best caught by trolling with heavy tackle.

A Wyoming fishing license is required; a nonresident 1-day license is available for $14; a full-year permit is $92. Special fishing regulations apply in the park, and changes are made annually regarding limits and waters open to fishing; check the current regulations.

Mountain climbing is a popular summer pastime. Authorized guide services are available, and because of the difficulty of the Teton peaks, climbers are urged to use them. Prospective climbers should consult rangers for information about routes and appropriate equipment. The Jenny Lake Ranger Station is the park's climbing information center.

© 2015 HERE

© AAA

To Yellowstone National Park

MOUNT BERRY EL 8,951 FT

WILDCAT PEAK EL 9,693 FT

Conant Creek

Caribou-Targhee

Grand

Teton

Teton

National

Lizard Creek

Jackson

Wilderness

Area

RANGER PEAK EL 11,355 FT

MOOSE MOUNTAIN EL 10,054 FT

EAGLES REST PEAK EL 11,257 FT

Colter Bay

Colter Bay Visitor Center

Two Ocean Lake

TRAIL

Emma Matilda Lake

National

BIVOUAC PEAK EL 10,825 FT

Grand Teton Lodge Company Wild and Scenic Rafting Trips

Jackson Lake

Barker-Ewing Scenic Float Trips

South Badger Creek

North Leigh Creek

TRIPLE GLACIERS

GREEN MOUNTAIN EL 9,614 FT

Forest

THOR PEAK EL 12,028 FT

MT MORAN EL 12,605 FT

Signal Mountain

Signal Mountain

Moran

Buffalo

Fork

Bridger-Teton

To Dubois

Lake

National

Leigh Lake

Teton Creek

PAINTBRUSH TRAIL

CASCADE CANYON TRAIL

MOUNT SAINT JOHN EL 11,430 FT

Jenny Lake

TETON PARK RD

Cunningham Cabin Historic Site

River

Snake

Spread

Creek

TETON GLACIER

GRAND TETON EL 13,770 FT

MIDDLE TETON EL 12,804 FT

SOUTH TETON EL 12,514 FT

BUCK MOUNTAIN EL 11,938 FT

NEZ PERCE EL 11,901 FT

Jenny Lake

Jenny Lake

Jenny Lake Visitor Center

AMPHITHEATER LAKE TRAIL

189 191 26 89

N

Triangle X Ranch Float Trips

MOUNT LEIDY EL 10,326 FT

National

DEATH CANYON TRAIL

FOSSIL MOUNTAIN EL 10,916 FT

HOUSETOP MTN EL 10,537 FT

MOUNT WISTER EL 11,490 FT

ROAD CLOSED IN WINTER

PROSPECTORS MTN EL 11,241 FT

Chapel of the Transfiguration

Menor's Ferry

Craig Thomas Discovery and Visitor Center

Lower Slide Lake

MOUNT HUNT EL 10,783 FT

GRANITE CANYON TRAIL

Phelps Lake

Moose

Park

Kelly

Gros Ventre

Gros Ventre Slide

TAYLOR RANCH RD

Atherton Creek

VENTRE

Gros

Ventre

River

RD

Forest

Grand Teton National Park Attractions

Jackson Hole Mountain Resort

Teton Village

Jackson Hole Airport (JAC)

Welcome Center

National Museum of Wildlife Art

390

National Elk

Jackson National Fish Hatchery

SHEEP MOUNTAIN EL 11,239 FT

Scale in Miles

3.8   0   3.8

See p. 6 - Map Legend

Bridger-Teton

Bar J Chuckwagon Supper & Western Music Show

National

Refuge

Flat Creek

CAMPGROUND SITE WITHIN NATIONAL PARK.

Jackson Hole Hist Society & Mus

Curtis Canyon

MILLERS BUTTE EL 6,775 FT

TETON PASS EL 8,431 FT

Wilson

Forest

22

Snow King Resort

JACKSON PEAK EL 10,741 FT

26 89 191 189

Sands Whitewater and Scenic River Trips

Jackson

2120-16

To Idaho Falls, ID

To Salt Lake City, UT

(See map & index p. 287.)

Standard alpine equipment is essential: ice axes, ropes and rubber-soled boots or climbing shoes. Two park-approved mountaineering schools offer lessons and guide service.

The climbing season in Grand Teton National Park ordinarily spans mid-June to mid-September, but conditions are best from July to early September. In most cases it is advisable to allow 2 days for an ascent of Grand Teton, Mount Owen or Mount Moran and 1 or 2 days for all the other peaks, depending upon your experience.

Riding on horses trained for mountain trails is another popular way to explore the park. From corrals at Colter Bay Village and Jackson Lake Lodge, the Grand Teton Lodge Company conducts daily guided 1- and 2-hour rides, half-day trail rides and wagon rides; phone (307) 543-2811.

Morning and evening horse or wagon rides with breakfast or dinner also are available for $39-$73. Guide fees vary according to trail, but all rates are regulated by the park and range from $40-$75. Restrictions apply to horseback riding.

CCInc. Auto Tape Tours allows drivers to set their own pace while a CD or cassette narrative describes the park's attractions and history. They are available at gift shops, RV campgrounds, Colter Bay Village, Jackson Lake Lodge, Jenny Lake, and by mail; phone (201) 236-1666.

If water levels allow, boat and canoe rentals, guided fishing trips and scenic boat trips can be arranged at the Colter Bay Marina at Colter Bay Village, the Bridge Bay Marina on Yellowstone Lake and the booking office at Jackson Lake Lodge. Canoe and kayak rentals are $18.50-$21 per hour, and boat rentals are $42 per hour or $175 per 8-hour day (including gas); there is a 2-hour minimum boat rental.

Jackson Lake boat cruises lasting 1 hour, 30 minutes leave the Colter Bay Marina several times daily, if water levels allow. Daily trout breakfast cruises to Elk Island as well as Monday, Wednesday, Friday and Saturday evening dinner cruises also are offered. Cruise rates range from $30 to $64; $13.50 to $37 (ages 3-11). Contact the Grand Teton Lodge Co. for schedules and exact fares; phone (307) 543-2811.

Jenny Lake Boating Co. offers scenic cruises and shuttle service to the west shore of Jenny Lake. Round-trip shuttle service $15; $12 (ages 65-79); $8 (ages 3-12); free (ages 80+). One-way shuttle service $9; $6 (ages 3-12). The booking office is at the south end of Jenny Lake near the ranger station; phone (307) 734-9227, mid-May through September 21.

Motorboats can be operated on Jackson and Jenny lakes, but motors more than 10 horsepower cannot be used on Jenny Lake. Hand-propelled craft are permitted on Bearpaw, Bradley, Emma Matilda,

▼ See AAA listing p. 265 ▼

(See map & index p. 287.)
Jackson, Jenny, Leigh, Phelps, String, Taggart and Two Ocean lakes and on the Snake River. Water skiing and windsurfing are permitted only on Jackson Lake.

Mandatory boating permits can be purchased at the visitor centers. Seven-day permits are $10 for nonmotorized craft and $20 for motorized craft; annual permits are $20 for nonmotorized craft and $40 for motorized craft.

Several companies offer scenic float trips on the Snake River from May through September (see attraction listings). Reservations for these relaxing excursions are recommended (and, in some cases, required).

Winter activities include cross-country skiing, snowshoe hikes and ice fishing. Marked trails for cross-country skiing also are provided.

Five campgrounds, Colter Bay, Gros Ventre, Jenny Lake, Lizard Creek and Signal Mountain, are open on a first-come, first-served basis. Opening dates vary from early May to early June; closing dates are from early September to mid-October. Rates are $22 per night and reservations are not accepted. See Recreation Areas Chart.

ADMISSION to the park is by private vehicle permit ($30), motorcycle permit ($25) and by single nonmotorized entry ($15), valid in Grand Teton and the John D. Rockefeller, Jr. Memorial Parkway for 7 days; a two-park pass for Grand Teton and Yellowstone private vehicle permit ($50), motorcycle ($40) and nonmotorized entry ($20), valid for 7 days. Park Annual Pass ($60) or Interagency Annual Pass ($80 for entrance to most federal sites) also is available. An Interagency Lifetime Senior Pass for U.S. citizens ages 62+ is $10; an Interagency Access Passport for physically impaired U.S. citizens provides free admission. Daily entrance fee mid-Dec. through Apr. 30, $5 per private vehicle, motorcycle or individual hiker, biker or skier.

PETS are permitted in the park only if they are on a leash or otherwise physically restricted at all times. They are not permitted on trails, in the backcountry or in any public building.

ADDRESS inquiries to Grand Teton National Park, P.O. Drawer 170, Moose, WY 83012-0170; phone (307) 739-3300.

AMPHITHEATER LAKE TRAIL extends up the eastern slope of Disappointment Peak to two alpine lakes, Surprise and Amphitheater, both at altitudes of more than 9,000 feet. Amphitheater Lake occupies a protected glacial cirque, or steep hollow. An overlook, reached by several trails climbing 3,000 feet above the valley floor, offers a sweeping panorama of Jackson Hole and a view extending eastward 80 miles to the Wind River Mountains. A branch from the trail leads into Garnet Canyon. Trail conditions are available at the visitor centers. **Time:** Allow 6 hours minimum.

CASCADE CANYON TRAIL, 25 mi. n. of Jackson in the center of the park, explores the deepest recesses of the Tetons, passing through a broad, glacier-carved canyon with walls that rise thousands of feet on either side. Lake Solitude, near the head of the canyon at the tree line, is a pristine example of an alpine lake. **Time:** Allow 7 hours minimum.

CHAPEL OF THE TRANSFIGURATION is off Chapel of the Transfiguration Rd. near Moose. Above the altar of the 1925 log chapel is a large window framing a view of the Teton Range. Episcopal services are held during the summer; schedules are posted on a board outside the chapel and in park newspapers. **Time:** Allow 30 minutes minimum.

COLTER BAY VISITOR CENTER is 25 mi. n. of Moose near Jackson Lake. Videos featuring local wildlife and scenery are shown daily in the amphitheater. **Hours:** Daily 8-7, first Mon. in June-Labor Day; 8-5, early May-day before Memorial Day and day after Labor Day-early Oct. **Cost:** Free. **Phone:** (307) 739-3594.

CRAIG THOMAS DISCOVERY & VISITOR CENTER is across the street from the park headquarters in Moose. The center orients visitors to the unique natural and cultural history of the area and features stories about conservation and stewardship. Maps and permits are available. **Hours:** Daily 8-7, early June-Labor Day; 8-5, May 1-early June and mid-Sept. through Nov. 1; daily 9-5, early Mar.-Apr. 30. **Cost:** Free. **Phone:** (307) 739-3399.

CUNNINGHAM CABIN HISTORIC SITE is 6 mi. s. of Moran Junction on US 26/89/191. The site was the base of pioneer Pierce Cunningham's Bar Flying U Ranch that once comprised some 560 acres. The site now contains the foundations of the house, barn, shed and outbuildings as well as the remains of a cabin. A leaflet outlining a self-guiding trail through the area also describes the life of the homesteader in Jackson Hole. **Time:** Allow 30 minutes minimum.

DEATH CANYON TRAIL, about 3 mi. s. of Moose, traverses the length of a canyon of profound depth and grandeur to broad meadows. No canyon better illustrates the contrasts of the Teton area. **Time:** Allow 6 hours minimum.

FLAGG RANCH INFORMATION STATION is at Flagg Ranch, 16 mi. n. of Colter Bay on US 89/191/287. The station provides information about John D. Rockefeller, Jr. Memorial Parkway and the Yellowstone area. **Hours:** Daily 9-4, June 1-Labor Day. The site may be closed during lunch hours; phone ahead to confirm schedule. **Cost:** Free. **Phone:** (307) 543-2372.

HIDDEN FALLS AND INSPIRATION POINT TRAILS lead from the southern shore of Jenny Lake off Teton Park Rd. A boat ride to the trailhead is available in the summer. Ranger-guided tours to Hidden Falls and Inspiration Point depart the trailhead daily

(See map & index p. 287.)

at 8:30 in season; departure time may vary. **Time:** Allow 2 hours minimum. GT

JENNY LAKE VISITOR CENTER is 8 mi. n. of Moose Junction on Teton Park Rd. The visitor center has exhibits about geology. **Hours:** Daily 8-7, early June-Labor Day; 8-5, mid-May to early June and day after Labor Day-late Sept. **Cost:** Free. **Phone:** (307) 739-3392.

MENOR'S FERRY is near the Chapel of the Transfiguration in Moose. The ferry is a reconstruction of the craft that was once the only means of crossing the Snake River in central Jackson Hole country. The original home of Bill Menor, one of the area's first settlers, is in the area; it contains historical objects and exhibits. **Time:** Allow 30 minutes minimum. **Hours:** Daily 10-4, early July-Aug. 31, weather and staff permitting. Phone ahead to confirm schedule.

PAINTBRUSH TRAIL starts near the outlet of Leigh Lake, follows the bottom of Paintbrush Canyon, crosses Paintbrush Divide and joins the Cascade Canyon Trail at Lake Solitude. The many wildflowers along this trail give the canyon its name. Wildlife, especially moose, can be seen near lakes and marshes. This trail affords several good views of Jackson and Leigh lakes. Since dangerous snow and ice remain on the divide until late in the year, check conditions at the visitor centers. Horses cannot be taken over the divide to Lake Solitude until late August.

SIGNAL MOUNTAIN is 3 mi. s. of Jackson Lake Junction on Teton Park Rd. The mountain affords a panorama of the valley, Jackson Lake, a portion of southern Yellowstone and the Teton, Gros Ventre and Hoback mountain ranges. A narrow, paved road that's 5 miles long leads to the summit. Trailers are not allowed on this road.

TETON CREST TRAIL traverses the Tetons from Teton Pass to Cascade Canyon. This high alpine country can be explored on foot or horseback.

VALLEY TRAIL runs parallel to the mountains from the e. shore of Leigh Lake s. to Teton Village. The trail is the point of origin of all trails into the Teton Range. From this point, trails run westward into Cascade, Death, Granite, Open and Paintbrush canyons; others encircle String Lake, Jenny Lake and Hermitage Point on Jackson Lake. A popular hike follows the south shore of Jenny Lake to Hidden Falls.

Float Trips

Float Trips, on the Snake River through Grand Teton National Park, are conducted by experienced guides who thread rubber rafts down the river. These trips, which offer spectacular mountain scenery and opportunities to view native wildlife, are carefully supervised by the National Park Service.

Note: A minimum weight of 35-40 pounds is required for most float trips.

BARKER-EWING SCENIC FLOAT TRIPS depart from the float-trip parking lot at Moose Village; transportation from the parking lot to the launch area is provided. Scenic 10-mile trips are conducted entirely within the park's natural environment and provide opportunities to view wildlife and the Teton peaks. **Hours:** Trips depart several times daily, mid-May to late Sept. **Cost:** $70; $50 (ages 6-15). Reservations are required. **Phone:** (307) 733-1800 or (800) 365-1800. GT

DORNAN'S SNAKE RIVER SCENIC FLOAT TRIPS originate at 185 N. Center St. in Jackson. Lasting 3 to 3.5 hours, the 14-mile scenic float trips provide good opportunities for photography and for observing elk, bear and other wildlife. **Hours:** Trips depart daily at 8, noon and 4, mid-May to late Sept. (weather and water conditions permitting). **Cost:** $70; $55 (ages 0-11, with a 40-lb. minimum weight). Reservations are recommended. **Phone:** (307) 733-3699. GT

GRAND TETON LODGE COMPANY WILD AND SCENIC RAFTING TRIPS is 5 mi. n.w. of Moran Junction on US 89/191/287. The company offers 3- to 4-hour float trips as well as luncheon and dinner trips; transportation to and from the river is provided.

Hours: Three- to 4-hour float trips and luncheon trips run daily, late May-early Sept. Dinner trips run Tues., Thurs. and Sat., late May-late Sept. Phone ahead to confirm schedule. **Cost:** Three- to 4-hour float trip $67; $45 (ages 6-11). Luncheon trip $77.44; $54.08 (ages 6-11). Dinner trip $84.16; $58.50 (ages 6-11). Fares may vary; phone ahead. Ages 0-5 are not permitted. **Phone:** (307) 543-2811. GT

SIGNAL MOUNTAIN LODGE FLOAT TRIPS meets at Signal Mountain Lodge, on Inner Park Rd. in Moran; transportation to and from the Snake River is provided. A 10-mile scenic float ride down the river lasts 3.5 hours and features wildlife viewing opportunities. **Hours:** Morning and evening trips depart daily (times vary), mid-May to late Sept. (weather and water conditions permitting). **Cost:** $70; $45 (ages 6-12). Fares may vary; phone ahead. **Phone:** (307) 543-2831. GT

SOLITUDE FLOAT TRIPS departs the float-trip parking lot across from the Moose Visitor Center. Ten-mile scenic trips are available. **Hours:** Trips are offered several times daily, May-Sept. (weather and water conditions permitting). **Cost:** $70; $52 (ages 6-17). Reservations are recommended. **Phone:** (307) 733-2871 or (888) 704-2800. GT

SAVE **TRIANGLE X RANCH FLOAT TRIPS** meets in the float-trip parking lot across from the Craig Thomas Discovery & Visitor Center. Ten-mile sunrise, mid-day and evening wildlife floats take visitors along the Snake River. Enjoy a hearty meal on the 12-mile scenic dinner float. **Hours:** Trips depart several times daily, May-Sept. **Cost:** Ten-mile float trip $68; $49 (ages 5-18). Twelve mile dinner float

(See map & index p. 287.)

$79; $62 (ages 5-18). Fares may vary; phone ahead. Reservations are required. **Phone:** (307) 733-5500 or (888) 860-0005. *(See ad p. 263, p. 270.)* GT

HEADWATERS LODGE & CABINS AT FLAGG RANCH
307/543-2861 **1**

◆◆ ◆ **Hotel.** Rates not provided. **Address:** Hwy 89 83013 **Location:** 25 mi n of jct US 89/191; 2.5 mi s of Yellowstone National Park south entrance. **Facility:** 92 units, some cabins. 1 story, exterior corridors. **Terms:** check-in 4 pm. **Activities:** fishing, recreation programs in summer. **Guest Services:** coin laundry.

JACKSON LAKE LODGE
307/543-2811 **2**

◆◆◆ ◆ **Resort Hotel.** Rates not provided. **Address:** US Hwy 89 83013 **Location:** 5 mi nw of jct US 89 and 191. **Facility:** This impressive lodge is set on spacious grounds. Numerous seating arrangements on and below the mezzanine have views that I guarantee will take your breath away; they are what postcards are made of. 385 units, some cabins. 1-3 stories, interior/exterior corridors. **Terms:** check-in 4 pm. **Amenities:** safes. **Dining:** 2 restaurants, also, The Mural Room, see separate listing. **Pool(s):** heated outdoor. **Activities:** recreation programs in summer, playground, trails. **Guest Services:** valet laundry, area transportation.

JENNY LAKE LODGE
307/543-3351 **4**

◆◆◆ ◆◆◆ **Cabin.** Rates not provided. **Address:** Jenny Lake Inner Park Rd 83012 **Location:** 3 mi off Inner Park Rd; jct N Jenny Lake. Located in a secluded area. **Facility:** At the foot of the majestic Tetons, log cabins are named after wildflowers and offer hardwood floors, area rugs, high-beamed ceilings, willow and pine furnishings and thoughtful amenities. 37 cabins. 1 story, exterior corridors. **Terms:** check-in 4 pm. **Amenities:** safes. **Dining:** Jenny Lake Lodge Dining Room, see separate listing. **Activities:** recreation programs in summer, bicycles, lawn sports, trails. **Guest Services:** valet laundry, area transportation.

SIGNAL MOUNTAIN LODGE
307/543-2831 **3**

◆◆◆
Hotel
$184-$386

Address: 1 Inner Park Rd 83013 **Location:** Jct US 26, 89 and 191, 3 mi s on Teton Park Rd. **Facility:** 79 units, some efficiencies, kitchens and cabins. 1-2 stories (no elevator), exterior corridors. **Terms:** closed 10/16-5/12, 7 day cancellation notice-fee imposed. **Dining:** 2 restaurants, also, The Peaks at Signal Mountain Lodge, see separate listing. **Activities:** motor boats, self-propelled boats, boat dock, fishing, recreation programs in summer, trails. **Guest Services:** coin laundry.

TOGWOTEE MOUNTAIN LODGE
(307)543-2847 **5**

◆◆ ◆ **Hotel** $179-$229 **Address:** 27655 Hwy US 26 & 287 83013 **Location:** 16.5 mi e of Moran; 38 mi nw of Dubois. Rural location. **Facility:** 88 units, some efficiencies and cabins. 1-3 stories (no elevator), interior/exterior corridors. **Terms:** closed 10/16-12/1, check-in 4 pm, cancellation fee imposed. **Dining:** Grizzly Grill & Red Fox Saloon at Togwotee Mountain Lodge, see separate listing. **Activities:** hot tub, snowmobiling, game room. **Guest Services:** coin laundry.

WHERE TO EAT

GRIZZLY GRILL & RED FOX SALOON AT TOGWOTEE MOUNTAIN LODGE
307/543-2847 **5**

◆◆ ◆◆ **American. Casual Dining.** $7-$28 **AAA Inspector Notes:** From high in the Grand Teton Mountain Range comes hearty meat and potato dishes packed with rich local flavors. Local, seasonal and organic ingredients are used when possible. Seafood dishes meet the sustainability practices of the Monterey Bay Aquarium Seafood Watch Program. While I enjoyed the edamame hummus, additional favorites are the beef and elk meatloaf, whiskey bison burger, blackened shrimp and sausage pasta, roasted red pepper quinoa burger and pan-seared Idaho trout. **Features:** full bar. **Address:** 27655 Hwy 26 & 287 83012 **Location:** 16.5 mi e of Moran; 38 mi nw of Dubois; in Togwotee Mountain Lodge. B L D

JENNY LAKE LODGE DINING ROOM
307/733-4647 **4**

◆◆◆◆ ◆◆◆◆ **Regional American. Fine Dining.** $10-$85 **AAA Inspector Notes:** Visit this intimate restaurant for a memorable dining experience. Some tables offer unparalleled views of the Tetons. The five-course menu might feature a wild game crepe, horseradish crusted lamb with garlic fried green tomato, coconut braised ono, grilled red trout with asparagus potato puree or pan seared elk with braised beet greens and port raisin syrup. Vegetarian items are available. For dinner, jackets are suggested, but sweaters and slacks are suitable. **Features:** full bar. **Reservations:** required. **Address:** Jenny Lake Inner Park Rd 83013 **Location:** 3 mi off Inner Park Rd; jct N Jenny Lake; in Jenny Lake Lodge. B L D CALL

LEEK'S MARINA & PIZZA
307/543-2494 **1**

◆ **Pizza Sandwiches. Quick Serve.** $10-$23 **AAA Inspector Notes:** At this spot, guests can create their own toppings or try the specialty pizza and calzones. Other menu items include salads, pasta, meatball sub on a sourdough hoagie and pesto chicken served on ciabatta bread. Do not miss a scoop, or two, of the organic ice cream. A children's menu is available. **Features:** beer & wine. **Address:** 89 National Park Dr 83013 **Location:** 11 mi n of jct US 89/191. L D

THE MURAL ROOM
307/543-2811 **2**

◆◆◆ **American. Casual Dining.** $12-$44 **AAA Inspector Notes:** Murals depicting the history of Jackson Hole and wonderful views of the Tetons set the stage for your dining experience. The extensive menu features some game dishes. The wine list is extensive. **Features:** full bar. **Reservations:** suggested. **Address:** US Hwy 89 83013 **Location:** 5 mi nw of Moran; in Jackson Lake Lodge. B L D

THE PEAKS AT SIGNAL MOUNTAIN LODGE
307/543-2831 **3**

◆◆◆ **American. Casual Dining.** $19-$38 **AAA Inspector Notes:** Situated on Jackson Lake with a great view of the Tetons, this popular dining room features a varied menu which includes a signature roasted garlic soup, bison and elk sliders, baked Idaho trout with a dill and sherry cracker crust, organic risotto primavera, wild-caught salmon piccata and sautéed elk medallions. Expect a wait at peak times. **Features:** full bar. **Address:** 1 Inner Park Rd 83013 **Location:** Jct US 89/191/287, 2 mi s on Teton Park Rd; in Signal Mountain Lodge. D

GREEN RIVER (E-2) pop. 12,515, elev. 6,082'

The northern gateway to the Flaming Gorge National Recreation Area *(see place listing p. 258)*, Green River developed as a stop along the Overland Trail in the mid-1800s. One prominent traveler was Maj. John Wesley Powell, who began his explorations of the Green and Colorado rivers in 1869. The town is a railroad center and the seat of Sweetwater County.

Green River Chamber of Commerce: 1155 W. Flaming Gorge Way, Green River, WY 82935. **Phone:** (307) 875-5711 or (800) 354-6743.

SWEETWATER COUNTY HISTORICAL MUSEUM is at 3 E. Flaming Gorge Way. The museum contains permanent and temporary exhibits with photographs and artifacts telling the story of the area's geology and the history of the American West and Sweetwater County. **Time:** Allow 30 minutes minimum. **Hours:** Mon.-Sat. 10-6. **Cost:** Free. **Phone:** (307) 872-6435.

HAMPTON INN & SUITES   (307)875-5300

Hotel $109-$199 **Address:** 1055 Wild Horse Canyon Rd 82935 **Location:** I-80 exit 89, 0.4 mi s, then 0.5 mi n. **Facility:** 106 units. 4 stories, interior corridors. **Terms:** 1-7 night minimum stay, cancellation fee imposed. **Pool(s):** heated indoor. **Activities:** hot tub, picnic facilities, exercise room. **Guest Services:** valet and coin laundry.

AAA Benefit: Members save up to 10%!

GREYBULL (B-3) pop. 1,847, elev. 3,788'

Greybull derives its name from a local Native American legend that claimed a great albino buffalo once roamed the area. The Native Americans revered the bull, considering it a sign from their Great Spirit. Native American arrowheads, fossils and semiprecious stones can be found around town. The site of widespread oil and mineral activity, Greybull recently has focused its attention on bentonite mining.

Scenic attractions in the vicinity include Shell Canyon and Falls *(see Bighorn National Forest p. 235)*, 24 miles east of US 14, and the drive over the Bighorn Mountains via scenic US 14 to Sheridan. Devil's Kitchen, a few miles northeast, and Sheep Mountain to the north are interesting geological formations.

Greybull Chamber of Commerce: 521 Greybull Ave., Greybull, WY 82426. **Phone:** (307) 765-2100 or (877) 765-2100.

GREYBULL MUSEUM is .2 mi. e. on US 14 at 325 Greybull Ave. The museum houses fossils, minerals, Native American artifacts and early Western memorabilia. Of interest are large ammonite fossils, which date from the Mesozoic era when the Greybull area was part of a large inland sea. **Hours:** Mon.-Fri. 10-8, Sat.

10-6, June 1-Labor Day; Mon.-Fri. 1-5, day after Labor Day-Mar. 31; Mon., Wed. and Fri. 1-4, rest of year. **Cost:** Free. **Phone:** (307) 765-2444.

WHEELS MOTEL   (307)765-2105

Motel
$62-$210

Address: 1324 N 6th St 82426 **Location:** On US 14/16/20, north end of town. **Facility:** 29 units. 1 story, exterior corridors. **Parking:** winter plug-ins. **Terms:** 3 day cancellation notice. **Activities:** limited exercise equipment. **Guest Services:** coin laundry.

WHERE TO EAT

BEIJING GARDEN   307/765-9826

Chinese. Casual Dining. $6-$14 **AAA Inspector Notes:** In a converted storefront building downtown, this restaurant offers a relaxed, casual dining experience. Asian dishes are well prepared and the service is friendly. **Address:** 510 Greybull Ave 82426 **Location:** 0.4 mi e on US 14. **Parking:** street only. L D

LISA'S   307/765-4765

American
Casual Dining
$9-$40

AAA Inspector Notes: Relax and unwind amid stucco walls and an adobe fireplace at this spot which serves up a mixture of Western and Southwestern courses as well as a number of microbrewed beers. Locally raised beef is featured on the varied steak menu. Farmer's pasta, fajitas, shrimp and hot sandwiches also are available. The salsa is always fresh. **Features:** full bar. **Address:** 200 Greybull Ave 82426 **Location:** On US 14, 0.4 mi e. *Menu on AAA.com* L D

GUERNSEY (D-6) pop. 1,147, elev. 4,361'

Just below the mouth of Platte River Canyon, Guernsey is in an area known for its limestone beds and a profusion of such artifacts as agricultural and war implements. Native Americans driven from their homes east of the Mississippi River and pioneers headed westward followed the river through this area.

During one of his expeditions in 1842, John C. Fremont camped near what is now the Oregon Trail Ruts State Historic Site *(see attraction listing)*. The small prairie next to the river (the present town site) impressed him as a good spot for a military installation because of its cottonwood trees, pines and abundant rock for building.

Prospectors discovered early that the rock formations around Guernsey were good for more than just building. Moss agate stone, unearthed from what is believed to be the first commercially developed deposit of moss agate in the nation, was found in the Guernsey-Hartville region and exported to Germany in the late 1800s. The additional discovery of copper led to the founding of nearby communities Hartville and Sunrise.

Guernsey Visitors Center: 90 S. Wyoming, P.O. Box 667, Guernsey, WY 82214. **Phone:** (307) 836-2715.

GUERNSEY STATE PARK MUSEUM is 1.2 mi. w. on US 26, then 2.7 mi. n. on SR 317 in Guernsey State Park *(see Recreation Areas Chart)*. Exhibits depict the natural and human history of the region

Time: Allow 30 minutes minimum. **Hours:** Daily 9-5, May-Sept. **Cost:** Park $6 (per private out-of-state vehicle); $4 (per private in-state vehicle). Museum free. **Phone:** (307) 836-2900.

OREGON TRAIL RUTS STATE HISTORIC SITE is 1 mi. s. on S. Wyoming Ave. from jct. US 26. The site presents well-preserved examples of mid-19th-century pioneer trails. Some of the ruts are 5 to 6 feet deep. Next to the ruts are footpaths used by muleteers and others who walked beside the wagons. Self-guiding trails provide an explanation of the site. No facilities are available. **Time:** Allow 30 minutes minimum. **Hours:** Daily dawn-dusk (weather permitting). **Cost:** Free. **Phone:** (307) 836-2334.

REGISTER CLIFF STATE HISTORIC SITE is 3 mi. s. on S. Wyoming Ave. from jct. US 26. The site contains a 100-foot cliff with the carved names of thousands of pioneers who journeyed past this point. Many of the inscriptions were made 1840-60. A walkway and an explanatory sign are at the base of the cliff.

HULETT pop. 383

BEST WESTERN DEVILS TOWER INN   (307)467-5747

Hotel
$80-$230

AAA Benefit: Save 10% or more every day and earn 10% bonus points!

Address: 229 Hwy 24 82720 **Location:** Center. **Facility:** 40 units. 2 stories (no elevator), interior corridors. **Parking:** winter plug-ins. **Pool(s):** heated indoor. **Activities:** hot tub, exercise room. **Guest Services:** coin laundry.

HULETT MOTEL

Motel
$88-$185

(307)467-5220
Address: 202 Main St 82720 **Location:** On SR 24 (Main St), north end of town. **Facility:** 15 units, some two bedrooms and cabins. 1 story, exterior corridors. **Terms:** cancellation fee imposed. **Activities:** picnic facilities.

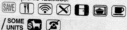
WHERE TO EAT

PONDEROSA CAFE & BAR   307/467-5335

American. Casual Dining. $7-$27 **AAA Inspector Notes:** The owner/chef at this local favorite hails from New Jersey, so patrons will find a few delicious Eastern specialties on the menu. However, he prepares Western cuisine like he has lived here all his life. Distinctive, local Western art is displayed in a rustic environment. **Features:** full bar, Sunday brunch. **Address:** 115 Main St 82720 **Location:** Center. **Parking:** street only. [B] [L] [D] [↘]

HYATTVILLE (B-3) pop. 75, elev. 4,447'

Hyattville, which began as an isolated frontier cow town, is at the confluence of Medicine Lodge and Paint Rock creeks in a region that mixes rolling foothills with

rugged canyons to create a series of caves, ledges and grassy knolls. The protective nature of this area is what lured its first inhabitants in prehistoric times.

Artifacts of early Paleo-Indian family groups were preserved in the layers of sediment beneath a sandstone cliff containing myriad petroglyphs and pictographs. Some of these can be seen at Medicine Lodge State Archeological Site, 6 miles northeast of town off SR 31 on Cold Springs Road; phone (307) 469-2234.

JACKSON (C-1) pop. 9,577, elev. 6,123'
• Hotels p. 272 • Restaurants p. 282
• Attractions map p. 262
• Hotels & Restaurants map & index p. 287
• Part of Jackson Hole Including Grand Teton National Park area — see map p. 285

The southern entrance to Grand Teton National Park *(see place listing p. 261)*, Jackson is on a scenic portion of US 89 that extends south 255 miles from Mammoth Hot Springs to Geneva, Idaho. It is the supply point and center of activity for ranchers and vacationers in Jackson Hole country. Recreation in the mountain-rimmed valley includes boating, fishing, hiking, horseback riding, mountain climbing, downhill and cross-country skiing, snowmobiling, white-water rafting and windsurfing on Jackson Lake.

Jackson's historic town square is the hub of activity, with plentiful dining and nightlife options. Visitors enjoy strolling amid a setting of Western architecture, with such accents as wooden sidewalks and elk antler arches. Shopping opportunities range from outdoor gear to trendy boutiques.

Live musical comedies are presented in summer at Jackson Hole Playhouse. The J.H. Rodeo also operates in the summer; phone (307) 733-7927. Gray Line of Jackson Hole offers tours of Grand Teton and Yellowstone national parks; for schedules and reservations phone (800) 443-6133.

While Snow King Scenic Chairlift provides uphill transportation for skiers in winter, summer passengers can enjoy scenic panoramas of Jackson Hole and the Tetons; phone (307) 733-5200 or (800) 522-5464.

Jackson Hole Chamber of Commerce: 112 Center St., P.O. Box 550, Jackson, WY 83001. **Phone:** (307) 733-3316.

BAR-T-5 COVERED WAGON COOKOUT & SHOW is 1 mi. e. on Broadway, then .5 mi. s. on Redmond to 812 Cache Creek Dr. A Western-style dinner show begins with a covered-wagon ride. Mountain men, Native Americans and Western musicians offer entertainment. **Hours:** Two shows nightly Mon.-Sat. and holidays at 5 and 6:30, mid-May through Aug. 24; at 4:30 and 6, Aug. 25-Sept. 30. **Cost:** $45; $37 (ages 5-12). Reservations are recommended. **Phone:** (307) 733-5386 or (800) 772-5386.

(See map & index p. 287.)

BRUSHBUCK GUIDE SERVICES, 400 US 89S, picks up passengers from the clock tower in Teton Village. With a knowl-

edgeable guide in the driver's seat, visitors ride in a safari-style van through scenic Grand Teton National Park. Among the wildlife that may be seen on this 4-hour tour are bison, grizzly and black bears, eagles, elk, moose, wolves and pronghorn antelope. The tour includes snacks and beverages and the use of binoculars, spotting scopes, blankets and rain gear. Yellowstone National Park tours, multiday tours and private tours also are offered.

Note: The tour may include a walk through sagebrush flats; comfortable, durable clothing is recommended. **Hours:** Grand Teton tour departs daily at dawn (between 6 and 6:30) and dusk (between 4:30 and 5:15). Phone for other tour schedules. **Cost:** Grand Teton tour $125, plus $15 park entrance fee. Yellowstone tour $299. Phone for other tour prices. Grand Teton tours require a minimum of two people. A 50 percent deposit is required for all tours. Reservations are required. **Phone:** (888) 282-5868 or (307) 699-2999. GT ⑪ ㊐

JACKSON HOLE HISTORICAL SOCIETY & MUSEUM, 225 N. Cache St., features exhibits about area history and sports and recreation. Firearms, tools and historical photographs are on display. During summer months, an additional museum showcasing Native Americans of Greater Yellowstone exhibits is open at 105 Glenwood St.

Guided walking tours of Jackson's historical downtown area are available. **Time:** Allow 1 hour minimum. **Hours:** Mon.-Sat. 10-6, Memorial Day weekend to mid-Sept. Schedule varies rest of year; phone ahead. **Cost:** $5; $4 (ages 60+ and students with ID); free (ages 0-11). **Phone:** (307) 733-2414. GT

JACKSON HOLE IDITAROD SLED DOG TOURS is 20 mi. s. on SR 191/189 at 11 Granite Creek; transportation to and from area hotels is provided. Sled dog trips in Bridger-Teton National Forest are offered. **Note:** Warm clothing is recommended. Meals and supplemental clothing are provided. **Hours:** Full-day trips pick up at 8 a.m. and return at 4:30 p.m.; half-day trips pick up at 8 a.m. and return at 1:30 p.m. or at 11:45 a.m. and return at 4:30 p.m. Trips depart mid-Nov. to mid-Apr. **Cost:** Full-day trip $325. Half-day trip $255. Reservations are required. **Phone:** (307) 733-7388 or (800) 554-7388. GT

JACKSON NATIONAL FISH HATCHERY is 4 mi. n. on US 26/89/191 at 1500 Fish Hatchery Rd. The hatchery raises predominantly Snake River cutthroat trout. A public fishing pond is available to those with a fishing license. **Time:** Allow 30 minutes minimum. **Hours:** Daily 8-4. Closed major holidays. **Cost:** Free. **Phone:** (307) 733-2510.

NATIONAL ELK REFUGE is 1 mi. e. on Broadway to Elk Refuge Rd. The 24,700-acre refuge is the winter home of 7,500 elk, one of the largest herds in North America. Elk can be seen November through April; during the summer they migrate to mountain meadows in Grand Teton and Yellowstone national parks and Bridger-Teton National Forest. The habitat also attracts other wildlife, including bighorn sheep and trumpeter swans.

The visitor center at 532 N. Cache St. offers exhibits and wildlife videos. **Hours:** Refuge open daily 24 hours. Visitor center open daily 8-7, Fri. before Memorial Day-Sept. 30; 9-5, rest of year. Closed

▼ See AAA listing p. 265 ▼

Request roadside assistance in a click — online or using the AAA or CAA apps

(See map & index p. 287.)

Thanksgiving and Christmas. **Phone:** (307) 734-9378.

Sleigh Rides depart from the visitor center at 532 N. Cache St. in the National Elk Refuge. Offered through Double H Bar, Inc., the 45-minute sleigh rides with knowledgeable guides provide up-close elk viewing. **Note:** Warm clothing is recommended. **Hours:** Daily 10-4, mid-Dec. through Mar. 31 (weather permitting). Closed Christmas. **Cost:** $20; $15 (ages 5-12). **Phone:** (307) 733-0277 or (800) 772-5386. GT

NATIONAL MUSEUM OF WILDLIFE ART is on Rungius Rd. across from the National Elk Refuge. The museum is in a stone building wedged into a hillside so that it appears to be part of its surroundings. The collection includes more than 5,000 paintings, sculptures and photos of wildlife. Artists include Albert Bierstadt, George Catlin, John Clymer, Bob Kuhn, Georgia O'Keeffe, Carl Rungius, C.M. Russell and Conrad Schwiering.

Of note are the JKM Collection of big game animals and the Conservation Gallery. The museum also houses a children's discovery gallery, a library and changing exhibits. **Hours:** Daily 9-5, mid-May to mid-Oct.; Mon.-Sat. 9-5, Sun. 11-5, rest of year. Closed Columbus Day, Thanksgiving and Christmas. **Cost:** $14; $12 (senior citizens); $6 (ages 5-18 with adult). **Phone:** (307) 733-5771 or (800) 313-9553. TI

RIPLEY'S BELIEVE IT OR NOT! MUSEUM is n. of jct. US 26/89/189/191 at 140 N. Cache St. The more than 200 oddities of this collection include such weird wonders as a shrunken head, a jeweled horse, Annie Oakley's pistol, a huge cigar, purportedly the world's largest ball of barbed wire, a bison made of nails, two-headed creatures, art created by using lint from the dryer and a gallery devoted to the mysteries of vampires.

Time: Allow 1 hour minimum. **Hours:** Daily 9 a.m.-10 p.m., Memorial Day weekend-Labor Day; times vary rest of year. Closed Jan. 1 and Christmas. **Cost:** $13.99; $12.99 (senior citizens); $9.99 (ages 5-11). **Phone:** (307) 734-0000.

TETON EXPEDITIONS SCENIC FLOATS departs from 650 W. Broadway. Thirteen- and 21-mile trips allow passengers to view the scenic Grand Teton area and its wildlife, including bald eagles and moose. **Time:** Allow 3 hours minimum. **Hours:** Trips depart daily, May-Oct. **Cost:** Thirteen-mile trip $70; $60 (ages 4-12). Twenty-one-mile trip $125; $105 (ages 6-12). **Phone:** (800) 700-7238. GT TI

TETON WAGON TRAIN AND HORSE ADVENTURE offers trips along back roads between Grand Teton and Yellowstone national parks. The 4-day, 3-night guided wagon train trips, which stop at a different camp each night, include chuck wagon meals,

evening entertainment, canoeing and horseback riding. Camping gear (including sleeping bags) is provided. **Hours:** Departures Mon. at 9, third week in June-third week in Aug. **Cost:** $970; $890 (ages 9-14); $840 (ages 4-8). Ages 0-3 are not permitted. Reservations are required. **Phone:** (307) 734-6101 or (888) 734-6101. GT

WAGONS WEST picks up passengers at the Antler Inn, 43 W. Pearl Ave. Tours traverse the Mt. Leidy Highlands in Jackson Hole. Hourly, 1-day and multiday horse pack rides are available. Marshaled by a wagon master, a covered-wagon train carries passengers along scenic mountain trails. Chuck wagon meals and campfire entertainment are provided.

Hours: Wagon trips depart in Aug. Horseback rides June-Sept. Phone ahead to confirm schedule. **Cost:** Two-day wagon trip $470; $395 (ages 4-13). Four-day wagon trip $820; $725 (ages 4-13). Horseback rides $50-$90 depending upon duration of ride. Prices may vary; phone ahead. Reservations are required. **Phone:** (800) 447-4711. GT

WILDLIFE EXPEDITIONS OF TETON SCIENCE SCHOOLS picks up passengers in Jackson or at area hotels. Seven-passenger safari-style vehicles take passengers on half-, full- and multiday expeditions through Yellowstone and Grand Teton national parks. Led by local wildlife biologists, the expeditions focus on wildlife observation and natural history. **Time:** Allow 6 hours minimum. **Hours:** Tours daily. Phone ahead to confirm schedule. **Cost:** Half- and full-day expeditions $130-$300; $99-$250 (ages 6-12). **Phone:** (307) 733-2623 or (888) 945-3567. GT

RECREATIONAL ACTIVITIES
Alpine Slides
- **Snow King Alpine Slide** is at 400 E. Snow King Ave. **Hours:** Daily, Memorial Day weekend and early June-Labor Day; Sat.-Sun., day after Labor Day-early Sept. (weather permitting). **Phone:** (307) 733-7680.

Hiking
- **Jackson Hole Llamas** departs from local trailheads. **Hours:** Trips daily, June-Sept. **Phone:** (307) 739-9582. GT

Mountain Biking
- **Teton Mountain Bike Tours** is at 545 N. Cache St. **Hours:** Tours daily. **Phone:** (307) 733-0712. GT

Skiing
- **Snow King Resort** is at 400 E. Snow King Ave. Other activities are offered. **Hours:** Winter activities Tues.-Sat. 10-8, Sun.-Mon. 10-4, late Nov.-late Mar. (weather permitting). **Phone:** (307) 733-5200, (307) 734-3136 or (800) 522-5464.

Snowmobiling
- **Jackson Hole Snowmobile Tours** picks up passengers from Jackson area accommodations. **Hours:** Tours offered Dec.-Mar. **Phone:** (800) 633-1733. GT

(See map & index p. 287.)

White-water Rafting

- **Barker-Ewing River Trips, Whitewater and Scenic Floats** meets at 945 W. Broadway. Other trips are offered. **Hours:** Trips depart daily, Memorial Day weekend to mid-Sept. **Phone:** (800) 448-4202. GT

- **Dave Hansen Whitewater and Scenic River Trips** operate from 225 W. Broadway. **Hours:** Five trips depart daily at various times, mid-May to late Oct. **Phone:** (307) 733-6295 or (800) 732-6295. GT

- **Jackson Hole Whitewater** is at 650 W. Broadway. Other activities are offered. **Hours:** Trips depart several times daily, May 15-Oct. 15. **Phone:** (307) 733-1007, or (800) 700-7238 out of Wyoming. GT

- **Lewis & Clark River Expeditions** is at 335 N. Cache Dr.; trips depart from 3 blks. n. of town square. Other activities are offered. **Hours:** Trips depart several times daily, mid-May to mid-Sept. **Phone:** (307) 733-4022 or (800) 824-5375. GT

- **Mad River Boat Trips** is at 1255 US 89S. Other activities are offered. **Hours:** Trips depart 15 times daily, mid-May to mid-Sept. **Phone:** (307) 733-6203 or (800) 458-7238. *(See ad this page.)* GT

- **Sands Whitewater and Scenic River Trips** is at 1450 US 89S. Other activities are offered. **Hours:** Trips depart daily, May 15-Sept. 30. **Phone:** (307) 733-4410 or (800) 358-8184. GT

- **Snake River Park Whitewater** is 12 mi. s. on US 89S. **Hours:** Trips depart four to five times daily,

May 15-Oct. 15 (weather permitting). **Phone:** (307) 733-7078 or (800) 562-1878. GT

▼ See AAA listing this page ▼

(See map & index p. 287.)

ANGLER'S INN

Motel
$90-$220

(307)733-3682 **27**

Address: 265 N Millward St 83001 **Location:** 0.3 mi n of US 89 and 191 (W Broadway Ave) and N Millward St; just nw of Town Square. **Facility:** 28 units, some cabins. 2 stories (no elevator), exterior corridors. **Terms:** 3 day cancellation notice-fee imposed.

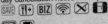

Anglers Inn

Jackson Hole, Wyoming

Conveniently located just a short walk to the Town Square, restaurants, and shops.

ANTLER INN

Motel
$90-$300

(307)733-2535 **38**

Address: 43 W Pearl St 83001 **Location:** Just w of S Cache and W Pearl sts; just s of Town Square. **Facility:** 106 units, some kitchens. 2 stories (no elevator), interior/exterior corridors. **Parking:** winter plug-ins. **Terms:** 4 day cancellation notice-fee imposed, resort fee. **Activities:** sauna, hot tub, exercise room. **Guest Services:** coin laundry, area transportation. *(See ad p. 275.)*

BUCKRAIL LODGE

Motel
$90-$199

307/733-2079 **44**

Address: 110 E Karns Ave 83001 **Location:** Jct S Cache St and Karns Ave, just e; 0.5 mi s of Town Square. At the foot of Snow King Mountain. **Facility:** 12 units. 1 story, exterior corridors. **Terms:** closed 10/16-5/5, cancellation fee imposed. **Activities:** hot tub. *(See ad this page.)*

▼ *See AAA listing this page* ▼

(See map & index p. 287.)

COWBOY VILLAGE RESORT (307)733-3121 **39**

♦♦♦
Cabin
$99-$284

Address: 120 S Flat Creek Dr 83001 **Location:** 4 mi w of Town Square. **Facility:** 84 efficiency cabin units. 1 story, exterior corridors. **Parking:** winter plug-ins. **Terms:** cancellation fee imposed, resort fee. **Pool(s):** heated indoor. **Activities:** hot tub, bicycles, picnic facilities, exercise room. **Guest Services:** coin laundry, area transportation. *(See ad this page.)*

ELK COUNTRY INN (307)733-2364 **36**

♦♦♦
Motel
$76-$284

Address: 480 W Pearl St 83001 **Location:** Just e of US 89 and 191 (W Broadway Ave) and Pearl St; 0.4 mi w of Town Square. **Facility:** 90 units, some efficiencies, kitchens and cabins. 1-2 stories (no elevator), interior/exterior corridors. **Parking:** winter plug-ins. **Terms:** cancellation fee imposed, resort fee. **Amenities:** *Some:* safes. **Activities:** hot tub, playground, picnic facilities, exercise room. **Guest Services:** valet and coin laundry, area transportation. *(See ad this page.)*

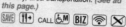

(See map & index p. 287.)

GOLDEN EAGLE INN

307-733-2042 **34**

Motel
$75-$170

Address: 325 E Broadway 83001 **Location:** 0.3 mi e of Town Square. **Facility:** 23 units. 2 stories (no elevator), exterior corridors. **Parking:** winter plug-ins. **Terms:** closed 11/1-4/30, 3 day cancellation notice-fee imposed.

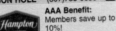

Golden Eagle Inn

Quiet residential neighborhood, clean & spacious rooms, larger rooms available, 1.5 blks to downtown!

HAMPTON INN JACKSON HOLE

(307)733-0033 **43**

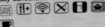

Hotel
$119-$359

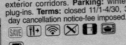

AAA Benefit:
Members save up to 10%!

Address: 350 S US Hwy 89 83002 **Location:** Just s of jct US 89 and 191 (W Broadway Ave) and SR 22 (Teton Pass); 1.7 mi sw of Town Square. **Facility:** 88 units. 3 stories, interior corridors. **Parking:** winter plug-ins. **Terms:** check-in 4 pm, 1-7 night minimum stay, cancellation fee imposed. **Amenities:** safes. **Activities:** hot tub, exercise room. **Guest Services:** valet and coin laundry. **Featured Amenity:** breakfast buffet. *(See ad this page.)*

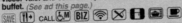

HOMEWOOD SUITES BY HILTON

(307)739-0808 **25**

Extended Stay Hotel
$119-$389 **Address:** 260 N Millward St 83001 **Location:** 0.3 mi n of US 89 and 191 (W Broadway Ave) and N Millward St; just nw of Town Square. **Facility:** 41 efficiencies. 3 stories, interior corridors. **Terms:** 1-7 night minimum stay, cancellation fee imposed. **Amenities:** safes. **Pool(s):** heated indoor. **Activities:** hot tub, bicycles, exercise room. **Guest Services:** complimentary and valet laundry.

AAA Benefit:
Members save up to 10%!

HOTEL JACKSON

(307)733-2200 **22**

Boutique Hotel
$299-$799

Address: 120 N Glenwood St 83001 **Location:** Just n of US 89 and 191. **Facility:** Guest rooms feature a surround-sound speaker system, fine bedding, leather headboards and luxurious bathrooms, some with a separate shower and deep soaking tub. 58 units. 4 stories, interior corridors. **Parking:** on-site (fee) and valet. **Terms:** 14 day cancellation notice-fee imposed, resort fee. **Amenities:** safes. **Dining:** Figs, see separate listing. **Activities:** exercise room. **Guest Services:** valet laundry, area transportation.

JACKSON HOLE LODGE

(307)733-2992 **33**

Motel
$89-$399

Address: 420 W Broadway 83001 **Location:** 0.3 mi w of town square. **Facility:** 59 units, some two bedrooms and kitchens. 3 stories (no elevator), exterior corridors. **Terms:** check-in 4 pm, 14 day cancellation notice-fee imposed. **Pool(s):** heated outdoor. **Activities:** hot tub, picnic facilities. *(See ad p. 277.)*

▼ See AAA listing this page ▼

(See map & index p. 287.)

THE LEXINGTON AT JACKSON HOLE HOTEL & SUITES
(307)733-2648

 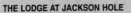 Hotel $109-$339 Address: 285 N Cache St 83001 Location: Just n of jct US 26, 89 and 191; at N Cache St and Mercill Ave; downtown. Facility: 91 units, some efficiencies and kitchens. 2-3 stories, interior/exterior corridors. Terms: check-in 4 pm, 3 day cancellation notice-fee imposed, resort fee. Pool(s): heated indoor. Activities: hot tub, bicycles. Guest Services: valet and coin laundry. (See ad p. 277.)

[amenity icons]

PAINTED BUFFALO INN   (307)733-4340

 Motel $100-$250

Address: 400 W Broadway Ave 83001 Location: On US 89 and 191 (W Broadway Ave); 0.3 mi w of Town square. Facility: 137 units, some two bedrooms. 2 stories (no elevator), exterior corridors. Terms: check-in 4 pm, cancellation fee imposed, resort fee. Pool(s): heated indoor. Activities: sauna. Guest Services: valet and coin laundry. Featured Amenity: continental breakfast. (See ad this page.)

[amenity icons]

THE LODGE AT JACKSON HOLE   307/739-9703

Hotel
Rates not provided

Address: 80 Scott Ln 83002 Location: 0.3 mi sw, just e of US 26/89/191. Facility: 154 units. 3 stories, interior corridors. Parking: winter plug-ins. Terms: check-in 4 pm. Amenities: safes. Pool(s): heated outdoor, heated indoor. Activities: sauna, hot tub, exercise room, massage. Guest Services: valet and coin laundry, area transportation. Featured Amenity: breakfast buffet. (See ad p. 279.)

[amenity icons]

Experience Effortless Travel

Save up to 20% on daily, weekend, weekly and monthly rentals.

Hertz.

▼ See AAA listing this page ▼

(See map & index p. 287.)

PARKWAY INN OF JACKSON HOLE

(307)733-3143 **30**

~~~~ ~~~~ ~~~~
Hotel
$119-$289

Address: 125 N Jackson St 83001 **Location:** Just n of jct US 89 and 191 (W Broadway Ave) and Jackson St; 0.3 mi w of Town Square. Across from Miller Park. **Facility:** 47 units. 2 stories (no elevator), interior/exterior corridors. **Parking:** winter plug-ins. **Terms:** 14 day cancellation notice-fee imposed, resort fee. **Pool(s):** heated indoor. **Activities:** sauna, hot tub, exercise room. **Guest Services:** valet laundry. **Featured Amenity: continental breakfast.**

(SAVE) (ⅰ+) (🏊) (BIZ) (📶) (✕) (🧳)
(📠)

RAWHIDE MOTEL

307/733-1216 **35**

~~~ **Motel.** Rates not provided. **Address:** 75 S Millward St 83001 **Location:** Just s of jct US 89 and 191 (W Broadway Ave) and S Millward St. **Facility:** 23 units. 2 stories (no elevator), exterior corridors.

(ⅰ+) (📶) (✕) (🧳) (📠)

THE RUSTIC INN CREEKSIDE RESORT & SPA AT JACKSON HOLE

307/733-2357 **24**

~~~~ ~~~~ ~~~~
Hotel
Rates not provided

Address: 475 N Cache St 83001 **Location:** 0.5 mi n of Town Square. Across from Visitor's Center. **Facility:** 157 units, some two bedrooms and cabins. 2 stories (no elevator), interior/exterior corridors. **Terms:** check-in 4 pm. **Amenities:** safes. **Pool(s):** heated outdoor. **Activities:** sauna, hot tub, self-propelled boats, fishing, recreation programs in summer, trails, exercise room, spa. **Guest Services:** valet and coin laundry, area transportation. **Featured Amenity: breakfast buffet.** *(See ad p. 281.)*

(SAVE) (✈) (ⅰ) (🍽) CALL (ⅿ) (🏊) (BIZ) (📶) (✕) (🧳)
(📠) (📺) / SOME UNITS (ﬆ)HS

Dream. Plan. Go.

Picture yourself on the ideal road trip.

TripTik® Travel Planner

AAA.com/ttp

RUSTY PARROT LODGE & SPA

(307)733-2000 **28**

~~~~ ~~~~ ~~~~
Boutique Country Inn
$195-$495

Address: 175 N Jackson St 83001 **Location:** Just nw of Town Square. **Facility:** This elegant lodge features pine-log beds and luxurious Southwestern-style decor. An outdoor deck with a rock hot tub offers stunning views. Guests will enjoy the gourmet cooked-to-order breakfast. 32 units. 3 stories (no elevator), interior corridors. **Parking:** on-site and valet. **Terms:** check-in 4 pm, 3 night minimum stay - seasonal and/or weekends, 14 day cancellation notice-fee imposed, resort fee. **Amenities:** *Some:* safes. **Dining:** The Wild Sage, see separate listing. **Activities:** hot tub, bicycles, spa. **Guest Services:** valet laundry.

(SAVE) (ⅰ) (🍽) (BIZ) (📶) (✕) / SOME UNITS (🧳)

SNOW KING HOTEL

(307)733-5200 **45**

~~~~ ~~~~ ~~~~ **Resort Hotel** $125-$599 **Address:** 400 E Snow King Ave 83001 **Location:** 0.4 mi s of E Broadway. **Facility:** Located at the foot of a mountain, this hotel has two cozy lobbies. Guest rooms feature lodgepole pine furnishings and bedding with comforters and multiple accents. Ask for a room with a balcony. 240 units, some two bedrooms, kitchens and condominiums. 7 stories, interior/exterior corridors. **Parking:** winter plug-ins. **Terms:** closed 4/6-4/30, check-in 4 pm, 14 day cancellation notice-fee imposed, resort fee. **Pool(s):** heated outdoor. **Activities:** hot tub, fishing, downhill & cross country skiing, snowboarding, ice skating, recreation programs in season, bicycles, trails, exercise room, spa. **Guest Services:** valet and coin laundry, area transportation.

(✈) (ⅰ) (🍽) CALL (ⅿ) (🏊) (BIZ) (📶) (✕) (📺)
/ SOME UNITS (ﬆ) (HS) (🐾) (🧳) (📦)

SPRING CREEK RANCH

(307)733-8833 **23**

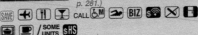

~~~~ ~~~~ ~~~~
Resort Hotel
$180-$2250

Address: 1800 Spirit Dance Rd 83001 **Location:** 2 mi w on US 26/89/191, 0.5 mi w on SR 22, then 1 mi n on Spring Gulch Rd. **Facility:** This activity-oriented ranch offers sweeping views of the majestic Grand Tetons. Rustic guest rooms are decorative, offer a wood burning fireplace, balcony or patio, and some have a washer and dryer. 113 units, some kitchens and condominiums. 2 stories, exterior corridors. **Parking:** winter plug-ins. **Terms:** check-in 4 pm, 22 day cancellation notice-fee imposed, resort fee. **Dining:** Granary, see separate listing. **Pool(s):** heated outdoor. **Activities:** hot tub, tennis, cross country skiing, recreation programs in summer, exercise room, spa. **Guest Services:** valet laundry, area transportation.

(SAVE) (✈) (ⅰ) (🎾) (🍽) CALL (ⅿ) (🏊) (BIZ) (HS) (📶)
(✕) (🐾) (🧳) (📺) / SOME UNITS (📦)

SUPER 8

(307)733-6833 **46**

~~~ ~~~ **Hotel** $60-$204 **Address:** 750 S US Hwy 89 83001 **Location:** 0.5 mi s of jct US 89 (W Broadway Ave) and SR 22. **Facility:** 91 units. 3 stories (no elevator), interior corridors. **Amenities:** safes. **Guest Services:** coin laundry.

(ⅰ+) (BIZ) (📶) (✕) (🧳) (📦) (📺)

VIRGINIAN LODGE

(307)733-2792 **41**

~~~ **Motel** $59-$129 **Address:** 750 W Broadway Ave 83001 **Location:** On US 89 and 191 (W Broadway Ave); 0.9 mi w of Town Square. **Facility:** 170 units, some two bedrooms and efficiencies. 1-2 stories (no elevator), interior/exterior corridors. **Terms:** check-in 4 pm, cancellation fee imposed. **Pool(s):** heated outdoor. **Activities:** hot tub, game room. **Guest Services:** coin laundry.

(ⅰ) (🍽) CALL (ⅿ) (🏊) (BIZ) (📶)
/ SOME UNITS (🧳) (📦) (📺)

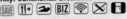

(See map & index p. 287.)

WHERE TO EAT

THE WORT HOTEL

(307)733-2190 **31**

WWWW WWWW
Historic Boutique
Hotel
$129-$999

Address: 50 N Glenwood St 83001 **Location:** Just n of US 89 and 191 (W Broadway Ave) and S Glenwood St; just w of Town Square. **Facility:** Expect an authentic Western lodging experience. Beautiful rooms and bathrooms are elegantly appointed with custom furnishings and ample amenities. Guests will appreciate the humidifier in each room. 55 units. 2 stories, interior corridors. **Parking:** onsite and valet, winter plug-ins. **Terms:** check-in 4 pm, 14 day cancellation notice-fee imposed, resort fee. **Amenities:** safes, video games. **Dining:** Silver Dollar Grill, see separate listing, entertainment. **Activities:** hot tub, exercise room, massage. **Guest Services:** valet laundry, area transportation. *(See ad this page.)*

 [icons] CALL 🔥M BIZ 🛜 ✕ 🖥 📠

WYOMING INN OF JACKSON HOLE

307/734-0035 **40**

WWWW Hotel. Rates not provided. **Address:** 930 W Broadway Ave 83001 **Location:** 0.3 mi e of SR 22 (Teton Pass) on US 89 and 191 (W Broadway Ave); 1.2 mi w of Town Square. **Facility:** 68 units. 3 stories, interior corridors. **Terms:** check-in 4 pm. **Activities:** exercise room, massage. **Guest Services:** complimentary and valet laundry.

[icons] ✈ [icons] CALL 🔥M BIZ 🛜 ✕ 🖥 📠

AMANGANI

307/734-7333

[fyi] Not evaluated. **Address:** 1535 NE Butte Rd 83001 **Location:** 2 mi w on US 26/89/191, 0.5 mi w on SR 22, then 1 mi n on Spring Gulch Rd, follow signs. Facilities, services, and décor characterize an upscale property. This elite resort features a beautiful frost-colored quartzite-tiled pool set on the edge of a bluff. Enjoy magnificent panoramic views of the valley, Grand Tetons and Snake River mountain ranges.

ATELIER ORTEGA

307/734-6400 **59**

WWW WWW Desserts. Quick Serve. $5-$15 **AAA Inspector Notes:** Pastry chef and master chocolatier Oscar Ortega, who was trained in Mexico City and Brescia, Italy, produces an extensive variety of hand-made chocolates, desserts and fine confections, which patrons can savor as they sip a fine artisan tea, espresso or the popular Mexican spiced coffee. Also offered is a small selection of breakfast items, savory quiche, salad, lunch or dessert crepes and homemade gelato. **Address:** 150 Scott Ln 83001 **Location:** 0.4 mi sw, just e of US 26/89/191. B L CALL 🔥M

BIN22 WINE BAR & TAPAS

307/739-9463 **47**

WWW Small Plates. Casual Dining. $7-$24 **AAA Inspector Notes:** In the back of a liquor and wine store is a hidden gem serving a variety of small plates, addictive entrees and high-end salami and cheese. Seasonal dishes may include medjool dates with chorizo and smoked pancetta, charred baby octopus or veal and Gulf shrimp with piquillo peppers. The fond memory of the pea and butter lettuce salad and grilled rib-eye with kale is still close to my heart. Try the chocolate salami for dessert. **Features:** full bar, patio dining. **Address:** 200 W Broadway Ave 83001 **Location:** Just w of Town Square at S Millward St. L D CALL 🔥M

THE BLUE LION

307/733-3912 **38**

WWWW American. Fine Dining. $19-$43 **AAA Inspector Notes:** This art-filled restaurant offers an intimate atmosphere in a quaint refurbished older home. Menu selections may include Santa Fe duck cakes, grilled wasabi elk, Thai seafood fritters, creative vegetarian dishes and the house specialty, rack of lamb with an addictive jalapeño mint dipping sauce. The signature mud pie, tiramisu and Russian cream fruit desserts are tempting and can be shared. A children's menu is available. **Features:** full bar, patio dining, early bird specials. **Reservations:** suggested. **Address:** 160 N Millward St 83001 **Location:** US 26/89/191, just n; opposite Miller Park. **Parking:** street only. D

▼ *See AAA listing this page* ▼

AAA Vacations® packages ...
exciting itineraries and exclusive values

(See map & index p. 287.)

BON APPE THAI
307/734-0245 [53]

◆◆ Thai. Casual Dining. $12-$22 **AAA Inspector Notes:** Just a few blocks from Town Square, this restaurant serves made-from-scratch Thai fare in a casual and cozy dining room. The express lunch special is hard to beat. **Features:** full bar, patio dining. **Reservations:** suggested. **Address:** 245 W Pearl St 83001 **Location:** Just w, then just s of Town Square. **Parking:** street only.

L D

BUBBA'S BAR-B-QUE RESTAURANT
307/733-2288 [52]

◆◆ Barbecue. Casual Dining. $8-$26 **AAA Inspector Notes:** This eatery offers a salad bar every day along with a variety of pit barbecue fare accented with homemade sauces. One of the local favorites is the sloppy Bubba sandwich, a combination of sliced beef and pork served with a side of curly fries. Expect to sign-in and wait during busy periods. **Features:** beer & wine. **Address:** 100 Flat Creek Dr 83001 **Location:** 0.5 mi w on US 26/89/191; jct Pearl St.

B L D

THE BUNNERY BAKERY & RESTAURANT
307/734-0075 [43]

◆◆◆ American. Casual Dining. $6-$15 **AAA Inspector Notes:** Locals love the light meals, fresh all-natural bakery items and sandwiches made on oats, sunflower and millet bread. The interior boasts pine walls, large windows and artwork depicting local wildlife. **Features:** beer & wine, patio dining. **Address:** 130 N Cache St 83001 **Location:** Just n of center. **Parking:** street only.

B L D CALL ♿M

CAFE GENEVIEVE
307/732-1910 [49]

◆◆ Comfort Food Soul Food. Casual Dining. $14-$38 **AAA Inspector Notes:** Diners can discover inspired home cooking in this darling log cabin. Stop in for a Spanish frittata or fried chicken and waffles for breakfast. For lunch there are such sandwiches as grilled cheese, pulled pork and a Cuban. Dinner brings out broiled Idaho trout, caramelized day boat scallops and dry-aged pork chops with black-eyed peas and kale. **Features:** full bar, patio dining, Sunday brunch, happy hour. **Address:** 135 E Broadway 83001 **Location:** Just e of Town Square. **Parking:** street only.

B L D

EL ABUELITO
307/733-1207 [44]

◆◆ Mexican. Casual Dining. $8-$18 **AAA Inspector Notes:** Looking for consistently good Mexican cuisine? This is it! This is the place locals frequent for tasty enchiladas, tacos, chimichangas and huge portions at reasonable prices. Also, a children's menu is available. The spacious dining room with wood accents is decorated with traditional Mexican art and colors. **Features:** full bar. **Address:** 385 W Broadway 83001 **Location:** 0.3 mi w on US 26/89/191.

L D

E.LEAVEN RESTAURANT & BAKERY
307/733-5600 [41]

◆ Sandwiches Breads/Pastries. Quick Serve. $11-$23 **AAA Inspector Notes:** Enjoy bagels, omelets, cold and hot sandwiches, salads and seasonal soups at this casual eatery which offers lots of windows with stunning views. The tarragon chicken salad is a big hit and the sunporch is a popular spot to eat, sit a spell, and return to the counter for a pastry. **Features:** beer & wine, patio dining. **Address:** 175 W Center St 83001 **Location:** Just e of town square, just n. **Parking:** street only.

B L

FIGS
307/733-2200 [62]

◆◆ Mediterranean. Casual Dining. $18-$39 **AAA Inspector Notes:** This chic and hip restaurant offers a beautiful décor, an intimate ambience and a cozy upscale bar next to an open kitchen. Featuring Wyoming-inspired fare combined with local ingredients, the harissa-rubbed lamb ribs make a great starter. Watch out for the pop pita bread and wild arugula salad with castelvetrano olives—they are addictive. My favorite was the chicken with shishito peppers and a powerfully flavored au jus. Also popular are the coffee-rubbed elk and Idaho rainbow trout. **Features:** full bar. **Address:** 120 N Glenwood St 83001 **Location:** Just n of US 89 and 191; in Hotel Jackson. **Parking:** valet and street only.

B L D CALL ♿M

GRANARY
307/733-8833 [34]

◆◆◆◆ Continental. Fine Dining. $8-$35 **AAA Inspector Notes:** For those in search of fine, upscale dining with a world-class view, then this is the right place. A favorite dish is the elk short loin. An extensive wine list featuring the finest California vintages, including Chalk Hill, is offered. **Features:** full bar, patio dining, happy hour. **Reservations:** suggested. **Address:** 1800 Spirit Dance Rd 83001 **Location:** 2 mi w on US 26/89/191, 0.5 mi w on SR 22, then 1 mi n on Spring Gulch Rd, follow signs; in Spring Creek Ranch.

B L D

GUN BARREL STEAK & GAME HOUSE
307/733-3287 [58]

◆◆◆ Regional Steak Wild Game. Casual Dining. $19-$47 **AAA Inspector Notes:** Feast on aged beef from Texas, venison, buffalo and elk cooked to perfection on an open-fire pit grill. A former wildlife museum and taxidermy studio, many mounts of bison, wild boars, rattlesnakes and birds can be seen, as well as dioramas with bighorn sheep. Rough-hewn wood floors and hand-peeled lodge pole pine beams and tables set the décor along with a large river rock wood-burning fireplace. **Features:** full bar. **Address:** 862 W Broadway 83002 **Location:** Just s on US 26/89/191; in Teton Plaza.

D CALL ♿M

THE KITCHEN
307/734-1633 [39]

◆◆◆ New American. Casual Dining. $12-$29 **AAA Inspector Notes:** This restaurant, with a knowledgeable staff, may become a habit-forming favorite. The menu changes seasonally and chefs prepare innovative dishes such as papaya-marinated Wagyu flank steak with carrot-kaffir lime puree, truffled yellowtail tuna, duck breast in peach-peanut mole, Mexican ceviche with Colorado striped bass, braised pork shoulder croquettes, and sea scallops with potato-habanero hash. **Features:** full bar, patio dining, happy hour. **Reservations:** suggested. **Address:** 155 N Glenwood St 83001 **Location:** Just n of SR 89 and 191. **Parking:** street only.

D CALL ♿M

LOCAL: RESTAURANT & BAR
307/201-1717 [46]

◆◆◆ Western Steak. Casual Dining. $18-$44 **AAA Inspector Notes:** The contemporary setting in this restaurant is the perfect backdrop to showcase the chefs' combined talents for creating house-cured charcuterie, in-house butchering of locally ranched game and meats and expertly prepared seafood. Brought to you by the same owners/chefs as Trio. **Features:** full bar, happy hour. **Address:** 55 N Cache St 83001 **Location:** Center; across from town square. **Parking:** street only.

L D CALL ♿M

LOTUS ORGANIC CAFE
307/734-0822 [42]

◆◆◆ International. Casual Dining. $12-$24 **AAA Inspector Notes:** The dishes presented at this jewel of a cafe are magical. It's hard to make a decision with so many well-prepared menu items but the teriyaki bowl, lentil tacos, bison burger, pesto chicken, tempeh sandwich or beef pho with mung bean sprouts and hoisin sauce are local favorites. Colorful and creative salads are loaded with goodness. In addition to raw, vegan, vegetarian and gluten-free choices, freshly extracted juices and smoothies are available. **Features:** full bar, patio dining. **Address:** 145 N Glenwood St 83001 **Location:** Just n of US 89 and 191. **Parking:** street only.

B L D CALL ♿M

THE MERRY PIGLETS MEXICAN GRILL AND CARRY-OUT
307/733-2966 [40]

◆◆ Mexican. Family Dining. $7-$26 **AAA Inspector Notes:** Since 1969, this eatery has served fresh Mexican fare in a fun and lively setting. Regulars like to meet for a snack of nachos or quesadillas as well as dine on fire-roasted, mesquite-grilled fajitas. The conqueso and ranchero Tex-Mex sauces merit a thumbs-up. **Features:** full bar, happy hour. **Address:** 160 N Cache St 83001 **Location:** Just n of town square; next to Ripley's. **Parking:** street only.

L D

Choose real ratings you can trust

from professional inspectors

who've been there

(See map & index p. 287.)

NANI'S CUCINA ITALIANA 307/733-3888 [35]

▽▽▽
Italian
Casual Dining
$13-$33

AAA Inspector Notes: Dining here is an event—a trip to Italy right in Wyoming. A nice selection of pasta is available with homemade sauces and risotto with jumbo scallops. The thick, crusty bread is hard to stop eating. **Features:** full bar, patio dining. **Address:** 242 N Glenwood St 83001 **Location:** 0.3 mi n, turn n on Glenwood St or w on Mercill Ave from US 26/89/191. **Parking:** on-site and street. [D]

NIKAI ASIAN GRILL & SUSHI BAR 307/734-6490 [36]

▽▽▽▽ Sushi. Casual Dining. $8-$25 **AAA Inspector Notes:** This restaurant has an upscale décor and bamboo accents. Along with beautifully presented sushi and sustainable fresh fish flown in daily, the chef serves Asian grilled items. Popular items include the sashimi blossom with escolar, red tuna, salmon and yellowtail, Kobe beef and lobster roll and sake sliders. The TNT and big kahuna rolls are favored by the locals. Children have their own menu. An elevator is available at this upstairs location. Parking is available across the street. **Features:** full bar. **Reservations:** suggested. **Address:** 225 N Cache St 83001 **Location:** Just n of Town Square.
[D] CALL [&][M]

PEARL ST. MEAT & FISH CO. 307/733-1300 [55]

▽ Specialty. Quick Serve. $8-$10 **AAA Inspector Notes:** Gourmet and specialty foods line the shelves in the aisles of this market, and the meat case is loaded with all-natural beef and fish, specialty baked goods and specialty cheeses. Meals are served in the evening only; otherwise, lunches are ordered at the counter or salad and soup are dished from gourmet bars. **Address:** 40 W Pearl Ave 83001 **Location:** Just w, just s of town square. **Parking:** street only. [B] [L] [D]

PEARL STREET BAGELS JACKSON 307/739-1218 [54]

▽ Coffee/Tea Sandwiches. Quick Serve. $3-$8 **AAA Inspector Notes:** Crusty on the outside and chewy inside are the hallmarks of these New York-style boiled bagels. Luckily for us, we can find them here and at the Wilson location. Other offerings include homemade chicken and tuna salad, cream cheese-lox spread and freshly roasted coffee. **Address:** 145 W Pearl Ave 83014 **Location:** Between S Millward and S Glenwood sts; just w of town square. **Parking:** street only. [B] [L]

PERSEPHONE BAKERY & CAFE 307/200-6708 [50]

▽ Breads/Pastries Sandwiches. Quick Serve. $8-$12 **AAA Inspector Notes:** This eatery offers a small but mighty menu featuring brioche and smoked salmon, bread pudding French toast, an addictive truffled prosciutto sandwich on ciabatta and grilled bacon-kale-ricotta on house bread. Guests perusing the decadent pastry choices through the glass cases may feel as if they are in a candy store. **Features:** wine only, patio dining. **Address:** 145 E Broadway 83001 **Location:** 0.3 mi n of town square. **Parking:** street only. [B] [L]

PIZZA ARTISAN & PASTA 307/734-1970 [61]

▽▽ Pizza Small Plates. Casual Dining. $12-$24 **AAA Inspector Notes:** This trendy eatery has two inviting patios and serves small plates, salads, oven-baked sandwiches served with a tasty pasta salad and red-and-white pizza. The hand-crafted meatballs, kale salad and prosciutto, arugula and mozzarella sandwich drizzled with lemon oil are well-liked by locals and travelers. Gluten-free crust and vegetarian items are available. **Features:** full bar, patio dining. **Address:** 690 S Hwy 89 83002 **Location:** Jct US 26/89/191 (Broadway Ave), just s. [D]

RENDEZVOUS BISTRO 307/739-1100 [60]

▽▽ Regional American. Casual Dining. $14-$34 **AAA Inspector Notes:** This energetic bistro has a raw oyster bar and prepares creative, imaginative and colorful appetizers, entrées, salads and desserts. Menu items change seasonally and might include sage and sweet potato ravioli, braised organic chicken and kale, goose leg confit, seared scallops and a popular pork adobe. The desserts are glorious. Note that it can get festive and some tables are close together. **Features:** full bar, patio dining. **Reservations:** suggested. **Address:** 380 S Broadway 83002 **Location:** 1.7 mi w of town square. [D]

SILVER DOLLAR GRILL 307/733-2190 [45]

▽▽▽
American
Casual Dining
$10-$35

AAA Inspector Notes: This restaurant specializes in American-style chophouse cuisine, such as black Angus beef, seafood specialties and local wild game dishes. When the weather permits, al fresco meals are an option. Be sure to try the Kobe burger. **Features:** full bar, patio dining, happy hour. **Reservations:** suggested. **Address:** 50 N Glenwood St 83001 **Location:** Center of downtown; in The Wort Hotel. **Parking:** street only. [B] [L] [D] CALL [&][M]

SNAKE RIVER BREWING 307/739-2337 [57]

▽▽ American. Gastropub. $8-$15 **AAA Inspector Notes:** Wood-fired oven pizza, calzone, elk burgers, a nice selection of pasta and daily homemade soup fill the menu at this popular brewpub as well as a variety of wild game items. Beer lovers can appreciate the wide array of ales and lagers and kids will be thrilled with their own menu. **Features:** beer & wine, patio dining, happy hour. **Address:** 265 S Millward St 83001 **Location:** Just s of W Broadway. [L] [D]

SNAKE RIVER GRILL 307/733-0557 [48]

▽▽ Regional American. Fine Dining. $20-$40 **AAA Inspector Notes:** On town square, this restaurant affords views of Snow King Mountain. Lending to the décor are three-dimensional paintings on the ceiling, booths of tapestry and leather, and a double-fireplace of moss-rock and log walls. Seasonal dishes may include white gazpacho with sweet crab, bacon-wrapped Idaho trout and melt-in-your mouth steak. **Features:** full bar, patio dining. **Reservations:** suggested. **Address:** 84 E Broadway 83001 **Location:** Jct King St; on town square. **Parking:** street only. [D]

SWEETWATER RESTAURANT 307/733-3553 [56]

▽▽ Regional American. Casual Dining. $10-$32 **AAA Inspector Notes:** *Historic.* Housed in a restored log cabin, this restaurant offers both indoor and outdoor seating. Attentive and well-trained staff members deliver out-of-the-ordinary daily specials, including fresh fish and steak, phyllo creations and vegetarian items. **Features:** full bar, patio dining. **Reservations:** suggested. **Address:** 85 S King St 83001 **Location:** Just se of town square; corner of King and Pearl sts. **Parking:** street only. [L] [D] [🅜]

TRIO, AN AMERICAN BISTRO 307/734-8038 [51]

▽▽▽ Regional American. Casual Dining. $16-$42 **AAA Inspector Notes:** Named for the local chefs who own the restaurant, innovative cuisine is prepared with seasonal ingredients. Starters and main courses can range from seared scallops, sauteed mussels, a BLT soup with arugula pesto and bacon lardons, grilled elk chop with butternut squash puree, pork osso buco and pan-roasted pheasant. Typically, a tasting menu is available. **Features:** full bar. **Reservations:** suggested. **Address:** 45 S Glenwood St 83001 **Location:** Between Broadway and Pearl St; just sw of town square. **Parking:** street only. [D]

THE WILD SAGE 307/733-2000 [37]

▽▽▽▽
Regional
American
Fine Dining
$28-$78

AAA Inspector Notes: This restaurant is a favorite for upscale, intimate dining with impeccable service. Through the open kitchen, diners can glimpse at the chefs' hard at work preparing their delectable meals. The seasonally changing menu might include lavender seared lamb loin, grilled bison short ribs, melt-in-your-mouth vanilla day boat scallops or porcini-dusted elk short loin. The seasonal desserts are delectable and hard to resist. **Features:** full bar. **Reservations:** suggested. **Address:** 175 N Jackson St 83001 **Location:** Just nw from Town Square; in Rusty Parrot Lodge & Spa. **Parking:** on-site and valet.
Menu on AAA.com [B] [D]

JACKSON HOLE INCLUDING GRAND TETON NATIONAL PARK

Visitors to the area often wonder exactly what "Jackson Hole" means. The "Hole" is actually a high mountain valley encompassed by the ranges of the Grand Tetons, bordered by the Teton Range on the west and the Gros Ventre Range on the east. Bisected by the Snake River, the valley is 80 miles long and 15 miles wide.

You'll rarely hear Jackson Hole Valley called anything other than Jackson Hole. Early trappers coined the term when they navigated the valley's steep slopes, which they likened to descending into an enormous hole. Although Jackson Hole is home to the town of Jackson and the Jackson Hole Mountain Resort, you'll notice that folks refer to both of these places as Jackson Hole, too—don't get confused since this isn't technically correct. The valley also boasts the pristine wilderness of Grand Teton National Park (including Moose and Moran) along with the small communities of Kelly, Teton Village and Wilson.

Mountain men sporting beaver hats started to explore this remote and rugged frontier in the early 1800s, as they trekked through the territory now known as Jackson Hole and Yellowstone on a quest to trap animals—in fact, the valley was named for David Jackson, a partner in a fur-trapping company. The Homestead Act eventually drew pioneers willing to take a chance on improving a free plot of land—Moran, Kelly and Wilson had a sprinkling of settlers by the 1890s. The harsh climate sent many packing, but those who stayed and toughed it out used the abandoned parcels to their advantage and developed large ranches.

By the late 1890s, the town of Jackson started to take root. A park, churches, bank, and shops sprang up, and ultimately a jail, saloons and rodeo added to the Old West intrigue. As the 20th century approached, residents made ends meet by hosting wealthy visitors at dude ranches and serving as guides for game-hunting and sport-fishing expeditions. The creation of Grand Teton National Park in 1929 launched Jackson Hole as a prime sightseeing destination and recreational paradise.

Outdoor enthusiasts flock to Grand Teton National Park to indulge in an enticing array of activities, including high-altitude hiking, float trips, wildlife viewing, boating and cross-country skiing. The park offers a habitat for many large mammals, while the rare trumpeter swan is among the resident bird life. Teton Park Road leads to Jenny Lake Lodge, campgrounds, fishing sites and many of the park's trails.

This map shows cities in Jackson Hole where you will find attractions, hotels and restaurants. Cities are listed alphabetically in this book on the following pages.

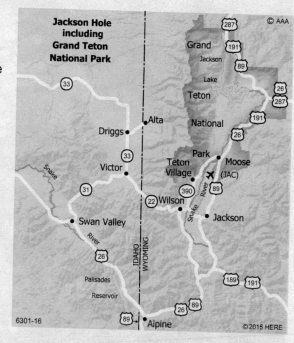

Jackson Hole including Grand Teton National Park

© AAA

6301-16

© 2015 HERE

East of the Snake River, Jackson Hole Highway (US 26/89/191) runs parallel to Teton Park Road between Moran and Moose and affords superb views of the Teton Range.

The town of Jackson retains vestiges of the Old West, yet manages to please the discriminating traveler. The old town square, adorned with elk horn arches, is dotted with a mix of historic buildings, upscale eateries and boutiques. You can see many of Jackson's historic structures on a walking tour sponsored by the Jackson Hole Historical Society & Museum (see attraction listing). Teton Village serves as adventure hub to downhill skiers attempting the daring slopes of Jackson Hole Mountain Resort, or sightseers wishing to ride the gondola to lofty heights.

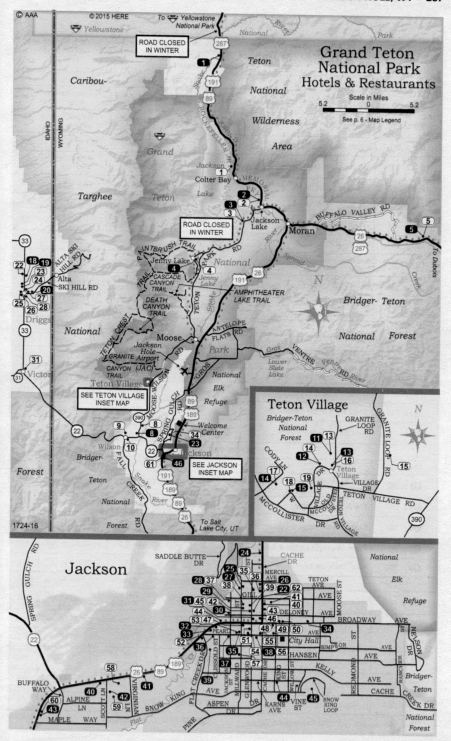

© AAA © 2015 HERE

Grand Teton
National Park
Hotels & Restaurants

Scale in Miles
5.2 · 0 · 5.2

See p. 6 - Map Legend

Teton Village

Jackson

Grand Teton National Park

This index helps you "spot" where approved hotels and restaurants are located on the corresponding detailed maps. Hotel daily rate range is for comparison only. Restaurant price range is a combination of lunch and/or dinner. Turn to the listing page for more detailed rate and price information and consult display ads for special promotions.

GRAND TETON NATIONAL PARK

Map Page	Hotels	Diamond Rated	Rate Range	Page
① p. 287	Headwaters Lodge & Cabins at Flagg Ranch	♦♦	Rates not provided	266
② p. 287	Jackson Lake Lodge	♦♦♦	Rates not provided	266
③ p. 287	**Signal Mountain Lodge**	♦♦♦	$184-$386 SAVE	266
④ p. 287	Jenny Lake Lodge	♦♦♦♦	Rates not provided	266
⑤ p. 287	Togwotee Mountain Lodge	♦♦	$179-$229	266

Map Page	Restaurants	Diamond Rated	Cuisine	Price Range	Page
① p. 287	Leek's Marina & Pizza	♦	Pizza Sandwiches	$10-$23	266
② p. 287	The Mural Room	♦♦♦	American	$12-$44	266
③ p. 287	The Peaks at Signal Mountain Lodge	♦♦♦	American	$19-$38	266
④ p. 287	Jenny Lake Lodge Dining Room	♦♦♦♦	Regional American	$10-$85	266
⑤ p. 287	Grizzly Grill & Red Fox Saloon at Togwotee Mountain Lodge	♦♦	American	$7-$28	266

WILSON

Map Page	Hotel	Diamond Rated	Rate Range	Page
⑧ p. 287	Bentwood Inn Bed & Breakfast	♦♦♦	$259-$399	313

Map Page	Restaurants	Diamond Rated	Cuisine	Price Range	Page
⑧ p. 287	Q Roadhouse & Brewing Co	♦♦	Barbecue	$13-$29	313
⑨ p. 287	Street Food at the Stagecoach	♦	Mexican	$8-$14	313
⑩ p. 287	Pearl Street Bagels Wilson	♦	Coffee/Tea Sandwiches	$5-$8	313

TETON VILLAGE

Map Page	Hotels	Diamond Rated	Rate Range	Page
⑪ p. 287	**Four Seasons Resort & Residences Jackson Hole**	♦♦♦♦♦	$375-$1600 SAVE	309
⑫ p. 287	**The Alpenhof Lodge**	♦♦	$124-$599 SAVE	309
⑬ p. 287	**Snake River Lodge & Spa**	♦♦♦	Rates not provided SAVE	310
⑭ p. 287	**Teton Mountain Lodge & Spa**	♦♦♦♦	$139-$3200 SAVE	310
⑮ p. 287	**Hotel Terra Jackson Hole**	♦♦♦♦	$149-$3500 SAVE	310

Map Page	Restaurants	Diamond Rated	Cuisine	Price Range	Page
⑬ p. 287	**Westbank Grill**	♦♦♦♦	Regional American	$18-$36	311
⑭ p. 287	**Alpenrose**	♦♦♦	Regional Swiss	$21-$34	310
⑮ p. 287	Teton Thai	♦♦	Thai	$14-$20	310
⑯ p. 287	Gamefish	♦♦♦	Regional American	$9-$47	310
⑰ p. 287	Spur Restaurant & Bar	♦♦♦	Regional American	$14-$35	310
⑱ p. 287	IL Villaggio Osteria	♦♦♦	Italian	$11-$49	310
⑲ p. 287	Mangy Moose Restaurant & Saloon	♦♦	New American	$9-$39	310

DRIGGS, ID

Map Page	Hotels	Diamond Rated	Rate Range	Page
18 p. 287	Super 8 - Teton West	◆◆	$65-$182 [SAVE]	61
19 p. 287	BEST WESTERN Teton West	◆◆	$105-$140 [SAVE]	60
20 p. 287	Teton Valley Cabins	◆◆	$69-$99	61

Map Page	Restaurants	Diamond Rated	Cuisine	Price Range	Page
22 p. 287	Seoul Restaurant - Korean Cuisine & Sushi	◆◆	Korean Sushi	$8-$18	61
23 p. 287	Agave Mexican Restaurant	◆◆	Mexican	$7-$18	61
24 p. 287	Big Hole Bagels & Bistro	◆	Breakfast Deli	$6-$10	61
25 p. 287	Pendl's Bakery & Cafe	◆	Breads/Pastries Deli	$7-$9	61
26 p. 287	Teton Thai	◆◆	Thai	$9-$16	61
27 p. 287	Forage Bistro & Lounge	◆◆◆	Regional American	$10-$29	61
28 p. 287	Provisions Local Kitchen	◆◆	American	$8-$14	61

JACKSON

Map Page	Hotels	Diamond Rated	Rate Range	Page
22 p. 287	Hotel Jackson	◆◆◆◆	$299-$799 [SAVE]	276
23 p. 287	Spring Creek Ranch	◆◆◆	$180-$2250 [SAVE]	280
24 p. 287	The Rustic Inn Creekside Resort & Spa at Jackson Hole (See ad p. 281.)	◆◆◆	Rates not provided [SAVE]	280
25 p. 287	Homewood Suites by Hilton	◆◆◆	$119-$389	276
26 p. 287	The Lexington at Jackson Hole Hotel & Suites (See ad p. 277.)	◆◆◆	$109-$339	278
27 p. 287	Angler's Inn	◆	$90-$220 [SAVE]	274
28 p. 287	Rusty Parrot Lodge & Spa	◆◆◆◆	$195-$495 [SAVE]	280
29 p. 287	4 Winds Motel	◆	$75-$150 [SAVE]	272
30 p. 287	Parkway Inn of Jackson Hole	◆◆◆	$119-$289 [SAVE]	280
31 p. 287	The Wort Hotel (See ad p. 282.)	◆◆◆◆	$129-$999 [SAVE]	282
32 p. 287	Painted Buffalo Inn (See ad p. 278.)	◆◆	$100-$250 [SAVE]	278
33 p. 287	Jackson Hole Lodge (See ad p. 277.)	◆◆	$89-$399 [SAVE]	276
34 p. 287	Golden Eagle Inn	◆◆	$75-$170 [SAVE]	276
35 p. 287	Rawhide Motel	◆	Rates not provided	280
36 p. 287	Elk Country Inn (See ad p. 275.)	◆◆	$76-$284 [SAVE]	275
37 p. 287	49'er Inn and Suites - Quality Inn (See ad p. 275, p. 273.)	◆◆◆	Rates not provided [SAVE]	272
38 p. 287	Antler Inn (See ad p. 275.)	◆◆	$90-$300 [SAVE]	274
39 p. 287	Cowboy Village Resort (See ad p. 275.)	◆◆	$99-$284 [SAVE]	275
40 p. 287	Wyoming Inn of Jackson Hole	◆◆◆	Rates not provided	282
41 p. 287	Virginian Lodge	◆	$59-$129	280
42 p. 287	The Lodge at Jackson Hole (See ad p. 279.)	◆◆◆	Rates not provided [SAVE]	278
43 p. 287	Hampton Inn Jackson Hole (See ad p. 276.)	◆◆◆	$119-$359 [SAVE]	276
44 p. 287	Buckrail Lodge (See ad p. 274.)	◆◆	$90-$199 [SAVE]	274
45 p. 287	Snow King Hotel	◆◆◆	$125-$599	280
46 p. 287	Super 8	◆◆	$60-$204	280

Map Page	Restaurants	Diamond Rated	Cuisine	Price Range	Page
㉞ p. 287	Granary	◆◆◆	Continental	$8-$35	283
㉟ p. 287	**Nani's Cucina Italiana**	◆◆◆	Italian	$13-$33	284
㊱ p. 287	Nikai Asian Grill & Sushi Bar	◆◆◆	Sushi	$8-$25	284
㊲ p. 287	**The Wild Sage**	◆◆◆◆	Regional American	$28-$78	284
㊳ p. 287	The Blue Lion	◆◆◆	American	$19-$43	282
㊴ p. 287	The Kitchen	◆◆◆	New American	$12-$29	283
㊵ p. 287	The Merry Piglets Mexican Grill and Carry-Out	◆◆	Mexican	$7-$26	283
㊶ p. 287	E.Leaven Restaurant & Bakery	◆	Sandwiches Breads/Pastries	$11-$23	283
㊷ p. 287	Lotus Organic Cafe	◆◆	International	$12-$24	283
㊸ p. 287	The Bunnery Bakery & Restaurant	◆◆	American	$6-$15	283
㊹ p. 287	El Abuelito	◆◆	Mexican	$8-$18	283
㊺ p. 287	**Silver Dollar Grill**	◆◆◆	American	$10-$35	284
㊻ p. 287	Local: Restaurant & Bar	◆◆◆	Western Steak	$18-$44	283
㊼ p. 287	Bin22 Wine Bar & Tapas	◆◆◆	Small Plates	$7-$24	282
㊽ p. 287	Snake River Grill	◆◆◆	Regional American	$20-$40	284
㊾ p. 287	Cafe Genevieve	◆◆	Comfort Food Soul Food	$14-$38	283
㊿ p. 287	Persephone Bakery & Cafe	◆	Breads/Pastries Sandwiches	$8-$12	284
(51) p. 287	Trio, An American Bistro	◆◆◆	Regional American	$16-$42	284
(52) p. 287	Bubba's Bar-B-Que Restaurant	◆◆	Barbecue	$8-$26	283
(53) p. 287	Bon Appe Thai	◆◆	Thai	$12-$22	283
(54) p. 287	Pearl Street Bagels Jackson	◆	Coffee/Tea Sandwiches	$3-$8	284
(55) p. 287	Pearl St. Meat & Fish Co.	◆	Specialty	$8-$10	284
(56) p. 287	Sweetwater Restaurant	◆◆	Regional American	$10-$32	284
(57) p. 287	Snake River Brewing	◆◆	American	$8-$15	284
(58) p. 287	Gun Barrel Steak & Game House	◆◆	Regional Steak Wild Game	$19-$47	283
(59) p. 287	Atelier Ortega	◆◆	Desserts	$5-$15	282
(60) p. 287	Rendezvous Bistro	◆◆◆	Regional American	$14-$34	284
(61) p. 287	Pizza Artisan & Pasta	◆◆	Pizza Small Plates	$12-$24	284
(62) p. 287	Figs	◆◆◆	Mediterranean	$18-$39	283

VICTOR, ID

Map Page	Restaurant	Diamond Rated	Cuisine	Price Range	Page
㉛ p. 287	Knotty Pine Supper Club	◆◆	American	$11-$25	104

KAYCEE (C-4) pop. 263, elev. 4,660'

Kaycee Area Chamber of Commerce: 100 Park Ave., P.O. Box 147, Kaycee, WY 82639. **Phone:** (307) 738-2444. ***(See ad p. 238.)***

HOOFPRINTS OF THE PAST MUSEUM is at 344 Nolan Ave. Exhibit topics highlight the Hole-in-the-Wall area's history and include the Bozeman Trail, Dull Knife Battlefield, Johnson County invasion and Fort Reno. Collections contain guns, historical pictures, utensils, Native American artifacts and timelines. A jail, schoolhouse, cabin and tool shed are on the grounds. **Time:** Allow 1 hour minimum. **Hours:** Mon.-Sat. 9-5, Sun. 1-5, Fri. before Memorial Day-Oct. 31. **Cost:** Donations. **Phone:** (307) 738-2381. ***(See ad p. 238.)***

KEMMERER (E-1) pop. 2,656, elev. 6,908'

One feature of the boom that followed the discovery of coal near Kemmerer in 1897 was the saloon of "Preaching Lime" Huggins, who maintained that he never sold a drink to a man already under the influence. Over the bar mirror hung such mottos as "Don't buy a drink before seeing that your baby has shoes." One of his patrons liked the establishment because he could do his repenting during his sinning and "get the whole thing over at once."

A nationwide retail chain originated in Kemmerer when James Cash Penney opened his first store, the Golden Rule, in 1902 with an initial investment of $500. The original home of the founder is now a museum at 107 JC Penney Dr.

Native fossils and historical artifacts are displayed at the visitor center in Herschler Triangle Park.

Kemmerer/Diamondville Area Chamber of Commerce: 921 Pine Ave., Kemmerer, WY 83101. **Phone:** (307) 877-9761 or (888) 300-3413.

FOSSIL COUNTRY MUSEUM is at 400 Pine Ave. Permanent exhibits in this museum include a replica of an underground coal mine and a moonshine still, mountain man artifacts, Union Pacific Railroad and World Wars I and II memorabilia, vintage clothing, fossils and a dinosaur footprint from a local coal mine.

Time: Allow 30 minutes minimum. **Hours:** Mon.-Fri. 9-5, Memorial Day-Labor Day; 10-4, rest of year. Closed Jan. 1, July 4, Thanksgiving, day after Thanksgiving and Christmas. **Cost:** Donations. **Phone:** (307) 877-6551.

BEST WESTERN PLUS FOSSIL COUNTRY INN & SUITES (307)877-3388

Hotel
$90-$160

AAA Benefit: Save 10% or more every day and earn 10% bonus points!

Address: 760 US 30/189 83101 **Location:** Jct US 30 and 189. **Facility:** 80 units. 3 stories, interior corridors. **Pool(s):** heated indoor. **Activities:** hot tub, picnic facilities, exercise room. **Guest Services:** coin laundry.

LANDER (D-3) pop. 7,487, elev. 5,372'
• Restaurants p. 292

Lander began around 1869 when Camp Augur was built to protect the settlers and Shoshone Native Americans. In 1884 Lander became the seat of newly created Fremont County, which is as large as some Eastern states. The county covers 5,861,120 acres and is an important wildlife habitat for moose, elk, bighorn sheep, deer and pronghorn antelopes.

North of Lander is the vast Wind River Mountain Range. Part of this range is now the Wind River Indian Reservation. Farther northwest near Dubois is an area that was the site of a horse ranch operated by George Parker, alias Butch Cassidy. Cassidy frequently sold his stock in Lander, whose citizens maintained he always had more to sell than he raised.

SR 131 follows the middle fork of the Popo Agie River southwest of Lander to Sinks Canyon State Park *(see attraction listing)* and Shoshone National Forest *(see place listing p. 307).* Lander contains the trailhead for the Continental Divide Snowmobile Trail.

Lander Area Chamber of Commerce: 160 N. 1st St., Lander, WY 82520. **Phone:** (307) 332-3892.

SINKS CANYON STATE PARK is 7.5 mi. s.w. on SR 131. Moose, bighorn sheep and other wild game often can be sighted. The Popo Agie River disappears into the sinks of the Madison Limestone and reappears in a rise one-quarter of a mile down the canyon in a large trout pool.

The Sinks Canyon State Park Visitor Center provides information about natural features and recreational opportunities. *See Recreation Areas Chart.* **Hours:** Park open daily dawn-dusk. Visitor center daily 9-6, Memorial Day-Labor Day. Campground daily, May-Oct. **Cost:** Day use free. Camping $11. **Phone:** (307) 332-6333.

GAMBLING ESTABLISHMENTS

• **Shoshone Rose Casino** is at 5690 US 287. **Hours:** Daily 24 hours. **Phone:** (307) 335-7529.

HOLIDAY INN EXPRESS & SUITES LANDER 307/332-4005

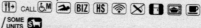

Hotel. Rates not provided. **Address:** 1002 11th St 82520 **Location:** 1 mi w on US 287, just w on Lincoln St. **Facility:** 78 units. 3 stories, interior corridors. **Parking:** winter plug-ins. **Pool(s):** heated indoor. **Activities:** hot tub, picnic facilities, exercise room. **Guest Services:** coin laundry.

THE INN AT LANDER 307/332-2847

Hotel
Rates not provided

Address: 260 Grand View Dr 82520 **Location:** Jct US 287 and SR 789. **Facility:** 101 units, some efficiencies. 2 stories, interior corridors. **Parking:** winter plug-ins. **Pool(s):** heated outdoor. **Activities:** hot tub, exercise room. **Guest Services:** coin laundry. **Featured Amenity:** continental breakfast.

Restaurant, Lounge, Pool HotTub, Ext Stay Suites, Hot Breakfast. Near Main Street Attractions & Park.

RODEWAY INN & SUITES PRONGHORN LODGE
(307)332-3940

Motel
$74-$125

Address: 150 E Main St 82520 **Location:** Just n of jct US 287 and SR 789. **Facility:** 56 units, some efficiencies. 1-2 stories (no elevator), exterior corridors. **Parking:** winter plug-ins. **Terms:** 3 day cancellation notice. **Dining:** The Oxbow Restaurant, see separate listing. **Activities:** hot tub, limited exercise equipment. **Guest Services:** coin laundry. **Featured Amenity:** continental breakfast.

SAVE ❍❍ CALL ❍❍ BIZ ❍ ❍ / SOME UNITS ❍❍

WHERE TO EAT

COWFISH RESTAURANT & BREWERY
307/332-8227

American. Casual Dining. $10-$29 **AAA Inspector Notes:** This restaurant and pub offers a wide selection of menu items consisting of a sirloin with grilled shrimp topped with caramelized lemon, panko-crusted pan-fried rainbow trout, ricotta gnocchi with pancetta and spring peas, and roasted pork shank mole verde. Creative desserts include a popular espresso and cardamom chocolate mousse. **Features:** full bar, patio dining. **Address:** 126 Main St 82520 **Location:** Downtown. **Parking:** street only.

L D CALL ❍❍

HITCHING RACK
307/332-4322

American. Casual Dining. $7-$29 **AAA Inspector Notes:** At this spot diners can feast on grilled mahi mahi with cilantro pesto, a juicy rib-eye, prime rib, fried jumbo shrimp, chicken or pasta, but leave room for one of the seasonal desserts such as pumpkin mousse with ginger snap cookies or apple pecan bread pudding. There is an extensive soup and salad bar offered as well as plenty of microbrewed beers. Attentive service from a well-trained staff rounds out the experience. **Features:** full bar, patio dining. **Address:** 785 E Main St 82520 **Location:** 0.5 mi s on US 287. L D

THE MIDDLE FORK
307/335-5035

American. Casual Dining. $9-$19 **AAA Inspector Notes:** This eatery has a serene and refreshing ambience, the perfect recipe for travelers. Expect colorful and thoughtful presentations. A few favorites include savory quiche, steak salad with greens and pork ragout. When available, the creamy parsnip soup drizzled with white truffle oil is a home run. Seasonal desserts are decadent and made in house. **Features:** full bar, Sunday brunch. **Address:** 351 Main St 82520 **Location:** Just w of center. **Parking:** street only. B L

THE OXBOW RESTAURANT
307/332-0233

American. Casual Dining. $6-$15 **AAA Inspector Notes:** You will appreciate the daily specials which include steak, pasta, chicken, seafood and ribs, in addition to the popular soup and salad bar. **Features:** full bar. **Address:** 170 E Main St 82520 **Location:** Just n of jct US 287 and SR 789; adjacent to Rodeway Inn & Suites Pronghorn Lodge. B L D

LARAMIE (E-5) pop. 30,816, elev. 7,171'
• Hotels p. 294 • Restaurants p. 294

Although Native Americans roamed the Laramie Plains as early as 8000 B.C., Laramie's recorded history began in the early 19th century with the arrival of the area's first white man, Jacques LaRamie, a trapper for American Fur Co. In his steps followed mountain men, trappers, emigrants, soldiers and explorers, many tracing the old Cherokee Trail.

Fort Sanders, a short distance south, provided protection for the Overland Stage Line and for the Union Pacific. The railroad brought the bulk of Laramie's citizenry—including a sizable population of

lawless riffraff who finally left town at the prompting of self-appointed vigilance committees. The first woman juror, Eliza Stewart, served in Laramie in March 1870. In the fall "Grandma" Louisa Swain became the first woman to vote in a general election.

Recreational opportunities abound nearby. Cross-country skiing is available east of Laramie, and downhill skiing and snowmobiling can be found in the Snowy Range of the Medicine Bow Mountains, west of the city on SR 130. Both regions are equally attractive to vacationers during the summer, with many camping and picnic areas.

Of geological interest is Sand Creek, a 6,000-acre natural landmark about 20 miles southwest of Laramie. Some of North America's finest examples of cross-bedded sandstone and "topple blocks" can be seen.

Laramie serves as the eastern end of a scenic portion of I-80, which runs 99 miles northwest to Walcott. Snowy Range Scenic Byway (SR 130), off the I-80 Snowy Range exit, offers a view of mountains, lakes and forests. At the summit, the Libby Flats Observatory and a viewing platform offer a panorama of the area.

Albany County Tourism Board Convention and Visitor Bureau: 210 E. Custer St., Laramie, WY 82070. **Phone:** (307) 745-4195 or (800) 445-5303. *(See ad p. 293.)*

Self-guiding tours: Brochures describing downtown and architectural walking tours are available at the Albany County Tourism Board Convention and Visitor Bureau.

ABRAHAM LINCOLN MEMORIAL MONUMENT is 10 mi. s.e. on I-80 exit 323, at the edge of a rest area. The 48.5-foot-tall monument, sculpted by Robert I. Russin, stands at an 8,640-foot summit off I-80 near Sherman Hill. The monument marks the highest point on this transcontinental route. I-80 follows the path of the first transcontinental railroad line.

AMES MONUMENT is 17 mi. s.e. on I-80, then 2 mi. s. on Ames Rd. The 60-foot granite pyramid honors Oliver and Oakes Ames, the two promoters of the transcontinental railroad. Built 1881-82, the monument marks the site of Sherman, a train inspection point before it became a ghost town with the relocation of the Union Pacific tracks. A plaque relates local history.

SAVE **LARAMIE PLAINS MUSEUM** is 1 blk. n. of I-80 and US 30 Business Loop at 603 E. Ivinson St. The museum is the restored 1892 Victorian mansion of Edward Ivinson, one of the city's original settlers. Period furnishings and thousands of artifacts from the area are displayed. The grounds include a carriage house and a one-room log schoolhouse. **Hours:** Guided tours are given Tues.-Sat. 9-5, Sun. 1-3, June-Aug.; Tues.-Sat. 1-4, rest of year. **Cost:** $10; $7 (senior citizens); $5 (students and military with ID); free (ages 0-5); $25 (family). **Phone:** (307) 742-4448. GT

UNIVERSITY OF WYOMING is between 9th and 30th sts. and Lewis and Grand aves. The university opened its doors in 1887. The 785-acre campus contains buildings of native sandstone. **Hours:** Cultural and fine arts programs and concerts are held year-round. **Phone:** (307) 766-4075.

American Heritage Center, 2111 Willett Dr. in the Centennial Complex of the University of Wyoming, is a repository for manuscripts, special collections, rare books and the university's archives as well as a site for lectures, concerts, symposiums and exhibits. The center features changing displays from its collections including the art of Henry Farny, Alfred Jacob Miller and Frederic Remington. **Hours:** Mon.-Fri. 10-5 (also Mon. 5-9). Closed major holidays. **Cost:** Free. **Phone:** (307) 766-4114.

Anthropology Museum is at 12th and Lewis sts. on the north side of the University of Wyoming campus. It chronicles the state's cultural history, including information about Northwest Plains Native Americans and other Native Americans of the U.S. and Canada. Collections include archeological and ethnological materials. **Hours:** Mon.-Fri. 8-5, Sept.-May; 7:30-4:30, rest of year. Closed major holidays. **Cost:** Free. **Phone:** (307) 766-5136.

Art Museum is at 22nd St. and Willett Dr. in the Centennial Complex of the University of Wyoming. The museum contains more than 7,000 sculptures, prints, paintings and artifacts from many cultures and periods. Exhibitions focus on contemporary pieces, art of the American West and works from various countries that have influenced American artists. Artworks by established artists as well as traveling exhibitions are displayed. **Hours:** Mon.-Sat. 10-5 (also Mon. 5-9 when school is in session). Closed major holidays. **Cost:** Free. **Phone:** (307) 766-6622.

Geological Museum is in the e. wing of the S.H. Knight Building at the University of Wyoming. The museum interprets the physical and historical geology of the state through displays of rocks, minerals and fossils. Of interest is a mounted skeleton of a brontosaurus, purported to be one of only five exhibited in the world. Other dinosaur displays include an allosaurus, tyrannosaurus and triceratops. **Hours:** Mon.-Sat. 10-4. Closed major holidays. **Cost:** Free. **Phone:** (307) 766-3386.

VEDAUWOO is 17 mi. s.e. via I-80 exit 329. The recreation area takes its name from the Arapaho Native American word meaning "earth born spirits." The picnic and camping areas are marked by rock formations developed during the ice age and rounded by weathering. Both expert and novice rock climbers practice their skills on the rocks. **Hours:** Daily 24 hours, May-Sept. (weather permitting). **Cost:** Day use/parking fee $5. Camping $10. **Phone:** (307) 745-2300.

▼ *See AAA listing p. 292* ▼

WYOMING TERRITORIAL PRISON STATE HISTORIC SITE is at 975 Snowy Range Rd. at jct. I-80 exit 311. The site features a restored 19th-century prison, a warden's house, a prison industries building, a homestead ranch display, museum exhibits, a nature trail and special events. The 1872 prison is said to be the only prison in which outlaw Butch Cassidy was incarcerated and an exhibit marks his time there.

Self-guiding museum and prison tours are available. **Time:** Allow 4 hours minimum. **Hours:** Daily 8-7, May-Oct. **Cost:** $5; $2.50 (ages 12-17). **Phone:** (307) 745-3733.

AMERICINN LODGE & SUITES OF LARAMIE (307)745-0777

Hotel $90-$229 **Address:** 4712 E Grand Ave 82070 **Location:** I-80 exit 310 (Grand Ave), just n. **Facility:** 59 units. 3 stories, interior corridors. **Parking:** winter plug-ins. **Terms:** cancellation fee imposed. **Pool(s):** heated indoor. **Activities:** hot tub, exercise room. **Guest Services:** coin laundry.

BEST WESTERN LARAMIE INN & SUITES
(307)745-5700

Hotel $89-$199

AAA Benefit: Save 10% or more every day and earn 10% bonus points!

Address: 1767 N Banner Rd 82072 **Location:** I-80 exit 310 (Curtis St), just n. Near truck stop. **Facility:** 61 units. 3 stories, interior corridors. **Pool(s):** heated indoor. **Activities:** hot tub, exercise room. **Guest Services:** coin laundry. **Featured Amenity:** full hot breakfast.

COMFORT INN LARAMIE (307)721-8856

Hotel $89-$205 **Address:** 3420 E Grand Ave 82070 **Location:** I-80 exit 316 (Grand Ave), 2.3 mi nw. **Facility:** 55 units. 2 stories, interior corridors. **Parking:** winter plug-ins. **Amenities:** safes. **Pool(s):** heated indoor. **Activities:** hot tub, exercise room. **Guest Services:** coin laundry.

DAYS INN (307)745-5678

Hotel $91-$151 **Address:** 1368 N McCue St 82072 **Location:** I-80 exit 310 (Curtis St), 0.3 mi e, then just s. **Facility:** 53 units. 2 stories (no elevator), interior corridors. **Parking:** winter plug-ins. **Pool(s):** heated indoor. **Activities:** hot tub, exercise room. **Guest Services:** valet and coin laundry.

FAIRFIELD INN & SUITES BY MARRIOTT (307)460-2100

Hotel $84-$162 **Address:** 1673 Centennial Dr 82070 **Location:** I-80 exit 310 (Curtis St), just w, then just s. **Facility:** 82 units. 3 stories, interior corridors. **Pool(s):** heated indoor. **Activities:** hot tub, exercise room. **Guest Services:** valet and coin laundry.

AAA Benefit: Members save 5% or more!

HAMPTON INN (307)742-0125

Hotel $80-$209 **Address:** 3715 E Grand Ave 82070 **Location:** I-80 exit 316 (Grand Ave), 2.2 mi nw to Boulder Dr. **Facility:** 84 units. 3 stories, interior corridors. **Terms:** 1-7 night minimum stay, cancellation fee imposed. **Amenities:** video games. **Pool(s):** heated indoor. **Activities:** hot tub, exercise room. **Guest Services:** valet and coin laundry.

AAA Benefit: Members save up to 10%!

HILTON GARDEN INN LARAMIE (307)745-5500

Hotel $99-$169 **Address:** 2229 Grand Ave 82070 **Location:** I-80 exit 316 (Grand Ave), 2.5 mi nw; at University of Wyoming Conference Center. **Facility:** 135 units. 5 stories, interior corridors. **Parking:** winter plug-ins. **Terms:** 1-7 night minimum stay, cancellation fee imposed. **Pool(s):** heated indoor. **Activities:** hot tub, exercise room. **Guest Services:** valet and coin laundry.

AAA Benefit: Members save up to 10%!

HOLIDAY INN 307/721-9000

Hotel. Rates not provided. **Address:** 204 S 30th St 82070 **Location:** I-80 exit 316 (Grand Ave), 2.5 mi w to 30th St. **Facility:** 100 units. 4 stories, interior corridors. **Amenities:** video games. **Pool(s):** heated indoor. **Activities:** hot tub, exercise room. **Guest Services:** valet and coin laundry.

QUALITY INN & SUITES (307)742-6665

Hotel $85-$169 **Address:** 1655 Centennial Dr 82070 **Location:** I-80 exit 310 (Curtis St), just w, then just s. **Facility:** 72 units. 3 stories, interior corridors. **Parking:** winter plug-ins. **Amenities:** safes. **Pool(s):** heated indoor. **Activities:** hot tub, picnic facilities. **Guest Services:** coin laundry.

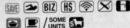

WHERE TO EAT

ALTITUDE CHOPHOUSE & BREWERY 307/721-4031

American. Casual Dining. $8-$27 **AAA Inspector Notes:** In the historic downtown area, this restaurant offers a varying menu of Choice steak and shrimp, cedar-plank salmon, orange-braised pork loin and signature burgers and pizza. With several hand-crafted beers brewed on the premises, there is no shortage of sudsy choices here. In fact, a brewery sampling menu offers patrons the opportunity to experience the various creations available. Weekly specials are offered. **Features:** full bar. **Address:** 320 S 2nd St 82070 **Location:** I-80 exit 313, 1 mi n to Grand Ave, then just w. **Parking:** street only.

ANONG'S THAI CUISINE 307/745-6262

Thai. Casual Dining. $10-$20 **AAA Inspector Notes:** Patrons can expect fresh ingredients and traditional Thai dishes at this popular restaurant. Choices include a variety of soups, salads, curries and noodle dishes including spicy kee mao noodles which comes highly recommended. **Features:** beer & wine. **Address:** 101 E Ivinson Ave 82070 **Location:** At 1st St and Ivinson Ave; downtown. **Parking:** street only.

JEFFREY'S BISTRO   307/742-7046

♦♦ ♦♦ New World. Casual Dining. $8-$21 **AAA Inspector Notes:** This popular eatery focuses on wholesome food and offers appetizers, seasonal soups and a nice variety of salads including sesame Thai carrot with baked tofu. Rounding out the menu are the tomato basil cheddar sandwich, grilled portobello with pesto and Brie, Thai curried chicken with bananas, and decadent desserts made in house. Vegan items are available. **Features:** beer & wine. **Address:** 123 E Ivinson Ave 82070 **Location:** I-80 exit 311 (Snowy Range Rd), 1.3 mi e to N 3rd St, just s to Ivinson Ave, then just w. **Parking:** street only.

L D

NEW MANDARIN RESTAURANT   307/742-8822

♦♦ Chinese. Casual Dining. $7-$13 **AAA Inspector Notes:** This restaurant offers all of your favorite traditional foods like sesame chicken, egg rolls, fried won tons, pu pu platter, mu shu beef, chicken or pork and more. **Features:** beer & wine. **Address:** 1254 N 3rd St 82072 **Location:** I-80 exit 310 (Curtis St), 1.3 mi e to N 3rd St, then just s. L D

SWEET MELISSA VEGETARIAN CAFE   307/742-9607

♦♦ ♦♦ Vegan Vegetarian. Casual Dining. $6-$13 **AAA Inspector Notes:** This café features an eclectic assortment of vegetarian offerings, including soups, salads, sandwiches and pasta dishes. Chili tacos, lasagna and vegetable stir-fry with tofu are some of the flavorful offerings that please a diverse clientèle, vegetarian and meat-eater alike. Desserts are divine. Many gluten-free options are available. **Features:** full bar. **Address:** 213 S 1st St 82070 **Location:** Between Grand and Ivinson aves; downtown. **Parking:** street only.

L D

LINGLE (D-6) pop. 468, elev. 4,171'

WESTERN HISTORY CENTER is 5 mi. w. at 2308 US 26. The center has displays about archeological excavations and the physical evidence left behind by the area's earliest citizens. In addition to a working lab, visitors can see fossils, mammoth bones and projectile points—items found in local digs that enable researchers to understand the lives of early residents of the Western plains.

Dig tours are available upon request. **Time:** Allow 1 hour minimum. **Hours:** Wed.-Thurs. and Sat. 10-4, Fri. 10-3, Sun. 1-4, Memorial Day-Labor Day; Mon.-Tues. and Sat. 10-3, Thurs.-Fri. 10-2, rest of year. Phone ahead to confirm schedule. **Cost:** Donations. Reservations are required. **Phone:** (307) 837-3052. GT

LITTLE AMERICA pop. 68

LITTLE AMERICA HOTEL   (307)875-2400

♦♦ ♦♦
Motel
$69-$109

Address: I-80, exit 68 82929 **Location:** I-80 exit 68, just n. **Facility:** 140 units, some two bedrooms. 1-2 stories (no elevator), interior/exterior corridors. **Terms:** cancellation fee imposed. **Amenities:** *Some:* safes. **Pool(s):** heated outdoor. **Activities:** playground, exercise room. **Guest Services:** coin laundry. *(See ad this page.)*

SAVE ⊡ BIZ 🛜 ✕ ▢
/ SOME UNITS S▢ HS ▢ ▢

LOVELL (B-3) pop. 2,360, elev. 3,837'

Lovell, founded by Mormons in 1900, serves as the southern gateway to Bighorn Canyon National Recreation Area *(see place listing p. 133)*. A recreation area visitor center offering interpretive displays and movies is at the junction of US 310 and scenic US 14A. Lovell is said to be the "Rose City" of Wyoming due to the exceptional climate for growing these flowers. Area recreational pursuits include camping, fishing, hunting, water sports, hiking, snowmobiling and trail riding.

Next to Bighorn Canyon is Pryor Mountain Wild Horse Range, a 38,000-acre refuge for wild horses and bighorn sheep.

Lovell Area Chamber of Commerce: 287 E. Main St., Lovell, WY 82431. **Phone:** (307) 548-7552.

HIDDEN TREASURE CHARTERS AND WYOMING ECO-TOURS departs from the Horseshoe Bend Marina, 1200 SR 37. Narrated boat rides on Bighorn Lake afford views of Bighorn Canyon National Recreation Area's wildlife and spectacular cliffs. Keep your eyes peeled for bighorn sheep and such birds as falcons, eagles, osprey, terns and swallows. Sunset dinner cruises also are available.

Time: Allow 2 hours minimum. **Hours:** Trips depart Fri.-Sat. and holidays at 10 and 2, Memorial Day-Labor Day. Sunset dinner cruises depart Fri.-Sat. at 6:30 p.m. **Cost:** $40; $25 (ages 1-12). Phone for sunset dinner cruise fares. Recreation area admission $5 per private vehicle. Reservations are required. **Phone:** (307) 899-1401, or (307) 548-7230 for the marina. GT 🏕 🍴 ⛱

LUSK (D-6) pop. 1,567, elev. 5,014'

Named for an early settler, Lusk is a trading center for a ranching and dry-farming district that also is involved in some oil production. To the west are red-colored cliffs from which Native Americans obtained material for paint. Through this area ran the Cheyenne and Black Hills Stage Line, whose route is marked by two rows of white posts. Three miles east on US 20, a marker indicates the location of a segment of the Texas Trail. The trail was used to herd cattle from Texas to the open ranges of Wyoming, Montana and the Dakotas.

Niobrara Chamber of Commerce: 224 S. Main St., P.O. Box 457, Lusk, WY 82225. **Phone:** (307) 334-2950. *(See ad this page.)*

STAGECOACH MUSEUM is 322 S. Main St. The museum displays many relics of pioneer and Native American days, including an original Concord stagecoach, which was the last running stagecoach. The coach's Cheyenne-Deadwood running mate is in the Smithsonian Institution in Washington, D.C. **Hours:** Mon.-Fri. 9-8, May-Oct.; 9-4:30, rest of year. **Cost:** $2; free (ages 0-12). **Phone:** (307) 334-3444. *(See ad this page.)*

AMERICAS BEST VALUE INN COVERED WAGON
(307)334-2836

Motel
$90-$165

Address: 730 S Main St 82225 **Location:** Just n of jct US 20/85. **Facility:** 51 units. 1-2 stories (no elevator), interior/exterior corridors. **Parking:** winter plug-ins. **Terms:** cancellation fee imposed. **Pool(s):** heated indoor. **Activities:** sauna, hot tub, playground, picnic facilities, limited exercise equipment. **Guest Services:** coin laundry. **Featured Amenity:** full hot breakfast.

SAVE 🅴 🍴 🛏 BIZ 🛜 🖥 / SOME UNITS 🔒 🖼

BEST WESTERN PIONEER   (307)334-2640

Motel
$99-$220

AAA Benefit:
Save 10% or more every
day and earn 10% bonus
points!

Address: 731 S Main St 82225 **Location:** Just n of jct US 20/85. **Facility:** 40 units. 1 story, exterior corridors. **Parking:** winter plug-ins. **Pool(s):** heated outdoor. **Activities:** bicycles, picnic facilities. **Guest Services:** coin laundry. **Featured Amenity: full hot breakfast.**

MEDICINE BOW (E-5) pop. 284, elev. 6,564'

Faced with no available lodgings when he arrived in Medicine Bow in 1885, American author Owen Wister was forced to spend his first night at the counter of the town's general store. Had he visited 26 years later, he could have slept at the Virginian Hotel, named after his well-known novel "The Virginian." Published in 1902, Wister's book became the inspiration for two stage plays, two silent films, a "talking" film and a television series in the 1960s.

Although Wister first described the modest town of Medicine Bow as a "wretched husk of squalor," he later wrote: "I don't wonder a man never comes back [East] after he has once been here a few years." Medicine Bow's still-operating Virginian Hotel now stands as a town landmark.

MEDICINE BOW MUSEUM is at 405 Lincoln Hwy. The museum is housed in a 1913 railroad depot. Local and traveling historical exhibits depict the history of Medicine Bow and the West. Among the displays are such Western items as cowboys' chaps and branding irons. A picnic area, restored caboose and Owen Wister's cabin are on the grounds. **Time:** Allow 30 minutes minimum. **Hours:** Mon.-Sat. 10-5, Memorial Day-Labor Day. **Cost:** Donations. **Phone:** (307) 379-2383.

MEDICINE BOW NATIONAL FOREST
(D-5)

Elevations in the forest range from 5,000 ft. north of the Laramie River to 12,013 ft. at Medicine Bow Peak. Refer to AAA maps for additional elevation information.

In southeastern Wyoming, Medicine Bow-Routt National Forest consists of three separate districts that together cover 1,093,618 acres. Scenic SR 130 (closed in winter) crosses the Laramie and Brush Creek/Hayden districts, which extend northward from Colorado along the Snowy Range.

The Brush Creek/Hayden District spans the Continental Divide in the Sierra Madre Mountains west of Encampment. Douglas District, the northernmost section, is high in the rugged Laramie Mountains south of Douglas. Between Cheyenne and Laramie

I-80 crosses the Pole Mountain Unit, noted for its unusual rock formations.

The Thunder Basin National Grassland *(see place listing p. 312)* lies in the energy-rich Powder River Basin north of Douglas. There also are four wilderness areas with 79,135 acres of forested land west of Laramie.

Opportunities for such winter sports as cross-country skiing and snowmobiling abound in the area. Camping, fishing, hiking and hunting also are available. For additional information contact the Forest Supervisor, 2468 Jackson St., Laramie, WY 82070. Phone (307) 745-2300. *See Recreation Areas Chart.*

MEETEETSE (B-2) pop. 327, elev. 5,798'
• **Hotels & Restaurants map & index p. 324**
• **Part of Yellowstone National Park area — see map p. 316**

Meeteetse has retained so much of its original western flavor that you might feel like you've stepped onto a John Wayne movie set, but this is the real McCoy. Downtown's turn-of-the-20th-century buildings house 21st-century cafés and antique shops fronted by awning-covered wooden sidewalks. Horse-watering troughs and hitching posts complete the Old West feel.

Established in 1880, this is a town where Butch Cassidy once lived and Amelia Earhart and Will Rogers once visited, staying at a local dude ranch. Lying along the scenic portion of SR 120, which runs 83 miles between Cody and Thermopolis, Meeteetse is located in the midst of mountains, rivers and valleys. Grizzly bears, deer, bighorn sheep, elk, moose and mountain lions consider this area the perfect home, presenting great opportunities for wildlife photography. The picturesque surroundings also suit humans who enjoy boating, camping, fishing, water skiing, snowmobiling, cross-country skiing and hunting.

CHARLES J. BELDEN MUSEUM AND MEETEETSE MUSEUM is at 1947 State St. Two separate museums are located within the building. The Charles J. Belden Museum features personal effects, sculpture and Western photography that led to Belden's fame. The far end of the building holds The Meeteetse Museum and includes artifacts gathered from local ranches and homesteads as well as a local wildlife collection.

Time: Allow 1 hour minimum. **Hours:** Mon.-Sat. 9:30-5, Sun. noon-4, May 1-Oct. 31; Tues.-Sat. 10-4, Feb.-Apr. and Nov. 1-Dec. 22. Closed Thanksgiving. **Cost:** Free. **Phone:** (307) 868-2423.

FIRST NATIONAL BANK MUSEUM is at 1033 Park Ave. in a 1901 former bank building. Artifacts and records document local and regional history. **Time:** Allow 1 hour minimum. **Hours:** Mon.-Sat. 9:30-5, Sun. noon-4, May 1-Nov. 1; Tues.-Sat. 10-4, Feb.-Apr. and Nov. 2-Dec. 22. Closed Thanksgiving. **Cost:** Donations. **Phone:** (307) 868-2423.

(See map & index p. 324.)

OUTLAW STEAK AND RIB HOUSE   307/868-2585 (55)

American. Casual Dining. $9-$24 **AAA Inspector Notes:** Known for its Captain Morgan's molasses and rum ribs and Jack Daniel's honey and whiskey ribs, this hometown café serves a variety of homemade dishes. Hand-tossed pizzas and thick sourdough sandwiches make for a hearty lunch. Fresh made-from-scratch pies round out the menu. Next door is the Cowboy Bar and Saloon, established in 1893—be sure to take a walk through and look at all the memorabilia. **Features:** full bar. **Address:** 1936 State St 82433 **Location:** Center. **Parking:** street only. ⓛ ⓓ 🛒 〽

MOOSE

• **Part of Jackson Hole Including Grand Teton National Park area — see map p. 285**

LOST CREEK RANCH & SPA   307/733-3435

[fyi] Not evaluated. **Address:** 1 Old Ranch Rd 83012 **Location:** 8 mi n. Facilities, services, and décor characterize an upscale property. This is a seasonal, all-inclusive luxury ranch and spa.

NEWCASTLE (C-6) pop. 3,532, elev. 4,321'

Founded in 1889 when coal was discovered in the area, Newcastle was named after its sister community in England, Newcastle-Upon-Tyne. Mining is a continuing industry, along with ranching, lumbering and petroleum exploration. The yield of Newcastle's oil field is processed by its own refinery.

Newcastle Area Chamber of Commerce: 1323 Washington Blvd., Newcastle, WY 82701. **Phone:** (307) 746-2739 or (800) 835-0157.

Self-guiding tours: Brochures about driving tours are available from the visitor center at the junction of US 85 and US 16.

ANNA MILLER MUSEUM is 3 blks. w. of US 16/85 at 401 Delaware St. The museum displays wildlife, antique firefighting apparatus, pioneer articles, fossils, minerals and Native American artifacts.

Also at the site is the Jenney Cabin, built in 1875 by the expedition sent into the Black Hills area by the U.S. government to investigate reports of gold. The structure is best known as a way station on the Cheyenne-Deadwood stage line, which began in 1876. **Hours:** Mon.-Fri. 9-5 and by appointment. Closed major holidays. **Cost:** Free. **Phone:** (307) 746-4188.

PINES MOTEL   307/746-4334

▼▼ ▼▼
Motel
$69-$145

Address: 248 E Wentworth St 82701 **Location:** Just se of center, just ne from Summit Ave (US 16) and Wentworth St. Located in a residential area. **Facility:** 11 units, some two bedrooms and kitchens. 1 story, exterior corridors. **Parking:** winter plug-ins. **Terms:** check-in 4 pm, cancellation fee imposed. **Activities:** hot tub. **Featured Amenity:** continental breakfast.

 (SAVE) (HS) 🛜 ✕ 🗄 🖭 ▣

SAGE MOTEL   307/746-2724

▼
Motel
$75

Address: 1227 S Summit Ave 82701 **Location:** 0.5 mi se of Main St on US 16 to Seneca Ave, then 0.3 mi e. **Facility:** 12 units. 1 story, exterior corridors. **Parking:** winter plug-ins. **Terms:** 3 day cancellation notice-fee imposed.

(SAVE) 🍴 🛜 ✕ 🗄 🖭 ▣

PAINTER

• **Hotels & Restaurants map & index p. 324**
• **Part of Yellowstone National Park area — see map p. 316**

HUNTER PEAK RANCH   307/587-3711 (49)

▼ Ranch $150-$215 **Address:** 4027 Crandall Rd 82414 **Location:** SR 296, 5 mi s of US 212; 40 mi n of SR 120. **Facility:** 8 units, some two bedrooms, three bedrooms, efficiencies, kitchens and cabins. 2 stories (no elevator), exterior corridors. *Bath:* some shared. **Terms:** closed 11/1-4/30, check-in 4 pm, check-out 9 am, 91 day cancellation notice-fee imposed. **Activities:** beach access, fishing, lawn sports, picnic facilities. **Guest Services:** coin laundry.

🛜 ✕ 〽 ▥ 🅿 🗄 🖭 / SOME UNITS 🖭

PINE BLUFFS (E-6) pop. 1,129, elev. 5,047'

Pine Bluffs, named for the stunted pine trees on the bluffs overlooking the area, was once an important watering place along the Texas Cattle Trail. In 1871 more than 600,000 head of cattle were herded through the Pine Bluffs Crossroads, making it the largest cattle shipping point in the world.

Texas Trail Museum preserves historic treasures of the area; phone (307) 245-3713. The University of Wyoming Archaeological Dig presents a look into civilization 10,000 years ago through extracted nomadic Native American artifacts displayed at the University of Wyoming Archaeological Educational Center, Second and Elm streets. Also of interest is the Our Lady of Peace Shrine. Reputed to be one of the largest Marian statues in the United States, it can be seen from the north side of I-80.

Pine Bluffs Visitors' Center: Milepost 401 on I-80 (at the rest area), P.O. Box 486, Pine Bluffs, WY 82082. **Phone:** (307) 245-3695.

PINEDALE (D-2) pop. 2,030, elev. 7,176'

With the majestic Wind River Range as a backdrop, Pinedale serves as an outfitting point for recreation in the Bridger-Teton National Forest *(see place listing p. 236).* Outdoor activities in the area include trout fishing and various water sports on nearby Fremont Lake, the second largest natural lake in Wyoming *(see Recreation Areas Chart).* Fishing float trips originate on the Green River, while camping, climbing, backpacking and cross-country and downhill skiing also are available.

Eleven miles southwest of town, Father DeSmet Monument designates the site where the first Catholic Mass in Wyoming was held in 1840.

Upper Green River Rendezvous National Historic Landmark is 6 miles west of Pinedale on US 191. Native Americans from throughout the West and such legendary mountain men as Jim Bridger and William Sublette gathered each year during the 1830s to meet the supply caravans from St. Louis and barter, trade for furs and cavort.

Sublette County Chamber of Commerce/Visitors' Center: 19 E. Pine St., P.O. Box 176, Pinedale, WY 82941. **Phone:** (307) 367-2242.

Self-guiding tours: Information about the Pinedale Walking Tour and day trips in the area is available at the visitor center.

MUSEUM OF THE MOUNTAIN MAN is at 700 E. Hennick St. The museum contains exhibits relating to the rugged individuals—Jim Bridger, Kit Carson, Thomas Fitzpatrick and William Sublette, to name a few—who opened the West to settlers. Displays focus on exploration, the fur trade, the Plains Native Americans and early settlement. Items of interest include Jim Bridger's rifle, a Shoshone sheep-horn bow and a collection of Rocky Mountain fur trade journals.

Time: Allow 30 minutes minimum. **Hours:** Daily 9-5, May-Oct.; by appointment rest of year. **Cost:** $7; $5 (ages 61+); $4 (ages 6-12). **Phone:** (307) 367-4101 or (877) 686-6266.

BAYMONT INN & SUITES   (307)367-8300

Hotel
$59-$109

Address: 1424 W Pine St 82941 **Location:** 1 mi n on US 191. **Facility:** 82 units. 3 stories, interior corridors. **Pool(s):** heated indoor. **Activities:** hot tub, limited exercise equipment. **Guest Services:** valet and coin laundry. **Featured Amenity: continental breakfast.**

BEST WESTERN PINEDALE INN   (307)367-6869

Hotel
$79-$160

AAA Benefit: Save 10% or more every day and earn 10% bonus points!

Address: 864 W Pine St 82941 **Location:** 0.5 mi n on US 191. **Facility:** 84 units. 2 stories (no elevator), interior corridors. **Parking:** winter plug-ins. **Pool(s):** heated indoor. **Activities:** hot tub. **Guest Services:** coin laundry. **Featured Amenity: full hot breakfast.**

Discover a wealth of savings and offers on the AAA/CAA travel websites

HAMPTON INN & SUITES   (307)367-6700

Hotel
$99-$179

AAA Benefit: Members save up to 10%!

Address: 55 Bloomfield Ave 82941 **Location:** 1.5 mi n on US 191. **Facility:** 102 units. 3 stories, interior corridors. **Parking:** winter plug-ins. **Terms:** 1-7 night minimum stay, cancellation fee imposed. **Pool(s):** heated indoor. **Activities:** hot tub, picnic facilities, exercise room. **Guest Services:** valet and coin laundry. **Featured Amenity: full hot breakfast.**

WHERE TO EAT

LAKESIDE LODGE BAR & GRILL   307/367-3555

American. Casual Dining. $9-$34 **AAA Inspector Notes:** Diners at this restaurant can take in beautiful views of the glacial lake and mountain peaks beyond while sampling steak, seafood and pasta dishes. **Features:** full bar, patio dining, happy hour. **Reservations:** suggested, in summer. **Address:** 99 Forest Service Rd 111 82941 **Location:** 3.2 mi n from US 191, then 0.6 mi e; on Fremont Lake; follow signs; in Lakeside Lodge Resort & Marina.

STOCKMAN'S RESTAURANT   307/367-4563

American
Casual Dining
$6-$17

AAA Inspector Notes: Locals favor the juicy prime rib, large prawns and lamb at this old-fashioned steakhouse where western hospitality is served with a smile. The Old West décor features a prize-winning saddle in a glass case and game adorns the walls. **Features:** full bar, happy hour. **Address:** 117 W Pine St 82941 **Location:** Center. Menu on AAA.com

WIND RIVER BREWING COMPANY   307/367-2337

American. Casual Dining. $10-$26 **AAA Inspector Notes:** A concise step-by-step guide note on the menu teaches diners how to taste handcrafted brews. You cannot go wrong with the variety of mouth-watering appetizers, salads, sandwiches and steaks. A few stand outs are the beer-b-q brisket sandwich served with fried pickles and a pan-seared sesame-encrusted ahi tuna with curried coconut fried rice. **Features:** full bar, patio dining, happy hour. **Address:** 402 W Pine St 82941 **Location:** Just e of center. **Parking:** on-site and street.

POWELL (B-3) pop. 6,314, elev. 4,365'
- Hotels p. 300
- Hotels & Restaurants map & index p. 324
- Part of Yellowstone National Park area — see map p. 316

Native Americans from the Blackfoot, Crow and Shoshone tribes inhabited the area exclusively until explorer John Colter arrived in 1807. Following his arrival came a stream of explorers, trappers and miners. Powell, located about 75 miles from Yellowstone National Park's east entrance, was named after Mayor John Wesley Powell, an early-day explorer. The town's proximity to the Bighorn, Pryor and Absaroka mountain ranges makes it a recreational hot spot. A variety of wildlife inhabits the area, and historic walking tours of the city are available.

Powell Valley Chamber of Commerce: 111 S. Day St., Powell, WY 82435. **Phone:** (307) 754-3494 or (800) 325-4278.

(See map & index p. 324.)

HEART MOUNTAIN INTERPRETIVE CENTER, 1539 Rd. 19, provides a glimpse into the lives of Japanese-Americans interned at the Heart Mountain Relocation Center following the Pearl Harbor bombing. Designed to look like tar paper barracks, the museum building features artifacts and interactive displays, a reflection room and a theater. A short interpretive trail on the grounds offers eight stopping points.

Hours: Grounds daily 24 hours. Interpretive Learning Center daily 10-5, Memorial Day weekend-Oct. 1; Wed.-Sun. 10-5, rest of year. **Cost:** Grounds free. Interpretive Learning Center $7; $5 (ages 62+ and students with ID); free (ages 0-12). **Phone:** (307) 754-8000.

HOMESTEADER MUSEUM is at 324 E.1st St. The museum celebrates the area's homesteading history and features a homestead cabin, a caboose and displays focusing on farming, domestic life and such notorious Western outlaws as Earl Durand. **Hours:** Tues.-Fri. 10-5, Sat. 10-2, June-Sept.; Tues.-Fri. 10-4, Apr.-May and Oct.-Dec. **Cost:** Free. **Phone:** (307) 754-9481.

Say YES to ERS text updates to stay posted when your tow truck is on the way

---

AMERICAS BEST VALUE INN   (307)754-5117 68

Motel
$90-$175

Address: 777 E 2nd St 82435 **Location:** 0.3 mi e on US 14A. **Facility:** 50 units. 2 stories (no elevator), exterior corridors. **Parking:** winter plug-ins. **Featured Amenity: continental breakfast.**

SAVE BIZ 🛜 🖥 💻 / SOME UNITS 🐾

RAWLINS (E-4) pop. 9,259, elev. 6,758'

In traditionally wool- and hay-producing Carbon County, Rawlins was a departure point for the Union Pacific Railroad and for miners bound for the gold-rich Black Hills. Nearby mines produced the "Rawlins Red" pigment that was used on the Brooklyn Bridge in 1874. The ruins of Fort Fred Steele, built in 1868 to protect early railroads and settlers, are 13 miles east of town off I-80.

During the 1870s Rawlins was a wild town with more than its share of outlaw activity. However, it came to an abrupt halt by the end of the decade when exasperated citizens employed vigilante tactics against two of the region's most notorious outlaws, Butch Cassidy and the Sundance Kid. After the lynching of "Big Nose" George Parrot, warnings were sent out to 24 other known outlaws, who left town the next morning.

▼ See AAA listing p. 256 ▼

On the southern edge of the Sweetwater jade fields and the eastern edge of the gem-riddled Red Desert, Rawlins is noteworthy for its geological features.

CARBON COUNTY MUSEUM is at 904 W. Walnut St. Displays tell the story of Wyoming's first female physician, Lillian Heath. Restored Western artifacts include a sheepherder's wagon, an original Wyoming flag, a 1920 hook-and-ladder fire truck, a 1900s buggy, a horse-drawn sleigh and shoes made from outlaw "Big Nose" George Parrott's skin. The Discovery Zone offers child-friendly, hands-on exhibits. Changing exhibits depict life in the West, Native American lore, ranching and the Union Pacific Railroad. **Hours:** Tues.-Sat. 10-6, May-Sept.; Tues.-Sat. 1-5, rest of year. **Cost:** Donations. **Phone:** (307) 328-2740.

WYOMING FRONTIER PRISON is at 500 W. Walnut St. The prison replaced the territorial prison in Laramie in 1901 and operated until 1981. A 1-hour guided tour includes three cell blocks, a cafeteria, an exercise yard, visiting rooms, a gas chamber and the death house. Three museums and a walking path also are on the premises.

Hours: Tours daily 8:30-4:30, Memorial Day-Labor Day; Mon.-Thurs. at 10:30 and 1:30, rest of year. Night tours are available by appointment. Closed Jan. 1, Thanksgiving, Christmas Eve, Christmas and day after Christmas. **Cost:** $8; $7 (ages 6-12 and 60+); $35 (family). Rates may vary; phone ahead. **Phone:** (307) 324-4422. (GT)

BEST WESTERN COTTONTREE INN   (307)324-2737

Hotel
$119-$249

AAA Benefit: Save 10% or more every day and earn 10% bonus points!

Address: 2221 W Spruce St 82301 **Location:** I-80 exit 211, just n. **Facility:** 122 units. 2 stories (no elevator), interior/exterior corridors. **Pool(s):** heated indoor. **Activities:** hot tub, exercise room. **Guest Services:** coin laundry. **Featured Amenity:** breakfast buffet.

COMFORT INN & SUITES   (307)324-3663

Hotel
$99-$160

Address: 2366 E Cedar St 82301 **Location:** I-80 exit 215 (Cedar St), 0.3 mi w. **Facility:** 65 units. 3 stories, interior corridors. **Pool(s):** heated indoor. **Activities:** hot tub, exercise room. **Guest Services:** coin laundry. **Featured Amenity:** continental breakfast.

FERRIS MANSION BED & BREAKFAST   (307)710-3961

Historic Bed & Breakfast $120 **Address:** 607 W Maple St 82301 **Location:** I-80 exit 211, 1.5 mi e to 7th St, just n, then just e; at W Maple and 6th sts. **Facility:** This mansion has a grand oak stairway which leads to the blue, gold, lavender and rose rooms which offer modern amenities. The personal touches and furnishings in each room will not go unnoticed. 4 units. 2 stories (no elevator), interior corridors. **Terms:** check-in 4 pm. **Guest Services:** area transportation.

PRONGHORN INN & SUITES   (307)324-5588

Hotel
$109-$180

Address: 812 Locust St 82301 **Location:** I-80 exit 214, 0.4 mi n on Higley Blvd, then just e. **Facility:** 59 units. 3 stories, interior corridors. **Terms:** cancellation fee imposed. **Guest Services:** coin laundry. **Featured Amenity:** full hot breakfast.

HAMPTON INN   307/324-2320

(fyi) Hotel Did not meet all AAA rating requirements for locking devices in some guest rooms at time of last evaluation on 10/22/2014. **Address:** 406 Airport Rd 82301 **Location:** I-80 exit 215 (Cedar St), 0.8 mi nw. Facilities, services, and décor characterize a mid-scale property.

AAA Benefit: Members save up to 10%!

WHERE TO EAT

ANONG'S THAI CUISINE   307/324-6262

Thai. Casual Dining. $9-$18 **AAA Inspector Notes:** This cute eatery features reasonably priced Thai cuisine including a popular lunch buffet. Most menu items are authentic and well prepared. Be aware that some of the dishes can be very spicy. **Address:** 210 5th St 82301 **Location:** Jct US 287; center. **Parking:** street only. (L) (D)

ASPEN HOUSE RESTAURANT   307/324-4787

American. Casual Dining. $11-$27 **AAA Inspector Notes:** The dining choices at this Victorian home reflect Eastern and Western influences. Enjoy fresh preparations of Szechuan, blackened and Cajun dishes, spring rolls, beef lettuce wraps, Korean style barbecue beef, chicken fried steak, grilled steaks, stir-fried selections and seafood. You may want to call ahead for winter hours. A kids' menu and vegetarian items are available. **Features:** full bar. **Address:** 318 5th St 82301 **Location:** Just s of center at W Buffalo and 5th sts. **Parking:** street only. (L) (D)

BUCK'S SPORTS GRILL   307/328-5581

American. Casual Dining. $8-$12 **AAA Inspector Notes:** Pine walls, nature photos and distinctive taxidermy add character to this eatery. The menu consists of standard American fare, including pizza, burgers and hot dogs. Start with the loaded potato skins topped with a choice of barbecue pulled pork or bacon. **Features:** full bar. **Address:** 401 W Cedar St 82301 **Location:** Corner of 4th St. **Parking:** street only. (L) (D)

RIVERTON (C-3) pop. 10,615, elev. 4,956'

Once part of Wind River Indian Reservation, the lower Wind River Basin now supports 130,000 acres of farmland surrounding Riverton. Castle Gardens, a state historical monument 45 miles east, is a formation of knobs, pinnacles and spires rising abruptly 10

---

to 100 feet above the prairie. Petroglyphs depicting warriors, hunters and animals decorate the soft sandstone formations.

Riverton Area Chamber of Commerce: 213 W. Main St., Suite C, Riverton, WY 82501. **Phone:** (307) 856-4801 or (800) 325-2732.

RIVERTON MUSEUM is at 700 E. Park Ave. The museum interprets the story of 20th-century homesteaders who brought the town to life in 1906. Displays include fixtures and merchandise from an early 20th-century general store, drugstore, school, beauty salon, dentist's office, church and post office. Northern Arapaho and Shoshone Native American artifacts also are exhibited.

An outdoor display features early 20th-century farm machinery. **Time:** Allow 1 hour, 30 minutes minimum. **Hours:** Mon.-Sat. 9-noon and 1-5, May-Aug.; Mon.-Sat. 10-4, rest of year. Closed major holidays. **Cost:** Free. **Phone:** (307) 856-2665.

WIND RIVER HERITAGE CENTER, 1075 S. Federal Blvd., displays 62 full-size mounts and 20-plus head mounts of bears, bighorn sheep, bison, deer, elk, moose, wolves and other animals. Other highlights include Native American art; an extensive collection of traps; and 50 period-dressed wax figures of such notable Westerners as Lewis and Clark, Jim Bridger, Big Nose George Parrot and Cattle Kate.

Time: Allow 1 hour minimum. **Hours:** Mon.-Sat. 10-4; otherwise by appointment. Closed federal holidays. **Cost:** Free. **Phone:** (307) 856-0706.
GT 🎫 🏞️

GAMBLING ESTABLISHMENTS

- **Wind River Casino** is at 10269 SR 789. **Hours:** Daily 24 hours. **Phone:** (307) 856-3964. *(See ad this page.)*

COMFORT INN & SUITES   (307)856-8900
◇◇ ◇◇ **Hotel** $119-$179 **Address:** 2020 N Federal Blvd 82501 **Location:** 1.5 mi ne on US 26/SR 789. **Facility:** 63 units. 3 stories, interior corridors. **Parking:** winter plug-ins. **Pool(s):** heated indoor. **Activities:** hot tub, exercise room. **Guest Services:** coin laundry.
🛎️ CALL 🅖M 🔒 BIZ HS 📶 🔲 📺 🔳 / SOME UNITS 🅢🄿

DAYS INN   (307)856-9677
fyi **Motel** $80-$105 Under major renovation, scheduled to be completed March 2015. **Last Rated:** ◇ **Address:** 909 W Main St 82501 **Location:** 0.5 mi nw on US 26. **Facility:** 33 units. 2 stories (no elevator), exterior corridors. **Parking:** winter plug-ins. **Amenities:** *Some:* safes.
🛎️ BIZ 📶 🔲 📺 📺 📺 / SOME UNITS 🅢🄿 HS

Stay connected with #AAA and #CAA

on your favorite social media sites

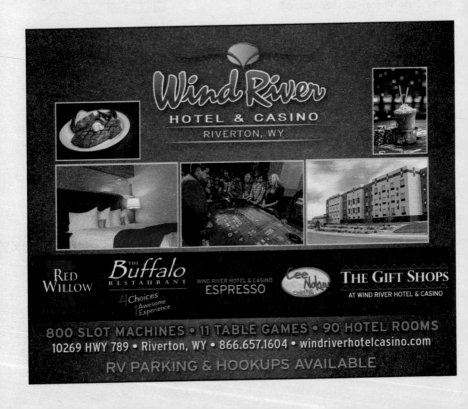

HAMPTON INN & SUITES RIVERTON   (307)856-3500

▼▼▼▼ Hotel $99-$189 **Address:** 2500 N Federal Blvd (US 26) 82501 **Location:** 2 mi ne on US 26/SR 789. **Facility:** 89 units. 3 stories, interior corridors. **Parking:** winter plug-ins. **Terms:** 1-7 night minimum stay, cancellation fee imposed. **Pool(s):** heated indoor. **Activities:** hot tub, exercise room. **Guest Services:** coin laundry.

AAA Benefit: Members save up to 10%!

CALL Ⓜ 🅿 BIZ HS 🛜 ⊠ 💻 / SOME UNITS 🛏 ⊟ ⬛

HOLIDAY INN RIVERTON CONVENTION CENTER   (307)856-8100

▼▼▼▼ Hotel $109-$169 **Address:** 900 E Sunset Dr 82501 **Location:** 0.8 mi ne on US 26/SR 789. **Facility:** 120 units. 2 stories, interior corridors. **Parking:** winter plug-ins. **Pool(s):** heated indoor. **Activities:** exercise room. **Guest Services:** coin laundry, area transportation.

➕ 🍴 🖥 ⛾ CALL Ⓜ 🅿 BIZ 🛜 ⊠ ⊟ ⬛ 💻

WIND RIVER HOTEL & CASINO   (307)856-3964

▼▼▼ Hotel $90-$149

Address: 10269 Hwy 789 82501 **Location:** 2 mi s from jct US 26. **Facility:** A colorful exterior depicts patterns from the Arapaho culture. A highlight of the lobby is the Discovery Room, a walk-through display depicting native history using pictures, artifacts and movies. 90 units. 3 stories, interior corridors. **Parking:** winter plug-ins. **Terms:** check-in 4 pm, resort fee. **Amenities:** safes. **Dining:** 2 restaurants, also, Red Willow, see separate listing. **Activities:** exercise room. **Guest Services:** coin laundry, area transportation. *(See ad p. 302.)*

SAVE 🐾 ➕ 🍴 CALL Ⓜ BIZ 🛜 ⊠ ⊟ 🖨 💻 / SOME UNITS 💲

WHERE TO EAT

THE BULL & BISTRO   307/240-1913

▼▼▼ Steak Seafood. Casual Dining. $9-$29 **AAA Inspector Notes:** Guests can get a good value at lunch here with such sandwiches as oregano-rubbed roast beef and pesto turkey. The dinner menu features a variety of steak, lamb, pork chop and chicken dishes as well as a nice selection of seafood and pasta. When available, try the gingerbread cream puffs or chocolate pot de creme. **Features:** full bar. **Address:** 1100 W Main St 82501 **Location:** 1.5 mi ne of US 26/SR 789, 1 mi w. Ⓛ Ⓓ

RED WILLOW   307/856-3964

▼▼ American. Casual Dining. $7-$28 **AAA Inspector Notes:** Diners receive incredible value in reasonably priced dishes of Maine lobster tail, Alaskan king crab and filet mignon. There are also may choices for the lighter appetite. No alcohol is served on the reservation. **Address:** 10269 Hwy 789 82501 **Location:** 2 mi s from jct US 26; in Wind River Hotel & Casino. *(See ad p. 302.)*

Ⓑ Ⓛ Ⓓ CALL Ⓜ

ROCK SPRINGS (E-2) pop. 23,036, elev. 6,261'
• Hotels p. 304 • Restaurants p. 305

Rock Springs began in 1862 as a way station along the Overland Stage route. The Union Pacific also chose this route because of the area's rich coal deposits that fueled the railroad's locomotives. Mining and refining are still major industries, with resources expanding to include trona and natural gas.

Some of the world's largest deposits of trona, used in the manufacture of glass, phosphates, silicates and soaps, lie 30 miles west of the city.

To the north and stretching more than 70 miles between the town of Eden and the Green Mountains is the Red Desert, an area of moving sand dunes second in size only to the Sahara Desert. Of archeological and geological interest, the Sands, as the region is known, has produced evidence of human habitation as far back as 5000 B.C.

Petroglyphs and pictographs adorn the walls of rock outcrops in Cedar, Pine and Killpecker canyons and White Mountain. Visitors also can see evidence of prehistoric Wyoming at Western Wyoming Community College, which maintains a collection of fossils.

Boars Tusk, a volcanic monolith, rises 400 feet above Killpecker Valley at the edge of the Sands. The rock tower, 28 miles north of Rock Springs, is visible from US 191.

The Red Desert is home to one of the nation's largest herds of wild horses. To control the size of the herds, the Bureau of Land Management (BLM) conducts roundups; Mustangs captured by the BLM are kept at Rock Springs' Wild Horse Holding Facility, which conducts an Adopt-a-Horse program; phone (307) 352-0292. The Pilot Butte Wild Horse Scenic Loop provides views of these creatures; the dirt road has markers and covers some 23 miles.

Note: When traveling in desert areas, be sure to start with a full tank of gas and plenty of food and water. Off-road vehicles and cellphones are recommended for travel in remote areas.

Rock Springs Chamber of Commerce: 1897 Dewar Dr., P.O. Box 398, Rock Springs, WY 82902. **Phone:** (307) 362-3771 or (800) 463-8637.

Self-guiding tours: A self-guiding walking tour of downtown Rock Springs covers sites related to the community's coal mining history. Brochures are available at the chamber of commerce.

COMMUNITY FINE ARTS CENTER is at 400 C St. The center contains a collection of more than 600 works by Wyoming and other Western artists as well as nationally and internationally known artists. Highlights include single works by Loren McGiver, Grandma Moses and Norman Rockwell. **Hours:** Mon.-Thurs. 10-6, Fri.-Sat. noon-5. **Cost:** Free. **Phone:** (307) 362-6212.

ROCK SPRINGS HISTORIC MUSEUM is at 201 B St. This museum describes area history, coal mining and the diverse nationalities that settled Rock Springs. The building was constructed in 1894 and restored in 1992. **Time:** Allow 1 hour minimum. **Hours:** Mon.-Sat. 10-5. Closed major holidays. **Cost:** Free. **Phone:** (307) 362-3138.

WESTERN WYOMING COMMUNITY COLLEGE NATURAL HISTORY MUSEUM is off I-80 exit 103, then 1 mi. s. to 2500 College Dr. The museum contains life-size replicas of dinosaurs, prehistoric fossil specimens and artifacts gathered from various formations around southwestern Wyoming. Exhibits, which are scattered throughout the campus, include reproductions of cave art from the Upper Paleolithic era and a 9-ton replica of an Easter Island statue. Maps are available at the entrance. **Time:** Allow 30 minutes minimum. **Hours:** Daily 9 a.m.-10 p.m., Aug.-May; Mon.-Thurs. 7 a.m.-9 p.m., rest of year. **Cost:** Free. **Phone:** (307) 382-1600.

BEST WESTERN OUTLAW INN   (307)362-6623

Hotel
$119-$179

AAA Benefit: Save 10% or more every day and earn 10% bonus points!

Address: 1630 Elk St 82901 **Location:** I-80 exit 104 (Elk St), 0.3 mi n. Next to gas stations and truck stop. **Facility:** 100 units. 1-2 stories, interior/exterior corridors. **Parking:** winter plug-ins. **Dining:** Open Range Restaurant, see separate listing. **Pool(s):** heated indoor. **Activities:** exercise room. **Guest Services:** valet laundry, area transportation. **Featured Amenity:** full hot breakfast. *(See ad this page.)*

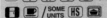

HAMPTON INN   (307)382-9222

Hotel $129-$299 **Address:** 1901 Dewar Dr 82901 **Location:** I-80 exit 102 (Dewar Dr), 0.5 mi se. **Facility:** 70 units. 3 stories, interior corridors. **Terms:** 1-7 night minimum stay, cancellation fee imposed. **Pool(s):** heated indoor. **Activities:** hot tub, exercise room. **Guest Services:** valet and coin laundry.

AAA Benefit: Members save up to 10%!

HOLIDAY INN   (307)382-9200

Hotel $129-$200 **Address:** 1675 Sunset Dr 82901 **Location:** I-80 exit 102 (Dewar Dr), just e, then 0.7 mi sw. **Facility:** 170 units. 4 stories, interior/exterior corridors. **Amenities:** *Some:* safes. **Pool(s):** heated indoor. **Activities:** hot tub, picnic facilities, exercise room. **Guest Services:** valet and coin laundry.

HOLIDAY INN EXPRESS & SUITES   307/362-9200

Hotel. Rates not provided. **Address:** 1660 Sunset Dr 82901 **Location:** I-80 exit 102 (Dewar Dr), just e, then 0.5 mi sw. **Facility:** 79 units. 3 stories, interior corridors. **Parking:** winter plug-ins. **Pool(s):** heated indoor. **Activities:** hot tub, exercise room. **Guest Services:** valet and coin laundry.

▼ *See AAA listing this page* ▼

HOMEWOOD SUITES BY HILTON   307/382-0764

▼▼▼ **Extended Stay Hotel.** Rates not provided. **Address:** 60 Winston Dr 82901 **Location:** I-80 exit 102 (Dewar Dr), 0.4 mi se, then just ne on Winston Dr. **Facility:** 84 efficiencies, some two bedrooms. 4 stories, interior corridors. **Parking:** winter plug-ins. **Pool(s):** heated indoor. **Activities:** hot tub, picnic facilities, exercise room. **Guest Services:** valet and coin laundry.

| **AAA Benefit:** Members save up to 10%! |

🍴 CALL ⊝M 🏊 BIZ HS 🛜 ✕ 🛄 🖥 ▭

LA QUINTA INN ROCK SPRINGS   (307)362-1770

▼▼ **Hotel** $64-$251 **Address:** 2717 Dewar Dr 82901 **Location:** I-80 exit 102 (Dewar Dr), just n. **Facility:** 129 units. 2 stories (no elevator), interior corridors. **Pool(s):** heated outdoor. **Activities:** picnic facilities, exercise room. **Guest Services:** valet and coin laundry.

🍴 CALL ⊝M 🏊 BIZ 🛜 ✕ 🛄 🖥 ▭ / SOME UNITS 🐾

MY PLACE HOTEL - ROCK SPRINGS   (307)362-5977

▼▼ **Extended Stay Hotel** $96-$99 **Address:** 700 Gateway Blvd 82901 **Location:** I-80 exit 102 (Dewar Dr), just se, then 0.6 mi n. **Facility:** 64 efficiencies. 3 stories, interior corridors. **Parking:** winter plug-ins. **Terms:** cancellation fee imposed. **Guest Services:** coin laundry.

CALL ⊝M BIZ 🛜 ✕ 🛄 🖥 ▭ / SOME UNITS 🆂

WHERE TO EAT

9 IRON ITALIAN GRILL & STEAKHOUSE   307/362-2561

▼▼ American. Casual Dining. $12-$24 **AAA Inspector Notes:** Specializing in Italian cuisine and steaks, this relaxing restaurant also serves a wide variety of specialty, build-your-own pizza and a nice selection of pasta, antipasto, salads, hot and cold sandwiches and some seafood. Locals favor the whiskey steak and blackened chicken Alfredo, while kids like the spaghetti with browned butter and cheese—everyone loves the spumoni. A kids' menu is available as well as protein diet choices. **Features:** full bar, patio dining. **Address:** 1501 Clubhouse Dr 82901 **Location:** I-80 exit 104 (Elk St), 0.8 mi n to Yellowstone Rd, then 1.7 mi nw; at White Mountain Golf Course. D

BITTER CREEK BREWING   307/362-4782

▼▼ American. Casual Dining. $9-$18 **AAA Inspector Notes:** This brewpub offers a nice selection of ice cold microbrews. Be sure to sample the beer flights. Menu offerings consist of Thai chicken nachos, stuffed mushrooms, a hearty daily soup, popular blackened chicken salad, some pasta dishes and hot and cold sandwiches. Kids have their own menu. **Features:** full bar. **Address:** 604 Broadway St 82901 **Location:** At Broadway and E sts; downtown. **Parking:** street only. L D

BONSAI   307/362-1888

▼▼ Asian Sushi. Casual Dining. $9-$19 **AAA Inspector Notes:** At this colorful eatery, expect an attentive staff, lovely presentations, a nice selection of soups, standard and specialty sushi rolls and a variety of popular combination plates. Expect a crowd during peak lunch and dinner hours. **Features:** beer & wine. **Address:** 1996 Dewar Dr 82901 **Location:** I-80 exit 102 (Dewar Dr), 0.4 mi se. L D

COYOTE CREEK STEAKHOUSE & SALOON   307/382-4100

▼▼ American. Casual Dining. $15-$29 **AAA Inspector Notes:** Enjoy a cocktail at the bar before dinner and then feast on a nice house salad, an appetizer such as jumbo Gulf shrimp cocktail, a juicy steak, half rack of lamb or baby back ribs. The atmosphere is casual and the food is spot on. **Features:** full bar. **Address:** 404 N St 82901 **Location:** I-80 exit 102 (Dewar Dr) eastbound; exit 107 (US 30 BL/Pilot Butee Ave) westbound; corner of N St and Pilot Butte Ave; downtown. **Parking:** on-site and street. L D

FIESTA GUADALAJARA   307/382-7147

▼▼ Mexican. Casual Dining. $7-$16 **AAA Inspector Notes:** The colorful and festive décor inside this restaurant soon replaces the first impression of the shabby entry to an abandoned historic hotel. Quesadillas, nachos, steak and chicken fajitas, tamales, enchiladas and chile relleno are available and the mole is good enough to drink. A children's menu is also available. **Features:** full bar. **Address:** 19 Elk St 82901 **Location:** I-80 exit 102 (Dewar Dr), 2 mi e to Grant St, then just e; downtown. L D

LEW'S   307/382-9894

▼▼ American. Casual Dining. $8-$28 **AAA Inspector Notes:** Diners can find a wide variety of menu items at this restaurant including filet mignon, pork chops, veal cutlets, chicken, chicken-fried steak, pan-seared halibut, tempura shrimp, Asian appetizers and entrées, pizza and sandwiches. Kids can appreciate their own special menu. Be sure to sample the pineapple upside-down cake or panna cotta. **Features:** full bar. **Address:** 1506 9th St 82901 **Location:** I-80 exit 107 (Pilot Butte Ave), 0.6 mi nw. B L D

OPEN RANGE RESTAURANT   307/362-6623

▼▼▼ American Casual Dining $8-$25

AAA Inspector Notes: Locals and travelers come together for choices that range from sandwiches, burgers and seafood to Angus beef, chops and cutlets, with prime rib and seafood specials offered every evening. Adventurous diners can appreciate the Rocky Mountain oysters appetizer, a great opportunity to prove power of the palate. For dessert, order the grilled carrot cake. **Features:** full bar. **Address:** 1630 Elk St 82901 **Location:** I-80 exit 104 (Elk St), 0.3 mi n; in BEST WESTERN Outlaw Inn. *Menu on AAA.com* B L D

WONDERFUL HOUSE   307/382-8800

▼▼ Chinese. Casual Dining. $8-$14 **AAA Inspector Notes:** This family-run restaurant is popular with the locals and serves authentic Chinese food made with fresh ingredients. **Features:** full bar. **Address:** 1676 Sunset Dr 82901 **Location:** I-80 exit 102 (Dewar Dr), just s, then just w. L D

SARATOGA (E-4) pop. 1,690, elev. 6,791'
• Hotels p. 306

Saratoga, named for Saratoga Springs, N.Y., is a supply center and access point for recreation on the North Platte River and in Medicine Bow National Forest *(see place listing p. 297).* The 64 miles of the North Platte River between the Colorado border and Saratoga are a nationally designated blue-ribbon trout fishery and include a stretch of white water rated as high as 10 on the U.S. Forest Service scale.

Saratoga Hot Springs offers a natural hot springs pool open free to the public. Fishing areas are available on the Platte and golf facilities are nearby.

Saratoga-Platte Valley Chamber of Commerce: 210 W. Elm St., P.O. Box 1095, Saratoga, WY 82331. **Phone:** (307) 326-8855.

SARATOGA MUSEUM is at 104 Constitution Ave. The museum, in the 1915 Union Pacific Railroad depot on SR 130, contains historical and archeological artifacts depicting the settlement and growth of the Platte Valley. Geological displays and a sheep wagon also are included. **Time:** Allow 1 hour minimum. **Hours:** Thurs.-Mon. 9-4, Memorial Day weekend-Oct. 15; by appointment rest of year. **Cost:** Donations. **Phone:** (307) 326-5511.

SARATOGA NATIONAL FISH HATCHERY is 2.5 mi. n. on SR 130, then 1.5 mi. e. on a dirt road (CR

207), following signs. Constructed in 1915, the hatchery produces lake and brown trout eggs for export. **Time:** Allow 1 hour minimum. **Hours:** Daily 8-4. **Cost:** Free. **Phone:** (307) 326-5662.

HACIENDA MOTEL   307/326-5751

fyi Not evaluated. **Address:** 1500 S 1st St 82331 **Location:** On SR 130, 0.4 mi s of center. Facilities, services, and décor characterize an economy property.

SAVERY (E-4) elev. 6,463'

LITTLE SNAKE RIVER MUSEUM is 1 blk. n. of SR 70 on CR 561. Until 1972, the main building of the museum was used as the Savery School. Exhibits pertain to the history of Little Snake River Valley, focusing on such subjects as area residents, outlaws, mountain men and cowboys. Also on the grounds is the Strobridge-Groshart-Hays House, built in 1888. The house has been restored to its original state since being donated to the museum site in 1993. **Time:** Allow 1 hour, 30 minutes minimum. **Hours:** Daily 11-5, Memorial Day-late Oct. **Cost:** Free. **Phone:** (307) 383-7262.

SHERIDAN (B-4) pop. 17,444, elev. 3,724'

Sheridan is located halfway between the Mount Rushmore National Monument and Yellowstone National Park in the valley of the Little and Big Goose. Access through the Bighorn Mountains via US 14 (Bighorn Scenic Byway) or US 14A (Medicine Wheel Passage) offers spectacular sightseeing opportunities. The majestic Bighorn Mountains rise to the west and rolling plains slope to the east.

Sheridan is rich in Western history. In 1866 the area was part of unreserved Native American territory that was home for the Sioux, Cheyenne and Arapaho. Native American chiefs such as Dull Knife, Red Cloud and Crazy Horse fought battles to keep the white man from their precious hunting grounds.

The Bozeman Trail, a shortcut scouted by John Bozeman through eastern Wyoming, cut across Native American hunting grounds to the rich gold fields of Montana. The trail, which ran south of Sheridan along part of what is now US 87, was the scene of so many battles that it became known as the Bloody Bozeman. The U.S. Cavalry forbade trains of fewer than 100 wagons to take this trail.

The discovery of gold in the Black Hills brought a new influx of fortune seekers and further confrontations, culminating in the Battle of the Little Bighorn just north of Sheridan in southern Montana *(see Little Bighorn Battlefield National Monument in Montana p. 187).*

Many battle sites are in the area, including those of the Wagon Box Fight and the Fetterman Massacre, near Fort Phil Kearny in Story *(see attraction listing p. 308)*; Dull Knife Battle, south of town; the Sawyer Fight, 20 miles north near Dayton; Rosebud Battle, north in Montana; and the Connor Battlefield in Ranchester, 15 miles north of Sheridan.

After the wars ended, Sheridan was incorporated and built up by the profitable businesses of cattle ranching, farming and coal mining. For today's outdoor enthusiast, recreational activities are nearly unlimited in the nearby Bighorn National Forest *(see place listing p. 235)* and include wildlife viewing, hiking, fishing, hunting, snowmobiling and cross-country and downhill skiing.

The town recaptures the flavor of the Old West during the Sheridan WYO Rodeo in mid-July; phone (307) 672-9715 for ticket information. In addition to several PRCA rodeo performances, highlights include a pancake breakfast, a carnival, concerts, parades and a golf tournament.

Sheridan Travel and Tourism: 1517 E. 5th St., P.O. Box 7155, Sheridan, WY 82801. **Phone:** (307) 673-7120. *(See ad p. 318.)*

Self-guiding tours: A walking tour of the city's historic Main Street District covers many original buildings from the late 1800s and early 1990s. A map is available from Sheridan Travel and Tourism.

▼ **THE BRINTON MUSEUM**—see Big Horn GEM p. 235.

FETTERMAN MONUMENT stands 20 mi. s. on US 87. On this site in 1866 Col. William J. Fetterman disobeyed orders to stay off the Bozeman Trail and took to the trail with only 81 men under his command. Crazy Horse and 2,000 warriors ambushed and killed the entire force. The site is near Fort Phil Kearny.

FORT PHIL KEARNY STATE HISTORIC SITE— see Story p. 308.

KING'S SADDLERY MUSEUM is at 184 N. Main St. This two-story facility highlights Western history and the life of cowboys. Native American artifacts, guns, photographs and leather saddles are displayed. **Time:** Allow 1 hour minimum. **Hours:** Mon.-Sat. 8-5. **Cost:** $2. **Phone:** (307) 672-2702 or (800) 443-8919.

TRAIL END STATE HISTORIC SITE is at 400 Clarendon Ave. The site is the former home of Sen. John B. Kendrick, the "Cowboy Senator." Set on 3.8 acres, the fully furnished 1913 Flemish-revival mansion has elaborate woodwork, stained-glass windows, chandeliers and hand-painted walls and ceilings. Exhibits reflect the period 1913-33. Self-guiding tours are available; guided tours also are available by appointment. **Time:** Allow 1 hour minimum. **Hours:** Daily 9-6, June-Aug.; 1-4, Apr.-May and Sept. 1-Dec. 14. **Cost:** $4; free (ages 0-17). **Phone:** (307) 674-4589. GT

WYO THEATER is at 42 N. Main St. The theater is an Art Deco structure built in 1923 and renovated in 1989. It is said to be the oldest operating vaudeville theater in the state. Musical entertainment, ballets and stage presentations are featured year-round. **Hours:** Box office open Tues.-Fri. noon-4 (also Sat. on day of shows). **Cost:** Varies depending on event. **Phone:** (307) 672-9084.

AMERICAS BEST VALUE INN   (307)672-9757

Motel
$69-$119

Address: 580 E 5th St 82801 **Location:** I-90 exit 23 (5th St), 0.4 mi w. **Facility:** 39 units. 2 stories (no elevator), exterior corridors. **Terms:** cancellation fee imposed. **Guest Services:** coin laundry. **Featured Amenity:** breakfast buffet.

BEST WESTERN SHERIDAN CENTER   (307)674-7421

Motel
$90-$209

AAA Benefit: Save 10% or more every day and earn 10% bonus points!

Address: 612 N Main St 82801 **Location:** I-90 exit 23 (5th St), 1 mi w, then just s. **Facility:** 139 units. 2 stories (no elevator), interior/exterior corridors. **Parking:** winter plug-ins. **Pool(s):** heated indoor. **Activities:** hot tub. **Guest Services:** valet and coin laundry, area transportation.

/ SOME UNITS

CANDLEWOOD SUITES   (307)675-2100

Extended Stay Hotel $109-$139 **Address:** 1709 Sugarland Dr 82801 **Location:** I-90 exit 25, just w, then just n. **Facility:** 71 efficiencies. 3 stories, interior corridors. **Parking:** winter plug-ins. **Activities:** picnic facilities, exercise room. **Guest Services:** complimentary and valet laundry.

COMFORT INN & SUITES   (307)675-1101

Hotel $169-$239 **Address:** 1950 E 5th St 82801 **Location:** I-90 exit 23 (5th St), just e. **Facility:** 66 units. 3 stories, interior corridors. **Parking:** winter plug-ins. **Amenities:** safes. **Pool(s):** heated indoor. **Activities:** hot tub, exercise room. **Guest Services:** valet and coin laundry.

HAMPTON INN SHERIDAN   (307)673-2734

Hotel $109-$249 **Address:** 980 Sibley Cir 82801 **Location:** I-90 exit 23 (5th St), just w. **Facility:** 65 units. 4 stories, interior corridors. **Terms:** 1-7 night minimum stay, cancellation fee imposed. **Pool(s):** heated indoor. **Activities:** hot tub, exercise room. **Guest Services:** valet and coin laundry.

AAA Benefit: Members save up to 10%!

HOLIDAY INN ATRIUM & CONVENTION CENTER
307)672-8931

Hotel
Rates not provided

Address: 1809 Sugarland Dr 82801 **Location:** I-90 exit 25, just w on Brundage, then just n. **Facility:** 212 units. 5 stories, interior corridors. **Dining:** Sugarland Mining Company, see separate listing. **Pool(s):** heated indoor. **Activities:** hot tub, game room, exercise room, massage. **Guest Services:** valet and coin laundry, area transportation.

/ SOME UNITS

SUPER 8 SHERIDAN   (307)672-9725

Motel $52-$97 **Address:** 2435 N Main St 82801 **Location:** I-90 exit 20, 0.7 mi n. **Facility:** 39 units. 2 stories (no elevator), interior corridors.

/ UNITS

WHERE TO EAT

FRACKELTON'S   307-675-6055

American. Casual Dining. $10-$31 **AAA Inspector Notes:** This restaurant with distinctive charm and a comfortable atmosphere offers daily market specials and a wonderful Sunday brunch. **Features:** full bar, Sunday brunch. **Address:** 55 N Main St 82801 **Location:** On US 87, just n of jct SR 331; downtown. **Parking:** street only. L D

JAVA MOON   307-673-5991

Coffee/Tea. Casual Dining. $6-$15 **AAA Inspector Notes:** Although popular for its many coffee choices, the restaurant also offers delicious sandwiches and pastries. **Features:** patio dining. **Address:** 170 N Main St 82801 **Location:** Center. **Parking:** street only.

B L

MIDTOWN CAFE   307-674-0800

Sandwiches Coffee/Tea. Quick Serve. $5-$10 **AAA Inspector Notes:** An espresso machine, freshly-prepared panini and flavorful soups are the highlights of this café. Friendly and attentive staff make for an enjoyable meal. Be sure to try their signature banana pastry! **Address:** 137 N Main St 82801 **Location:** Center. **Parking:** street only. B L CALL

SUGARLAND MINING COMPANY   307-672-8931

American
Casual Dining
$12-$28

AAA Inspector Notes: Tucked in a quiet area of the hotel, this intimate restaurant displays metal wall art depicting a mine and rail in addition to historical pictures of the city. Varied menu offerings include mahi mahi, lobster and steaks as well as such comfort foods as fried chicken. **Features:** full bar. **Address:** 1809 Sugarland Dr 82801 **Location:** I-90 exit 25, 0.3 mi nw; in Holiday Inn Atrium & Convention Center. D CALL

WYOMING'S RIB & CHOPHOUSE   307-673-4700

American. Casual Dining. $7-$32 **AAA Inspector Notes:** Historic. Reservations are a must at this popular and casual chophouse, where the meat falls off the bones of the succulent ribs. Also delicious are the steaks and burgers. Most dinners include an appetizer. **Features:** full bar. **Reservations:** required. **Address:** 847 N Main St 82801 **Location:** Jct 5th St; west end of town. L D

SHOSHONE NATIONAL FOREST (C-2)

Elevations in the forest range from 4,600 ft. at Clarks Fork Canyon to 13,804 ft. at Gannett Peak. Refer to AAA maps for additional elevation information.

In northwestern Wyoming, the Shoshone National Forest was established by presidential proclamation in 1891 as the nation's first forest reserve. It occupies nearly 2.5 million acres. Its boundaries extend south from Montana and include parts of the Beartooth, Absaroka and Wind River mountains. The forest includes the state's highest mountain, Gannett Peak.

Forest watersheds and glacial runoff feed several rivers of the Missouri River Basin and serve as a major water source for many communities and ranches within or near the forest.

Scenic drives include Buffalo Bill Cody Scenic Byway (US 14/16/20) through the North Fork of the Shoshone River canyon en route to the east entrance of Yellowstone National Park *(see place listing p. 316)*; the Wyoming Centennial Scenic Byway over Togwotee Pass on US 287/26 between Dubois and Moran Junction; the Beartooth Scenic Highway (US 212) over the Beartooth Plateau; and the Chief Joseph Scenic Highway (SR 296) from its junction with SR 120 to the junction of US 212. SRs 296, 291 and 131 also travel past spectacular mountain scenery.

Backcountry hiking, trail riding, fishing and primitive camping are available in the Fitzpatrick Wilderness, which has two of Wyoming's highest peaks and some of the nation's largest glaciers; the Popo Agie Wilderness, dotted by more than 200 lakes; the Absaroka-Beartooth Wilderness, containing many lakes and granite peaks; and the North Absaroka Wilderness, scored by steep canyons. Cross-country skiing also is available.

Information and maps (a fee is charged) can be obtained by writing the Forest Supervisor, 808 Meadow Ln., Cody, WY 82414-4516. Phone (307) 527-6241. *See Recreation Areas Chart.*

SOUTH PASS CITY (D-2) elev. 7,805'

When early travelers traversed South Pass, the gradual incline often left them unaware that they were crossing the Continental Divide. From 1840 to 1860 an estimated 300,000 settlers traveled through the gap.

Gold was discovered at a site about 12 miles north of the pass in 1842, but takings were not impressive at first. In 1867 the Carissa, a hard-rock lode, was found and a boom began. By 1871 South Pass City boasted 2,000 inhabitants and was the seat of Carter County, which encompassed a third of Wyoming.

William H. Bright, a South Pass City saloon keeper and Wyoming senator, introduced a bill granting women the right to vote, hold office and own property. With passage in 1869, Wyoming women became the first in the nation to participate in government, and Wyoming became nicknamed the "Equality State." One town citizen was Esther Hobart Morris, who in 1870 became the city's justice of the peace, the first woman in the country to hold any political office.

Despite its successes, South Pass City was not to escape the usual fate of boom towns: By 1875 the city was nearly deserted. The death of the mines did not, however, mean the end of South Pass City. In the 1950s a new boom came—one that involved not gold but iron ore. While the iron mines are now closed, the gold mines periodically operate, helping the town's economy. Tourism also has enabled the town to capitalize on its rambunctious past.

SOUTH PASS CITY STATE HISTORIC SITE encompasses the entire town; turn off SR 28 at Milepost 43 and follow signs. This ghostly reminder of South Pass City's mining era is being restored. Thirty-one log, frame and stone structures—

including the Carissa Saloon, the South Pass Hotel, a jail, a livery stable, mill and a butcher shop—remain on 200 acres of land. A visitor center has interpretive displays depicting the town's past. Living-history programs also are offered. The site has a historic nature trail.

Time: Allow 2 hours minimum. **Hours:** Buildings open daily 9-6, May 15-Sept. 30. **Cost:** $4; $2 (Wyoming residents); free (ages 0-18). **Phone:** (307) 332-3684. ♿

STORY (B-4) pop. 828, elev. 5,079'

Story took its name from Charles P. Story, an early mayor of nearby Sheridan who was related to Nelson Story, one of the first to drive Texas cattle over the Bozeman Trail into Montana in 1866. His northbound trip was the only significant use of the trail. Because the costs of maintaining the forts along the trail were immense in terms of both money and lives lost, the U.S. government eventually abandoned them and closed the Bozeman Trail.

Nestled at the base of the Bighorn Mountains in thick stands of Ponderosa pine and aspen, Story offers abundant recreational activities. Camping, hiking, fishing, hunting and horseback riding are readily available.

FORT PHIL KEARNY STATE HISTORIC SITE is reached by following signs from I-90 exit 44. The site preserves the remains of Fort Phil Kearny. Of the three forts built along the Bozeman Trail, Fort Phil Kearny suffered the worst. A visitor center houses displays and photographs. Markers identify the sites of the Fetterman interpretive trail and Wagon Box fights.

A self-guiding tour is available. **Time:** Allow 2 hours minimum. **Hours:** Visitor center open daily 8-6, May-Sept.; Wed.-Sun. noon-4, rest of year. Phone ahead to confirm schedule. **Cost:** $4; free (ages 0-17). **Phone:** (307) 684-7629 or (307) 684-7687. *(See ad p. 238.)*

THE STORY FISH HATCHERY is 2 mi. w. to end of SR 194. The hatchery was built 1907-08 and is the oldest operating fish hatchery in the state. The hatchery raises lake, rainbow and brook trout. Besides incubating and hatching fish eggs, the hatchery serves as a holding facility for fish and eggs destined for other stations throughout Wyoming. It includes an indoor hatchery and outdoor raceways and ponds. **Hours:** Daily 8-5. **Cost:** Free. **Phone:** (307) 683-2234.

SUNDANCE (B-6) pop. 1,182, elev. 4,750'

Sundance lies at the foot of Sundance Mountain, so named because the Sioux Native Americans held their councils and religious ceremonies at a place called Wi Wacippi Paha, or Temple of the Sioux. It is believed that Harry Longabaugh, better known as "The Sundance Kid," assumed his nickname in Sundance during his 18-month sentence in the Crook County jail for horse stealing.

Sundance is a convenient departure point for trips to nearby Devils Tower National Monument *(see place listing p. 253)* and Black Hills National Forest *(see place listing p. 235).* An 82-mile circle tour via US 14, SRs 24 and 111 and I-90 circles a portion of the national forest and offers opportunities to see the volcanic core of Devils Tower as well as prong-horns, wild turkeys and white-tailed deer.

Sundance Area Chamber of Commerce: P.O. Box 1004, Sundance, WY 82729. **Phone:** (307) 283-1000.

CROOK COUNTY MUSEUM AND ART GALLERY

is on the lower level of the courthouse at 309 Cleveland St. The gallery contains more than 20,000 items from the Old West, including a re-creation of the original county courtroom. Photographs and legal papers of the Sundance Kid, who was incarcerated in the county jail for 18 months, also are displayed. Works by local artists are exhibited. **Hours:** Mon.-Fri. 8-4 (also Sat. 8-4, June-Aug.). **Cost:** Free. **Phone:** (307) 283-3666.

BEST WESTERN INN AT SUNDANCE   (307)283-2800

Hotel
$124-$167

AAA Benefit: Save 10% or more every day and earn 10% bonus points!

Address: 2719 E Cleveland St 82729 **Location:** I-90 exit 189, just n, then just w; 1.5 mi ne of SR 585. **Facility:** 44 units. 2 stories (no elevator), interior corridors. **Parking:** winter plug-ins. **Pool(s):** heated indoor. **Activities:** hot tub. **Guest Services:** coin laundry.

BEARLODGE MOUNTAIN RESORT   307/283-3235

fyi Not evaluated. **Address:** 1615 E Cleveland St 82729 **Location:** I-90 exit 189, just w. Facilities, services, and décor characterize an economy property.

TEN SLEEP *(B-4)* pop. 260, elev. 4,513'

Because Native Americans who traversed the Big Horn Basin of Wyoming reckoned time and distance in "sleeps," this midway point across the Big Horn Basin became known as Ten Sleep.

Range wars between cattle and sheep ranchers—quite common in the West during the 1890s and early 1900s—reached a climax with the Ten Sleep-Spring Creek Raid in 1909. This attack on the camp of an ex-cattleman who had brought a large herd of sheep into Big Horn Basin resulted in an investigation that eventually led to a peaceful arbitration.

Nearby Ten Sleep Canyon, on the western side of the Bighorn Mountains, is an outstanding feature of Bighorn National Forest *(see place listing p. 235).* Near the mouth of the canyon are a trout hatchery and a fish-rearing station; visitors are welcome at both stations. A scenic section of US 16 runs between Ten Sleep and Buffalo *(see place listing p. 237).*

TETON VILLAGE *(C-1)* pop. 330, elev. 6,329'

- **Restaurants p. 310**
- **Attractions map p. 262**
- **Hotels & Restaurants map & index p. 287**
- **Part of Jackson Hole Including Grand Teton National Park area — see map p. 285**

Situated at the base of Jackson Hole Mountain Resort *(see attraction listing),* Teton Village serves as a hub of activity during ski season. It is the site of many area lodgings and restaurants, and offers visitors the opportunity to browse in an assortment of specialty shops. An aerial tram in the village lifts passengers to the mountaintop, boasting one of North America's steepest and longest vertical drops.

Celebrate the joys of music at the Grand Teton Music Festival, which brings orchestra and chamber concerts in summer and winter months; phone (307) 733-1128 for ticket information.

RECREATIONAL ACTIVITIES

Skiing

- **Jackson Hole Mountain Resort** is 12 mi. w. via SRs 22 and 390. Other activities are offered. **Hours:** Daily 9-4, last Sat. in Nov.-first Sat. in Apr. **Phone:** (307) 733-2292 or (888) 333-7766.

THE ALPENHOF LODGE   (307)733-3242 12

Country Inn
$124-$599

Address: 3255 W Village Dr 83025 **Location:** At the base of Jackson Hole Mountain Resort; Lower Village. **Facility:** 42 units, some two bedrooms. 4 stories (no elevator), interior corridors. **Parking:** winter plug-ins. **Terms:** closed 4/10-5/10 & 10/20-11/25, 10 day cancellation notice, in summer; 30 day in winter-fee imposed, resort fee. **Dining:** Alpenrose, see separate listing. **Pool(s):** heated outdoor. **Activities:** sauna, hot tub, downhill & cross country skiing, snowboarding, picnic facilities, trails, massage. **Guest Services:** valet and coin laundry, area transportation. **Featured Amenity:** breakfast buffet.

FOUR SEASONS RESORT & RESIDENCES JACKSON HOLE   (307)732-5000 11

Resort Hotel
$375-$1600

Address: 7680 Granite Loop Rd 83025 **Location:** At base of Jackson Hole Mountain Resort; Lower Village. **Facility:** A ski concierge is along for every step at this ski-in/ski-out resort, where fine Western decor epitomizes rustic elegance. The luxurious guest rooms feature a gas fireplace. 158 units, some two bedrooms and condominiums. 10 stories, interior corridors. **Parking:** on-site (fee) and valet. **Terms:** closed 4/3-5/4 & 10/30-11/22, check-in 4 pm, 30 day cancellation notice-fee imposed, resort fee. **Amenities:** safes. **Dining:** 3 restaurants, also, Westbank Grill, see separate listing. **Pool(s):** heated outdoor. **Activities:** hot tub, steamroom, downhill & cross country skiing, snowboarding, sledding, recreation programs, game room, lawn sports, trails, spa. **Guest Services:** valet laundry, boarding pass kiosk, area transportation.

(See map & index p. 287.)

HOTEL TERRA JACKSON HOLE (307)739-4000 **15**

Boutique Hotel
$149-$3500

Address: 3335 W Village Dr 83025 **Location:** At base of Jackson Hole Mountain Resort; Mid Village. **Facility:** "Upscale" and "eco luxury" best describe this full-service, ski-in/walk-out condominium hotel featuring bamboo furnishings and luxurious 100 percent organic cotton sheets. 132 units, some condominiums. 5 stories, interior corridors. **Parking:** on-site (fee) and valet. **Terms:** check-in 4 pm, 30 day cancellation notice-fee imposed, resort fee. **Amenities:** safes. **Dining:** IL Villaggio Osteria, see separate listing. **Pool(s):** heated outdoor. **Activities:** hot tub, steamroom, downhill skiing, snowboarding, bicycles, trails, exercise room, spa. **Guest Services:** complimentary and valet laundry, area transportation.

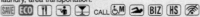

SNAKE RIVER LODGE & SPA 307/732-6000 **13**

Resort Hotel
Rates not provided

Address: 7710 Granite Loop Rd 83025 **Location:** At base of Jackson Hole Mountain Resort; Lower Village. **Facility:** Set alongside the slopes for easy ski-in access, this resort offers endless recreational activities. A variety of guest rooms and condominiums are available; some rooms have restricted floor space. 149 units, some condominiums. 5 stories, interior corridors. **Parking:** on-site and valet. **Terms:** check-in 4 pm. **Amenities:** safes. **Dining:** Gamefish, see separate listing. **Pool(s):** heated outdoor, heated indoor. **Activities:** sauna, hot tub, steamroom, downhill skiing, snowboarding, bicycles, trails, spa. **Guest Services:** valet and coin laundry, area transportation.

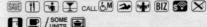

TETON MOUNTAIN LODGE & SPA (307)734-7111 **14**

Resort Hotel
$139-$3200

Address: 3385 W Cody Ln 83025 **Location:** At base of Jackson Hole Mountain Resort; Upper Village. **Facility:** Nestled among the majestic Tetons, this resort features an upscale lobby with the coziest of seating arrangements and mesmerizing appointments and artwork. 145 units, some condominiums. 5 stories, interior corridors. **Parking:** on-site (fee) and valet. **Terms:** check-in 4 pm, 30 day cancellation notice-fee imposed, resort fee. **Amenities:** safes. **Dining:** Spur Restaurant & Bar, see separate listing. **Pool(s):** heated outdoor, heated indoor. **Activities:** hot tub, steamroom, downhill skiing, snowboarding, trails, exercise room, spa. **Guest Services:** valet and coin laundry.

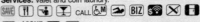

ALPENROSE 307/733-3242 **14**

Regional Swiss Fine Dining
$21-$34

AAA Inspector Notes: The atmosphere here is European and includes game dishes. A professional staff assists diners with the extensive wine list that features finer California and European varieties as well as a nice selection of after-dinner drinks. Dessert favorites include warm apple strudel and chocolate fondue served with fresh fruit. There is a parking fee in the winter. **Features:** full bar. **Reservations:** suggested. **Address:** 3255 W Village Dr 83025 **Location:** At the base of Jackson Hole Mountain Resort; Lower Village; in The Alpenhof Lodge. [D]

GAMEFISH 307/732-6040 **16**

Regional American. Fine Dining. $9-$47 **AAA Inspector Notes:** Windows on three walls afford views of the mountains in the upscale dining room, where guests savor expertly prepared game, meats and seafood. Creativity marks the desserts. **Features:** full bar, patio dining. **Reservations:** required. **Address:** 7710 Granite Loop Rd 83025 **Location:** At base of Jackson Hole Mountain Resort; Lower Village; in Snake River Lodge & Spa. **Parking:** on-site (fee) and valet. [B] [L] [D]

IL VILLAGGIO OSTERIA 307/739-4100 **18**

Italian. Fine Dining. $11-$49 **AAA Inspector Notes:** At this spot, I find it hard to decide between the home-made pizza with gourmet toppings or the grilled quail stuffed with pears, pine nuts and panettone. No matter what is on the plate, diners can enjoy great wines and beautiful scenery. Al fresco dining is available in season. Lunch is served only during the ski season. **Features:** full bar. **Address:** 3335 W Village Dr 83025 **Location:** At base of Jackson Hole Mountain Resort; Mid Village; in Hotel Terra Jackson Hole. **Parking:** on-site and valet. [D]

MANGY MOOSE RESTAURANT & SALOON 307/733-4913 **19**

New American. Casual Dining. $9-$39 **AAA Inspector Notes:** You will enjoy watching all of the people and activities buzzing about in Teton Village while eating prime rib, trout or beef stroganoff. The bison filet, buffalo meatloaf and elk top sirloin are popular too. The two-level dining room is covered with nostalgic antiques. Lunch and dinner are also served in the laid-back saloon. **Features:** full bar, patio dining. **Address:** 1 McCollister Dr 83025 **Location:** Center of village. [L] [D]

SPUR RESTAURANT & BAR 307/734-7111 **17**

Regional American. Fine Dining. $14-$35 **AAA Inspector Notes:** This classic lodge-inspired restaurant specializes in seasonal creations, many grilled over an open fire. Among examples are roast leg of Colorado lamb, porcini-dusted salmon and kale and goat cheese polenta cakes. For the forager, some sugar snaps and heirloom carrots or shrimp and grits are good choices. The dark chocolate pudding with peanut butter bark and lemon olive oil cake are a few of the dessert favorites. **Features:** full bar. **Address:** 3385 Cody Ln 83025 **Location:** Upper Village; in Teton Mountain Lodge & Spa. [B] [L] [D]

TETON THAI 307/733-0022 **15**

Thai. Casual Dining. $14-$20 **AAA Inspector Notes:** This family-run spot serves authentic Thai cuisine in a full-service setting. Space and seating is very limited. This restaurant has a sister location in Driggs, Idaho. **Features:** full bar, patio dining. **Address:** 7342 N Granite Loop Rd 83025 **Location:** Center; west of ranch lot. [L] [D]

Request roadside assistance in a click —

online or using the AAA or CAA apps

(See map & index p. 287.)

WESTBANK GRILL
307/732-5000 [13]

Regional
American
Fine Dining
$18-$36

AAA Inspector Notes: After a day skiing or white-water rafting, guests can savor a creatively presented, regionally influenced meal made all the more enjoyable by warmth from a massive stone fireplace. The grand dining room continues the resort's elegant rustic theme featuring floor-to-ceiling windows which offer panoramic views of the slopes and the mountains. **Features:** full bar. **Reservations:** suggested. **Address:** 7680 Granite Loop Rd 83025 **Location:** At base of Jackson Hole Mountain Resort; Lower Village; in Four Seasons Resort & Residences Jackson Hole. **Parking:** on-site (fee) and valet.

[] B [] D CALL []M

THERMOPOLIS (C-3) pop. 3,009, elev. 4,326'

• Restaurants p. 312

A treaty between the Shoshone and Arapaho nations and the United States specified that the waters of the hot mineral springs at Thermopolis would be available to everyone free of charge. The agreement continues to be honored at the State Bath House in Hot Springs State Park. Petroglyphs, 30 miles northwest of Thermopolis and about 8 miles off SR 120, are etched on a south-facing cliff at Legend Rock State Petroglyph Site.

Thermopolis is a favorite destination for hunters in search of pronghorn antelopes, game birds, elk and deer. South of Thermopolis on US 20 is Boysen Reservoir, with developed recreational facilities at Boysen State Park *(see Recreation Areas Chart).*

Thermopolis provides access to two scenic highways—US 20 along Wind River Canyon and SR 120 traveling north to Cody.

Thermopolis-Hot Springs Chamber of Commerce: 220 Park St., P.O. Box 768, Thermopolis, WY 82443. **Phone:** (307) 864-3192.

HOT SPRINGS COUNTY MUSEUM AND CULTURAL CENTER is at 700 Broadway. The museum complex contains period rooms, a cherry-wood bar said to be visited by the Hole in the Wall gang, Native American artifacts, a restored country school, wildlife and mining exhibits, arts and crafts and geological, agricultural and oil industry displays. **Hours:** Mon.-Sat. 8-5, Memorial Day-Labor Day; Tues.-Sat. 9-4, rest of year. Closed Jan. 1, Thanksgiving and Christmas. **Cost:** $4; $2 (ages 6-12 and 60+); free (military veterans with ID). **Phone:** (307) 864-5183.

HOT SPRINGS STATE PARK is at the n.e. edge of town on US 20 and SR 789. The park contains mineral baths, pools, hot mineral springs, terraces and hot waterfalls, and is home to the state's bison herd. Of particular interest is Bighorn Hot Spring, which releases 3.6 million gallons daily and is one of the largest hot mineral springs in the world. Black Sulphur Springs and White Sulphur Springs are other springs within the park. *See Recreation Areas Chart.* **Hours:** Daily 6 a.m.-10 p.m. **Cost:** Free. **Phone:** (307) 864-3765. [] [] []

WIND RIVER CANYON is 5 mi. s. via US 20. The canyon is a channel carved more than 2,000 feet deep by the rushing waters of the Wind River. Rock was blasted to create US 20, which tunnels through solid granite in three places. At the south end of the canyon is Boysen Dam.

Remarkable rock formations highlight the canyon walls, which are identified in terms of geological era and formation by strategically placed highway signs. One of the canyon's most prominent landmarks is Chimney Rock, about 10 miles south of Thermopolis.

WIND RIVER CANYON WHITEWATER is at 210 US 20S, Suite 5. Scenic float trips as well as whitewater, lunch and fishing trips are offered. **Hours:** Daily 7-5, Memorial Day-Labor Day. **Cost:** Scenic trip $39. Age requirements may vary depending on river conditions. Reservations and a deposit are required. **Phone:** (307) 864-9343 in season, or (888) 246-9343 year-round. [GT]

THE WYOMING DINOSAUR CENTER AND DIG SITES is at 110 Carter Ranch Rd. on the e. side of town. The 16,000-square-foot complex houses interpretive displays, dioramas and more than 30 full-size skeletons. Visitors may view the preparation lab, where bones are prepared for display, and take a 1-hour tour of the paleontological dig site.

Hours: Daily 8-6, May-Sept.; 10-5, rest of year. **Cost:** Museum $10; $5.50 (ages 4-12, ages 60+ and military veterans with ID). Dig site $12.50; $8.75 (ages 4-13, ages 65+ and military veterans with ID). Combination museum and dig site $18.50; $11.75 (ages 4-13, ages 60+ and military veterans with ID). **Phone:** (307) 864-2997. [GT]

BEST WESTERN PLUS THE PLAZA HOTEL
(307)864-2939

Historic Hotel
$127-$167

Best Western PLUS

AAA Benefit:
Save 10% or more every day and earn 10% bonus points!

Address: 116 E Park St 82443 **Location:** In Hot Springs State Park. **Facility:** There is a year round outdoor hot springs spa in the courtyard of this hotel. Guest rooms are beautifully appointed. Some rooms have a fireplace. 36 units. 2 stories (no elevator), interior corridors. **Parking:** winter plug-ins. **Terms:** cancellation fee imposed. **Pool(s):** heated outdoor. **Activities:** hot tub. **Featured Amenity:** full hot breakfast.

[SAVE] [][+] [] [BIZ] [] [] []
/SOME UNITS [HS] [] []

DAYS INN HOT SPRINGS CONVENTION CENTER
(307)864-3131

[][] Hotel $77-$159 **Address:** 115 E Park St 82443 **Location:** In Hot Springs State Park. **Facility:** 80 units. 2 stories (no elevator), interior/exterior corridors. **Parking:** winter plug-ins. **Terms:** cancellation fee imposed. **Dining:** The Safari Club Restaurant & Lounge, see separate listing. **Pool(s):** heated outdoor. **Activities:** sauna, hot tub, game room, exercise room, massage. **Guest Services:** coin laundry.

[] [] [] [BIZ] [] [] [] /SOME UNITS [S][] []

WHERE TO EAT

FRONT PORCH BISTRO   307/864-3494
▼▼▼ ▼▼▼ American. Casual Dining. $8-$15 **AAA Inspector Notes:** Gourmet sandwiches and hand-formed, made-in-house burgers on buns are just some of the reasons this place is recommended by locals. Travelers truly can enjoy cozy candlelight dinners. **Features:** full bar. **Address:** 536 Arapahoe St 82443 **Location:** Downtown. **Parking:** on-site and street. [L] [D] CALL [&M]

THE SAFARI CLUB RESTAURANT & LOUNGE   307/864-3131
▼▼▼ ▼▼▼ American. Casual Dining. $10-$30 **AAA Inspector Notes:** Hundreds of types of mounted fish, birds and animals decorate the restaurant and lounge, where house specials such as prime rib and pork chops are served in a fun, lively atmosphere. **Features:** full bar, patio dining, happy hour. **Address:** 115 E Park St 82443 **Location:** In Hot Springs State Park; in Days Inn Hot Springs Convention Center. [D]

STONES THROW RESTAURANT & BAR   307/864-9464
▼▼▼ ▼▼▼ American. Casual Dining. $9-$32 **AAA Inspector Notes:** A fireplace and large windows with spectacular views of the golf course are offered at this restaurant where diners can enjoy a flavorful steak or the house favorite Jagerschnitzel pork platter. **Features:** full bar. **Reservations:** suggested, Fri & Sat. **Address:** 143 Airport Rd 82443 **Location:** US 20, just w on Park St, just n on 7th St to airport Rd, then 1 mi on golf course grounds. [D]

THUNDER BASIN NATIONAL GRASSLAND (C-5)

Thunder Basin National Grassland is in Campbell, Converse, Crook, Niobrara and Weston counties. Covering 1,800,339 acres, the national grassland was once a dust bowl. Settlers from the East, familiar only with the homesteading methods for a humid climate, met with disaster when they tried to establish farms in Wyoming's semiarid plains. Poor soil and recurrent droughts foiled attempts to cultivate the land, which soon deteriorated into dust bowls.

The grassland serves as an example of the regenerative use of land deemed unsuitable for cultivation. Sheep and cattle graze on the grassland's vast acreage, which also supports one of the world's largest herds of pronghorns. The Bozeman and Texas trails traverse a portion of the grassland.

The grassland lies within the Powder River Basin and contains a wealth of natural resources for energy development, including oil, gas and coal. The Black Thunder Mine, 9 miles from SR 59 on east SR 450, is one of the largest coal mines in the country. It operates on the grassland under a special state permit with forest service consent and produces more than 30 million tons of coal per year. For further information phone (307) 358-4690.

TORRINGTON (D-6) pop. 6,501, elev. 4,098'

Traversed by the Oregon, Mormon and California trails and the Overland Stage, Pony Express and overland telegraph lines, Torrington served as a Western gateway for pioneers. Named after settler William Curtis' hometown in Connecticut, Torrington is primarily a livestock exchange center, with cattle raising and agriculture as its main economic contributors.

Goshen County Chamber of Commerce: 2042 Main St., Torrington, WY 82240. **Phone:** (307) 532-3879.

HOMESTEADERS MUSEUM is s. on US 85 at 495 Main St. The museum is in the former Union Pacific depot and contains artifacts that depict the homestead period, which occurred from 1882-1929. **Hours:** Mon.-Wed. 9:30-4, Thurs.-Fri. 9:30-5, Sat. noon-4, June-Aug.; Mon.-Fri. 9:30-4, rest of year. **Cost:** Donations. **Phone:** (307) 532-5612.

AMERICAS BEST VALUE INN   307/532-7118
◆ **Motel.** Rates not provided. **Address:** 1548 S Main St 82240 **Location:** Just s of jct US 26 (W Valley Rd) and 85 (Main St). **Facility:** 57 units. 2 stories (no elevator), interior corridors. **Pool(s):** heated indoor. **Activities:** hot tub. **Guest Services:** coin laundry.
[⫙] [⇌] [📶] [🛏] [▢] [▭] / SOME UNITS [🐾]

HOLIDAY INN EXPRESS & SUITES   307/532-7600
▼▼▼ ▼ **Hotel.** Rates not provided. **Address:** 1700 E Valley Rd 82240 **Location:** On US 26 (E Valley Rd), 0.4 mi e of US 85 (Main St). Across from train tracks. **Facility:** 67 units. 2 stories, interior corridors. **Parking:** winter plug-ins. **Pool(s):** heated indoor. **Activities:** hot tub, exercise room. **Guest Services:** coin laundry.
[✈] [⫙] CALL [&M] [⇌] [BIZ] [HS] [📶] [✕] [🛏] [▢] [▭] / SOME UNITS [🐾]

UCROSS

THE RANCH AT UCROSS   307/737-2281
▼▼▼▼ ▼ **Ranch.** Rates not provided. **Address:** 2673 US Hwy 14 E 82835 **Location:** Jct US 14/16, 0.5 mi w. Located in a rural area. **Facility:** Big Horn Mountain scenery and a manicured lawn dotted with cottonwood trees create an appealing setting at this ranch, which offers annex rooms in a historic house and four cabins. 31 units, some cabins. 1-2 stories (no elevator), interior/exterior corridors. **Pool(s):** heated outdoor. **Activities:** fishing, tennis, game room, limited exercise equipment.
[⫙] [🍴] [⇌] [BIZ] [📶] [✕] [📺] / SOME UNITS [🐾]

WAPITI (B-2) elev. 5,641'

- Hotels & Restaurants map & index p. 324
- Part of Yellowstone National Park area — see map p. 316

The Wapiti Valley was popularized by William F. "Buffalo Bill" Cody. He brought guests to the area to enjoy the beauty of the valley and Yellowstone National Park. Wapiti Valley provides a scenic byway into or out of Yellowstone National Park (see place listing p. 316). Among wildlife inhabiting the valley are elk, deer, buffalo, moose, bighorn sheep, bears, coyotes, bald and golden eagles, and even mountain lions.

Characterized by historic resorts, the valley also offers abundant recreational activities, including hiking, horseback riding, fishing, windsurfing, snowmobiling and skiing.

(See map & index p. 324.)

BILL CODY RANCH   307/587-2097 71

▼▼▼ Cabin. Rates not provided. Address: 2604 N Fork Hwy 82414 Location: US 14, 25 mi from eastern entrance to Yellowstone National Park. Facility: 17 cabins, some three bedrooms and kitchens. 1 story, exterior corridors. Activities: fishing, game room, trails.

⊟ ▣ ⊞ ⊠ ⊞ ⊞ ⊞ ⊟ ⊟
/ SOME UNITS ⊟

WHEATLAND (D-6) pop. 3,627, elev. 4,738'

Attracted by the cheap land and irrigation water that were made available by the Carey Act of 1894, settlers streamed into Platte County and transformed its dry landscape into productive farmland, dotted with such aptly named towns as Wheatland.

Wheat continues to be the region's principal crop, sustained in part by the Wheatland Irrigation Project, one of the largest privately owned enterprises of its type in the country. Wheatland also is the home of a white marble quarrying business and Laramie River Power Station, which supplies electric power to Wyoming and six neighboring states.

Recreational opportunities include camping and winter sports in nearby Medicine Bow National Forest (see place listing p. 297). Grayrocks Reservoir, 16 miles northeast, is stocked with game fish and offers boating.

Platte County Chamber of Commerce: 65 16th St., Wheatland, WY 82201. Phone: (307) 322-2322.

LARAMIE PEAK MUSEUM is 2 mi. n. on 16th St. from exit 78 off I-25. The museum displays items relating to the early settlers of Platte County, the Oregon Trail and the cattle baron era. Some artifacts date from the late 1800s. Time: Allow 30 minutes minimum. Hours: Mon.-Fri. 10-5, Sat. 10-3, mid-May to mid-Sept.; by appointment rest of year. Closed major holidays. Cost: Donations. Phone: (307) 322-3765.

BEST WESTERN TORCHLITE MOTOR INN
                                       (307)322-4070

Motel
$120-$150

AAA Benefit:
Save 10% or more every day and earn 10% bonus points!

Address: 1809 N 16th St 82201 Location: I-25 exit 80, just e, then 0.6 mi s. Facility: 50 units. 2 stories (no elevator), exterior corridors. Parking: winter plug-ins. Terms: check-in 4 pm. Pool(s): heated outdoor. Activities: hot tub, picnic facilities. Featured Amenity: full hot breakfast.

SAVE ⊟ ⊟ ⊟ BIZ HS ⊞ ⊟
⊟ ⊟ / SOME UNITS S⊟

SUPER 8   (307)322-2224

▼▼ Hotel $75-$120 Address: 2401 16th St 82201 Location: I-25 exit 80, just e, then just s. Facility: 58 units. 2 stories (no elevator), interior corridors. Pool(s): heated indoor. Activities: hot tub, picnic facilities. Guest Services: coin laundry.

⊟ BIZ HS ⊞ ⊠ ⊟ ⊟ ⊟

WILSON (C-1) pop. 1,482, elev. 6,152'
• Hotels & Restaurants map & index p. 287
• Part of Jackson Hole Including Grand Teton National Park area — see map p. 285

BAR J CHUCKWAGON SUPPER & WESTERN MUSIC SHOW, 1 mi. e. on SR 390 to 4200 W. Bar J Chuckwagon Rd., offers a chuck wagon supper and a live Western-style stage show. The Bar J Wranglers entertain guests with songs, stories and biscuit-baking and steak-grilling demonstrations. Time: Allow 4 hours minimum. Hours: Daily 5:30-10, Memorial Day-last Sat. in Sept. Cost: (Includes dinner and show) $24-$34; $12 (ages 4-12). Reservations are recommended. Phone: (307) 733-3370. ⊟

BENTWOOD INN BED & BREAKFAST   (307)739-1411 8

▼▼▼ Bed & Breakfast $259-$399 Address: 4250 Raven Haven Rd 83014 Location: 0.5 mi n of jct SR 22 (Teton Pass) and SR 390 (Moose Wilson Rd), just w. Facility: A short drive from Jackson, this beautiful log structure features a three-story river-rock fireplace offering a nice place to congregate in the living room. Guest rooms are tastefully decorated. 5 units. 2 stories (no elevator), interior corridors. Parking: winter plug-ins. Terms: check-in 4 pm, 2 night minimum stay - seasonal, 31 day cancellation notice-fee imposed. Activities: bicycles, trails.

⊟ CALL ⊞ ⊞ ⊠ ⊠ ⊟

WHERE TO EAT

PEARL STREET BAGELS WILSON   307/739-1261 10

▼ Coffee/Tea Sandwiches. Quick Serve. $5-$8 AAA Inspector Notes: A crusty outside and chewy inside are the hallmarks of these New York-style boiled and baked bagels. Other offerings at this little eatery include homemade chicken and tuna salad, cream cheese-lox spread and freshly roasted coffee. Daily soups made in house are not to be missed. Address: 1230 Ida Ln 83014 Location: 5.5 mi w from US 26/89/191 (Broadway Ave). B L

Q ROADHOUSE & BREWING CO   307/739-0700 8

▼▼ Barbecue. Casual Dining. $13-$29 AAA Inspector Notes: This restaurant hones its focus on an eclectic menu ranging from lamb sliders to a hummus platter and wonderful, fragrant smoked meats. Buckets of peanuts on the table complete the roadhouse experience. Features: full bar, happy hour. Reservations: suggested. Address: 2550 Moose Wilson Rd 83014 Location: Jct SR 22 and 390 (Moose Wilson Rd), 1 mi ne. D

STREET FOOD AT THE STAGECOACH   307/200-6633 9

▼ Mexican. Quick Serve. $8-$14 AAA Inspector Notes: This cantina serves habit-forming food including a Wagyu steak sandwich and chicken satay with coconut sauce. Tacos and quesadillas consist of marinated mahi mahi with cilantro, shredded chicken with chipotle or roasted pork with pineapple. It does not matter what you order—you will be back for more. A children's menu is available. Features: full bar, patio dining. Address: 5755 W SR 22 83014 Location: 0.3 mi w on SR 22; at the base of Teton Pass. L D CALL ⊞

WIND RIVER INDIAN RESERVATION (C-2)

Wind River Indian Reservation spans 2.2 million acres in western Wyoming; the tribal information office is at 15 North Fork Rd. in Fort Washakie. Of different linguistic stock and cultural background, the Shoshone and Arapaho tribes occupy different sections of the reservation. The graves of Chief Washakie and of Sacajawea, as well as the Shoshone Cultural Center, which offers displays and tours, are in Fort Washakie. Arapaho artifacts are displayed in the Arapaho Cultural Museum in Ethete.

Sun Dances are performed near Fort Washakie and Ethete for 3 days in July and August. Photography is prohibited. Powwows and rodeos are held throughout the summer. Christmas dances are performed Christmas Eve through Jan. 1.

The information office is open Mon.-Fri. 8-4:45. Phone (307) 332-3040.

WORLAND (B-3) pop. 5,487, elev. 4,061'

Worland is in a rich farming and stock-feeding area in the center of Wyoming's Big Horn Basin. Sugar beets, beans, malt barley and hay are harvested on irrigated lands; local industries produce aluminum cans, soft drinks, beet sugar and cat litter.

On the grounds of the county courthouse is a 260-year-old Douglas fir that has been carved into a monument honoring Native Americans, part of sculptor Peter Toth's "Trail of the Whispering Giants." Among the city's nine parks is Pioneer Square, which has statues honoring the area's early settlers. A nearby drinking fountain offers artesian mineral water from the Bighorn Mountains.

The Bighorn Mountains are popular with campers, hikers, hunters, skiers and snowmobilers. Passing through the city is Bighorn River, offering abundant fishing opportunities.

Vestiges of a far earlier time are the Gooseberry Formations and Painted Desert west on SR 431. In this area of dramatically eroded formations were found the remains of eohippus (dawn horse), the earliest known equine. Wild horses still can be viewed north of town.

Worland-Ten Sleep Chamber of Commerce: 120 N. 10th St., Worland, WY 82401. **Phone:** (307) 347-3226. *(See ad p. 322.)*

SAVE **WASHAKIE MUSEUM & CULTURAL CENTER** is at 2200 Big Horn Ave.; a 25-foot-tall bronze mammoth greets visitors at the entrance. Fossils, mammoth bones and rock art are on display in The Ancient Basin, an exhibit that explores the archeology, geology and paleontology of the Big Horn Basin. The Last West exhibit chronicles area history, highlighting events like the Johnson County War, the Spring Creek Raid and the harsh winter of 1886-87.

Visitors can watch movies about cattle barons and global climate change, hear stories about the Old West and the railroad era, and use a touch screen to design their own cattle brand. Changing exhibits, special events and educational programs are offered throughout the year.

Time: Allow 1 hour minimum. **Hours:** Mon.-Fri. 9-5:30, Sat. 9-5, Sun. noon-4, mid-May to mid-Sept.; Tues.-Sat. 9-4, rest of year. Closed Jan. 1, Presidents Day, Easter, Thanksgiving and Christmas. **Cost:** $8; $7 (ages 62+); $6 (ages 7-12). **Phone:** (307) 347-4102.

COMFORT INN OF WORLAND   (307)347-9898

▽▽ Hotel $95-$165 **Address:** 100 N Road 11 82401 **Location:** On US 16, 1.4 mi e. **Facility:** 50 units. 2 stories (no elevator), interior corridors. **Parking:** winter plug-ins. **Pool(s):** heated indoor. **Activities:** hot tub. **Guest Services:** coin laundry.

🍴➕ 🏊 BIZ 🛜 ✖ 🔌 📷 💻

DAYS INN   (307)347-4251

▽▽ Motel $94-$111 **Address:** 500 N 10th St 82401 **Location:** 0.5 mi n on US 20. **Facility:** 42 units. 1 story, exterior corridors. **Parking:** winter plug-ins. **Activities:** limited exercise equipment. **Guest Services:** coin laundry.

🍴➕ BIZ 🛜 ✖ 🔌 📷 💻

WRIGHT (C-5) pop. 1,807, elev. 5,121'

WRIGHT MUSEUM is at 104 Ranch Ct. Windmills, World War I artifacts, heavy mining equipment, wood-working implements and antique dishes are on display; there also are exhibits about oil drilling and coal mining. **Time:** Allow 30 minutes minimum. **Hours:** Mon.-Fri. 10-5, Sat. 10-2, mid-May to early Oct. **Cost:** Free. **Phone:** (307) 464-1222.

WRIGHT HOTEL   (307)464-6060

▽▽▽ Hotel $129-$139 **Address:** 300 Reata Dr 82732 **Location:** Just w of jct SR 59 and 387. **Facility:** 71 units. 3 stories, interior corridors. **Parking:** winter plug-ins. **Terms:** 3 day cancellation notice. **Amenities:** safes. **Dining:** Open Range Steak House, see separate listing. **Guest Services:** coin laundry.

🍴 CALL 📵 HS 🛜 ✖ 🔌 📷 💻 /SOME UNITS 🔒

WHERE TO EAT

OPEN RANGE STEAK HOUSE   307/464-6161

▽▽ Steak. Casual Dining. $9-$30 **AAA Inspector Notes:** Although Durham Ranch buffalo and certified Angus beef stand out on the menu of this popular steakhouse, diners also can order seafood, pasta, burgers and sandwiches. **Features:** full bar, patio dining. **Address:** 350 Reata Dr 82732 **Location:** Just w of jct SR 59 and 387; in Wright Hotel. L D CALL 📵

YELLOWSTONE NATIONAL PARK (B-1)

- Hotels p. 329 • Restaurants p. 329
- Attractions map p. 319
- Hotels & Restaurants map & index p. 324

Elevations in the park range from 5,314 ft. at the north entrance in Gardiner, Mont., to 11,358 ft. at Eagle Peak in the southeastern side of the park. Refer to AAA maps for additional elevation information.

Yellowstone National Park has five entrances: Gardiner, Mont. (north); West Yellowstone, Mont. (west); Jackson Hole via Grand Teton National Park (about 60 miles south); Cody (about 53 miles east); and Cooke City, Mont. (northeast).

The first national park, Yellowstone was established by an act of Congress in 1872. The region took its name from the dramatic gold-hued cliffs lining the river canyon, known by the Minnetaree Native Americans as *mi tse a-da-zi* (Yellow Rock River).

Though its mountain forests and meadows are beautiful in their own right, Yellowstone is unique for its geysers, hot springs, mud pools and fumaroles—the largest concentration of geothermal features in the world. The park sits atop one of the largest active volcanoes on earth, a "hot spot" that last erupted some 640,000 years ago, carving out a caldera 30 miles wide and 45 miles long. Heated by this vast subterranean magma chamber, the Yellowstone valley continues to steam and vent.

Fountains of scalding water burst high into the air from some geysers, while others bubble and spit in murky depths. Hot springs gleam in shades of emerald green and blue. Algae and bacteria withstand boiling temperatures to create these vivid colors; vigorous steam vents emit uncanny sounds and smells.

Miles of boardwalks, paved trails and driving loops allow visitors to come within close proximity of these active volcanic formations. Despite their cool

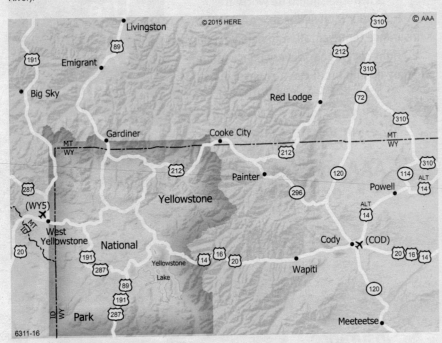

This map shows cities in Yellowstone National Park where you will find attractions, hotels and restaurants. Cities are listed alphabetically in this book on the following pages.

(See map & index p. 324.)

colors, mineral springs are boiling hot, and the solid-looking crusts around geyser formations can be remarkably fragile—keep a close watch over children while in these areas, and be sure to stay on boardwalks or formal paths.

In addition to its geologic wonders, Yellowstone National Park is also one of the most successful wildlife sanctuaries in the world. Grizzly and black bears can be sighted occasionally in the backcountry and sometimes from park roadways (a traffic situation known as "bear jam"). The park also has several thousand elk; many mule deer, pronghorn antelopes and moose; bands of bighorn sheep; and about 4,600 bison. Gray wolves were reintroduced to Yellowstone 1995-97, and several packs now roam the park and surrounding areas; the wolf population is estimated to be between 400 and 450.

General Information

Most park roads are open to automobile travel from May through October (weather permitting). The 60-mile road between the north entrance at Gardiner, Mont., and the northeast entrance at Cooke City, Mont., is open all year. During the off-season this road is accessible only from the north entrance near Gardiner, Mont.; the northeast entrance via Red Lodge, Mont., is usually open from Memorial Day weekend through September 30. The east entrance from Cody usually opens in mid-May and remains open as weather permits.

The approach to Cooke City, Mont., from Red Lodge, Mont., via the Beartooth Scenic Highway (US 212) negotiates Beartooth Pass at an elevation of almost 11,000 feet. From Cody the approach to Sylvan Pass follows US 14/16/20 through the carved red walls of Wapiti Valley.

The road between Canyon and Tower-Roosevelt runs over Dunraven Pass and along Mount Washburn and passes Tower Fall, where the spectacles of the gorge, the falls on Tower Creek and the palisades of rock high above the Yellowstone River can be viewed.

Although most of the park's 3,472 square miles lie in northwestern Wyoming, they also extend into Montana and Idaho. The central portion of the park is essentially a broad, elevated volcanic plateau that lies between 6,500 and 8,500 feet above sea level. On the south, east, north and northwest are mountain ranges with peaks and ridges rising between 2,000 and 4,000 feet above the enclosed tableland.

Most park facilities are open mid-May to mid-October, but food and lodging facilities are limited after October 1. During the off-season manned gas stations are available only at Gardiner and Cooke City, Mont. Unstaffed, credit card-only gas stations are available at developed locations when the roads are open. Interior park roads are open to guided snowcoach and snowmobile tours from mid-December through the first week in March. During the summer, rental cars are available at Cody and

Jackson as well as at Billings, Bozeman, Livingston and West Yellowstone, Mont.

The roads through the park make many of the most prominent attractions readily accessible. During the summer travel season visitors may encounter slow traffic. Be especially alert for others stopped in the road to watch wildlife; if you must stop, pull well off the highway onto a marked wayside.

Note: According to National Park Service figures, about 80 percent of the park roads are "in a structurally deficient state...including narrow shoulders and rough surfaces." The roads are being gradually repaired under a 20-year program. For up-to-date road information phone (307) 344-2117.

The park headquarters is at Mammoth Hot Springs, 5 miles from the north entrance. The main post office is at Mammoth; ranger stations are at Old Faithful, Grant Village, Tower-Roosevelt, Mammoth Hot Springs, Lake, Madison, Bechler, Canyon and the south entrance. The Mammoth ranger station, open all year, is accessible by car in winter via the north entrance. West Thumb Information Center is located at junction Grand Loop and South Entrance roads.

Park information can be received by tuning radios to 1610 AM. Low-powered transmitters broadcast from entrance stations.

From Memorial Day through Labor Day ranger-naturalists conduct geyser walks, natural- and living-history talks, photographic workshops and children's programs at Bridge Bay, Canyon, Fishing Bridge, Grant Village, Lake, Madison, Mammoth Hot Springs, Norris Geyser Basin, Old Faithful, West Thumb Geyser Basin and West Yellowstone. Free evening programs are given at most park campgrounds during the summer season.

ADMISSION to the park is by private vehicle permit ($30), motorcycle permit ($25) and nonmotorized entry ($15), valid for 7 days; a two-park pass for Grand Teton and Yellowstone by private vehicle ($50), motorcycle ($40) and nonmotorized entry ($20), valid for 7 days. Park Annual Pass ($60) or Interagency Annual Pass ($80 for entrance to most federal sites) also is available. An Interagency Lifetime Senior Pass for U.S. citizens ages 62+ is $10; an Interagency Access Passport for physically impaired U.S. citizens provides free admission.

PETS are permitted in the park only if they are on a leash, crated or otherwise physically restricted at all times. They are not permitted more than 100 feet from the roads and parking areas, and are not permitted on trails, boardwalks, in the backcountry or in hydrothermal areas. It is illegal to leave pets unattended.

ADDRESS inquiries to the Superintendent, Yellowstone National Park, P.O. Box 168, Yellowstone National Park, WY 82190; phone (307) 344-7381. For lodging and guest service information phone (307) 344-7311 or (866) 439-7375.

▼ See AAA listing p. 306 ▼

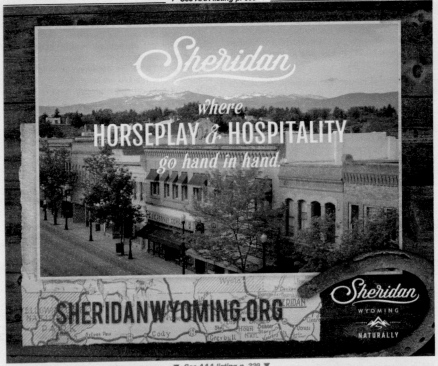
▼ See AAA listing p. 329 ▼

(See map & index p. 324.)

Activities

Not all of Yellowstone's grandeur can be seen from the boardwalks. More than 1,000 miles of backcountry trails lead to many of the park's less accessible attractions. A free backcountry use permit, obtainable from any area ranger station, is required for those who wish to camp in the backcountry. The permit can be obtained in person and no more than 48 hours in advance. Advance backcountry reservations for a limited number of campsites can be obtained by mail or at a backcountry office for a $25 fee.

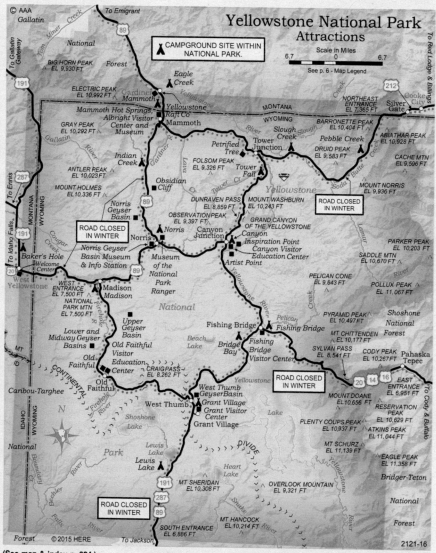

Yellowstone National Park
Attractions

(See map & index p. 324.)

There is no better way to explore the park than on horseback over the trails. Private stock can be ridden, or 1- or 2-hour guided rides are available at Mammoth Hot Springs, Tower-Roosevelt and Canyon from Xanterra Parks & Resorts. Horses cannot be rented without a guide.

Motorboats and rowboats can be rented from Xanterra Parks & Resorts at the Bridge Bay Marina on Yellowstone Lake. Guided fishing trips also are available. A permit is required for all vessels (motorized and nonmotorized, including float tubes) and must be obtained in person. The fee is $10 for motorized vessels and $5 for nonmotorized vessels; the permits are valid for 7 days. Private boats

launched in Yellowstone require an AIS (Aquatic Invasive Species) inspection in addition to a boat permit

Jet skis, airboats, submersibles and similar watercraft are prohibited in Yellowstone National Park. All vessels are prohibited on park rivers and streams except the channel between Lewis and Shoshone lakes, where only hand-propelled vessels are permitted.

Guided snowcoach tours by Xanterra Parks & Resorts to the interior of the park are available mid-December to early March from Mammoth Hot Springs, the south and north entrances to Yellowstone and Old Faithful Snow Lodge. Guided cross-country ski trips also are offered.

(See map & index p. 324.)

Most of the streams and lakes below the timberline contain one or more species of trout. Roadside streams and Yellowstone Lake offer some of the best fishing in the park. Fishing tackle is sold by Delaware North general stores located throughout the park.

Anglers ages 16+ are required to purchase a Yellowstone National Park fishing permit. A 3-day permit costs $18; a 7-day permit is $25. Children under 16 may fish without a permit under the direct supervision of an adult who has a valid park fishing permit, or they may obtain a free permit signed by an adult. For further information phone (307) 344-2107. Fishing regulations and permits can be obtained at any ranger station, visitor center or Yellowstone Park General Stores. Fishing permits also are available at many businesses in the greater Yellowstone area. No state fishing license is required in Yellowstone National Park. The opening of the season varies from the Saturday of Memorial Day weekend to July 15 for different lakes and streams; it closes the first Sunday in November.

Check at visitor centers or ranger stations for season variations and legal limits. *See Recreation Areas Chart.*

Note: It is not only against park regulations but also dangerous to feed, touch or tease any wildlife. Animals in the park are wild and should be viewed only from a safe distance. According to park regulations, you must stay at least 100 yards (the length of a football field) away from bears and wolves and at least 25 yards away from all other animals. The following items (whether new, used, clean, dirty, empty or full) may not be left unattended on picnic tables, in tents or tent trailers, in the back of pickups or in any other outdoor location at any time: food, beverage containers, cooking and eating utensils, stoves and grills, coolers and ice chests, cosmetics and toiletries, pet food and bowls, buckets and washbasins. All trash should be disposed of in bear-proof garbage cans.

ALBRIGHT VISITOR CENTER & MUSEUM is at Mammoth Hot Springs. Housed in one of the original U.S. Cavalry buildings, the headquarters museum focuses on those who shaped the history of Yellowstone, including Native Americans, mountain men, early explorers, the U.S. Army and the National Park Service. An art gallery displays the works of photographer William Henry Jackson and painter and explorer Thomas Moran. Films chronicle Moran's life and the park's development. An orientation area has interactive displays to help with trip planning, and park rangers offer talks and tours.

Hours: Daily 8-7, Memorial Day weekend-Sept. 30; 9-5, rest of year. Closed Thanksgiving and Veterans Day. Phone ahead to confirm schedule. **Cost:** Free. **Phone:** (307) 344-2263. GT

CANYON VISITOR EDUCATION CENTER is at Canyon Village. A room-size relief map illustrates Yellowstone's volcanic activity, and a variety of interactive exhibits describe the formation of geysers, hot springs and other geologic features here and around the world. A giant lava lamp demonstrates how magma rises with heat convection. Murals, dioramas and panoramas show how glaciers and volcanic eruptions have shaped the landscape.

A 20-minute film explores the connection between the park's geological origins and its wildlife. **Hours:** Daily 8-8, Memorial Day weekend-Labor Day; 8-6, day after Labor Day-Sept. 30; 9-5, Oct. 1-12. **Cost:** Free. **Phone:** (307) 344-2550.

FISHING BRIDGE VISITOR CENTER is 1 mi. off the main park road on the east entrance road. The 1931 stone-and-log building houses exhibits about biological life in the park. Mounted specimens include a regional collection of birds, as well as a grizzly sow and cubs and a family of river otters. **Hours:** Daily 8-7, Memorial Day weekend-Sept. 30. **Cost:** Free. **Phone:** (307) 344-2450.

▼ *See AAA listing p. 248* ▼

Ask about on-the-spot vehicle battery testing and replacement

▼ See AAA listing p. 314 ▼

Ask about AAA/CAA Associate membership
to share the benefits you value

(See map & index p. 324.)

GRAND CANYON OF THE YELLOWSTONE is a section along the Yellowstone River between Canyon and Tower-Roosevelt. Noted for its spectacular yellow coloring, the deep river canyon offers striking views of the Yellowstone falls. Among the best vistas are Artist's Point on the south rim and Inspiration Point on the north rim. Lookout Point provides the best view of the Lower Falls. Uncle Tom's Trail descends about halfway and ends at the base of the Lower Falls on the south side. The Upper Falls are visible from several trails and lookouts.

GRANT VISITOR CENTER is on the shore of the West Thumb of Yellowstone Lake. Exhibits depict fire's role in shaping the environment. The film "Ten Years After Fire" recounts the 1988 blaze that scorched 1.2 million acres. **Hours:** Daily 8-7, Memorial Day weekend-Sept. 30. **Cost:** Free. **Phone:** (307) 344-2650.

LOWER AND MIDWAY GEYSER BASINS are n. of the Old Faithful area on the main park road. Covering 12 square miles, this area features clusters of thermal features including the Fountain Paint Pots. These boiling pools of red, yellow and brown mud change with the seasons and the water table. The 3-mile Firehole Lake Drive leads to Great Fountain Geyser, which erupts about twice a day from a beautiful travertine terrace. Excelsior Geyser, one of the largest features in the Midway Basin, discharges thousands of gallons of water per minute into the Firehole River.

MAMMOTH HOT SPRINGS is near the park headquarters at the north entrance. The springs are characterized by terrace-like formations created by limestone deposits. Well-marked trails and boardwalks allow the safe viewing of the formations at close range. **Note:** Visitors must stay on the marked trails and boardwalks at all times, since in many places the thin crust is dangerous.

MUSEUM OF THE NATIONAL PARK RANGER is at the entrance to the Norris Campground. Housed in a 1908 soldier station, this small museum chronicles the role of national park rangers, from early military roots to today's specialized profession. A 25-minute film, "An American Legacy," traces the history of the National Park Service. **Hours:** Daily 9-5, Memorial Day weekend-Sept. 27. **Cost:** Free. **Phone:** (307) 344-7353.

NORRIS GEYSER BASIN is just n. of Norris Junction on the main park road. Boardwalks and trails lead across this barren valley of steam vents and rainbow-colored pools. This is the oldest and hottest geothermal area in the park, with water temperatures above 200 degrees.

Steamboat Geyser, the world's tallest geyser, has reached heights of 300-400 feet but often remains quiet for months or years between major eruptions.

Echinus Geyser was long considered the only predictable geyser at Norris, though its performance has fluctuated in the past decade. **Note:** Due to new seismic activity, some trails in this area may be closed.

NORRIS GEYSER BASIN MUSEUM & INFORMATION STATION is just off the main park road at Norris Junction. Exhibits describe the park's geothermal features, particularly in the active Norris area. **Hours:** Daily 9-6, Memorial Day weekend-Sept. 30. **Cost:** Free. **Phone:** (307) 344-2812.

OLD FAITHFUL is on the main park road between Madison and West Thumb, just beyond the Old Faithful Inn. Though not quite as predictable as its name suggests, this 120-foot waterspout erupts every 80-90 minutes. A paved walkway and benches surround the cone geyser, keeping visitors about 300 feet away from the massive spray. Daily geyser predictions are posted at the Old Faithful Visitor Education Center and the lodge.

OLD FAITHFUL VISITOR EDUCATION CENTER is off the main park road between Madison and West Thumb, just beyond the Old Faithful Inn. Visitors can view Old Faithful through the center's massive front windows. Exhibits describe the park's geyser activity and Yellowstone history. Predictions are posted daily for eruptions throughout the park. **Hours:** Daily 8-8, Memorial Day weekend-Sept. 30; 9-5, Oct. 1-Nov. 1. **Cost:** Free. **Phone:** (307) 344-2751.

UPPER GEYSER BASIN is on the main park road between Madison and West Thumb. The area surrounding Old Faithful Lodge contains the world's largest concentration of geysers, including the star of the show, Old Faithful. Other geysers such as Grand and Riverside are less frequent but equally spectacular. Boardwalks and paved trails allow visitors to walk within safe distance of geysers, fumaroles, hot springs and mud pots across the basin. **Time:** Allow 2 hours minimum.

YELLOWSTONE LAKE is e. and s. of the park road between West Thumb and Fishing Bridge. Covering 132 square miles at 7,733 feet above sea level, this lake is the largest body of water in North America at so high an altitude. It is also home to the continent's largest population of wild cutthroat trout. The mountain lake has 110 miles of shoreline and a maximum depth of more than 400 feet. Boating and fishing are popular summer sports, but because the water stays so cold, swimming is not advised; the lake freezes over completely in winter.

RECREATIONAL ACTIVITIES
Hiking

• **Adventure Yellowstone** picks up at area hotels. Other activities are offered. **Hours:** Trips depart daily. **Phone:** (406) 585-9041.

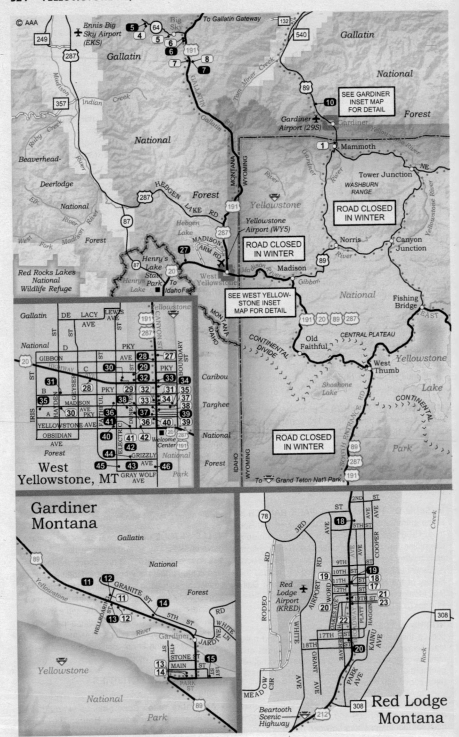

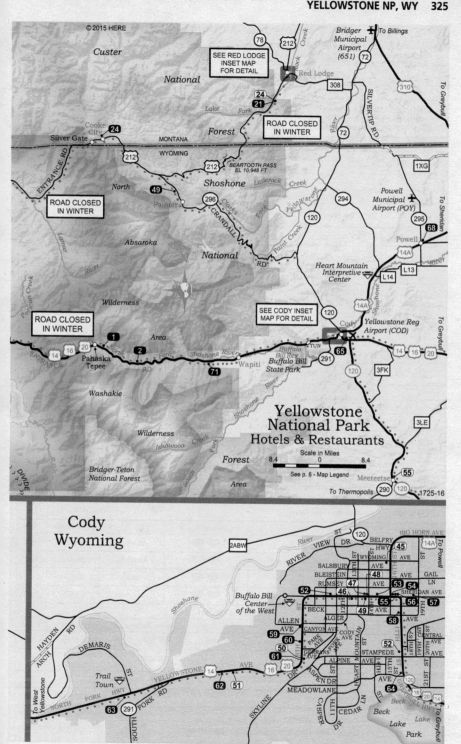

Yellowstone
National Park
Hotels & Restaurants

Scale in Miles

See p. 6 - Map Legend

Cody
Wyoming

Yellowstone National Park

This index helps you "spot" where approved hotels and restaurants are located on the corresponding detailed maps. Hotel daily rate range is for comparison only. Restaurant price range is a combination of lunch and/or dinner. Turn to the listing page for more detailed rate and price information and consult display ads for special promotions.

YELLOWSTONE NATIONAL PARK

Map Page	Hotels	Diamond Rated	Rate Range	Page
1 p. 324	Shoshone Lodge	◆◆	$140-$330	329
2 p. 324	**Elephant Head Lodge** (See ad p. 318.)	◆◆	$150-$350 SAVE	329

Map Page	Restaurant	Diamond Rated	Cuisine	Price Range	Page
① p. 324	Mammoth Hot Springs Hotel Dining Room	◆◆	Regional American	$8-$28	329

BIG SKY, MT

Map Page	Hotels	Diamond Rated	Rate Range	Page
5 p. 324	The Lodge at Big Sky	◆◆◆	Rates not provided	134
6 p. 324	Buck's T-4 Lodge	◆◆	$149-$209	134
7 p. 324	Rainbow Ranch Lodge	◆◆◆	Rates not provided	134

Map Page	Restaurants	Diamond Rated	Cuisine	Price Range	Page
④ p. 324	The Cabin Bar & Grill	◆◆	Regional American	$10-$38	134
⑤ p. 324	Lotus Pad	◆◆	Thai	$14-$24	134
⑥ p. 324	Buck's T-4	◆◆◆	Regional American	$11-$39	134
⑦ p. 324	**The Corral Steakhouse**	◆◆	Steak	$9-$35	134
⑧ p. 324	Rainbow Ranch Lodge	◆◆◆	Regional American	$26-$55	134

GARDINER, MT

Map Page	Hotels	Diamond Rated	Rate Range	Page
10 p. 324	Yellowstone Basin Inn	◆◆	$205-$450	161
11 p. 324	Yellowstone Village Inn	◆◆	Rates not provided	161
12 p. 324	Comfort Inn Yellowstone North	◆◆	$125-$275	161
13 p. 324	**BEST WESTERN By Mammoth Hot Springs**	◆◆◆	$94-$239 SAVE	161
14 p. 324	Yellowstone Super 8-Gardiner	◆◆	$50-$210	161
15 p. 324	**Yellowstone River Motel**	◆	$65-$134 SAVE	161

Map Page	Restaurants	Diamond Rated	Cuisine	Price Range	Page
⑪ p. 324	The Antler Pub & Grill	◆◆	American	$9-$28	161
⑫ p. 324	**Yellowstone Mine Restaurant**	◆◆	American	$9-$22	161
⑬ p. 324	Teddy's Yellowstone Cafe	◆◆	Italian	$8-$16	161
⑭ p. 324	The Raven Grill	◆◆	American	$9-$26	161

RED LODGE, MT

Map Page	Hotels	Diamond Rated	Rate Range	Page
18 p. 324	Comfort Inn of Red Lodge	◆◆	$104-$220	200
19 p. 324	The Pollard	◆◆	Rates not provided	200
20 p. 324	Yodeler Motel	◆	$72-$165	200
21 p. 324	**Rock Creek Resort**	◆◆	$130-$390 SAVE	200

Map Page	Restaurants	Diamond Rated	Cuisine	Price Range	Page
⑰ p. 324	The Dining Room at The Pollard	◆◆◆	Regional American	$10-$36	200

Map Page	Restaurants (cont'd)	Diamond Rated	Cuisine	Price Range	Page
18 p. 324	The Pub at the Pollard	◆◆	American	$7-$20	200
19 p. 324	Bogart's	◆◆	American	$9-$24	200
20 p. 324	Carbon County Steakhouse	◆◆◆	Steak	$12-$36	200
21 p. 324	Bridge Creek Backcountry Kitchen & Wine Bar	◆◆	American	$10-$34	200
22 p. 324	Red Lodge Pizza Co.	◆◆	Pizza	$9-$25	200
23 p. 324	China Garden	◆◆	Chinese	$8-$17	200
24 p. 324	Old Piney Dell	◆◆◆	American	$16-$32	200

COOKE CITY, MT

Map Page	Hotel	Diamond Rated	Rate Range	Page
24 p. 324	Elk Horn Lodge	◆	$120-$140	152

WEST YELLOWSTONE, MT

Map Page	Hotels	Diamond Rated	Rate Range	Page
27 p. 324	Super 8 - West Yellowstone	◆◆	$82-$186 SAVE	209
28 p. 324	BEST WESTERN Weston Inn	◆◆	$149-$319 SAVE	208
29 p. 324	One Horse Motel	◆	$79-$161 SAVE	209
30 p. 324	Evergreen Motel	◆	Rates not provided	208
31 p. 324	Lazy G Motel	◆	$89-$120 SAVE	209
32 p. 324	Crosswinds Inn	◆◆	$85-$234 SAVE	208
33 p. 324	Brandin' Iron Inn	◆◆	Rates not provided SAVE	208
34 p. 324	BEST WESTERN Desert Inn	◆◆	$90-$290 SAVE	208
35 p. 324	Yellowstone West Gate Hotel	◆◆◆	$180-$300	210
36 p. 324	Days Inn West Yellowstone	◆◆	$100-$219 SAVE	208
37 p. 324	Stage Coach Inn	◆◆	$49-$329 SAVE	209
38 p. 324	West Yellowstone City Center Motel	◆	Rates not provided SAVE	210
39 p. 324	Alpine Motel	◆◆	$95-$175 SAVE	208
40 p. 324	Holiday Inn West Yellowstone Conference Hotel	◆◆◆	$119-$319 SAVE	209
41 p. 324	Three Bear Lodge	◆◆	$99-$259 SAVE	209
42 p. 324	Clubhouse Inn	◆◆◆	$129-$299	208
43 p. 324	Yellowstone Park Hotel	◆◆◆	$99-$299 SAVE	210
44 p. 324	Explorer Cabins at Yellowstone	◆◆◆	$109-$479 SAVE	209
45 p. 324	Yellowstone Lodge	◆◆	$89-$269	210
46 p. 324	Gray Wolf Inn and Suites	◆◆	$89-$279 SAVE	209

Map Page	Restaurants	Diamond Rated	Cuisine	Price Range	Page
27 p. 324	Cafe Madriz	◆◆	Spanish Small Plates	$8-$30	210
28 p. 324	Ernie's Bakery, Sandwich Shop & Deli	◆	Breakfast Sandwiches	$7-$14	210
29 p. 324	Euro Cafe	◆◆	Breakfast Sandwiches	$9-$12	210
30 p. 324	Running Bear Pancake House	◆◆	Breakfast Sandwiches	$7-$15	211
31 p. 324	Bullwinkle's Saloon & Eatery	◆◆	American	$9-$29	210
32 p. 324	Pete's Rocky Mountain Pizza & Pasta	◆◆	Pizza Sandwiches	$8-$22	211

Map Page	Restaurants (cont'd)	Diamond Rated	Cuisine	Price Range	Page
(33) p. 324	Beartooth BBQ	◆◆	Barbecue	$8-$15	210
(34) p. 324	Madison Crossing Lounge	◆◆	American	$13-$25	211
(35) p. 324	Red Lotus	◆◆	Chinese	$9-$28	211
(36) p. 324	The Gusher Pizza and Sandwich Shoppe	◆◆	American	$8-$16	210
(37) p. 324	Wild West Pizzeria & Saloon	◆◆	Pizza Sandwiches	$9-$25	211
(38) p. 324	Arrowleaf Ice Cream Parlor & Grill	◆	Burgers	$6-$9	210
(39) p. 324	Canyon Street Grill	◆◆	Burgers Sandwiches	$8-$15	210
(40) p. 324	Serenity Bistro	◆◆	New French	$12-$38	211
(41) p. 324	**Three Bear Restaurant**	◇◇	American	$8-$25	211
(42) p. 324	Timberline Cafe	◆◆	American	$8-$19	211

PAINTER

Map Page	Hotel	Diamond Rated	Rate Range	Page
(49) p. 324	Hunter Peak Ranch	◆	$150-$215	298

CODY

Map Page	Hotels	Diamond Rated	Rate Range	Page
(52) p. 324	**Moose Creek Lodge & Suites** *(See ad p. 252.)*	◇◇	Rates not provided [SAVE]	252
(53) p. 324	**Cody Motor Lodge**	◇	Rates not provided [SAVE]	252
(54) p. 324	Comfort Inn at Buffalo Bill Village Resort	◆◆	$123-$278	252
(55) p. 324	Holiday Inn at Buffalo Bill Village Resort	◆◆◆	Rates not provided	252
(56) p. 324	Buffalo Bill Village	◆	$100-$199	251
(57) p. 324	A Western Rose	◆	Rates not provided	251
(58) p. 324	Buffalo Bill's Antlers Inn	◆	$80-$165	251
(59) p. 324	Sunrise Motor Inn	◆	Rates not provided	252
(60) p. 324	**BEST WESTERN Sunset Motor Inn**	◇◇	$155-$185 [SAVE]	251
(61) p. 324	**BEST WESTERN PREMIER Ivy Inn & Suites**	◇◇◇	$139-$300 [SAVE]	251
(62) p. 324	**AmericInn Lodge & Suites of Cody**	◇◇	$99-$219 [SAVE]	251
(63) p. 324	The Cody	◆◆◆	Rates not provided	251
(64) p. 324	**Rodeway Inn**	◇	$54-$250 [SAVE]	252
(65) p. 324	**Beartooth Inn of Cody**	◇◇	Rates not provided [SAVE]	251

Map Page	Restaurants	Diamond Rated	Cuisine	Price Range	Page
(45) p. 324	Heritage Bakery & Bistro	◆◆	American	$9-$14	253
(46) p. 324	Adriano's Italian Restaurant	◆◆	Italian	$9-$26	253
(47) p. 324	Wyoming's Rib & Chop House	◆◆	American	$8-$32	253
(48) p. 324	La Comida	◆◆	Mexican	$8-$18	253
(49) p. 324	Zapata's	◆◆	Mexican	$9-$18	253
(50) p. 324	**8th Street at the Ivy**	◇◇◇	Western American	$13-$29	253
(51) p. 324	Bubba's Bar-B-Que Restaurant	◆◆	Barbecue	$7-$25	253
(52) p. 324	The Breadboard	◆	Sandwiches	$4-$15	253

POWELL

Map Page	Hotel	Diamond Rated	Rate Range	Page
68 p. 324	**Americas Best Value Inn**	◈◈	$90-$175 SAVE	300

WAPITI

Map Page	Hotel	Diamond Rated	Rate Range	Page
71 p. 324	Bill Cody Ranch	◈◈	Rates not provided	313

MEETEETSE

Map Page	Restaurant	Diamond Rated	Cuisine	Price Range	Page
55 p. 324	Outlaw Steak and Rib House	◈	American	$9-$24	298

ELEPHANT HEAD LODGE 307/587-3980 **2**

◈◈ Historic Cabin $150-$350

Address: 1170 Yellowstone Hwy 82414 **Location:** 11.7 mi e of Yellowstone National Park east gate on US 14/16/20. **Facility:** Cozy wilderness cabins, including three with lofts, are featured at this small mountain lodge. All have decks for watching wildlife and spectacular views. 15 cabins. 1 story, exterior corridors. **Terms:** 30 day cancellation notice-fee imposed. **Activities:** fishing, recreation programs in season, playground, trails. (See ad p. 318.)

SAVE 🍴 🍷 BIZ 📶 ✕ 🎿 🐾 ☎ 🖥

/SOME UNITS 🛏 🔌 🖥

SHOSHONE LODGE 307/587-4044 **1**

◈◈ Cabin $140-$330 **Address:** 349 North Fork Hwy 82190 **Location:** 3.5 mi e of Yellowstone National Park east gate on US 14/16/20. Located in a quiet secluded area. **Facility:** 17 cabins. 1 story, exterior corridors. **Terms:** closed 10/2-5/19, 2 night minimum stay, 30 day cancellation notice-fee imposed. **Activities:** fishing, trails. **Guest Services:** coin laundry.

🍴 🍷 BIZ 📶 ✕ 🎿 ☎ 🔌 🖥

/SOME UNITS 🛏 🐾 🖥

CANYON LODGE 307/344-7311

fyi Not evaluated. **Address:** Canyon Jct 82190 **Location:** Jct Norris Canyon Lp and Grand Loop Rd. Facilities, services, and décor characterize an economy property.

LAKE LODGE & CABINS 307/344-7311

fyi Not evaluated. **Address:** 1 Grand Loop Rd 82190 **Location:** 1.5 mi s of Lake Jct. Facilities, services, and décor characterize an economy property.

LAKE YELLOWSTONE HOTEL & CABINS 307/344-7311

fyi Not evaluated. **Address:** 1 Grand Loop Rd 82190 **Location:** 1 mi s of Lake Jct. Facilities, services, and décor characterize an economy property.

MAMMOTH HOT SPRINGS HOTEL & CABINS 307/344-7311

fyi Not evaluated. **Address:** Mammoth Hot Springs 82190 **Location:** Jct Hwy 89 and Hwy 212. Facilities, services, and décor characterize an economy property.

OLD FAITHFUL INN 307/344-7311

fyi Not evaluated. **Address:** West Thumb & Madison 82190 **Location:** Opposite Old Faithful Geyser; between West Thumb and Madison. Facilities, services, and décor characterize an economy property. This property is accessible from West Yellowstone, Flagg Ranch and Mammoth Hot Springs.

WHERE TO EAT

MAMMOTH HOT SPRINGS HOTEL DINING ROOM 307/344-7901 **1**

◈◈ Regional American. Casual Dining. $8-$28 **AAA Inspector Notes:** The large dining room accommodates the many summer visitors that frequent this area for fresh regional seafood and meats. Efficient, friendly staff members deliver well-prepared meals off of a varied menu. For those visiting in spring and fall, phone for exact hours. **Features:** full bar. **Address:** Mammoth Hot Springs 82190 **Location:** In Mammoth Hot Springs Hotel & Cabins.

ECO B L D CALL 🅖🅜

Take Your Imagination to New Destinations

Use AAA Travel Guides online to explore the possibilities.

Go to AAA.com/travelguide today.

Offices

Main office listings are shown in **BOLD TYPE** and toll-free member service numbers appear in *ITALIC TYPE*.
All are closed Saturdays, Sundays and holidays unless otherwise indicated.
The addresses, phone numbers and hours for any AAA/CAA office are subject to change.
The type of service provided is designated below the name of the city where the office is located:

✛ Auto travel services, including books and maps, and on-demand TripTik® routings.
● Auto travel services, including selected books and maps, and on-demand TripTik® routings.
■ Books/maps only, no marked maps or on-demand TripTik® routings.
▲ Travel Agency Services, cruise, tour, air, car and rail reservations; domestic and international hotel reservations; passport photo services; international and domestic travel guides and maps; travel money products; and International Driving Permits. In addition, assistance with travel related insurance products including trip cancellation, travel accident, lost luggage, trip delay and assistance products.
○ Insurance services provided. If only this icon appears, only insurance services are provided at that office.
◖ Car Care Plus Facility provides car care services.
▣ Electric vehicle charging station on premises.

AAA NATIONAL OFFICE: 1000 AAA DRIVE, HEATHROW, FLORIDA 32746-5063, (407) 444-7000

IDAHO

BOISE—AAA OREGON/IDAHO, 7155 W DENTON ST, 83704. WEEKDAYS (M-F) 8:00-5:30. (208) 342-9391, *(800) 999-9391.* ✛▲○

COEUR D'ALENE—AAA WASHINGTON, 296 W SUNSET AVE #33, 83815. WEEKDAYS (M-F) 8:30-5:30. (208) 664-5868, *(800) 407-2020.* ●▲○

LEWISTON—AAA WASHINGTON, 802 BRYDEN AVE, 83501. WEEKDAYS (M-F) 8:30-5:30. (208) 798-5555 ○

MERIDIAN—AAA OREGON/IDAHO, 2310 E OVERLAND STE 110, 83642. WEEKDAYS (M-F) 8:30-5:30. (208) 884-4222 ✛▲○

POCATELLO—AAA OREGON/IDAHO, 1000 POCATELLO CRK RD #E5, 83201. WEEKDAYS (M-F) 8:30-5:30. (208) 237-2225, *(800) 574-4222.* ✛▲○

TWIN FALLS—AAA OREGON/IDAHO, 1239 POLE LINE RD E #315, 83301. WEEKDAYS (M-F) 8:30-5:30. (208) 734-6441, *(800) 999-6441.* ✛▲○

MONTANA

BILLINGS—AAA MOUNTAINWEST, 3220 4TH AVE N, 59101. WEEKDAYS (M-F) 8:30-5:30. (406) 248-7738, *(800) 391-4222.* ✛▲○

BOZEMAN—AAA MOUNTAINWEST, 1530 N 19TH AVE STE B, 59718. WEEKDAYS (M-F) 8:30-5:30. (406) 586-6156, *(800) 391-4222.* ✛▲○

BOZEMAN—AAA MOUNTAINWEST, 3509 LARAMIE DR STE 1, 59718. WEEKDAYS (M-F) 9:00-5:00. (406) 586-4334 ■○

GREAT FALLS—AAA MOUNTAINWEST, 1219 13TH ST S, 59404. WEEKDAYS (M-F) 8:00-5:00. (406) 454-8888 ○

GREAT FALLS—AAA MOUNTAINWEST, 1520 3RD ST NW STE G, 59404. WEEKDAYS (M-F) 8:30-5:30. (406) 727-2900, *(800) 391-4222.* ✛▲○

HAMILTON—AAA MOUNTAINWEST, 1265 N 1ST ST UNIT B, 59840. WEEKDAYS (M-F) 8:30-5:30. (406) 363-3407 ○

HELENA—AAA MOUNTAINWEST, 2100 11TH AVE, 59601. WEEKDAYS (M-F) 8:30-5:30. (406) 447-8100, *(800) 332-6119.* ✛▲○

HELENA—AAA MOUNTAINWEST, 2100 11TH AVE, 59601. WEEKDAYS (M-F) 8:30-5:30. (406) 447-8100 ✛▲○

KALISPELL—AAA MOUNTAINWEST, 135 HUTTON RANCH RD #106, 59901. WEEKDAYS (M-F) 8:30-5:30. (406) 758-6980, *(800) 391-4222.* ✛▲○

MISSOULA—AAA MOUNTAINWEST, 1200 S RESERVE STE B, 59801. WEEKDAYS (M-F) 8:30-5:30. (406) 829-5500, *(800) 391-4222.* ✛▲○

MISSOULA—AAA MOUNTAINWEST, 2704 BROOKS STE 1, 59801. WEEKDAYS (M-F) 9:00-5:00. (406) 926-1282 ○

WYOMING

CASPER—AAA MOUNTAINWEST, 341 EAST E STREET #150, 82601. WEEKDAYS (M-F) 9:00-5:00. (307) 439-2222 ■○

CHEYENNE—AAA MOUNTAINWEST, 2316 DELL RANGE BLVD #B, 82009. WEEKDAYS (M-F) 8:30-5:30. (307) 634-8861, *(800) 391-4222.* ✛▲○

ROCK SPRINGS—AAA MOUNTAINWEST, 157 K ST, 82901. WEEKDAYS (M-F) 8:30-5:30. (307) 362-1222 ○

Metric Equivalents Chart

TEMPERATURE

To convert Fahrenheit to Celsius, subtract 32 from the Fahrenheit temperature, multiply by 5 and divide by 9.
To convert Celsius to Fahrenheit, multiply by 9, divide by 5 and add 32.

ACRES

1 acre = 0.4 hectare (ha)   1 hectare = 2.47 acres

MILES AND KILOMETRES

Note: A kilometre is approximately 5/8 or 0.6 of a mile.
To convert kilometres to miles multiply by 0.6.

Miles/Kilometres		Kilometres/Miles	
15	24.1	30	18.6
20	32.2	35	21.7
25	40.2	40	24.8
30	48.3	45	27.9
35	56.3	50	31.0
40	64.4	55	34.1
45	72.4	60	37.2
50	80.5	65	40.3
55	88.5	70	43.4
60	96.6	75	46.6
65	104.6	80	49.7
70	112.7	85	52.8
75	120.7	90	55.9
80	128.7	95	59.0
85	136.8	100	62.1
90	144.8	105	65.2
95	152.9	110	68.3
100	160.9	115	71.4

Celsius °		Fahrenheit °
100	BOILING	212
37		100
35		95
32		90
29		85
27		80
24		75
21		70
18		65
16		60
13		55
10		50
7		45
4		40
2		35
0	FREEZING	32
-4		25
-7		20
-9		15
-12		10
-15		5
-18		0
-21		-5
-24		-10
-27		-15

LINEAR MEASURE

Customary	Metric
1 inch = 2.54 centimetres	1 centimetre = 0.4 inches
1 foot = 30 centimetres	1 metre = 3.3 feet
1 yard = 0.91 metres	1 metre = 1.09 yards
1 mile = 1.6 kilometres	1 kilometre = .62 miles

WEIGHT

If You Know:	Multiply By:	To Find:
Ounces	28	Grams
Pounds	0.45	Kilograms
Grams	0.035	Ounces
Kilograms	2.2	Pounds

LIQUID MEASURE

Customary	Metric
1 fluid ounce = 30 millilitres	1 millilitre = .03 fluid ounces
1 cup = .24 litres	1 litre = 2.1 pints
1 pint = .47 litres	1 litre = 1.06 quarts
1 quart = .95 litres	1 litre = .26 gallons
1 gallon = 3.8 litres	

PRESSURE

Air pressure in automobile tires is expressed in kilopascals. Multiply pound-force per square inch (psi) by 6.89 to find kilopascals (kPa).

24 psi = 165 kPa   28 psi = 193 kPa
26 psi = 179 kPa   30 psi = 207 kPa

GALLON AND LITRES

Gallons/Litres				Litres/Gallons			
5	19.0	12	45.6	10	2.6	40	10.4
6	22.8	14	53.2	15	3.9	50	13.0
7	26.6	16	60.8	20	5.2	60	15.6
8	30.4	18	68.4	25	6.5	70	18.2
9	34.2	20	76.0	30	7.8	80	20.8
10	38.0	25	95.0	35	9.1	90	23.4

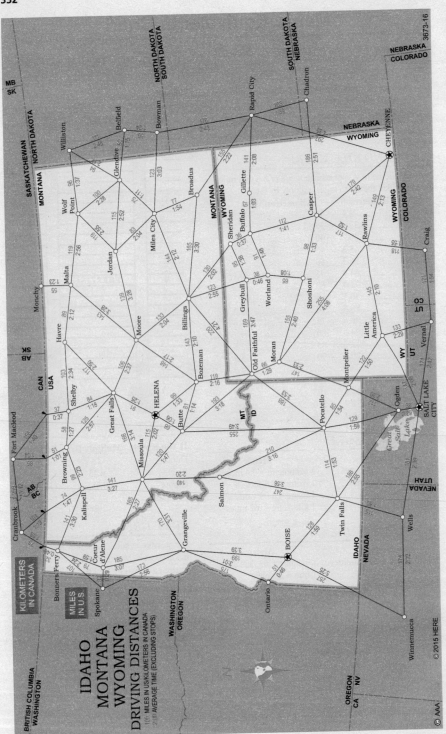

IDAHO
MONTANA
WYOMING
DRIVING DISTANCES

100 MILES IN U.S./KILOMETERS IN CANADA
2:00 AVERAGE TIME (EXCLUDING STOPS)

© 2016 HERE

3673-16

Border Information

U.S. Residents Traveling to Canada

Border crossing requirements: Travelers are required to present proper travel documents in order to enter Canada and return to the U.S.

Air travel: A U.S. passport is required.

Land or sea travel: Proof of citizenship and proof of identity are required. Approved documents include a passport or passport card, Enhanced Driver's License or NEXUS trusted traveler program card. Visit the U.S. Department of State website travel.state.gov for the most current information on these requirements. Canadian citizens should refer to the Canada Border Services Agency website www.cbsa-asfc.gc.ca.

U.S. resident aliens: An Alien Registration Receipt Card (Green Card) as well as a passport from the country of citizenship is required.

Children: All children must provide their own travel documents. In lieu of a U.S. passport or passport card, children under 16 traveling to Canada by land or sea may present an original or copy of their birth certificate, a Report of Birth Abroad obtained from a U.S. consulate or a Naturalization Certificate. Minors must be accompanied by both parents; if one parent is absent, a notarized

letter of consent from the absent parent giving permission to go on the trip is required.

Legal Issues: Persons with felony convictions, DUI convictions or other offenses may be denied entry into Canada.

Firearms: Canada has strict laws regarding the importing, exporting, possession, use, storage, display and transportation of firearms. These are federal laws that apply across the country. Firearms are divided into classes: non-restricted (most ordinary rifles and shotguns); restricted (mainly handguns) and prohibited (full and converted automatics and certain handguns, among others).

To bring a non-restricted or restricted firearm into Canada you must:
- Be 18 years of age or older
- Declare firearm(s) at the first point of entry
- Obtain an Authorization to Transport (ATT) from a provincial or territorial Chief Firearms Officer prior to arrival at the point of entry; contact the Canadian Firearms Centre at (800) 731-4000 for additional details.

Hunters may bring in, duty-free, 200 rounds of ammunition; a valid license or declaration to purchase ammunition is required. Those planning to hunt in multiple provinces or territories must obtain a hunting license from each one.

Firearms are forbidden in many of Canada's national and provincial parks, game reserves and adjacent areas. For additional information regarding the temporary importation and use of firearms consult the Canada Border Services Agency website.

Personal items: Clothing, personal items, sports and recreational equipment, automobiles, snowmobiles, cameras, personal computers and food products appropriate for the purpose and duration of the visit may be brought into Canada duty and tax-free. Customs may require a refundable security deposit at the time of entry.

Tobacco products: Those meeting age requirements (18 years in Alberta, Manitoba, Northwest Territories, Nunavut, Saskatchewan, Quebec and Yukon; 19 years in other provinces) may bring in up to 50 cigars, 200 cigarettes, 200 grams of tobacco and 200 tobacco sticks.

Alcohol: Those meeting age requirements (18 years in Alberta, Manitoba and Quebec; 19 years in other provinces and territories) may bring in limited alcoholic beverages: 40 ounces of liquor, 1.6 quarts of wine or 9 quarts of beer or ale (equivalent to 24 12-ounce bottles or cans).

- Amounts exceeding the allowable quantities are subject to federal duty and taxes, and provincial/territorial liquor fees.
- Provincial fees are paid at customs at the time of entry in all provinces and Yukon.
- It is illegal to bring more than the allowable alcohol quantity into the Northwest Territories or Nunavut.

Purchases: Articles purchased at Canadian duty-free shops are subject to U.S. Customs exemptions and restrictions; those purchased at U.S. duty-free shops before entering Canada are subject to duty if brought back into the United States.

Prescription drugs: Persons requiring medication while visiting Canada are permitted to bring it for their own use. Medication should be in the original packaging with a label listing the drug and its intended use. Bring a copy of the prescription and the prescribing doctor's phone number.

Gifts: Items not exceeding $60 (CAN) in value (excluding tobacco, alcoholic beverages and advertising matter) taken into or mailed to Canada are allowed free entry. Gifts valued at more than $60 are subject to regular duty and taxes on the excess amount.

Pets: You must have a certificate for a dog or cat 3 months and older. It must clearly describe the animal, declare that the animal is currently vaccinated against rabies and include a licensed veterinarian signature.

- Collar tags are not sufficient proof of immunization.
- Be sure the vaccination does not expire while traveling in Canada.
- The certificate is also required to bring the animal back into the U.S.

Exemptions: Service animals; healthy puppies and kittens under 3 months old with a health certificate signed by a licensed veterinarian indicating that the animal is too young to vaccinate.

Vehicles

- Vehicles entering Canada for leisure travel, including trailers not exceeding 8 feet 6 inches (2.6 m) in width, are generally subject to quick and routine entry procedures.
- To temporarily leave or store a car, trailer or other goods in Canada if you must leave the country, you must pay an import duty and taxes or present a valid permit. Canadian Customs officials issue vehicle permits at the point of entry.
- You are required to carry your vehicle registration document when traveling in Canada.
- If driving a car other than your own, you must have written permission from the owner.
- If driving a rented car, you must provide a copy of the rental contract.
- A valid U.S. driver's license is valid in Canada.
- In all Canadian provinces and territories except Alberta, British Columbia and Saskatchewan, it is illegal to use radar detectors, even if unplugged.
- Seat belt use is required for the driver and all passengers.

Financial Responsibility Laws in Canada: When an accident involves death, injury or property damage, Canadian provinces and territories require evidence of financial responsibility.

U.S. motorists should check with their insurance company regarding whether they are required to obtain and carry a yellow Non-Resident Inter-Province Motor Vehicle Liability Insurance Card (accepted as evidence of financial responsibility throughout Canada). Those not carrying proper proof may be subject to a substantial fine. If renting a vehicle, check with the rental car company.

U.S. Residents Returning to the U.S.

U.S. citizens returning to the U.S. from Canada by air must have a valid passport. Those returning by land or sea are required to present the appropriate travel documents outlined above.

Every individual seeking entry into the United States—foreign visitors, U.S. citizens or lawful permanent residents—must be inspected at the point of entry. Random searches may be conducted by U.S. Customs and Border Protection agents.

U.S. Exemptions for a Stay in Canada of 48 Hours or More

- Each individual may bring back tax- and duty-free articles not exceeding $800 in retail value.
- Any amount over the $800 exemption is subject to duty.
- The exemption is allowed once every 30 days.
- A family (related persons living in the same household) may combine purchases to avoid exceeding individual exemption limits.
- Exemptions are based on fair retail value (keep receipts of all purchases as proof).
- Exemptions apply to articles acquired only for personal or household use or as gifts and not intended for sale.
- The exemption may include 100 cigars, 200 cigarettes and 1 liter of liquor per person over age 21 (state liquor laws are enforced).
- All articles must accompany you on your return.

U.S. Exemptions for a Stay in Canada Less Than 48 Hours

- Each individual may bring back tax- and duty-free articles not exceeding $200 in retail value.
- The exemption may include no more than 50 cigarettes, 10 cigars, 5 fluid ounces (150 milliliters) of alcoholic beverage or 150 milliliters of perfume containing alcohol.
- A family may not combine purchases.
- If purchases exceed the $200 exemption, you forfeit the exemption and all purchases become subject to duty.
- All articles must be declared and accompany you upon return.

Gifts

- Gifts up to $100 fair retail value may be sent to friends or relatives in the United States provided no recipient receives more than one gift per day (gifts do not have to be included in the $800 exemption).
- Gifts of tobacco products, alcoholic beverages or perfume containing alcohol valued at more than $5 retail are excluded from this provision.
- Mark the contents, retail value and "Unsolicited Gift" on the outside of the package.

Prohibited: Narcotics and dangerous drugs, drug paraphernalia, obscene articles and publications, seditious or treasonable matter, lottery tickets, hazardous items (fireworks, dangerous toys, toxic or poisonous substances) and switchblade knives. Also prohibited are any goods originating in embargoed countries.

Canadian Residents Traveling to the U.S.

Canadian citizens entering the U.S. by air must have a valid passport. Canadian citizens entering the U.S. by land or sea are required to present the appropriate travel documents; refer to the Canada Border Services Agency website www.cbsa-asfc.gc.ca for the most current information on these requirements.

If traveling to the United States with a minor, carry documentation proving your custodial rights. A person under age 18 traveling to the United States alone or with only one parent or another adult must carry certified documentation proving that the trip is permitted by both parents.

U.S. Customs permits Canadian residents to bring—duty-free for personal use and not intended for sale—the following: clothing, personal items and equipment appropriate to the trip, up to 200 cigarettes, 50 cigars or 2 kilograms of tobacco, and 1 liter of alcoholic beverage.

Canadian Residents Returning to Canada

Canadian residents may bring back, free of duty and taxes, goods valued up to $400

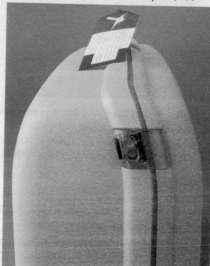

(CAN) any number of times a year, provided the visit to the United States is 48 hours or more and all goods accompany the purchaser (a written declaration may be required).

You may claim a $50 (CAN) exemption on goods, excluding alcoholic beverages and tobacco products, if returning after an absence of less than 48 hours and not using any other exemption. If bringing back more than $50 worth of goods, the regular duty and tax rate is levied on the entire value. This exemption may apply any number of times in a year. No tobacco or alcohol may be brought back if returning from a visit of less than 48 hours.

If returning after 7 days or more (not counting the departure day from Canada)

you may claim up to a $750 (CAN) exemption. Goods other than alcohol and tobacco products need not accompany you (a written declaration may be required).

Permitted within the $400 and $750 exemptions: up to 50 cigars, 200 cigarettes, 200 tobacco sticks and 6.4 ounces of tobacco, and up to 40 ounces of liquor or 1.6 quarts of wine or 9 quarts of beer or ale (the equivalent of 24 12-ounce bottles or cans). You must meet the minimum age requirement of the province or territory entered to claim alcohol or tobacco products.

While AAA makes every effort to provide accurate and complete information, AAA makes no warranty, express or implied, and assumes no legal liability or responsibility for the accuracy or completeness of any information contained herein.

Points of Interest Index

Attractions appear at the top of each category and offer a Great Experience for Members®.

Index Legend

NB.	national battlefield	NR.	national river
NBP.	national battlefield park	NS.	national seashore
NC.	national cemetery	NWR.	national wildlife refuge
NF.	national forest	PHP.	provincial historic(al) park
NHM.	national historic(al) monument	PHS.	provincial historic(al) site
NHP.	national historic(al) park	PP.	provincial park
NHS.	national historic(al) site	SF.	state forest
NL.	national lakeshore	SHM.	state historic(al) monument
NME.	national memorial	SHP.	state historic(al) park
NMO.	national monument	SHS.	state historic(al) site
NMP.	national military park	SME.	state memorial
NP.	national park	SP.	state park
NRA.	national recreation area	SRA.	state recreation area

EVENTS & FESTIVALS

HISTORIC SITES & EXHIBITS

OUTDOORS & SCIENCE

SHOPPING & NIGHTLIFE

SPORTS & RECREATION

TOURS & SIGHTSEEING

Photo Credits

Page numbers are in bold type. Picture credit abbreviations are as follows:
- (i) numeric sequence from top to bottom, left to right ▪ (AAA) AAA Travel library.

- (Cover) Logan Pass, Glacier National Park, MT / © Inge Johnsson / Alamy Stock Photo
- **2** (i) © Stephen Saks Photography / Alamy Stock Photo
- **2** (ii) © Photri Inc. / age fotostock
- **2** (iii) © Wolfgang Kaehler / age fotostock
- **12** (i) Courtesy of Berry Manor Inn
- **12** (ii) © Chris Dew / Killarney Lodge
- **12** (iii) Courtesy of Hyatt Hotels
- **12** (iv) Courtesy of Montpelier Plantation and Beach
- **12** (v) © Elisa Rolle / Wikimedia Commons
- **12** (vi) Courtesy of The Shores Resort & Spa
- **12** (vii) Courtesy of All Star Vacation Homes
- **12** (viii) Courtesy of Bryce View Lodge
- **12** (ix) Courtesy of Vista Verde Guest Ranch
- **13** Courtesy of Divi Resorts
- **18** (i) © Bob Rowan Progressi / age fotostock
- **18** (ii) © steve bly / Alamy Stock Photo
- **19** © George Ostertag / age fotostock
- **20** (i) Courtesy of Wikimedia Commons
- **20** (ii) Courtesy of Wikimedia Commons
- **23** (i) © Kevin Griffin / Alamy Stock Photo
- **23** (ii) © FOTOSEARCH RM / age fotostock
- **23** (iii) © Lane Erickson / Alamy Stock Photo
- **23** (iv) © George Ostertag / age fotostock
- **23** (v) © Andre Jenny / Alamy Stock Photo
- **24** (i) © Jon Sullivan / Wikimedia Commons
- **24** (ii) © Anna Gorin Travel / Alamy Stock Photo
- **24** (iii) © Wolfgang Kaehler / age fotostock
- **24** (iv) © Andre Jenny / Alamy Stock Photo
- **108** (i) © Douglas Lander / Alamy Stock Photo
- **108** (ii) © Visions of America, LLC / Alamy Stock Photo
- **109** © Tetra Images / Alamy Stock Photo
- **110** (i) Courtesy of Wikimedia Commons
- **110** (ii) Courtesy of Wikimedia Commons
- **113** (i) © Ami Vitale / Alamy Stock Photo
- **113** (ii) © America / Alamy Stock Photo
- **113** (iii) © Richard Cummins / Alamy Stock Photo
- **113** (iv) © FOTOSEARCH RM / age fotostock
- **113** (v) © Terrance Klassen / age fotostock
- **114** (i) © Stephen Saks Photography / Alamy Stock Photo
- **114** (ii) © SuperStock / age fotostock
- **114** (iii) © Yunner / Wikimedia Commons
- **114** (iv) © Patti McConville / Alamy Stock Photo
- **216** (i) © Henk Meijer / Alamy Stock Photo
- **216** (ii) © Dennis MacDonald / age fotostock
- **217** © franzfoto.com / Alamy Stock Photo
- **218** (i) Courtesy of Wikimedia Commons
- **218** (ii) Courtesy of Wikimedia Commons
- **221** (i) © Zoonar GmbH / Alamy Stock Photo
- **221** (ii) © RGB Ventures / SuperStock / Alamy Stock Photo

(cont'd)

- **221** (iii) © Joe Mamer / age fotostock
- **221** (iv) © SuperStock / age fotostock
- **221** (v) © SuperStock / age fotostock
- **222** (i) © Ian Dagnall Commercial Collection / Alamy Stock Photo
- **222** (ii) © Ian Dagnall Commercial Collection / Alamy Stock Photo
- **222** (iii) © SuperStock / age fotostock
- **222** (iv) © Photri Inc. / age fotostock
- **333** © Garry Gay / Alamy Stock Photo
- **335** © image100 / age fotostock

LET'S GET SOCIAL

Stay connected with #AAA and #CAA

Visit with us on your favorite social media sites for the latest updates on hot discounts, cool destinations and handy automotive know-how.

Talk with us!

AAA.com/Facebook

AAA.com/Googleplus

AAA.com/Twitter

YouTube.com/AAA

CAA Social Media: CAA.ca/social